W9-BFE-500

# Rock and Roll
## An Introduction

SECOND EDITION

**Michael Campbell**

with **James Brody**
University of Colorado, Boulder

SCHIRMER
CENGAGE Learning™

Australia • Brazil • Japan • Korea • Mexico • Singapore • Spain • United Kingdom • United States

# SCHIRMER
## CENGAGE Learning

**Rock and Roll: An Introduction,**
**Second Edition**
**Michael Campbell, James Brody**

Publisher: Clark Baxter

Development and Media Editor:
Julie Yardley

Assistant Editor: Emily Perkins

Editorial Assistant: Nell Pepper

Executive Marketing Manager:
Diane Wenckebach

Marketing Assistant: Marla Nasser

Project Manager, Editorial Production:
Trudy Brown

Creative Director: Rob Hugel

Art Director: Maria Epes

Print Buyer: Nora Massuda

Permissions Editor: Bob Kauser

Production Service: Melanie Field

Text and Cover Designer: Lisa Langhoff,
One Good Dog Design

Photo Researcher: Eric Schraeder

Copy Editor: Jennifer Gordon

Compositor: International Typesetting
and Composition

© 2008, 1999 Schirmer, Cengage Learning

ALL RIGHTS RESERVED. No part of this work covered by the copyright herein may be reproduced, transmitted, stored, or used in any form or by any means graphic, electronic, or mechanical, including but not limited to photocopying, recording, scanning, digitizing, taping, Web distribution, information networks, or information storage and retrieval systems, except as permitted under Section 107 or 108 of the 1976 United States Copyright Act, without the prior written permission of the publisher.

For product information and technology assistance, contact us at
**Cengage Learning Customer & Sales Support, 1-800-354-9706**

For permission to use material from this text or product,
submit all requests online at **cengage.com/permissions**
Further permissions questions can be emailed to
**permissionrequest@cengage.com**

Library of Congress Control Number: 2006936559

ISBN-13: 978-0-534-64295-2

ISBN-10: 0-534-64295-0

**Schirmer**
25 Thomson Place
Boston, MA 02210-1202
USA

Cengage Learning is a leading provider of customized learning solutions with office locations around the globe, including Singapore, the United Kingdom, Australia, Mexico, Brazil, and Japan. Locate your local office at:
**international.cengage.com/region**

Cengage Learning products are represented in Canada by Nelson Education, Ltd.

For your course and learning solutions, visit **academic.cengage.com**

Purchase any of our products at your local college store or at our preferred online store **www.ichapters.com**

Printed in Canada
3  4  5  6  7  11  10  09  08

*to my wife Marie Jo De Maestri and our son Gabriel Campbell*
MICHAEL CAMPBELL

*to my wife Kim*
JAMES BRODY

# CONTENTS

3

12

13

14

# Rock Is Music/Rock as Music

■ Before it is anything else, rock is music. For us, an inescapable corollary of this most basic observation is that a text for an introductory music course in rock music should enable readers to observe, describe, and interpret musical events with greater insight. That was the primary objective of the first edition, and it remains the primary objective of this edition.

In preparing the first edition of this book, we discovered that the licensing practices of record companies and some rock artists made it impossible to offer a representative selection of rock music at a reasonable price. That circumstance was the single biggest challenge we faced: it was simply not reasonable to expect readers to study a detailed discussion of a song without having the song available for repeated listening, nor was it reasonable to ask them to spend hundreds or even thousands of dollars to acquire a representative selection of music.

However, in the eight years since the publication of the first edition, online delivery modalities have revolutionized the distribution of recorded music. Systems such as the iTunes Store enable buyers to purchase single tracks instead of entire albums, while subscription services such as Rhapsody give users access to an enormous body of rock-era music for a reasonable monthly fee. By combining these services with a CD package, it is now possible to offer a truly representative selection of rock-era music at a price comparable to the CD sets that accompany traditional music appreciation texts.

*Rock and Roll: An Introduction* has been almost completely reconceived and rewritten, to take advantage of online delivery of recorded music. The fundamental design remains the same, but the discussion is even more focused on rock as music. This in turn permits more extensive discussion of not only stylistic connections and contrasts but also ways in which the music reflects and shapes society and culture. New features include:

- An extensive and representative playlist of 115 rock-era songs.
- More detailed, yet non-technical musical analyses of all the rock-era listening examples, including an annotated list of key features.

- An accessible opening chapter that defines and illustrates basic rock concepts and key terms.
- A comprehensive overview of rock's roots and antecedents, supported by twenty-seven excerpts of pre-rock music.
- More extensive discussion of the connection between rock music and its social and cultural context, smoothly integrated into the narrative.
- A more richly developed historical perspective on the music of the rock era, with emphasis on evolutionary, revolutionary, and devolutionary trends, patterns of influence, and connections and contrasts between musical examples.
- Activities and features that encourage readers to go beyond course content. Each chapter ends with Applying Chapter Concepts activities; the Outro highlights important themes in rock at the beginning of the twenty-first century.
- Far more extensive coverage of recent music: 34 percent of the songs on the playlist were released since 1976, 10 percent since 1990.
- A "heritage" two-CD set that includes not only twenty-seven excerpts of pre-rock music but also a decided majority of the musical examples discussed in the first half of the book.
- Extensive website support, including active listening guides, a multimedia-enhanced glossary, links to chapter playlists on both iTunes and Rhapsody for those songs not included on the CD set, and clearly organized recommendations for further listening.

## The Second Edition

In organizational terms, the overviews found in the first edition have been disassembled; much of this content now appears in those chapters where it is most germane to the song and style under discussion. Chapter organization is more thematic, so that major trends within a period stand out more clearly. Brief overviews in the form of part openers introduce the three main periods of the rock era; each includes a chronologically ordered list of the tracks discussed in that part, to help readers become aware of concurrent developments during that period. Website content—which includes timed listening guides, more in-depth discussion of key features, a multimedia glossary, and more—complements the musical discussions in the text and encourages further exploration.

All of this is in the service of the primary goal of the text: an enrichment of the experience of listening to rock. To that end, *Rock and Roll: An Introduction* encourages perceptive listening to rock-era music through five complementary and integrated strategies. The heart of the book is the series of discussions of the songs on the playlist. On a case-by-case basis, these help readers become more aware of the musical events in a song and their connection to the lyrics.

Supporting these discussions is a set of clearly defined and illustrated terms that help readers call to mind and identify distinct musical features. Terms like *rock beat*, *riff*, and *refrain* acquire specific meanings for readers, and the ability to identify a musical feature by name helps heighten awareness of it.

The discussions are typically embedded in a larger setting, which also includes contextualizing observations that draw connections among the musical events, their musical function, and the audience for the music. Cumulatively, the discussions help readers form a sound framework of the rock era into which they can add other music of their own (or their instructor's) choosing. As the semester progresses, readers create a rich network of musical connections, contrasts, and patterns of influence that provides a music-based historical context for rock music. Finally, there are extensive and specific suggestions for further musical exploration at the end of each chapter.

We are confident that those who read the text carefully and use the resources in the book and on the web as they listen to the musical examples will come away with a much clearer picture of the history of rock-era music; they will also be more aware of the salient features of the numerous rock styles that have emerged in the last fifty years. Finally, they will be better able to perceive the place of music not discussed in the text within this historical framework and to absorb its meaning more fully. For a book that serves as a text for an introductory course in rock music, these are the paramount objectives.

## Listening to the Music

The rapidly developing technology of the last decade has made it possible to deliver more music at a reasonable cost and provide interactive, multimedia support for its presentation. Information about music delivery and web support follows below.

There are 115 rock-era musical examples and twenty-seven pre-rock excerpts discussed in the book and on the web. To make this music available at the lowest possible cost, we have created a CD set that includes almost all of the examples from the first six chapters, plus those that we were able to license from subsequent chapters. (We recommend the CD set because it contains tracks not available on either online service at this time.)

To access the remaining examples, we suggest obtaining the music online, through the iTunes Store (*www.apple.com/itunes/store*) and/or Rhapsody—Real Network's online subscription service. Rhapsody's service is cross-platform, costs $9.99 per month as of this writing, and offers listeners access to over 2 million songs, including almost all of the music discussed in the latter two-thirds of the book (*http:// rhapsody.com*). As of this writing, the only songs discussed in the book that are not available online are those of the Beatles, Led Zeppelin, and Radiohead.

We will update information about available music periodically on the website. Please consult the site for news concerning the availability of recordings and recent developments in online delivery.

## Acknowledgments

We would like to thank the many people who have helped turn our manuscript drafts into the second edition of this text: our editors Sue Gleason and Julie Yardley; copyeditor Jennifer Gordon, whose enthusiasm and meticulousness were much appreciated; Trudy Brown and Melanie Field, who oversaw production of the book; Emily Perkins, assistant editor; our publisher Clark Baxter, who always sees the big picture; and the following reviewers whose valuable input was instrumental in the reconception of this second edition: Steve Allen, Rider University; Frank Daniels, Great Basin College; Steve Davis, Kingwood College; John Irish, Angelo State University; Mark Lochstampfor, Capital University; Melanie Lowe, Vanderbilt University; Alex J. Lubet, University of Minnesota; Mark D. Maxson, Weber State University; Peter J. Mercer-Taylor, University of Minnesota; Rick Mook, Arizona State University; Julian Onderdonk, West Chester University; and Nico Schüler, Texas State University.

Finally, we want to thank our families—for their support and because they make our work worthwhile: Michael's wife Marie Jo De Maestri, her daughters Eva and Helena Kranjc, and their son Gabriel; James's wife Kim and her two children, Lindsie and Jeremy.

MICHAEL CAMPBELL
JAMES BRODY

# Rock Is

■ **ROCK IS ...** *The most brutal, ugly, desperate, vicious form of expression it has been my misfortune to hear.*
FRANK SINATRA

*A type of sensuous music unfit for impressionable minds.*
TIP O'NEILL, FORMER SPEAKER OF THE HOUSE

*A combination of good ideas dried up by fads, terrible junk, hideous failings in taste and judgment, gullibility and manipulation, moments of unbelievable clarity and invention, pleasure, fun, vulgarity, excess, novelty, and utter enervation.*
GREIL MARCUS, NOTED ROCK CRITIC

*Dead. The attitude isn't dead, but the music is no longer vital. It doesn't have the same meaning. The attitude, though, is still very much alive—and it still informs other kinds of music.*
DAVID BYRNE

*Not so much a question of electric guitars as it is striped pants.*
DAVID LEE ROTH

*To dress up to.*
FRANK ZAPPA

*[A music that] can change things. I know that it changed our lives.*
BONO

# It's Only Rock and Roll

## Rock Is

Before it is anything else, rock is music. Everything else that is part of its world—the attitudes it communicates, its cultural impact, the musicians from around the world who continue to produce it, and the comparably broad audiences who listen to it—grows out of this inescapable fact. From our twenty-first-century perspective, rock is a rich musical tradition over a half-century old. In the deeply interwoven relationships among its numerous and disparate forms, it resembles an extended family that spans several generations and includes all of the in-laws. Rock can be vocal or instrumental, soft or loud, acoustic or electric, cobbled together in a garage or generated on a computer. It can stimulate your brain, touch your heart, and move your hips and feet.

Songs like the Rolling Stones' "It's Only Rock 'n Roll (But I Like It)" define rock in sound the way a dictionary entry defines rock in words. But the music that we call rock embraces far more than this most characteristic version of the style. From this core set of values, rock radiates out in every conceivable direction, as we will discover in the course of this book. It includes not only music that is unquestionably rock but also music that is rock simply because it was recorded by rock musicians (for example, some of the more esoteric music of Frank Zappa; Beatles' songs like "Michelle") and music that shows the influence of rock, however tangentially (such as Santana's Latin rock or rock musicals like Andrew Lloyd Webber's *Jesus Christ, Superstar*). The remainder of the book is an exploration of what rock has been and what it can be. Here, we explore what we mean by "rock"—and "rock and roll."

Most centrally, "rock" refers to the core style that coalesced in the years around 1970 and has remained largely unchanged since. It requires no substyle-defining label (such as "heavy metal" or "punk"), although it is often referred to as "rock and roll" (as in "the World's Greatest Rock and Roll Band") or "hard rock." As we move outward from this center, we find the boundaries between music that is rock and music that is not rock drawn more inclusively. There are temporal boundaries: we distinguish between rock, the music of the mid-sixties and beyond, and rock and roll, the music of the fifties from which rock evolved. There are boundaries shaped largely by race: we distinguish between rock (music performed mainly by white musicians) and rhythm and blues (music performed by black musicians). There are boundaries drawn mainly by provenance and personality: much of the music of Dylan and the Beatles is not *rock* in the most limited sense of the term, but it is rock because it was created by

2

these seminal rock musicians. Conversely, the music of Burt Bacharach is considered pop, not rock, although the influence of rock is often clearly evident.

Most generally, *rock* refers to all of the music of the last half century or so that exhibits the musical features we associate with rock music, or has some connection with or influence from this music. In this broadest meaning of rock, we find not only rock and its numerous substyles (such as heavy metal, new wave, Brit pop), but also rhythm and blues, soul, reggae, techno, and various fusions with established traditions, like musical theater, jazz, and Latin music. To reduce the confusion that may result from these multiple meanings of *rock*, we will use the term **rock era** to refer to this most inclusive understanding of rock. **Rock** will refer to music by white performers or played in the style most associated with white performers. We will use **rock and roll** in two ways: to refer to the music of the fifties that evolved most directly into rock and, more informally, to designate the most characteristic form of rock music.

Finally, rock is the reason for our journey together. As Mick Jagger, Keith Richards, and the rest of the Rolling Stones remind us again and again: "I know it's only rock 'n roll but I like it, like it, yes, I do."

We begin our discussion of rock in the center. Our goal is to describe music that could *only* be rock, music that evidences its most fundamental and prevalent elements, painting rock in primary colors. We start with a song that is a staple of classic rock playlists: the Rolling Stones' "It's Only Rock 'n Roll (But I Like It)." This song illustrates salient features of rock music, which will serve as our primary points of reference throughout the historical survey that follows.

---

"It's Only Rock 'n Roll (But I Like It)" is the title track from the Rolling Stones' 1974 album, *It's Only Rock 'N Roll*. At the time of the recording, the Rolling Stones consisted of Mick Jagger, vocals; Keith Richards and Mick Taylor, guitar; Bill Wyman, bass; and Charlie Watts, drums. The pianist on this track is Ian Stewart, who played on many of the band's recordings.

---

# Form in Rock: The Anatomy of a Rock Song

Music happens in time. Because it does, our auditory perception is fundamentally different from our visual perception. We can take in an image—for example, a photograph or painting—in a single glance and look at it for as long as we want. By contrast, what we hear in one instant is gone in the next. To help listeners navigate their way through a song, rock songwriters have made use of a time-honored two-step strategy: invent short, memorable, and easily retained melodic ideas (often called **riffs**), then bring them back several times during the course of the song. Riffs can be sung or played on an instrument. When sung, they become even more memorable because they often set the same words each time. A section of the song in which both words and music are repeated is called a **chorus**, or **refrain**.

Repeated riffs, especially sung ones, serve as milestones on the road from the beginning of the song to the end. Typically, they stress the main theme of the song and create a framework into which songwriters can insert other musical material that

"It's Only Rock 'n Roll (But I Like It)," the Rolling Stones (1974)

L. Trievnor/Express/Getty Images

The Rolling Stones in 1969, just after Mick Taylor joined the band. From left to right: drummer Charlie Watts, guitarist Mick Taylor, lead singer Mick Jagger, guitarist Keith Richards, and bassist Bill Wyman.

amplifies the main message of the song. This additional material almost always includes multiple statements of the **verse**—sections in which the same melody is used for different parts of the lyrics. The verse typically precedes the chorus, and it usually tells a story or presents images that explain the title phrase of the refrain lyric. The listening guide below highlights verse and chorus as they occur in "It's Only Rock 'n Roll."

| Listening Guide:"It's Only Rock 'n Roll (But I Like It)," the Rolling Stones (1974) | | |
|---|---|---|
| **0:00** | Intro | Instrumental |
| **0:08** | Verse | If I could stick my pen . . . |
| **0:44** | Chorus | I know it's only rock 'n roll |
| **1:17** | Verse 2 | If I could stick a knife . . . |
| **1:53** | Chorus | I know it's only rock 'n roll |
| **2:26** | Interlude | And do ya think that you're the only girl around? |
| **3:00** | Chorus | I know it's only rock 'n roll |
| **3:31** | Outro | Vocal, then instrumental jam over a section of the chorus |

Note: A more detailed version of this listening guide can be found on the website for this book: *academic. cengage.com/music/campbell*. The website offers comprehensive listening guides and other resources for all the tracks in the book that are discussed in detail.

The basic pattern—instrumental intro and outro framing multiple statements of the verse and chorus—has been used in thousands of rock and roll songs. Indeed, if you've ever sung the chorus of a song along with the band, then you are aware of the verse/chorus pattern. The realization of this basic plan in "It's Only Rock 'n Roll" is more elaborate than many, but the landmarks are still easy to locate, and the basic outline is clearly apparent.

## Verse/Chorus Form

We use the word **form** to describe the organization of music in time. We most easily recognize the form of a musical work—whether it's a rock song or Romantic symphony—when musical events return periodically. The pattern created by the periodic return of important musical events is generally the key element in determining form. Because the central formal events in "It's Only Rock 'n Roll" are the verse and chorus, we identify its form as **verse/chorus form**. This form is typical of rock-era songs. Certain details may make it distinctive—even unique—but the general outline is the most widely used strategy for organizing a rock song. We will encounter other forms, such as blues form, but none more frequently than the verse/chorus form heard in "It's Only Rock 'n Roll."

"It's Only Rock 'n Roll" also epitomizes other aspects of rock style, most notably its rhythms, instrument choice, and approach to melody.

# The Rhythms of Rock

In the excellent documentary *Rock and Roll: The Early Years*, there is a clip of a white preacher ranting and raving about the evils of rock and roll. He asks his congregation what it is about rock and roll that makes it so seductive to young people, then immediately answers his own question by shouting, "The BEAT! The BEAT! The BEAT!" thumping the pulpit with each "beat."

He was right. It *was* the beat that drew teens to rock and roll during the fifties and has continued to draw listeners to rock ever since. The beat is at the heart of our experience not only of rock rhythm but also of rock music. It is the music's most compelling feature, as the anonymous preacher so vigorously pointed out. Chances are that it would take a conscious decision for you to resist tapping your foot, bobbing your head, or otherwise moving your body to "It's Only Rock 'n Roll."

In this most meaningful way, we all know what the **beat** is—it is that aspect of the music that makes you want to move. However, we can deepen our understanding of the beat, and of the rhythms of rock, by also understanding beat conceptually. Our objective here is to translate this kinesthetic experience into words.

However, when we use the word *beat* in connection with rock songs like "It's Only Rock 'n Roll," we often imply three distinct, if interrelated, meanings. Consider, for example, the following three sentences:

- The tempo of "It's Only Rock 'n Roll" is about 125 beats per minute.
- "It's Only Rock 'n Roll" has a rock beat.
- "It's Only Rock 'n Roll" has a great beat; it makes you want to move to the groove.

The meaning of *beat* in each of these sentences is distinct from the other two. The first refers to the regular measure of time, the second refers to the rhythmic foundation of the style, and the third refers to the interaction of other rhythms with the regular measure of time and the rock beat. We consider each in turn.

## Beat, Rhythm, and Tempo

Listen to the beginning of "It's Only Rock 'n Roll" and start tapping your foot as soon as you find the beat. Once you find it, you will probably notice that you are marking off time at regular intervals, in time with the music. In other words, the time between foot taps is the same from one beat to the next. This rhythm moves at a steady pace, rather than speeding up or slowing down.

**Beat and Rhythm**  In this context, *beat* refers to a regular rhythm that moves at a speed to which you can comfortably respond with physical movement. A regular **rhythm** is a rhythm that measures time in equal increments. The tapping of your foot is a regular rhythm because the time that elapses between one tap and the next is always the same. In "It's Only Rock 'n Roll" there are other regular rhythms, both faster and slower than the beat, but we identify this particular regular rhythm as the beat because it lies in our physical comfort zone. It is the rhythm to which we time our movements when we dance, exercise, or simply tap our foot or bob our head in time with the song.

**Tempo**  We use the word **tempo** to refer to the *speed* of the beat. We generally measure tempo in beats per minute: the tempo of "It's Only Rock 'n Roll" is about 125 beats per minute. In rock songs, tempos generally range between 110 and 140 beats per minute. Tempos outside this range may connect powerfully to the musical message: the frenetic tempos of punk (often around 160 to 170 beats per minute) reinforce the confrontational nature of the style; by contrast, the languid tempos (often between 60 and 70 beats per minute) of so many doo-wop songs (such as "I Only Have Eyes for You") encourage the slow dancing that is often the prelude to the romance expressed in the lyrics.

**The Measure**  In rock, beats almost always coalesce into groups of four, although other groups—2, 3, or even 5—are also possible. We call a consistent grouping of beats a **measure**, or **bar**. The measure represents a slower regular rhythm. And because it is slower, it is a more convenient form of rhythmic reference for longer timespans: we refer to a 12-bar blues, for instance, rather than a 48-beat blues.

In "It's Only Rock 'n Roll," we can hear the relationship between beat and measure right from the start. The song begins with Mick Taylor's strummed rhythm guitar. Four beats later, Richards plays a two-note riff. Four beats after that, he plays it again. This immediately establishes the 4:1 relationship between beat and measure that is customary in rock music.

So far we have identified the most generic meaning of *beat*, which could be applied to a wide range of music—rock, pop, jazz, classical, and any other music with a steady pulse. (So do the terms *tempo, measure,* and *bar*). We consider next a more specific meaning of *beat*.

## Rock Beat and Rock Style

As you tap the beat to "It's Only Rock 'n Roll," you may notice that there is another regular rhythm that moves twice as fast as your foot. It is the first rhythm that we hear, in the acoustic guitar, and it continues through the entire song. Charlie Watts's drumming reinforces it, especially during the chorus. This faster regular rhythm is the primary component of a rock beat.

A song has a **rock beat** when the *fastest* regular rhythm moves twice as fast as the beat. This extra layer of regular rhythm is not universal in rock music; there are songs that use a different kind of rhythmic organization. But in rock music from the sixties and seventies, most songs have a rock beat; it occurs far more frequently than any other kind of rhythm.

### Style Beats

A rock beat is an example of a **style beat**, the rhythmic foundation of a style or family of styles—even a generation of music. Throughout much of the twentieth century, many in the music industry have named style beats using not only descriptive labels (rock beat, fox-trot) but also numerical labels. The numbers indicate the number of times one hears the fastest regular rhythm per measure. The fox-trot (which we encounter beginning in the next chapter) has been called a two-beat rhythm, because the fastest regular rhythm is heard twice in each measure. Similarly, a swing rhythm (heard in Chapter 3) has also been called a four-beat rhythm, because the fastest regular rhythm moves at beat speed, or four sounds per measure. More recently, one finds references to 16-beat rhythms, for example, on high-end electronic keyboards that have a bank of percussion tracks. In a 16-beat rhythm, the fastest regular rhythm moves four times as fast as the beat, producing 16 sounds per measure. The numerical label for a rock beat is an **eight-beat rhythm**: the fastest layer moves twice as fast as the beat, or eight sounds per measure. We will use rock beat and eight-beat rhythm more or less interchangeably throughout this text.

Numerical labels help clarify the rhythmic relationship among style beats and highlight the evolutionary direction of rhythm in twentieth-century popular music. For an interactive demonstration of style beats and other information, please visit the website: *academic.cengage.com/music/campbell*.

A footnote: The first well-known reference to an eight-beat rhythm occurred well before the rock era: "Beat Me Daddy, Eight to the Bar" was a big hit for the Andrews Sisters in 1940. The song title hints at the rhythmic feel of boogie-woogie, the blues style that would ultimately give rock its characteristic rhythmic foundation. However, the Andrews Sisters' "eight-to-the-bar" rhythm was not yet what we would call either rock beat or eight-beat rhythm, although it is on the way. Interestingly, several rock-era covers of the song do use a real rock beat/eight-beat rhythm.

Bands can present this steady rhythm in infinitely varied ways. It can be intrusively explicit: much of the power of punk derives from the entire band's playing this rock rhythmic layer fast and loud. It can be subtle, as it was in so many songs by James Taylor, Carole King, and other singer-songwriters from the early seventies. In these and other circumstances, the musicians *feel* this rhythm, whether they play it loudly or softly, consistently or intermittently, plainly or elaborated with other rhythmic patterns. In all cases, however, the *expectation* of this steady rhythm moving twice as fast as the beat serves as an aural graph paper, a temporal grid onto which rock musicians draw their sonic designs.

More than any other single feature, a rock beat identifies music as being rock. A song can have electric or acoustic instruments; it can be loud or soft; it can have a long, flowing, tuneful melody or layers of riffs; it can feature sweet-voiced singers like Karen Carpenter, soulful singers like Aretha Franklin, men singing high like Led Zeppelin's Robert Plant, or rough-voiced singers like Bob Dylan or Mick Jagger. However, if it has a rock beat, then we can place it chronologically sometime after 1956. The rock beat allows us to situate soft rock and hard rock under the same stylistic umbrella. We recognize it more easily in songs like "It's Only Rock 'n Roll," though, because it is clearly and constantly present; indeed, we expect it in such a rock-defining song.

**The Backbeat**  There is one other regular rhythm in "It's Only Rock 'n Roll": the backbeat. The **backbeat** is a sharp, percussive sound on the second of each pair of beats. In this song, Watts teases us at the beginning by playing it intermittently. However, it is heard more consistently once the song arrives at the chorus. It is strongest there: a sharp rap on the snare drum on the second and fourth beats of each measure.

In rock-era music, the backbeat is even more pervasive than the rock-defining rhythmic layer. Virtually every rock song has a backbeat; as Chuck Berry sang in "Rock 'n Roll Music": "It's got a backbeat, you can't lose it." The backbeat is a constant, even in those songs that do not use a rock beat. Together, the backbeat and the rock rhythmic layer (which moves twice as fast as the beat) form the foundation of rock rhythm.

## Syncopation: "It Has a Good Beat, and You Can Dance to It"

Among the most popular segments on *American Bandstand*, the television show that brought rock and roll into millions of homes from 1957 (when ABC began to broadcast the show nationally) to 1990 (when it finally went off the air), was "Rate-a-Record." In this segment, three participants would listen to a new song while the others danced, then give the song a numerical rating somewhere between 35 and 98. Ratings were often based on the perceived quality of the beat: when asked why a song received a high rating, one of the participants might answer something like "It has a good beat, and you can dance to it." "It's Only Rock 'n Roll" has a good beat, and you can dance to it—indeed, it makes you want to dance or at least move to the beat. Why? What is it about the rhythm of the song that invites us to respond physically? To address that question, we introduce another common feature of rock rhythm: syncopation.

A **syncopation** is a rhythm or accent that does not line up in an expected way with the beat or other regular rhythm. We hear a syncopation right at the beginning of "It's Only Rock 'n Roll": the second, and longer, note of Richards's opening riff comes *between* beats, rather than lining up with one of them. Syncopations pervade the rhythm in the song: the most accented notes in the vocal part are syncopations ("spill it all over the STAGE"; "ain't he STRA-A-ANGE"); Bill Wyman's bass line moves freely on and off the beat, both guitars play syncopated riffs, and Watts occasionally breaks free of the steady rock beat. All of this activity conflicts with the regular rock rhythm in the rhythm guitar and drums. The tension created by the interplay between the regular rhythms and the rhythms that fall off the beat creates much of the rhythmic interest in the song—more than any other aspect of the rhythm, it is what gives the song a "good beat."

This meaning of *beat* is more subjective and less precise than either of the other two meanings. Those we can quantify easily enough, and they will be the same to every listener: the tempo is 125 beats per minute, and the drummer and rhythm guitar player are marking off a rock beat. However, listeners may differ regarding what defines a good beat. Some may prefer the more straightforward rhythms of U2, whose music has relatively little syncopation, to the more syncopated rhythms heard in the music of the Rolling Stones, Led Zeppelin, Aerosmith, and other like-minded bands. Still, just about any consensus opinion regarding the quality of the beat in a group of rock songs will favor more syncopated rhythms. It's likely that a decided majority of rock fans would acknowledge that the interplay among the steady rock rhythm, the backbeat (which is actually the most basic syncopation of all), and the other syncopations gives "It's Only Rock 'n Roll" a great beat.

Rock is about rhythm, and rhythm in rock starts with the beat, in all three of its meanings. The time-measuring beat is at the center of our rhythmic experience, in mind and body. The rock beat is the rhythmic backdrop of the music and the source of much of its power, as we will discover again and again during our survey of rock-era music. And a good beat is one of the things that can draw us to the music. "It's Only Rock 'n Roll" offers clear illustrations of all three meanings of *beat*. In rhythm as well as sound, it serves as an ideal point of reference for further explorations of rock and roll.

# The Instrumentation of Rock

As in so many rock songs, in "It's Only Rock 'n Roll" the musicians enter one by one. We hear in short order the rhythm guitar, the drums, and the lead guitar. The bass enters at the beginning of the verse. These instruments are the core instruments of the band; others are optional.

## The Rhythm Section

These core instruments comprise what is commonly called a **rhythm section**. The rhythm section is a twentieth-century invention. The practice of combining at least one chord instrument, one bass instrument, and one percussion instrument into a section that provides steady rhythmic and harmonic support began around 1920 in the jazz bands and dance orchestras of the period. The first rhythm sections consisted of a banjo and/or piano (chord instrument), a tuba (bass), and a primitive drum set (percussion). From the twenties on, it was an integral part of the sound of popular music and jazz. During the thirties, the acoustic guitar replaced the banjo as one of the chord instruments, and the string bass replaced the tuba as the bass instrument.

After World War II, the rhythm section became part of the sound of blues, rhythm and blues, and country music. Especially in these styles, the newly developed electric guitar replaced the acoustic guitar. With rock, the rhythm section became even more electric, with the electric bass replacing its acoustic counterpart. This step transformed not only the sound of the rhythm section but also its role: instead of supporting the band, it *became* the band. These instruments are so integral to rock that it is no exaggeration to say that rock music would not have come into being without them.

**The Electric Guitar**  The solid-body guitar—the defining instrument of rock—is the product of a two-stage evolution that transformed the acoustic guitar into a new instrument with unimagined capabilities. The first stage, which got underway in the thirties, involved fitting an acoustic guitar with a *pickup*, a device that converted the vibration of a steel spring into an electrical signal, which could then be amplified. These instruments retained the hollow body of the acoustic instrument, although they relied mainly on amplification for sound. Chuck Berry used a Gibson hollow-body guitar in his best-known recordings.

The solid-body guitar took its shape from the acoustic guitar, but it took its technology from the electric lap steel guitar. Inventors working for Adolph Rickenbacker in southern California produced the first commercial electric steel guitars in the early thirties. Called "frying pans" because of their circular body and long neck, these were solid-body instruments. In the early forties, Leo Fender founded Fender Musical Instruments to make electric lap steel guitars. He would soon adapt the technology to other instruments: in 1951, his company introduced the first mass-produced solid-body guitar, the Broadcaster, which soon became the Telecaster. Other manufacturers soon followed suit, most notably Gibson, which in 1952 introduced a series of solid-body guitars designed by Les Paul, a superb guitarist as well as a technological wizard. (Paul was also a recording pioneer who helped develop multitrack recording and overdubbing). By the early sixties, the solid-body guitar was the instrument of choice for rock guitarists.

Although the playing techniques are similar enough that guitarists like Eric Clapton move easily between acoustic and electric instruments, the solid-body guitar is a fundamentally different instrument from its acoustic cousin. The conventional acoustic guitar gets its sound exclusively from its hollow body, which serves as a resonating cavity. Compared to other popular instruments, it does not make much sound—that is why inventors sought to amplify it. Moreover, the sound dies away quickly.

Without amplification, the solid-body guitar makes even less noise than the acoustic guitar. Plug it in, however, and it becomes a completely different instrument. The vibration of the string is converted into an electric signal, which can be processed in infinitely varied ways and converted back into sound at ear-splitting volumes. Guitarists can sustain sounds indefinitely, distort them beyond recognition, and add a host of other effects.

With this new technology, the guitar went from an intimate, informal instrument suitable for front porches, coffee houses, or a background role in a big band to the powerhouse instrument of a new music, capable of filling arenas and stadiums with heavily distorted sound—all in less than two generations. The speed of its transformation and the extent of its impact are without precedent in the history of music.

**The Electric Bass**  The electric bass was an instrument that had to be invented, not transformed. Improvements in amplification during the postwar years opened a loudness gap between the amplified electric guitar and the unamplified string bass. Leo Fender anticipated the need for such an instrument: he introduced the first solid-body electric bass in 1951, which he called the Precision Bass, the same year he introduced the Broadcaster. The instrument took longer to catch on than the electric guitar, in part because it required bassists to learn a new instrument: the switch from string bass to electric bass involved reorienting from a vertical to a horizontal fingerboard and learning new playing techniques.

Its guitarlike shape soon became an asset, not a liability. The string bass had to be big, because as an acoustic bass instrument it needed a large resonating cavity, and it had to be played with the strings aligned vertically. Fender's guitarlike design made the instrument more comfortable to play and easier to transport—even with the amplifiers of the fifties. The instrument caught on during the latter part of the decade; by 1960, it was the standard bass instrument in a rock band.

The solid-body guitar and the electric bass were truly rock and roll–era innovations—effectively new instruments that made a new kind of music possible. So were the exponential gains in amplification during the sixties, especially those that came about through the application of solid-state technology, which used transistors instead of tubes. By contrast, the drum kit (or drum set) used by rock drummers was already fully developed by the fifties. We consider it next.

**The Drum Kit**  The standard drum kit in the early sixties (see the 1965 photo of the Stones on page 12) contained at least four drums and four cymbals: a snare drum, a bass (or kick) drum, a smaller tom-tom mounted on the bass drum, and a larger floor tom-tom, plus two or more freestanding cymbals and the hi-hat—a pair of cymbals operated by a foot pedal.

In essence, the drum kit consolidates the percussion section of a marching band or theater orchestra, enabling a single musician to fill several different roles. The modern drum kit required two inventions: a foot pedal that enables a drummer to beat the bass drum and the hi-hat mechanism. Around the turn of the century, numerous drummers attempted to devise a functional bass drum pedal. The most commercially successful was the one developed by William Ludwig in 1909 and manufactured by him beginning in 1910. By the twenties, it was a standard part of the drum kit used in dance orchestras and jazz bands. The first foot-operated cymbal pair appeared in the twenties. Called a "low-boy" or "low-sock cymbal," this device placed the cymbals about 30 inches above the floor. The hi-hat, which appeared in the latter part of the twenties and became a standard part of the drum kit in the thirties, was tall enough for the drummer to play on the cymbals with sticks or brushes.

By 1940, the modern drum kit was in place. Most of the changes in the drum kit since that time have been cosmetic—for instance, transparent bodies—and some drummers use extensively expanded sets, with multiple toms, additional cymbals, and

Sunset Boulevard/Corbis

The Rolling Stones, New Year's Day, 1965. The musicians include (from left to right) Bill Wyman, bass; Brian Jones, guitar; Mick Jagger, vocal; Charlie Watts, drums; Keith Richards, guitar. Watts's drum kit is basic: we can see clearly the bass drum and the small tom-tom above and to the right of the bass drum, plus two freestanding cymbals and the hi-hat, which Watts operates with his left foot.

other percussion instruments. However, Charlie Watts has propelled the Rolling Stones for four decades using a traditional four-drum kit.

The drum kit was the last instrument in the rhythm section to go electric. Although the first electronic drum prototypes date back to the seventies, the electronic drum kit became a viable commercial product around 1980. It became a popular alternative to the conventional drum kit, first among pop-oriented drummers, then among rock and R&B drummers in numerous styles.

**Additions and Alternatives to Conventional Rock Rhythm Sections** These three instruments—electric guitar, electric bass, and drum kit—are the nucleus of a rock band. Indeed, they may *be* the rock band, as power trios like the Jimi Hendrix Experience and Cream amply demonstrated. However, other instruments can also provide rhythmic support and (in the case of pitched instruments like the piano) harmonic support as well. In "It's Only Rock 'n Roll," we hear Ian Stewart's piano occupying the highest register, and we hear acoustic guitar in the background maintaining a steady rhythm.

Other instruments can substitute for these core instruments: for example, an acoustic piano or electric keyboard can serve as the primary chord instrument (as most Elton John songs demonstrate). In recent years, digitally generated sounds have often served as an alternative to conventional instruments, especially in styles like rap and techno. Still, the instrumental *roles* have remained constant through these remarkable technological innovations: recordings from 2005 still typically feature at least one chord instrument (real or virtual), a bass instrument, and a percussion instrument, just as they did in 1955.

## Voices and Instruments Together

The other prominent sounds in "It's Only Rock 'n Roll" are the vocal parts. When he is singing, Jagger's vocal line is the most prominent part. However, Jagger's vocal does not push the other parts into the background. Instead, it seems to ride on top of the propulsive groove set up by the rhythm section. The sections of the song that include vocals and piano highlight two key features of the sound of classic rock. One is the distinction among core, customary, and optional sounds; the other is the quality of the sounds themselves.

In classic rock, there are core sounds, customary sounds, and optional sounds. The guitar, bass, and drum sounds are *core* for two reasons. First, the three instruments sound throughout the song. Second, the sound of a typical rock song is incomplete without all three instruments. One or more vocal parts are *customary* in rock; most rock songs have some singing. However, in "It's Only Rock 'n Roll" the vocal part comes and goes. In a song that lasts approximately 5 minutes, the vocal part is in the forefront only half of the time: there is about a minute of music without any vocals (the very beginning, in the middle, and at the end) and another minute (toward the end of the song) where the vocal part is simply part of the mix and subordinate to Richards's guitar. The piano part is *optional*. Although pianists Ian Stewart and Nicky Hopkins frequently appeared on Rolling Stones recordings, they were not an integral part of the band; nor is piano or other keyboard an integral part of rock. Rather, adding an instrument like the piano to the overall sound of the band is much like adding a tasty spice to a stew.

That "It's Only Rock 'n Roll" has a vocal doesn't surprise us; rock instrumentals are rare. That the song has sections for instruments alone also doesn't surprise us; this is customary in a rock song. What the shifting role of the vocal in "It's Only Rock 'n Roll"—in the spotlight, in the background, sometimes out of the picture—implies is that the meaning of the song resides much more in the sounds, riffs, and rhythms of the band than it does in the lyric.

## Rock's Approach to Sound

"It's Only Rock 'n Roll" is a basic rock song—the kind of song that defines the essence of rock. It focuses more on affirming core values than it does on extending boundaries. In terms of instrument choice, that means building the sound of the band around the three most basic instruments of rock music: the guitar, the bass, and the drum kit.

# Melody in Rock Music

> I said I know it's only rock 'n roll but I like it
> I know it's only rock 'n roll but I like it, like it, yes, I do

If we are at all inclined to sing along with Mick and Keith, it's all but certain that this is one part of the song where we would join in. One reason is that it includes the title phrase. Another might be the way the vocal line enhances the normal inflection of the words, so that the singing delivers the words with much more impact. However, there are strictly musical reasons why we might be drawn more to the chorus than to the verse; we explore the reasons in the context of a discussion of melody in rock music.

## Riffs and Hooks

We previously described a riff as a short, memorable, and easily retained melodic idea. Here we consider why riffs tend to be short, what makes them memorable, and how their length and shape help make them easy to remember.

Riffs are short: most riffs contain between two and seven notes. In this song, the chorus grows out of three riffs. The first—which sets "I know"—contains just two notes. The second, "it's only rock 'n roll," has six. The third, "but I like it," has four. Other memorable melodic fragments—such as "ain't he strange" and Richards's guitar riffs—also contain just a few notes.

There is a valid psychological reason for keeping riffs short. In a famous paper published in 1956, Harvard psychologist George Miller established that humans are able to retain in short-term memory only about seven unrelated bits of information—the equivalent of a local phone number. Add an area code and it's harder to retain, unless the person chunks the information in some way. That's why companies and agencies so often select phone numbers that can convert to words or simple phrases. For example, the American Red Cross obtained the number 1-866-438-4636 for their local toll-free help line, but it was much easier to remember when presented as 1-866-GET-INFO. Similarly, it is harder to retain longer musical ideas, at least until the notes are grouped in some way: odds are that you find the chorus easier to remember than the verse.

Riffs are inherently memorable if they have a distinctive rhythmic or melodic shape. In the case of the chorus of "It's Only Rock 'n Roll," the emphasis is on the rhythm rather than on the melody: the rhythm enhances the natural inflection of the lyric as spoken. It makes the declamation of the words more emphatic. The instrumental riffs have distinctive melodic patterns as well as syncopated rhythms.

Riffs are typically set off by silence. This is most apparent in the chorus, where there are gaps between each segment of the title phrase. Similarly, almost all of the riffs have at least a small gap between question and answer, or between statement and its repetition. These gaps—short or long—*frame* the riff; they help it stand out even more clearly.

Good songwriters create riffs that catch listeners' interest; they implant riffs in listeners' ears through frequent repetition. The repetition can be exact, or there can be some variation of the riff; in either circumstance, the riff retains its identity. The most memorable riffs are often called **hooks**: they become embedded in listeners' memory much as the hook at the end of a line gets snagged in the mouth of a fish. The chorus of the song, especially the title phrase, is likely to be a hook. However, any riff that stands out and is repeated frequently enough can become a hook: rock-defining songs like Roy Orbison's "Pretty Woman," the Stones' "Satisfaction," the Kinks' "You Really Got Me," Jimi Hendrix's "Purple Haze," and Aerosmith's "Walk This Way" begin with a guitar riff that is repeated several times.

The hook is the closest thing to a melodic constant in rock and roll; it is to melody what the rock beat is to rock's rhythm or the rhythm section is to rock's instrumentation.

Its prominence and pervasiveness point to rock's dramatic departure from conventional melodic practice, as we know it from patriotic anthems, hymns, familiar folksongs, and pre-rock popular song. Rock is often both less melodic and more melodic than these other kinds of music, as we explore next.

## From Riff to Melody

In talking about music, we use **melody** in two distinct ways. The more general meaning is the most prominent and individual musical line. Generally, this is the vocal part. However, it isn't always, as the end of the song evidences. The more limited meaning of *melody* refers to a musical line that is coherent, distinctive, and interesting enough to be performed meaningfully without accompaniment. "The Star-Spangled Banner" is a familiar illustration of this more limited meaning of melody.

We should begin any discussion of melody in "It's Only Rock 'n Roll" by noting that the song does not *have* a melody in the more limited meaning of the term. None of the sections in the song contain melodic material that would hold together without the band underneath.

The absence of a conventional melody should be understood as a choice, not a shortcoming. Richards and the other members of the Rolling Stones were certainly capable of writing tuneful melodies, as in "Ruby Tuesday," a late sixties hit. Rather, it would seem that they opted for the riff-repeating melodic approach used here because it was a better fit with the terrific rhythmic groove that runs through the song. Viewed in isolation, songs like "It's Only Rock 'n Roll" are less melodically interesting than pre-rock pop. However, the larger issue is the appropriateness of a particular melodic approach to the song as a whole. In this song, we hear a shift in emphasis away from melody and toward rhythm.

In the sense that it does not have a standalone melody, "It's Only Rock 'n Roll" offers less melodically than do other kinds of music. But it also offers more melodically, because most of its instruments play melodic ideas. The vocal line and Richards's guitar are the most prominent riffs, but they are not the only ones. At several points in the song, most notably in the chorus, Mick Taylor answers Richards's riffs with one of his own, and Bill Wyman's bass lines also have considerable melodic interest. As a result, there is a great deal of melodic material in this song. However, it is spread around among the members of the band, rather than concentrated in the vocal line.

Both dimensions of the approach to melody used in this song—the assembling of melody by repeating riffs and spreading melodic material throughout the band—came into sixties rock from the urban blues bands of Muddy Waters and others. Rock musicians recontextualized this approach, just as they did with other aspects of the blues. Their reworking of this aspect of blues style was one of the major innovations of rock and roll.

# Key Elements of Rock Style

To summarize the main points of our discussion, we expect a rock-defining song like "It's Only Rock 'n Roll" to have the following features:

- A verse/chorus form, framed by an instrumental introduction and ending. Each statement of the form has a verse that tells part of a story or describes a scene, followed by a chorus that repeats the same words and music several times to emphasize the main theme of the song.

- A steady beat that moves at a tempo of 125–130 beats per minute.
- A rock beat and a strong backbeat.
- A good beat, created by the interaction of the beat and rock beat with lots of syncopated rhythms.
- A core instrumentation of at least one electric guitar, electric bass, and drums (the rhythm section), filling the roles of chord, bass, and percussion instruments and providing much of the essential musical information of the song.
- Other instruments filling a secondary role, with no particular expectations regarding instrument choice or instrument roles.
- An abundance of riffs, both played and sung; hooks, the most prominent riffs, appear in the chorus and in the lead guitar part.
- The melodies of sections within the form, like the chorus and instrumental introductions, assembled by repeating a riff two or more times.

These are among the most prominent features of the song—and of rock music at its most typical. There are other prominent features of "It's Only Rock 'n Roll" that either require no explanation—the song is loud—or are easy to identify but difficult to describe precisely—the sound quality of Mick Jagger's singing or the edge to Richards's guitar sound. These, too, are typical of rock style: we expect that a rock song will be loud, not soft, and that both voices and instruments will be more abrasive than soothing.

Other features heard in this song—such as the chords played by the guitars and piano and the way in which the instruments work together—are more in the background. We will discuss *harmony*, the study of chords and how they connect, and *texture*, the interrelationship of all the parts, in some detail in the chapters that follow. Our goal in this chapter has been to highlight the most prominent features of rock style—the customary points of entry into a song.

## Rock Style and Rock Attitude

The musical features outlined above are central to the message that songs like "It's Only Rock 'n Roll" communicate. In the case of the Stones, it projected their swagger in sound. From the start, the Rolling Stones projected a "bad boy" image. They and their music were provocative, rebellious, and insolent, and their fans loved it. We can certainly construct the attitude that they projected during the early part of their career from sources beyond the music. We can read accounts of how Andrew Loog Oldham, their co-manager at the beginning of their career, deliberately positioned them as the anti-Beatles, as well as accounts of their drug use and sexual adventures. We can read the titles of their albums and songs and scan the lyrics. We can look at images of the band members: Jagger's leer, Richards's sneer, or simply the Stones logo.

The lyrics of "It's Only Rock 'n Roll" are characteristically provocative: if Jagger actually did what he asks in the lyric, there would be a bloody mess (and only one performance). Still, it is in the music that we *feel* most powerfully what the Stones are trying to communicate in this song. Perhaps the most obvious clue is Jagger's singing.

His rough voice and half-sung, half-spoken delivery inflate the impact of the lyrics as spoken: the words are louder and more resonant, and the rhythm is slower than speech. Similarly, the band plays with an edge to the sound: guitar and piano mimic Jagger's aggressive vocal style.

It is the rhythm that conveys the character of the song most strongly. By its very nature, a medium-tempo rock beat is intrusive: in a song like "It's Only Rock 'n Roll," the rhythm comes at us at a rate of over four times per second. (Try tapping on a table top, first at beat speed, or even every other beat, and then at rock beat speed to sense the impact of this faster layer). Played as vigorously as it is in this song, the rock rhythm invades one's auditory space. Listeners can either welcome it or reject it, but it is difficult to simply tune out. Even more compelling is the trademark groove—the good beat—that the Rolling Stones create. The groove invites erotic movement. In live performance, Jagger makes the erotic aspect explicit, but one needn't see him to get the musical message. The erotic invitation can in turn conjure up a host of associations, all of which seem to promise a good time. We receive this message beginning with Richards's first riff and continue to receive it throughout the song, even when Jagger isn't singing.

The key point here is this: in "It's Only Rock 'n Roll" and so many other rock songs, words, music, and (in live performance) visual images work together to send a message and convey an attitude. Our main objective here has been to identify those aspects of the music that most strongly convey the message.

We began this book with a series of quotations that complete the sentence "Rock is . . ." Some of them were serious, some derogatory, some whimsical. However, none of them said very much about what one might expect to hear in a rock song. If we pose "Rock is" as a question, then this chapter is an answer, but it is not *the* answer: rock is too rich and too diverse to be limited to the features that we described. Our summary can serve as a point of departure and central reference for further discussion of rock-era music. We continue that discussion with an exploration of rock's deepest roots in Chapter 2. As we do, keep in mind that the music, even if "it's only rock 'n roll," is the main reason for our journey together.

## Terms to Remember

| | | |
|---|---|---|
| rock era | verse/chorus form | style beat |
| rock | beat | eight-beat rhythm |
| rock and roll | rhythm | backbeat |
| riff | tempo | syncopation |
| chorus, refrain | measure, bar | rhythm section |
| verse | rock beat | hook |
| form | | |

## Applying Chapter Concepts

Both of these projects can be completed individually or in small groups. We recommend coming together in groups to gather more examples.

1. Go through your music collection and find one song that has *all* of the key features described in "It's Only Rock 'n Roll." Then make a listening chart similar to this chapter's Listening Guide, in which you identify the sections of the form and note their timing. When you've finished the guide, compare the form of the two songs—does your song have similar proportions, the same number of verses, an instrumental solo, and so forth? On the basis of this limited sample, construct a theory about the ways in which rock bands treat verse/chorus form.

2. Find examples of rock-era songs that *lack* the following features, choosing a different song for each feature:

   a. Does *not* have verse/chorus form
   b. Does *not* have a tempo around 125–130 beats per minute
   c. Does *not* have a rock beat
   d. Does *not* feature electric guitar prominently
   e. Does *not* have a melody created from a riff
   f. Does *not* have an instrumental hook

Then ask yourself why the songs that you have chosen are examples of rock music, even though they miss at least one key feature of rock style.

# PART TWO

# Before Rock: Roots and Antecedents, Evolution and Revolution

Those who chart the history of rock work with a mountain of artifacts: films and videos, anecdotal accounts, media coverage, physical evidence such as instruments and equipment, and—above all—recordings. Indeed, the quest for the first rock and roll *record* has been a key element in bringing the early years of the rock era into focus. By contrast, those who chart the history of the *roots* of rock must work largely by inference much of the time: the farther back in time they search, the skimpier and less reliable the musical evidence becomes. Indeed, rock's deepest roots are in music that seems timeless, because we have so little direct information on the music and the cultures that created and preserved it.

The roots of rock music are as richly varied and deeply intertwined as the music itself. They grow out of music from the African diaspora throughout the New World and out of music from several strata of European culture, in Europe and the New World. These origins date back centuries, not decades. And they show that rock, despite its revolutionary impact on music and culture, was also the most recent stage in a long evolutionary process within popular music.

Accordingly, two major objectives of the next two chapters are to identify and describe the varied roots of rock and note their interaction along the evolutionary path toward rock. By way of introduction, here are three significant stages:

1. *The beginning of the slave trade.* The slave trade, which dates back to the early sixteenth century in Latin America and the early seventeenth century in the United States, brought together Europeans and Africans in the New World, albeit in a horribly inhumane relationship. The integrative process began when blacks in the New World created music that drew on their own cultural memory as well as the music of their white masters.

2. *The emergence of blackface minstrelsy.* The first minstrel troupes, which appeared in the United States during the 1840s, mixed caricatures of blackness with decidedly white music that nevertheless displayed the indirect influence of black music. After the Civil War, black minstrels supplanted whites; in the process they introduced a black sensibility, however distorted by the conventions of minstrelsy, into mainstream culture.

3. *An infusion of black music into the popular music mainstream.* In the first years of the twentieth century, ragtime, then commercial blues, hot dance music, and jazz created a revolutionary and fully modern kind of popular music. The impact of these new black musical styles is evident in the numerous musical features that also occur in rock, though significantly transformed: for example, the backbeat, the rhythm section, riffs, and a black rhythmic feel.

The other major objectives in Chapters 2 and 3 are to describe the most direct antecedents of rock-era music and contrast them with the increasingly conservative music of the popular mainstream after World War II. At the dawn of the rock era, there was a wide gap, musically and culturally, between the inside and outside of the music industry. The most commercially dominant and most critically acclaimed popular styles were mainstream pop and musical theater. Much of this music retreated from the progressive musical developments of the twenties and thirties. By contrast, outsider styles like country and western, folk, and rhythm and blues, which existed mainly on the fringes of the music industry, continued to evolve toward rock. The differences between these two bodies of music at the dawn of the rock era will help us understand why rock seemed so revolutionary.

We begin by linking the distant past with the present in samples of music from the British Isles and Africa.

# Before Rock

## An Evolutionary Perspective

Rock is a fully integrated music. It has strong musical and social connections to the cultures of Europe and West Africa, whose musical traditions are so contrasting as to seem almost mutually exclusive. As rock came together in the sixties, it seamlessly blended musical elements from these quite different and often antagonistic cultures into a new kind of music.

We hear rock as a revolutionary music because of its innovations, because its most immediate sources came from largely marginalized music, because it brought not only new sounds but also new attitudes into popular music, and because it used technology to redefine what popular music was. But rock was also the product of a long evolution that began with the arrival of African slaves in the New World.

A balanced view of the relationship of rock to the music that preceded it takes both perspectives into account. Accordingly, we document the evolutionary perspective in this chapter and portray the musical circumstances that made rock seem so revolutionary in Chapter 3. We begin by contrasting European and African musical traditions.

## EUROPEAN AND AFRICAN MUSICAL TRADITIONS IN THE NEW WORLD

Rock became possible only with extensive contact between Europeans and Africans. Most of the contact between European and African cultures occurred in colonies in North and South America and in the Caribbean, under the most inhospitable circumstances. In the New World, European and African immigrants may have inhabited the same geographical space, but they lived in two different worlds—socially, culturally, and musically. Further, in the United States there was a sharp division between working-class and middle- and upper-class whites through the early twentieth century.

CD 1:1

"Barbara Allen" excerpt, Rebecca Tarwater (1936)

# Folk Music from the British Isles

The members of the lower classes who emigrated from the British Isles to North America brought their music with them: there are songs and dances that are still sung and played that date back centuries. For those people living in more isolated areas, such as the Appalachians and Newfoundland, the traditions remained largely untouched by outside influences until well into the twentieth century. We hear excerpts from two early recordings: a British ballad recorded in 1936 by Rebecca Tarwater (1908–2001), a woman from Tennessee; and an American dance tune recorded in 1927 by Ben Jarrell, a fine old-time fiddler from North Carolina. The music and the performance of it represent traditions that date back decades, even centuries.

## "Barbara Allen"

"Barbara Allen" is a folk ballad, one of the most common types of folksongs. A **ballad** is a simple song with a lyric that tells a story. The stories were often morbid, even grisly, and they usually had a moral. In this respect, "Barbara Allen" is typical: It intertwines love and death—two of the most enduring themes in art and life—in a most understated and succinct way, as we can learn from the lyric. It was typically sung without accompaniment.

"Barbara Allen" dates back to at least the seventeenth century. Samuel Pepys describes it as a "little Scotch song" in his diary entry from January 2, 1665, but it must have been popular well before that date. It almost certainly came to North America with the first colonists. The version recorded here is one of hundreds of variants found throughout the Southeast. Rebecca Tarwater came to Washington, DC, at the urging of the folklorists John and Alan Lomax to record the song and help preserve a heritage that was rapidly disappearing.

The song is a simple four-phrase melody that forms a graceful arch: up, then down. It is constructed from a **pentatonic** (five-note) scale, one that is common in the folk music of Ireland and Scotland. It is **strophic**: that is, several stanzas are sung to the same melody. (We hear two in this excerpt; there are seven in this recording of the song.) Tarwater's singing is unpolished by classical standards, but her voice is pleasant and exceptionally true. There is no accompaniment.

### ROCK CONNECTIONS

- Storytelling song
- "Real" story, although apparently based on a long-forgotten incident
- Strophic form (this led to verse/chorus form)
- Unpolished but effective vocal style

CD 1:2

"Old Joe Clark" excerpt, Ben Jarrell, vocal and fiddle (1927)

## "Old Joe Clark"

The most popular dances brought from the British Isles were up-tempo jigs and reels, played by a fiddler. We have no way of knowing exactly how this music sounded in the early nineteenth century, but we do know some of the songs and can infer some of the key features of the style from the earliest country recordings and contemporary accounts. This early recording of "Old Joe Clark"—one of the first country music recordings—reveals musical features that were almost certainly present in Americanized versions of British folk music, as heard in the nineteenth century.

Ben Jarrell, who sings and plays the fiddle on this recording, lived in a rural part of North Carolina. Because Jarrell's son Tommy also played in much the same style, it is likely that Ben Jarrell's singing and playing typify a traditional approach that had been substantially unchanged for generations.

This song is somewhat unusual in that it combines song and dance. Many fiddle tunes were strictly instrumental. Here, vocal and instrumental statements of the melody alternate (note: in the interest of highlighting the verse/chorus pattern, we have truncated instrumental statements of the melody). Each statement of the melody includes a verse and a refrain. Their relationship is apparent from the lyric: the refrain retains the same words and melody, while the verses give unflattering snapshots of Betsy Brown. Fiddle, banjo, and voice play different versions of the melody; there is no chordal accompaniment. The song has a fast tempo and a clear, danceable beat.

> ## ROCK CONNECTIONS
>
> - Down-home, good-humored attitude
> - Story told in everyday language
> - Melody set to a danceable beat
> - Rough, untrained singing voice
> - Verse/chorus form

## Music of the Urban Middle and Upper Classes

Throughout the eighteenth and nineteenth centuries, the upper and middle classes in Europe and America shared a common musical language. We know its most sophisticated statements as classical music: the music of Bach, Handel, Haydn, Mozart, Beethoven, Schubert, among others. However, there was also a vast body of "popular" song and music for social dancing that used a simpler form of the same musical language, as well as patriotic music (for example, national anthems such as "God Save the King") and hymns and other church music. Through the middle of the nineteenth century, there was a smooth stylistic continuum among these different types of music.

The genre that connected classical and commercial music most smoothly was the song with piano accompaniment. Songs in this format appeared only in the latter years of the eighteenth century, for two main reasons. The first was the widespread adoption of the piano as the keyboard instrument of choice; in almost every circumstance, it replaced the harpsichord, a much less flexible and more brittle-sounding instrument. The second was the economic growth of the middle class, who bought the songs as sheet music and paid instructors to teach them to sing and play. Music publishing and music instruction were key steps in the growth of the music industry, as was the construction of pianos.

In the British Isles, the most popular kinds of songs were gentrified versions of regional folksongs: Irish, Scottish, and Welsh. Poets and musicians, most notably Thomas Moore, would collect folksongs, supply them with modest piano

CD 1:3

"Woodman,
Spare That
Tree" excerpt,
Henry Russell
(1830s), vocals
by Richard Lalli

accompaniments, and perform them in a genteel manner. This was the musical counterpart to bringing a farmer or shepherd into the city, bathing and grooming him, then dressing him well to make him presentable to "polite" society.

These middle-class versions of folksongs helped spawn new kinds of popular music, including the most popular genre in nineteenth century America: the **parlor song**. These songs told sentimental stories, set to simple melodies with generally modest accompaniment. They were written for performance in the home by amateur musicians. We encounter a slightly more elaborate version of this genre in an especially popular song from the 1830s: Henry Russell's "Woodman, Spare That Tree."

Henry Russell (1812–1900) was the Elton John of the nineteenth century: an English songwriter, singer, and pianist who enjoyed extraordinary success in America. Russell claimed to have studied composition with the Italian opera composers Rossini and Bellini before emigrating briefly to the United States; "Woodman, Spare That Tree" clearly shows the influence of Italian operatic style.

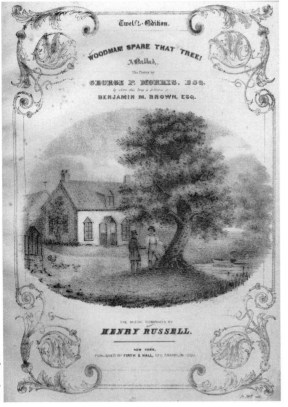

Like "Barbara Allen," "Woodman, Spare That Tree" has a simple melody supporting a lyric that tells a story. The most noticeable difference is the piano accompaniment, which outlines simple chords. Although "Woodman, Spare That Tree" may seem miles away from rock, the musical tradition that it exemplifies is the source of the harmony used in "It's Only Rock 'n Roll."

"Woodman, Spare That Tree" is a very early example of the two-stage process through which outsider styles were brought into the popular mainstream. The first stage was the transformation of the folk style into commercial music by blending it with the prevailing popular style; the second was the creation of a new style by combining the commercial folk style with the prevailing style. We will encounter this several times: for example, the music of the minstrel show, the first commercial blues and their reshaping of popular song, the rise of country music, and—in the rock era—the reworking of rhythm and blues and the transformation of deep blues into hard rock and heavy metal. This process can also work in reverse: "Wildwood Flower," one of the Carter Family's best-loved recordings, began life as a parlor song; it

Library of Congress

The cover of the original version of "Woodman, Spare That Tree." The image that dominates the cover depicts the central theme of the song and matches its sentimental tone. Through the early 20th century, sheet music was the principal way to disseminate popular song, and the principal way of making money from its dissemination.

eventually found its way into the mountains, where it was completely reworked.

### ROCK CONNECTIONS

- Use of chords to support a melody
- Use of chords to establish slow regular rhythms, such as the measure, and to outline the form

Classical music, from which Henry Russell borrowed so freely, embodied cultural prestige. Throughout the twentieth century, new popular styles have assumed classical trappings to "legitimize" themselves. A few examples: Scott Joplin's ragtime opera, *Treemonisha*; Paul Whiteman's concert of "symphonic jazz," which included the premiere of George Gershwin's *Rhapsody in Blue*; the Beatles' concept albums; art rock; the Who's *Tommy*; Metallica's *S & M*, with the San Francisco Symphony.

# The African Influence

The published sheet music of "Woodman, Spare That Tree" is a reliable guide to the performance of the song. By contrast, we don't know much about the music of the slaves in the United States during the early nineteenth century. We have some anecdotal evidence, mostly written by white observers who found their music baffling. But we do know that drums were largely outlawed on the southern plantations, because slave owners feared that blacks were using them as a means of communication. As a result, extensive use of percussive instruments, perhaps the most crucial element of African music making, was all but eliminated. In Cuba, Brazil, and elsewhere in Latin America, African retentions were stronger, because slaves were allowed to re-create their drums, rattles, and other instruments.

Because we have virtually no hard evidence of the music made by people of African descent during the years of slavery, we must infer the nature and extent of the musical connection. The most informative path has been to compare field recordings of African folk musicians with those of musicians of African descent living in the New World. Often there are striking correspondences or retentions: Cubans singing in an old Yoruba dialect as they drum and dance during a Santería ceremony; a Mississippi bluesman sounding uncannily like a man from Senegal. We hear each in turn.

## Santería

**Santería** is the adaptation of Yoruba religious practices by Cuban descendants of African slaves, mainly from what is now Nigeria. In the traditional religions of the Yoruba people, initiates seek to establish a personal relationship with a patron spirit, called an *orisha*. An *orisha* is a minor deity who serves as an intermediary between the person on earth and God. In this respect, an *orisha* functions much the same as a saint in the Catholic Church; for believers, both are intercessors. Because

CD 1:4

"Song for Odudua" artists unknown

## ROCK CONNECTIONS

- Prominent percussion: more specifically, drums similar to conga drums
- Complex rhythms, with constant syncopations in the percussion parts
- **Call-and-response** between leader and group
- Melody built on a pentatonic scale (although both this scale and the scale heard in "Barbara Allen" contain five notes within the octave, they are in different arrangements; for more information, visit the website: *academic. cengage.com/music/campbell*)

of the close association of *orishas* and saints, this adaptation of Yoruba religious practice in Cuba has become known as Santería, or the way of the saints. Music and dance are integral components of Santería ceremony; it is through music and dance that initiates communicate with their personal *orisha*.

In the example presented here, the leader is singing in an old-fashioned dialect of Yoruba: he is inviting Odudua, an *orisha*, to aid them. Soon, drums, then voices, enter. The music settles into a steady rhythm, with the leader singing in alternation with the group. In this recording we hear several musical features that will be assimilated into rock-era music.

CD 1:5

"Louisiana/Field Song from Senegal" excerpt; Henry Ratcliff, vocals, and artist unknown, vocals

## From Senegal to Mississippi

The next recording combines the singing of Henry Ratcliff, a Mississippi prison inmate at the time of the recording, with the singing of a fieldworker in Senegal to show a remarkable similarity in vocal style between the folk music of the two cultures. Many of these shared features find their way into rock-era music.

Taken together, the two examples demonstrate the extraordinarily faithful retention of African musical practices in the New World. The Cuban example is more richly African, because slave overseers allowed slaves to retain much more of their culture and because a significant percentage of the slaves brought from Africa during the nineteenth century came from Nigeria. Although it lacks the rhythms and percussion instruments that we associate with African music, the American example is in some ways even more remarkable. Southern slave masters vigorously suppressed such musical practices as drumming and sold slaves without regard to family or tribal bonds. In effect, African Americans have had to re-create the African aspects of their musical heritage from scratch. The next example shows how successful they have been.

## ROCK CONNECTIONS

- Vocal timbre: basic sound and inflection of the voice
- Melodic shape: most phrases begin high and finish low
- Rhythmic freedom of the delivery
- Pitch choice: reliance on pentatonic (five-note) scales
- Use of **melismas**: several notes sung to a single syllable

## Reconstructing a Heritage: African Retentions in Contemporary Rhythm and Blues

During the course of the twentieth century, African-derived musical features became increasingly prominent in popular music. The rise of Afro-pop in the

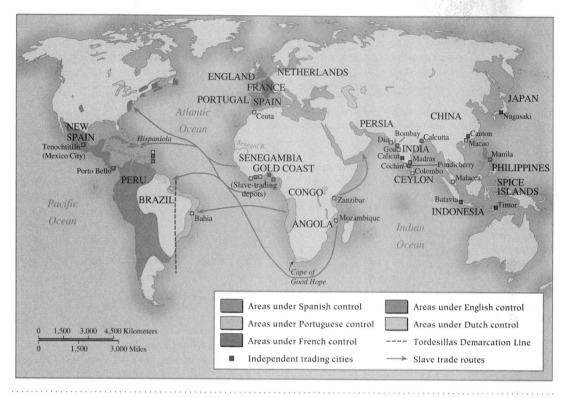

A map showing the routes that slave ships followed from Africa to the New World.

seventies strongly suggested extensive common ground; so did African musicians' enthusiasm for James Brown's music. We can sense the close affinity between African music and contemporary popular music in this short excerpt, which joins a field recording from Nigeria with the beginning of Kool & the Gang's hit song "Ladies Night."

The African excerpt comes from a Smithsonian Folkways album, *Africa, South of the Sahara*, which was released in 1957. The actual recording probably predates the release date by several years; there is no apparent evidence of external influence in the performance. Kool & the Gang was a top rhythm-and-blues (R&B) group in the seventies and early eighties. They enjoyed considerable crossover success: "Ladies Night" reached number 8 on the pop charts in 1979, and "Celebration," their biggest hit, topped both the R&B and pop charts the following year.

Some of the correspondences between the African recording and Kool & the Gang's "Ladies Night" are uncanny in their similarity:

- A dense, syncopated rhythmic texture built around what is a rock beat in "Ladies Night" and what could be a rock beat in the African recording with a more contemporary setting

CD 1:6

"Untitled" excerpt (1957 release of Smithsonian Folkways album), Yoruba chorus, vocals; and "Ladies Night" excerpt, Kool & the Gang (1979), merged recording

## ROCK CONNECTIONS

These two examples are an exceptional fit; not all African music matches up so well with contemporary popular music. Nevertheless, rock's debt to African music is extensive and unmistakable. It includes key features of rhythm, including

- An unvarying beat and/or other regular rhythm
- Several other layers of rhythmic activity, which often create syncopations and other forms of rhythmic conflict

It also inherited other elements, including

- Percussion instruments and percussive playing techniques
- Rifflike melodic ideas
- Layered textures
- Open forms

- Melismatic vocal lines—Note that the opening melisma in "Ladies Night" starts high and ends low
- A layered texture made up of voices, percussion, and pitched instruments

Perhaps the most interesting aspect of the evolution of popular music is the gradual, but relentless, infiltration of African musical values into mainstream pop. That this has occurred—despite suppression of African rhythms and instruments during slavery, then strong resistance from the culturally dominant white majority—is extraordinary. We will observe this infiltration throughout this chapter and in the remainder of the book.

# European Versus African Musical Traditions

If we compare the musical examples we have just heard, we can gain a clear picture of the deep contrast between the two musical traditions, and especially between the urban European music popular during the first part of the nineteenth century and West African music. Table 2.1 highlights some of the key differences.

In short, there is virtually no common ground between the two traditions. Indeed, accounts written by European explorers and missionaries make clear that African music is beyond their experience or comprehension. However, as the excerpt from "Ladies Night" demonstrates, all of the African musical elements eventually found their way into popular music, and especially into rock-era music. Two centuries ago,

|  | Urban European | West African Folk |
|---|---|---|
| **Harmony** | Chords | No chords |
| **Instrumentation** | Chord instrument (piano) is the only instrument | Several percussion instruments (including handclaps) are the most prominent; also a plucked instrument |
| **Melody** | Long, flowing melodies | Short phrases connected by long notes |
| **Rhythm** | Gentle beat keeping | Strong beat keeping |
| **Rhythm** | No syncopation | Lots of syncopation in drum parts |

**Table 2.1** EUROPEAN VERSUS AFRICAN MUSICAL TRADITIONS

these features would have been unknown to whites. By the middle of the nineteenth century, white audiences could *see* the influence of African American culture more than they could *hear* it. By the turn of the twentieth century, they heard the first incontrovertible evidence of African influence. We trace this gradual evolution of popular music toward rock next.

# THE EVOLUTION OF POPULAR MUSIC, FROM MINSTRELSY TO MODERN POPULAR SONG

The blending of African and European musical traditions in American popular music has been a three-stage process. In the first stage, the *inspiration* of African American music and culture reshaped the sound and style of popular music. In the second stage, the *influence* of African American music transformed popular music. In third stage— the rock era—African and European traditions were thoroughly *integrated*. We consider the first and second stages next.

## Minstrelsy, the First Synthesis

If American popular music has a birthday, it could easily be March 7, 1843. On that evening, the Virginia Minstrels, a four-man troupe of experienced blackface performers, presented the first complete minstrel show at the Masonic Temple in Boston. Blackface entertainers had been fashionable in England since the end of the eighteenth century; they and their songs were wildly popular in the United States during the 1820s and 1830s. But it wasn't until the 1840s that several banded together to create a new, truly American form of entertainment. In *America's Music*, a comprehensive history of musical life in the United States, Gilbert Chase described the Virginia

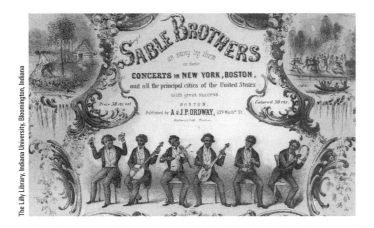

The Lilly Library, Indiana University, Bloomington, Indiana

An advertisement for a minstrel troupe, around 1850. Notice the instruments depicted in the drawing: the *endmen* are playing bones (on the left) and tambourine (on the right); there are two minstrels playing banjo, and one playing the fiddle.

Minstrels' show as a freewheeling affair, "a combination of singing, dancing, and instrumental music... interspersed with jokes, anecdotes, and repartee in pseudo-Negro dialect."

The music of the minstrel show was the first *American* popular music genre. There had been music that was "popular" in the commercial sense. Russell's songs, for example, were widely known, and they sold well. And there had been songs that were simply popular, such as "Yankee Doodle." But the minstrel show brought qualities into popular music that stamped it as distinctively American. Two stand out: an irreverent attitude that had little tolerance for the airs of genteel society; and a vibrant new sound synthesized from both African music and European traditions.

The main source of minstrel-show music was Anglo-American folk music. It infused these new popular songs with the energy and high spirits of its jigs and reels—indeed, some of the early minstrel-show songs were simply adapted from dance tunes that were in the air. These songs became lively alternatives to the slow and sentimental songs of Russell and others like him.

**CD 1:7**

"De Boatmen's Dance" excerpt, Dan Emmett; performed by Robert Winans's troupe (1985)

Blacks provided **minstrelsy** images and instruments. White and, after the Civil War, black entertainers used to perform in "blackface." That is, they applied burnt cork to their faces to simulate the appearance of blacks, or at least a black stereotype. Their depiction of black speech and movement was comparably stereotyped. Three of the core instruments of the minstrel show gave the music an African tinge. The banjo is, by most accounts, an instrument of African origin; bones and tambourine add percussion to the texture. Only the fiddle comes from white folk music.

Dan Emmett (1815–1904), a native of Ohio, was one of the original Virginia Minstrels. He is best remembered as the composer of "Dixie," which became the Confederate anthem during (and after) the Civil War. His song "De Boatmen's Dance," re-created here in Robert Winans's conscientious 1985 recording, was one of the first minstrel songs. It is a synthesis on two levels. First, it mixes folksong and folk dance: we hear the fiddle playing a reel-like tune while the singer(s) tell a story. Second, it blends elements of European classical/urban music and black music into the Anglo-American folk style: it took harmony and regular form from urban music, and, as we have noted, most of its instruments come from African American culture.

"De Boatmen's Dance" also exemplifies the most fundamental creative process in popular music: forging new styles by blending together musical elements that are seemingly incompatible, both musically and socially. This synthetic process is also part of the minstrel show's legacy to rock.

Post–Civil War popular song shows the influence of minstrelsy in two innovations: the use of dance rhythms and forms that alternate storytelling sections with a recurrent chorus.

## ROCK CONNECTIONS

The list below identifies those elements heard in "De Boatmen's Dance" that were also heard in "It's Only Rock 'n Roll" but were not present in "Woodman, Spare That Tree."

- Down-home attitude
- Verse/chorus form
- Song set to a dance rhythm
- Percussion instruments

Popular songs prior to 1840 seldom had either, while the majority of the songs written between the Civil War and the 1910s had both. In other respects, however, popular song retreated from the freshness and vitality of the early minstrel songs. Around 1900, the most popular songs of the time were **waltz songs**, such as "Take Me Out to the Ball Game," a big hit in 1908. To be sure, these songs had verse/chorus form and a dance beat, but there was little else in the style that we associate with the minstrel show, or rock. Popular music was still miles away from rock and roll.

## A New Century–and New Sounds

The next revolutionary change in popular music began around the turn of the twentieth century with a healthy infusion of African American music—ragtime, blues, and jazz—into the prevailing popular styles. By 1930, when this revolution would be complete, popular music and the industry that supported it would have changed more substantially than at any time before or since.

This transformation of popular music began in the 1890s, when the **cakewalk** (a social dance fad borrowed from the minstrel show) and the **coon song** (also borrowed from the minstrel show) introduced syncopation into popular song and dance.

### WALKING FOR DAT CAKE.

PERFORMED BY

**HARRIGAN & HART.**

WORDS BY
ED. HARRIGAN.

MUSIC BY
DAVE BRAHAM.

NEW YORK:
Published by WM. A. POND & CO., 25 Union Square, (Broadway, between 15th and 16th Sts.)

Morgan Collection

The cover of the first published cakewalk. It appeared in 1877, about 20 years before the cakewalk fad took off. The Englishmen Harrigan and Hart, along with Harrigan's father-in-law Dave Braham, were instrumental in establishing musical comedy as a new and distinct entertainment genre. The scene portrayed on the sheet music cover is a curious mixture of images: the smaller figures, presumably children, are dressed formally, but the setting is a rustic, run-down cabin.

The 1890s were probably the low point in post–Civil War race relations. Few whites seemed bothered by racial slurs such as "coon," the grotesque caricatures of blacks on sheet music covers, or *Plessy v. Ferguson*, the 1896 Supreme Court decision that legitimized the "separate but equal" practice in so many aspects of southern life.

CD 1:8

"Maple Leaf Rag" excerpt, Scott Joplin (1899)

### Ragtime and Its Impact

Ragtime, a more syncopated style, caught on around 1900, soon after the publication of Scott Joplin's "Maple Leaf Rag" (1899). Although published by

California State Library

This sheet music cover is typical of the era in its depiction of African Americans. Contrast the obviously white minstrel who has "blacked up" with the representations of African Americans on the note heads at the top of the page.

### ROCK CONNECTIONS

- Syncopations based on an African rhythmic conception
- Dance music based on a black beat
- Popular style based on a black rhythm

the obscure St. Louis publisher John Stark, the rag was an overnight sensation. Both whites and blacks bought the sheet music to play in their homes. This gave white Americans their first contact with an authentic black style. Soon, **ragtime** was in the air: not only piano rags, but also ragtime songs and dances. Any music with a hint of syncopation, or even with a bouncy beat but no syncopation at all, was considered ragtime. (Irving Berlin's 1911 hit, "Alexander's Ragtime Band," is a good example of an unsyncopated "ragtime" song.)

The piano rags of Joplin (1867/1868?–1917) and others were, in essence, black interpretations of the European march, performed on the piano. They retained the form, beat, and harmony of the march but "ragged" (that is, syncopated) the melody. This was the first prominent and documented instance of a black reinterpretation of white music; whites quickly reciprocated with an avalanche of ragtime, much of which was ragtime in name only. This pattern—black innovation followed by white response—would drive the evolution of popular music in the twentieth century.

Ragtime also provided music for the notorious **animal dances** of the 1900s and 1910s: among them, the turkey trot, chicken scratch, monkey glide, and bunny hug. These watered-down versions of black social dances became popular with many white youths during the first years of the century. As such, they were the forerunners of the social dances popularized on Dick Clark's *American Bandstand*.

Ragtime was a crucial step on the road to rock. It introduced authentic black rhythms into popular music; out of this would eventually come the rhythms of rock. Moreover, it gave black music a commercial presence. Still, even at the peak of its popularity, ragtime remained a minority music, commercially as well as racially. But it was a start. And, like rhythm and blues in the forties, it was the first harbinger of another major revolution in popular music.

## Early Commercial Blues Styles

We know virtually nothing about the earliest history of the **blues**. We find anecdotal accounts of blues and blues singing from shortly after the turn of the century; however, the first tangible evidence, mainly in the form of sheet-music versions of blues songs, doesn't appear until the early teens. Within a decade, however, the blues had made a decisive impression on popular music.

Blues entered popular music in three waves. The first blues appeared as popular songs and dance music, most notably the songs of W. C. Handy, such as "St. Louis Blues." These songs introduced some blues basics: its melodic and harmonic form, and a little of its feeling. Jazz bands followed with their own instrumental blues. Finally, in the early twenties, record companies began to record black blues singers, most notably "classic blues" singers such as Ma Rainey and Bessie Smith.

Blacks, especially women, had been singing the blues professionally since just after the turn of the century. However, "classic" blues—vocal blues songs that had blues form, style, and feeling—didn't appear on record until the twenties. In 1920, Mamie Smith recorded "Crazy Blues." Like many so-called blues songs of the era, it was not really a blues, but a vaudeville-type song sung in a bluesy style. Its success made record companies aware that there was a substantial market for black music. Other more authentic blues songs soon found their way onto disc.

CD 1:9

"Empty Bed Blues" Bessie Smith (1927)

Recordings featuring black performers and directed mainly to the black community were called **race records**. This term for recordings by blacks for blacks remained in use through 1945; it wasn't until 1949 that "rhythm and blues" caught on.

Bessie Smith (1894–1937), nicknamed the empress of the blues, was the most popular and artistically successful of the women blues singers. Her audience included both blacks and whites. Her recordings, of which "Empty Bed Blues" (1927) is a good example, put real blues feeling and style on record.

Smith's classic blues originated first-person music in American culture. When Smith sings "I woke up this morning with a awful aching head," we sense that she is talking about herself; the events in the song could have happened the night before. The lyric swings back and forth between the joys of love and the pains of love lost and love betrayed. It is this emotional range and the intimacy of the subject that suggests to us that Smith is singing from the heart, that she is using the blues to talk about *her* good and bad times—not the feelings of a character in a musical or some romantic illusion.

This was the first "real" music—music that was deeply felt, emotionally honest, and frank. It seems drawn from Smith's personal experience; her account of good-loving and two-timing partners is credible, and the expressive capacity of blues style makes the feelings more vivid and powerful than the words alone would be. The roots of rock's realness are mainly in the blues; we hear this realness first in the blues recordings from the twenties.

In addition, "Empty Bed Blues" offers a clear illustration of 12-bar blues form, in words and music. The poetic form is a rhymed couplet, with the first line repeated. Each line of text begins a phrase that lasts four bars. The harmony

## ROCK CONNECTIONS

In the song, we hear all the elements we associate with blues singing:

- Gritty vocal quality
- Speechlike rhythm in the delivery of the melody
- Inflection that heightens the normal accentuation of speech
- **Blue notes**
- Phrases that start high and finish low
- A narrow melodic range
- "Real" music: music that conveys deep feelings frankly

These qualities invest the somber lyric with the emotion of deep blues, and most of these elements found their way into rock singing, as we heard in "It's Only Rock 'n Roll."

supporting Smith's singing is conventional blues harmony. (A more detailed discussion of blues harmony appears in Chapter 4, in the discussion of Jackie Brenston's "Rocket 88.")

Smith's singing has the emotional commitment we expect from the blues. This depth of feeling is familiar to rock-era audiences. However, from the perspective of a white American, around 1925, it was pretty strong stuff. A generation that has grown up on rap may find it difficult to understand that the infusion of black musical values into music that was lily white in 1900 was a long, gradual, and often reluctant process.

## Jazz

**Jazz** took shape in New Orleans around the turn of the century. It remained a regional music until the late teens when, almost overnight, two developments made jazz the most notorious new music of the era.

The first jazz records, by the Original Dixieland Jazz Band (a group of white musicians), were released in 1917. That same year the federal government closed down Storyville, the district in New Orleans where prostitution was legal and where many jazz musicians found employment. This resulted in an exodus of jazz musicians from New Orleans over the next several years. By the early twenties, many had migrated north to Chicago, where they found work in dance halls and speakeasies, the illegal clubs that flourished during Prohibition. By the early twenties, jazz had become the most popular and influential of the new black musical genres. More than ragtime or blues, it reshaped popular music. Indeed, it lent its name to the era: the twenties were the Jazz Age, much as the sixties were the Age of Rock.

Jazz got more than employment from brothels. The word *jazz* was originally a verb—slang for having intercourse. *Rock* has a related etymology. In the twenties, *rock and roll* also referred to the sex act, as in Trixie Smith's 1922 blues recording where she sings "my man rocks me with a steady roll."

The greatest of the New Orleans jazz bands was the one led by King Oliver—first in New Orleans, then in Chicago. Their recordings demonstrate the ebullient and expressive new sounds that energized and transformed popular music. Like the ragtime pianists, jazz musicians had transformed the march into an African American music. Indeed, jazz kept more of the march sound, at least in its instrumentation: The early jazz band—cornet, clarinet, trombone, brass bass, drums, banjo, and piano—is nothing more than the nucleus of a marching band plus two chord instruments. (It is also the predecessor of the soul bands of the sixties and the funk bands of the seventies and beyond. Change clarinet to saxophone, brass bass to electric bass, and banjo to electric guitar, and you have the Blues Brothers' backup band.)

At the same time, jazz transferred the expressive feeling of classic blues singing to instruments. A passage from Oliver's 1923 recording "Dippermouth Blues" shows how close blues and jazz could be—and how they remained different. At the beginning of Oliver's solo one can almost imagine Bessie Smith moaning "My man's gone" to the opening riff. But as the solo develops, Oliver goes beyond what a vocalist would do. Blues-based instrumental improvisation begins in jazz; the extended jams of Jimi Hendrix and Eric Clapton are part of that legacy.

CD 1:10

"Dippermouth Blues" King Oliver's Creole Jazz Band (1923)

The novel elements in ragtime, blues, and jazz would become part of the sound of rock, although in different forms. However, their impact was felt most immediately in a new kind of popular music.

# A Modern Era in Popular Music

In the twenties, America got a new kind of popular song: the fox-trot. It was a song created for both singing and dancing. It had lyrics that spoke conversationally, using everyday speech. They were set to syncopated riff-based melodies, which were played by dance orchestras and jazz bands, who laid down a black beat with a backbeat. All of these features came from the new African American music: ragtime, blues, and jazz. As

## ROCK CONNECTIONS

The jazz of the twenties anticipates many of the key features of rock-era music. Among the most outstanding are these:

- Adaptation of blues sensibility (expressive inflection, speechlike rhythmic delivery, and so on) to instruments
- Formation of the rhythm section
- Instrumental improvisation
- African-derived rhythm: the four-beat swing rhythm of jazz
- Backbeat
- Use of riffs
- Extensive syncopation
- Cultivation of new sounds

they appeared in popular song, these innovations were toned down from their original black forms. Still, they completely transformed the sound of popular music in less than a generation. Sentimental ballads were out; syncopated, danceable popular song was in. We hear this up-to-date sound in a 1927 recording of "The Varsity Drag" by the George Olsen Orchestra.

This recording makes clear the extent to which black musical influence reshaped popular music. The most compelling evidence is the rhythm. It is obvious in the syncopation of the melody: each riff ends on an off-beat. However, it is also present in the underlying rhythm. This is the sound of a **fox-trot**, or **two beat**: bass note alternating with crisp backbeat, played here by the banjo. The fox-trot was the first **style beat**: a black-inspired rhythmic foundation for the music of an era. Most of the popular songs of the twenties and early thirties were fox-trots. (Chuck Berry's

CD 1:11

"The Varsity Drag" George Olsen Orchestra (1927)

"Maybellene" presents a far more aggressive version of this two-beat rhythm, which we hear in Chapter 5.)

### Tin Pan Alley

Fox-trot songs are often identified as **Tin Pan Alley** songs. The term refers to the popular songs published from the end of the nineteenth century to the dawn of the rock era.

   Fox-trot songs are the most familiar examples of this kind of song, but the term also identifies songs published before the emergence of the fox-trot. Monroe Rosenfeld, a songwriter and journalist, coined the term in 1899 as he walked down West 28th Street, where the offices of many of the top music publishers were located. Most publishers retained pianists, called "song pluggers," to play songs for customers. Before air conditioning, New Yorkers stayed cool—or at least less hot—by opening windows. The sound of several song pluggers, wafting through the open windows and playing at the same time, reminded Rosenfeld of the clank of tin pans banging together, so he named that stretch of West 28th Street "Tin Pan Alley." Over time, the term came to refer not only to the place, but also to the popular music publishing industry and the styles of songs that they published.

### ROCK CONNECTIONS

Dominant popular style with the following features:

- Riff-based melody
- Backbeat
- Full rhythm section
- A style beat: two-beat rhythm of the fox-trot
- Syncopation

Almost as significant as these new sounds was their gradual acceptance. Through the first quarter of the century, the new black-inspired sounds of popular music aroused considerable hostility: magazine and newspaper articles linked ragtime and jazz to moral depredation, and girls lost their jobs or went to jail for dancing the turkey trot. However, by the early thirties, the hectic animal dances of the 1900s had been transformed by a kind of musical alchemy into elegant fox-trots. Dancing "Cheek to Cheek" (a 1935 Irving Berlin hit song) was about as classy and elegant as Americans could get, as Fred Astaire and Ginger Rogers showed us in a series of film musicals. Most found the image quintessentially romantic; only the most hidebound traditionalists objected.

   Accompanying these musical and social changes was a technological advance. Electrical recording and amplification, both adapted from radio broadcasting, not only made for better-sounding performances but also opened the door for new kinds of singers. Vocalists no longer had to belt out their songs. Instead, **crooners** like Bing Crosby and jazz singers like Louis Armstrong could sing in a more intimate, personal manner. Indeed, these new singing styles would have been impossible without the microphone. This popular music was the first whose sound was crucially shaped by modern technology; it would not be the last.

# Taking Stock

Almost a century separates the publication of Henry Russell's "Woodman, Spare That Tree" and the release of "The Varsity Drag." A brief review of the changes in popular music during that time will help bring the evolution toward rock into perspective.

The most significant change was the very idea of popular music as a completely different family of styles. For the first time in history, a music infused with black elements was the most popular music in America. Popular music still had miles to go before it would become rock, but it is important to note how many elements of rock were already in the air by the end of the twenties.

New technology made popular music and its performance accessible in ways barely imagined by those living in the early nineteenth century. People could now sit in their living room and turn on their radio or phonograph to hear their favorite singers and bands, or they could go to the local theater to see one of those new talking films. These films brought singers and bands to the silver screen, allowing small-town audiences in Depression-ravaged America to imagine themselves in swanky supper clubs. With the advent of commercial radio broadcasting and more widespread recording, many people learned songs by ear, rather than from sheet music.

For a generation that has grown up with MTV, car sound systems, portable CD players, iPods, satellite radio, and Internet access, it may be difficult to imagine daily life without instant access to popular music. However, in the nineteenth century, if you wanted to hear popular music, you usually had to perform it yourself, and you usually learned songs from the sheet music. The transition from visual to aural dissemination of popular music—from sheet music to recordings, radio, and films—took place in the first part of the century. It was the most profound consequence of technological change in the history of popular music. Subsequent developments—television, portable radios, cassettes, CDs, massive amplification, and multitrack recording—have improved the quality of the product and made access easier, but they did not fundamentally change the way people encountered popular music. All that happened before 1930.

Popular music also led the way in improving race relations. In the twenties, even as Ku Klux Klan klaverns were forming throughout much of the nation, black performers were recording extensively and performing on Broadway stages and in cabarets, ballrooms, and speakeasies. Through this widespread exposure, whites could experience black music firsthand—on record and in live performance—and even, in some cases, perform with blacks. Bing Crosby, a good jazz singer and the first great crooner, learned how to swing from listening to Louis Armstrong sing and play. As a result, the influence of black music was far more direct than it had been throughout the nineteenth and early twentieth century. This was an important step forward in the interaction between races—an interaction crucial to the development of rock.

Both popular music and the technology that supported it would change dramatically during the early years of the rock era. Nevertheless, by 1930 popular music was well along the road to rock. It's important to keep this point in mind, because there has been a tendency in rock histories to privilege the blues as the main source of rock: to uncover rock's roots mainly in the music of Robert Johnson, Muddy Waters, and some honkers and shouters from the late forties. While there is no question of the importance of the blues to rock and roll and to rock, it does both the blues and rock an injustice to view them so monolithically. For example, there is not a lot of blues influence in the music of Buddy Holly, the Beatles, or even Motown. Moreover, both the labels *blues* and *rock* represent not one style but several. Rock-era popular music grew out of several different kinds of music: eclecticism has been its hallmark.

From our twenty-first-century perspective, it might seem that rock was inevitable and that it was simply a matter of time before the musical integration that shaped rock would take place. Both are true. That being the case, one may wonder why rock fomented a revolution. There are two reasons. First, the music that most directly shaped rock-era music—blues, country, black gospel, authentic Latin music—survived on the fringes of the popular music world, or even outside it; most listeners would not have been familiar with this music in its original form. Second, the main branch of mainstream popular music grew increasingly conservative over the ensuing twenty-five years, and especially after World War II. So, as outsider styles took on a more African cast, popular music turned back the clock toward a more European kind of song. By the fifties, the gulf between mainstream popular song and rhythm and blues and rock and roll was substantial, both culturally and musically. We present this revolutionary perspective on rock in the next chapter.

### Terms to Remember

| | | |
|---|---|---|
| ballad | minstrelsy | race records |
| pentatonic | waltz song | blue notes |
| strophic | cakewalk | jazz |
| parlor song | coon song | fox-trot (two beat) |
| Santería | ragtime | style beat |
| call-and-response | animal dance | Tin Pan Alley |
| melisma | blues | crooner |

### Applying Chapter Concepts

1. Using Table 2.1, which contrasts African and European musical traditions as a reference, select musical examples from four different twenty-first-century styles (for example, rap, techno, country, alternative) and evaluate the relative influence of urban European and African folk traditions on each example. Then order them from most European to most African, justifying the reasons for your ordering.

2. To get some sense of the evolution of popular music toward rock, try the following. Locate the "Key Elements of Rock Style" summary in Chapter 1, on page 15. Then, us as a reference, listen to the excerpts from Russell's "Woodman, Spare That Tree," Emmett's "De Boatmen's Dance," and the Olsen recording of "Varsity Drag." Focus particularly on melody (riffs, riff-based melody), rhythm (dance rhythm and tempo, backbeat, style beat, syncopation), and instrumentation (percussion instruments, rhythm section). Use a three-part rating system:

    a. No connection
    b. On the way (explain why)
    c. Close (explain connections)

# Before Rock

## A Revolutionary Perspective

By the mid-thirties, popular music had come to an evolutionary fork in the road. One path, built on blues and jazz, would eventually lead to rock. The other, the increasingly conservative pop of the same era, would become the music that rock would react against. The music that led most directly to rock and rhythm and blues existed well outside the mainstream, far from the Broadway stage, Hollywood studios, and—after 1950—network television. Much of it remained unfamiliar or unknown to the majority of white listeners. Its sudden emergence and transformation into rock and roll, then rock and soul, had much to do with making rock seem revolutionary. So did the contrast with the increasingly conservative popular music of the fifties and early sixties.

## THE ROOTS OF ROCK

Muddy Waters summed it up a long time ago: "The blues had a baby, and they called it rock and roll." Waters's famous remark highlights the strong connection between blues and rock: the deepest roots of rock are in the blues. But both rock and blues are a family of styles, rather than a single style. In its formative years, rock and roll drew on several blues styles—taking its rhythm from one, its vocal style and texture from another, and its riffs and form from a third; somewhat later, rock would gain power through a deeper infusion of blues.

## The Sounds of the Blues, 1929–1945

Changing taste, continuing evolution, and the Depression completely transformed the sound of blues, as preserved on recordings. The barely blue pop songs and the up-tempo blues of the syncopated dance orchestras went out of fashion. The Depression, which hit blacks especially hard, eroded their support of Bessie Smith and the other classic blues singers. The careers of these artists were effectively over by 1930.

In their place came a number of blues styles—some old, some new. Among the old—but new to records—was country blues. In the latter part of the twenties, Paramount Records advertised the country blues of Blind Lemon Jefferson, the first major country blues singer to record, as "real old-fashioned blues by a real old-fashioned blues singer." Among the new styles were hokum and boogie-woogie, both blues styles with a strong beat. We sample them next.

## Country Blues

From 1926, the year of Jefferson's first recording, until about 1940, **country blues**—so called because it flourished in rural settings throughout the South—created a small but viable niche in the record industry. The bluesmen who recorded in the twenties and thirties came from all over the South and Southwest. Blind Lemon Jefferson and Huddie Ledbetter ("Leadbelly") came from Texas, Blind Willie McTell from Georgia. However, the spiritual center of the blues, then and now, was the Mississippi Delta region, just south of Memphis. It was home to a host of legendary bluesmen, including Robert Johnson and Muddy Waters. We discuss Johnson here and Waters in the next chapter.

Johnson (1911–1938) is the most compelling personality in the history of the blues. His is the kind of story that fans, musicians, historians, and just about anyone else interested in popular music find irresistible: unsurpassed musical genius coupled with a "live hard, die young" life about which we know very little.

If his life is a mystery, his music is not: no one has sung and played the blues better than Johnson. He excelled at each phase: writing, singing, playing. His music communicates on an elemental level. It speaks to us directly, almost unfiltered by musical conventions; Johnson wouldn't be constrained by such "rules" as "this blues has to have 12 bars," or "it needs to have a dance beat." Its power is present in both words and music, in both singing and playing.

His lyrics can speak about life issues in vivid, to-the-point language ("If she gets unruly and thinks she don't wan' do/Take my 32-20, now, and cut her half in two" is about as direct as it gets) or powerful metaphors ("Blues coming down like hail...hellhound on my trail").

CD 1:12

"Come on in My Kitchen" Robert Johnson (1937)

Johnson's performing style intensifies the already potent message of his lyrics. The lyrics may tell us what the message is, but his delivery helps us feel the emotions behind the words—or, at times, beyond the words. "Come on in My Kitchen" is an especially good example of his style. Most of the time he sings clearly and comprehensibly, so we can savor his words. However, he occasionally slurs words, drops spoken asides, or simply hums a line, as he does at the outset. His singing intensifies speech, like so much great blues singing. Similarly, his nonverbal sounds amplify the feelings we express without words—a sigh, a moan, a laugh.

Johnson modeled his melodic playing on his singing. In the opening of "Come on in My Kitchen," the guitar line not only matches the notes of the sung melody fairly closely (a good example of blues-style **heterophony**) but also parallels the inflection of his voice. Johnson's singing and playing are different forms of a more basic expressive conception. In particular, the use of **vibrato**—slight oscillations in pitch—in his melodic guitar playing increases the intensity of the sound. The technique was widely used by electric blues guitarists and, through their example, by rock guitarists.

In his blues singing and playing, Johnson sets up the fundamental rhythmic tension of African music. His accompaniment sets up a strong beat, sometimes through a note or chord on the beat, other times via a lazy **shuffle rhythm**. (A shuffle rhythm divides each beat into two parts; the first part is twice as long as the second. The shuffle beat was widely used in postwar rhythm and blues and continues to be the most frequently used alternative to rock rhythm, as we'll hear in subsequent chapters.) He alternates between marking the beat and suspending beat keeping. Over this steady rhythm, Johnson sings and plays the melody, which moves beyond simple syncopation—a reaction against the beat—to real rhythmic freedom that owes more to the rhythms of highly inflected speech than its does to the beat.

## ROCK CONNECTIONS

- Music that's real
- Blues elements: free rhythm, intense inflection of voice and instrument, rough voice, edge to the guitar sound
- Lazy shuffle rhythm
- Static harmony: one chord

Johnson's music is self-consistent in a way that very little music—of any kind—is. In every respect, it resonates with life experience of the most elemental kind and at the same time transcends it. Perhaps it is this elemental quality that has given his music such universality, and it may explain how music from one of the least known and appreciated American subcultures—blacks in the Mississippi Delta—could reach across oceans and generations.

Eric Clapton says of Johnson's singing, "His music remains the most powerful cry that I think you can find in the human voice." Keith Richards recalls hearing Johnson for the first time, wondering "who's the other guy playing with him?" and not realizing until much later that what sounded like two guitars was actually one person—Johnson—playing two parts, often simultaneously.

By the time Johnson made his last recordings in 1937, country blues had peaked as a commercial style, at least in the eyes of the record executives. It went into decline for about two decades, resurfacing as part of the folk revival around 1960. Johnson's recordings were among those reissued on LP about this time.

Country blues, and especially Johnson's music, hit British blues-based rock bands like a heavyweight's right hand, partly because it leapfrogged a generation and partly because it defined the essence of the blues. Its impact on rock was sudden and dramatic: Johnson inspired rock musicians to get real. Other blues styles would trace a more continuous path to rock. Among them were two upbeat sounds: hokum and boogie-woogie.

## Hokum

New, more urban blues styles also began to appear on record in the late twenties. They featured singers who sounded bluesier than pop or jazz singers but not as emotionally charged as Bessie Smith or as raw as the country bluesmen. The accompaniment, typically piano and guitar, gave the music a stronger, more consistent beat than country blues, but it was not as elaborate as the jazz accompaniments of the classic blues singers.

Among these new blues styles was **hokum**, a blues novelty style that was popular between the two world wars. Hokum songs showed an entirely different side of the blues: upbeat, salacious, good-humored, light-hearted. They were miles away from the elemental power of Johnson's blues.

CD 1:13

"It's Tight Like That" Tampa Red and Georgia Tom (1928)

Perhaps the most famous hokum blues is "It's Tight Like That," a 1928 recording featuring pianist Georgia Tom (1899–1993) and guitarist Tampa Red (1904–1981), who advertised themselves as the Hokum Brothers. Its naughty good humor connects with much forties rhythm and blues, not to mention the original uncensored version of Little Richard's "Tutti Frutti." It is also an early example of a verse/refrain-type blues form. Here, the first four bars of each chorus tell a story; the last eight repeat a refrain. Verse/refrain blues forms resurfaced in the jump band rhythm and blues of Louis Jordan and others and in many of Chuck Berry's breakthrough hits. Other elements of the song—most notably the bright tempo and the humorous lyric with sexual overtones—were common in fifties rhythm and blues. Joe Turner's "Shake, Rattle and Roll," discussed in Chapter 4, has its roots in songs like "It's Tight Like That."

The song also had another strong—if less direct—link with the music of the rock era. Georgia Tom was Thomas A. Dorsey, who gave up performing on Saturday nights for preaching on Sunday mornings shortly after making this recording. We discuss his seminal role in the development of black gospel music later in the chapter.

### ROCK CONNECTIONS

- Up-tempo blues
- Good humored lyric with sexual innuendo
- Verse/chorus blues form

## Boogie-Woogie

**Boogie-woogie**, an idiomatic blues piano style, emerged in the twenties, mainly in the cities north of the Delta: Chicago, St. Louis, Memphis, and New Orleans. It took root in nightclubs, bars, and barrelhouses, where pianists needed a powerful two-fisted piano style to be heard over noisy crowds.

CD 1:14

"Pine Top's Boogie Woogie" Pine Top Smith (1928)

The recording that put boogie-woogie on the popular music map was Pine Top Smith's eponymous "Pine Top's Boogie Woogie." Smith (1904–1929) recorded the song in 1928, less than a year before his death at 24 from an accidental shooting. The song was an early crossover hit and became an even bigger hit in 1938, when Tommy Dorsey recorded it as "Boogie Woogie."

It is understandable that Dorsey would want to redo Smith's famous boogie-woogie, because it anticipates two key elements of swing style: a strong four-beat rhythm and a melody constructed by repeating a riff. The rhythm laid down by Smith's left hand is a shuffle rhythm: each beat divided into long and short parts. This rhythm is identical in proportions and feel to the shuffle rhythm in Johnson's blues, but the tempo is faster, and the rhythm more consistently present.

The other feature that would soon find its way into swing, and then into rock and roll, was the practice of creating a melody by playing a riff, then repeating it with little or no variation, either at the original pitch or at a higher or lower pitch. The choruses without the stop time typically use this approach, whether Smith is just playing or talking over his playing. We will hear a similar example in Chapter 5; Chuck Berry's "Johnny B. Goode" is a familiar example of the same melodic style.

ROCK CONNECTIONS

- Shuffle rhythm in boogie-woogie left-hand pattern brings rhythmic foundation closer to rock
- Melodies constructed from repeated riffs
- Conventional blues form and harmony

CD 1:15

"Roll 'Em, Pete" Joe Turner and Pete Johnson (1938)

In 1938, at the first of the famous "Spirituals to Swing" concerts, singer Joe Turner (1911–1985) and pianist Pete Johnson (1904–1967) presented a more up-tempo version of boogie-woogie that would eventually give rock music its most defining musical feature: its beat.

In Turner and Johnson's song, later released commercially as "Roll 'Em, Pete," Johnson used his left hand to play a repetitious figure low on the keyboard that outlines basic blues harmony. The pattern is strong and relentless, a rock-solid foundation for everything else that happens. Johnson's right hand is almost as active; he plays repeated riffs or running lines; both typically feature double notes or chords. These patterns are as idiomatic to this style of piano playing as Robert Johnson's guitar lines are idiomatic to country blues.

At this fast tempo, Johnson's left-hand pattern divides each beat into two more or less equal parts. *This up-tempo boogie pattern is the direct source of rock rhythm.* Chuck Berry would learn it from another Johnson—pianist Johnny Johnson, who played with him on his seminal recordings from the fifties—and adapt it to the guitar. "Rock and roll" became "rock" when everyone in the band understood Berry's new rhythmic conception, which he had adapted from Johnson's left-hand patterns.

ROCK CONNECTIONS

- Blues form
- Melody created by repeating a riff
- Original source of rock rhythm: boogie-woogie pattern played by Johnson's left hand

The recordings of Robert Johnson, the Hokum Brothers, and Joe Turner and Pete Johnson link directly to rock style. In their own time, however, they were little known outside the black community. In fact, Robert Johnson was hardly known outside of the Delta. Better known was the big-band swing of Count Basie, and the jump band music of Louis Jordan, which helped shape rhythm and blues in the fifties.

## Swing and Jump Bands

Through most of the twenties, jazz was strictly an instrumental music, played mainly by small groups. Some of it was danceable, but it was not strictly dance music, at least in the minds of its best musicians. In the thirties, it became a truly popular music for the first and only time in its history when it introduced a new, vibrant dance music: swing.

### Swing

**Big-band swing** broke out in 1935. It coalesced in the late twenties and early thirties, mainly in the music of urban black dance orchestras, most notably those of Duke Ellington and Fletcher Henderson, and Midwest territory bands, like Bennie Moten's,

Bettmann/Corbis

Count Basie and His Orchestra, circa 1940. Note the standard big-band instrumentation: four trumpets, three trombones, five saxophones (the photo shows just the left arm and leg of the baritone saxophonist), and rhythm section. Basie's famous rhythm section included guitarist Freddie Greene, drummer Jo Jones, bassist Walter Page, and Basie himself at the piano.

which used Kansas City as their base, then suddenly crossed over to the mainstream in mid-decade.

Benny Goodman was the first bandleader to find a large white audience. Other white bands quickly followed his example: both Dorsey brothers, Glenn Miller, and Artie Shaw. Count Basie (1904–1984), who took over Moten's band after Moten's death, Duke Ellington, and other black bandleaders also found a wider audience, although it wasn't as big as that of the white bands. For the rest of the thirties and into the forties, a line was drawn. It was swing, the energetic new dance music, versus **sweet**, the fox-trot song, now grown more melodious, less syncopated, and (usually) slower.

Swing moved popular music several steps closer to rock, as we can hear in Count Basie's 1938 recording of "Jumpin' at the Woodside." In this song, we notice several of the features already heard in the jazz and blues discussed previously. In this recording, they are present in a popular style—Basie's recording was far better known by mainstream audiences than any of the earlier recordings.

CD 1:16

"Jumpin' at the Woodside" Count Basie and His Orchestra (1938)

### ROCK CONNECTIONS

Among the swing-style elements that anticipate important features of rock style are:

- Four-beat rhythm
- A complex, syncopated rhythmic texture
- Call-and-response exchanges between horn sections
- A melody built from a repeated riff
- Simple, slowly changing harmony

The presence of these elements in a popular style lets us observe this important stage in the continuing evolution toward rock. All of the features listed previously represent a substantial infusion of African-derived elements. We can connect them to the African examples in the previous chapter:

- The dense, syncopated rhythmic texture is present in the Yoruba examples, from Africa and Cuba; here it results from the interplay between horns and rhythm section.
- Call-and-response occurs between leader and group in "Song for Odudua"; here it occurs between horn sections.
- The extensive use of repeated riffs is heard in both Yoruba examples (and all of the blues examples); here repeated riffs generate the melody.
- The African examples lack harmony; the static harmony of the first phrase of the melody is a way of adapting that principle to a harmonic context (we heard it in Robert Johnson's blues and will hear much the same approach in some post-1965 black music, beginning with the music of James Brown).

Of particular interest is the four-beat swing rhythm: timekeeping by bass and guitar on every beat. This four-beat rhythm is the intermediate step between the two-beat rhythm of the fox-trot (the first black-derived rhythm in mainstream popular music) and the eight-beat rhythm of rock. It is particularly propulsive in this example. Indeed, Rolling Stones drummer Charlie Watts has repeatedly expressed his admiration for the Basie rhythm section.

Blues and jazz would continue to recombine in new ways during the forties. Out of these cross-pollinations came several postwar rhythm-and-blues styles. In the late forties, the most popular form of rhythm and blues was the jump band music of groups like Louis Jordan's Tympany Five.

## Jump Bands

**Jump bands** stripped down big-band swing and souped it up with a stronger beat, even more riffs, and a bluesy vocal style. They kept the rhythm section of the big band but reduced the horn section from twelve or thirteen to two or three. They appropriated the shuffle rhythm of medium-tempo boogie-woogie, strengthened the backbeat, and overlaid all of this with layers of syncopated riffs.

The shuffle rhythm is an intensified form of the four-beat rhythm of swing, because the long/short rhythm makes each beat stronger. The interaction of the shuffle rhythm, which intensifies the beat, with a stronger backbeat and syncopated riffs, produced unprecedented rhythmic energy. This was real foot-tapping music.

CD 1:17

"Choo-Choo-Ch-Boogie"
Louis Jordan
(1946)

The man most responsible for putting the rhythm in rhythm and blues was Louis Jordan (1908–1975). People danced to Jordan's music; he was the most popular rhythm-and-blues artist during the forties. There were other R&B artists at the time, but none had Jordan's sustained commercial impact. From 1943 to 1950, he had a string of hits, many of which crossed over to the pop charts: his 1944 hit "G.I. Jive" topped both pop and R&B charts.

In songs such as his 1946 hit, "Choo-Choo-Ch-Boogie," we can hear the shuffle rhythm in the piano part, especially during the piano solo. Riffs now permeate the entire texture. All the melodic material—not just the tune and horn accompaniments but the solos as well—grow out of simple riffs. The simplest and most memorable is the refrain: "Choo-choo-ch-boogie." Almost every other melodic idea is either a riff or a more extended but riff-based figure that is repeated with little or no variation. (The opening phrase of the verse is a good example of an extended phrase built on a repeated pattern.)

The form of "Choo-Choo-Ch-Boogie" expands the verse/refrain blues heard in "It's Tight Like That." Here, the storytelling verse sections are set over a 12-bar blues form. But the refrain does not use blues form: it is a simple eight-bar section that lines up exactly with the last eight measures of a standard blues progression. Songs such as "Choo-Choo-Ch-Boogie" (and there were many) link Georgia Tom's hokum blues to Chuck Berry's blues-based storytelling forms, which began to appear about a decade later.

In the space of about twenty years, from about 1930 to 1950, popular music received a serious infusion of rhythm and blues. The more active rhythms of swing, the shuffle rhythms of several blues styles, and the eight-to-the-bar rhythms of fast boogie-woogie all move popular music closer to the rhythms of rock-era music. Key elements of blues style—a rough vocal style; call-and-response between voice and instrument; melodies made from repeated riffs; rich, syncopated rhythmic textures; plus blues harmony and form—become more popular and more prevalent, although they were still on the fringes of mainstream pop music. Electric blues, another influential blues style, would take hold around 1950; we encounter it in the next chapter. For now, we turn to other music that helped shape rock.

Hulton-Deutsch Collection/Corbis

Louis Jordan playing alto saxophone. A publicity photo from the fifties. Jordan was the most popular R & B performer during the forties.

# Black Gospel Music

**Black gospel** blends white Protestant hymnody, the black spiritual, and more fervent religious music with a touch of the blues. It emerged as a new style around 1930 and flourished over the next several decades.

Gospel came by its blues tinge naturally. Thomas A. Dorsey, the father of gospel music, had begun his musical career as the blues pianist Georgia Tom, whom we met performing "It's Tight Like That." Dorsey didn't turn his back on the blues when he

## ROCK CONNECTIONS

"Choo-Choo-Ch-Boogie" offers more modern versions of the following features:

- Verse/chorus blues form: verse uses 12-bar blues chord progression; refrain uses the last part of the progression
- Shuffle rhythm
- Riff-based melody

In addition, it previews the backup band for fifties R&B, sixties soul, and seventies funk in two ways:

- Basic R&B/soul/funk band instrumentation: full rhythm section plus small mixed horn section (saxes, brass)
- Saxophone is the featured solo instrument

devoted himself to gospel music. The opposite is closer to the truth. In *The Gospel Sound*, his seminal survey of black gospel music, Anthony Heilbut observed that:

> Dorsey says he didn't deliberately use blues melodies and rhythms but "You see, when a thing becomes a part of you, you don't know when it's gonna manifest itself. And it's not your business to know or my business to know."

The message of gospel was quite different from the blues. Blues comments on everyday life. Sometimes it is a lament; on other occasions, it talks about good times. Gospel, by contrast, is good news. Again in Dorsey's words:

> This music lifted people out of the muck and mire of poverty and loneliness, of being broke, and gave them some kind of hope anyway. Make it anything [other] than good news, it ceases to be gospel.

Dorsey gave the new music its name:

> In the early 1920s I coined the words "gospel songs" after listening to a group of five people one Sunday morning on the far south side of Chicago. This was the first I heard of a gospel choir. There were no gospel songs then, we called them evangelistic songs.

Although Dorsey considered C. A. Tindley the first gospel songwriter, he himself was the person most responsible for creating both the music and the environment in which it flourished. His first gospel hit "If You See My Savior, Tell Him That You Saw Me," written in 1926, was a sensation at the 1930 Baptist Jubilee convention. After it caught on, Dorsey devoted himself full time to gospel.

In its first two decades, gospel was a world unto itself. Performers traveled from stop to stop along the "Gospel Highway," churches and conventions where black believers congregated. The music remained virtually unknown outside the black community. Some white southerners knew and liked Dorsey's songs, but the rest of the country knew little or nothing about this new music.

Gospel represented both a repertoire and a way of performing. Gospel songs included traditional hymns such as "Amazing Grace" and newer compositions by Tindley, Dorsey (such as "Precious Lord"), and W. Herbert Brewster ("How I Got Over"). There were two distinct performing traditions in early gospel music: male quartets and female solo singers. Mixed gender groups were not unheard of, but they were the exception, even in the forties and fifties.

One reason that male gospel singers formed into groups while females generally sang solo is that a male quartet can present complete harmonies in low and middle registers, which eliminates the need for accompanying instruments—as we hear in the Golden Gate Jubilee Quartet's recording. By contrast, an *a cappella* female group would not have a voice in the lower ranges, so that a performance would virtually demand some kind of instrumental accompaniment.

## Male Quartets

Black male quartets were not unique to black gospel music. The Dinwiddle Colored Quartet had recorded in 1902, and the Mills Brothers, a popular pre-rock vocal group, began their career in the early thirties, about the time gospel was getting off the ground. However, gospel quartets, who often sang **a cappella**—without instrumental accompaniment—developed their own approach, which would often add rhythm-sectionlike support to the lead vocal: not only harmony, but also a strong beat.

CD 1:18

"The Golden Gate Gospel Train" Golden Gate Jubilee Quartet (1937)

We hear this in "The Golden Gate Gospel Train," a song recorded by the Golden Gate Jubilee Quartet in 1937. The recording shows how resourceful such groups could be in depicting images in sound: the group replicates the sound of the train whistle and bell, as well as the chug of the engine. More important, the singers back up the lead vocalist with an accompaniment that supplies more rhythm than harmony. Both the static harmony and the percussive vocal sounds anticipate rock-era music, especially funk and rap. Other prominent African-derived elements include a melody of mostly descending phrases constructed from a pentatonic scale, blueslike inflection, and an active rhythmic texture.

## Female Soloists

Women were the brightest stars on the gospel circuit. Female vocalists such as Mahalia Jackson, Clara Ward, and Shirley Caesar sang alone, or at least in the forefront. Their accompaniment often included both piano and Hammond organ, both popular instruments in black churches; backup vocalists were optional.

The best gospel solo singers during this era sang with rich, resonant voices. They occasionally colored their singing with blueslike

ROCK CONNECTIONS

- Percussive vocal sounds
- Pentatonic scale
- Syncopated rhythms in the accompaniment
- Riff-based melody with phrases that start high and end low
- Static harmony

inflection and, more distinctively, expressive melismas (a melisma is a group of pitches sung on a single syllable). During the thirties and forties, it was a sound distinct from every other kind of singing related to popular music: pop, jazz, country, blues, and others. Only with the migration of singers from gospel into R&B did this vocal style enter the popular mainstream.

Mahalia Jackson's 1947 recording of "Move On Up a Little Higher" showcases her rich, blues-inflected voice. Dorsey may have brought the blues into gospel, but it

CD 1:19

"Move On Up a Little Higher" Mahalia Jackson (1947)

was Mahalia Jackson (1911–1972) who adapted the feeling and style of her idol, Bessie Smith, to gospel singing. She would in turn influence Aretha Franklin, the queen of soul, who heard her sing at her father's church.

Black gospel, especially when sung by women, gave the Hammond organ an early toehold in a style related to popular music. The **Hammond organ** was invented in the thirties and immediately found a home in churches, white and black, that could not afford a pipe organ. By contrast, it was a novelty instrument in popular music and jazz: one heard it playing background music on radio soap operas and in cocktail lounges. It became a viable jazz instrument around 1960 and in rock and soul toward the end of the sixties.

## Gospel Harmony

As it developed during the thirties and forties, gospel took its harmonic language from nineteenth-century European hymns and colored it with blues harmony. This produced a distinctive harmonic vocabulary: richer than blues, country, and rhythm and blues, yet distinct from the pop music of the same era.

Implicit in this distinctive harmonic approach is a message of hope. Even in "Move On Up a Little Higher," which has relatively static harmony throughout much of the song, there is a slight harmonic digression just before the end and a quick, straightforward return to the home key. This seems to suggest that no matter how lost we are—harmonically or in life—we will find happiness when we go home—to the Lord, to heaven, and to the tonic. This kind of harmonic tension and release—drift away from the tonic chord, then return to it—is not present in conventional blues harmony in the same way; indeed, in one-chord songs like "Come on in My Kitchen," there is no possibility of harmonic tension.

The harmonic tension and release found in many gospel songs parallels the tension and release used in pre-rock pop. It has survived in rock-era music mainly in songs about love and happiness, most notably mainstream pop, by black and white acts.

Gospel's legacy to rock-era popular music is substantial. Most black popular music of the fifties and sixties—doo-wop, Motown, soul, and the like—is inconceivable without gospel. Singing—the presence of both lead and backup singers, the vocal sounds and styles of the lead singers, call-and-response between lead and choir—is its most obvious contribution. In addition, its distinctive rhythms (especially the heavy backbeat), the Hammond organ, and rich harmony also filtered into rock-era music, both black and white. It is an impressive contribution.

---

### ROCK CONNECTIONS

- Vocal style, including basic timbre and the use of melismas
- Use of Hammond organ
- Rich, blues-tinged harmony

---

# Country and Folk Music

The influence of Anglo-American folk music on rock dates back to the minstrel show, as we have noted. More recently, it shaped rock through two direct antecedents: country music and the music of the folk revival. Country music began in the early twenties, when white southerners began to perform their traditional music on radio and records. This converted a true folk music into a commercial music, although it was certainly small time at first. The impetus for the folk revival (usually called "folk music") came about a decade later, when John and Alan Lomax began recording white and black folk performers throughout the South.

The wellspring for both was the folk music of the British Isles. Both country and folk wrestled with the ever-present creative tension between tradition and innovation. In country music, this tension was mainly in the music; for folk music it was in the words. Innovation in country music meant absorption of outside musical influences: pop, jazz, blues, swing. Tradition meant holding onto country music's defining qualities. Innovation in folk music meant writing about what happened yesterday, while tradition was rediscovery and presentation of the past. As we will hear, country brought the music of the Anglo-American folk tradition into the twentieth century; folk music brought the words into contemporary society.

There was also an insider/outsider difference. **Country music** was created by southerners. Those most responsible for the folk revival came from outside the South. Even Woody Guthrie came from the Southwest. Country moved away from its musical roots; the first folk revivalists tried to preserve them. They would cross paths at the beginning of the rock era: the folk revival took off just as rockabilly began to fade away.

# Country Music

The transformation of Anglo-American folk music into country music began in Atlanta: a local radio station broadcast the first country music performance in 1922, and Ralph Peer recorded Fiddlin' John Carson there the following year. The music that they played was not new. The songs and dance music of the first country musicians had been passed down through several generations, as had the singing and playing styles.

What was new was the idea that **old-time music** (as it was called) was commercially viable. Both the record companies and the newly established radio stations found an audience for this music. It was small by pop standards, but the audience was enthusiastic and supportive enough to justify opening up this new market.

The success of country music on records and radio had three far-reaching consequences. It created a nucleus of professional—or at least semi-professional—musicians. (Most didn't give up their day jobs, at least early on.) It improved the access of country musicians to one another: a guitarist in Oklahoma could now learn Maybelle Carter's innovative guitar style from her recordings. It also enlarged country musicians' contact with other kinds of music. This outside contact gave country music its evolutionary momentum.

## Country Music's First Stars

Jimmie Rodgers and the Carter Family, the two biggest and most influential acts in early country music, began their recording careers in the same place and on the same day: Bristol, Tennessee, on August 4, 1927. Talent scout Ralph Peer recorded them on one of his many forays through the southern Appalachians. It was one of the most remarkable coincidences in the history of popular music. The Carter Family and Jimmie Rodgers represented two enduring, and conflicting, trends in country music.

CD 1:20

"Wildwood Flower" the Carter Family (1928)

The Carters preserved its heritage, in both repertoire and style. By contrast, Rodgers pointed the way to the future with his assimilation of blues, jazz, and pop influences.

The Carters' best-selling record was "Wildwood Flower." A popular song published in the northern United States in the 1860s, "Wildwood Flower" had been familiar in oral tradition throughout the South for several generations. Recorded in 1928, it sold over a million copies, one of a very few early country recordings to do so.

Its three most traditional features are the song itself, Maybelle's singing, and the absence of contemporary influences. The singing of Maybelle (1909–1978)—nasal, unadorned, with no vibrato or other vocal devices, and straightforward in its presentation of the melody—is a sound that we associate exclusively with country music. Moreover, there are no drums, horns, riffs, or other evidence of pop or jazz influence. Nor is there fiddle—the most characteristic country instrument—or banjo. Instead, Maybelle accompanies herself using her trademark **thumb-brush** style: she plays the melody on the lower strings and interpolates chords using the upper strings. This guitar style would be copied by dozens of other folk and country players.

By contrast, Rodgers (1897–1933) embraced the musical world around him. He learned the blues from blacks and performed with jazz musicians. His willingness to open his music to the musical world outside country music—white and black—inspired others to follow suit. The assimilation of elements from noncountry styles would be the main force for change in country music.

## ROCK CONNECTIONS

- Guitar style: to folk revival, folk rock, and singer-songwriters

CD 1:21

"Blue Yodel No. 11" Jimmie Rodgers (1929)

"Blue Yodel No. 11" (1929), one of thirteen "blue yodels" that Rodgers recorded, is a blues, pure and simple—in its lyrics, melodic style, harmony, and form. More significantly, it is a blues in style. Rodgers sounds natural and very much at ease singing a blues. He captured essential elements of the blues singing style: a rhythmically free and unstilted delivery of the text; a highly inflected phrasing (listen to the extra emphasis on the word *presents* in the third phrase of the first section); and a vocal style more expressive than pretty.

In the thirties and early forties, the boldest new country sound was **western swing**, a style popularized by Bob Wills and his Texas Playboys. Wills fleshed out the sound of country music with the sound of a full rhythm section (much to the chagrin of the tastemakers at the Grand Ole Opry, who wouldn't let him perform with his drummer visible) and was instrumental in adding the sound of the electric steel guitar. Wills's innovations led directly to **honky tonk**, the new country sound of the forties and fifties.

## ROCK CONNECTIONS

- First "white man with a Negro feel": a quarter century before Elvis
- Enormous influence opens up country music to outside influences, especially black: road to rockabilly began here

## Honky Tonk

A *honky-tonk* is a place where working-class people go to drink and dance. (There were honky-tonks for whites and separate honky-tonks for blacks.) Following the repeal of

Underwood & Underwood/Corbis

Hank Williams Sr. performing with his band at a square dance. Notice the steel guitar player in the back left corner and the fiddle player, partly shown on the right. Steel guitar and fiddle are the new and old "traditional" instruments in country music.

Prohibition in 1933, honky-tonks sprang up all over the South and Southwest and in northern cities where southern whites had moved. Honky-tonks were usually rough places, with loud, often unruly crowds. In order to be heard above the crowd, country musicians working in such places soon learned to fill out the sound of their band by adding drums and replacing acoustic guitars and Dobros (an acoustic steel guitarlike instrument) with electric guitars and pedal steel guitars.

They wrote songs that related to the lives of their audience. The most common were songs about woman–man troubles, told from varying points of view. Other popular themes included the trials of living in a new place (usually in or near a city) and homesickness, drinking, and traveling, especially trucking.

"Your Cheatin' Heart," a 1952 recording by Hank Williams Sr. (1923–1953), epitomizes honky-tonk style, as well as the best country music has to offer. The words to "Your Cheatin' Heart" say what they have to say in plain, no-frills language. Williams's singing, which he called "moanin' the blues," invests the words with an intense emotion that brings them to life and makes them meaningful: the effect is almost cinematic.

The instrumental accompaniment features fiddle and steel guitar, country's old and new instrumental trademarks. Features

"Your Cheatin' Heart" Hank Williams Sr. (1952)

## ROCK CONNECTIONS

- Down-to-earth lyric
- Country/pop/blues fusion: prelude to rockabilly
- Moanin' the blues: Williams's intensely expressive vocal style

not associated with traditional country music include a full rhythm section (guitar, string bass, and drums) to give rhythmic and harmonic support. This particular blend of country and pop instruments helped define the sound of honky tonk. So did the beat: a honky-tonk beat is a fox-trot beat with a crisp, emphatic backbeat.

Honky tonk and western swing brought country music to the verge of rock and roll. Bill Haley, Elvis, and the other rockabilly artists would take the next step. They would follow much the same strategy as their progressive country predecessors: rockabilly would be, in Carl Perkins's words, "blues with a country beat."

While progressive country evolved from old-time music into honky tonk and rockabilly, country traditionalists like the Carter Family retreated to a niche within the country music world. The Carters' songs would resurface during the folk revival in cover versions by Joan Baez and others; Maybelle's guitar style would turn up again much sooner, in the music of Woody Guthrie.

## Folk Music

The folk revival that got underway in the thirties had two main agendas. One was the preservation of Anglo-American folk music, both in print and on record. The other was the use of a simple folk style to talk about the life of everyday people, to further a politically progressive populism. Five men gave the contemporary folk tradition its sound and its message: John and Alan Lomax, Leadbelly, Woody Guthrie, and Pete Seeger. Beginning in 1933, under the auspices of the Library of Congress, John Lomax and his son Alan recorded white folk musicians in the South (as well as many others, both white and black, throughout the United States). In addition, they transcribed many of the songs, which they published in a series of songbooks. The Lomaxes discovered Leadbelly (Huddie Ledbetter) in a Louisiana prison, helped get him a pardon, recorded him extensively, and promoted his career.

CD 1:22

"Do-Re-Mi"
Woody Guthrie
(1937)

Woody Guthrie (1912–1967) brought **folk music** into the twentieth century. In the course of his career, he wrote or adapted over a thousand songs. Some were new songs; others simply fitted old songs with new lyrics, in true folk tradition. Nearly all were influenced by his travels, the people he met, the situations he encountered. There were storytelling ballads and incisive commentaries on hard times, political injustices, and social inequities. They covered a wide range of topics, from the hardships of the Great Depression (many of which romanticized the role of the labor union) to simple children's songs. Although Guthrie was constantly on the move, his branch of folk music found a home in New York's Greenwich Village and a following among the political left.

In "Do-Re-Mi," a song Guthrie wrote in 1937, we can hear what drew Lomax, Seeger, and working-class folk to his music. We don't listen to Guthrie's songs for the beauty of his singing; what Robert Christgau calls his "vocal deadpan" was the opposite of the crooning of Bing Crosby, whom Guthrie openly despised. And we don't listen for the sophistication of the accompaniment; Guthrie was fond of saying that three chords were one too many. We listen for the words.

With no sugarcoating, Guthrie tells the tough-times story of the desperate people who migrated west in search of a decent life. He gets his point across with a wry humor that, if anything, intensifies the grim circumstances that he describes. This is a funny song that isn't funny at all.

Guthrie's music is centuries old and brand-new at the same time. In his music are echoes of British broadside ballads, a tradition that dates back to the sixteenth century. (A **broadside** is a topical text sung to a well-known tune. Broadsides were, in effect, urban folk music with printed words.) In fact, Guthrie occasionally fashioned new words to familiar songs, in true

ROCK CONNECTIONS

- Song as social commentary
- Voice and acoustic guitar: link from Carter Family to folk revival

broadside and folk tradition. But in the musical context of the thirties—the world of silver screen pop, swinging big-band jazz, singing cowboys, and crooners—Guthrie's songs stood apart. From the late thirties through the end of World War II, there was no sharper musical commentator on the inequities of life in America, no more persistent musical voice for social justice, no more prolific musical advocate for the cause of the working class than Guthrie.

Guthrie wrote and delivered his songs in a folk style, but the songs were new, not old. In so doing, he made folk music a commercial music—even if much of the time his songs had an anti-commercial message. He also made folk a living music. Others, most notably the Weavers, would follow in his footsteps. However, it remained for Bob Dylan to fully realize Guthrie's legacy.

Beginning in 1939, Pete Seeger worked closely with both the Lomaxes and Guthrie and provided the strongest link to the folk revivals after World War II. In 1948, he helped found the Weavers, a traditional-style folksinging group. They enjoyed tremendous commercial success as the fifties began, but their politics cut their career short. Senator Joseph McCarthy's House Un-American Activities Committee brought them in for questioning in 1955. Their subsequent blacklisting turned them into pariahs within the music industry, although Seeger would return as a major figure in the civil rights movement.

The use of music as a vehicle for social commentary and protest was the most important contribution of this urban folk movement to rock. Guthrie's music inspired the new voices of the sixties folk revival, most notably Bob Dylan, who in turn raised rock's consciousness.

## Afro-Cuban Music

The Rolling Stones' "Honky Tonk Women" begins with a **habanera rhythm** played on a cowbell. The habanera was a Cuban dance that eventually morphed into the tango in Argentina and lent its rhythm to the cakewalk. The cowbell is a **found instrument**—that is, a nonmusical object that is converted into a musical instrument; it is most strongly associated with Afro-Cuban music. Rhythms and percussion instruments are the two most important contributions of Afro-Cuban music to rock; both often go unacknowledged. Indeed, the familiarity of "Honky Tonk Women" and its country theme may cause us to overlook these clear, if not obvious, Afro-Cuban influences. Afro-Cuban music was the "silent partner" in the rock revolution. Its influence is often present, sometimes directly, as in the Stones' song, but more often indirectly and rarely acknowledged.

Afro-Cuban musical groups typically include a battery of percussion instruments: conga drums, timbales, bongos, maracas, claves, and cowbell. Of these, the most widely used outside of Afro-Cuban music are the **conga drums**. They have been especially popular in black music: for example, they were part of the Motown sound almost from the beginning. They were used to thicken the rhythmic texture or provide a gentler alternative to the drum set. Other instruments appear less frequently. And when they do, they are often woven discreetly into the fabric of the song. Still, there are conspicuous examples on occasion: Bo Diddley's use of maracas is a noteworthy early instance of this practice.

## Mambo

During the first half of the twentieth century, Latin music infiltrated popular music in America in three waves. The first was the tango, an Argentine dance that was enormously popular during the 1910s. In 1930, Don Azpiazú, a white Cuban bandleader, had a surprise hit with a song entitled "El Manisero" ("The Peanut Vendor"). The song introduced Afro-Cuban rhythm and instruments to American audiences and sparked a new dance craze, the rumba, prompting many Tin Pan Alley songwriters to write Latin songs.

The final pre-rock Afro-Cuban dance fad was the **mambo**. Unlike earlier Latin dance fads, the mambo was homegrown, not imported; it was developed during the early forties in uptown New York. Latin musicians, some of whom had worked in the swing bands, cross-bred big-band swing with Latin rhythms and percussion instruments and came up with a hot new dance music. By the late forties, non-Latins were filling up ballrooms. The mambo craze peaked in the fifties. By the end of the decade, the much simpler cha-cha-chá had become the Latin dance of choice.

Among the top Afro-Cuban bandleaders was Machito (Frank Grillo [1912–1984], an American-born Cuban singer). We hear the sound of mambo in an excerpt from "Carambola," a recording from around 1950 of Machito and his Afro-Cuban orchestra.

The most characteristic feature of Afro-Cuban rhythm is the **clave pattern**. Its relation to the beat and to the pervasive faster rhythms is shown in Figure 3.1.

Clave is to Afro-Cuban rhythm what the backbeat is to American dance rhythms: its most elemental feature and main point of reference. Playing in clave is to Afro-Cuban music what rocking is to rock or swinging is to swing. In stylistically authentic Cuban music, other rhythms conform to clave or react against it in a specific way. In "Carambola" we can most easily hear the way other rhythms line up with the clave rhythm in the section about 2 minutes into the song: background vocalists sing a rifflike figure that is in clave.

The asymmetrical nature of clave rhythm highlights the fundamental difference between Afro-Cuban rhythm and the black rhythms heard in jazz, blues, and popular song. In American black rhythms the beat is typically marked, such as by a walking bass or a strummed guitar. In Afro-Cuban music, the attention is on the faster rhythms and the clave pattern; the beat is felt but not kept by any particular instrument. This approach is much closer to the African example heard in Chapter 2 (the untitled Yoruba chorus that was merged with Kool & the Gang's "Ladies Night") than any of the American examples.

American musicians tended to hear Afro-Cuban rhythm in terms of their own experience. The clave rhythm popped up occasionally in rhythm and blues songs; the Bo Diddley beat almost certainly has roots in Afro-Cuban music, although the path

CD 1:23

"Carambola"
Machito
(ca. 1950)

Frank Driggs Collection

Machito, fronting his big band. The instrumentation is typical: a swing-style big band (five saxophones, three trumpets, two trombones, plus a rhythm section of piano, bass, and drums) augmented by a conga player (far left) and a bongo player (left center, in the back). In addition, Machito is playing maracas.

from Havana to Mississippi—probably via New Orleans—is not clear. More common were Americanized versions of Afro-Cuban rhythms. These often ignored the clave pattern but kept the faster overlay rhythm and something of its rhythmic density, which mapped onto rock rhythm perfectly. By the late fifties, Latin rhythms would be an occasional alternative to rock rhythm, as in the Champs' "Tequila" (1958) and Ray Charles's "What'd I Say" (1959).

| (Beat) | 1 | | | 2 | | | 3 | | | 4 | | | 1 | | | 2 | | | 3 | | | 4 | | |
|---|---|---|---|---|---|---|---|---|---|---|---|---|---|---|---|---|---|---|---|---|---|---|---|---|
| **Fast regular rhythm** | x | x | x | x | x | x | x | x | x | x | x | x | x | x | x | x |
| **Clave rhythm** | X | | | X | | | X | | | | X | | X | | | | | |

**Figure 3.1**  A representation of clave rhythm. The top line shows two four-beat measures, with each beat numbered. The middle line shows the division of each beat into two equal parts. The bottom line shows the clave rhythm. Notice that the pattern is asymmetrical $(3 + 3 + 4 + 2 + 4)$, which is one reason American musicians have had some trouble assimilating it. Experience the clave pattern by tapping the fast regular rhythm with your right hand and the clave pattern with your left. If you find this challenging, try counting out the rhythm (1-2-3-1-2-3-1-2-3-4-1-2-1-2-3-4-) as you tap.

ROCK CONNECTIONS

- Dense rhythmic texture, with lots of rhythmic conflict
- Extensive use of percussion instruments
- Clave rhythm leads to "Bo Diddley beat"
- Call-and-response
- Freer approach to timekeeping

# The Roots of Rock Versus Mainstream Pop

Almost all of this music—the several blues styles discussed previously, plus country, folk, black gospel, and Afro-Cuban music—existed on the fringes of the popular music world. Swing was a popular music, but most of it was much tamer than the Basie example we heard earlier. The energy and immediacy projected through this music was largely foreign to mainstream pop. So was the down-to-earth dimension of blues, country, and folk. We bring into focus the contrast between these several styles that led to rock and the most popular music of the post–World War II era in the remainder of the chapter.

## THE POP MUSIC ESTABLISHMENT

The conventional wisdom about winners writing history certainly seems to apply to popular music. Ask the proverbial person on the street to name the top acts in popular music during the fifties, and you're likely to get a list that reads like the maiden class of inductees into the Rock and Roll Hall of Fame: Chuck Berry, Ray Charles, Sam Cooke, Fats Domino, the Everly Brothers, Buddy Holly, Jerry Lee Lewis, Elvis Presley, Little Richard. Mention Perry Como, Frankie Laine, Patti Page, or Eddie Fisher, and you may elicit only a quizzical glance or a fleeting memory—Perry Como, didn't he have a TV show? Eddie Fisher, wasn't he married to Liz Taylor?

The reality was quite different. Of these first-generation rock stars, only Elvis topped the singles charts on a regular basis. Albums were largely the province of classical music, musical theater, jazz, and what we now call "easy listening." For much of the fifties, radio stations that programmed the new music were few and far between; Buddy Holly and his friends drove around Lubbock late at night to find a spot where they could pick up a clear-channel radio station that played rhythm and blues. Television occasionally featured rock-and-roll acts. Carl Perkins appeared on Perry Como's popular television show, but Como—a smooth-voiced pop singer–turned–television personality—*had* the show; audiences tuned him in every week. Even among teenagers, enthusiasm for real rock and roll was far from unanimous. Pat Boone—a pop singer in every respect except age (he was a year older than Elvis) and occasionally material (for instance, his disastrous cover of Little Richard's "Tutti Frutti," which still reached number 12)—was more successful than any rock-and-roll act besides Elvis. Most rhythm-and-blues artists were even less known; only Fats Domino charted on a regular basis.

Early on, rock and roll aroused hostile reactions from the majority of Americans: a sizeable percentage of teens, and most of their parents and grandparents. (Many of the older generations had apparently forgotten the hostility that the new music of their youth had aroused.) To appease censors, Elvis was shown only from the waist up on his last appearance on *The Ed Sullivan Show* in 1956. By the end of the decade, the federal government had gotten into the roll-over-rock-and-roll act; the moral degradation caused by rock and roll was an unspoken subtext to the payola hearings at the end of the decade. It was in this climate that rock and roll and rhythm and blues emerged and eventually fomented a musical revolution. We briefly describe American society in the fifties, major developments in media-related entertainment, and sample the pop music that dominated musical life in the early years of the rock era.

## American Values in the Fifties

Among the dominant values in American life during the fifties were a belief in unending progress and prosperity and a political conservatism that in mid-decade mutated into paranoia. A postwar boom gave economic relief to a generation that had suffered through the Great Depression and the deprivations of the war effort. With this economic growth came an abiding faith that science and technology had all the answers, whether it was developing weapons to destroy the world (the nuclear arms race), improving on nature (the use of baby formula instead of mother's milk), or building better automobiles (cars got larger and more ostentatious every year) and highways (Congress passed the Interstate Highway Act in 1956). Hand in hand with material progress came materialism. Conspicuous consumption—a brand-new tract house in the suburbs, a new car with big tailfins, or the latest model television set—was the fifties counterpart to the "greed is good" mentality of the eighties.

At the same time, war was very much part of social consciousness: the vivid memory of World War II, the most terrible war in history; the frustration of the Korean War; and the Cold War, in which both American and Soviet citizens lived with the threat of nuclear annihilation. The specter of war was an oppressive presence throughout the fifties; families stocked bomb shelters in anticipation of nuclear attacks. It created a politically conservative climate that too often spilled over into paranoia. The most notorious expression of this was the Communist witch hunt led by Wisconsin Senator Joseph McCarthy, which ruined numerous lives and careers before McCarthy's censure in 1954.

Television, the new entertainment medium of the fifties, brought all of this home in a powerful new way. During the fifties, television went from a novelty to a fixture in the American home. In 1949, less than a million households owned a TV; four years later, over 20 million had a set. By 1960, it was almost as common in American homes as a refrigerator or stove.

Television quickly became the dominant mass entertainment. Variety shows, news, situation comedies, mysteries, westerns, children's shows, cartoons, soap operas, talk shows, sports, and more: all became part of television programming. In most of the country, choice was limited mainly to the three networks—NBC, CBS, and ABC—throughout the fifties and early sixties. For the most part, programming catered to majority taste; controversial topics and personalities typically got a wide berth. So did popular music: on television, in films, and on radio and records.

## Mainstream Popular Music

We understand the evolution of popular music toward rock as the gradual assimilation of African elements into the prevailing popular style, which began as music brought from Europe (recall that Henry Russell was an Englishman who claimed to have studied in Italy). In Chapter 2 we traced this evolution from the middle of the nineteenth century through the twenties and noted that it was not a smooth, gradual process. Rather, it was more akin to two steps forward and one back: in the latter part of the nineteenth century, popular song lost the spunk of the mid-century minstrel show song but kept a dance rhythm in the accompaniment.

The thirties saw not only the continuing evolution of popular music in swing but also the beginning of a devolutionary trend: a reversal of the assimilation of African elements that typified the music of the twenties. In the latter part of the thirties, this branch of popular song and its performance, called "sweet" by commentators, placed more emphasis on melody and less on rhythm. Melodies flowed more, with less syncopation. Tempos slowed, and bands supported these tuneful melodies with a straightforward fox-trot beat, rather than the more active four-beat rhythm of swing. Vocal and instrumental styles acquired a silky smooth patina, in strong contrast to the more jazz- and blues-oriented sounds of swing bands. For the bands of the time, it was usually swing versus sweet: most were better at one style than the other, although a few, such as the bands led by Glenn Miller and Tommy Dorsey, moved easily between the two styles.

CD 1:24

"Heart and Soul" Eddy Duchin (1938)

## ROCK OPPOSITIONS

- Light two-beat rhythm and less syncopation than in "Varsity Drag"
- More moderate tempo
- More smoothly flowing melody
- Rhythm section plays gently in the background; melody stands out
- Sweet-voiced singing

We can hear this opposition by comparing Count Basie's "Jumpin' at the Woodside" with Eddy Duchin's 1938 recording of Hoagy Carmichael's evergreen "Heart and Soul." Duchin, a pianist, led one of the most popular sweet bands of the thirties. His band's performance of "Heart and Soul" typifies the sweet style: a lilting fox-trot at a moderate tempo, with Carmichael's melody, which forms a graceful arch, sung and played elegantly. The rhythm still has a bounce, and there is a hint of swing occasionally. But in terms of drive and energy, it pales in comparison to the Basie recording.

Although sweet music would eventually morph into the music that rock and roll would rebel against, it also has a strong rock connection. Slow doo-wop was essentially a black take on sweet music: there are dozens of doo-wop and black pop songs that recycle the famous "Heart and Soul" chord progression, including "Sh-Boom," "Earth Angel," and Sam Cooke's "You Send Me." So do seminal rock ballads like the Everly Brothers' "All I Have to Do Is Dream."

More generally, the form used in songs like "Heart and Soul" (and "Varsity Drag") carried over into pop-oriented R&B and early rock and roll. This popular pop-song form contains four phrases: the first, second, and fourth are identical or at least similar; the third is contrasting. This form is often identified as AABA form (A = the first phrase and its repetition; B is the contrasting third phrase).

During the swing era, swing and sweet competed more or less equally for public favor: Hit Parade charts show a fairly balanced ratio of swing and sweet songs and bands. After World War II, however, the popular music mainstream continued the devolutionary trend: up-tempo swing virtually disappeared, crooners flourished, and rhythmic enervation replaced rhythmic excitement.

By the fifties, the dominant popular music was as conservative musically as its audience was politically. In general, the most effective and enduring expression of this conservative outlook came in the musical—on stage and in films. The postwar years were the golden age of the American musical. *Oklahoma!* (1943), the first collaboration by Richard Rodgers (1902–1979) and Oscar Hammerstein (1895–1960), marked the beginning of this golden age; *The Sound of Music* (1959), their last collaboration, marked the beginning of the end. Film musicals, whether original or adapted from stage musicals, also flourished. Both typically traded the energy and excitement of swing-era music for symphonic sophistication and dramatic substance. Songs like "Do-Re-Mi," "Edelweiss," "Climb Ev'ry Mountain," and "The Sound of Music," all from this beloved and supremely popular musical, are engagingly melodious, but they retreat to a musical world that has almost no connection with the new popular music of the twenties, thirties, and forties.

In the case of a musical such as *The Sound of Music*, it could be argued that current-sounding music would have been dramatically inappropriate. The argument would have more cogency if the musical had not been such a conservative musical genre. (Leonard Bernstein's extensive use of jazz, the rebel music for adults in the fifties, to characterize the Jets, the white gang, in *West Side Story*, is a noteworthy exception to this trend.) No such excuse is available for pop songs like the hit "Hot Diggity," by Perry Como (1912–2001), which bumped Elvis's "Heartbreak Hotel" from the top of the charts in 1956. The song is the musical counterpart of Wonder Bread; both were bland fare and staples in the middle-class American home.

Como's hit was not an isolated instance, either for him or for popular music. Other pop singers delivered comparably tuneful and innocuous songs. Among the number 1 hits of the late fifties were Pat Boone's sentimental "April Love" and the McGuire Sisters' pseudo-country "Sugartime." Even good jazz-influenced singers like Frank Sinatra, Nat Cole, and Ella Fitzgerald slowed down tempos and swung more lightly.

These two short excerpts—one from a musical, the other a number 1 pop hit—show the extent to which mainstream popular musicians had turned their back on recent history. There is almost nothing in either excerpt that shows the influence of the new popular music of the twenties, not to mention anything since. There is no syncopation in the rhythm; what rhythmic energy there is comes from the brisk tempos. The instrumentation connects more to a classical symphony orchestra than a jazz band, and the singing and playing styles have no connection with the modern styles of the twenties and thirties. The focus is squarely on the melodies. It is as if the creators of this music whitewashed the last thirty years of progressive popular music and tried to turn back the clock to a time before ragtime, blues, jazz, and syncopated popular song. This is popular music *devolution*, twenty-five years before Devo.

Although musicals like Rodgers and Hammerstein's *Sound of Music* and songs like "Hot Diggity" enjoyed the support of the pop music establishment and the dominant media, the threat of rock and roll and rhythm and blues was real enough that they took

"Do-Re-Mi" excerpt from Rodgers and Hammerstein's The Sound of Music (1959), vocals by Mary Martin

"Hot Diggity" excerpt, Perry Como (1956)

## ROCK OPPOSITIONS

- Even more emphasis on flowing melody
- No influence of blues or jazz in singing or playing
- Rhythmically bland; no syncopation
- Instrumentation favors symphony orchestra, not swing band or similar ensemble
- Insipid lyrics in popular song; lightweight if clever lyrics in "Do-Re-Mi"

action. To protect their turf from the onslaught of rock and roll—and other outsider music—the pop music establishment mounted a two-pronged attack. On one front, they attacked rock and roll and the small-time industry that nurtured it. They denigrated rock and roll as debased music, suitable only for primitives. They attacked BMI, the agency that licensed most of the music. And they went after the disc jockeys who promoted rock and roll.

At the same time, they offered teen audiences bleached alternatives to rock and roll. One was cover versions of rhythm and blues hits by pop-oriented white performers: Pat Boone became Elvis's G-rated counterpart. Another was "titular" rock and roll: songs, such as Georgia Gibbs's "Rock Right," that were rock and roll in name only. The artists were pop performers who had no understanding of the new style but were simply trying to climb on the bandwagon. By the end of the decade, another strategy was in place: recruit teen singers who more or less looked the part—Fabian is a good example—but sang in a pop style palatable to parents and teenagers without taste. However, all were rearguard actions, and none of them worked. After the British invasion, popular music belonged to a new generation.

In the years after World War II, the popular music establishment turned back the clock musically. While rhythm and blues became bluesier and more rhythmic, pop retreated from the rhythmic vitality found in the popular music of the swing era and before. The contrast between old-fashioned pop and the new music of the fifties made rock and roll seem revolutionary. We survey the start of the rock revolution in the next two chapters.

......................................................................................................

### Terms to Remember

| | | |
|---|---|---|
| country blues | jump band | honky tonk |
| heterophony | black gospel | folk music |
| vibrato | a cappella | broadside |
| shuffle rhythm | Hammond organ | habanera rhythm |
| hokum | country music (old-time music) | found instrument |
| boogie-woogie | | conga drums |
| big-band swing | thumb brush | mambo |
| sweet | western swing | clave pattern |

......................................................................................................

### Applying Chapter Concepts

1. The lyrics of Woody Guthrie's "Do-Re-Mi" and "Do-Re-Mi" from *The Sound of Music* make clear that the two songs send quite different messages. Explore how the music also

sends different messages by comparing the two performances, focusing on the following features:

   a. Vocal quality and style
   b. Instrumentation
   c. Melody (especially the pattern of rise and fall and the length of phrases)
   d. Rhythm (focusing on the underlying rhythm and presence or absence of syncopation)

Then consider in what ways they are most similar and in what ways they are most different. In your opinion, which of the features have the greatest impact on the musical message of each song?

2. The blues songs in this chapter include those by Robert Johnson, the Hokum Brothers, Pine Top Smith, Joe Turner and Pete Johnson, Louis Jordan, and Jimmie Rodgers. To deepen your sense of the blues as a family of styles capable of expressing a wide range of moods, compare the blues songs heard in this chapter, focusing on these features:

   a. Vocal style
   b. Instrumentation
   c. Tempo
   d. Strength of the beat

Then arrange them along a continuum with "blues" at one end and "rhythm" at the other, according to the extent to which blues feeling and rhythmic energy are present in the song.

3. Locate two recordings by Glenn Miller: one should exemplify swing, the other sweet. Then compare these features of the two recordings:

   a. Tempo
   b. Style beat
   c. Amount of syncopation
   d. Melodic style (how does the melody develop?)
   e. Loudness
   f. Performing style (smooth or more rough-edged?)

Then consider how your comparison matches up with the Basie and Duchin recordings.

# THREE

# Becoming Rock:
# The Rock Era, 1951–1964

■ In discussions of rock music, "rock and roll" has two distinct, if related, musical usages. One is an informal way of identifying music that affirms rock's core musical values: the Rolling Stones' "It's Only Rock 'n Roll (But I Like It)" is an archetypical example. This use of the term *rock and roll* surfaced in the late sixties, around the time the Stones began referring to themselves as "the World's Greatest Rock and Roll Band." In its other more widely known usage, *rock and roll* (or *rock 'n' roll*) refers to the new black-influenced music of the fifties that teens embraced so enthusiastically.

The two uses of the term are the opposite of each other with respect to style over time. As used by the Stones and other like-minded bands, "rock and roll" refers to a consistent sound over an open-ended period of time: it identifies much the same kind of music at the beginning of the twenty-first century as it did in 1974, when the Rolling Stones released their hit song. By contrast, in its original musical usage, "rock and roll" refers to music from a delimited time period—the fifties—that was constantly evolving: the sound of the music called "rock and roll" in 1959 is far different from the music that Alan Freed called "rock and roll" in 1951.

In our survey of the early years of the rock era (1951–1964), we distinguish four stages in the evolution of rock and roll. They are:

- 1951–1955: "Rock and roll" was code for "rhythm and blues."
- 1955–1957: "Rock and roll" identified not only rhythm and blues but also R&B-influenced songs by Elvis and other white performers.
- 1957–1959: "Rock and roll" emerges as a new kind of music different from rhythm and blues; by the end of the decade, it seems to be no more than a passing fad.
- 1959–1964: "Rock and roll" rises phoenixlike from its apparent death; it becomes one of several paths to rock.

To chart the rise, fall, and rebirth of rock and roll and to cast into relief its relationship to other significant rock-related musical developments during the fifties and early sixties, we present rhythm and blues and rock and roll in separate chapters. Chapter 4 covers rhythm and blues in the fifties. Chapter 5 discusses rock and roll during the same timespan, emphasizing its distinct path, both racially (for the most part) and then musically. Chapter 6 covers the adolescence of rock. It is the most diverse chapter in the book, addressing everything from folk music and the most famous rock dance of all time to girl groups and surf music. Integrated into the musical commentary are discussions of pertinent social issues (such as race relations during the fifties and early sixties; the empowerment of teens), developments in the music industry (independent labels; the Brill Building), and technological innovations (stereophonic recording and playback; the invention of the electric bass).

We begin with the emergence of rhythm and blues.

## Songs Discussed in Chapters 4–6, Ordered Chronologically

| YEAR | CHAPTER | GROUP | TITLE |
|------|---------|-------|-------|
| 1951 | 4 | Jackie Brenston and His Delta Cats | Rocket 88 |
| 1953 | 4 | Fats Domino | Mardi Gras in New Orleans |
| 1954 | 4 | Joe Turner | Shake, Rattle and Roll |
|      | 4 | Muddy Waters | (I'm Your) Hoochie Coochie Man |
|      | 4 | The Chords | Sh-Boom |
|      | 5 | Bill Haley | Rock Around the Clock |
| 1955 | 4 | Bo Diddley | Bo Diddley |
|      | 5 | Elvis Presley | Mystery Train |
|      | 5 | Chuck Berry | Maybellene |
| 1957 | 4 | The Coasters | Young Blood |
|      | 4 | Sam Cooke | You Send Me |
|      | 5 | Elvis Presley | Jailhouse Rock |
|      | 5 | Little Richard | Lucille |
|      | 5 | Jerry Lee Lewis | Great Balls of Fire |
|      | 5 | Buddy Holly | Not Fade Away |
| 1958 | 5 | Chuck Berry | Johnny B. Goode |
|      | 5 | The Everly Brothers | All I Have to Do Is Dream |
| 1959 | 4 | The Flamingos | I Only Have Eyes for You |
|      | 4 | Ray Charles | What'd I Say |
| 1960 | 6 | Chubby Checker | The Twist |
|      | 6 | The Shirelles | Will You Love Me Tomorrow? |
| 1963 | 6 | The Crystals | Da Doo Ron Ron |
|      | 6 | The Kingsmen | Louie Louie |
|      | 6 | Bob Dylan | Blowin' in the Wind |
| 1964 | 6 | Roy Orbison | Oh, Pretty Woman |
|      | 6 | Beach Boys | I Get Around |

# Rhythm and Blues, 1951–1959

In January 1922, Okeh Records placed an advertisement in the *Chicago Defender*, a black newspaper, that announced "All the greatest race phonograph stars can be heard on Okeh Records . . . Ask your neighborhood dealer for a complete list of Okeh race records." Okeh had recorded Mamie Smith's "Crazy Blues" at the end of 1920; its success opened the door for other classic blues singers, most notably Bessie Smith. "Down Hearted Blues," Smith's first recording for Columbia Records (now Sony), in 1923, reputedly sold over 1 million copies.

During the twenties, recordings by black musicians mainly for a black audience occupied a small but important niche within the recording industry. Other major companies, most notably Victor and Columbia (which would ultimately merge into Sony BMG), created branches of their catalog to serve the "race" market. Joining them in catering to the black community were small labels like Paramount and W. C. Handy's Black Swan, which was bought by Paramount in 1924. However, the **race record** part of the music industry almost went under during the first years of the Depression: sales of race records, which had been as high as 5 percent of total sales at the end of the twenties, dropped to only 1 percent in the early thirties, and several record companies went out of business or stopped recording black musicians.

Business began to pick up toward the end of the thirties; by 1942, *Billboard*, then and now the bible of the entertainment industry, began charting "race record" hits. The magazine dubbed the chart the "Harlem Hit Parade"; reportedly chart position was determined by an informal poll of a handful of record stores in Harlem. After World War II, *Billboard* reverted to "race records" to refer to the chart. In 1949, Jerry Wexler, then a staff writer at the magazine, suggested the more politically correct and musically appropriate term *rhythm and blues*.

## The Emergence of Rhythm and Blues

By the time the renamed chart made its first appearance on June 25, 1949, **rhythm and blues (R&B)** had become a small but significant part of the record industry. During World War II, what we now call rhythm and blues was just an occasional blip on the radar screen of popular music. After the war ended, rhythm and blues took off—maybe not as fast as Jackie Brenston's "Rocket 88"—but quickly enough to get the attention of *Billboard's* staff. However, it was in the fifties that rhythm and blues began to expand its niche in the pop marketplace, even as it carved out its distinctive sound identity. In less than a decade, rhythm and blues became an integral part of a new pop world.

The commercial growth of rhythm and blues during the fifties was mainly a product of four factors: the economic and social empowerment of blacks, a media revolution that introduced new recording formats and redefined the role of radio, the growing interest of whites in black music, and the crossover appeal of the music itself.

## Black Social and Economic Issues in the Fifties

The central issue for blacks after World War II was equality: racial, economic, and social. Black and white soldiers had fought for the United States during World War II, sometimes side by side, but more often in segregated units. The irony of blacks fighting to defend freedom in a country that did not treat them as free men was not lost on President Truman. In 1948, he signed an executive order demanding an end to discrimination in the armed services. This was one of numerous postwar developments that moved the United States—however painfully—closer to an integrated society.

If World War II brought the question to the fore, the postwar economic boom, the massive emigration of blacks from the rural South, and the Cold War gave the United States the reasons to respond to it. The flourishing postwar economy meant more and better-paying jobs. It put more money in the pockets of blacks, although not at the same rate as whites, and it reduced competition for jobs, which was one reason for trying to maintain the status quo, especially in the South. The migration of blacks to the North and West, which had begun in earnest after the turn of the century, accelerated during and especially after World War II. There they had the right to vote, which enabled them to exert pressure on politicians. Another factor was the evident hypocrisy between the United States presenting itself to other nations as a defender of freedom and denying it to some of its citizens. During the Cold War, schoolchildren recited the Pledge of Allegiance every day, reiterating that the republic was "one nation under God, indivisible with liberty and justice for all." Observers outside of the South, as well as those in other countries, were increasingly reminded that so long as all Americans were not equal under the law this pledge—what the nation professed to believe and practice—was in fact a lie.

The two events that catalyzed the civil rights movement occurred within a year of each other. The first was the Supreme Court's 1954 decision, *Brown v. Board of Education of Topeka*, which rescinded the "separate but equal" policy sanctioned by the Court's 1896 decision in *Plessy v. Ferguson*. In *Plessy*, the Court had held that blacks could be educated in separate (or segregated) schools as long as they were "equal" in quality to the schools whites attended. Now, the Court said that there could be no equality unless blacks and whites had equal access to all schools.

Following this decision, the civil rights movement gained momentum in the courts and on the streets. In 1955, Montgomery, Alabama, native Rosa Parks refused to give up her bus seat to a white person. When she was arrested and sent to jail, blacks in Montgomery boycotted the municipal bus service for a year. Two years later, Dr. Martin Luther King Jr. organized the Southern Christian Leadership Conference, which advocated nonviolent protest modeled after that used by Mahatma

Gandhi in India. All of this laid the foundation for the major advances in civil rights during the sixties.

Unlike jazz musicians such as Charles Mingus, rhythm-and-blues artists did not lift their voice in support of the civil rights movement during the fifties. Their contribution was indirect: the appeal of their music helped heighten awareness of black culture. At the same time, rhythm and blues benefited from the increased attention given to race relations in the media; it was a two-way street.

## The Media Revolution

Two major developments—the emergence of commercial television and the development of new record formats—triggered a media revolution during the fifties. The ripple effect from their impact helped open the door for rhythm and blues.

**Television and Radio**   The television industry mushroomed after the war. In 1946, the industry was in its infancy; only 6,000 television sets were sold that year. Three years later, sales topped 2 million sets. By the mid-fifties, television was a household staple, and the first color sets were on the market. Television quickly took over radio's role as the primary source of all-purpose entertainment. Soap operas, situation comedies, variety shows, mystery shows—all of these and more moved from radio to television.

As a result, radio redefined itself as a medium. To fill the void left by the migration of these shows to television, radio stations began programming recorded music—most prominently, pop. Some stations, however, began to offer programs that provided an alternative to the bland pop fare. Not surprisingly, these programs were broadcast at odd times—late at night, early in the morning. Still, many attracted a small but fervent following.

**Disc jockeys (DJs)**, a new breed of radio personality created by the more extensive use of prerecorded material, hosted these shows. Listeners tuned in for the DJ as well as the music. During these early years of radio programming, disc jockeys chose their own music. As rhythm and blues and rock and roll caught on, their ability to choose the music that they played gave them enormous clout, which they abused on occasion. (We discuss Alan Freed's rise and fall, the most familiar instance of this abuse, in Chapter 5.)

**Record Formats**   After World War II, the major record companies fought a format war. For decades, shellac **78 rpm** (revolutions per minute) recordings had delivered about 3 minutes of popular music on 10-inch discs and about 4 minutes of classical music on 12-inch discs. In 1948, Columbia Records began issuing **long-playing (LP) records**, or **33 rpm**. These were vinyl discs that held over a half-hour of music and didn't break when you dropped them. The next year, RCA brought out the 7-inch **45 rpm single**. This disc was also vinyl and, despite its much smaller size, also held about 3 minutes of music.

It took a while for these new formats to catch on because they required new record players. However, by the mid-fifties, the new 45 rpm format had largely replaced the 78. Record companies used the 45 for singles targeted at teens, who liked the convenience and durability of the new format and had enough money to buy them.

Rhythm-and-blues and rock-and-roll 45s, found their way into more and more teenage bedrooms; they also turned up on jukeboxes and radio stations more frequently.

**Indies**  The music market was there, thanks to the postwar economic boom. The way to make money was there, thanks to radio, jukeboxes, and record stores. The way to bring the money in was there, thanks to Broadcast Music Incorporated—a music licensing agency formed in 1939 to collect fees on behalf of those clients (blues and country musicians) not represented by ASCAP, the licensing organization for pop songwriters and performers. All that was needed was someone to record the music.

The growth of **indie** (independent) **music** in recent years, in opposition to the major recording companies, relives the rise of independent labels in the late forties and early fifties. Today's technology is different: sophisticated, inexpensive, digital technology versus primitive but costly tape recorders. The distribution is different: Internet and cooperative download sites versus selling records from the trunk of a car (as forties indie pioneer Leonard Chess did). And the music is different. Many of today's indie bands, mostly white, explore peripheral retro styles and style fusions, like ska and punk. More than half a century ago, legendary independent labels recorded blacks whose music was the cutting edge of popular music.

What the indies of yesterday and today have in common is an entrepreneurial spirit and a desire to bring the music to which they are passionately devoted to a larger audience—and make some money in the process. For Leonard Chess, a Polish immigrant, it was another potential source of income. Chess and his brother Phil owned several nightclubs on Chicago's South Side, including the Macomba, a club that featured some of the best black performers in the city. In 1947, sensing that the recording industry offered another good business opportunity, the Chess brothers bought into a newly formed independent label, Aristocrat Records. Like most other independents, Aristocrat concentrated on music outside of the pop mainstream. The first releases on the new label featured jazz and jump band performers. Over the next several years, they added such key figures as Muddy Waters and Chuck Berry to their roster.

The story of Chess Records was replicated with some variation in cities around the country. Ahmet Ertegun, a Turkish immigrant living in New York, founded Atlantic Records in 1947; Jerry Wexler bought in six years later. Art Rupe's Specialty Records based in New Orleans, Lew Chudd's Imperial Records based in Los Angeles, Syd Nathan's King Records based in Cincinnati—all helped preserve and disseminate the sound of rhythm and blues (and country and western). So did Sam Phillips's Sun Records. His recording studio, the only place that blacks could record in Memphis, also recorded top rockabilly acts, beginning with Elvis Presley. Starting and running an independent label was a risky business. Some folded. Labels like Imperial, Chess, and King carved a niche in the market on the strength of a few good acts. Only Ertegun's Atlantic grew into a major label. Still, all the independent labels left later generations an impressive legacy.

## Crossover Appeal

From 1951 to 1955 the only black performers to top the charts were established pop stars Nat Cole and the Mills Brothers. In 1956, the Platters, a slick doo-wop group supported by sumptuous instrumental arrangements, broke through with two number 1 hits. Sam Cooke's "You Send Me" topped the charts for three weeks in 1957. The Platters returned in 1958 with another hit; they were joined by the Coasters, whose novelty hit "Yakety Yak" also made it to number 1. In 1959, the Platters returned again; joining them were Lloyd Price and Wilbert Harrison, both of whom scored with "big-beat" hits.

Although the number 1 songs of the fifties are an extremely small sample of the music available during the decade, they highlight the growing commercial presence of rhythm and blues and describe the path that the music took to **crossover** success. There is no rhythm and blues at the top of the charts for the first half of the decade. The three hits by the Platters exemplify the most pop-oriented form of doo-wop. Cooke's song is in essence a pre-rock pop tune; the setting features white backup singers and light rhythm; Cooke's singing is the only distinctively black element. However, the Coasters' song mixes together barbed humor, a strong honky-tonk beat, and a honking sax with the Coasters' distinctive vocal sound. The hits by Price and Harrison demonstrate the most rhythmic kind of rhythm and blues during the fifties. The sound had been around for over a decade—we will hear an early example of it shortly—but didn't find a wider audience until the end of the fifties.

The career of Fats Domino confirms the timeline for the deepening interest of whites in rhythm and blues. Before 1950, Domino was all but unknown outside New Orleans. Beginning with his 1950 hit, "The Fat Man," he began to develop a nationwide following, mainly among blacks. Still, between 1950 and 1955, only two of his long string of R&B hits crossed over to the pop charts. After 1955, however, almost all of his R&B hits also charted on pop.

Domino's commercial success—he sold over 65 million records in his career and was the most popular black recording artist during the early years of the rock era—is evidence of the changing taste of whites, or at least young whites. Domino's songs and style remained remarkably consistent throughout his career. He made little effort to modify any aspect of his music in order to attract a wider audience. Domino let the white audience come to him, rather than catering to their taste.

On the one hand, it is clear that in rhythm and blues the road to pop success began by mixing black style with mainstream popular music. On the other, the audience outside the black community became increasingly receptive to this new black music. In a few more years, music and audience would meet in the middle; *Billboard* discontinued their R&B chart from 1963 to 1965

Bettmann/Corbis

Fats Domino at the piano, in a publicity photo taken in 1956.

because it had become virtually identical to the pop charts. In less than a generation, rhythm and blues had grown from a commercial afterthought to a major player in popular music.

## The Range of Rhythm and Blues

Like "race records," "rhythm and blues" came into use as a marketing term: it identified music made by black musicians mainly for a black audience. Jerry Wexler's label implied that this new black music was a family of styles. Indeed, "rhythm and blues" embraced far more than basic blues and music with a big beat. Among the most important developments in rhythm and blues during the fifties were:

- Up-tempo good-time blues styles with a strong beat and/or backbeat
- Electric blues, a transformation of country blues through the use of amplified guitar and the addition of a rhythm section
- The introduction of gospel vocal styles into pop singing and a gospel-type approach to popular song
- The incorporation of **Latin rhythms** and instruments

These trends were like colors on an artist's palette; they could be mixed together in countless ways. For example, Latin-tinged rhythm and blues included such diverse examples as Professor Longhair's "Tipitina," Ruth Brown's "Mambo Baby" (a number 1 R&B hit for her in 1954), Bo Diddley's "Bo Diddley," and Ray Charles's "What'd I Say." We sample music from all of these sources, beginning with the music that put a lot of rhythm in rhythm and blues.

# Heavy Rhythms: Big-Beat Rhythm and Blues

In one strain of rhythm and blues, rhythm came to the forefront. The rhythms weren't new; they dated back to the twenties. What was new was their prominence. With the aid of amplification and an amplified guitar, the increased prominence of rhythm section instruments, and a fair amount of muscle, the rhythms of the rhythm section came out from behind the rest of the band. We take a closer look at three prominent rhythmic features, then hear how they sound in two songs from the first part of the fifties.

## The Rhythms of Up-Tempo Rhythm and Blues

The three rhythmic features that became prominent in fifties rhythm and blues were the backbeat, the shuffle beat, and triplets. They combined in numerous ways to give rhythm and blues a big beat. We review each in turn.

**The Backbeat**   The **backbeat** had been part of popular music and jazz since the early twenties; surprisingly, it was not prominent in any of the blues styles of the twenties and thirties. However, in the latter part of the forties and into the fifties, it came in with a vengeance. The majority of up-tempo rhythm-and-blues recordings featured a strong backbeat, played on the drums and often reinforced with a handclap.

**Shuffle Rhythm**  In music with a four-beat rhythm, the rhythm section marks every beat. Melody lines that move faster than the beat typically divide each beat into two unequal parts: the first is twice as long as the second. In a **shuffle rhythm**, this long/short division of the beat moves into the rhythm section: typically at least the chord instrument and the drums consistently mark off this pattern.

The shuffle rhythm has been around since the mid-twenties. It was (and is) the rhythmic foundation of medium-tempo boogie-woogie: Pine Top Smith's eponymous 1928 recording "Pine Top's Boogie Woogie" is a well-known early example of this. One also hears this long/short rhythm in the accompaniments of country blues singers; Robert Johnson used it more than any other rhythm. About the same time that Johnson made his recordings, the rhythm surfaced in big-band swing, most often in songs inspired by boogie-woogie, like Tommy Dorsey's remake of Smith's song, which was titled simply "Boogie Woogie," and the Andrews Sisters' "Boogie Woogie Bugle Boy." It became more and more prominent in the songs of the postwar jump bands; we heard it in Louis Jordan's hit "Choo-Choo-Ch-Boogie." By the early fifties, it was the most widely used rhythm in rhythmic rhythm and blues; it would remain the most popular rhythmic option through the end of the decade.

**Triplets**  The term **triplet** identifies a rhythmic pattern that divides each beat into three equal parts. In the respect that they divide each beat into equal time segments, triplets are like rock rhythm and unlike the shuffle rhythm. Before the early fifties, triplets were seldom used in blues, jazz, and pop, and when they were used it was mainly in slower tempos. After 1950, triplets became a staple in slow rhythm and blues and were also used for emphasis in medium-tempo songs, as we hear next.

## The Sound of Up-Tempo Fifties R&B: Hard Shuffles and Honking Saxophones

Jackie Brenston's "Rocket 88" (1951) was a big rhythm-and-blues hit with a big beat. Although Brenston (1930–1979) was the singer on this date, it was the band of pianist Ike Turner (b. 1931) that Brenston fronted, and the most distinctive sound on this recording is Willie Kizart's distorted guitar, not Brenston's singing. The story of how it found its way onto a record is the stuff of rock-and-roll legend.

CD 1:25

"Rocket 88,"
Jackie Brenston
and His Delta
Cats (1951)

According to most accounts of the making of this record, the band was driving from Mississippi to Memphis, with their instruments strapped on top of the car. At some point, the guitar amp fell off, or was dropped, and the speaker cone was torn. As a result, the guitar produced a heavily distorted sound, even after Kizart had stuffed it with paper. When recording engineer Sam Phillips heard it, he decided to make an asset out of a perceived liability, so he made the guitar line, which simply adapts a shuffle-style boogie-woogie left hand to the guitar, stand out.

Both the **distortion** and the relative prominence of the guitar were novel features of this recording—these are the elements that have earned "Rocket 88" so many nominations as "the first" rock-and-roll record. From our perspective, "Rocket 88" wasn't the first rock-and-roll record, because the beat is a shuffle rhythm, not the distinctive rock rhythm heard first in the songs of Chuck Berry and Little Richard. Still, the distortion and the central place of the guitar in the overall sound certainly anticipate key features of rock style.

In other respects, the song is right in step with the up-tempo songs of postwar rhythm and blues. The lyric tells a story over a blues progression. Its subject touches on a recurrent theme: cars. "Rocket 88" was inspired by Joe Liggins's 1947 recording, "Cadillac Boogie," and it is one link in a chain that passes through Chuck Berry's "Maybellene" to the Beach Boys' "Little Deuce Coupe." There is the obligatory honking sax solo—a good one—and a nice instrumental out-chorus (the final statement of the blues progression) that's straight out of the big-band era.

**Shuffle Rhythm**    Kizart's guitar line provides an explicit outline of the shuffle rhythm.

Notice the way in which the shuffle rhythm lines up with the piano triplets: the long note in each beat lasts as long as the first two notes of the triplets, while the short note lasts as long as the third triplet. The triplets enable us to hear precisely the 2:1 ratio between the long and short notes of a shuffle rhythm.

As the figure shows, the shuffle rhythm is *not* a rock rhythm. However, as it is heard here—played loudly on a guitar with a distorted sound—it conveys much the same kind of energy as a rock rhythm, because there are insistent rhythms that move faster than the beat. This rhythm is in the foreground throughout the song; it is this feature— loud, insistent, active rhythms—that seemed to attract teens, both black and white, and repel so many adults, who wanted such rhythms heard gently in the background.

**Blues Progression**    Blues can be a *feeling*: music to convey sadness, like Bessie Smith's "Empty Bed Blues," or music to chase the blues away, like "Roll 'Em, Pete" or "Rocket 88." Blues can be a *style* of singing and playing, as we heard most powerfully in the singing of Smith and Robert Johnson and in the playing of King Oliver and Johnson.

Blues can also be a *form*, a consistent way of organizing music in time. In the discussion of Smith's song, we pointed out the most common pattern of a blues lyric: a rhymed couplet with the first line repeated. Each phrase of the lyric and vocal silence that follows takes up four measures; together, the three phrases add up to twelve measures. This is the poetic form of one chorus of a 12-bar blues.

The chords that underpin this form follow a predictable pattern. This pattern, commonly referred to as a **blues progression**, is typically present in blues songs, whether they are vocal or instrumental and whether the lyric is a rhymed couplet or some other pattern. We have heard the blues progression in these songs:

- Bessie Smith's "Empty Bed Blues"
- King Oliver's "Dippermouth Blues"
- Tampa Red and Georgia Tom's "It's Tight Like That"
- Joe Turner and Pete Johnson's "Roll 'Em, Pete"
- Louis Jordan's "Choo-Choo-Ch-Boogie" (in the verse)

We have saved the discussion of the blues progression until "Rocket 88" because it is easier to hear the progression in this song than any other song that we have discussed or will discuss in the text: the guitar part outlines the progression clearly and unmistakably.

The 12-bar blues progression consists of three four-measure phrases. The first phrase begins on the I chord and typically stays on it through the phrase. The second phrase begins on the IV chord and returns to the I chord halfway through. The third phrase begins on the V chord; it also arrives back on the I chord halfway through. Thus, each phrase *begins* on a different chord and *returns* to the I chord halfway through. In blues songs with a rhymed couplet, the beginning of each four-measure phrase lines up with a phrase of the lyric: that is what we heard in "Empty Bed Blues" and "Roll 'Em, Pete." However, the progression remains the same even when the lyric follows another pattern, as it does here during the vocal, or when there is no vocal at all, as is the case during the saxophone solo.

**Honking Saxophones**   Rhythmic rhythm-and-blues bands were as consistent in their approach to instrumentation as they were in their approach to rhythm and harmony. "Rocket 88" is typical: the band behind Jackie Brenston consists of a full early-fifties-style rhythm section—electric guitar, piano, bass, and drums—plus two saxophones, one of which takes an extended solo. In a fifties rhythm-and-blues song we expect to hear bands with a rhythm section and at least one saxophone; the saxophone will be a solo instrument as well as an accompanying instrument; and both accompaniments and solo passages will feature repeated riffs.

> The online glossary, which contains multimedia-enhanced definitions of musical terms, uses examples presented in this chapter to define terms like "shuffle" and "blues progression." The glossary can be found on the website for the text at *academic.cengage.com/music/campbell*.

### ♪ KEY FEATURES

**"Rocket 88," Jackie Brenston (1951)**

- Strong shuffle rhythm with occasional triplets adding to rhythmic activity
- Distorted guitar sound (a happy accident!)
- Clear outline of blues progression and blues form
- Standard jump band instrumentation: rhythm section with electric guitar plus saxophones; saxophone in the spotlight
- A song about cars: a popular topic in the postwar era

## The Sound of Up-Tempo Fifties R&B: Backbeats, Blues, and Sex

When we last encountered Joe Turner (1911–1985), he was a young man singing the blues as Pete Johnson pounded out boogie-woogie behind him. Turner, commonly identified as "Big" Joe Turner because of his girth, grew up in Kansas City, Missouri, which was a wide-open city and a major center for jazz and blues during the thirties. During the forties, Turner's career gathered momentum; he became a popular R&B recording artist, hopping from one independent label to the next. His career peaked in the mid-fifties: "Shake, Rattle and Roll" topped the R&B charts in 1954. Perhaps

CD 1:26

"Shake, Rattle and Roll," Joe Turner (1954)

Joe Turner singing at the Newport Jazz Festival, 1958.

Ted Williams/Corbis

because of its lyrics, Turner's version never crossed over to the pop charts; a cover version by Bill Haley with some less suggestive lyrics reached number 7 that same year.

**Blues Talking About Sex** The blues has always been a personal music, and there is no more personal subject in secular culture than man–woman relationships. We heard one frank account in Bessie Smith's "Empty Bed Blues" and another in Robert Johnson's "Come on in My Kitchen." In "Shake, Rattle and Roll," Turner talks about a woman in his life, and it's not pretty: she's lazy, trashy, loose with money and her favors, and diabolical.

The most intimate aspect of a relationship is sexual intercourse. In our time, lyrics can and do discuss this explicitly. By contrast, blues lyrics have usually talked about sexual relations indirectly, typically through metaphor. We heard this in Bessie Smith's song: her partner is a "coffee grinder" who's got a brand new grind. In Blind Lemon Jefferson's "Black Snake Moan," one of the very early country blues recordings, it's easy to imagine what the black snake is, especially when he sings "black snake crawling in my room/and some pretty mama better come and get this black snake soon." Hokum was a blues genre dedicated to the double entendre; songs like "It's Tight Like That" are laced with "wink-wink" lyrics. It was the exceptional bluesman who did not deal with sexual relations in at least one of his songs. In Robert Johnson's "Terraplane Blues," the woman is a car; he continues the metaphor when describing intercourse: "when I mash down on your little starter/then your spark plug would give me fire."

The lyrics of many postwar rhythm-and-blues songs continued to explore all aspects of man–woman relationships. On some blues recordings the lyrics were so raunchy that they were not issued commercially (a few circulated as bootleg recordings). Others approached the matter implicitly, as in Roy Brown's 1947 classic "Good Rockin' Tonight," when he says "I'm gonna hold my baby as tight as I can/Tonight she'll know I'm a mighty mighty man." Here, the "rockin'" in the title refers to sex, not music. In "Shake, Rattle and Roll," Turner describes foreplay in this line: "I'm like a one-eyed cat peeping in a seafood store." It was a metaphor that eluded not only the censors but apparently the musicians who redid the song: in his cover version, Bill Haley changed some of the lyrics in an effort to clean them up but left that line in.

What the blues started, rap has finished. Rap lyrics can talk about sex in the most explicit terms; some leave nothing to the imagination. It is now possible to discuss sexual matters openly, although recordings must wear the record industry's scarlet letter. But perhaps this freedom has come at a price: the music has lost some of the fun that goes along with describing sexual matters elliptically or metaphorically. The good humor that seems to accompany indirect references to sex is a thread that runs from the earliest blues recordings through rhythm and blues and into rock. It seems to have disappeared in recent years.

**Heavy Rhythm: The Backbeat** Among the most distinctive musical features of "Shake, Rattle and Roll" is the heavy backbeat. Here it is much stronger than in any earlier recording we've studied. Upbeat rhythm-and-blues songs like "Shake, Rattle and Roll" were the direct source of the heavy backbeat that is such an important component of rock rhythm. One hears a strong backbeat in many of the hits of Chuck Berry and Little Richard, who quite clearly borrowed it from R&B. From there it went directly into rock.

**Verse/Chorus Blues Form** The song offers another approach to a refrain-based blues form. In "It's Tight Like That," the second and third phrases of each chorus formed the refrain. In "Choo-Choo-Ch-Boogie," the refrain was not in blues form, but the verses were. In "Shake, Rattle and Roll," the first three choruses are scene-painting verses. The fourth chorus functions like the chorus in a verse/chorus form. It is simple, repetitive, and highlights the title phrase. Both words and music return two more times in alternation with new verses. This is another instance of an inventive manipulation of blues form.

**Rich, Layered Sound** Perhaps because the guitar is more in the background, we hear a more balanced version of the postwar jump band in "Shake, Rattle and Roll" than we did in "Rocket 88": full rhythm section, with the bass **walking** (when a bass player **walks**, he plays one note on each beat), the piano playing consistently in a high register, and saxophones typically playing riffs behind Turner's vocals. Both the vocal line—and especially the title phrase—and the saxophone line are mainly repeated riffs. Rock is, in general, a denser-sounding music than pre-rock pop; we hear the transition to a thicker sound in recordings like this.

♪ **KEY FEATURES**

**"Shake, Rattle and Roll," Joe Turner (1954)**
- Heavy backbeat
- Verse/chorus blues form
- Thick layered sound

## Rhythm and Blues, Rock and Roll, and the Beat

Much of this **big-beat music** was considered rock and roll, especially when it crossed over to the pop charts and/or was covered by white bands. And many critics and commentators have claimed that "Rocket 88" was the first rock-and-roll record, largely because of the prominent distorted guitar sound. In 1956, these songs and others like them, such as Fats Domino's "Ain't That a Shame," would have been labeled "rock and roll." As Domino told an interviewer, "What you call rock and roll is what we've been playing in New Orleans for 15 years." However, if we understand rock and roll as the music that led directly to rock, and agree that the most fundamental and pervasive feature of rock music is its beat, then this strain of rhythm and blues is not rock and roll: these songs and others like them have the wrong beat.

The fascinating aspect regarding the emergence of rock rhythm is that white bands adopted it before black bands. What makes this fascinating is that the impetus for denser and more active rhythms in popular music has come from Afro-centric musical cultures, especially those in the United States, Cuba, and Brazil, and that the beat that would soon distinguish rock and roll from rhythm and blues would come from Little Richard and Chuck Berry. Despite this, the vast majority of black acts retained the four-beat rhythms—either the standard swing beat or the more active shuffle rhythm—of earlier rhythm and blues through the end of the decade, even as white rock-and-roll bands jumped on the rock-beat bandwagon. Wilbert Harrison's "Kansas City" and Lloyd Price's "Stagger Lee," both number 1 pop hits in 1959, feature a shuffle rhythm, not a rock beat. We revisit the connection between the rhythms of fifties rock and roll and sixties rock in Chapter 5.

# Blues in the Fifties

Attend any of the many blues festivals throughout North America and you will hear band after band take the stage. Most will feature a full rhythm section with one or more electric guitars; horns are optional. For most contemporary listeners, this is the sound of the blues: the classic blues style that has remained largely unchanged for half a century. The sounds of these bands are unlike the blues of the twenties and thirties, and it is different from the rhythm and blues that we have just heard. It came together in the early fifties, when deep blues moved north from Mississippi to Chicago and went electric.

## Electrifying the Blues

The electric guitar, already a staple in country music and jazz by the early forties, soon began to find its way into the blues. Muddy Waters began playing electric guitar in 1944, so that he could be heard over the crowd noise in the bars where he performed; others followed suit. At the same time, bluesmen like Waters surrounded themselves with other instrumentalists—another guitarist, a drummer, a bass player, and in Waters's case, Little Walter, the soulful master of the harmonica. This new sound has been called electric blues; now it is just the blues.

**Electric blues** came of age in the fifties. It completed its transformation from a rural to an urban music and its migration from the juke joints and street corners of Mississippi to the bars of Chicago's South Side. Blues kept its soul through the journey, most notably in the music of Muddy Waters.

**Muddy Waters**  Muddy Waters (1915–1983), born McKinley Morganfield, grew up in Clarksdale, Mississippi, the northwest part of the state in the heart of what is called the Delta region. The population was mostly black, and for the vast majority, life was brutal. Both males and females worked as sharecroppers, often from childhood; Waters was a farm laborer as a boy. Some men made a little more money working as stevedores loading riverboats along the Mississippi, but there too, the days were long, the work hard, and the pay meager. Most lived at subsistence level, trapped in an unending cycle of economic dependence. From this harsh and isolated environment came what Robert Palmer called **deep blues**, a powerful music that gave expression to, and release from, the brutal conditions of the Delta.

Waters heard this music while he was growing up and began to play it in his teens. He started on the harmonica, then took up the guitar, because, "You see, I was digging Son House and Robert Johnson." By his late 20s, Waters had become a popular performer in the region.

Like many other southern blacks, Waters moved north during World War II, settling on Chicago's South Side. He continued to play, first at house parties, then in small bars, and recorded for Columbia in 1946. (The recordings were not released until many years later.) Still, it was not enough to pay the rent, and Waters was working as a truck driver when he approached Aristocrat Records about recording for them.

**The Sound of Electric Blues** Muddy Waters's singing and playing retained its earthiness and passion after he moved north; however, he added the power of amplification and a full rhythm section during his first years in Chicago. Both voice and guitar gained a presence not possible with the "man and his guitar" setup of country blues.

In the music of Waters and other like-minded Chicago bluesmen, electric blues found its groove during the fifties. By the end of the decade, it had evolved into its classic sound, which it has retained to this day. Its most consistent features include:

- Regular blues form (or an easily recognized variant of it)
- Rough-edged vocals
- Vocal-like responses and solos from the lead guitar or harmonica
- A dense texture, with several instruments playing melody-like lines behind the singer
- A rhythm section laying down a strong beat, usually some form of the shuffle rhythm popularized in forties rhythm and blues

At the same time, its stars attracted a loyal following, mostly in the black community. Records by Muddy Waters, B. B. King, Howlin' Wolf, Lowell Fulson, Elmore James, and Bobby Bland consistently found their way onto the R&B charts. They were not as well known as the pop-oriented groups, but far better known—within and outside the black community—than their country kin from previous generations. We hear a famous example of this sound next.

CD 1:27

"(I'm Your) Hoochie Coochie Man," Muddy Waters (1954)

## The Sound of Electric Blues

"(I'm Your) Hoochie Coochie Man," the 1954 recording that was Muddy Waters's biggest hit, epitomizes the fully transformed electric blues style. It retains the essence of country blues in Waters's singing and playing yet creates a far richer and more powerful sound than we heard in Robert Johnson's blues. Blues singer Big Bill Broonzy described Waters's appeal in this way:

> It's real. Muddy's real. See the way he plays guitar? Mississippi style, not the city way. He don't play chords, he don't follow what's written down in the book. He plays notes, all blue notes. Making what he's thinking.

And certainly it is all of a piece: Waters's singing brings Willie Dixon's lyrics to life. It makes the references to love potions and voodoo charms, sexual prowess and special status seem believable. It is easy to conjure up such a world and him as the hoochie-coochie man. That much remained virtually unchanged from the rawest country blues of the twenties and thirties.

The great achievement of electric blues, however, is that everything else that goes on amplifies Waters's message. Instrumental support includes what amounted to Chess Records' house blues band—bassist (and blues songwriter) Willie Dixon, pianist Otis Spann, and drummer Fred Below—plus guitarist Jimmy Rogers and harmonica player Little Walter, Waters's musical alter ego. Together they weave a dense musical fabric out of riffs and repeated rhythms.

The song alternates between two textures: the stop time of the opening (an enormous expansion of the first four bars of the standard 12-bar blues form), where an instrumental riff periodically punctuates Waters's vocal line, and the free-for-all of the refrain-like finish of each chorus. The stop-time opening contains two competing riffs—one played by the harmonica, the other by the electric guitar. In the refrain, everybody plays—harmonica trills; guitar riffs; piano chords, either lazy Fats Domino–style triplets or on speed; thumping bass; shuffle pattern on the drums—all are woven together with Muddy's singing.

These different melodic and rhythmic strands are an important part of the mix, but none is capable of standing alone. This kind of dense texture, with independent but interdependent lines, was almost unprecedented in small-group music before rock. The closest parallel would be early New Orleans jazz band recordings, such as those by King Oliver. And it works. No one gets in anyone else's way. There is no stylistic inconsistency, as is so often the case when country blues singing is mixed with horns or strings.

The electric blues of the fifties also brought nastier guitar sounds into popular music. The distorted guitar in "Rocket 88" may have been an accident, but the overdriven guitar sounds that jumped off numerous blues records were intentional. Almost as soon as they went electric, blues guitarists began to experiment with distortion in order to get a guitar sound that paralleled the rawness of singers like Muddy Waters and Howlin' Wolf. Among the leaders in this direction were Buddy Guy and Elmore James, both based in Chicago through much of the fifties.

## Electric Blues' Legacy to Rock

What electric blues gave to rock came in two installments. The first arrived in the mid-fifties, when Chuck Berry adapted the basic blues band instrumentation—prominent lead guitar, second chord instrument, bass, and drums—to his influential brand of rock and roll.

> ## ♪ KEY FEATURES
>
> ### "(I'm Your) Hoochie Coochie Man," Muddy Waters (1954)
>
> - Expanded blues form: the first phrase is twice as long as in a conventional blues; the last two phrases serve as a refrain.
> - Rough-edged vocals: Waters's singing is especially passionate in the refrain-like part of the song.
> - Vocal-like responses and solos from the lead guitar or harmonica: Little Walter almost sings through his harmonica.
> - A dense texture: high piano chords, Little Walter's harmonica, Waters's voice, plus guitars playing riff figures, bass, and drums.
> - A slow, strong shuffle rhythm.

The second arrived a decade later, when rock musicians dipped so deeply into the blues. The Rolling Stones took their name from a 1950 Muddy Waters recording. Rockers adapted the blues attitude, as expressed in words and music. The Stones covered Muddy Waters' "I Can't Be Satisfied," then reworked it into "(I Can't Get No) Satisfaction" (even though the story behind the title came out differently). Bluesmen like Howlin' Wolf inspired the onstage persona and singing of Jagger and countless others.

Rock also took its dense texture most directly from electric blues and found inspiration in the sounds of blues guitarists. The sounds of the Rolling Stones, the Who, Jimi Hendrix, Eric Clapton, and other major sixties acts have deep blues roots.

Although it was innovative and influential in many other ways, electric blues was certainly in the R&B rhythmic mainstream. The tempos were slower, but the shuffle rhythm heard in so many jump band recordings was also the mainstay of electric blues. More active rhythms that paralleled the rock beat came via Afro-Cuban music.

# The Latin Tinge

The rhythmic evolution of rhythm and blues during the fifties began conservatively and ended innovatively. Even as rock and roll broadcast a new beat, most rhythm and blues held onto the shuffle beat of the forties, as we have noted. The rock-preparing music of Chuck Berry and Little Richard immediately stands apart from the music of most other black artists of the mid-fifties because of its rhythm. By the end of the decade, however, Latin-inspired rhythms were used increasingly as an alternative to rock and shuffle rhythms in a wide range of R&B styles. These were generally richer and more complex than the straightforward timekeeping of rock and roll. We trace the gradual infiltration of Latin rhythm into rhythm and blues next.

## New Orleans and Latin Influence

Rhythm and blues influenced by Afro-Cuban music first surfaced in New Orleans. It blended Afro-Cuban rhythmic elements with the feel of rhythm and blues. Afro-Cuban rhythm and rock rhythm have this essential feature in common: a rhythmic layer that moves twice as fast as the beat. This even division of the beat immediately distinguishes both rhythms from the long/short shuffle rhythm. This "Latin tinge" had been part of the New Orleans R&B mix almost from the beginning. It is evident as early as 1949 in a series of recordings by Roy Byrd, better known as Professor Longhair.

Professor Longhair was arguably the most important musical influence in New Orleans rhythm and blues, although he was virtually unknown outside of the city. His only hit was the 1950 recording "Bald Head," which briefly visited the R&B charts. In town, however, his influence was considerable. Many of the great New Orleans piano players—Huey Smith, Allen Toussaint, Mac Rebbenack (Dr. John)—acknowledge his impact on their playing. Professor Longhair, Byrd's professional name, confirms his stature: among New Orleans musicians, a "professor" is a skilled pianist.

Longhair's influence on the rhythms of New Orleans music was even more far-reaching. In several of his early recordings, Professor Longhair blended Afro-Cuban rhythms with rhythm and blues. The most explicit is "Longhair's Blues-Rhumba," where he overlays a straightforward blues with a **clave rhythm**.

**CD 1:28**

"Mardi Gras in New Orleans," Fats Domino (1953)

We hear an important stage in the Americanization of Afro-Cuban rhythms in the 1953 recording by Fats Domino (b. 1928) of a popular New Orleans R&B song: "Mardi Gras in New Orleans." Perhaps because it was so regionally oriented, the song was not one of his hits; it failed to make either the pop or R&B charts. The theme of the lyric is about as New Orleans as one could get: it describes events one would see during the annual parade. Domino would soon chart extensively—first on the R&B charts, then on the pop charts. He would continue to release new hits until the British invasion.

**Latin-Tinged Rhythms in R&B**  Our interest in this song is mainly in the rhythm. There are two noteworthy features: one specific and one general. The specific feature is the clave rhythm tapped out on the claves. As we noted in the discussion of the mambo in the previous chapter, this rhythm is the rhythmic reference for Afro-Cuban music, much as the backbeat is for black rhythms. Here, the clave rhythm is accurate, but it simply adds another interesting layer of rhythmic activity. Unlike the mambo, the other rhythms do not conform to it.

However, there is a kind of rhythmic trickle-down effect from Latin music, because the other rhythms are busy, and they create a dense, active rhythmic texture that recalls the rhythmic interplay of Latin music. The contrast in rhythmic approach between this song and the two "big-beat" songs is especially striking because they are so alike in other respects: vocal sound, use of blues form, jump band instrumentation.

---

♪ **KEY FEATURES**

**"Mardi Gras in New Orleans," Fats Domino (1953)**
- Clave rhythm played on claves
- Dense, active rhythms that create complex patterns
- Blues form
- Jump band/fifties R&B instrumentation: vocal, small horn section, rhythm section

"Mardi Gras in New Orleans" was not popular around 1950, when several New Orleans artists recorded it; it has since been recorded many times. The next example offers a paradox: it presents the most overt and distinctive merging of Afro-Cuban rhythm and rhythm and blues during the fifties, yet there is no evidence of a musical trail from Cuba to that part of Chicago's South Side, where Bo Diddley grew up.

## The Bo Diddley Beat

The circuitous transformation of the clave rhythm into the **Bo Diddley beat** is just one of several unanswered questions about one of the most fascinating musicians of the rock era. The questions begin with his name. He was born in McComb, Mississippi, in 1928. His father's name was Bates, but he was adopted by a relative, Gussie McDaniel; by most accounts, his real name is Elias McDaniel. In the mid-thirties, the McDaniels family moved to Chicago and settled on the South Side. Like many other black performers (such as the bluesmen Muddy Waters and Howlin' Wolf) he acquired a stage persona, but he claims it came from his schoolmates. As he tells it, students started calling him "Bo Diddley" during his teens and it stuck. (Given McDaniel's Mississippi roots, the name would seem to connect to the diddley bow, a homemade instrument popular in the deep South. However, there is no evidence of such a connection.)

There are musical questions as well. How do we reconcile the extent of his influence with his lack of commercial success? In his fifty-year career, he has had only a few R&B hits and only one Top 40 hit—"Say Man," which reached number 20 in 1959. Yet he is, without question, a rock icon; among his many distinctions, he was a second-year inductee into the Rock and Roll Hall of Fame (1987). And he is a celebrity: he returned to the spotlight in the 1990s in a famous commercial with Bo Jackson.

There is one aspect of his music about which there is no question: his interest in rhythm. Bo Diddley was fascinated by rhythms and percussion. (The story goes that he added **maracas** to his street-corner band because he wanted a percussive sound but didn't want to lug a drum set around town. Still, he kept the maracas when he added drums.) Not surprisingly, then, his most important and memorable contribution to popular music is not a song but a beat—the Bo Diddley beat—which appears in the aptly titled 1955 song "Bo Diddley," the first of his R&B hits.

The source of the Bo Diddley beat is the biggest question of all. Although the Bo Diddley beat is virtually identical to the clave rhythm we encountered in the mambo and Fats Domino's song, there is no clear connection between the two. We can infer that this is from a long-standing African American tradition. The practice of beating out rhythms on one's body dates back to slavery; slaves could not make or play percussion instruments, so they used their body. The practice was called **patting juba**; one such rhythm was apparently the **hambone rhythm**. Whether there is a link between the rhythm as it was heard in the American South and Cuban rhythm is an open question: keep in mind that New Orleans is close to the Delta and also the original gateway for Cuban music into the United States.

Provenance of the Bo Diddley beat aside, the song "Bo Diddley" is all about rhythm. It consists mainly of rifflike vocal fragments alternating with the Bo Diddley rhythm, played on guitar and drums. All of this happens over one chord. The lyric is

CD 1:29

"Bo Diddley,"
Bo Diddley
(1955)

Frank Driggs Collection/Getty Images

Bo Diddley and his trademark rectangular guitar, circa 1955, around the time that he recorded "Bo Diddley."

true stream of consciousness: diamond rings, private eyes, animals slaughtered for Sunday clothes, now-you-see-them-now-you-don't people; there is no story. In this respect, it is a grown-up version of a child's song and Bo Diddley's rhythmic take on the one-chord Delta blues style.

Rhythms and chords provide a continuing undercurrent to a repetitious, sing-song melody. Even in an era of genuine novelty, Bo Diddley's music stands apart.

## Latin Music and R&B

Afro-Cuban influence on other fifties R&B artists was generally less direct but still evident. For many, it came by way of the mambo. With the mambo craze in full swing by the early fifties, most rhythm-and-blues bands included a few Latin numbers in their repertoire. Ruth Brown topped the R&B charts in 1954 with "Mambo Baby." She was not alone. Both of Ray Charles's two live sets recorded in the late fifties, from the 1958 Newport Jazz Festival and a 1959 concert in Atlanta, feature one Latin number among rhythm-and-blues and jazz songs.

♪  **KEY FEATURES**

**"Bo Diddley," Bo Diddley (1955)**
- Bo Diddley beat, a slightly altered version of the clave rhythm (in this recording; in a television performance, Bo Diddley and his band play the clave pattern)
- Use of maracas, in addition to conventional blues-band instrumentation
- Almost exclusive emphasis on rhythm

Recall that Afro-Cuban rhythms and rock rhythm both divide the beat into two equal parts. However, the rhythmic foundation of Afro-Cuban rhythm is more complex than the rhythmic foundation of rock. Its basic texture is richer, yet more open, and the beat is marked less explicitly than in rock and roll. When black music eventually assimilated rock rhythm in the early sixties, it often gravitated to more Latin rhythmic textures, instead of simply aping the prevailing rock style. Afro-Cuban influence is apparent in both the more "open" sound of the Motown songs and the new rhythmic approach that James Brown announced in "Papa's Got a Brand New

Bag" (1965). Indeed, both occasionally used the clave pattern (for instance, the Miracles' "Mickey's Monkey" and Brown's "Get It Together").

The frequent use of Latin percussion instruments (conga, bongos, and others), especially in Motown recordings, provides additional evidence of Afro-Cuban influence. The rhythms of black music from the mid-sixties on are generally more intricate, complex, and active than those heard in the music of white rock bands. Afro-Cuban music was not the sole source of these new rhythms, but its influence—however indirect—was certainly significant, even though it is generally not acknowledged.

## Gospel and Rhythm and Blues: Doo-Wop

"Life could be a dream, life could be a dream"; "doo, doo, doo, doo, sh-boom." The first part of the lyric is typical of the romantic pop of the era, the second is the signature of **doo-wop**, the most popular kind of fifties rhythm and blues. As the song unfolds, the lyric alternates between explaining why life could be a dream and nonsense syllables like "hey, nonny ding dong, shalang alang alang." "Sh-boom" returns regularly between phrases of the lyric; it is like a gentle prod that keeps the rhythmic momentum going. Periodically, an entire phrase of nonverbal sounds interrupts the romantic scene unfolding in the rest of the lyric, and the nonverbal sounds from the introduction also serve as the vocal part behind the saxophone solo. Significantly, the title of the song comes from one of these nonsense syllables, not from the first phrase of the lyric.

The function of the nonsense syllables is to inject rhythmic energy into the song. The syllables are typically rich in consonant sounds that explode (*b*) or sustain (*sh* or *m*). In the "sh-boom"-like parts of the song, the voices become instruments. They are not percussive instruments per se, because they have pitch, but the vocal sounds have a percussive quality, like the plucking of a string bass or the slapping of an electric bass.

The practice of using the voice to imitate instruments, especially percussive-sounding instruments, is a distinctively black practice. In jazz, the practice is called **scat singing**. The first familiar examples come from Louis Armstrong's late twenties recordings; there is no difference in conception between Armstrong the trumpeter and Armstrong the vocalist. Armstrong's vocalizations influenced black performers like Cab Calloway, famous as the "hi-de-ho" man. ("Hi-de-ho" were nonsense syllables woven into his account of "Minnie the Moocher," a big hit for him in 1931; the parallel with "Sh-boom" should be clear!) Scat singing gave **bebop** (later shortened to **bop**), new jazz sound of the forties, its name: "be-bop" are the syllables that end a scatted stream of notes. Male gospel quartets were a more direct influence. Most sang *a cappella* (that is, without instrumental accompaniment), so backup vocal parts often assumed a rhythmic as well as a harmonic role.

The practice became part of the sound of rhythm and blues in the forties, in such hit songs as Lionel Hampton's "Hey! Ba-Ba-Re-Bop" and "Stick" McGhee's "Drinking Wine Spo-Dee-O-Dee." With doo-wop the practice became so integral to the music that it gave the style its name. The term *doo-wop*—borrowed from songs that used the phrase (we will hear one following)—was applied retrospectively to this music to acknowledge its most salient feature.

Doo-wop was the more popular of two gospel-influenced R&B styles from the fifties. We briefly survey doo-wop and then turn our attention to solo singing.

## Doo-Wop and Black Singing Groups

Group singing by blacks has a history in sound that extends back to the nineteenth century: there are recordings by vocal groups such the Unique Quartet, the Oriole Quartette, and the Standard Quartette from as early as 1893. These are among the earliest recordings by black performers. Such groups sang a little of everything, from minstrel-show routines to sacred songs.

The first black vocal group to enjoy widespread popular success was the Mills Brothers, who charted regularly from the mid-thirties. Other black vocal groups followed in their wake, most notably the Ink Spots. These groups sang in a smooth pop style quite different from the gospel male quartets active around the same time.

**The Doo-Wop Era**    After World War II, pop, gospel, and rhythm and blues came together in a new family of styles that featured male or mostly male singing groups. The styles ranged from gospel-tinged pop ideally suited for slow dancing to up-tempo numbers and novelty songs. The common threads seem to be the gospel and pop influences (the male gospel quartets and pop vocal groups like the Mills Brothers) and the names, which identify the groups as a unit: the Platters, the Penguins, the Cadillacs, the Drifters, and countless others. The first recordings of these new sounds appeared in the late forties, many by "bird" groups such as the Ravens and the Orioles.

From the mid-fifties to the early sixties, doo-wop crossed over to the pop market more consistently and with greater success than any other rhythm-and-blues style. The Orioles' 1953 hit, "Crying in the Chapel," blazed the trail. Its history highlights the blurred genre boundaries in the early rock era: "Crying in the Chapel" was a country song that crossed over to the pop charts, which was then covered by an R&B group whose version also made the pop charts!

The breakthrough hit "Sh-Boom" came the following year. The original R&B version by the Chords hit both pop and rhythm-and-blues charts the same week: July 3, 1954. A cover version by the Crew Cuts, a white singing group, hit number 1 on the pop charts a week later. Other doo-wop hits soon crossed over. The first and most enduring was the Penguins' "Earth Angel." The song blended old (Tin Pan Alley–style melody, harmony, and form plus the swing rhythm in bass and drums) and new (triplet rhythm overlay and the refreshingly untutored singing of Cleveland Duncan and the rest of the Penguins). This distinctive mix transformed "Earth Angel" into one of the most recognizable sounds of the fifties. Others mined the same lode countless times—from the Moonglows' "Sincerely," which followed on the heels of "Earth Angel," to the appropriately titled 1961 hit "Beat of My Heart," the first big hit for the Pips, and beyond.

The most popular of the doo-wop groups was the least typical. The Platters were not only the most successful by far, but also the slickest, most sophisticated, and most symphonic. Guided by their vocal coach Buck Ram, who wrote or adapted most of their material, they found commercial success with a real middle-ground style. Their four number 1 pop hits were among fifteen songs that made the Top 40 between 1955 and 1959. In effect, they were doo-wop by association, simply because they were a black vocal group. Stylistically, they owed much more to pop than rhythm and blues; indeed, they were more popular on the pop charts than on the R&B charts.

For whites, doo-wop put a fresh coat of paint on familiar-sounding material. For the majority of white teens who had heard their parents' Tin Pan Alley pop growing up, the familiar elements must have made the music more accessible. They also made it easier for white singers to copy. The success of these black vocal groups and the even greater success of white groups like the Crew Cuts spawned countless other white imitators, from Danny and the Juniors to Dion and the Belmonts. The sound and the style died out in the early sixties with the rise of the girl groups, Motown, and other fresh black pop sounds. Somewhat after the fact, this music came to be known as doo-wop; at the time, it was simply the most popular form of rhythm and blues.

## Cover Versions and Commercial Success

The higher chart position of the Crew Cuts' cover of "Sh-Boom" has often been hauled out as Exhibit A in the case against white covers of early rock-and-roll hits. Certainly, the financial and racial implications of white covers give an unflattering picture of the practice.

### Cover Versions

A **cover** is a recording of a song by an act other than the first act to record the song. For example, "Sh-Boom" was originally by a black vocal group called the Chords. The Crew Cuts, a white Canadian group, *covered* the song almost immediately; their version charted higher than the Chords'. White covers of black songs occurred frequently in the early years of rock and roll: Pat Boone's covers of Little Richard's "Tutti Frutti" and Fats Domino's "Ain't That a Shame," both of which outsold the originals, are particularly egregious examples. Because of these and other similar instances, cover versions have acquired racial baggage: commentators have viewed them as white acts riding on the coattails of black acts and enjoying the success that should have gone to the black act.

However, details of the "Sh-Boom" story show that the business of covers was not as one-sided as it may seem. "Sh-Boom" was the "B" side of the Chords' single—almost an afterthought. The "A" side was their cover of Patti Page's hit from earlier that year: "Cross Over the Bridge." Page, like the Crew Cuts, recorded on Mercury. So, from the point of view of Mercury Record executives, the Crew Cuts' cover simply returned the favor.

The notion of a cover version is a rock-era concept; it depends on a recording being understood as the song, and not simply a version of the song. The record—whether bought outright or heard on the air—was becoming the primary document. Increasingly, the recording was not simply a version of the song; it *was* the song. By contrast, pop songs from the prewar era usually existed independently of any particular version of it.

Many doo-wop songs were, in effect, cover versions—that is, remakes of existing songs—before the idea of covers surfaced. Many of the songs reconceived by the early doo-wop groups were standards that had been around for a while. However, "Cross Over the Bridge," like "Crying in the Chapel," was a current hit. In doo-wop, at least, song covering was a two-way street. The repertoire that doo-wop groups recorded clearly suggests that they were trying to locate the pop middle ground.

The injustice of covers is not so much a musical issue. The blacks who sang doo-wop were borrowing liberally from white pop. The greatest *musical* injustice in white covers of black recordings is bad taste: the pop music establishment superimposing their conception of a sound with mass appeal, and enervating the music as a result. (RCA won the bad taste contest hands down, having sugarcoated both Elvis and Sam Cooke.) Instead, it's a financial and racial issue: that blacks did not have easy access to the pop market, that many were naive about the music business and never saw the money that their records made, that the labels that signed and recorded them could not compete with the majors, and that white versions sold better than the black originals. Covers became less common as white audiences opened up to black music of all kinds. Perhaps the poster child for this shift in consciousness would be the Marcels, whose raucous version of the standard "Blue Moon" topped the pop charts in 1961. It was a sound that no white group could imitate.

## The Sound of Up-Tempo Doo-Wop

CD 1:30

"Sh-Boom," the
Chords (1954)

In any event, the Chords' eye toward the pop charts is clearly evident in "Sh-Boom." We might describe "Sh-Boom" as jump band lite. From the jump band it took the shuffle rhythm and instrumentation: rhythm section plus saxophone. But the beat is discreet—very much in the background—and the good saxophone solo straddles the boundary between jazz and honking R&B. Moreover, the song is not a blues; its form and underlying harmony use "Heart and Soul" as a model.

The song focuses on the voices; the instrumental accompaniment is very much in the background. The Chords' sound is typical: a lead singer (Carl Feaster) with a pleasant but untrained voice, plus four backup singers, including the requisite bass voice (William "Ricky" Edwards), who steps into the spotlight briefly. When singing behind Feaster, the backup singers alternate between sustained chords and the occasional rhythmic interjection—"Sh-boom." During the saxophone solo, the voices mimic a big-band horn section playing a riff underneath a soloist.

---

♪   **KEY FEATURES**

**"Sh-Boom," the Chords (1954)**

- Jump band shuffle rhythm, medium tempo, and instrumentation
- Doo-wop vocal sound: lead singer plus three or four backup vocalists
- Use of nonsense syllables to provide rhythmic energy

---

The Chords' song exemplified another phenomenon of the early rock era: the **one-hit wonder.** The Chords recorded on Cat Records, an obscure subsidiary of

Atlantic Records; the company released only eighteen discs. This is undoubtedly one reason the group never reached either the pop or R&B charts again. Another factor was their frequent name-changing. After "Sh-Boom" hit, they discovered that another group already owned the name, so they became the Chordcats, then the Sh-Booms. Neither name worked for them, although they remained active as the Sh-Booms through the mid-sixties.

Although "Sh-Boom" was the first doo-wop song to cross over to the pop charts, the sound that is more strongly associated with the style is the slow romantic ballad. We hear a doo-wop take on the pop standard "I Only Have Eyes for You" next.

## The Sound of Slow Doo-Wop

The link between doo-wop and pre-rock pop is implicit in songs like "Sh-Boom," in which an original song uses pop-song form and style as a point of reference. The link between doo-wop and pop is explicit when doo-wop groups remake pop standards (a **standard** is a pop song that has retained its appeal well after its initial release). What also becomes clear is the extent to which doo-wop groups transformed pop style into something new and distinctive by drawing on gospel and R&B. A 1959 remake of "I Only Have Eyes for You" by the Flamingos is a fine late example of this hybrid style.

The Flamingos were one of the countless "bird" groups: Orioles, Ravens, Penguins, and so on. The group, made up of two pairs of cousins and lead singer Sollie McElroy, came together in 1952. They enjoyed modest success in the middle of the decade; "I Only Have Eyes for You" was the only recording that would cross over to the pop charts during the fifties.

"I Only Have Eyes for You" dates from the thirties: it was a hit in 1934 and became a favorite of Frank Sinatra and many other singers over the years. However, the Flamingos' version reworks it so extensively that it becomes virtually a new song.

CD 1:31

"I Only Have Eyes for You," the Flamingos, (1959)

The vocal sound comes straight out of one strain of gospel: it is pleasant but not silky smooth. So does the slow tempo: black gospel choirs typically sing a hymn like "Amazing Grace" at a much slower tempo than their white counterparts. To energize this slow tempo, the pianist plays repeated chords in a triplet rhythm.

The influence of both gospel and rhythm and blues is evident in the opening of the song, where we hear static harmony and two riffs—one sung and played in a low register, the other the signature riff of the song. The static harmony replaces more conventional chords. This is clearly by choice, as most of the song retains the lush harmonies of the original—beautifully sung. The "doo-wop-chi-bop" riff stands in counterpoint to the lead vocal and low riff during the opening. By adding the signature riff, dropping the tempo to a snail's pace, and changing the harmony so drastically, the Flamingos give the song a completely new identity.

The presence of a signature riff here shows a crucial stage in the evolution of doo-wop into the black pop of the sixties. Memorable riffs outside of the main melody were common in much fifties rhythm and blues, including up-tempo doo-wop, but not in earlier doo-wop ballads. The "doo-wop-chi-bop" riff of this song puts rhythm in this, the most melodic R&B style of the era. Although it died out in the early sixties, doo-wop was the main source of the new black pop styles of the sixties. It would inspire both the popular girl groups of the early sixties and Motown, which was just getting started as doo-wop was dying out.

> ♪ **KEY FEATURES**
>
> **"I Only Have Eyes for You," the Flamingos (1959)**
> - New vocal timbre: pleasant blend of a doo-wop singing group, rather than the smooth crooning of a pop singer
> - Tempo that is about half the speed of the original version
> - Bipolar harmony: long stretches of a single chord contrasting with lush harmonies, most notably on the title phrase
> - Insistent triplet rhythm played on the piano in a high register
> - Rhythmic nonsense syllables: "doo-wop-chi-bop"

The Flamingos' recording is classic doo-wop: slow, well sung, beautifully harmonized, and with "doo-wop" always in the background. It is an especially good example of the mainstream black vocal group style. By contrast, the most distinctive style belonged to the Coasters, a group produced by Jerry Leiber and Mike Stoller. We consider the rise of music production, as exemplified in one of their songs.

## The Coasters and Music Production in the Fifties

The Coasters—so named because they came from the west coast, unlike most of the other doo-wop groups—were really doo-wop in name only, because their music was so different from almost all the other groups of the time. They had formed as the Four Bluebirds in 1947 and became the Robins in 1950, singing backup behind Little Esther. They reformed in late 1955, renaming themselves the Coasters.

The group's fortunes changed when they met Jerry Leiber and Mike Stoller in 1953. Leiber and Stoller were a white songwriting and (later) producing team, also from Los Angeles, who had grown up listening to rhythm and blues. Active from 1950, they had scored big in 1953 with "Hound Dog," recorded initially by Big Mama Thornton and later covered by Elvis, for whom they later wrote several other songs, including "Jailhouse Rock." By the time the Coasters recorded "Young Blood" in 1957, they were independent producers for Atlantic Records, often writing the songs and supervising all aspects of the recording.

**Songwriting and Production** Sam Phillips's inspired decision to record Willie Kizart's distorted guitar was an early hint of what would soon become an important creative dynamic in popular music: the interplay between artist and producer. This in turn reflected a reconception of what a song was and where it existed. In pre-rock popular music, songs existed independently of any particular version of the song. For example, "I Only Have Eyes for You" was sung by Dick Powell, a popular singer and actor during the thirties, in the film *Dames*. In short order, several other recordings of the song appeared on the market; at least three were hits. The song continued to be recorded over the next several decades; the Flamingos' distinctive rendition was still only one of many versions of the song.

By contrast, in the new music of the fifties—rhythm and blues and rock and roll— the song was often what was on the recording; it was not *independent* of the recording.

A remark by Leiber and Stoller sums up this new approach: "We don't write songs, we write records." In many fifties recordings, the sound on the recording owes as much to the producer as the featured artists.

The first producers wore several hats—artist and repertoire (A&R) man, songwriter, arranger, contractor—as well as recording engineer, in several cases. Because producers controlled so many elements, they often put their own stamp on the sound of a recording. For example, the **New Orleans sound** was the product of a distinctive arranging style played by the same nucleus of musicians. Dave Bartholomew at Imperial Records (who produced Fats Domino's sessions) and "Bumps" Blackwell at Specialty Records (who produced so many of Little Richard's hits) favored a heavy sound. To achieve this, they would have saxes, guitar, and bass all play a low-register riff: Little Richard's "Lucille" (discussed in Chapter 5) is a clear example. It could be part of the sound, regardless of the featured artist. Indeed, behind virtually all of the major fifties stars was an important producer, who often doubled as recording engineer. Sam Phillips oversaw Elvis's early career and Jerry Lee Lewis's rock-and-roll records, while Leonard Chess produced Chuck Berry's hits and Norman Petty most of Buddy Holly's.

Leiber and Stoller were among the first to elevate record production to an art. They were meticulous in both planning and production, often recording up to sixty takes to obtain the result they sought. Their most distinctive early songs were what Leiber called "playlets"—songs that told a funny story with serious overtones; Stoller called them "cartoons." As with print cartoons, the primary audience was young people—of all races—who identified with the main characters in the story. These were humorous stories, but with an edge.

CD 1:32

"Young Blood,"
the Coasters
(1957)

**"Young Blood"** Through the mid-fifties, the Robins/Coasters were the vehicle for these songs. Their list of hits includes "Smokey Joe's Cafe," "Charlie Brown," "Yakety Yak," and "Young Blood," which topped the R&B charts and reached the Top 10 in the pop charts in 1957.

The story told in "Young Blood" deals with youthful infatuation, but it is a far cry from the starry-eyed romance found in songs like "Earth Angel"—and with no happy ending. As "Young Blood" shows, the Coasters' songs were the opposite of most doo-wop: steely-eyed, not sentimental, and darkly humorous. The Coasters' singing sounds slick, but not sweet. Although the Coasters have a black sound, the theme of the song is universal: teens of all races could relate to it, and did.

The musical setting is a distinctive take on fifties rhythm and blues. The core instrumentation is typical: full rhythm section plus saxophone behind the vocal group. However, there are other instruments in the background. A shuffle rhythm with a heavy backbeat provide the underlying rhythmic framework. But the most prominent rhythm is the repeated guitar riff, which has a distinct rhythmic profile, and there are numerous shifts in the rhythmic flow—breaks that showcase the Coasters' trademark humorous asides that drop down the vocal ladder, with bass singer Bobby Nunn getting in the last word, and sections where the rhythm players sustain long chords instead of marking the beat. These and other features separate "Young Blood" musically from more straightforward R&B songs (like "Shake, Rattle and Roll"), just as the lyrics separate the song from both blues-oriented lyrics and romantic doo-wop.

---

### ♪ KEY FEATURES

**"Young Blood," the Coasters (1957)**

- Wry tone of lyrics: youthful infatuation that leads nowhere but trouble
- Distinctive approach to shuffle rhythm: guitar riff, breaks, sustained chords
- Sound of the Coasters, especially the down-the-ladder breaks

---

Leiber and Stoller's work with the Coasters evidences the growing role of the producer and the shift in perception of the relationship between song and recording: the recording *is* the song, not just a performance of the song that happened to be recorded. The role of the producer would continue to grow, to the point where in some cases the most identifiable feature of the music would be the background sounds, rather than the featured artists. We return to this in Chapter 6.

# Gospel-Influenced Solo Singing

Ray Charles (born Ray Charles Robinson, 1930–2004) lost his sight at age 7 to an undiagnosed case of glaucoma. The onset of blindness may well have stimulated what was already a voracious appetite for music. Charles grew up listening to and playing everything: blues, gospel, country, jazz, classical, pop. He launched his professional career in the late forties; in his first recordings he emulated the style of Nat Cole, the most popular black vocalist of the era and a fine jazz pianist. In 1952, Atlantic Records bought his contract from Swingtime, the label that had released his first recordings. For about two years, he recorded rhythm-and-blues songs distinguished mainly by the unique quality of his voice. However, late in 1954, Charles made one of those abrupt shifts in musical direction that characterized his career.

The song that signaled this sudden shift was "I Got a Woman." Charles did not write the song; rather, he gave the gospel hymn "Jesus Is All the World to Me" new words and a new beat. His transformation of the sacred into the profane scandalized members of the black community. The blues singer Big Bill Broonzy summed up what Charles had done and why it outraged so many when he said: "He's crying, sanctified. He's mixing the blues with the spirituals. He should be singing in a church."

Charles had mixed rhythmic rhythm and blues with the most fervent kind of gospel singing, the kind one might hear in black Pentecostal churches. It was a defining moment in the assimilation of gospel music into rhythm and blues, for at least two reasons: first, it transformed a hymn into a pop song, and second, it introduced the vocal style that would define soul music. However, by the time "I Got a Woman" charted in early 1955, the influence of gospel on solo singing was evident in a wide range of music, from Charles's proto-soul to gospel-flavored pop.

Gospel's influence on rhythm and blues went far beyond doo-wop's gospel/pop/R&B blends. The full range of its influence becomes apparent only in the work of gospel-influenced solo singers. Three performers whose careers took off in the mid-fifties demarcated innovative paths. Each blended gospel with another style. Cooke and Charles are discussed following; the profile of Little Richard more properly belongs in the discussion of rock and roll (see Chapter 5).

- Pop/gospel—Sam Cooke blended smooth-voiced gospel singing with pop, defining a new black pop solo-singing style in the process.
- Gospel/rock and roll—Little Richard combined gospel's ecstatic side with the old/new beat of boogie-woogie/rock and roll.
- Gospel/blues—Ray Charles secularized the uninhibited passion of the sanctified church and mixed it with the deep feeling of the blues.

The careers of Sam Cooke and Ray Charles run parallel in several important respects and opposite in others. Both were commercially successful, especially within the black community. They were also the best at what they did. In the late fifties, their music epitomized the possibilities within black pop solo singing and the blues/gospel merger that would soon become soul.

However, the paths of their careers ran in opposite directions. Cooke started on the outside (with gospel, a noncommercial style), and came "inside" in search of pop success. Charles, on the other hand, started out on the inside by emulating the popular style of Nat "King" Cole, then made his mark by creating a new "outside" style.

They also differed in the amount of adversity they had overcome. Cooke, whose looks matched his talent, seemed to be sailing through life, as much as any black man could in the fifties and sixties—signing with a major label, headlining at the Copacabana—until his sudden, shocking death. By contrast, Charles had to battle through numerous problems—most obviously his blindness, but also a well-publicized drug problem. He overcame both to become one of the icons of the rock era.

## Sam Cooke

The son of a minister, Sam Cooke (born Sam Cook, 1931–1964) grew up singing in church. His family moved from Mississippi to Chicago in 1933, and in 1950 he joined one of the top gospel groups of the era, the Soul Stirrers, as the lead singer. In 1956, he began recording secular material under the direction of Bumps Blackwell, the producer at Specialty Records who also recorded Little Richard. Blackwell determined the course of Cooke's career early on by packaging him in a purely pop setting. This hybrid sound bothered Art Rupe, the owner of Specialty Records, enough that he agreed to let Cooke and Blackwell keep the record masters in exchange for a release from their contract.

**"You Send Me"** Among the recordings they took to Keen Records was a Cooke original, "You Send Me" (1957). The song is yet another take on the "heart and soul" ballad style so popular in rhythm and blues, and the setting includes an understated rhythm section accompaniment and a choir of white pop singers, which adult listeners of the time would typically hear in easy-listening recordings.

The distinctive element in "You Send Me" was Cooke's singing, which was admired throughout the music industry. Jerry Wexler, who by this time was a partner in Atlantic Records—the label that had Charles, the Coasters, and several other top R&B acts on their roster—commented on Cooke's singing:

Frank Driggs Collection/Getty Images

Sam Cooke at the RCA Recording Studios. Cooke moved from Keen to RCA in 1960.

Sam was the best singer who ever lived, no contest. . . . he had control, he could play with his voice like an instrument, his melisma, which was his personal brand—I mean, nobody else could do it—everything about him was perfection.

In "You Send Me," two features of Cooke's singing stand out. First and foremost, there is his beautiful, effortless sound, a rock-era analogue to Nat Cole. Second, there are the elements he brought from gospel, most notably the melisma that Wexler found so distinctive and the rhythmic freedom that allows him to soar over the beat. Aside from Cooke's singing, however, "You Send Me" is pop. Both the song and the setting—discreet backup, white chorus—are closer to Patti Page or Perry Como material than to rhythm and blues.

Cooke seemed to have it all: looks, charm, and one of the truly superb voices in popular music history. Recognizing this in 1960, RCA brought him to their label, where he produced a stream of hits. But his career

"You Send Me," Sam Cooke (1957)

## ♪ KEY FEATURES

**"You Send Me," Sam Cooke (1957)**
- New song composed on the old pop models, like "Sh-Boom"
- Discreet, bland accompaniment: white choir, quiet rhythm section, with subtle triplets and backbeat
- Cooke's glorious singing

ended abruptly one night in 1964 when he was shot and killed by a woman in a Los Angeles hotel room. Everyone connected with the event seems to have a different story, and his death remains a mystery.

Cooke's tragically short career followed a mainstream, pop path. The disparity between the expressiveness of his singing and the treacly pop settings widens. Cooke's voice never finds a perfectly complementary accompaniment on his commercial pop recordings. For most of this material there is only one reason to listen: Cooke's singing. For every "Bring It on Home to Me" there seem to be ten trite songs, like "Sad Mood" and "Ain't That Good News." Even on his most soulful studio recordings, the background never measures up to the quality of his singing. If it had, Cooke's legacy as a pop singer would have been far more substantial. Still, we are grateful for what we have.

Because his voice was all but inimitable and because his music usually looked to the past, rather than the future, Cooke had almost no influence on the course of rock-era music. Just the opposite is true in the case of Ray Charles, whose music we consider next.

## Ray Charles

The music of Ray Charles presents a puzzle of a different kind: why did a man who had created such an important new musical direction suddenly turn his back on it? Unlike Cooke, who simply brought his voice, Charles brought the whole gospel package to rhythm and blues: the songs, his uninhibited singing, the open-ended "getting happy" exchanges, the beat, the feel of the music.

"I Got a Woman," the 1955 recording that integrated this full gospel sound into rhythm and blues, marked an abrupt change from his earlier recordings. For him, and for the world of popular music, it was a brand-new sound, as new in its own way as rock and roll. It brought him a measure of success, especially within the black community—much more than he had enjoyed previously. For about five years, he refined and expanded this new concept, producing some of the definitive music of the decade.

Then, just as abruptly, he switched gears again—not once, but three times—with excursions into pop (1960), jazz (1961), and country music (1962). These detours brought him unprecedented success: while his gospel/blues fusions made him a top artist among blacks, his gospel/blues/jazz/pop/country fusions made him one of the most successful and influential artists in all of popular music during the early sixties.

Each of his chameleon-like changes broadened his audience significantly. However, financial considerations did not seem paramount. In each case, he found distinctively new ways of interpreting his material: no one had ever sung "Georgia on My Mind" or "Your Cheatin' Heart" like him. Instead, his style shifts seemed to come from his restless, curious musical mind. For Charles, there were no boundaries or limits: he was equally at home singing and playing with soul partner Aretha Franklin, country great Willie Nelson, pop-rocker Billy Joel, jazz vibraphonist Milt Jackson, or gospel legend Andrae Crouch.

By his own account, Charles listened to, and absorbed, all kinds of music when he was growing up, and it has all come out in his music over the course of his career. He brought to popular music one of the most unusual dualities in its history: one of the most personal, immediately identifiable voices in all of popular music, paired with an eclecticism that embraces almost every popular style of his generation.

Charles's two live recordings from the fifties, from performances at the 1958 Newport Jazz Festival and in Atlanta a year later, show how he filtered a broad array of music through his gospel experience—and vice versa—to come up with a range of new sounds. There is blues, rhythm and blues, Latin dance music, jazz, secularized gospel, even minstrel songs (Stephen Foster's "Old Folks at Home" becomes "Swanee River Rock").

These recordings also document the range and power of his blues/gospel synthesis. In effect, he infuses all the blues strains in rhythm and blues with a gospel

Hulton Archive/Getty Images

Ray Charles at the piano, around the time that he recorded "What'd I Say," in 1959.

tinge and updates their sound. It is not that Charles's blues become more powerful than Bessie Smith's or Robert Johnson's; rather, it is that they are powerful in a different way. The sad blues find a new way to communicate their melancholy, while the happy blues convey a heaven-on-earth ecstasy that could arrive only by way of gospel.

Some of his most emotionally charged music comes out at a slow tempo. Perhaps the best example is "A Fool for You." In this song, he sings with the deep feeling of the blues, enriched with the most expressive devices of gospel singing—the melismas, the soaring phrases, the high-pitched wails—all set to the stately swing of slow gospel. Charles's fusion of blues feeling with gospel style in slow songs was a unique synthesis and an expressive milestone in the history of popular music. Few popular performers have communicated with such emotional intensity, and only Aretha Franklin followed in Charles's footsteps with comparable artistic success.

**"What'd I Say"**   Perhaps the song that best summarizes the many facets of Charles's musical personality during the fifties was his only Top 10 hit from that decade: "What'd I Say." There are two recordings of the song from 1959—a live performance in Atlanta and a studio recording that lasts about 6½ minutes— both sides of a 45. It combines not only blues and gospel—musically, verbally, and in spirit—but also draws on Latin music and jazz. The extended length of the studio recording allows Charles to let the song unfold slowly. It begins with a comprehensive instrumental introduction and adds musical layers one by one—Charles's singing, the horn section, and then the Raelettes, his backup vocal group—as it builds to an orgasmic climax.

"What'd I Say," Ray Charles (1959)

In the instrumental section we hear Charles's take on Latin rhythm. The opening piano figure evokes the piano parts of Afro-Cuban music, and the drum part is much closer to Americanized Latin drumming than standard rock drumming, circa 1959. Charles was not the first to blend Latin rhythms into rhythm and blues—recall the New Orleans songs—but his Americanized Latin rhythm was certainly a catalyst in pointing rhythm and blues toward the more rhythmically free approach to the rock rhythm heard in black music during the sixties.

The solo vocal section alternates between stop time and a more continuous flow in which the vocal line soars over the instrumental riffs. Although the solo vocal section uses the by-now venerable verse/chorus blues form, it does not tell a story. Instead, it alternates between images of a dancing woman with all the right moves and Charles's need for sexual satisfaction. His need is fulfilled in the final section, in which Charles's exchanges with the Raelettes depict sexual ecstasy about as graphically as one can in music.

---

♪ **KEY FEATURES**

**"What'd I Say," Ray Charles (1959)**

- Americanized Latin rhythm, heard in the drums and lower part of the electric piano, which parallels rock rhythm in that it divides beats into two equal parts, but is more active
- Extended instrumental introduction and interlude, unusual for a pop song but typical of a jazz performance
- Merger of happy blues with ecstatic gospel style
- Charles's soulful singing, especially during the call-and-response section with the Raelettes

---

"What'd I Say" defined a crucial juncture in the relationship between gospel and blues, and in black music during the rock era. The song revisits a blues tradition—in subject matter (the pleasures of sex), narrative style (pictures, not a story), upbeat mood, and form (verse/chorus blues)—that began with songs like Thomas A. Dorsey's "It's Tight Like That" (see Chapter 3). Soon after Dorsey recorded "It's Tight Like That," he brought the blues into black sacred music. Charles closes that particular circle by bringing gospel music into a "It's Tight Like That"–type blues song. The use of the fervent gospel style is functional: it adds a dimension to the blues that was not there before. Sexual relations (and the lack of them) have been the most recurrent theme in blues, as we have noted. The infusion of ecstatic gospel style communicates the experience of sex more powerfully than is possible in traditional blues. Songs like this are the bridge between blues and soul.

**The Influence of Ray Charles**  Charles's influence has come in two installments. The first grew out of his work in the late fifties, when he mapped out new directions in the gospel/rhythm and blues synthesis that was already well underway. It was his musical example, more than anyone else's, that led black music to soul and inspired numerous white musicians along the way. The second resulted from his recordings of popular song and country music. In particular, the country recordings opened up expressive possibilities to a new generation of country performers.

# Rhythm and Blues and Rock and Roll

In the decade between 1949 and 1959, rhythm and blues got a name, a host of new styles, and a much bigger audience. Electric blues, jump bands, Latin R&B from New Orleans, doo-wop, and the blues/gospel fusions of Ray Charles were all new sounds. All these styles sounded black, but they covered a lot of territory. There's a big gap between doo-wop ballads and electric blues or New Orleans R&B. Still, there was also a lot of interplay among the styles. From one perspective, the blues got rhythm, rhythm got the blues, and much of it got the spirit via gospel. Country blues became electric blues when it moved to the city and added an electric guitar and a heavier beat, via a full rhythm section. Slow doo-wop applied black gospel style to pop ballads;

up-tempo doo-wop did the same to jump band R&B. Among solo singers, gospel also mixed with pop and blues.

For the first half of the fifties, rhythm and blues and rock and roll were the same. They began to diverge with the emergence of white performers working in this new style—artists such as Bill Haley, Elvis, and Carl Perkins. Still, the main criterion that distinguished rock and roll from rhythm and blues was where they charted. If a black act appeared regularly on the pop charts, then their music was rock and roll; if their success was limited to the black audience, like Muddy Waters, then they were rhythm and blues. However, toward the end of the decade, clear musical differences between rock and roll and rhythm and blues begin to emerge. We explore these and other aspects of the relationship between rock and roll and rhythm and blues in Chapter 5.

## Terms to Remember

| | | |
|---|---|---|
| race record | triplet | patting juba |
| rhythm and blues (R&B) | distortion | hambone rhythm |
| disc jockey (DJ) | blues progression | doo-wop |
| 78 rpm, 33 rpm, 45 rpm | I, IV, and V chords | scat singing |
| long-playing (LP) record | walking, walk | bebop (bop) |
| single record | big-beat music | cover |
| indie music | electric blues | one-hit wonder |
| crossover | deep blues | standard |
| Latin rhythm | clave rhythm | New Orleans sound |
| backbeat | Bo Diddley beat | |
| shuffle rhythm | maracas | |

## Applying Chapter Concepts

1. To clarify in your own mind both the difference between a shuffle rhythm and a rock beat and the affinity between Latin rhythms and rock rhythm, revisit the Rolling Stones' song from Chapter 1 (and/or rock songs discussed in subsequent chapters) and compare it with the shuffle rhythm in "Rocket 88," "(I'm Your) Hoochie Coochie Man," and "Sh-Boom," and the Latin-tinged rhythms of "Bo Diddley" and "What'd I Say." Note how the even division of the beat in "It's Only Rock 'n Roll" lines up with the Latin-tinged songs but *not* with the shuffle rhythm—at any tempo.

2. It can be argued that doo-wop and black pop such as "You Send Me" are neither rhythm nor blues. Explore the connection of doo-wop to pop by comparing "Sh-Boom" and "You Send Me" to "Heart and Soul," especially in the song form and the chord progression. Then discuss similarities and differences in style between Eddy Duchin's pop and the two R&B songs, focusing particularly on rhythm, vocal style, and instrumentation. And if you can gain access to a thirties recording of "I Only Have Eyes for You," compare that recording with its remake by the Flamingos.

3. Using Bessie Smith's "Empty Bed Blues" as a model for conventional blues form, in words and music, write a rhymed couplet. It can be as simple as this:

> *My teacher says I gotta write a blues*
> *Yeah, my teacher says I gotta write a blues*
> *I got to say it sure was some good news*

(Hopefully it will be more inspired!) Then say (or sing) it over the first chorus of "Rocket 88," making sure to coordinate the repetition of the first line with the move to the IV chord and coordinate the second line with the move to the V chord. This should give you an experiential understanding of conventional blues form.

4. "Rocket 88," "Shake, Rattle and Roll," "(I'm Your) Hoochie Coochie Man," and "What'd I Say" are the four songs that use some variant of blues form, either in the form of the lyric or in the underlying chord progression. Make a chart that details the way(s) in which each of these songs varies this conventional form.

Then compare these four songs according to the following criteria:

  a. Subject and style of the lyric
  b. Vocal style
  c. Connection between tempo and mood
  d. Instrumentation and texture

# 5

# Rock and Roll

In 1986, the Rock and Roll Hall of Fame Museum in Cleveland, Ohio, admitted its first class of inductees: Chuck Berry, James Brown, Ray Charles, Sam Cooke, Fats Domino, the Everly Brothers, Buddy Holly, Jerry Lee Lewis, Elvis Presley, and Little Richard. Performers become eligible for induction twenty-five years after the release of their first record. Selection criteria include "the influence and significance of the artist's contributions to the development and perpetuation of rock and roll."

If the complete list of inductees can be used as a reliable guide, *rock and roll* is, for the Rock and Roll Hall of Fame, more or less equivalent to our *rock era* as an umbrella term for the rock-related music of the last several decades. In this chapter, we describe another more specific understanding of "rock and roll." Our central point of reference will be those artists who were *not* discussed in the previous chapter, or—in the case of James Brown—whose most important work would come in the sixties. We look to the music of Chuck Berry, the Everly Brothers, Buddy Holly, Jerry Lee Lewis, Elvis Presley, and Little Richard to lead us to a *musical* understanding of rock and roll.

The music of these six musicians is the heart and soul of this more time-limited understanding of rock and roll. Although their music represents only a small fraction of the new music of the late fifties, it defines the core and the boundaries of rock and roll, as a style distinct from both pop and rhythm and blues in the fifties, and the rock of the sixties. Rock and roll grew out of rhythm and blues; in the latter part of the fifties, it acquired an increasingly distinct identity. Our primary objective in this chapter is to trace the evolution of rock and roll from its first use as a "cover" label for rhythm and blues to its premature "death" in 1959, by which time it had laid the foundation for sixties rock. We begin in 1951.

## The Beginnings of Rock and Roll

When did rock and roll begin? The answer depends a great deal on the context in which the question is asked. Does it have to do with the term itself? Did rock and roll begin when people labeled rhythm and blues "rock and roll"? Or did it begin when young white singers began covering rhythm-and-blues songs? Or when the media acknowledged a new kind of music and its new stars? Or when what was called "rock and roll" brought new sounds to the pop charts? The answers to all of these questions shed light on the emergence of rock and roll.

## Alan Freed

"Rockin' and rollin'" was originally a euphemism for the sexual act, as we have noted. The expression had been in use on recordings for almost thirty years by the time disc jockey Alan Freed attached "rock and roll" to a musical style. Freed was an early and influential advocate of rhythm and blues. Unlike most of the disc jockeys of the era, he refused to play white cover versions of R&B hits, a practice that gained him respect among black musicians but made him enemies in the business. While broadcasting over WJW in Cleveland in 1951, he began using "rock and roll" as a euphemism of a different kind: through him, the term became a code word among whites for "rhythm and blues."

Freed's "Moondog's Rock and Roll Party" developed a large audience among both whites and blacks, so he took his advocacy of rhythm and blues one step further, into promotion. He put together touring stage shows of rhythm-and-blues artists, which played to integrated audiences. His first big event, the Moondog Coronation Ball, took place in 1952; 25,000 people, the majority of them white, showed up at a facility that could accommodate only a small fraction of that number. The ensuing pandemonium was the first of many "incidents" in Freed's career as a promoter.

Freed linked the term *rock and roll* to rhythm and blues, so it's no wonder that Fats Domino and producer Dave Bartholomew, the mastermind of so many New Orleans R&B hits, commented that rock and roll was rhythm and blues. Bartholomew said, undoubtedly with some bitterness, "We had rhythm and blues for many, many a year, and here come in a couple of white people and they call it rock and roll, and it was rhythm and blues all the time!"

In 1954, Freed moved to New York in order to offer his rock-and-roll radio show on WINS. By that year, rock and roll took its first steps toward an identity distinct from rhythm and blues, with white takes on rhythm and blues. In 1954, the best-known example of this was the Crew Cuts' cover of "Sh-Boom." However, in Memphis and in small towns in Pennsylvania and neighboring states, **rockabilly**, a more significant white reinterpretation of R&B, was taking shape.

# Rockabilly

Carl Perkins, perhaps the truest of the rockabilly stars, once explained his music this way: "To begin with . . . rockabilly music, or rock and roll . . . was a country man's song with a black man's rhythm. I just put a little speed into some of the slow blues licks." As Perkins described it, rockabilly was the latest take in a long line of country takes on black music. It continues a trend that began with Jimmie Rodgers's blue yodels, and ran through Bob Wills's western swing, and Hank Williams' "moanin' the blues."

Rockabilly was a state of mind—and body. It was the music of liberation for southern white males: what they danced to on Saturday nights when they wanted to "get real, real gone." As Glenn Gass observed, "Rockabilly was distinctly and proudly southern." Its capital was Memphis, and its capitol building a small storefront located at 706 Union Avenue, where Sam Phillips operated Sun Records. A legion of Johnny B.

Goodes, many of whom sang and played with the abandon of black rhythm-and-blues musicians, beat a path to Phillips's door. However, even as southern rockabilly was taking shape in Memphis, other musicians outside the South were following a similar path.

## Bill Haley and Rockabilly

CD 2:1

"Rock Around the Clock," Bill Haley (1954)

The first big rockabilly hit came from an unlikely source, by way of an unlikely place, and took an unlikely path. Bill Haley (1925–1981), who recorded it, grew up in Pennsylvania listening to the Grand Ole Opry and dreaming of country music stardom. By the late forties he had begun fronting small bands—one was called the Four Aces of Western Swing—and enjoyed some local success. Over the next few years, he began to give his music a bluesier sound and chose—or wrote—songs with teen appeal. "Crazy, Man, Crazy" (1953) was his first hit. In 1954, he had some success with a song called "Rock Around the Clock"; it reached number 23 on the pop charts.

> ### Black and White/R&B and Rockabilly
>
> Rockabilly gives one perspective on the musical relationship between black and white in the early years of the rock era. However, musical exchange went both ways: "Rock Around the Clock" was the work of the white songwriters Jimmy DeKnight and Max Freedman, who had previously scored with "Rock the Joint," an R&B hit in 1949 for saxophonist Jimmy Preston and a song that Haley covered in 1952. This white/black/white sequence would be repeated several times over, most notably in Leiber and Stoller's "Hound Dog" and "Kansas City," both of which were originally hits for R&B artists and were soon covered by white artists.

A year later, "Rock Around the Clock" resurfaced in the film *The Blackboard Jungle*. The connections among film, song, and performer were tenuous. The film portrays juvenile delinquents in a slum high school, but "Rock Around the Clock" is exuberant rather than angry, and Haley, at almost 30, looks nothing like a rebel. But it was music for and about teens (parents weren't likely to rock around the clock); that was enough for the producers. With the release of the film, the song returned to the charts and skyrocketed to number 1. It was Haley's big moment. He had a few other minor hits but never repeated his chart-topping success.

"Rock Around the Clock" might be characterized as a lite version of rhythmic R&B: it has the shuffle beat that we associate with so much fifties rhythm and blues, but the tempo is faster, and the beat keeping is more subtle. The sound is also less aggressive: the vocal style is not as rough, and the instruments play in a higher register; the saxophonist doesn't honk a solo—the electric guitar is the featured instrument. Overall, it's a brighter sound.

"Rock Around the Clock" also takes its form and harmony from rhythm and blues. Like so many songs of the era, it is a 12-bar blues. As in songs like "It's Tight Like That," the first four bars function as the verse, and the last eight as the refrain.

♪ **KEY FEATURES**

**"Rock Around the Clock," Bill Haley (1954)**
- Light-hearted lyric: "rocking" here is simply about dancing the night away; nothing suggests a more intimate involvement between partners.
- Light-hearted music: the brisk tempo, discreet shuffle beat, and generally high register of Haley's voice and the guitar give the song a bright feel.
- Blues form with a built-in refrain.

While Haley nibbled at the charts, a grittier form of rockabilly was taking shape in Memphis. We encounter it in the music of the performer who would eventually become rock and roll's biggest star.

## Elvis, Sam Phillips, and Rockabilly

In the summer of 1953, a young truck driver named Elvis Presley (1935–1977) walked into the Sam Phillips Recording Service to make a demo record. Phillips wasn't in, so his assistant, Marion Keisker, handled the session. Perhaps to make him feel at ease, she asked him about himself. The conversation went something like this:

*Marion:* What kind of singer are you?

*Elvis:* I sing all kinds.

*Marion:* Who do you sound like?

*Elvis:* I don't sound like nobody.

*Marion:* Hillbilly?

*Elvis:* Yeah, I sing hillbilly.

*Marion:* Who do you sound like in hillbilly?

*Elvis:* I don't sound like nobody.

This now-legendary encounter gives us some insight into Elvis's success. Imagine yourself—barely out of high school and with no professional experience—having such a clear sense of who you are and what you can do. Elvis truly didn't sound like anyone else; he was the "white man with the negro feel" that Sam Phillips had been seeking for several years.

Presley recorded his first local hit for Phillips's Sun Records in 1954. The record, a cover of bluesman Arthur Crudup's "That's All Right," sparked interest on country-western radio (although some stations wouldn't play it because Elvis sounded too black). Within a year he had reached number 1 nationally on the country-and-western (C&W) charts with "Mystery Train"—one of Elvis's most enduring early hits. Elvis's Sun sessions are quintessential rockabilly. In Junior Parker's 1953 version—the one Presley covered—"Mystery Train" is a boogie-based rhythm-and-blues song; it chugs along at a slow pace underneath Parker's bluesy vocal and the occasional saxophone train whistle. Elvis's version is brighter and more upbeat (recall Perkins's remark), and

CD 2:2

"Mystery Train,"
Elvis Presley
(1955)

it uses a more country-style beat. The rhythm section sets a honky-tonk, two-beat bass alternating with a heavy backbeat on the electric guitar. But the backbeat is modified with a quick rebound that begins alternately on, then off, the beat. In form, the song is a modified blues; it has the poetic and melodic form of a blues song, but its harmony and phrase length are slightly irregular.

Elvis's singing is the magical element. In both its basic timbre and its variety, his sound is utterly unique—the purest Elvis. It ranges from a plaintive wail on the opening high notes to the often-imitated guttural singing at the end of each chorus. Elvis positions himself not only between country and rhythm and blues, but beyond them. We don't hear the nasal twang so common in country music, nor do we hear the rough-edged sound of a blues singer. Elvis draws on both but sounds like neither ("I don't sound like nobody").

---

### ♪ KEY FEATURES

**"Mystery Train," Elvis Presley (1955)**

- Fast tempo, with a modified two-beat rhythm; drums maintain a light, fast rhythm very much in the background
- Elvis's soulful singing and unique sound
- Another fresh take on blues form: modified version of the blues progression

---

The distinctive sound of Elvis's voice is only part of the magic. Just as remarkable is his ability to adapt his sound to suit the material. He can emulate the "high lonesome" sound of bluegrass singers like Bill Monroe or croon when he sings pop songs like "Harbor Lights" and "Blue Moon." Elvis could evoke almost any style and still sound like himself. Although he didn't play much guitar, he played the radio really well. He was an equal opportunity listener with an insatiable appetite for music. And what he heard he used.

**Sam Phillips, Sun Records, and Rockabilly** Elvis was not the only rockabilly artist to get his start at Sam Phillips's Sun Studio. In 1950, while still working as a DJ, Phillips (1923–2003) started his Memphis Recording Service. Initially, he recorded rhythm-and-blues artists like Jackie Brenston and Ike Turner, as well as important Memphis-based bluesmen like B. B. King and Howlin' Wolf. Phillips's studio was by far the best place in the region for black musicians to record. Phillips treated the musicians with respect and approached his work with them imaginatively, as we heard in "Rocket 88." Phillips saw the growing market for rhythm and blues from the inside and formed Sun Records after problems with other record companies. He stayed on the lookout for the "white man with the negro feel" until Elvis walked in his door in 1953. In the wake of Elvis's regional success, other top rockabilly acts soon showed up at his studio: Carl Perkins, Jerry Lee Lewis, and somewhat later, Roy Orbison. He also recorded some of the top hard-country acts of the era, including Johnny Cash.

Like so many other men behind the scenes during the early years of rock, Phillips wore many hats. As he built up the Memphis Recording Service into Sun Records, he became not only the engineer but also the producer and promoter of the recordings on his label. In recognition of his seminal role in shaping rock and roll and rhythm and blues, Phillips was, with Alan Freed, the first nonperformer inducted into the Rock and Roll Hall of Fame.

## Rockabilly and Rock and Roll

In rockabilly songs like "Rock Around the Clock" and "Mystery Train," we hear the first stage in the separation of rhythm and blues and rock and roll. Unlike the pop-oriented covers of rhythm-and-blues (and country-and-western) songs (such as the Crew Cuts' version of "Sh-Boom," a dated-sounding cover of the original), rockabilly was a genuinely new sound. It drew on rhythm and blues, but it was distinctly different. In 1955 "Rock Around the Clock" was rock and roll: the first number 1 hit that was neither pop nor a white cover of a rhythm-and-blues song. But it lacked crucial features that would soon distinguish rock and roll not only from pop but also from rhythm and blues, and that would ultimately define rock.

Bill Haley would never really go beyond rockabilly; for the rest of his career he essentially relived his early hits. His star faded about the time Elvis's soared. For Elvis, the defining moment in his career came late in 1955 when, with the help of his manager-to-be Colonel Tom Parker, Elvis moved from Sun Records to RCA. Although Elvis's records were selling well, Phillips was in a financial bind, so he was willing to sell Elvis's contract to the highest bidder, because he was sure that Carl Perkins, another one of his up-and-coming acts, would be just as popular. RCA paid Phillips $35,000 for the contract, $10,000 more than Atlantic Records had offered. Almost overnight, Elvis became a national celebrity.

# Elvis Presley: The First Rock-and-Roll Star

RCA quickly got Elvis in the studio. "Heartbreak Hotel," his first number 1, topped the charts in March 1956. Later that year, he made his first Hollywood film, *Love Me Tender*; he would make three more, including *Jailhouse Rock*, before his induction into the army. Within a few months, Elvis had become a national phenomenon. Within two years, he had recorded several number 1 hits and appeared on numerous television programs, including *The Ed Sullivan Show*, the Sunday night staple for so many Americans during the fifties.

Elvis's sound caught the attention of radio listeners, but it was his looks and his moves that propelled him to stardom. He became the symbol of rock and roll for millions—both those who idolized him and those who despised him. With his totally uninhibited stage manner, teen-tough dress, greased hair in a pompadour, and energetic singing style, Elvis projected a rebellious attitude that many teens found overwhelmingly attractive. By contemporary standards, Elvis seems tame—almost wholesome. But in his day, this was bold stuff, and he took a lot of heat for it. For this, we can admire Elvis's courage. He was rock and roll's lightning rod. For teens, he was all that was right with this new music; for their parents, he symbolized all that was wrong with it. And, for all intents and purposes, he stood alone.

The *Billboard* charts reflect his singular status. Except for Elvis's hits, rock and roll represented only a modest segment of the popular music market. The top-selling

Bettmann/Corbis

Elvis Presley on stage, circa 1957, showing one of his patented moves. Guitarist Scotty Moore is behind Elvis; drummer D. J. Fontana and bassist Bill Black are to his right.

albums during this time were mostly soundtracks from Broadway shows and film musicals. Even sales of singles, which teens bought, show that rock and roll did not enjoy the unconditional support of America's youth. The top singles artists during the same period were either pre-rock stars (Frank Sinatra and Perry Como), younger artists singing in a pre-rock style (Andy Williams or Johnny Mathis), teen stars like Pat Boone, who covered early rock-and-roll songs, or vocal groups like the Platters, whose repertoire included a large number of reworked Tin Pan Alley standards. Among the lesser figures—from a commercial perspective—were such important and influential artists as Buddy Holly, Chuck Berry, Little Richard, and Ray Charles. Elvis was, by far, the most important commercial presence in rock and roll; no one else came close.

## The King of Rock and Roll?

Here's a heretical thought: Elvis Presley, the king of rock and roll, sang very little rock and roll. Such a statement would have been literally incredible to teenagers living in 1956 or 1957; for them, and their parents, Elvis embodied rock and roll. In his discussion of Elvis in *The Story of Rock*, Carl Belz writes:

Elvis Presley is the most important individual rock artist to emerge during the music's early development between 1954 and 1956. His extraordinary popularity surpassed that of any artist who appeared in those years, and it remained as a standard for almost a decade . . . . For the music industry, Presley was "king" for almost ten years. He was the first rock artist to establish a continuing and independent motion picture career, the first to have a whole series of million-selling single records—before 1960 he had eighteen—and the first to dominate consistently the tastes of the foreign record market, especially in England, where popularity polls listed him among the top favorites for each year until the arrival of the Beatles.

Belz equates importance almost exclusively with popularity. His list of Elvis's firsts contains no musical innovations; importance is strictly numbers and visibility. However, Elvis's contributions to rock and roll (and rock) extend beyond his remarkable commercial success. He brought a fresh look, a fresh attitude, and a fresh sound to popular music. All three proved to be enormously influential.

Elvis gave rock and roll its most memorable visual images. His looks sent girls into hysteria and guys to the mirror, where they greased their hair and combed it into Elvis-like pompadours. His uninhibited, sexually charged stage persona scandalized adults even as it sent teen pulses racing. These images endure, as the legion of Elvis imitators reminds us. There had been flamboyant black performers, like T-Bone Walker, whose stage antics included playing his guitar behind his head while doing the splits, but no popular white entertainer had ever moved like Elvis did, and no one had ever looked like he enjoyed it as much. Even now, when we watch clips of Elvis performing, we sense that he is having fun. This was an extraordinarily liberating presence for a new generation of pop stars.

We get some sense of his presence and his appeal in the scene from his 1957 film *Jailhouse Rock* where he sings the title song. In staging the scene, choreographer Alex Romero wisely asked Elvis to perform some of his songs, then choreographed the movements of the other dancers to mesh with Elvis's moves. In the scene, we see that for Elvis, all of this is fun. He moves freely, spontaneously; the other dancers seem routine by comparison. Elvis's uninhibited movement, evident in film and television clips, contrasts sharply with pop singers—white and black—who simply stand in front of microphones and croon their songs.

CD 2:3

"Jailhouse Rock," Elvis Presley (1957)

"Jailhouse Rock," which was released as a single in conjunction with the film, highlights the qualities that made Elvis so appealing, evidences the craft of Leiber and Stoller, who wrote the song, and shows rock and roll on the road to musical differentiation from rhythm and blues.

"Jailhouse Rock" begins with guitar and drums marking off a stop-time rhythm, which continues as Elvis begins to sing. The beginning of the song is, practically speaking, all Elvis, and he makes the most of it. There is an exuberance and a lack of inhibition in his singing that jumps out of the speakers. In this song, Elvis communicates fun—the exhilaration of moving to the beat (even when it can only be felt)—in a way that was unprecedented in pop. Especially when compared to songs like Perry Como's "Hot Diggity," there is an emotional honesty to Elvis's singing that transcends the staginess of the scene in the film. The story may be fake, but Elvis's enthusiasm is real. Elvis found this kind of realness in the blues, and in songs like "Jailhouse Rock" he brought it into the mainstream.

When viewed in the context of the music that he recorded before his induction into the army, Elvis's performance is even more remarkable, because it is only one of many dimensions to his musical personality. In slow songs like "Love Me Tender" and "Don't," he becomes rock's first crooner; his voice is lower, sweeter, and more intimate. Even a quick sampling of his early hits and Sun recordings shows his almost chameleon-like ability to adjust his vocal style to the musical and lyrical context. Few rock-era singers have matched either the innate quality or the expressive range of his voice.

Leiber and Stoller's song shows the same kind of imagination that we heard in the Coasters' "Young Blood." Like Muddy Waters's "Hoochie Coochie Man," "Jailhouse Rock" is a verse/chorus blues form in which the first phrase is doubled in length. To make the verse (and Elvis) stand out and highlight the verse/chorus distinction, Leiber and Stoller provide minimal accompaniment—just enough to sustain the momentum under Elvis's singing. In the chorus part of the form, when the rhythm instruments play continuously, the guitar pumps out the boogie-based pattern that is almost identical in pitch to that used in "Rocket 88." It operates just above the electric bass—still a new instrument in 1957. By contrast, the piano is in a very high register. The wide separation leaves the mid-range completely to Elvis; the prominence of guitar and bass gives the texture a dark sound that helps project the message of the song: we're in jail (dark), but we're still going to have a good time (Elvis).

Rhythmically, "Jailhouse Rock" shows rock and roll in transition. The most rocklike feature is the guitar pattern, which divides the beat into two equal parts. The difference between this version and the same pattern in a shuffle rhythm (as heard in "Rocket 88") is striking; it shows rock and roll moving away from the shuffle rhythm heard in so much rhythm and blues. But Elvis is not fully committed to this new rhythmic approach. By accenting and slightly lengthening the first note of each pair, Elvis creates a rhythmic feel (evident especially in the stop-time verse sections) that is somewhere between a standard rock rhythm and a shuffle rhythm. And even though the bass player is playing an electric bass, he is still **walking**—one note on each beat, like a swing-era or jazz bassist. Most strikingly, the band switches to a swing rhythm in the instrumental interlude; we can almost hear a sigh of relief from the guitarist and drummer as they let go in a rhythm that they know how to feel. Because of the rhythmic inconsistencies, "Jailhouse Rock" is rock and roll commercially but not quite rock and roll rhythmically.

"Jailhouse Rock" also gives us some sense of the relative innocence of the fifties. In the third verse, Elvis sings "Number forty-seven said to number three/You're the cutest jailbird I ever did see. I sure would be delighted with your company, Come on and do the jailhouse rock with me." Few if any took it as a real-life depiction of homosexual relations inside a prison; that kind of awareness would only come much later.

The most influential and musically significant part of Elvis's career lasted only three years. It ended in 1958, when he was inducted into the army. Although still a major public figure in the sixties and seventies, he seldom recaptured the freshness of his earlier years. His fans still call him the king of rock and roll, but is that a reflection

> ♪ **KEY FEATURES**
>
> **"Jailhouse Rock," Elvis Presley (1957)**
> - Elvis's exuberant and uninhibited singing
> - Full rhythm section with prominent electric guitar
> - Expanded verse/chorus form
> - Rhythmic variety: stop time in the verse versus consistent timekeeping in the chorus
> - Different rhythmic conceptions: swing, rock and roll, and in between

of his enduring popularity or his contribution to the development of rock and roll? We consider this question in our discussion of Chuck Berry.

# Chuck Berry: The Architect of Rock and Roll

Sometime early in 1955, well before Elvis's fateful meeting with Colonel Parker, Chuck Berry (b. 1926) "motorvated" (to use a Chuck Berry word) from St. Louis to Chicago to hear Muddy Waters perform at the Palladium Theater. Waters had been Berry's idol for years, although when Berry performed with the Johnny Johnson Trio, they played many different kinds of music. After the concert, Berry went backstage to meet his idol. When he asked Waters how to find a record deal, Waters suggested that he get in touch with Leonard Chess. Two weeks later, Berry was back in Chicago, to give Leonard Chess a demo tape containing four songs. Among them was Berry's remake of a song called "Ida Red." Chess liked the song, Berry recorded it, retitled it "Maybellene," and Chess released it on August 20, 1955.

"Maybellene" caught the ear of Alan Freed, who promoted the song by playing it frequently on his radio show after negotiating a share of the songwriting credits—and the royalties that went with them. With Freed's considerable help—legend has it that Freed played the song for 2 hours straight on one broadcast—"Maybellene" quickly jumped to number 5 on the *Billboard* "Best Seller" chart.

It would take Berry almost a year to get another song on the pop charts. "Roll Over, Beethoven" reached the charts in the fall of 1956. However, over the next two years, Berry had four Top 10 singles, from "School Days" to "Johnny B. Goode." In the hits from "Roll Over, Beethoven" to "Johnny B. Goode," Berry assembled the distinctive sound of rock and roll, step by step. When he was done, rock and roll was well along the road to rock: bands like the Beach Boys, the Beatles, the Rolling Stones, and the Dave Clark Five covered far more Chuck Berry songs than any other rock-and-roll artist.

## "Maybellene," His First Hit

Berry's musical innovations were a synthesis of the music that he liked and played. Waters's music was a big influence, although Berry took his music in a quite different direction. Berry's musical apprenticeship also included singing and playing not only blues, but also rhythm and blues, pop, and what he called **hillbilly**—his take on country music. These numbers were especially popular with the patrons at the Cosmopolitan Club in East St. Louis, where Berry fronted a trio. Another key element was his long-time association with Johnny Johnson, a fine blues pianist who was a master of boogie-woogie. Johnson originally hired Berry to join his trio, but Berry, the more flamboyant entertainer by far, soon took over as leader.

Because Chess's featured artist was Waters, Berry included tapes of blues numbers to his meeting with Chess. But Chess thought that "Ida May," Berry's reworking of the old-time country song "Ida Red," had a much better shot at crossing over to the pop market. Berry claimed that he had learned the song from Bob Wills's recording of "Ida Red." (Some years later Wills provided his own sequel: "Ida Red Likes the Boogie"). Berry's version, which became "Maybellene" (allegedly after the cosmetic company) at the recording session, was a transformation of the original so drastic that the connection between the two songs is not at all clear.

**CD 2:4**

"Maybellene,"
Chuck Berry
(1955)

Chess was right: "Maybellene" was an immediate success, and Berry was on his way to rock-and-roll fame. In "Maybellene" we can hear several of the features that distinguished Berry's music throughout the latter part of the fifties. Here they are, in order of appearance:

**An Aggressive Guitar Sound** The song begins with an unaccompanied guitar riff. There are two features of the riff that stand out. One is the edge to the sound—not as distorted as Kizart's guitar in "Rocket 88" but far from mellow. It is a much more aggressive sound than that heard in pop, country, or even most rhythm and blues. The exception, of course, is electric blues; Berry's sound is closer to the guitar style of electric blues guitarists like T-Bone Walker and Muddy Waters than any other guitar style of the era. This is one important area of influence.

The other is a Berry trademark: the use of double notes. When Berry plays two notes simultaneously, it makes the sound thicker, which in turn gives it more impact. His way of bending the notes (heard here mainly in the guitar solo) is reminiscent of the slide (or bottleneck) guitar style of blues guitarists.

**A Full Rhythm Section** Almost immediately, the other instruments enter: piano, string bass, drums, and maracas (played by Jerome

Bettmann/Corbis

Chuck Berry having a good time on stage, circa 1959.

Green, who also played them with Bo Diddley). Maracas aside, this is, with Berry, the instrumentation of the fifties electric blues band: full rhythm section but with no saxophone. And as in the electric blues band, the electric guitar is the most prominent instrument. That the recording would feature blues-band instrumentation is not surprising: Berry brought pianist Johnny Johnson, his long-time associate, with him from St. Louis; bassist Willie Dixon, who wrote Waters's "(I'm Your) Hoochie Coochie Man," and drummer Fred Below were Chess house musicians during the fifties.

**A Souped-Up Honky-Tonk Beat** "Maybellene" features Berry's take on the two-beat rhythm used in honky tonk. Except for the guitar solo, where the band shifts into a four-beat swing rhythm, the song features a two-beat rhythm. The difference between Berry's version of a two-beat rhythm and the one in general use is mainly in the backbeat, which is far stronger than in a pop or country two beat. With both Berry and the drummer emphasizing it, it is more prominent than the beat. It stands out more in the two-beat sections than it does in the swing beat sections because it is in opposition to the beat, rather than in addition to a beat. The heavy backbeat would be one component of Berry's revolutionary rock beat.

**Verse/Chorus Blues Form** The title-phrase refrain frames several episodes in Berry's humorous account of a car chase. The refrain is a straightforward 12-bar blues. The verses are also twelve bars in length, but the accompaniment stays on one chord throughout. Almost all of Berry's fifties hits use some kind of blues form.

**Teen-Themed Lyrics** The refrain of "Maybellene" seems to set up a story about lost love. However, the verses are strictly car talk. We learn much more about the two cars—a Coupe de Ville Cadillac and a V8 Ford—than we do about their drivers, and we never do find out what happens when Berry finally catches Maybellene.

The lyrics are key to the success of Berry's song. They tapped into the fifties teen enthusiasm for cars—this was the age of the so-called hot rod (think *Grease*). And the idea of a working-class car overtaking the far more expensive car of the era made the story even more appealing. (Ironically, Chuck Berry has a garage filled with vintage Cadillacs in pristine condition.)

### ♪ KEY FEATURES

**"Maybellene," Chuck Berry (1955)**
- Aggressive guitar sound
- Full rhythm section with prominent electric guitar, like an electric blues band
- Fast two-beat rhythm with a heavy backbeat
- Verse/chorus blues form
- Teen-themed lyrics

What is absent from "Maybellene" is the most critical component of Berry's conception of rock and roll. He would add and perfect it in a series of hits, beginning with "Roll Over, Beethoven."

## Rock Rhythm and Rock Style

Berry's hit recordings between "Roll Over, Beethoven" (1956) and "Johnny B. Goode" document the synthesis that eventually produced rock and roll's beat and texture. Berry's instrumental contribution was twofold: he provided both the first important model for lead guitar playing and the first definitive rock rhythm guitar style.

The lead guitar style came first. In "Roll Over, Beethoven," the guitar introduction builds on the thick double-note style that Berry used in "Maybellene." It becomes even more insistent because it is now based on rock rhythm. Berry was not a virtuoso guitarist, like many of those who followed him, such as Jimi Hendrix or Eric Clapton. But his playing was perfectly suited to broadcast the new rhythm that would define rock and roll: the repeated notes made the rhythm insistent; the double notes gave it density.

In the long nights at the Cosmopolitan Club, Berry must have heard hours and hours of Johnny Johnson's boogie-woogie. What Berry did was transfer boogie-woogie left-hand patterns, similar to the ones heard on "Roll 'Em, Pete," to the guitar. The repetitive boogie-woogie patterns became, in Berry's adaptation, the first authentic rock-based rhythm guitar style; even in medium-tempo songs, he typically divides the beat into two equal parts. In "Roll Over, Beethoven," this pattern is very much in the background. In "Rock and Roll Music," it is more prominent, but there is no lead guitar.

Finally, in "Johnny B. Goode" (1958), Berry—presumably through the miracle of overdubbing; there is no other guitar player credited on the recording date—puts the whole package together: great solo breaks, plus the boogie pattern prominent under both lead guitar and vocal lines. This recording brings together some of the essential features of rock style: backbeat; the eight-beat rhythm, completely purged of any swing influence; strong rhythm guitar; and assertive lead guitar. It was this sound, above all, that would inspire the next generation of rockers.

What is fascinating and somewhat surprising is that neither the drummer nor bass player seemed to grasp Berry's new conception and adapt it to their instruments. Below, the drummer continues to pound out the backbeat but does not try to match up with Berry's rock rhythm. Throughout most of "Johnny B. Goode," bassist Willie Dixon plays a walking bass line, more appropriate for swing or rhythm and blues. Occasionally he interjects a fast-moving line, but the overall feel is still the walking bass. This may have been due in part to his instrument: it is hard to play loud and play fast on an unamplified string bass. Musically, "Johnny B. Goode" is rock and roll and not rock because the bass is acoustic, not electric, and because both bass and drums are playing a swing rhythm with a strong backbeat, similar to that heard in "Shake, Rattle and Roll." Berry was sending the message in his vocal and in his guitar playing, but the rest of the band wasn't receiving it. Rhythmically, rock and roll became rock only when the entire band bought into a rock rhythmic conception. That would not happen until the early sixties—at times in covers of Berry's songs.

Like most of Berry's fifties hits, "Johnny B. Goode" is a verse/chorus blues. Here, the song begins with a storytelling verse, which consists of six two-measure phrases set to the blues progression. By contrast, the chorus repeats the refrain "Go, go Johnny go" five times before concluding with "Johnny B. Goode."

CD 2:5

"Johnny B. Goode," Chuck Berry (1958)

Berry was remarkably inventive in his approach to blues form: there are subtle differences from song to song, yet all clearly build on the basic blues progression. His use of refrain-type blues form offers additional takes on this now-venerable practice. Still, his seemingly limitless variations keep both his sound and the form fresh.

♪ **KEY FEATURES**

**"Johnny B. Goode," Chuck Berry (1958)**
- Rock rhythm guitar patterns
- Rock lead guitar patterns
- Verse/chorus blues form
- Lead and rhythm guitars playing simultaneously + patter-style vocal = clear projection of rock rhythm

## Berry and His Audience

In "Johnny B. Goode," Berry might be describing a rockabilly, or a bluesman—we don't know the race. What is clear is that the hero of the song comes from the outside. As with "Maybellene," the subject resonated with teens. Like so many songs of the mid-fifties, Berry's hits have teen themes: cars, school, rebellion, rock and roll. But that's where the similarity ends. Unlike "Earth Angel" and its countless clones, Berry's lyrics were not sentimental pop watered down for teens. Nor were they the barely articulate sentiments of Gene Vincent ("Be-Bop-A-Lula, she's my baby... don't mean maybe") or the personal reflections of Buddy Holly.

His lyrics are accessible, yet sophisticated: "Roll Over, Beethoven, and tell Tchaikovsky the news." They have catchy new words, like "motorvatin'." They talk about relationships but not love: "Maybellene" is a good example. They're instructive: the lyric to "Rock and Roll Music" not only lays out a key ingredient of the style "got a backbeat, you can't lose it" but also distinguishes rock and roll from all the other music in the air.

How did a black man speak so easily to white teens without either compromising his dignity or threatening the establishment during a period of real racial tension? (1957, the year that Berry recorded "Rock and Roll Music," was also the year that President Eisenhower forcibly integrated the Little Rock schools.) Perhaps it's because the lyrics speak with such detachment and humor about their subjects. Berry is usually an impersonal commentator. Even when he is (presumably) the subject of the song, he deflects attention away from himself toward events (the car chase in "Maybellene") or activities (going dancing in "Carol"). Even in "Brown-Eyed Handsome Man," possibly his most autobiographical song, he writes in the third person.

There are no real precedents for Berry's lyrics. They are as clever in their own way as the most sophisticated Cole Porter lyrics, but they speak to a different audience with a different language. Their most direct antecedents are, of course, the lyrics of blues and rhythm and blues. But there is none of the self-deprecation so common in jump band lyrics: no one is out of work, getting arrested, or getting drunk. And they contain none of the posturing ("tonight you'll know I'm a mighty man") or the personal passion ("the sky is cryin'") heard in so much blues and rhythm and blues.

Berry's lyrics talked about new ideas in a new way to a new audience. As such, they were both a model for sixties rock musicians and a standard to be measured against. Yet, as influential as his lyrics were, Berry's music was even more innovative.

Berry's groundbreaking work was done by 1958. Most of his subsequent recordings—"Carol," "Sweet Little Rock and Roller," and "Back in the USA"—mine this same rhythmic and textural vein. They are great songs but add nothing significant. "Memphis," which features a more delicate texture and subtle presentation of rock rhythm, is an intriguing exception.

Still, in his early hits, Chuck Berry was the architect of rock and roll and the musician who laid the foundation for rock. He assembled rock and roll out of blues, boogie-woogie, rhythm and blues, and country, blending them into the sound that most distinctively defines rock and roll as the music that leads to rock. He gave rock and roll its two most distinctive features: its beat and its most prominent instrumental sound: an assertive guitar.

Today, Berry is a bitter man, touring with only his guitar and replaying his hits for the umpteenth time. He will stop in the middle of a performance if necessary to correct his pickup band. Even Keith Richards was not exempt from his criticism: an episode in the documentary *Hail, Hail, Rock and Roll* shows Berry scornfully correcting Richards's rendition of a guitar lick in "Carol." His attitude makes clear that he knows his place in the history of rock and roll: at the top. No other musician contributed more.

## Little Richard and Jerry Lee Lewis

Little Richard and Jerry Lee Lewis were among the few true kindred spirits of rock and roll. Both

- Grew up poor in the South
- Were manic performers: if Elvis stretched the boundaries of acceptable performance, Jerry Lee Lewis and Little Richard broke through them and kept on running
- Played the piano, not the guitar
- Found a narrow groove and stayed in it during their brief moment in the sun

Their most obvious differences were their race and their sexual orientation. Little Richard was black, Jerry Lee Lewis was white. Little Richard was flamboyantly homosexual; Jerry Lee Lewis decidedly heterosexual. In this matter, both strayed well outside the sexual norms of the time. Little Richard was overtly gay during a time when few men, and even fewer black men, were out of the closet. Lewis went through a string of wives—three before he reached 24! It was his third marriage, to his 13-year-old cousin Myra Gale Brown, that caused the scandal that torpedoed his career. Not only was she underage, but he had neglected to divorce his previous wife.

Little Richard was the first to hit nationally: "Tutti Frutti," released in late 1955, reached number 17 on the pop charts in early 1956 and caused enough of a sensation to merit a Pat Boone cover. Lewis's first hit, "Whole Lot of Shakin' Going On," appeared on the charts about a year and a half later—not much time in the larger view of things but half a lifetime in the brief flourishing of rock and roll.

## Little Richard

Little Richard (born Richard Penniman, 1932) was the first and the loudest of the early rock and rollers. His flamboyant personality, outrageous appearance (wearing eyeliner decades before Michael Jackson), dynamic stage presence, and jet-propelled energy established a standard for rock-and-roll performance that only Elvis and Jerry Lee Lewis approached. He took the stage, literally throwing himself into his work; at one moment casting a leg up onto the top of the piano, then leaping to the ground in a leg split. Little Richard embodied the new style: wild, uninhibited, and sexually charged. From the moment he sang "Womp-bomp-a-loo-bomp, a-lomp-bomp-bomp!" to start "Tutti Frutti," popular music would never be the same.

Little Richard brought substance as well as style to rock and roll. He introduced several of its most characteristic musical features: its volume, a vocal style that valued power over prettiness, and its beat. His music started loud and stayed that way. It was a conscious decision, as he acknowledged:

> I came from a family where my people didn't like R&B. Bing Crosby and Ella Fitzgerald was all I heard. And I knew that there was something that could be louder [sic] than that, but I didn't know where to find it. And I found it was me.

He sang with a voice as abrasive as sandpaper. He hurled his lyrics at the microphone, periodically interrupting them with his trademark falsetto howls and whoops. His singing, like his piano playing, is more percussive than anything else: we are more aware of rhythm than melody, which in most cases is minimal.

Rhythm is where Little Richard made his greatest contribution. He brought the new rock beat—the one that Chuck Berry would consolidate—into rock and roll. Listen to a group of mid-fifties rhythm-and-blues songs and interpolate a Little Richard hit: it immediately stands out because of its beat. Rock and roll had a name before Little Richard hit; after "Tutti Frutti," however, it also had its beat.

Little Richard has acknowledged the source of the beat: boogie-woogie. His two major contributions were

1. To keep the beat division even at all tempos (recall that medium-tempo boogie-woogie typically features a shuffle rhythm).
2. To take a two-handed approach to the rhythm; Little Richard often played patterns with his right hand that also reinforce this new rock rhythm, which typically pop out in the piano's high register.

His gospel roots are evident in every one of the melismatic flourishes. But his combination of boogie, gospel, blues—and his own personality—gave the mix an unprecedented aggressiveness. His music was loud, fast, and in the face of everyone who listened to it.

Little Richard made his mark in a series of songs released between late 1955 and early 1958. Many of them were about girls: "Long Tall Sally," "The Girl Can't Help It" (the girl in this case was blonde bombshell Jayne Mansfield, the star of the film for which the song was written; Little Richard also appeared on screen), "Lucille," "Good Golly, Miss Molly," and "Jenny, Jenny" stand out.

He found his sound right away in "Tutti Frutti" and kept it pretty much the same throughout his three years in the limelight. His songs seem to offer little variation, mainly because his vocal style is so consistent but also because they are fast and loud and rely so heavily on standard blues form. "Long Tall Sally" could be grafted onto "Tutti Frutti" without dropping a beat—they are that much alike.

CD 2:6

"Lucille," Little Richard (1957)

**"Lucille" and a New Orleans Conception of Rock and Roll**  The changes in Little Richard's music are due mainly to the musicians behind him. Unlike Chuck Berry's backup band, they quickly adapted to Little Richard's new rhythm. In his first hits, such as "Tutti Frutti," the band plays in a rhythm-and-blues style: walking bass, heavy backbeat on the drums, and so on. However, in some of his later hits, such as "Lucille" (1957), the entire band is thinking and playing rock rhythm. Bass, guitar, and sax play a repetitive riff in a low register, while Little Richard hammers away, and the drummer taps out a rock beat and a strong backbeat. The contrast with Berry's songs from the same year is clear: Berry is single-handedly trying to establish the new beat; in songs like "Lucille," the entire band is on the same page as Little Richard.

The low-register riffs and the interplay between them and a strong, active, and steady beat are among the most distinctive elements in the music coming from New

Little Richard, performing with his band on the set of an unidentified film. Note the characteristic one-leg-on-the-piano pose and the instrumentation of the band: full rhythm section with electric bass, plus three saxophones.

Orleans during the fifties, whether heard in rhythm and blues or Little Richard's rock and roll. In particular, the heavy bass line and slower tempo forecast the rhythmic feel of sixties rock.

Like so many early rock-and-roll songs, "Lucille" is a verse/chorus blues. The scene-setting sections feature stop-time breaks (when the band stops playing underneath Little Richard) and no change in harmony. The lyric tells the tale of the wayward "Lucille," but the song is really about Little Richard's voice and the beat. We don't listen to Little Richard songs for the lyrics, as we do with Chuck Berry. It would seem that they're there simply because he has to sing *something*.

There is no questioning Little Richard's importance to rock and roll. He embodied its spirit more outrageously and flamboyantly than any other performer of the era. He gave it one of its most identifiable and influential vocal sounds. And he blazed its rhythmic trail. If he had been a good-looking white heterosexual guitar player, he would have been the undisputed king of rock and roll. His music found a slim groove and stayed there, but what a groove it was! And is!

♪ **KEY FEATURES**

**"Lucille," Little Richard (1957)**

- Little Richard's abrasive vocal sound, complete with whoops
- Strong rock beat, played by the entire band
- Verse/chorus blues form
- Darker sound because most instruments are in a low register

### Rock and Roll, Rhythm and Blues, and Race: Chuck Berry and Little Richard

The most apparent distinction between rock and roll and rhythm and blues is racial: rhythm and blues is black music; rock and roll is, for the most part, white music. The most prominent of the early rock-and-roll stars were white, and through the latter part of the decade, the rock-oriented hits on the pop charts came mainly from white acts.

The success of white rock and roll acts vis-à-vis black rhythm-and-blues acts, especially with respect to cover versions of R&B hits, may suggest that the difference between the rock and roll and rhythm and blues was a matter of race. In the middle of the fifties, this may have been true to some extent. However, by the end of the decade, there was also a musical difference. The most compelling evidence of this is the music of Little Richard and Chuck Berry. Both are black, and—as we have heard—they were the musicians most responsible for formulating rock rhythm. Berry played the more important role because he not only presented the new beat but also showed how it should be played on the most important rock instrument, the electric guitar.

Their music demonstrates that the *musical* difference between rhythm and blues and rock and roll has to do mainly with rhythm, not race. A simple exercise bears this out: mix "Lucille" and "Johnny B. Goode" into a playlist of fifties rhythm-and-blues songs, such as those discussed in the previous chapter. The two songs should clearly stand apart from the rhythm-and-blues songs because of their beat. And because of this difference, we consider them to be rock-and-roll musicians, rather than rhythm-and-blues musicians.

## Jerry Lee Lewis

Of the ten rock-era acts inducted into the Rock and Roll Hall of Fame in 1986, the first year of induction, no one had a shorter career, fewer hits, or less influence than Jerry Lee Lewis (b. 1935). So why was he a member of the inaugural class?

For all intents and purposes, Lewis's rock-and-roll career lasted just over a year. He began recording late in 1956 with a country song, "Crazy Arms." He recorded his first rock-and-roll song, "Whole Lot of Shakin' Going On," in March 1957 and scored big. It went to the top of the R&B and C&W charts and reached number 3 on the pop chart. He had three more big hits—"Great Balls of Fire," "Breathless," and "High School Confidential"—within a year. Then he watched his career go down in flames after he married his underage cousin.

Still, if any performer ever deserved rock immortality for a single song, it would be Lewis for "Great Balls of Fire." It was rock and roll's first recorded orgasm, or as close to it as anyone could get in the fifties: "kiss me, baby . . . HOOOOOO . . . feels good!" The recording was overtly sexual to a degree that surpassed even Elvis and Little Richard; it anticipated Ray Charles's comparably orgasmic "What'd I Say" by more than a year.

Bettmann/Corbis

Jerry Lee Lewis at the piano in 1957, around the time he recorded "Great Balls of Fire."

**"Great Balls of Fire"**  The song is 1 minute 48 seconds of ecstasy, from the opening words of the lyric to the last four chords. Unlike most of the impersonal, teen-themed songs of the period, this song shouts its message loud and clear. And the music, with its pulsing beat, sends the same message, just as loudly and just as clearly.

"Great Balls of Fire" was the aural counterpart to Elvis's gyrations. It made the link between the original and musical meanings of rock and roll explicit. Songs with strong sexual overtones were common in blues and rhythm and blues, but most were different from Lewis's song. The lyrics often talk about what will happen: for example, in "Good Rockin' Tonight," Elvis (and others) sing "Tonight you'll know . . ." By contrast, Lewis's lyric is of the moment; he's right in the middle of the experience he's describing. Moreover, his singing and playing imply that he's experienced—that he knows what he's talking about. Lewis was a white man singing blatantly about lust and using rock and roll as a subtext. It was a moment of liberation for rock and roll: a prelude to the sixties.

---

### ♪ KEY FEATURES

**"Great Balls of Fire," Jerry Lee Lewis (1957)**
- Lyrics with strong sexual overtones
- Vocal style that conveys the pleasures of sex
- Strong, fast rock beat pounded out by Lewis on the piano

---

Among the first great rock and rollers, only Lewis matched Little Richard's musical frenzy. His voice was not as assertive as Little Richard's, whose sound cut through a band like a buzz saw, but he made up for it by attacking the piano, pounding out rock-and-roll chords and swooping up and down the keyboard with his trademark glissandos. For that alone, he's worth remembering.

Both Little Richard and Jerry Lee Lewis were so outside the mainstream that they could not have Elvis's impact. Girls could develop crushes on Elvis because he was enough like their schoolmates (many of whom tried to copy Elvis's looks and mannerisms). Little Richard and Lewis were far less likely to attract adoring fans: Richard because of race and sexual preference, Lewis because of his well-documented marital issues. More fundamentally, however, it was because the world was not ready for them: Little Richard's overt homosexuality (gays were "queers" in the fifties) and Lewis's overt sexuality. Still, their music and their stage personas were crucial in liberating rock—and American culture.

# The Everly Brothers and Buddy Holly

It's hard to imagine two rock-and-roll acts more different in temperament from Jerry Lee Lewis and Little Richard than the Everly Brothers and Buddy Holly. They were shy where Jerry Lee and Little Richard were flamboyant. Their music was different, too—Holly's was more varied and innovative, the Everly Brothers' more melodic. Together, they showed that rock and roll also had a gentler and more introspective side.

## The Everly Brothers

The Everly Brothers—Don (b. 1937) and his younger brother Phil (b. 1939)—stand out in the history of rock and roll for two related reasons: they continued rock and roll's country connection, and they popularized melodious song with a rock beat.

The brothers had begun their career as country entertainers not long after they started school. Their parents, Ike and Margaret Everly, had featured the boys on their radio show, broadcast from Iowa, during the mid-forties. After their parents retired, the brothers went to Nashville, where they wrote songs and tried to secure a recording contract. They finally did, with Cadence Records, a small label that recorded mostly pop and jazz. Their first hits were teen-themed country songs that crossed over to the pop charts. "Bye, Bye, Love" and "Wake Up, Little Susie" were among the biggest hits of 1957. These songs relate to rock and roll mainly in their subject matter. Musically, they relate much more to country music—especially their sweet-voiced close harmony.

CD 2:8

"All I Have to Do Is Dream," Everly Brothers (1958)

Quickly, their music moved closer to rock and roll. As it did, they created—with the help of Felice and Boudleaux Bryant, who wrote most of their early hits—a new sound: the **rock ballad**. As we have heard in the music of Chuck Berry, Little Richard, and Jerry Lee Lewis, early rock-and-roll songs—real rock and roll—were set over a driving, up-tempo rock rhythm. Slower songs were usually "Earth Angel"–type songs, with muted triplets in the background.

With their 1958 hit "All I Have to Do Is Dream," the Everly Brothers changed that. There is much about the song that links it to pre-rock pop. The theme of the lyrics is romantic love—commonplace in pop but increasingly on the wane in rock-era music. The form of the song is the venerable pop-song form of the twenties, thirties, and forties, not a blues-based form or even the verse/chorus form used in so many country songs. The song has a flowing melody (the melody is the dominant strand in the texture), and the tempo is slow—all like "Earth Angel."

The modern elements include the gentle rock beat, kept mainly by an acoustic rhythm guitar and subtle drums. The singing of the brothers is the perfect complement to the melody—sweet but not saccharine. The key element in integrating old and new into this brand-new rock ballad style is the lyric.

**Lyrics, Speech Rhythm, and the Melodious Rock Song**   In the discussion of the modern popular song in Chapter 2 we noted that one of the important new developments was the creation of lyrics that spoke everyday language and melodies that captured, then amplified the inflection of speech. When we sing the opening phrases of "Varsity Drag" ("Here is the drag, see how it goes/Down on the heels, up on the toes"), the rhythm and accentuation of the melody closely approximate speech rhythm and accentuation.

By contrast, the phrase "All I Have to Do Is Dream" has minimal inflection and accentuation when spoken. It is much more natural to say them over a gentle rock rhythm than it is to say them in the loud-long/soft-short rhythm of pre-rock pop. As a result, the song works as a melodious *rock* song because the rhythm and inflection of the lyrics are much better suited to a rock rhythm than a fox-trot or swing rhythm.

This was a major innovation—one that added an important new dimension to rock-and-roll music. Out of this subtle adjustment came songs like the Beatles' "Yesterday," arguably the most popular song of the rock era, and Carole King's "You've Got a Friend." The gentler inflection helped the music create a more intimate and personal atmosphere. The mood is miles away from "Lucille" and "Great Balls of Fire," but the song marks the beginning of the path that will lead through the Beatles and Bob Dylan to the singer-songwriters of the early seventies.

♪ **KEY FEATURES**

**"All I Have to Do Is Dream," Everly Brothers (1958)**

- Song with message (romantic love) and form (AABA song form) inspired by pre-rock pop
- Melodious rock song: the melody is more important than the beat
- Up-to-date accompaniment: subtle rock rhythm, acoustic guitar, electric bass
- Sweet-sounding vocal harmony by the Everly Brothers
- Lyrics suited to rock rhythm

The Everly Brothers' music represented the quietest side of the rock revolution, but its impact was nevertheless almost as revolutionary as the louder music. Songs such as "All I Have to Do Is Dream" marked the real beginning of the end for pre-rock pop. Prior to these songs, pop traditionalists could dismiss rock and roll as crude, noisy, vulgar dance music for tasteless teens. But these songs signal the emergence of a new, rock beat-based pop: rock and roll was meeting pop on its own terms—and holding its own. By the early seventies, songwriters like Lennon and McCartney, Burt Bacharach, Paul Simon, Joni Mitchell, and others had created a body of melody-first songs that certainly rival, even surpass, the best songs of earlier generations.

The hard rockers may have represented rock and roll's cutting edge, but it was groups such as the Everly Brothers that would ensure rock's complete domination of popular music within a decade. Their music guaranteed that there was something for almost everyone.

## Buddy Holly

Buddy Holly (born Charles Holley, 1936–1959) occupies a unique position in the history of rock: he is the musical bridge between fifties rock and roll and sixties rock. In the music of Chuck Berry, Elvis, Little Richard, and Jerry Lee Lewis, rock and roll coalesced out of several diverse styles, as we have seen. Their achievement was to form a new style out of existing sources. Buddy Holly's achievement was just the opposite. Using this newly formed style as his point of departure, he opened up rock and roll to new sounds, forms, harmonies, and rhythms. All would resurface in the sixties, especially in the music of the Beatles and Bob Dylan, and would become the main inspiration for the eclecticism that characterized so much sixties rock.

What makes Holly's achievement even more remarkable is that it happened in such a short time. He began rock and roll's second generation less than two years after the style had begun to come together. By the time he began recording, he had assimilated the music of his heroes and was using it as a springboard for rock-based innovations. Moreover, his career as a major rock-era artist lasted only a year and a half, from August 1957, when "That'll Be the Day" topped the charts, to February 1959, when he died at age 22. No one got more done in less time.

CBS Photo Archive/Getty Images

Buddy Holly and the Crickets on Ed Sullivan's *Toast of the Town,* a Sunday night staple during the fifties. The Crickets include guitarist Niki Sullivan, drummer Jerry Allison, and bassist Joe B. Maudlin. Holly's two-guitar/bass/drums instrumentation would become the standard rock band in the sixties.

Holly was an unlikely rock star. With his horn-rimmed glasses, he looked more like a nerd than a sex symbol. His singing voice was high, somewhat thin and reedy—the most ordinary sound of the rock-and-roll greats. Saturated with hiccups, stutters, and other Elvis-isms, Holly's sound could have been Elvis-lite: a gifted teen who wanted to sound like Elvis but lacked Elvis's vocal presence or expressive range. (Of course, that was true of many other early rock stars.) Curiously, all this seemed to work in his favor. His looks, voice, and reserved stage manner gave him an everyman quality. Seeing him perform, the implicit message was that one didn't need super looks, a great voice, and a total lack of inhibition to be a rock star.

This image resonated beautifully with the images portrayed in the lyrics. From "That'll Be the Day" to "Think It Over," so many of the songs deal with the insecurities of teen relationships. Male teens may have wanted to be another Elvis, but they could put themselves in Buddy Holly's shoes much more easily. Many did, in garages around the United States and in England.

Holly hid a curious, open, and imaginative mind beneath his shy, rather gawky exterior. It was fueled by the diverse musical influences that he encountered growing up. The first was country music. Lubbock, Holly's hometown, is in west Texas, just below the panhandle and close to the New Mexico border. Texas had been home to Jimmie Rodgers toward the end of his life and the home base of western swing king Bob Wills, so progressive country music was definitely in the air.

Holly also listened to rhythm and blues intently. A friend recalls sitting with him in his car late on Saturday nights so that they could hear an R&B show on a station out of Shreveport, Louisiana. Not surprisingly, then, numerous R&B elements pop up in his songs: the Bo Diddley beat of "Not Fade Away" is an obvious example.

Elvis was a more powerful and immediate influence. He performed in Lubbock twice during 1955, in the spring and fall, and both times Holly and his friend Bob Montgomery opened the show. This direct contact not only influenced his singing but also strengthened his resolve to pursue a career in music. By the time Elvis returned for his second engagement, Holly was pumping him about how to get a recording contract.

In 1956, Holly went to Nashville to record for Decca Records, with indifferent results. After returning home, he headed west, to Clovis, New Mexico, where Norman Petty operated a well-equipped studio—the best in the region. In Petty, Holly found a soul mate, someone interested in record production and in expanding the sound world of rock and roll. Although their relationship ended badly, their work together helped lay the groundwork for the recording innovations of the Beatles and other major sixties artists.

Country, Elvis-isms, rock and roll, and rhythm and blues all figure in Holly's music, but it was more than just a synthesis of these styles. His hit recordings are a catalog of innovations and adaptations, but perhaps the most daring was a song that did not chart: "Not Fade Away."

**Rock and Roll: Beyond Dance Music** Its rhythmic point of departure was not rock rhythm, but was the Bo Diddley beat—itself firmly rooted in the clave rhythm of Afro-Cuban music. In this song, the rhythm is a slight alteration of the typical clave pattern. The persistent call-and-response exchanges between Holly and the backup singers also recall Bo Diddley's self-titled hit.

CD 2:9

"Not Fade Away," Buddy Holly (1958)

However, despite this connection to rhythm and blues, "Not Fade Away" is *philosophically* different from the rock and roll of Berry, Little Richard, and the others. Their rock and roll is dance music—loud, assertive dance music. This song is not. A typical rock-and-roll song reinforces three regular rhythms: the eight-beat rock rhythm (for instance, Berry's guitar), the beat (usually kept by the bass), and the backbeat. Here, none of these rhythms is consistently present.

Jerry Allison's drumming is especially unconventional here. He marks the clave rhythm on the hi-hat and keeps time intermittently on a deadened drum, a sound that suggests the conga drum much more than the standard drum set.

Throughout the song, almost all of the accents play against the beat and measure instead of confirming it. The backup vocalists don't sing on the first note of the clave pattern, so they never mark the beginning of the measure. And Holly gives a strong accent on the last beat of the second measure of the pattern. Moreover, there is no bass or rhythm guitar. No one marks time, so we don't get our rhythmic bearings until Holly sings the lead vocal line. This kind of rhythmic ambiguity was unprecedented in rock and roll.

"Not Fade Away" introduces into rock and roll the idea that a song can be more than dance music. It can tell a story—here, at something less than full volume. It's an about-face from the music's original message and a door opening to a new sound world.

In its approach to rhythm and percussive sounds, "Not Fade Away" is arguably Holly's most experimental song. Interestingly, Holly's more conventional songs, from "That'll Be the Day" on, were key in establishing the standard rock band instrumentation: two guitars, bass, and drums. This instrumentation was another of Holly's important contributions.

Buddy Holly stands apart among the early rock and rollers. If the others showed the world what rock and roll was, he showed them what it could—and would—become. His

♪ **KEY FEATURES**

**"Not Fade Away," Buddy Holly (1958)**

- Teen lyrics with feeling: lyrics such as these project a more vulnerable image than the "mighty, mighty man" lyrics heard in so many rhythm-and-blues songs.

- Beyond dance music: it's obvious from the start that this is not a song for dancing. In a single stroke, Holly opens the door to a new world of musical possibilities; he elevates rock and roll from the dance floor to music just for listening.

- The rapid evolution of rock and roll: Holly's apparent adaptation of the Bo Diddley beat suggests that recordings sped up the evolutionary pace: musicians would listen to a song, then use it as a point of departure for a new direction. "Bo Diddley" was a hit two years previously; Holly's songs would in turn strongly influence the Beatles.

songs were an obvious inspiration for the innovative music of the Beatles, Dylan, Simon & Garfunkel, and many others. Add to his impressive musical achievement the sense of loss that his death created, and it's easy to understand the veneration that he has enjoyed.

## The Birth, Death, and Resurrection of Rock and Roll

In this chapter, we have charted the rise and fall of rock and roll during the fifties. To summarize the emergence and evolution of rock and roll, we offer the following timeline.

| | Rock and Roll, 1951–1959 |
|---|---|
| **Pre-1951** | *Rock* and *roll* are black euphemisms for sex. |
| **1951–1954** | *Rock and roll* is Alan Freed's code phrase for rhythm and blues. The term does not represent a new kind of music. |
| **1954–1956** | Rock and roll begins to develop an identity: an image, in the appearance and movements of Elvis, Little Richard, Chuck Berry, and others; a sound, beginning with rockabillies like Bill Haley, Carl Perkins, and Elvis; white cover acts like the Crew Cuts and (yes) Pat Boone; black crossover acts like the many doo-wop groups and Fats Domino; and in the initial rock-defining songs of Little Richard and Chuck Berry; a fresh, impudent, attitude expressed in image, lyrics, and sound that teens find appealing; and a commercial presence, most prominent in the overwhelming success of Elvis Presley. |
| **1957–1959** | Rock and roll solidifies its distinct musical identity, most significantly in the music of Chuck Berry, and begins to grow beyond teen dance music, most notably in the music of Buddy Holly. |

## Rock and Roll's Hall of Fame Acts

We have chosen to focus in this chapter mainly on five solo acts and one duo who were among the first class of inductees to enter the Rock and Roll Hall of Fame. Collectively, they did more than any other acts to give rock and roll an image, an attitude, and a musical identity, and they played the most decisive roles in defining both its essence and its range:

- Elvis Presley personified rock and roll: he gave the music its most memorable voice, its most indelible image, and its strongest commercial presence.
- Little Richard brought in the beat and performed with an outrageousness that inspired generations of rockers.
- Chuck Berry put together its key musical elements: the beat and the sound and style of lead and rhythm guitar. He contributed more than anyone else to the distinct musical identity of rock and roll.
- Jerry Lee Lewis reinforced the beat and brought unrestrained abandon into rock and roll.
- The Everly Brothers introduced melodious rock song.
- Buddy Holly was the most important bridge between rock and roll and rock: he gave rock its basic instrumentation, new forms and harmonies, and its primary way of creating the future out of the past. He also led the way in showing that rock and roll could be more than teen dance music.

Five of them seemed to share a common karma, finding success very quickly and then suffering death or a career-damaging experience almost as quickly. In 1955, Berry had his first hit, "Maybellene." His rock-and-roll-defining records, such as "Roll Over, Beethoven," would begin to appear in the following year. Little Richard gave 1956 a wake-up call with "Tutti Frutti." Elvis became a national celebrity with "Heartbreak Hotel" a few months later. Lewis and Holly would score with number 1 hits the following year.

Their decline was just as sudden. Little Richard traded the stage for the pulpit in the middle of a 1957 Australian tour. It was the first of several vacillations between secular and sacred careers. The next year, Lewis married his 13-year-old cousin and saw his career go into a tailspin. Elvis's induction into the army that same year put a huge two-year hole in his career. In 1959, Holly died in a plane crash, while Berry had a scrape with the law that eventually put him in jail for two years. Only the Everly Brothers escaped the fifties more or less unscathed; their career remained strong until the British invasion. In that brief window of time, however, the six acts defined rock and roll, put it on the map, and set it on its course.

## The Death and Resurrection of Rock and Roll

The silencing of rock and roll's most important acts seemed to be one sign that rock and roll was just a fad that had run its course. (Hindsight is the great clarifier: it may be hard to believe that in 1959 many Americans thought that rock and roll was ready to disappear from the pop music scene.) Another indicator that rock and roll would not survive was a multipronged attack on the music and those responsible for it. Leading figures denigrated it: Steve Allen, host of a popular late-night television show, mockingly read the lyrics to Gene Vincent's "Be-Bop-A-Lula" with tinkly music in the background; Frank Sinatra spoke for the pop-music establishment when he derided rock and roll as "the most brutal, ugly, desperate, vicious form of expression it has been my misfortune to hear." At the same time, as soon as the music industry saw that there was money to be made, the major labels began churning out their versions of rock and roll, none of which had any lasting impact. After the British invasion, popular music would belong to a new generation.

**Payola**    The pop establishment, in conjunction with the government, launched their heaviest attack on the men who played the records: the disc jockeys. **Payola** is the practice of paying disc jockeys for playing records. Rewarding people for promoting songs is almost as old as the popular-music business. Indeed, two bribes—money and the promise of a good review for the singer who introduced it—greased the wheel that made "After the Ball" (1893) Tin Pan Alley's first big hit.

In the fifties, disc jockeys were the people to bribe, because they controlled airplay. Representatives of the small independent labels often resorted to bribes of one kind or another in order to get their records on the air. Sometimes it was money, but there were other favors. Alan Freed got partial songwriting credit—and royalties—for Chuck Berry's "Maybellene" and many other rock-and-roll songs in return for promoting them on his shows. In many cases, payola was the only leverage that the indies had, because the big labels were firmly entrenched.

In 1958, the pop music establishment, and in particular the members of **ASCAP**, the licensing agency that represented traditional pop songwriters and publishers, pressured Congress to study abuses with the pop music industry, particularly among purveyors of rock and roll. Payola was part of the investigation. The results from the congressional report released in 1960 were less than satisfactory, as far as the pop establishment was concerned; teens were still listening to the new music. The most publicized casualty was Alan Freed, whose career was ruined. He died in 1965. By contrast, Dick Clark, whose *American Bandstand* was the cornerstone of his growing publishing/production empire, came out of the hearings with reputation and power intact.

ASCAP members had an ulterior motive for seeking an investigation: they felt threatened by the growing market share of **BMI**, the licensing agency that represented virtually all of the rock-and-roll and rhythm-and-blues songwriters, and had convinced themselves that rock and roll was being kept afloat by payola. The payola hearings had no discernible impact on BMI.

Ultimately, condemnation, co-opting, and the congressional investigation had no effect on the rise of rock and roll. What seemed like the death of rock and roll was in fact the beginning of the last stage of its transformation into rock. We trace that leg of the journey in the next chapter.

# Rock and Roll: A New Attitude

In spite of the death or decline of its first heroes, rock and roll helped engineer a major cultural shift—first in the generation that listened to it and ultimately in the English-speaking world. Like the civil rights movement, rock and roll entered mainstream consciousness slowly, often through disruptive events. In the latter part of the fifties, the majority of Americans were more concerned with the Cold War and the threat of nuclear annihilation than they were with civil rights, despite television coverage of such troublesome issues as the integration of the Little Rock public schools, when President Eisenhower had to send in federal troops to maintain order and enforce the law.

Some Americans chose to escape through film and stage musicals, many of which depicted different times and places; or through television, which offered situation comedies like *Father Knows Best*, in which problems were solved on a weekly basis in 30 minutes—minus a few minutes for commercials—or westerns, which distorted life in the nineteenth-century West as severely as situation comedies distorted reality in America during the fifties.

Most of the parents and grandparents of fifties teens had lived through the Great Depression and two major wars. With the specter of the Cold War and the chance to make some good money after decades of deprivation, many did not want to concern themselves with unresolved issues, like segregation. They sought comfort, not challenge, in their entertainment. They wanted their listening easy, gentle, and smooth, not hard, loud, and rocking. But their children, most of whom had not endured their parents' trials, were ready for music that was more vigorous, more challenging, and more "real."

It is against this background that we can understand rock and roll as the soundtrack for the first steps in a seismic shift in western culture. This environment planted the seeds of the rock revolution—and the social and cultural revolution of which rock was such an integral part. Rock and roll was not overtly political, like the music that would soon emerge from the folk revival. It did not champion social causes, criticize segments of society, or comment on controversial events, as Bob Dylan, Marvin Gaye, Neil Young, and so many others would. Still, implicit in the images, words, and above all in the sounds of the music were values that confronted and challenged the status quo.

The images remain vivid: Elvis's gyrating pelvis, Little Richard in full makeup with one leg up on the piano, Chuck Berry's duck walk. There were certainly plenty of bad lyrics in early rock and roll (as there have been in any generation of popular music), but there were also lyrics that set the tone for the next generation: Berry's good-humored defiance; the unabashed directness of Jerry Lee Lewis's feeling good; Buddy Holly's honest portrayals of teen angst. All of these foreshadowed the "realness" of rock.

Ultimately, however, it was the music that delivered the heart of the message. It was often loud; listeners couldn't avoid it. It was aggressive—Berry's guitar sound from "Maybellene" on, Little Richard's abrasive voice, Jerry Lee Lewis's piano pounding. It blurred racial boundaries: Elvis was the white man with the Negro feel. And most of all, it was the new beat: the first 5 seconds of "Johnny B. Goode," where Berry pumps out two strings of two-note chords, distill the essence of this new, more insistent beat. Here is where the impact of this new music is felt most powerfully. As the decade came to an end, more and more acts were harnessing this power. We follow this path into the sixties, in the next several chapters.

### Terms to Remember

| | | |
|---|---|---|
| rockabilly | rock ballad | BMI |
| walking | payola | |
| hillbilly | ASCAP | |

### Applying Chapter Concepts

1. In this chapter, we have presented a specific music view of rock and roll: it is the music that would lead directly to rock. However, in the fifties, the term *rock and roll* identified all of the black-influenced music that teens (and a few adults) listened to: the music heard in both this and the previous chapter, plus much more. Pair up with a classmate (or form a group) and draft position papers that justify each understanding of "rock and roll."

2. Armed with the position papers, listen to a Fats Domino hit, such as "Blueberry Hill" or "Ain't That a Shame," and decide whether it should be considered rock and roll or simply rhythm and blues. Support your decision musically and historically.

3. Listen to the original of a rock-and-roll song covered by Pat Boone (for example, "Tutti Frutti," "Ain't That a Shame"), then his cover. Then decide whether you think Boone's recording is also rock and roll, and consider why you think it is or isn't. Take into account both Boone's singing and the instrumental background.

# 6

# On the Roads to Rock

## From Girl Groups and Garage Bands to Folk and Surf Music

● If Buddy Holly's death on February 3, 1959, symbolized the death of rock and roll, then the appearance of the Beatles on *The Ed Sullivan Show* on February 9, 1964, signaled the birth of rock. Certainly it was perceived that way in the years that followed. Robert Christgau, one of the most authoritative and outspoken critics of the rock era, wrote in 1973 that rock—as distinguished from rock and roll—"signifies something like 'all music deriving primarily from the energy and influence of the Beatles....'" The transformation of rock and roll into rock was one product of an ongoing musical evolution that lasted half a decade. Our focus in this chapter is charting the development of rock-era music between these two milestones.

## Pop, Rock, and Rhythm and Blues in the Early Sixties

In the early sixties, rock did not rule. Especially when compared to the previous five years, when rock and roll exploded on the national consciousness, and the subsequent five years, when rock came of age, the early sixties seem to be a time of transition. There were no new acts that were supremely popular or influential, like Elvis was or the Beatles would be, nor were there the kinds of wholesale changes in the pop music landscape that accompanied the emergence of rock and roll and the coming together of rock.

Still, the five years between Holly's death and the Beatles' American debut were an eventful time in the history of rock and rhythm and blues, in much the same way that the years of adolescence are an eventful time in the development of a person. There were occasional moments of brilliance—and moments of silliness. Above all, there was the gradual maturation of the music: rock and roll became rock, and rhythm and blues became Motown and soul.

## Pop Versus Rock and Rhythm and Blues

A new generation of rock and R&B musicians scrambled to find room at the top of the singles charts. They competed with the postmilitary Hollywood Elvis; a group of young pop singers that included Johnny Mathis, Connie Francis, Bobby Vinton, and

129

Bobby Darin; sedate bandleaders like Percy Faith and Lawrence Welk; and the occasional one-hit wonder. The album charts were foreign territory for rock musicians, except for two giants who defected: albums by Elvis and Ray Charles did very well. Everyone bought the soundtrack to *West Side Story*—or so it seemed; in general, soundtracks from films and Broadway shows did well. The two most commercially successful new styles were the pop-oriented folk music of acts like the Kingston Trio and Peter, Paul, and Mary and the Brazilian bossa nova. Both would filter into rock-era music, but through circuitous paths.

Many of the developments that would reshape popular music were occasional blips on the radar screen, or seemed to slip under the radar entirely. They took place in Liverpool and London and Hamburg, Germany; near the beaches of southern California; at 2845 West Grand Boulevard in Detroit; in the Brill Building and Greenwich Village cafes in New York; and countless garages throughout the United States—most notably in Portland, Oregon.

## The Integration of Popular Music

On November 30, 1963, *Billboard* suspended its R&B singles chart. Their decision was a sensible reaction to the enormous crossover between the R&B and pop charts; for the previous few years, they had become so similar that the R&B chart had become redundant. The brief merging of the two charts—they would separate again just over a year later—was one aspect of a wholesale shift toward a more integrated musical world and the drive toward a more integrated society. It was apparent not only on the charts but also in the recording studio, in the sound of the music, and in the lyrics of folk-inspired protest songs.

Rock and R&B also opened the door to women a little wider. Rock and roll was music for "guys": all its early stars were male. So was rhythm and blues, for the most part. Doo-wop groups were, with few exceptions, male, and so were most of the top solo acts. However, the early sixties saw the emergence of girl groups such as the Shirelles and Ronettes, as well as Motown stars such as Mary Wells and Martha and the Vandellas. Behind the scenes, Carole King, Cynthia Weil, and other female songwriters turned out hit after hit, while Deborah Chessler trailblazed the path for women producers.

There was a kind of generational coming together as well. One catalyst was a new dance made popular not once, but twice, by a Fats Domino fan. It helped bring parents and their children together, at least on the dance floor.

## Twisting the Night Away

In the fifties, rock and roll was dance music for teens. Most adults were still fox-trotting and cha-cha-chá-ing. The song that would change all that was "The Twist," a two-time hit for Chubby Checker.

Checker (born Ernest Evans in 1941) was part of pop promoter Dick Clark's stable of artists. Clark was always on the lookout for new dance sensations, because he hosted the popular *American Bandstand*, a dance-oriented television program for teens. "The Twist" first appeared on the rhythm-and-blues charts in 1959 as a minor hit for Hank Ballard and the Midnighters, a Detroit-based doo-wop group that had had several R&B hits during the fifties. When Clark discovered Ballard's song, he had Checker record it for a local Philadelphia label. Clark, who had a financial interest in the label, then promoted the song vigorously on his show. The song was an immediate sensation, and it had staying power as well: it was the only rock-era song to reach the top of the charts twice—first in 1960/1961, then again in 1962.

"The Twist" got everybody dancing to rock and roll. It was easy to learn, even for adults—and they did. Suddenly, dancing the **twist** (and the frug, watusi, and subsequent dance sensations) was the "in" thing to do. John F. Kennedy watched dancers twist the night away in the East Room of the White House; his bad back kept him on the sidelines. Christopher Lawford, Kennedy's nephew, recalls dancing the twist with Marilyn Monroe.

### Dance-Instruction Songs

"The Twist" continues the tradition of dance-instruction songs by black popular musicians. The earliest of these date back to the teens: "Ballin' the Jack" is a still-familiar example; "Pine Top's Boogie Woogie" is a slightly more recent example. The lyrics to "The Twist" show the crucial role television played in popularizing this new dance (and most others of the era). Earlier dance-instruction songs had given verbal directions. The lyrics for "Ballin' the Jack" describe the steps of the dance: "First you put your two knees close up tight..." Pine Top assumes that his dancers already know how to "boogie-woogie" and "mess around"; he cues them when to start and stop. Checker's instructions depend on visual evidence: he only asks that the dancers "Do like this." He presumes that his listeners will have seen him, or be able to see him, do the dance.

## "The Twist"

"The Twist" shows its rhythm-and-blues provenance in most of its features. We hear the standard fifties R&B instrumentation: lead and backup vocals, plus rhythm section and honking saxophone. The song is a straightforward blues, in lyrics and form. It has a bright tempo, set by a walking bass. There is one significant difference: the persistent rock rhythm pounded out on the drums and the piano. This energizes the accompaniment underneath Checker's vocal. There is nothing subtle about the rock beat; it is as simple and straightforward as the dance itself.

CD 2:10

"The Twist," Chubby Checker (1960)

With the exception of Little Richard and Chuck Berry, black musicians were reluctant to embrace rock rhythm through most of the fifties. Most stayed with the shuffle rhythm that had served them well. Others, like Ray Charles, substituted a Latin rhythm to get a rocklike feel but with more complexity. That changed around 1960: "The Twist" was one of many rhythm-and-blues songs to make use of rock rhythm, not only in dance songs like "The Twist" but also in new kinds of doo-wop style hits, such as the Marcels' outlandish take on the pop standard "Blue Moon," Gene Chandler's "Duke of Earl," and Ernie K-Doe's "Mother-In-Law." Rhythm in black music would soon take a great leap forward: the approach becomes subtler and much

Hulton-Deutsch Collection/Corbis

Chubby Checker in 1962, showing the couple behind him how to do the twist. The couple is old enough to be the parents of Checker's *American Bandstand* fans; the twist helped get adults dancing to rock.

more complex in so many Motown songs and in James Brown's music after he finds his new bag, as we will find out in Chapter 8.

"The Twist" is one of those right-time/right-place moments that are so much a part of rock history. Neither the song nor Checker's performance were exceptional, but its timing was impeccable. It also provides another demonstration of the enormous power wielded by DJs during the early years of the rock era. Just as Alan Freed helped make "Maybellene" a hit by playing it over and over, Clark (who, like Freed, had a financial interest in the song) pumped up "The Twist" by featuring it on his show. Clark's impact was more far-reaching because the medium was television, not radio. For so many teens, *American Bandstand* was obligatory after-school viewing; they couldn't miss it.

The twist was the most popular (and least athletic) of the dance fads of the early sixties. It was the signature dance of the early rock era, much as the Charleston (the most popular of the black-inspired dances of the early 1920s) was the signature dance of the early modern era. And like the Charleston, but unlike the fox-trot, the twist was a "do-it-alone" dance. Interestingly, none of the popular dances of the sixties ever evolved into a

> ♪ **KEY FEATURES**
>
> **"The Twist," Chubby Checker (1960)**
> - R&B instrumentation: lead and backup vocals, saxophone, rhythm section with acoustic bass, drums, and piano most prominent
> - Conventional blues form in lyrics and harmony
> - Strong, basic rock beat: beat, backbeat, and rock rhythm in drums; piano chords reinforce rock rhythm

real partner dance, where a couple could enjoy the "lingering close contact" that had scandalized bluenoses during the first decades of the twentieth century.

The dance also shows the complex way in which black and white drew together. The roots of the song and the dance are black. But the new rhythm, while also of black origin, had become prominent mainly through white performers. The song went from a relatively obscure R&B hit to the only two-time number 1 pop song in the early rock era largely through the influence of a white powerbroker. Chubby Checker's role in making the song a hit is relatively inconsequential; others could have easily filled the role. It was all but inevitable that a new dance would signal the mainstreaming of a new kind of popular music. The twist fulfilled that role.

## Girl Groups, Young Songwriters, and Celebrity Producers

In the early sixties, the best evidence of musical integration came from the songs of the **girl groups**. We can understand girl groups like the Shirelles, the Crystals, and the Ronettes as a continuation of doo-wop, but there are several differences. The most noteworthy include:

- The vocal group is exclusively female, not completely or mostly male.
- Race is not really a factor in the message of the words or the music.
- The songs, written mainly by young white songwriters, belong to the rock era. They are not remakes of Tin Pan Alley songs or new songs in an older style.
- The musical weight is more in the production than in the vocals. Although they are in the forefront, the singers are virtually interchangeable; the song and— even more—the sounds behind the vocals are often the more distinctive characteristics of the style.

The girl groups are a true musical fusion of white and black, not simply a black take on white music (like most doo-wop hits) or a white take on black music (such as Pat Boone covering Little Richard). This fusion marked the first time that a black-sounding *style*—not just a black artist—was competing on equal terms with white music.

We consider these points in more detail.

## Gender and Race

All-female vocal groups were a novelty in rock-era music but not in popular music. They first appeared on recordings in the late twenties, when bands began to record with vocalists. Groups like the Boswell Sisters and the Andrews Sisters were very popular in the thirties and forties; so were the Chordettes and the McGuire Sisters in the fifties. Three things made the Shirelles and the other girl groups different: they sang rock-era songs, they were not family, and they were black.

Girl groups broke through the gender barrier—in black music and in rock. Black female groups were rare in all genres. In gospel, there were countless male quartets; women typically appeared as soloists, although they often had backup vocalists in performance. In pre-rock pop, the most popular black vocal groups were also male: the Mills Brothers, the Ink Spots. Doo-wop, which emerged from the merger of gospel and pop, also remained almost exclusively male.

The same held true in rock and roll and rhythm and blues. There were no white female rock-and-roll stars in the fifties, and only a few successful female R&B singers: for example, LaVern Baker, Ruth Brown, Etta James. Both genres were largely a man's world.

The breakthrough of the girl groups evidences a shift in consciousness yet resounds with the echoes of longstanding racial and sexual attitudes. The songs of the girl groups are typically about love: both of the songs discussed in the following feature young ladies talking to their peers. Up until 1960, it was rare in any branch of the entertainment industry—popular song, stage musicals, films, or television—for black women to talk or sing about love in the first person, and when they did, they directed their attention to black males. Far more common were the stereotypical roles, like Butterfly McQueen in *Gone with the Wind*. Any suggestion of an interracial relationship was taboo. Lena Horne, a wonderful singer/actress and an ideal candidate for the role of Julie, a light-skinned black in the landmark musical *Show Boat*, was passed over in the thirties and again in the fifties. It is against this background that we can understand the girl groups as a sign that the times were "a changin'."

The girl groups represent a chink in the armor of racism. One sees them with the beehive hairdos fashionable in the early sixties among white women, wearing matching prom dresses. The look is designed to break down the barrier between white and black, not build it up. The stories that they tell in their songs and the questions that they ask—"Will you still love me tomorrow?"—are universal; they are not delimited by race. Their voices sound black, but not Muddy Waters or Ray Charles black. In image, words, and sound, they met their intended audience—teens of all races—more than halfway.

All of this opened the door for white males to imagine black partners and for white females to see their black counterparts as kindred spirits. At least one white male walked through the door: Phil Spector courted Ronnie Bennett of the Ronettes, one of the girl groups that he produced, and married her in 1968. That the marriage ended disastrously should not obscure the fact that American society was gradually growing more receptive to the idea of interracial relationships, although miscegenation was still illegal in the South for most of the sixties.

Of the two possible interracial relationships—white male/black female versus black male/white female—the white male/black female was less controversial by far, unless it involved marriage. White male/black female relationships were part of the fabric of life in the South; most looked the other way, even when such a relationship produced offspring. By contrast, a black man caught with a white woman too often ended up at the end of a rope, a victim of a lynching. The popularity of the girl groups, and the Motown acts that featured female performers such as the Supremes, owe something to this imbalanced dynamic.

The girl groups were both a sign and a catalyst for the social change well underway during the early sixties. It was—and is—a slow process, although those who have grown up seeing Denzel Washington romance women of many races may not understand the mindset of the couple portrayed by Spencer Tracy and Katharine Hepburn in the 1967 film *Guess Who's Coming to Dinner*, which featured Sidney Poitier as the black fiancé of the couple's white daughter.

## Songs and Production

The music of the girl groups represents a pivotal moment in the history of rock, for two reasons. First, a new kind of song emerges: in attitude, form, and approach. Second, a new definition of what a song is emerges. The two songs discussed following illustrate these developments.

**A New Kind of Song** Many of the girl group hits came from young songwriters working for publishers in New York's Brill Building. In the sense that they were songwriters writing songs for others to sing, they connect back to Tin Pan Alley. However, the songs that they created represent a decisive break with pre-rock song, in words and music. Many of the songs, like "Da Doo Ron Ron," make use of verse/chorus form, and even those that do not still adapt older forms: "Will You Love Me Tomorrow?" unfolds slowly, with the main phrase building to the title riff at the end.

"Will You Love Me Tomorrow?," co-written by Carole King and Gerry Goffin, her husband at the time, continues the kind of intimate, personal, and real feelings hinted at in the music of Buddy Holly. Even more significant, it expresses these feelings from a woman's perspective. Its message—the emotional uncertainty of a new relationship: is this love at first sight or a one-night stand?—is presented in plain, direct language. This kind of candor presages the realism of sixties rock.

### The Brill Building

The **Brill Building** was Tin Pan Alley's (that is, traditional pop music's) last stand. Located at 1619 Broadway in New York, it was home to several publishers whose songwriting staffs supplied teen idols and others with a string of hits in the late fifties and early sixties. Among the notable songwriters who worked for Brill Building publishers in the years around 1960 were King and Goffin, Hal David and Burt Bacharach, Neil Sedaka, and Bobby Darin. The "Brill Building sound" became associated with the lighthearted, teen-pop hits that were crafted there and then issued by the many small labels located in and around New York City.

The hiring of songwriters just to write songs was business as usual for music publishers. However, these songwriters were young, and the songs that they wrote were directed at a young audience. Further, they wrote songs mainly for recording; sheet music sales continued to diminish in importance. Indeed, for many of these songwriters, their Brill Building employment was simply an apprenticeship. Darin, Sedaka, and King all went on to important careers as performers and recording artists. Bacharach and David found a unique alternative to performing their own material: they wrote most of their hits for Dionne Warwick—with her sound in mind.

By contrast, "Da Doo Ron Ron" is mindless. With its nonsense syllables and dumbed-down lyric, it recalls songs like Gene Vincent's "Be-Bop-A-Lula." We explore the implications.

**The Producers**  Here are the lyrics for the first verse and chorus of the Crystals' "Da Doo Ron Ron," a huge hit for them in 1963:

> *Met him on a Monday and my heart stood still*
> *Da Doo Ron Ron Ron, Da Doo Ron Ron*
> *Somebody told me that his name was Bill*
> *Da Doo Ron Ron Ron, Da Doo Ron Ron*
> *Yes, my heart stood still*
> *Yes, his name was Bill*
> *Yes, when he walked me home*
> *Da Doo Ron Ron Ron, Da Doo Ron Ron*

Compared to the cleverness of Chuck Berry's lyrics, or the honesty and emotional commitment of "Will You Love Me Tomorrow?" these lyrics seem the work of an uninspired third-grader. One can argue that sophisticated, interesting, or even emotionally honest lyrics would have worked at cross purposes to the message of the song. Instead, the lyrics seem to be there simply because songs have lyrics. The song is not about the message of the words, or even the Crystals' singing of it. Rather, it is about the **wall of sound** behind the vocals. That wall of sound was the work of Phil Spector, the first celebrity producer.

From the start, producers played an integral role in shaping the sound of records. In previous chapters, we heard the impact of seminal rock producers like Sam Phillips (Jackie Brenston, early Elvis), Dave Bartholomew (Fats Domino and Little Richard), and Norman Petty (Buddy Holly). We encountered the work of Jerry Leiber and Mike Stoller, who wrote songs for specific acts, then produced them: not only several of Elvis's hits, but also virtually all of the Coasters' hits. Recall their remark: "We don't write songs; we write records."

Among the musicians who worked briefly with Leiber and Stoller in New York was Phil Spector. Spector soon formed his own record company, Philles (for Phil and Les [Sill], his partner at the time), and began churning out a string of hits in the early sixties, mainly with two girl groups: the Crystals and the Ronettes.

Although the songs appeared on the charts, in record stores, and on radio as the music of the Crystals or Ronettes, they were really about Spector and his radically new conception of what a rock-and-roll record could be. Spector crafted what he called a "Wagnerian approach to rock and roll." "Wagnerian" refers to the mid-nineteenth-century German opera composer Richard Wagner, whose music was noted for, among other things, bombastic orchestral writing, and—more important—embedding more of the *musical* meaning in the orchestral background than the vocal lines.

Spector was on target with his self-assessment. His songs were not about the words, the melody, or even the singers—the Crystals and the Ronettes were as interchangeable as the anonymous session musicians behind them. Spector would gather several of the finest available freelance musicians in a small room with hard walls and record them with extensive echo and reverb to create an almost tangible mass of sound. It is this feature, which was ideal for AM radio, with its relatively low fidelity, that gave the songs that Spector produced their distinctive character. Indeed, in songs like "Da Doo Ron Ron," there would seem to be a kind of arrogance in the use of simpleminded lyrics and melodies. It is as if Spector is saying, "I can transform even the most mundane material into a hit that everyone will want to hear." Even though he never sang on his recordings and seldom played an instrument, the records that he produced captured *his* sound.

During his run in the first half of the sixties, Spector raised the status of the producer. People knew that the "wall of sound" recordings were by Spector, in a way that they didn't know that Dave Bartholomew was behind the New Orleans sound or that, somewhat later, George Martin was behind the sound of the Beatles' music. More important, Spector's work added a symphonic dimension to rock music. He showed that the final result and the musical message could be far more powerful than that predicted by the most obvious elements—words, melodies, singers.

## Style and Commerce

The result of this activity—white songwriters and producers creating songs sung by young black women, backed by musicians of both races—was a unique moment in pop music history. The girl group recordings represent a style in which black and white elements are evident, yet all of a piece: it is a sound in which everything blends together seamlessly. In this respect, it goes further than Elvis's singing and further than the rock and rollers who built on the foundation laid down by Chuck Berry and Little Richard.

The listening audience for this music seemed as integrated as the music itself. The many girl group hits played a major role in collapsing pop and rhythm and blues into a single chart. Whites and blacks seemed to buy them in comparable numbers. Indeed, the girl groups' recordings often did as well or better on the pop charts than they did on the R&B charts before they were merged. Musically, it was a fresh new sound, with something for everyone.

## The Songs

We contrast two girl group recordings: the Shirelles' "Will You Love Me Tomorrow?" and the Crystals' "Da Doo Ron Ron." In one, the song is important; in the other, the wall of sound is preeminent.

**The Shirelles** The Shirelles were a female vocal quartet—Shirley Owens (b. 1941), Micki Harris (b. 1940), Beverly Lee (b. 1941), and Doris Coley (b. 1941)—who first came together as the Poquellos in 1958 while still in high school. Their rise to the top of the charts is another of the happy accidents of the rock era. The group had won over the crowd at a high school talent show with a song they wrote themselves: "I Met Him on a Sunday." A classmate, Mary Jane Greenberg, introduced them to her mother Florence, who after some haggling, signed them to record the song for her fledgling label—Tiara Records. It was a local hit—big enough to be picked up by Decca Records. When released by Decca, the song charted nationally; it became the Shirelles' first hit.

After a few more Decca-released recordings that went nowhere, Greenberg re-formed Tiara as Scepter Records and brought in Luther Dixon to produce the group. From 1960 to 1963, the group was almost always on the charts. Their biggest hit came in 1960, in a song written by Carole King and Gerry Goffin: "Will You Love Me Tomorrow?"

The song and its creation give us a wonderful preview of the tumultuous changes to come in the sixties. It was written and performed by women; the lyric gives us a woman's perspective on the fragility of new love.

Before rock, there had been few women songwriters (Kay Swift, who wrote the 1930 hit "Fine and Dandy," stands out). Moreover, most of the songs that they and their male counterparts wrote were gender-neutral; there is no obvious clue in words or music that a song is written by a woman for women. Even songs written for a female

CD 2:11

"Will You Love Me Tomorrow?" the Shirelles (1960)

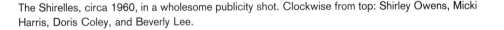

The Shirelles, circa 1960, in a wholesome publicity shot. Clockwise from top: Shirley Owens, Micki Harris, Doris Coley, and Beverly Lee.

Pictorial Press Ltd./Alamy

role in a musical—such as "My Funny Valentine," written by Richard Rodgers and Lorenz Hart for the 1937 musical *Babes in Arms*—would be performed by male singers, with a little tweaking of the lyrics. Before rock, we get the woman's perspective mainly from female blues singers (Bessie Smith's "Empty Bed Blues") and country songs like Kitty Wells's "It Wasn't God Who Made Honky Tonk Angels" (1952), her famous retort to Hank Thompson's "The Wild Side of Life."

Carole King's song gives us the other side of boastful, male, R&B songs ("Good Rockin' Tonight"). The man thinks only of tonight; the woman worries about tomorrow. There is no mistaking the message of the song; the lyrics are simple and clear. This kind of frankness became possible in mainstream popular music only when society, or at least the audience for this kind of song, could accept this straight talk. That change in attitude was underway by 1960. We hear this song as a transitional step between the Donna Reed–ish façade of fifties pop and the confessional songs of early seventies female singer/songwriters such as Joni Mitchell.

The music reinforces the message of the lyrics, not because it presents a coherent setting, but because its main components send such different messages. There are three groups of sounds: the rhythm section, the string section, and the Shirelles. The rhythm section lays down a rather mundane rock beat, one that was fashionable during these years in rock-influenced pop. It remains constant throughout the song; there is almost no variation. But the string writing is bold and demanding—the most sophisticated part of the sound. The intricate string lines stand in stark contrast to the Shirelles' vocals, especially Shirley Owens's straightforward lead.

And therein lies the charm. The instrumental backup, and especially the skillful string parts, contrast with the naive schoolgirl sound of the Shirelles (none of them was 20 years old when the song was released). All this meshes perfectly with King's lyrics, the song's simple melody, and the look of the group. Owens sounds courageous enough to ask the question—and vulnerable enough to be deeply hurt by the wrong answer. She, like the lyric, sounds neither worldly nor cynical.

The song and the singers were both a product and an agent of change—helping to close the gap between black and white. As a product, the song reflected the changes in rock-era music. As an agent of change, the song was written by a white woman, produced by a black man, supported with white-sounding string writing, and sung by young black women. The message of the song is colorblind. Teens of all races could relate to its theme. The Shirelles crossed over more consistently and successfully than

## ♪ KEY FEATURES

**"Will You Love Me Tomorrow?" the Shirelles (1960)**

- Vulnerable lyrics, vulnerable girls? young girls singing about the morning after
- Dressing up: sophisticated string writing
- Simple rock rhythm: the state of rock rhythm in pop, circa 1960
- Rock, R&B, and pop: a new synthesis of all three

any of the black acts of the fifties in part because of the changing racial climate (the civil rights movement was gathering steam) and in part because they were teens like their audience. In "Will You Love Me Tomorrow?" they sing peer-to-peer about a meaningful issue.

**Phil Spector and the Crystals**   Like the Shirelles, the Crystals were a female vocal group made up of black teens. At the time they recorded "Da Doo Ron Ron," the five members of the group were Barbara Alston, Dee Dee Kennibrew, Mary Thomas, Patricia Wright, and La La Brooks, who sang lead on the recording.

The Crystals had caught the ear of Spector while they were rehearsing in the Brill Building. Spector signed them up, then proceeded to jerk them around. After he and the group scored hits with "There's No Other (Like My Baby)" and "Uptown," Spector, who was at odds with the group about who should sing lead, took matters into his own hands and recorded Darlene Love as "the Crystals." In 1963, the actual group was back in the studio with Spector to record two of their biggest hits: "Da Doo Ron Ron" and "Then He Kissed Me."

"Da Doo Ron Ron," the Crystals (1963)

Perhaps "Da Doo Ron Ron" was the product of a war of wills. Spector had shown the group how dispensable they were by recording another singer under their name, which he owned. It galled them to have to sing songs that they didn't record during their constant touring in 1963. Given Spector's volatile personality—as of this writing, he awaits trial on a murder charge—it was certainly possible that he would find another way to show the group how small a part they were in the equation for success. Certainly, their relationship grew more strained when Spector became enamored with the Ronettes and their lead singer, Ronnie Bennett. In 1965, the group bought out their contract and moved to Imperial Records, a move that ended in failure. The group disbanded in 1966.

In any event, the most striking feature of "Da Doo Ron Ron" is the sound behind the singers. Spector's wall of sound is tall: it extends from the strong bass line, low-pitched drums, and sustained low saxophone chords to the high-register piano part—an oscillation between a single note and a chord that at once confirms and conflicts with the triplet rhythm that energizes the song.

Much of its impact comes from the fact that the rhythm, like the instrumentation, is clearly stratified. At the center is the beat, marked firmly by the bass instruments, the bass drum, and handclaps. There is a slower rhythm created from the sustained chords in the saxophones. On top, there is the triplet rhythm heard throughout in the piano part and occasionally reinforced in the drum part. This triplet rhythm obviously derives from the Fats Domino–style triplets heard in many of his medium- and slow-tempo hits. Here, the tempo is so fast that the pianist must play an oscillating pattern instead of simply repeating the chords. The oscillation, because it groups the notes of the triplets in pairs, creates a constant rhythmic conflict. It is one of the signature elements of the sound of this recording.

The vocal line is heavily syncopated. In particular, the title phrase is almost completely off-beat. The syncopated accents highlight the fact that the phrase is about rhythmic excitement—syncopations literally in the middle of several layers of rhythm. The title-phrase syllables sung by the Crystals are meaningless as words; they are used simply to make the rhythm of the vocal line more emphatic.

♪ **KEY FEATURES**

**"Da Doo Ron Ron," the Crystals (1963)**

- Stratified rhythm: low and slow chords; beat marking in bass, handclaps, and drums; fast triplet rhythm in the piano part; syncopation in the vocal line
- Wall of sound: massive blocks of sound, mostly in low and middle registers
- Silly lyrics, slick production: Spector's song is tailored to AM radio

## Redefining Song: The Recording as the Document

"Da Doo Ron Ron" offers an ideal illustration of one of the most significant changes of the rock era: a radically new conception of song. Every crucial element of a song—what it is, how it is created, and how it reaches its audience—underwent major revision. To appreciate the magnitude of this reconception, we need to examine how popular music reached its audience before the rock era.

**Popular Song Before Rock** The popular songs of the twenties, thirties, and forties generally went from inspiration to hit in several stages:

1. A songwriter or songwriting team (composer and lyricist) wrote the song.
2. An arranger scored the song for the group that would perform it: the orchestra for a Broadway or Hollywood musical; a dance band or a studio orchestra supporting a singer such as Frank Sinatra.
3A. Once a song caught on, it was "out there," for anyone to perform. Typically, several bands would record different versions of the song, all at about the same time. Live performances—in a nightclub, at a dance, over the radio—would be even more varied.
3B. At the same time, the song's publisher would print a piano/vocal setting of the song. This would offer a simplified version of the melody and harmony of the song, appropriate for home use.

As a result, the song would exist simultaneously in several forms. For instance, listeners in 1935 could hear Irving Berlin's hit song "Cheek to Cheek," featured in the film *Top Hat*, on records by Fred Astaire, Ginger Rogers, and several others, performed live on radio broadcasts and in night clubs and restaurants, or they could buy the sheet music and play it themselves.

Two aspects of this process stand out. First, there was no one person who controlled the sound of the song. Second, there was no authoritative version. The songwriter and the lyricist wrote the words, melody, harmony, and basic rhythms of the song. However, their published version of the song did not specify the instruments to be used in an ideal performance, the vocal style of the singer, the overall form of the performance, and many other features. Moreover, the songwriter effectively lost artistic control of the song when he or she finished it. Arrangers and performers could change almost any aspect of the song—and usually did.

By the early sixties, however, every aspect of this process had changed. Increasingly, the progress of a song from idea to finished product typically went like this:

1. Songwriters—either professional songwriters like Carole King and Gerry Goffin, producers like Spector, or musicians like Roy Orbison—would write a song, either for a band in which they played or (in the case of the girl groups) for a specific act. They would then flesh out the basic features of the song with the rest of the band in rehearsal or prepare an arrangement that added distinctive features that would become part of the song's identity, like the string lines in "Will You Love Me Tomorrow?" or the piano oscillation in "Da Doo Ron Ron."
2. They would bring it into the recording studio, where a producer would oversee the entire recording process: the basic recording, overdubbing, mixing, and so forth.
3. A record company would release the song as a single.
4. If the song became a hit, it would be played on the radio and bought in record stores throughout the country. Any other version of the song would be identified as a cover.

A simplified sheet music version might appear. However, most people learned the sound and style of a song from the recording. If they used the sheet music at all, it was only as a bare-bones guide.

This new process produced two far-reaching changes. First, the creators of the song generally retained some control of the end result throughout the entire creative process. Second, there was, as a result, a *definitive* version of a song: the original recording by the group or team that conceived it. The song became the sound captured on record: not just the melody and chords, but the complete sound experience. Unlike earlier popular songs, *the recording was the document.*

Everything about the recording—its beat, the choice of instruments, the sound of the singer(s), signature riffs, accompaniments—helped define the song. Any other version of the song, whether a cover recording or a sheet music reduction, lacked the authority of the original.

Moreover, songs often represented a more unified conception. It could be the musical vision of one individual or a collaboration among songwriter, performer, and producer, with one person often filling two of the roles. In either circumstance, the song represented a collectively conceived viewpoint, worked out mainly in one place (a recording studio) within a narrow timeframe (over the course of a recording session).

Steady improvement in recording technology made this new creative process possible. The most far-reaching innovation was **multitrack recording**, which enabled producers to assemble a song layer by layer. Experimentation through trial and error was possible on a much broader scale at every stage of the process, from initial idea to final mix. This more-or-less continuous evolution of a song was a far cry from the severely segmented assembly of a recorded performance in pre-rock pop.

Spector was not the first producer to craft a record. From Sam Phillips's inspired use of a broken speaker cone through Leiber and Stoller's hits for the Coasters and Luther Dixon's work with the Shirelles, producers had come to play an increasingly important role in the creative process. However, Spector turned the traditional relationship between song and sound on its head. Before the sixties, a song was mainly the words, the melody, and the person singing it—Elvis's numerous hits exemplify this perfectly. Everything else is in the service of the song and the singing of it. However, with Spector, the song and the singers are in the service of the sound. The most important element in his girl group hits is the wall of sound.

That was what teens heard when they listened to the songs on their car radios or on the tinny transistor radios that were flooding the market in the early sixties. These first-generation transistor radios—the predecessors of the Walkman—could receive only AM radio stations, and they had a limited frequency range. Spector designed his wall of sound to maximize the impact of the song *as it would be heard on a transistor or car radio*. (If your playback device has an equalizer, try reducing the very lowest and highest frequencies to replicate this experience as you listen to the song.) It was a revolutionary, and extremely influential, strategy.

Songs like "Da Doo Ron Ron" represent an extreme position in the relationship between song and sound. We might surmise that Spector's ego—his need to show the world who was the most important player in the song-creating game—clouded his judgment. As fascinating as his wall of sound is in songs like this, it doesn't make up for the lack of substance in other areas. Still, Spector's symphonic conception of rock offered subsequent producers a roadmap for expanding rock's sound world. It was a major contribution.

# From Folk to Rock

The folk revival that began in the late fifties had a short lifespan, even by pop standards. As a movement with mass appeal, it began in 1958, when the Kingston Trio's recording of "Tom Dooley" topped the pop charts. It ended seven years later, when Dylan went electric at the Newport Folk Festival, and Alan Lomax and Pete Seeger went ballistic.

In its revived form, **folk music** was an urban music. The earlier folk revival of the 1940s and early fifties, sparked by the work of the Lomaxes, Woody Guthrie, and—most popularly—the Weavers, had brought folk music into the city. The second revival, which began in the late fifties, made the separation between country roots and contemporary urban performance even wider. By 1960, this old/new folk music was flourishing in coffeehouses, often located in the more bohemian parts of major cities (Greenwich Village in New York, North Beach in San Francisco) or near college campuses.

The folk revival was apolitical at first. Its audience liked the tuneful melodies, pleasantly sung. That soon changed, as this new folk revival quickly rediscovered its past. Historic preservation and social commentary, the two main directions of the folk movement of the thirties and forties, resurfaced within a year.

## Restoring the Past

The restoration of traditional music during this folk revival had two branches. One was the rediscovery of folk musicians, white and black. The other was the re-creation of folk music by contemporary performers. The blues revival of the early sixties was one dimension of the folk revival. Delta bluesmen who hadn't sung professionally in twenty-five years were suddenly touring college campuses and appearing at folk festivals. Equally important was the reissue of early recordings. This helped folk traditionalists try to replicate the country and blues styles that they heard on folk recordings. Their search for authenticity went far beyond learning a song out of a songbook.

The most notable and popular of these traditionalists was Joan Baez. Her covers of traditional songs, such as those recorded by the Carter Family, show a conscientious attempt to re-create not only the songs but also the sound of traditional folk music. It is most evident in the accompaniment: Baez's guitar playing closely resembles that of Maybelle Carter. However, her pure-toned singing has none of the Carters' nasal quality or country twang. It is as far from their style as New York is from the southern Appalachians. Still, it is far more connected stylistically to the Carters than it is to the rock and popular music of the early sixties.

## Social Commentary: The Legacy of Woody Guthrie

The folk revival also gave voice to the protest movement. The drive for racial equality had been gathering momentum since the end of World War II. The gradual dismantling of the "separate but equal" policy and the confrontations that ensued brought the issue into the national spotlight. In the early sixties, both performers and audiences embraced this and other social issues of the day. The image of ex-Weaver Pete Seeger, the strongest link between the folk revivals of the 1940s and the sixties, leading the masses in singing "We Shall Overcome" is still vivid. He became godfather to a new generation of activists. Other folk performers, like Bob Dylan (born Robert Zimmerman, 1941) and Phil Ochs, were even more outspoken. Their songs would prod a generation of young people into thinking, then acting: massive rallies, marches on Washington, sit-ins.

In effect, this new folk revival relived the history of the music that inspired it. That is, it began by re-creating folksongs and classic "folk" performances (such as those by the Carters). However, just as Woody Guthrie gave the folk sound a contemporary focus, so did folksingers like Dylan begin to write topical songs. These were social commentaries with more sting, such as Dylan's "Talkin' John Birch Paranoid Blues." Indeed, Guthrie was the patron saint of the folk revival; Dylan's visit to Guthrie as he lay dying in a New York hospital was a momentous event in his life.

Social commentary presented in folk-style songs gushed forth from the coffeehouses of New York's Greenwich Village and college towns around the United States. The audience was young and idealistic. They turned to these songs, despite their musical simplicity, because no other music was comparably relevant.

## Bob Dylan and the Folk Revival

Dylan's music from the early sixties epitomizes the substance and spirit of the activist branch of the folk movement. The repertoire on his first few recordings includes mostly original songs as well as the occasional folk or blues cover—for instance, "House of the Rising Sun," popularized by the Almanac singers (Guthrie, Seeger, and others) in 1941, or "See That My Grave Is Kept Clean," a blues by Blind Lemon Jefferson. The original material ranged from songs like the aforementioned "Talkin' John Birch Paranoid Blues," which he delivered in his distinctive folk/rap style—resonant speaking over a strummed guitar accompaniment, with an occasional harmonica interlude—to anthemic songs like "Blowin' in the Wind." In either case, the words were pre-eminent; the guitar accompaniment typically consisted of simple strumming of the I, IV, and V chords, the three basic chords of common practice tonality. The main musical variable was the melody—including whether there was one.

"Blowin' in the Wind," Bob Dylan (1963)

**Dylan's "Blowin' in the Wind"**    Bob Dylan's first big hit—although it would be a hit for someone else, not him—was "Blowin' in the Wind," the first track on his 1963 album *The Freewheelin' Bob Dylan*. (The album rose as high as number 22 and eventually went gold.) It is hard to imagine a more striking contrast between "Blowin' in the Wind" and "Da Doo Ron Ron," although, ironically, they were released only a few months apart. Dylan's song is all about the words. The melody is simple, repetitive, and catchy, an ideal backdrop for important lyrics. The guitar strumming supports the melody unobtrusively, sustaining the flow when Dylan is not singing or playing the harmonica. In an indirect way, Dylan's voice also draws attention to the words. It is a grating sound, not a pretty one; listeners are not likely to be so seduced by its beauty that they would ignore the words. At the same time, his voice has an urgency that amplifies the message of the lyrics.

♪ **KEY FEATURES**

**"Blowin' in the Wind," Bob Dylan (1963)**

- Words are pre-eminent: Dylan's thought-provoking lyrics demand careful attention from listeners.
- Simple, repetitious melody: gives Dylan's presentation of the words more resonance; the clear form helps listeners retain the words.
- Guitar accompaniment: an unobtrusive sound cushion for the words and melody; it is there mainly for support and continuity.

The lyrics of "Blowin in the Wind" challenge listeners, both in their message and in the way Dylan presents the message. The song is strophic: three stanzas set to the same melody, with the title phrase as a short refrain. Dylan begins generally: he alludes to the long road to maturity, the dove of peace, and an archaic armament in the first stanza. In the second stanza, he juxtaposes the glacial pace of erosion with the lingering effects of racism; by implication, change comes much too slowly. In the third stanza, he focuses on the terrible cost of racism, for the victims and the perpetrators. Dylan avoids specifics in the images and—even more—in the refrain. By simply stating that the answer is there for everyone to see, rather than stating the theme of the song specifically, Dylan demands that his listeners respond actively.

We can hear the importance of Dylan's acerbic singing and harmonica playing to the message of the song if we compare Dylan's version to the cover version by Peter, Paul, and Mary. Peter, Paul, and Mary (Peter Yarrow, Noel Paul Stookey, and Mary Travers) were the Kingston Trio of the early sixties: commercial, but with a conscience. They rode the crest of the protest movement: "Blowin' in the Wind" was a number 2 hit for them in 1963. Their straightforward presentation of the

Bettmann/Corbis

Bob Dylan in the recording studio making his first album, circa 1962.

melody made the words easily comprehensible; their pleasant voices and subdued guitar accompaniment made it palatable to a broad audience. However, their sound related to the message of the song far less than Dylan's, and only in a generic way. Their other number 2 hit, "Puff (The Magic Dragon)," sounds virtually identical, although the lyric is ostensibly a children's story (some have interpreted it as an invitation to smoke marijuana) rather than a call to action. Still, the clean, careful, sweet-voiced singing seems out of sync with the message of Dylan's song.

We accept this music as part of rock history mainly because of its message and the way in which it invited rock to matter, and—more important—because of Dylan's subsequent gravitation toward rock. Dylan's song has virtually no musical connection with the other music of this chapter, or—for that matter—with the music of the two previous chapters. Dylan would address precisely this issue by going electric.

## From Rockabilly to Rock:
## The Music of Roy Orbison

Roy Orbison (1936–1988), a shy Texan, was the last rockabilly, the first country rocker, and one of the architects of the symphonic pop-rock sound of the early sixties. After recording his first sides at Norman Petty's studio in Clovis, New Mexico,

Orbison migrated to Tennessee in 1956. During stops in Memphis and Nashville, he rubbed shoulders with all of the important figures in white rock and roll by the end of the decade: Elvis, Buddy Holly, Jerry Lee Lewis, Sam Phillips, Norman Petty, the Everly Brothers.

His music—especially that produced at the peak of his career—would blend all these influences. Indeed, Orbison's major hits from the early sixties summarize and update the country elements of rock and roll and provide a fascinating early glimpse of the transformative changes that distinguish the rock of the sixties from rock and roll. Orbison's partner in these significant developments was producer Fred Foster, who worked with him at Monument Records.

Their summarizing work took two forms. In songs such as "Only the Lonely" (1960), they cultivated a more melodramatic version of the rock ballad introduced by the Everly Brothers. In "Meanwoman Blues" (1963), Orbison simultaneously updates rockabilly—the song is a country take on rock and roll, not rhythm and blues—and lays the foundation for country rock. The song is a musical stew: Orbison's singing with gentle overtones of Jerry Lee Lewis, backup vocals and saxophone borrowed from rhythm and blues, a bluesy guitar solo over the riff from the Surfari's "Wipeout," played on a saxophone. These were part of the sound world of the early sixties. Underpinning this is a rhythmic conception that would become the rhythmic foundation of country rock: a honky-tonk two-beat rhythm—electric bass alternating with heavy drum backbeat—with a clean rock beat layered on top. Along with the dense texture, this driving rhythm amplifies the swagger of the lyric. All of this happened several years before the idea of country rock surfaced, and almost a decade before the release of the Eagles' "Take It Easy," the song that clearly defined the genre.

## "Oh, Pretty Woman"

Orbison's masterpiece was "Oh, Pretty Woman" (more commonly known as "Pretty Woman"). Although the song was released after the onset of the British invasion, we include it in this chapter because the early sixties were the most successful stretch of Orbison's career.

CD 2:12

"Oh, Pretty Woman," Roy Orbison (1964)

The song evidences several features that would become trademarks of sixties rock. Among the most significant are:

- A straightforward rock rhythm
- A signature guitar riff to open the song and serve as an instrumental refrain
- A bass line that moves in a free rhythm, rather than a walking pattern or other narrowly defined role

Among the most distinctive features of the song is its form. More than any other song discussed to this point, "Pretty Woman" illustrates the more flexible approach to form that characterizes rock music. More than that, the memorable musical events in the song seem to respond almost cinematically to the images described in the lyric. Like a good soundtrack, they capture the basic mood of the story and highlight the constantly shifting emotions.

The story is a cliché of romantic comedies, music videos, and television commercials: boy sees beautiful girl, boy makes some kind of contact with girl, boy is apparently rebuffed, but gets the girl in the end. Here are the musical events that help tell the story:

The opening guitar riff is assertive, yet the chord that it outlines, and the silence that follows, asks a question that is not answered conclusively until the final notes of the song. The periodic return of the guitar riff not only outlines the form of the song but keeps us focused on the main issue in the song: will the pretty woman like the hero?

The first two sections of the vocal line begin by setting the scene. But both end by dangling on the V chord. The second time, the suspenseful ending highlights the crucial question: "Are you lonely, just like me?"

In the section that follows, the hero of the song hits on the pretty woman. A new melody, with short, pleading phrases in a higher register, underscores the intensity of his interest. Orbison extends the pleading section by dropping down into a lower register as he attempts to persuade her more intimately, in both words and music. This extension is the first clear signal that Orbison is molding the form to fit the pacing of his story: a more conventional song would have returned to the opening section before the extension.

He continues to press his case as the opening vocal section returns. However, the suspenseful ending is expanded enormously as the hero seems to lose the pretty woman, then discovers that she's returning. The sudden ending after the big buildup is, in effect, a quick fade to black as the hero and the pretty woman come together.

In "Pretty Woman," Orbison molded the form to the story, not the other way around. He underscored the feelings of his protagonist musically, in both the guitar riff and the melody. His hero's success with the pretty woman owes much to the persuasiveness of the music. Orbison's flexible approach to form and musical reinforcement of the story line would become increasingly common in rock. However, few would connect the music with the story as closely and powerfully as Orbison did here.

♪ **KEY FEATURES**

### "Oh, Pretty Woman," Roy Orbison (1964)

- Signature guitar riff to open the song
- Rock rhythm and rock instrumentation: electric guitar, electric bass, drums
- Liberated bass line: loping, not walking
- Orbison's haunting tenor
- Sprawling form that highlights key events of the lyric

With songs such as "Pretty Woman," Orbison survived the first wave of the British invasion. But the arrival of the second wave, a switch to MGM records, and personal tragedy (the death of his first wife and son in a fire at his Nashville home in the late sixties) sent his career into a tailspin.

Hulton-Deutsch Collection/Corbis

Roy Orbison in 1964, resting backstage during a British tour. (Orbison was invading England while the British bands were invading the United States.)

In the early sixties, folk music and country music seemed worlds apart: one flourished in Greenwich Village and other urban areas, the other mainly in the South. Orbison and Dylan would play key roles in bringing country and folk into rock: Orbison first with his recordings, and Dylan soon after, when he went electric. In 1988, just before Orbison's death, there was a symbolic celebration of both men's roles in bringing together folk, country, and rock in the almost accidental formation of the Traveling Wilburys: this famous supergroup included not only Orbison and Dylan, but also George Harrison, Jeff Lynne, and Tom Petty.

Orbison's "Pretty Woman" is among the memorable songs from 1963 and 1964 that line up on the rock side of the rock and rock-and-roll boundary. We encounter two more from the same period next.

## Garages and Cars and Surf and Sun

Rock and roll came from the center of the United States: New Orleans, Memphis, Texas, Chicago. However, it quickly spread to both coasts and beyond. While Dick Clark was filling the airwaves with teen idols and Philadelphia teens were twisting the night away, rock and roll was taking root elsewhere, most notably on the west coast of the United States and in England. We consider two locales in the United States in this chapter and England in the next.

The two songs considered here are the Kingsmen's version of "Louie Louie" and the Beach Boys' "I'll Get Around." The Beach Boys are forever linked to southern California, while the Kingsmen were based several hundred miles up the coast, in Portland, Oregon. In the sense that both bands were based on the west coast, away from the geographical center of rock, there is some geographic connection. There is also a clear musical affinity; in such basic features as instrumentation and rhythm, the songs are more like each other (and Orbison's "Oh, Pretty Woman") than they are like other songs discussed in the chapter.

However, there is a striking contrast in the way that they prepared for the recording sessions and the quality of the recording. The Kingsmen were the first big-time **garage band**; their recording of "Louie Louie" was one of only three songs by the band that charted; the other two rode its coattails. By contrast, the Beach Boys' song is carefully worked out and recorded with comparable care. Under the "fun in the sun" surface is a well-crafted song.

Together, however, the two songs show the two main facets of a revolutionary change in the creative process that took place during the early years of the rock era. One was the increased use of recordings as a tool for the transmission of music, the other was multitrack recording.

## Rock and Recordings: A New Mode of Musical Transmission

All music is an aural art. However, before the twentieth century, there were only two ways to create music and transmit it from one person to another. One way was by ear. A musician could invent a song or dance. When he or she performed it, others could listen to the musician's music and learn it. This is how folksongs and dances were passed around and passed down through generations. There were two limitations on this process. One involves location: the listener had to be in the same place at the same time as the person performing the music in order to learn it. The other has to do with difficulty. Musical notation (a set of visual symbols that represent musical sounds with varying degrees of precision) becomes a necessary tool when the music is too complex to work out strictly by ear—because the piece is too long, too difficult to execute, too complex, and/or involves too many musicians. Beethoven could have composed the melody we know as the "Ode to Joy" without notation, and we can learn it without reading music, but the symphony of which it is a part, his *Ninth Symphony*, absolutely demands notation. The work is about 70 minutes long (it was this piece that determined the storage capacity of the compact disc; the people responsible for its development wanted to be able to include the entire symphony on a single disc!) and requires four vocal soloists, a large choir, and an orchestra of about a hundred musicians.

Recording, radio, and talking films offered another way to pass music on. People could learn music via these new technologies. Recordings in particular offered the possibility of repeated scrutiny during the learning process. Folksingers like Bob Dylan and Joan Baez could learn songs by the Carter Family, Blind Lemon Jefferson, and dozens of other folk and blues performers. Jazz, rhythm-and-blues, and rock-and-roll musicians could steal licks from recordings and work them into their own performances.

During the early years of the rock era, the recording gained in authority. Aspiring rock-and-roll musicians understood that the record was the song. One can imagine the Wilson brothers listening to Chuck Berry's "Sweet Little Sixteen" countless times, then reworking it into "Surfin' USA." Implicit in their recording is the idea that the song is more than the melody; among its most distinctive features is a band-wide realization of Berry's conception of rock rhythm.

In the case of the Kingsmen's "Louie Louie," the path is more circuitous. The original version of the song was by Richard Berry, a Los Angeles–based R&B singer; he recorded the song in 1956 with his band the Pharaohs. By Berry's account, he drew on several sources for the song: Chuck Berry's "Havana Moon" was a principal source for the pseudo-Jamaican style of the lyric, while the repeated riff that is the song's signature came from a Latin song—Berry had been working with an R&B band that also played a lot of Latin music. Over the next several years, several bands covered Berry's song. One of them was Rockin' Robin Roberts and the Fabulous Wailers, a small-time band based in the Pacific Northwest; the group recorded their version in 1961. This is the version from which the Kingsmen crafted their memorable version.

This is the rock-era analogue to the folksong-style creation, re-creation, and dissemination. One can easily imagine newly formed rock-and-roll bands setting up in garages across the country working out three-chord songs like "Louie Louie." As each band works through it, it assumes a different form. The Kingsmen's version is noticeably different from Berry's original; the Wailers' version is somewhere in between. And there are numerous other versions of the song, enough to warrant two "Best of 'Louie Louie'" anthologies—just as there are multiple versions of folksongs. The main difference, of course, is the recording, which eliminates the need for personal contact and which provides a more reliable reference. But a simple song like "Louie Louie" quickly spawned many different renditions, including the one that made the Kingsmen famous.

## Multitrack Recording

"I Get Around," by contrast, is a sophisticated song supporting teen-themed lyrics. Brian Wilson, the mastermind of the Beach Boys' sound, took considerable care in shaping the harmony, rhythm, instrumentation, and texture of the song. His main tool in this enterprise was a multitrack tape recorder. According to his personal website, *www.brianwilson.com*, Wilson worked out the Beach Boys' distinctive sound before their first recording:

> It was a unique fusion that Wilson had been tinkering with in the family garage where, inspired by The Four Freshman and their complex vocal blends, and armed with a multi-track tape recorder, he'd spent hours exploring the intricacies of harmony and melody. By overlapping his own dynamic voice (which peaked in a soaring falsetto) and various instruments, he could create the effect of a full group.

Wilson's early exercises in multitrack recording show a new creative process at work. Before multitrack tape recorders, musicians had to imagine the sound that they wanted in their head, perhaps try it out on an instrument, such as the piano, then write out what they heard and assemble a group of musicians to hear the actual sound of the musical mental image. If the final result was not to their liking, they rewrote the composition or arrangement and reassembled the musicians. In most stages of the process, the musicians had to convert sounds—real or imagined—into notation, which is necessarily an imperfect rendering of the musical sound. Then they had to rely on the musicians to not only play what was written but also supply those elements of the performance that could not be notated. However, in multitrack recording, musicians like Wilson are working with actual sounds throughout the entire creative process. Further, they are able to experiment with their work at every stage of the process: they can add a part, and if it is not the desired result, they can remove it.

Today, creating music in a sound-only environment is commonplace. Buy an Apple computer; open up Garage Band (the audio workstation software that comes with the computer), drag and drop a few times: you have an instant dance track. Wilson's work is among the most noteworthy early examples of this process; it would soon become the *modus operandi* in rock music, as we discover in the next chapter. It is a process that belongs to the rock era; it is the result of technology responding to musical needs, much as the technology of the 1920s responded to the musical needs of that time. It is a revolutionary change in the creative process, one that is as far-reaching as the invention of musical notation and one whose possibilities are still being expanded. For those who have come of age in the twenty-first century, it may be hard to imagine a musical world without this technology. But fifty years ago, Wilson was on the cutting edge.

## A Garage-Band Triumph: "Louie Louie"

The success of "Louie Louie" is due largely to incompetence. The great attraction of the song seems to have been the incomprehensibility of the lyrics. The original lyrics are innocuous enough, although by today's standards, the pseudo-Jamaican dialect would probably be deemed politically incorrect. However, it has been impossible to reconstruct the lyrics of the song as sung by lead singer Jack Ely on this recording. The absence of a definite text led teens to imagine their own lyrics, led parents to wonder what their sons and daughter were listening to, and led the FBI to investigate the song; 31 months later the FBI could only conclude that the song was "unintelligible at any speed." Of course, in the absence of intelligible lyrics, randy teens supplied their own, some of which were documentably raunchy.

The recording took place late at night. It was supposed to have been a demo to help the band land a gig on a cruise ship; the session cost the band $36. Why were the lyrics unintelligible? The two most likely culprits are Robert Lindahl, the engineer for the session at Northwestern Inc., a recording studio in Portland, and the lead singer Jack Ely. The record sounds like it was recorded live at a fraternity party, rather than in a studio. The quality is so bad, especially when compared with the version recorded by Paul Revere and the Raiders at the same studio not long after, that some have speculated that the band thought that they were simply playing through the song to warm up rather than recording the final take. Some responsibility has to fall on Lindahl. However, most of the blame must fall on Ely—various accounts have him hung over or simply drunk, wearing braces, or hoarse from singing; the actual reason remains a mystery.

CD 2:13

"Louie Louie,"
the Kingsmen
(1963)

Whatever the reason, a rumor spread from Portland throughout the country that the song contained obscene lyrics; this seems to be the main reason for the popularity of the Kingsmen's version of the song. (Recall that this song foreshadows the era when fans believed that there were subliminal messages hidden in song lyrics that only became audible when the record was played backward. Both the Beatles and Led Zeppelin were accused of this practice.)

In 1963, the Kingsmen were a more-or-less basic garage band. The members of the band at the time of the recording were Ely, who played guitar as well as sang, drummer Lynn Easton, keyboardist Don Gallucci, guitarist Mike Mitchell, and bassist Bob Nordby. This is the standard rock band lineup—two guitars, electric bass, and drums—augmented by Gallucci's keyboard.

The most easily remembered parts of the song are Ely's vocal and the high-register riff, played on keyboard and guitar. However, the more interesting aspects of the song, at least from an evolutionary perspective, are the bass and drum parts. The bass part stands out because the other instruments are in a high register; the drums stand out because of the informal recording technique. Both Nordby and Easton, the bassist and drummer, break away from the rather mechanical roles typically assigned to them in rock-and-roll and rhythm-and-blues songs through the early sixties: compare the bass and drum parts here with their counterparts on "Will You Love Me Tomorrow?" Similarly, the guitar solo ("Let's give it to 'em right now!"), built exclusively on the pentatonic scale heard so often in Delta blues recordings, helped usher in a more blues-oriented solo guitar style. The greater freedom of the rhythm section and a blues-influenced guitar solo style were among the features that distinguish rock from the music that came before it. Their use by the Kingsmen shows that they were becoming common practice.

> ♪ **KEY FEATURES**
>
> **"Louie Louie," the Kingsmen (1963)**
> - Garbled vocals
> - Standard rock rhythm
> - Blues-influenced guitar solo based on pentatonic scale
> - Active bass line with a sometimes free rhythm

Rock critic Dave Marsh claimed that "Louie Louie" was the "world's most famous rock and roll song" and argued his case in a book that examined both the history and (as he put it) the mythology of the song. Most famous or not, "Louie Louie" was one of the first real rock songs, in style and attitude. It brought back the edge of early rock and roll even as it updated its conception. In the process, it assured the Kingsmen of a small slice of immortality. Ironically, Ely, whose garbled vocals were the main reason for the success of the song, left the group shortly after they recorded the song.

## Surf Music

When I arrived at college in Massachusetts in the fall of 1963, two dorm mates from the east coast asked me these three questions: What's your name? (Mike) Where are you from? (California) Do you surf? (No—I'm from northern California.)

**Regional Rock**   For teens who had grown up with snowy winters and dreary, late-arriving springs, the beaches of southern California seemed like a hedonist's dream: sun, surf, cars, babes—the endless summer. Although *Beach Party*, the first in a series of films celebrating the surfing lifestyle, had been released just a month earlier, most teens, including my dorm mates, learned about the southern California lifestyle from the lyrics of songs by the Surfaris, the Ventures, Jan and Dean, and—above all—the Beach Boys. These bands created the soundtrack for the "fun in the sun" lifestyle.

**Surf music** was responsible for two important firsts in rock history. It was the first post-1959 rock style to add significantly to rock's sound world. Perhaps the most distinctive new sound was the high-register close harmony vocals of the Beach Boys and, to a lesser extent, Jan and Dean. More influential, however, were the array of new guitar sounds—intense reverb, single line solos in a low register (most famously in the Ventures' "Walk, Don't Run"), and above-the-rapid, down-the-escalator tremolos and other virtuosic effects popularized by Dick Dale, the "king of the surf guitarists" and one of rock's first cult figures, and those who imitated him. Indeed, Dale is arguably rock's first virtuoso guitarist—Hendrix, who like Dale was left-handed, copied Dale's guitar setup.

In large part because of these distinctive sounds—high vocals, "surf guitar"—surf music acquired an indelible regional identity. A single vocal harmony or descending tremolo was all that was needed to put a listener on a Malibu beach watching the waves or cruising along the strip in a little deuce coupe or a station wagon with real wood paneling.

This was the first time in the short history of rock where the music evoked a strong sense of place. Rock and roll developed first in the center of the country, from Chicago through Memphis to New Orleans. There was a New Orleans sound, but the songs of Little Richard don't call to mind gumbo or wrought-iron railings the way jazz does. The music coming from Sam Phillips's studio had a distinct sound identity, but our images are of the performers, not the place; the same is true with Chuck Berry. By contrast, the name says it all: surf music is a sound about a place and a lifestyle. It would not be the last. A few years later, a street corner in San Francisco would become the geographic center of another rock-driven lifestyle; others would follow.

More generally, the new sounds coming out of California were the first clear signal of the geographic diffusion of rock. The British invasion would be a far more potent sign, because it made an American music international. It is in this early sixties development that we see the first stages in what would become the global reach of contemporary rock-era music.

**The Beach Boys**   The most important and innovative of the surf music bands was the Beach Boys. Their band was a family affair. The original group consisted of three brothers, Carl (1946–1988), Dennis (1944–1983), and Brian Wilson (b. 1942); their cousin, Mike Love (b. 1941); and a friend, Al Jardine (b. 1942).

The Beach Boys' first recordings point out their debt to rock's first generation. They feature Chuck Berry riffs—even entire songs—borrowed almost note-for-note. (However, they combined Berry's riffs with a completely new vocal sound.) In their recordings released between 1963 and 1965, they glorified the surfer lifestyle in songs that subtly varied their innovative, immediately recognizable sound.

"I Get Around," a song that reached the top of the charts in June 1964, shows key elements of their style and the variety possible within it. The song begins with just voices, presenting the essence of the Beach Boys' vocal sound. In order, we hear unison singing, tight harmonies, and a soaring single line melody juxtaposed with harmonized riffs: all sung with no vibrato.

The refrain follows, its split melody supported by a driving rock rhythm played by the entire band. Unlike this rhythm, the distinctive vocal sound of the Beach Boys came from outside rock: its source was the Four Freshmen, a slick, skilled, jazz-flavored vocal group who navigated complex harmonies as nimbly as Count Basie's saxophone section. Wilson, who admired the group and acknowledged them as a source of inspiration, used their sound as a point of departure. The song is harmonically richer than any other song that we have heard to this point; Wilson charts a distinctly new path in the fresh new chord progressions underneath the vocal.

The scene-painting verse sections are set off from the chorus by the substitution of an open-sounding, loping rhythm for the straightforward rock rhythm of the refrain. Even the instrumental solos have a characteristic, clearly defined sound. The short interlude in the verse combines a doubled organ and bass line with double-time drums, while the guitar solo is supported with sustained vocal harmonies.

The "fun in the sun" lyrics of the song suggest a mindless hedonism—enormously appealing not only to southern Californians but to teens everywhere. They belie the considerable sophistication of the music: not only the harmonies and key changes that range well beyond the three-chord rock progressions of so many bands, but also the beautifully interwoven vocal parts, sharp contrasts in texture that outline the form of the song, varied timekeeping, and other subtle features. This sophistication was mainly the work of Brian Wilson, who wrote the song, sang and played in the band,

Sunset Boulevard/Corbis

The Beach Boys performing in 1964. The band includes drummer Dennis Wilson, guitarists Al Jardine and Carl Wilson, bassist Brian Wilson, and vocalist Mike Love.

CD 2:14

"I Get
Around," the
Beach Boys
(1964)

and produced the recording. In their peak years, the sound of the Beach Boys was Brian Wilson's conception.

♪ **KEY FEATURES**

**"I Get Around," the Beach Boys (1964)**

■ Distinctive vocal sound: high lead singing with intricate, important backup vocal parts

■ Clear rock rhythm, with considerable variation: strong rock beat in the chorus of the song; open, loping rhythm in the verses

■ Considerable sound variety in the instrumentation and texture: overall low register of the instruments balances high register vocals; innovative sound combinations, such as the organ doubling the guitar in the verse

■ Strong bass line throughout the song

# Coming Together: From Rock and Roll to Rock and Soul

Brian Wilson might be the poster boy for the rock of the early sixties. He was 19 when he and his brothers recorded their first Beach Boys song. The songs that they recorded exemplify rock in late adolescence. The teen-themed lyrics sound innocent when compared to those of Dylan, the Beatles, the Who, the Rolling Stones, and so many other bands just a few years later. The music is clearly rock, not rock and roll, but it is not as muscular as the rock of the late sixties and early seventies. Like the basketball stars who jump from high school to the NBA, it took a little while for the bodies to fill out. Wilson's influences are obvious: "Surfin' USA" is naive in its aping of Berry's song. Yet there is also significant innovation: Wilson's use of the multitrack recorder as a dynamic new creative tool and the musical new directions in harmony, instrumentation, and production.

In differing ways, all of the music surveyed in this chapter suggests the late adolescence of rock-era music. The twist becomes a dance for adults as well as teens. The two girl group (not woman group) songs mix naiveté and immaturity (what does "Da Doo Ron Ron" mean?) with sophistication and innovation. Dylan's "Blowin' in the Wind" captures the high-mindedness and idealism of his peers. The songs of Orbison, the Kingsmen, and the Beach Boys show rock on the verge of maturity and significance.

In most cases, we hear the transformative impact of the new recording technology. Indeed, in Spector's recording, we hear the beginning of the divorce between live and recorded performance: it would have been difficult to emulate the sound of the Crystals' song in live performance with early sixties technology. Dylan's minimalist song is the striking exception to this trend.

## Common Musical Features of Early Sixties Music

Despite the significant differences in style, there are some common musical features that stamp virtually all of this music as from the early sixties, not the fifties. Among the most prominent and pervasive are these:

- *The use of electric bass and the liberation of the bass line.* The switch from acoustic to electric bass boosted the low register of the rock band. The use of an amplifier made it much easier to play loudly. This in turn freed the bass player from working hard simply to produce a walking bass line. Rock bass players could now take a more flexible approach to the bass line—active or laid back, on the beat or rhythmically independent. We get hints of this in the majority of the songs.

- *A collective conception of rock rhythm.* Musically, the clearest indication that rock and roll had become rock could be heard in the rhythm section. Guitarists like Chuck Berry had shown how rock rhythm should sound. When drummers and especially bass players (now playing electric bass exclusively) also think in terms of this faster rhythm, then rock and roll became rock—and rhythm and blues became a new kind of black pop. We hear this on the Shirelles' song and on the recordings by Chubby Checker, Orbison, the Kingsmen, and the Beach Boys.

- *Diffusion of melodic interest.* Dylan's "Blowin' in the Wind" is the exception that proves the rule. That song is a simple melody with a simple, straightforward accompaniment. In so many other songs, and especially the last three, melodic interest is diffused throughout the band, rather than concentrated in the vocal lines. "Pretty Woman" and "Louie Louie" begin with distinctive and memorable instrumental riffs; the one used in "Louie Louie" continues with virtually no change. In "I Get Around," Wilson distributes melodic material to both vocal lines and the instruments. The piano tremolo in "Da Doo Ron Ron" is an even more basic expression of this principle.

These were the most pervasive musical innovations of the early sixties. A new generation of rock and R&B acts would build on them during the mid-sixties. We meet them in the next several chapters.

## Terms to Remember

| | | |
|---|---|---|
| twist | wall of sound | garage band |
| girl groups | multitrack recording | surf music |
| Brill Building | folk music | |

## Applying Chapter Concepts

1. Using the Chords' "Sh-Boom" and the Shirelles' "Will You Love Me Tomorrow?" as reference points, discuss the changes in black group singing from doo-wop to the girl groups. Your comparison should include discussion of the lyrics, the vocal style, the form and length of the song, the basic rhythm, and the instruments used.

2. To explore the transition from rock and roll to rock, compare the following two pairs of songs: Elvis Presley's "Mystery Train" versus "Oh, Pretty Woman" (first and last rockabillies) and Chuck Berry's "Sweet Little Sixteen" and the Beach Boys' "Surfin' USA." In each comparison, focus particularly on the basic beat (is it a rock beat or something else?) and the role of each rhythm instrument in laying down the beat.

seven songs on the playlist for this chapter are unusually diverse: they range from an ..ion to dance to an invitation to think, then act. Please listen to each of the songs, paying ..icular attention to the content of the lyrics, the melody and the singing of it, and the ..ccompaniment. Briefly describe the message and function of the song, as you understand it, and note the contribution of the three features to the message and function: is the message mainly in the lyrics? in the background? some combination of two or three?

Then find three post-2000 songs that you feel are comparable to songs discussed in this chapter, in terms of the message of the song and where the message is embodied. Detail the reasons for your choices.

# PART FOUR

# Rock: The Rock Era, 1964–1977

On June 2, 1967, Capitol Records released the U.S. version of the Beatles' *Sgt. Pepper's Lonely Hearts Club Band*, the group's magnum opus. The album was a commercial success—it topped the charts for fifteen weeks. More significantly, it was also a critical success across the board: it received praise from critics inside and outside of rock. It remains arguably the most important recording of popular music ever released. For example, it sits atop *Rolling Stone*'s list of the 500 greatest albums of all time.

No other single artifact better embodies the nature and the impact of the rock revolution. Everything about it—the group, the concept, the music and the way it was created, the cover, its enormous appeal, its place in the Beatles' discography—exemplifies some significant aspect of the rock revolution. Coming less than three and a half years after the U.S. release of *Meet the Beatles*, it evidenced not only the Beatles' astounding musical growth but also the suddenness of the rock revolution.

From our vantage point at the beginning of the twenty-first century, the rock revolution remains one of the most momentous cultural developments of the previous century. Because of its all-encompassing nature, it had an enormous impact, not only on popular music but also on the entire musical world, on other arts, and on society and culture. The speed with which it occurred only magnified its impact. Among the reasons for its influence are these:

• *The rock revolution was commercially important.* Even on the eve of the British invasion, rock and R&B were a just a slice of the music industry. Traditional musicals, established pop singers, post-bop jazz, the Nashville sound, and novelties like the Brazilian bossa nova were also an important part of the popular music scene. By *Sgt. Pepper*, rock dominated both the singles and album charts, as well as AM and FM radio. By the time the Beatles disbanded, rock ruled the entertainment industry. Rock and black music consolidated their dominance of the marketplace. Many of those working in more traditional genres hopped on the rock bandwagon: the late sixties and early seventies saw a string of rock musicals, the emergence of jazz fusion, and the use of rock music in film soundtracks. By 1970, if music didn't rock, at least to some degree, it was out of date—and out of step with the music business.

• *The rock revolution was comprehensive in its scope.* Rock blurred the musical, social, racial, and geographical boundaries that it inherited from earlier generations. Even as musicians perfected its new groove, others aspired to art status—but on rock's terms.

Records by blacks and whites competed on the charts; black and white musicians played together and learned from one another. The result was the blurring or dissolving of the class and racial boundaries within popular music. Moreover, rock became the first truly international popular style, with much innovative music coming from the United Kingdom. By the middle of the sixties, rock was as much a British music as an American one.

• *The rock revolution was culturally significant.* Rock was the music most in step with the social and cultural challenges to the authority of dominant Euro-centric culture. At the very least, it was the most visible and audible evidence of these changes. And one can argue that simply by its pervasive presence, it helped transform the social, cultural, and intellectual climate of the last part of the twentieth century. Such key trends as minority rights, an expanded understanding of art and greater openness to the contributions of world cultures, and postmodernism certainly reflect and benefit from rock's inherent values.

The eight chapters in Part 4 explore dominant themes during this key period in the history of the rock era. Chapter 7 covers the ascendancy of rock, mainly in the music of Bob Dylan and the Beatles. Chapter 8 surveys the new black music of the sixties. Chapter 9 describes the maturation of its rhythmic essence and the affirmation of its core values. Chapter 10 highlights the extraordinary diversity of rock by surveying the San Francisco musical scene in the late sixties and early seventies. Chapter 11 samples diverse examples of art-oriented rock. Chapter 12 focuses on melodic rock, often far more personal and understated than the music of the previous chapters. Chapter 13 continues the survey of black music into the seventies, while Chapter 14 highlights the music that exemplified rock's reshaping of the popular music mainstream.

## Songs Discussed in Chapters 7–14, Ordered Chronologically

| YEAR | CHAPTER | GROUP | TITLE |
|------|---------|-------|-------|
| **1964** | 8 | The Temptations | My Girl |
| | 9 | The Kinks | You Really Got Me |
| **1965** | 7 | Bob Dylan | Mr. Tambourine Man |
| | 7 | Byrds | Mr. Tambourine Man |
| | 7 | Bob Dylan | Like a Rolling Stone |
| | 8 | Otis Redding | I Can't Turn You Loose |
| | 8 | James Brown | Papa's Got a Brand New Bag |
| | 9 | The Rolling Stones | (I Can't Get No) Satisfaction |
| **1966** | 7 | The Beatles | Eleanor Rigby |
| | 8 | Percy Sledge | When a Man Loves a Woman |
| **1967** | 7 | The Beatles | A Day in the Life |
| | 8 | Marvin Gaye | I Heard It Through the Grapevine |
| | 8 | Aretha Franklin | Respect |
| | 9 | Cream | Strange Brew |
| | 10 | Jefferson Airplane | White Rabbit |
| | 11 | The Doors | Light My Fire |
| | 11 | Velvet Underground | I'm Waiting for the Man |

| | 11 | Frank Zappa and the Mothers of Invention | *We're Only in It for the Money* (excerpts) |
|---|---|---|---|
| **1968** | 9 | The Rolling Stones | Jumping Jack Flash |
| | 9 | The Jimi Hendrix Experience | Voodoo Child (Slight Return) |
| | 10 | Janis Joplin | Piece of My Heart |
| **1969** | 10 | Creedence Clearwater Revival | Proud Mary |
| | 10 | Sly and the Family Stone | Thank You (Falettinme Be Mice Elf Agin) |
| | 11 | The Who | *Tommy* (excerpts) |
| **1970** | 10 | Grateful Dead | Uncle John's Band |
| | 9 | Black Sabbath | Paranoid |
| | 13 | Jackson 5 | ABC |
| **1971** | 10 | Santana | Oye Como Va |
| | 9 | Led Zeppelin | Black Dog |
| | 9 | The Who | Won't Get Fooled Again |
| | 12 | Carole King | (You Make Me Feel Like a) Natural Woman |
| | 12 | Joni Mitchell | All I Want |
| | 12 | James Taylor | You've Got a Friend |
| | 13 | Marvin Gaye | Inner City Blues |
| | 13 | Al Green | Tired of Being Alone |
| | 14 | Tiny Dancer | Elton John |
| **1972** | 9 | Deep Purple | Highway Star |
| | 11 | David Bowie | Hang on to Yourself |
| | 11 | Yes | Roundabout |
| | 12 | Randy Newman | Sail Away |
| | 13 | Stevie Wonder | Superstition |
| | 13 | The O'Jays | Backstabbers |
| | 13 | Curtis Mayfield | Superfly |
| | 14 | Eagles | Take It Easy |
| | 14 | Chicago | Saturday in the Park |
| **1973** | 11 | Pink Floyd | *Dark Side of the Moon* (excerpts) |
| **1975** | 12 | Neil Young | Tonight's the Night |
| | 14 | Queen | Bohemian Rhapsody |
| | 14 | Bruce Springsteen | Born to Run |
| | 14 | Aerosmith | Walk This Way |
| **1976** | 12 | Paul Simon | Still Crazy After All These Years |
| **1977** | 14 | Fleetwood Mac | Dreams |
| | 14 | Steely Dan | Peg |

# 7

# Bob Dylan and the Beatles
## Making Rock Matter

• On August 28, 1964, Bob Dylan and the Beatles met face to face for the first time. The Beatles were on tour in the United States and staying at the Delmonico Hotel in New York. They had acquired *The Freewheelin' Bob Dylan* while in Paris in January 1964; according to George Harrison, they wore the record out, listening to it over and over. John Lennon in particular seemed drawn to Dylan's gritty sound and rebellious attitude. Somewhat later during that same year, Dylan was driving through Colorado when he heard the Beatles for the first time over the radio. Later he would say, "I knew they were pointing the direction where music had to go." Each had something that the other wanted, and perhaps found intimidating: the Beatles, and especially Lennon, wanted Dylan's forthrightness; Dylan responded to the power of their kind of rock and envied their commercial success. It was Lennon who requested the meeting, through Al Aronowitz, a columnist for the *New York Post*, who brought Dylan down from Woodstock.

Whatever initial uneasiness Dylan and the Beatles may have felt with each other went up in smoke. Upon learning that none of the Beatles had tried marijuana, Dylan promptly rolled a couple of joints and passed them around. As Paul McCartney later recalled, "Till then, we'd been hard Scotch and Coke men. It sort of changed that evening."

The Beatles' encounter with cannabis is credited with helping to change the course of their music. Ian McDonald, author of *Revolution in the Head*, a track-by-track account of the Beatles' recordings, observed: "From now on, the superficial states of mind induced by drink and 'speed' gave way to the introspective and sensual moods associated with cannabis and later LSD."

Still, there was more to this meeting than turning the Beatles on. It seemed to further motivate both parties to learn from the other. For the Beatles, Dylan raised the bar—the standard to which the Beatles would hold their music. More specifically, his music occasionally served as a model for their songs, especially those in which Lennon provided the more significant creative input. Later, in explaining their musical breakthrough in the mid-sixties, McCartney said, "We were only trying to please Dylan." Without question, the music they created after the meeting, especially from *Rubber Soul* on, represents a far more substantial legacy than their earlier work.

As for Dylan, the experience gave him additional motivation to go electric. His next album, *Bringing It All Back Home*, which he recorded in January 1965, featured acoustic tracks on one side and electric tracks on the other. After that, he never looked back. In retrospect, his years as a folksinger, as important as they were to his career, and to rock, were simply a prelude to his more substantial career as a rock musician.

There are obvious differences between Dylan and the Beatles: solo performer versus group; private versus public persona; seat-of-the-pants versus state-of-the art record production; talking, barely melodic songs versus tuneful melodies.

However, they were alike in at least two crucial ways: they came to rock from the outside, and they stretched rock to its outer limits. Outside for Dylan meant starting his professional career as a folksinger. Outside for the Beatles meant, more than anything else, Liverpool, England. The idea of foreigners redefining American popular music—and thereby internationalizing it—was without significant precedent.

We focus on the most significant period in the careers of both acts—from the date of the meeting through the release of *Sgt. Pepper's Lonely Hearts Club Band*. We begin with Dylan.

# Dylan Goes Electric

Unlike CDs, vinyl albums contain content on both sides of the disc. So it was convenient, and perhaps expedient, for Dylan to dedicate one side of an LP to where he was coming from and the other side to where he was going. In *Bringing It All Back Home*, his first album of 1965, Dylan moves forward by returning to his roots: his first musical experiences were with a rock-and-roll band. To Alan Lomax, Pete Seeger, and the folkies who thought he'd committed musical blasphemy, this was the beginning of the end. But looked at in relation to the rest of his career, it was the end of the beginning. From that point on, Dylan was a rock musician, not a folksinger.

## From Folk to Rock

If Dylan needed any additional incentive to put his folk phase behind him, he received it from the Byrds' cover of "Mr. Tambourine Man," one of the acoustic songs on the album. The Byrds converted Dylan's elusive and elliptical ramble into a tight pop song. In the process, they inspired Dylan to seek out a more commercially promising path.

"Mr. Tambour-ine Man," Bob Dylan (1965)

Dylan's version of "Mr. Tambourine Man" features just his singing, harmonica and guitar accompaniment, plus another guitar playing an obbligato line. The song combines a catchy melody and memorable refrain ("Hey Mr. Tambourine man, play a song for me") with impressionistic lyrics ("evening's empire," "magic swirlin' ship," "skippin' reels of rhyme," twisted reach of crazy sorrow," "circled by the circus sands"), and the perfect sixties symbol: a pied piper leading a group of hip individuals to a new level of consciousness. "Mr. Tambourine Man" opened popular music up to a radically new kind of lyric. Country, folk, and blues lyrics were direct, as we have seen. Pop-song lyrics could be sophisticated, rock-and-roll lyrics could talk nonsense ("Da Doo Ron Ron") or capture the essence of teenage angst ("Not Fade Away"). But none had been surreal.

Agence France Presse/Getty Images

Bob Dylan performing in Paris, in May 1966. Note that Dylan has traded his acoustic guitar of 1962 for an electric guitar.

CD 2:15

"Mr. Tambour-ine Man," the Byrds (1965)

However, surrealism did not spark success. For all his critical acclaim, Dylan was still on the outside looking in, at least on the singles charts. (The albums fared far better.) "Subterranean Homesick Blues," a track from the electric side, was the first of his recordings to chart as a single—it reached number 39. For all its easy appeal, "Mr. Tambourine Man" did not chart—in Dylan's version. As with "Blowin' in the Wind," it was another group that would bring his song to the top of the charts. This time it was the Byrds, whose version hit number 1 in June 1965.

**The Byrds** The Byrds came together in the summer of 1964 to form what would become the first folk-rock band. The original lineup included guitarists Jim (later Roger) McGuinn, Gene Clark, and David Crosby; bassist Chris Hillman; and drummer Mike Clarke. McGuinn, Clark, and Crosby had formed a folk trio in Los Angeles in late 1963, which went nowhere. Adding Hillman and Clarke changed their sound and put them on the cutting edge of the mix between folk and rock.

A comparison of the two versions of "Mr. Tambourine Man" is instructive. Dylan's version is acoustic. The Byrds' cover uses a full band, including McGuinn's electric 12-string guitar. Dylan's version lasts 5 minutes 30 seconds; the Byrds' version lasts only 2 minutes 29 seconds. And even that difference is deceptive, because the Byrds' recording has a slower tempo and includes McGuinn's introductory riff, which also serves as an extended tag.

The Byrds' version is also much more like a rock song in form. Two statements of the refrain frame just one of the four verses. This truncated version cut out over half of the lyrics—precisely the element that had made the song so special for Dylan fans. But the expanded instrumentation, simpler form, and slower tempo gave the song much wider appeal. McGuinn's famous opening riff, played on a 12-string guitar, seemed to evoke the "jingle-jangle" of the refrain.

## Dylan Rocks

Judging by his next record, the connection between accessibility and commercial success was not lost on Dylan. He officially entered the rock era with his next album, *Highway 61 Revisited*. Recorded in the summer of 1965, the album brought into full flower the power latent in the electric side of *Bringing It All Back Home*. The songs mix

---

♪ **KEY FEATURES**

**"Mr. Tambourine Man," the Byrds (1965)**

■   From folk to rock: opening guitar riff, rock beat, and full rock rhythm section, including prominent electric bass, connect the song stylistically to the new sounds of the sixties.

■   Not much of the story: we only hear one verse of the song, so we know less of the story than we do in Dylan's original.

■   From words to music: in Dylan's version of the song, the melody and accompaniment are in the service of the words, which is where the real interest is. By contrast, the Byrds' version, with its richer accompaniment, distinctive guitar sound and riff, and emphasis on the refrain, shifts attention to the music. As presented in their version, Dylan's catchy melody and its setting seem more important than the lyrics.

---

blues, country, rock—and even pop, in "Ballad of a Thin Man"—into a new Dylan sound. The title of the album suggests this roots remix. U.S. Highway 61 runs through the heart of the Mississippi Delta, and the title track is a hard shuffle with strong echoes of deep blues.

"Like a Rolling Stone," Bob Dylan (1965)

"Like a Rolling Stone," the first track to be recorded, shows how he harnessed his verbal virtuosity to write an accessible rock song. The words still have sting: the song paints an "I told you so" portrait of a young girl who's gone from top to bottom. But they tell a story that we can follow, even on the first hearing.

The song sounds like a rock song from the start: a free-for-all of riffs overlay Dylan's vigorous electrified strumming and a straightforward rock beat on the drums. This sound is maintained throughout the song, with Dylan's harmonica competing with Mike Bloomfield's guitar in the instrumental interludes.

The body of the song consists of four long sections. Within each section, verse and refrain alternate, as they do in many rock songs. However, Dylan immediately puts his own spin on this rock convention: each section has, in effect, two verses and two hooks. The first verse of each section consists of two rapid-fire word streams, saturated with internal rhymes—typical Dylan. But each word stream paints only one picture, and each phrase ends with a short, rifflike idea (such as "Didn't you, babe?"), followed by a long pause. The slower pacing of the images and the break between phrases help the listener stay abreast of Dylan's lyric.

The second verse serves as a long introduction for the first of two melodic hooks: Dylan's voice drips scorn as he sings "How does it feel?" followed by a memorable organ riff; this is repeated, the question left hanging in the air. Dylan then gives a series of equally scornful responses that fill out our picture of the girl's plight. These culminate in the title phrase. By expanding each section internally, Dylan also expands the dimensions of the song: it lasts over 6 minutes, twice the length of a typical song.

"Like a Rolling Stone" established Dylan's rock credentials and his originality as well as any one song could. No one else could have written a song like this: a cinematic portrayal of a privileged princess who's strung out and trying to survive on the streets.

♪ KEY FEATURES

**"Like a Rolling Stone," Bob Dylan (1965)**

- Primacy of the words: in "Like a Rolling Stone," the lyrics are in the forefront. The music is clearly subordinate to the words. The large band behind Dylan—two guitars, piano, organ, electric bass, drums, and tambourine—remains in the background. There are no extended instrumental passages, and the musical materials—both melody and background—are commonplace. Despite the simple and catchy hook "How does it feel," the song would not make a very good instrumental. The relative lack of melodic or rhythmic interest helps focus attention on the words, which are what make the song special.

- Rock enhancing the message: at the same time, the spontaneous interaction of the band behind Dylan—who was extremely casual about the accompaniment—gives the music an edge that enhances the lyric and the grating sound of Dylan's voice. The overall impact of the song is far greater than it would have been with just an acoustic guitar accompaniment.

- Mind-expanding rock: in subject and style, Dylan's lyric obliterated the conventions of pop and rock before June 16, 1965 (the date of the recording). The lyrics were provocative, not pleasant. They challenged listeners to think, then feel. They were *cinéma vérité,* rather than beach movies or James Bond. By integrating such thought-provoking lyrics into a rock song, *and* scoring big with it, Dylan essentially freed rock from its self-imposed limitations. After songs like this, rock could be anything; it could say anything, as the Beatles and others would soon prove.

Despite its length, the song would become one of Dylan's most successful singles, briefly reaching number 2 in the summer of 1965.

However, it was the album, taken as a whole, that would fully reveal what Dylan would bring to rock. The next five songs on the album are extraordinarily diverse:

- "Tombstone Blues," an up-tempo song with a hard honky-tonk beat
- "It Takes a Lot to Laugh, It Takes a Train to Cry," a Dylanesque transformation of the blues, set to a medium groove shuffle rhythm
- "From a Buick 6," a blues-form song with piles of riffs and a honky-tonk beat
- "Ballad of a Thin Man," a ballad with slithery pop-ish harmony and a light shuffle beat
- "Queen Jane Approximately," an early sixties-style rock ballad

There are no recurrent stylistic conventions, such as a basic beat, harmonic approach, or formal plan. Instead, Dylan used these and the other songs on the album to invest rock with a freewheelin', anything-goes attitude. In the album, Dylan thumbed his nose at the conventions of pop music, and the pop music business. Songs ranged in length from just over 3 minutes to well over 11 minutes; most were 5 minutes or more. The song titles could be descriptive, evocative—or not: the title of one song, "From a Buick 6," has no apparent connection to the song itself. These are outward signs that the songs themselves are unconventional: shockingly original, despite their deep roots in rock and roll, blues, folk, country, and **Beat poetry**.

The songs seem to have come about almost by spontaneous combustion: they would take shape in the recording studio, with seemingly arbitrary decisions—such as Al Kooper playing organ for the first time on "Like a Rolling Stone"—crucially shaping the final result. The songs juxtapose the sublime and the ridiculous and package elusive ideas in images that brand themselves on your brain. Above all, they democratize popular music while elevating its message in a way that had never been done before: with Dylan, high art did not have to be high class.

The music was comparably original, in a much more subtle way. His most far-reaching innovation was the evocative use of musical style. He used beats, instruments, harmonies, forms, and the like to create an atmosphere: in "Highway 61 Revisited," for example, the rough-and-tumble ensemble sound recalls Delta blues, which contextualizes the title. Earlier generations of pop artists had used style evocatively, but no one before Dylan had let it penetrate so deeply into the fabric of the music. *Highway 61 Revisited* became one of the most influential rock albums of all time.

*Blonde on Blonde*, his next album, offers an even more spectacular example of his eclectic electric style. Dylan recorded it in Nashville during early 1966, at the suggestion of his producer, Bob Johnston. Several of his collaborators were veteran Nashville session men, most of whom knew nothing about Dylan's music. After an awkward adjustment period, they worked splendidly together, in large part because Dylan brought them into the creative process. He gave very little guidance before they started taping, preferring to let the song take shape as they recorded.

It worked. *Blonde on Blonde* expands Dylan's range in every way: verbally, musically, and—most important—emotionally. The contrasts are even more pronounced: in "Visions of Johanna," he follows doggerel-like quick rhymes—gall/all/small/wall/hall—with the thought-provoking "Infinity goes up on trial" and the searing "Mona Lisa had the highway blues, you can tell by the way she smiles."

Each song on the album has a distinct musical identity. Dylan's eclecticism embraces an even broader range of mood and style: a funky Salvation Army–type band ("Rainy Day Women #12 & 35"), the delicate rock ballad ("Visions of Johanna"), a gritty electric blues/R&B mix in "Obviously 5 Believers."

The constant element throughout all of this music is Dylan's voice, his most personal innovation. When he sings, it is not pretty, by conventional pop standards, and much of the time he talks/shouts/rants instead of singing. But his singing serves to remind rock that expressive power and personality could count for far more than prettiness. His blues and blues-influenced songs on *Highway 61 Revisited* and *Blonde on Blonde* show this better than any comparable group of songs. In them, Dylan sings with the spirit and feel of the blues. His sound is completely original, yet perfectly appropriate: he sounds like himself, not a white guy trying to sound black.

After a serious motorcycle accident in the summer of 1966 that prompted him to retire briefly, he resumed recording in 1967 with *John Wesley Harding*. Since 1967, his work has taken many twists and turns and shaped important trends in rock-era music: for example, his late sixties albums strongly influenced country rock. But none of his later work has had the pervasive impact of the first three electric albums, and the electric half of *Bringing It All Back Home*, if only because these albums were available as a standard of comparison.

It is in these albums that we can best gauge the fact and the nature of Dylan's importance. His lyrics raised the level of discourse in rock in a completely original way. Drawing on blues and folk, the topical songs of Woody Guthrie, and the Beat poets—after hearing Dylan, beat poet Allen Ginsberg said, "The world is in good hands"—he synthesized all of this into something radically new. The contrast between Dylan's lyrics and the songs that we heard in Chapter 6—even Dylan's "Blowin' in the Wind," is so pronounced that it is hard to conceive of them as part of the same musical tradition.

Similarly, Dylan's musical settings opened up new sound worlds, and—more important—new possibilities for the integration of words and music. Precisely because the lyrics were often so provocative and challenging, Dylan used musical settings to evoke mood—to convey the general character of the song without over-powering the words.

In both words and music, it was not just that Dylan made rock a music that mattered almost overnight. His songs were significant in a way that popular song had never been: they were profound, not clever, and they were without compromise. They approached the standards typically reserved for music considered art—for example, classical art songs, bop, and post-bop jazz. Just as important, Dylan made his music important completely on its own terms, rather than by emulating an established style.

Dylan challenged his audience to meet him at his level, rather than playing down to them, as, for example, Phil Spector did. As a result, he never enjoyed the kind of broad commercial success of so many other top acts: "Like a Rolling Stone" and "Rainy Day Women #12 and 35" reached number 2 on the singles charts; "Lay Lady Lay," released in 1969, was his only other song to reach the Top 10. However, his music profoundly influenced many of the important acts of the sixties and beyond. Nowhere is Dylan's influence more evident than in the music of the Beatles.

## The Beatles

The Beatles are rock's classic act, in the fullest sense of the term. Their music has spoken not only to its own time but to every generation since. Their songs are still in the air; they remain more widely known than any other music of the rock era. Beatles' music is a cultural artifact of surpassing importance. No single source—of any kind—tells us more about the sixties than the music of the Beatles.

Not surprisingly, no rock-era act has received more attention—from fans, fellow musicians, and scholars. The brief span of their career encourages this. Their recordings represent a largely finite legacy, like Beethoven's symphonies and sonatas. And like Beethoven's compositions, their recordings document a musical evolution that continued until death—in the Beatles' case, the death of the group.

We can trace the beginning of the Beatles back to the summer of 1957, when John Lennon (1940–1980) met Paul McCartney (b. 1942) and soon asked him to join his band, the Quarrymen. George Harrison (1943–2001) joined them at the end of year; the group was then known as Johnny and the Moondogs. They went through one more name change, the Silver Beetles, and one more drummer, Pete Best, before settling on the Beatles and Ringo Starr (born Richard Starkey, 1940), who joined the group after they had signed a recording contract.

The major phase of the Beatles' career lasted just under eight years. For all intents and purposes, it began on June 6, 1962, when they auditioned for George Martin, the man who would produce most of their records. It ended on April 10, 1970, when Paul McCartney announced that the Beatles had disbanded. After their breakup, all continued their careers as solo performers. But we remember the Beatles mainly through their recordings, and those were made between 1962 and 1970.

## The Music of the Beatles

Our discussion of the Beatles begins and ends with two musical questions: what made their music unique; and how did their music change over the course of their career? Other questions about their music—for example, who were their major influences, and what was the nature and extent of their influence—come out of these questions.

It is difficult to gauge the impact and importance of the Beatles' music in a small sampling of songs. There are two reasons for this difficulty: the rapid evolution of their music and its unparalleled emotional and musical range. If we didn't know their history so well, it would be hard to believe that the band that recorded "Love Me Do" in 1962 and "I Want to Hold Your Hand" in 1963 had become the retro band of "Back in the USSR," the groove merchants of "Get Back," or the soul-, gospel-, and folk-influenced creators of "Don't Let Me Down," "Let It Be," and "Here Comes the Sun"—all recorded between 1969 and 1970. No group changed so much in so short a time. More than any artists of the last forty years, the Beatles elude one-dimensional description, even though their career lasted less than eight years.

The five late recordings also hint at the Beatles' range. What other group could shift moods and styles so drastically—from the parody of "Back in the USSR" and the pathos of "Don't Let Me Down" to the (yes) sunniness of "Here Comes the Sun," the spaciness of "Get Back," and the soulfulness and universality of "Let It Be"—and still sound like themselves? And this is just a sample.

As a point of departure, we can make the following observations about their music:

1. The Beatles had their own sound, right from the start.
2. Their uniqueness grew out of their collaborative approach to music making; they were a *group*, in the fullest sense of the word.
3. Their music is both simple and sophisticated. Their songs always provide easy points of entry that hook us, yet also contain subtle details that set them apart from the mundane. This blend of simplicity and sophistication is one key to their commercial and artistic success.
4. They had the uncanny ability to absorb outside influences—sometimes almost overnight—and integrate them seamlessly into their music.
5. The Beatles' music went through four phases, each lasting about two years:

Bettmann/Corbis

The Beatles appearing on *The Ed Sullivan Show*, February 9, 1964. More than any other single event, this appearance triggered Beatlemania—it remains rock's top TV moment.

- **Beatlemania**: from 1962 to the end of 1964
- Dylan-inspired seriousness: 1965–1966
- **Psychedelia**: late 1966–1967
- Return to roots: 1968–1970

Not surprisingly, transitions from one phase to the next were gradual. Still, the differences between representative examples are easily heard. Our discussion of the Beatles' music describes each of these phases. We mention several songs in passing and discuss two songs in greater detail: "Eleanor Rigby" and "A Day in the Life." These two songs highlight how the Beatles' innovations expanded the range of rock music and invested it with the kind of significance associated with high art. Both qualities were among the most important musical contributions of the Beatles to rock and popular music.

### The Beatles and Drugs

Drugs were an inescapable fact of musical life in the sixties. Again, the Beatles were not the first. Dylan turned the Beatles on to marijuana, and a friend sent Lennon on his first acid trip by spiking a drink, well after Dylan and others had been tripping regularly. However, the Beatles were among the most prominent drug users.

While we can never know all the details of the Beatles' drug use, it's clear that drugs actively shaped their music. Indeed, it's not too much to say that the Beatles' shifts in style are a direct consequence of the drug they were taking: alcohol and speed until 1964; marijuana until 1966, acid during the *Sgt. Pepper* and *Magical Mystery Tour* years, and a cutting down or, in Lennon's case, a switch from acid to heroin in the last few years.

Moreover, the Beatles essentially advertised drug use, at least indirectly. For example, one of the most persistent rumors of the sixties was that "Lucy in the Sky with Diamonds" was a coded reference to LSD. Lennon's adamant denial only helped strengthen everyone's conviction that it was so. In any case, the group's use of drugs made them "cool"—if far from legal or beneficial.

**Beatlemania** The first phase of the Beatles' Martin-produced recording career spanned a little more than two years. It began in September 1962, when they recorded their first song, "Love Me Do," and ended early in 1965, with songs like "Ticket to Ride" clearly indicating that their music was exploring new territory.

During this first phase, the Beatles could be characterized as a rock band with a difference. Their instrumentation was conventional. Like so many bands of the early sixties, they were a Holly-esque quartet: two guitars, bass, and drums, with most of the band singing as well as playing. However, their singing was rougher than that of most other bands, especially the pop pap that was standard fare on British radio.

### The Beatles' Voices

The Beatles' singing gives us one clue to their popularity. In rock and roll's first decade (1955–1965), there were three overwhelmingly popular singles sources: Elvis, the Beatles, and the various Motown groups. All sang tuneful songs with voices that were not as sweet as those of pop singers, but not so rough that mainstream youth would find them unpleasant.

The difference also shows up in the songs. It seemed that even their first hits had at least one feature that was special to that song, and specific to the Beatles. It might be an element that carries through the entire song, or a little detail—or both. In "Love Me Do," for example, the opening phrase of the vocal melody is harmonized mainly with raw-sounding open fifths. "Please, Please Me," their first song with a rock beat, features McCartney's active bass line, a novelty for the time.

**Dylan-Inspired Seriousness (and Humor)** *Rubber Soul* (released in December 1965), *"Yesterday"...and Today* (released June 1966), and *Revolver* (released in August 1966) are the three American albums from this second phase of their career. Dylan's influence is evident in the lyrics, which were more meaningful, less teen-oriented, and wider-ranging in subject matter and tone. It is also evident in the music, although it takes a quite different form. Like Dylan, the Beatles were expanding their sound world but in a more adventurous and more encompassing way. Dylan drew mainly on existing popular styles and used them evocatively. By contrast, the Beatles reached farther afield, into musical traditions far removed from rock and its roots, such as classical Indian music (for instance, the sitar and finger cymbals heard in "Norwegian Wood") and string playing reminiscent of classical music. Moreover, they synthesized these extraneous sounds seamlessly into their music; they became part of the fabric of sound behind the vocals.

As their music matured, it became bolder and more individual. The songs are more clearly the work of the (new) Beatles—no one else could have made them—and less like each other. The contrast from song to song had clearly deepened. One can almost reach into a bag filled with song titles, pull out any five, and marvel at the distinctive identity in meaning and sound of each song and the pronounced differences from song to song. A representative sample: the soul-influenced and sharply tongued "Drive My Car"; the alternately positive and philosophical "We Can Work It Out," colored nicely with harmonium and a brief shift into a heavy-footed waltz; "Norwegian Wood," the one-night stand that wasn't, in which Harrison's East Indian sitar saturates the track, like the smell of incense in the bird's apartment; "Yesterday," which simultaneously evokes and updates the popular songs of "yesterday" (that is, pre-rock popular song), and the somber "Eleanor Rigby." We discuss "Eleanor Rigby" in more detail next.

**"Eleanor Rigby"** A song about the unlamented death of a relationship is unusual enough in popular music. A song about an unlamented death was unprecedented. "Eleanor Rigby," recorded in June 1966, for the album *Revolver*, broke sharply with pop song conventions in both words and music. McCartney relates the story of Eleanor Rigby with a detachment rare in popular music. There is no "you" or "I," even of the generic kind. The story is told strictly in the third person. Her tale is as gloomy as a cold, damp, gray day. Even the refrain is as impersonal as a Greek chorus. They simply ask: "Ah, look at all the lonely people." There's no particular empathy for either Eleanor Rigby or Father McKenzie.

The musical setting is as bleak as the words. A string octet (four violins, two violas, and two cellos), scored by George Martin from McCartney's instructions, replaces the rock band; there are no other instruments. The string sound is spare, not lush—the chords used throughout emulate a rock accompaniment, not the dense cushions of sound heard in traditional pop. Like Eleanor Rigby herself, the melody of both chorus and verse don't go anywhere. Set over alternating chords, the chorus is just a sigh. The melody of the verse contains longer phrases, but they too mostly progress from higher to lower notes. The harmony shifts between chords; there is no strong sense of movement toward a goal. Lyric, melody, harmony, and the repetitive rhythm of the accompaniment convey the same message: time passes, without apparent purpose.

## ♪ KEY FEATURES

**"Eleanor Rigby," the Beatles (1966)**

- Bleak lyrics: a song about seemingly pointless lives, told in an emotionally detached manner
- String group as rock band: for rock, this is a completely novel instrumentation; for popular music, this is a completely novel way of playing strings
- Portraying misery musically: the long melodic sighs, static harmony, and restless string accompaniment amplify the mood of the lyric; it captures the desperate lives of Eleanor Rigby and Father McKenzie

With "Eleanor Rigby," the Beatles announced that their music—and, by extension, rock—was, or could aspire to be, art. The most obvious clue was the classical-style string accompaniment. However, the subject of the song and the detachment with which it is presented have more in common with classical art songs than pop or rock songs. Having recorded rock's answer to the **art song**, the Beatles soon created rock's answer to the art song *cycle*: the **concept album**.

### *"Good Vibrations"*

Although *Sgt. Pepper* seems a logical next step in the Beatles' musical evolution, it can also be understood as a response to the Beach Boys' album *Pet Sounds*. The album, and especially the song "Good Vibrations," represented a major step forward in the use of multitrack recording technology. Wilson recorded "Good Vibrations" in four studios over a period of six months. The song, his wonderfully imaginative setting of it, the novel instrumentation, and—above all—the superb production (a remarkable achievement in the days before 24-track boards) made "Good Vibrations" unique, and a challenge to the Beatles and all who aspired to a higher standard of production.

**Psychedelia** The cover to *Sgt. Pepper's Lonely Hearts Club Band* tells the story. In a "group portrait," the Beatles appear twice—"live" and dressed in band uniforms and in wax-museum-style likenesses. They are surrounded by icons of high and popular culture, mainly from earlier generations: Karl Marx, Laurel and Hardy, and Marilyn Monroe are but a few; Dylan is their only contemporary. That they represent themselves as wax figures or in costume suggests that the Beatles no longer see themselves publicly as they had been in *A Hard Day's Night*. Instead, they are playing a role.

> Although the costumes and wax effigies connect most directly to the conceit
> of the album, the decision by the Beatles to mask their identity might also
> symbolize their retirement from live performance. On August 25, 1966,
> shortly after the release of *Revolver*, the Beatles gave their last performance as
> a touring band.

Further, by placing themselves among several generations of cultural icons, they seem to imply that their music is culturally significant—that it connects to the past even as it promises a new postmodern future and that the division between high and low art is not divinely ordained. Indeed, the message seems to be that gaps—both generational and cultural—implode, leaving artistic significance in the eye and ear of the beholder.

LSD helped fuel this relativistic vision of reality. Indeed, this vision is part of the underlying concept of the album. Throughout the album, there are contrasts between the everyday world and the heightened sensibility experienced while tripping on acid.

This contrast is most sharply drawn in "Lucy in the Sky with Diamonds." In this song, Lennon and McCartney put a truly original spin on verse/chorus form. The verse evokes a dreamy state. The lyric contains numerous psychedelic images ("marmalade skies"), and the music floats along in waltz time. It gives the impression of a person in the middle of an acid trip. By contrast, the chorus is straight-ahead rock and roll, which conveys a sense of normalcy. The repetition of the title phrase suggests a second persona in the song: a detached outsider who is watching the "verse" person while he's tripping.

However, the song that best sums up the *Sgt. Pepper* worldview is "A Day in the Life." Here, the contrast between the mundane, everyday world and the elevated consciousness of acid tripping is made even more dramatic. It is projected by the most fundamental opposition in music itself, other than sound and silence: music with words versus music without words. The texted parts of the song are everyday life, while the strictly instrumental sections depict tripping—they follow "I'd love to turn you on" or a reference to a dream.

This contrast is made even more striking by the nature of the words and music. The text of the song, and the music that supports it, paints four scenes. The first scene is Lennon's response to a newspaper account of a man who dies in a horrible automobile accident while, Lennon suspects, he was tripping. The second pictures Lennon attending a film—perhaps an allusion to the film *How We Won the War*, in which he'd acted a few months prior to recording the song. The third depicts Lennon in the rat race of the workaday world. The last one is a commentary on another even more mundane news article. In Lennon's view, it is news reporting—and, by extension, daily life—at its most trivial: who would bother counting potholes?

The music that underscores this text is, in its most obvious features, as everyday as the text. It begins with just a man and his guitar. The other instruments layer in, but none of them makes a spectacular contribution. This everyday background is opposed to the massive orchestral blob of sound that depicts, in its gradual ascent, the elevation of consciousness. The dense sound, masterfully scored by George Martin, belongs to the world of avant-garde classical music—it recalls the Polish composer Krzysztof

Penderecki's *Threnody for the Victims of Hiroshima* (1960) and other works of that type, works familiar to classical music insiders but not well-known generally. This creates another strong opposition: well-known versus obscure, and by implication, the unenlightened masses (that is, those not turned on) versus those few who are enlightened.

The apparent simplicity of the vocal sections obscures numerous subtle touches. Starr's tasteful drumming and McCartney's inventive bass lines are noteworthy. So is the doubling of the tempo in the "Woke up" section. What had previously been the rock beat layer is now the beat. This expresses in music the narrator's frantic preparation for work without disturbing the underlying rhythmic fabric of the song. Perhaps the nicest touches, however, are found in the vocal line: the trill heard first on "laugh" and "photograph," then expanded on "nobody was really sure" before floating up to its peak on "lords." It is precisely this melodic gesture—the trill, now set to "turn you on"—that presages the move from the vocal section to the orchestral section and by extension the beginning of an acid trip. When the trill/leap material returns in the film-viewing vignette, this connection becomes explicit: the melodic leap is followed by the trill, which blends seamlessly into the orchestral texture. As a melodic gesture, the trill/leap sequence is also a beautiful surprise, strictly on its own terms—a sequel of sorts to the leap to "hand" in "I Want to Hold Your Hand."

The final chord is an instrumental "*OM*," suggesting the clarity of enlightenment after the transition, via the orchestral section, from mundane life in the "normal" world. It is a striking ending to a beautifully conceived and exquisitely crafted song, a song that is one of the most powerful metaphors for the acid experience ever created.

**Return to Roots**   The Beatles reached a pinnacle with *Sgt. Pepper's Lonely Hearts Club Band*. Their subsequent efforts, most significantly *Magical Mystery Tour*, were not as successful, either artistically or commercially. By 1968, they had begun to retreat from the grandiose. Instead of attempting to make yet another major artistic statement, they created music that responded to the music around them. From one perspective, the songs from this period are their unique reinterpretations of the styles that were "out there." Gone, for the most part, are the big orchestras, electronic collages, crowd noises. In its place, more often than not, is some straight-ahead, high-class rock and roll.

But there are two crucial differences. First, they brought to their task what seems like a lifetime of experience and exposure. Second, the music around them had also grown up. Rock—in all its manifestations, black and white—was now an established family of styles, in a way it hadn't been five years previously, so they had much more to draw on. Their maturity, and the maturation of rock, gave their music a depth and breadth that it could not have had at the beginning of the decade.

Yet, despite the more modest scale of their efforts (although *The Beatles* was a double album), the songs of their last period continued to expand the emotional range of their music. Influences come from everywhere. Here's a sampling:

- "Back in the USSR" is twice-fried rock and roll: it recalls both Chuck Berry and the Beach Boys (the pseudo–Beach Boys harmonies and allusions to "Moscow girls" ironically recall the sunny surf music that the Beach Boys popularized).

Bettmann/Corbis

The Beatles on the front steps of Brian Epstein's home preparing to meet the press and preview their *Sgt. Pepper's Lonely Hearts Club Band* album.

- "Ob-La-Di, Ob-La-Da" is the Beatles' take on West Indian music. The song is touched by calypso and ska, the Jamaican precursor of reggae, which was known in England all through the sixties.
- "The Ballad of John and Yoko" owes part of its sound to country rock—appropriately enough, since ballads (long storytelling songs) have deep country roots.
- "Something" is a pop ballad: "the greatest love song of the past fifty years," according to Frank Sinatra—who should know.
- "Let It Be" comes straight out of black gospel.

The fact of the Beatles' familiarity with—and comfort in—so many different kinds of music is remarkable enough. However, it is their ability to personalize any style they absorb into their music—to make it work for a particular song—that sets their music apart from everyone else's.

Ironically, one reason for the greater range of these songs was the growing divisions within the Beatles. Their increasingly fractious relationship meant that they did as little as possible together. Typically, they would come together to record the basic tracks, and the person who wrote the song would supervise its production. That they created so much high-quality music in the midst of this turmoil is remarkable.

## The Beatles: Impact and Influence

In the documentable history of music, there has been one composer and one composing/performing group who have enjoyed widespread popularity and critical acclaim during their career, and whose music has never gone out of favor. The composer was Ludwig van Beethoven; the group was the Beatles. Beethoven and the Beatles have more in common than commercial and critical success. The music of Beethoven and the Beatles is remarkable for its range: both were able to create music of widely varying moods without forsaking their musical identity, significantly more than was the case with their predecessors or contemporaries. It is remarkable for its substantial evolution during the course of their careers. Both elevated the social status of the creator: Beethoven was the man most responsible for the perception of the composer as artist, with the commensurate upgrade in social standing. The Beatles invested rock with artistic stature. And both had a profound impact on the music of subsequent generations: Beethoven's influence was evident throughout the nineteenth century and well into the twentieth; the Beatles' music continues to influence rock-era music, through its continuing popularity—every generation discovers it anew—and by example—demonstrating what is possible in rock.

The impact and influence of the Beatles reshaped every aspect of rock music: what it was and what it could be, how it was created, what it stood for, its place in the music business. The early Beatles recordings helped draw the boundary between rock and roll and rock. However, from 1965 on, Beatles songs really begin to sound different from one another, yet they all sound like Beatles songs. Furthermore, they stretched the boundaries of rock: rock became whatever the Beatles produced, simply because it was by the Beatles.

**The Musical Breadth of the Beatles**  How do we account for their extraordinary boundary-stretching growth as a group? Here are three important reasons.

1. *Knowledge of styles.* They had firsthand familiarity with a broad range of styles. In their dues-paying years, the band performed not only rock-and-roll covers and original songs but also pop hits of all kinds. Unlike the vast majority of contemporary groups, they had a thorough knowledge of pop before rock, and they clearly absorbed styles along with songs.
2. *Melodic skill.* Along with the Motown songwriting teams, the Beatles were the first important rock-era musicians to write melody-oriented songs that were in step with the changes in rhythm, form, and other elements that took place during this time. No one since has written so many memorable melodies.
3. *Sound imagination.* Aided by the development of multitrack recording and the consummate craftsmanship of George Martin, their producer, the Beatles enriched their songs by startling, often unprecedented, combinations of instruments and—occasionally—extraneous elements, such as the crowd noises and trumpet flourishes of "Sgt. Pepper."

**Creating a Record**  The Beatles were *the* major players in the transformation of the recording industry. They influenced several developments that made popular music recording in 1970 substantially different from what it had been in 1960. Among the most significant were:

1. *The record becomes the document.* This process was well underway by 1965. The Beatles confirmed this trend by divorcing recorded performance from live performance.

2. *The first studio band.* Beginning with *Rubber Soul*, Beatles' records explored a sound world built on cutting-edge recording technology—including more than an orchestra's worth of instruments, everyday sounds such as crowd noises, and special effects such as tapes run in reverse. The result was a stream of recordings that would be difficult, if not impossible, to replicate in live performance.

3. *Multitrack recording.* The Beatles were not the first band to make use of this technology; **overdubbing** had been around for over a decade. However, they achieved the most spectacular results with it, especially on albums such as *Sgt. Pepper's Lonely Hearts Club Band*, and they inspired legions of imitators. Just as important, they used this still-new technology to help redefine the creative process: musicians could create a song in stages, through trial and error, rather than conceiving of it completely before entering the studio or improvising it in the moment.

Because of their work, rock records—by the Beatles and others—sounded a lot different in 1970 than they did in 1962. They were better produced, and they offered a broader palette of sounds.

**Popularity**  Elvis put rock and roll on the cultural map by his unprecedented success on the singles charts. The commercial breakthrough, for the Beatles and for rock, was their *total* domination of the album charts, in addition to their success on the singles charts. Although Dylan introduced the idea that the album was the appropriate medium for significant rock, it was the Beatles who made it the more meaningful medium for all of rock. Before the Beatles, rock records were promoted mainly as singles; albums were compilations of singles. However, with the Beatles, from *Rubber Soul* on, the process was reversed: the singles now typically came from the album. Part of the message in this reversal of form was that this music was important (that is, adult) enough to be released in album format. Indeed, Beatles' albums became rock milestones.

Record sales were only one dimension of their popularity. When their career took off, Beatlemania gripped the western world. At concerts, their fans would drown out the group with their screaming. Beatle sightings would inevitably produce a crush of fans. Their first film, *A Hard Day's Night*, shows the intensity of fan adulation. The film, acclaimed as innovative in its "day in the life" portrayal of the group and refreshing in its lack of pretense, only fanned the flames of their popularity. All this audience attention eventually backfired; the incessant pressure was a major factor in their decision to stop touring.

The mere fact of the Beatles' popularity gave weight to everything they did. Their work was both inspiration and model to a generation of rock musicians. It is likely that even without the Beatles, rock would have eventually become the dominant language of popular music. Because of the Beatles, however, it happened almost overnight. By the end of the decade, rock ruled—in the record stores, on the radio, and on stage.

# Rock That Matters

1965 was the year that rock matured, the year that it went well beyond a good-time music, as well as becoming an even better good-time music than before. The two acts most responsible for elevating its level of discourse and expanding its horizons were Bob Dylan and the Beatles. Dylan did it mainly with words. The musical backdrop might suggest a mood or call to mind an association, but it was always subordinate to the lyrics. The Beatles did it with both words and music; there is typically a beautiful and precise coordination between the lyrics and the significant musical features—for example, the shape of the melody (for example, the verse and chorus of "Eleanor Rigby" or the slow oscillation that serves as the bridge between everyday and heightened reality in "A Day in the Life"), the rhythms (the double-time third verse in "A Day in the Life"), the imaginative sound choices (such as the string group in "Eleanor Rigby"). This was music that could challenge listeners as well as entertain them, that could ask them to stretch their minds as well as shake their hips.

The music of Dylan and the Beatles in the mid-sixties was part of an explosion of innovation that created a new sound world and took over the popular music marketplace. There were other significant developments during that same period—among them the emergence of an important new black pop, soul music, the consolidation of rock style, the proliferation of numerous rock substyles. And there were other groups working along the same path, or at least in somewhat the same direction: for instance, Brian Wilson, the Who, Frank Zappa and the Mothers of Invention. But no one did more to legitimize rock as a compelling form of expression than Dylan and the Beatles.

## Terms to Remember

| | | |
|---|---|---|
| Beat poetry | psychedelia | concept album |
| Beatlemania | art song | overdubbing |

## Applying Chapter Concepts

The subtitle of this chapter is "Making Rock Matter." We explore further in two ways:

1. Compare "Like a Rolling Stone" and "A Day in the Life" to songs by any of the rock/R&B icons discussed in the previous chapters: for instance, those of Elvis, Chuck Berry, or Buddy Holly. Describe briefly what you feel are the three most significant reasons—in words, in music, and/or in the relationship between words and music—that the songs by Dylan and the Beatles matter more than the earlier songs.

2. Pick one song each by Dylan and the Beatles that is mentioned in the text but not discussed in detail (there are many). Then analyze the lyrics, the music, and the way(s) in which words and music work together to communicate the meaning of the song. Then explain why you feel that the song is important; support your argument with observations from your analysis.

3. To become more aware of the Beatles' extraordinary musical evolution, compare a song from 1963 or 1964 to a post-1966 song. Focus on the content and tone of the lyrics and the musical setting, with particular attention to form, instrumentation, length, and rhythm.

# Black Music in the Sixties
## Motown and Soul

"Ain't No Mountain High Enough." For black music in the sixties, this was finally true. By 1960, the influence of black culture had been evident in popular music for more than a century. The sounds of black music had been in the air for more than a half century. Black performers had begun to achieve stardom in the twenties. Black styles had become increasingly prominent during the next several decades. But it was not until the sixties that the obstacles that had kept black music on the lower rungs of the pop music ladder seemed to disappear. By mid-decade, the Supremes, the Temptations, and other Motown acts routinely kept pace with the British bands at the top of the charts. Aretha Franklin, James Brown, and the Stax soul stars also found a large, integrated audience. It was a glorious period in American music.

Black music reached this artistic and commercial peak just as the civil rights movement crested. The sixties began full of promise as much of the nation—from President John F. Kennedy on down—finally joined civil rights crusaders in the march toward racial equality. Many Americans were inspired by the words and deeds of Martin Luther King Jr., and other civil rights leaders. When racial equality became the law, racial harmony seemed possible.

However, the afterglow from these legislative successes was short lived. In 1968, everything went sour. The pivotal event was the assassination of Dr. King, which left many wondering whether "the dream died with the dreamer," as Stax producer Al Bell put it. Race riots in Detroit and Watts and the confrontation between liberals and radicals during the 1968 Democratic Convention replaced the idealism of the civil rights movement with disillusionment. The nation quickly discovered that laws do not change attitudes overnight. Nevertheless, the civil rights movement and the legislation it prompted profoundly redefined race relations in the United States.

The new black music of the sixties reshaped the popular music landscape just as profoundly. Even as it carved its new identity, it penetrated deeply into the fabric of popular music. The sounds of soul would resonate through much of the music of the late sixties and seventies—black and white—and they have continued to shape popular music into the present.

Moreover, black popular music had just about shed the racial stigma that it had carried for generations. The first black popular styles—for example, coon songs and ragtime—had been considered by many to be low-class, wrong-side-of-the-tracks music, capable of corrupting the morals of whites who came in contact with it. With the emergence of jazz and crossover black performers such as Lena Horne and Nat Cole, this attitude was neither as prevalent nor as hostile. Still, fifties rhythm and blues carried heavy racial baggage: recall that Alan Freed used "rock and roll" as code for "rhythm and blues." However, by the sixties, black music, and especially Motown, had lost any negative connotation, at least among the younger generation. In theory, at least, the playing field had become level.

In the seventies, the popular music audience would realign along racial lines to some degree. Nevertheless, popular music did not retreat to a pre-soul past, just as the nation could not return to the federally sanctioned injustices of segregation.

The great black music of the sixties came mainly from two cities, Detroit and Memphis. Detroit was the home of Berry Gordy's Motown empire. Memphis was "soul city" in the sixties, just as it had been the mecca for rockabillies in the fifties. As before, it was a single recording studio that was the magnet: in the sixties, Jim Stewart and Estelle Axton's Stax Records eclipsed Sam Phillips's Sun Records as the cutting-edge sound from Memphis.

Two stars transcended these geographical boundaries. Aretha Franklin, a Detroit native whose career took off with the support of the Stax house band, linked the two, symbolically and musically. James Brown followed his own path, geographically (from Georgia to the world via Cincinnati's King Records) and musically.

All of this music was called "soul" at the time. In fact, however, there were two distinct, if related, style families: the black pop of Motown and the real soul music of Aretha, James Brown, and the Stax artists.

# Motown

When Berry Gordy Jr. (b. 1929) got out of the army in 1953, he returned to Detroit, his home town, and opened a record store. He stocked it with jazz, a music he loved, but refused to carry rhythm-and-blues records, in spite of a steady stream of customers coming in to ask for them. Two years later, he was out of business. He would learn a crucial lesson from that experience: there was much more money to be made from pop.

After a couple of years working on an assembly line at the Ford plant, Gordy returned to the music business. In 1957, Gordy began writing songs for Jackie Wilson, at the beginning of Wilson's solo career; several of his songs were hits. Although encouraged by his songwriting success, Gordy realized that the only way he could gain complete artistic control of his music was to form his own record company.

Gordy started **Motown** in 1959 with little more than his dream and his drive. He knew that storytelling songs sold, and he soon learned how to sell them: Motown's first number 1 R&B hit (the Miracles' "Shop Around") came in 1961; the label had a number 1 pop hit the following year (the Marvelettes' "Mr. Postman"). By 1964, the roster of Motown performers included Mary Wells, Martha and the Vandellas, the Supremes, Stevie Wonder, Marvin Gaye, the Miracles, the Temptations, and the Four Tops. By mid-decade, three out of every four Motown releases charted—unprecedented success for a record label.

Motown was a unique phenomenon in popular music. Gordy was the first black to create and manage a major record label, and the empire that he created was like no other. The Motown sound was a collective effort. It was hundreds of people—Gordy, his singers, songwriters, producers, musicians, plus all the business and clerical staff—all working together to produce a reliable product.

## The Motown Formula

Gordy's Motown empire blended careful planning and tight control over every aspect of the operation with inspiration and spur-of-the-moment decisions. As it developed during the early sixties, Motown's organizational structure was a pyramid. At the top of the pyramid was Gordy. Underneath him were those who wrote and produced the songs, like Smokey Robinson and the Holland/Dozier/Holland team. Underneath them were the arrangers and house musicians. Berry recruited his core players from Detroit's jazz clubs. He relied on the skill and inventiveness of musicians such as bassist James Jamerson (the man most responsible for the freer bass lines of sixties rhythm and blues and rock), keyboardist Earl Van Dyke, drummer Benny Benjamin, and guitarists Robert White and Joe Messina to bring to life the songs brought down to the garage–turned–recording studio by the arrangers. The fourth level were the acts themselves: Stevie Wonder, Smokey Robinson and the Miracles, the Supremes, the Four Tops, Martha Reeves and the Vandellas, Mary Wells, and the two we consider here: the Temptations and Marvin Gaye.

There is no question that the acts were the most visible part of Motown. Gordy, who ran what amounted to a finishing school for his groups, made sure they were well dressed, well rehearsed, and presentable in every way. And there is no question that they were essential to the artistic and commercial success of the label. However, in terms of defining the **Motown sound**—the qualities that often identified the style before a note was sung—they were among the most interchangeable parts. Indeed, one act would often cover another act's hit. The essence of the sound was in the songwriting, the producing, the conception of the studio musicians, and—above all—in Gordy's overriding vision.

## The Motown Sound

In many respects, the Motown sound was predictable; fans knew pretty much what to expect from a Motown record. Yet the individual songs were usually different enough, and imaginative enough, to avoid becoming predictable in every respect. Within the general design, there was room for variation, as we hear following in comparing two enduring Motown hits: the Temptations' "My Girl" (1964) and Marvin Gaye's version of "I Heard It Through the Grapevine" (1967).

**The Temptations**  The Temptations were the premier Motown male group act. In sound and image, they embodied the Motown esthetic: five elegantly dressed men moving smoothly in skillfully choreographed steps, and singing with the grit and soulfulness of street-corner singers but with perfectly polished harmonies. It was the Motown blend of soul and class.

The group was a vocal quintet that originally came together in 1961 from members of two aspiring vocal groups, the Primes and the Distants, to audition for Gordy. Their career took off when David Ruffin replaced original member Eldridge Bryant as the lead singer. Ruffin would stay for four years, from 1964 to 1968. This now-classic version of

Hulton Archive/Getty Images

A publicity photo of the Temptations, circa 1965. From left to right: Melvin Franklin, Paul Williams, Eddie Kendricks, David Ruffin (with his trademark glasses), and Otis Williams. Motown acts typically wore formal attire in performance.

the quintet included—from high to low, Eddie Kendricks, David Ruffin, Otis Williams, Paul Williams, and Melvin Franklin, the deep bass voice of the group.

Their first number 1 hit on both the pop and R&B charts was the 1964 song "My Girl." It is one of the best early examples of the assembly-line process of hit making that served Motown so well in the sixties. The first stage in the process was the writing of the song itself. "My Girl" was one of several hits that Smokey Robinson (b. 1940), the lead singer in the Miracles and one of the top Motown songwriters, wrote for the Temptations. Robinson, a long-time associate of Gordy, recalled that Berry Gordy told him very early in their association that a song must tell a story. Motown songs do that—or at least paint pictures. The lyric of "My Girl" offers a succession of images that give us a character portrait of "my girl." The language is simple; the message is universal.

The song begins with a simple bass riff that is distinctive enough to be memorable: if you are familiar with the song, it's likely that you'll recognize it just from this riff. The guitar enters with another more elaborate—and even more

CD 2:16

"My Girl," the Temptations (1964)

memorable—riff; like the bass riff, it is repeated several times. Lead vocalist David Ruffin enters, singing the two short phrases of the verse. On the second phrase, the other Temptations discreetly support his vocal with gentle background harmonies. The chorus begins with a short, simple transition that builds to the title phrase, which is repeated several times. Horns reinforce the vocal harmonies, although they stay in the background. Lush string parts soar over the several statements of "my girl."

The second verse is virtually identical to the first melodically. However, the background is much richer, with strings and horns present throughout. In most of the background parts there are little snippets of melody—trumpet flourishes, string countermelodies. After the second set of "my girls," the violins play an elaborate interlude that moves the melody to a higher key. Like the second verse/chorus statement, the melody remains the same, and the instrumental background remains rich and active. The song ends with an extended tag that hammers home the main point of the song. In this song, we hear key components of the Motown sound.

These features work together to provide multiple points of entry for a widely varied audience. The instrumentation dissolves class and racial boundaries—all of the sounds, from the fingersnap (the easiest homemade percussion sound of all) to the symphonic strings (members of the Detroit Symphony moonlighted on these

## ♪ KEY FEATURES

### "My Girl," the Tempations (1964)

- A warm vocal and instrumental mix that has something for everyone: sounds include not only voices and rhythm instruments, but also violins, horns (mainly trumpets), and fingersnaps. The most prominent instrumental sounds are the bass, the fingersnap on the backbeat, and the strings.
- An abundance of melody: the song is exceptionally tuneful. Virtually every instrument capable of playing melodically does so—not only the lead vocal, but the bass, guitar, backup vocal parts, horns, and strings.
- A discreet rock rhythm: rock rhythm is heard faintly in the drum part; there is no rhythm guitar or keyboard pumping out a rock beat. The most prominent rhythmic feature is the backbeat.
- An easy-to-follow form: basic form of the song is verse/chorus. The verses flow into the chorus; the chorus consists of a transition and the title phrase. The gradual accumulation of activity within the verse/chorus statement highlights the arrival at the title phrase. This rich instrumental support and the frequent repetition of "my girl" essentially hands the form of the song to listeners on a silver platter. It is not hard to keep one's bearings.
- A rich, varied texture: there is a lot going on in the song. The melody is in the forefront, but the background parts, from the opening bass riff to the elaborate string lines, are also interesting.

recordings) mix together easily. There are abundant melodic hooks—the bass and guitar riffs, the many iterations of "my girl," and more. The rhythm is catchy but not overpowering; the tune remains the dominant element. The form is easy to navigate, not only because of the lyrics and melody but also because of the texture, which helps shine the spotlight on the title phrase.

This is the Motown sound template. It is predictable enough that listeners would find new songs familiar, yet customizable enough to give each song a distinct identity, not only in melody but other features as well. The flexibility of the Motown template is evident when we compare "My Girl" with Marvin Gaye's "I Heard It Through the Grapevine."

**Marvin Gaye**  Of all the Motown artists, none sang with more emotional intensity than Marvin Gaye (1939–1984). His turbulent life—stormy relationships with his wife and other women, drug and alcohol abuse, and his death by his father's hand—seemed to find expression in his music. Whether singing about love, as in "I Heard It Through the Grapevine," or contemporary life, as in several songs from his groundbreaking 1971 album *What's Going On*, he communicated an almost tangible range of feeling: pain, hope, joy, frustration.

"I Heard It Through the Grapevine" (1967) is one of the great recorded performances in the history of popular music. It is beautifully integrated: every element blends seamlessly to convey the sense of the text, which gradually unfolds the story of love gone wrong. The opening keyboard riff, harmonized with open intervals, immediately establishes a dark mood. Other instruments enter in stages, leading to the entrance of the voice. Each statement of the melody of the song contains four sections. The first two are blueslike, in that they generally stay within a narrow range and go down more than up. The third builds to the final section for the hook of the song: "I heard it through the grapevine." It is the emotional center of each statement. A Greek-chorus commentary by the backup singers ends each section.

We hear all of the key elements of the Motown sound in this recording as well. The song begins with a memorable instrumental hook. It has a muted rock rhythm. There are lots of melodic ideas woven into the texture. The rich instrumental accompaniment includes rhythm instruments, horns, and strings. "I Heard It Through the Grapevine" also has a verse/chorus form that builds to a title-phrase hook. As in "My Girl," these features provide easy entry into the song and provide enough interest to keep our attention.

Within these general parameters, we hear the variation in detail that keeps the Motown formula from being formulaic. The mood of the song is the mirror image of "My Girl": the bitter end of love, rather than the anticipation of it. This is conveyed most directly in the melody of the song, written by Norman Whitfield, another of the many fine songwriters on the Motown staff, and in Gaye's singing. The instrument choices and instrumental roles also help convey the mood. The opening electric piano riff is a dark sound; so is the drumming—tom-toms rather than the hi-hat—and the addition of a conga drum. The form is extended by the commentary of the backup singers at the end of each chorus. Together, the two songs demonstrate that both emotional and musical variety were possible within a consistent overall plan.

As before, the appeal of the song comes from an exquisite balance between melody and rhythm; a form that is not rigid but still easy to track; a rich vocal and instrumental

CD 2:17

"I Heard It Through the Grapevine," Marvin Gaye (1967)

♪ KEY FEATURES

**"I Heard It Through the Grapevine," Marvin Gaye (1967)**

- Depicting mood musically: dark mood of the song is established at the outset by such features as the ominous opening riff, the choice of an electric keyboard to play it, the open harmony, and the subtle, open-sounding rhythm. The melody of the song, which moves mainly from high to low, reinforces the mood.

- Flexible template: Motown template is predictable in its general features but accommodates considerable variation in detail and mood, as a comparison of "My Girl" and "Grapevine" reveals.

- Gaye's singing: strained sound of Gaye's high-register singing also helps communicate the despair described in the lyrics.

backdrop; and, most prominently, Gaye's singing. The gospel-inflected yet pop-oriented singing style of Motown acts like the Temptations and Gaye was a new black pop sound, one that struck a balance between novelty and familiarity.

## Motown and Black Pop

Motown updated **black pop**. From Armstrong and Ethel Waters, through Nat Cole and the Mills Brothers, into doo-wop and the girl groups, one direction in black music had been a distinctly black take on popular song. Motown offered not just a new take on pop, but a new, black popular style—and a new kind of romantic music.

In this sense, Motown was heading in the opposite direction from rock. Rock tended to look at love cynically (the Beatles' "Norwegian Wood" comes to mind), lustfully (such as the Rolling Stones' "Satisfaction"), or not at all. Motown songs preserved the romance present in the popular songs of the thirties and forties, even as they brought both lyrics and music into the present. It's evident not only in the sound—the rich string writing, the understated playing of the rhythm section—but also in the look. The groups wore tuxedos and gowns, like Las Vegas acts, not tie-dyed shirts and jeans, like the Woodstock crowd.

Motown was one of the remarkable success stories of the sixties. A black entrepreneur with fine musical instincts and an equally fine business sense created an empire. For the first time in history, a black style was on equal footing with white music. Motown's success was no accident. Rather, it was the result of Berry Gordy's carefully calculated strategy: he created a style positioned to appeal to as broad an audience as possible. He was lucky to be in the right place at the right time. But in his case, luck was largely the residue of design.

Gordy billed the music coming from his Motown studio as "the sound of young America." He was right. During the mid-sixties, the Motown sound spoke to young Americans of all races and backgrounds. Two generations later, many of the songs are classics, known not only to those who grew up with them, but also to their children and grandchildren.

# Soul

In 1969, almost after the fact, *Billboard* changed the name of its R&B chart from "Hot Rhythm and Blues Singles" to "Best Selling Soul Singles." "**Soul** " had replaced "rhythm and blues" as the umbrella term for the new black music that had emerged during the mid-sixties; the change in chart name belatedly acknowledged this. Much of this music was popular, by any measure. The Motown success story was the most spectacular evidence of the ascendancy of black music, but Motown artists shared the charts with other black performers, as well as whites: twelve of the top twenty-five singles acts during the decade were black. It was a diverse group that included James Brown, Aretha Franklin, Ray Charles, Dionne Warwick, and the Supremes; they represented not one style but several.

## Black and White Music in the Sixties

Black music charted musical paths that were different from (mostly) white rock. The Motown examples follow one route; the diverse examples of soul music discussed following highlight another. Although much black music crossed over to the pop charts and influenced musicians of all races (Paul McCartney claims Motown bassist James Jamerson as a primary influence), black performers created music distinctly different from that of most of their white counterparts.

There are three main reasons for this. The first and most significant is the strong gospel tradition. Most of the major black performers of the sixties had grown up singing in church. There is no better example than Aretha Franklin, the queen of soul: Aretha's father was pastor of one of the largest churches in Detroit, and she sang at his services from early childhood.

Another was the increasing musical distinction between rock and roll and rhythm and blues. As we heard in the previous chapters, the differences between the two styles increased toward the end of the fifties, not only because of the gospel influence in the singing, but also because of differences in rhythm, instrumentation (for example, horn sections were the rule in black music; they were rare in white music), and texture (the bass was in the foreground in black music, the guitar typically more in the background; the reverse was true in white rock). The trend continued with black artists whose careers began in the sixties.

A third reason for the array of distinctly black styles in the sixties was the artistic control of a few key producers. Berry Gordy, the emperor of Motown, was one. Another was Jerry Wexler, who had helped build Atlantic Records into a major pop label. Memphis-based Stax Records relied more on the musical intuition of its house musicians—which included Booker T. and the MGs and the Memphis horns—to create a "house" sound.

## Soul Power

*Soul* was more than a musical term. It came into use as an expression of the positive sense of racial identity that emerged during the decade: "black is beautiful" was the slogan of many politically active members of the black community. This shift in attitude, among both blacks and some whites, was the social dimension of the relentless pursuit of racial equality. It went hand in hand with the enfranchisement of so many blacks through the Civil Rights Act of 1964 and the Voting Rights Act of 1965.

**Black Music and Civil Rights**  Black music was both an agent and a product of the enormous social changes that grew out of the civil rights movement. For whites, it opened the window into the black community a little bit wider: now it was not so much a matter of individual performers, like Louis Armstrong or Nat Cole, as it was styles: the girl groups, Motown, Stax/Volt (Volt was a subsidiary label of Stax Records). The cultural penetration of black music during the sixties was unprecedented.

As the drive for racial equality peaked, then deflated in the wake of the assassination of Martin Luther King Jr., black music occasionally became a vehicle for social commentary. James Brown released a series of exhortations, beginning with the 1968 song "Say It Loud—I'm Black and I'm Proud." Marvin Gaye's landmark album *What's Going On* appeared in 1971. But most of the music did not contain overt references to social conditions or racial issues. More often, it dealt with the subjects that so often transcended race: love won and lost, and the good and bad times that resulted.

Black music benefited from white America's increased awareness of and sensitivity to racial issues. Open-mindedness toward black cultural expression paralleled open-mindedness toward political and social concerns. It didn't hurt that the music provided such accessible points of entry.

Another important factor in the popularity of black music in the sixties was the deepening influence of black music on mainstream pop. Fifties rock and roll represented a major infusion of both the rhythm and the blues elements of rhythm and blues. Because of this, black music—even music without a strong pop orienta-tion—sounded less different to sixties ears than Muddy Waters would have sounded to fifties ears. It is hard to imagine James Brown finding his new bag or finding a substantial white audience in the mid-fifties. A decade later, both happened.

With the passage of time, our view of soul has changed. In retrospect, *soul* refers to the emotionally charged black music of the sixties, music that draws deeply on the blues and on gospel. It is best exemplified by the music that came from two southern cities, Memphis and Muscle Shoals, Alabama, and two performers, Aretha Franklin and James Brown. This was music of real commitment: Percy Sledge bares his soul when he sings "When a Man Loves a Woman," and James Brown was, among other things, "the hardest working man in show business." The music expressed deep feelings, with little or no pop sugarcoating: when Aretha asks for respect, she spells it out.

# Soul Music

Like most of the music from the mid-sixties, soul music was a synthesis, a new sound created from several sources. What makes it virtually unique is the fact that the sources were almost exclusively black. Soul combined the emotional depth and range of the blues, the fervor of gospel, and the energy of rhythm and blues and rock. The result was one of the most memorable and influential styles of the rock era.

## Southern Soul Music

If Gordy's Motown operation was as sleek and well-oiled as a Cadillac, the **southern soul** scene was more like a souped-up, beat-up Chevy pickup that, despite appearances, ran exceedingly well. Owners and musicians learned the music business as they went, usually the hard way. Yet, despite all the internal bickering, late-night partying, session-skipping, and other unprofessionalisms, some great music was made and recorded.

Southern soul generally came in two speeds: fast and slow. Up-tempo songs built on the groove found in the rock-influenced rhythm and blues of the early sixties. Some are upbeat as well as up-tempo, while others sermonize or upbraid. The slow songs almost always deal with the pain of love. We introduce soul with one example of each: Otis Redding's "I Can't Turn You Loose," recorded for Stax Records, and Percy Sledge's "When a Man Loves a Woman," recorded in Muscle Shoals at the Fame Recording Studio for Atlantic Records.

**Stax Records**  Memphis, Tennessee, rockabilly's home base in the fifties, became soul's spiritual center in the sixties, mainly through Jim Stewart and Estelle Axton's Stax Records (Stax is an acronym for <u>St</u>ewart and <u>Ax</u>ton). In many respects, Stax Records was set up like Motown: it had owners, producers, staff songwriters, a house band, and interchangeable singers. (This organizational arrangement distinguished their operations from most of the rock produced by white bands, such as the Beatles and Rolling Stones. These groups wrote their own material; there was no such thing as a "house sound" for their record label.)

Nevertheless, there were key differences from Motown. The Stax sound seemed more a collective effort than a decision from above. Instead of playing from written arrangements, the Stax musicians would listen to a song a few times and construct what amounted to a **head arrangement** (that is, created on the spot—off the top of their heads). They would play the song through and briefly discuss among them-selves who should do what. Then, often within minutes, they would be ready to record.

Moreover, the operation was thoroughly integrated. Stewart and Axton (who were brother and sister) were white. Producer Al Bell, songwriters Isaac Hayes and David Porter—who penned "Soul Man" and many other Stax hits—and the headliners—Otis Redding, Rufus and Carla Thomas, Sam and Dave, and others—were black. The house rhythm section, which recorded under its own name as Booker T. and the MGs, included two blacks, keyboardist Booker T. Jones and drummer Al Jackson, and two whites, guitarist Steve Cropper and bassist Donald "Duck" Dunn. The horn players—who became famous on their own as the Memphis Horns—were all white. In the cocoon that was the Stax recording studio, race didn't seem to matter, even if it mattered a great deal as soon as they stepped out onto the street.

**Otis Redding**  The king of southern soul singers was Otis Redding (1941–1967). Redding, who grew up in Georgia, first tried to break into the music business in Macon; he eventually ended up singing behind Little Richard. After he secured an Atlantic recording contract, he turned out a string of R&B hits at Stax. He broke through to the pop market with a scintillating performance at the 1967 Monterey Pop Festival, where he won over a new, largely white audience for his music. Tragedy struck soon after: he died in a plane crash later that year. The posthumously released "(Sittin' on the) Dock of the Bay," written with Steve Cropper in Monterey, was his biggest hit. (Ironically, it was one of his least soulful recordings.)

Redding's singing calls to mind a fervent black preacher. Especially in up-tempo numbers, his singing is more than impassioned speech but less than singing

CD 2:18

"I Can't Turn You Loose," Otis Redding (1965)

Tony Frank/Sygma/Corbis

Otis Redding performing in Paris, 1962. We can see Redding's energy even from this still photo, just as we can hear his energy on recordings.

with precise pitch. It is as if the emotion of the moment is too strong to be constrained by "correct" notes. "I Can't Turn You Loose," one of his classic soul recordings, showcases his unique delivery, sandwiched between the Memphis Horns and the MGs.

The song is the quintessential illustration of the southern soul sound. The song begins with not one, but two, memorable melodic hooks, both of them instrumental. The first is the bass/guitar riff; the second is played by the horn section. There is a wide-open space between the low range guitar/bass riff and the horn riff: that's the range in which Redding sings. This is the typical instrumental backdrop for an up-tempo soul song: heavy on the bottom and top and basically empty in the middle (except, of course, for Redding's singing). The only chord sounds come from the piano, heard faintly in a high register.

The rhythm is also typical of sixties Memphis soul:

- Marking of the rock rhythm layer by the bass and guitar
- Strong beat keeping from the drums
- Frequent syncopations in both riffs that fight against the beat (the famous offbeat horn riff at the end of each big section is the classic example of this)
- Redding darting in and out of a steady rhythm with the kind of rhythmic freedom that all the great soul singers had

This performance has a harder edge than many soul recordings, not only because of Redding's gritty singing but also because the guitar is so prominent and has a little distortion. Perhaps the edge comes from rock: one of Redding's big hits was a cover of the Rolling Stones' "Satisfaction."

**Bittersweet Soul Music**   In soul music, tempo usually sends a direct message. Fast tempos signal an upbeat mood, or at least something to get excited about. By contrast, slow tempos typically reinforce a down mood; usually these tempos help convey a story involving love lost. One of the classic examples of this branch of sixties soul music is Percy Sledge's "When a Man Loves a Woman," a lament of love gone wrong.

Sledge (b. 1940) was born in Leighton, Alabama, a small town not far from Muscle Shoals, where he recorded "When a Man Loves a Woman" in 1966. Quin Ivy, a local disc jockey and all-around entrepreneur, had discovered Sledge singing in a local group called the Esquires. Ivy engineered a solo artist contract

♪ **KEY FEATURES**

**"I Can't Turn You Loose," Otis Redding (1965)**

- Redding as a singing preacher: Redding finds a rough midpoint between impassioned oratory and conventional singing. His delivery overflows with emotion.

- Updated jump band: the typical backup band for soul music is an updated version of the rhythm and horns bands of forties and fifties rhythm and blues. The big difference is in the rhythm section: electric bass replaces acoustic bass and becomes the dominant instrument.

- Strong, syncopated rock rhythm: soul traded in the hard shuffle of fifties R&B for a strong rock beat and overlaid it with extensive syncopation.

If we think of the sound world of Motown as comparable to an artist's palette, then the sound world of Memphis soul would be an 8-pack box of thick crayons. Up-tempo soul emphasizes power and impact over subtlety and refinement.

with Atlantic and arranged the recording date that produced Sledge's first and biggest hit.

Sledge's rapid rise to stardom proved once again that the black church was a very fertile training ground for soul. It seemed that many blacks (and not a few whites) sang gospel—not just the suave stylings of groups like Sam Cooke's Soul Stirrers but the raw, impassioned singing first secularized by Ray Charles. Enough sang well to provide a seemingly endless stream of talent.

Like the Motown acts who were lucky enough to live in Detroit, stardom for a soul singer seemed to be as much a matter of timing as talent. While there was no question that Otis Redding, Percy Sledge, and Wilson Pickett deserved their fame, there were certainly other talented southern blacks who could have achieved stardom if they had found themselves around people in the music business who could nurture their talent.

**Soul ballads**, of which "When a Man Loves a Woman" is perhaps *the* classic example, have an entirely different dynamic from up-tempo songs. Here the band is accompanist rather than partner, more like a frame to a painting than an indivisible part of the mix. The opening is about as unobtrusive as it can be in the rock era: walking bass, slow triplets and backbeat on the drums, sustained chords on a Farfisa organ (one of the wave of **electronic keyboards** that came on the market during the sixties). Other layers accumulate during the course of the song: guitar noodles, backup vocals, then horns on the final chorus. Their accompanying role is defined not so much by their volume—eventually the band all but overpowers Sledge—as by the complete lack of rhythmic or melodic interest in their parts. Only the guitarist is doing anything other than sustaining a chord or marking time, and his part remains pretty much in the background. As a result, the sound spotlight shines straight on Sledge.

Although this was Sledge's first recording, he "let it all hang out." He held nothing back; there is no emotional reserve in his singing. What you hear is what he

CD 2:19

"When a Man Loves a Wo- man," Percy Sledge (1966)

feels, with no buffer in between. Previously, such naked emotion had been heard almost exclusively in the blues—and Ray Charles's blues/gospel synthesis. Here, as in Charles's best work, it is amplified through gospel style. Like the blues, the phrases start high and finish low, but the strain from singing so high in his range projects the pain that is inherent in the song.

The powerful emotion captured in this song touched a lot of hearts, black and white, here and abroad. The song was number 1 on both the R&B and pop charts in 1966 and remains one of the great soul anthems.

---

### ♪ KEY FEATURES

**"When a Man Loves a Woman," Percy Sledge (1966)**
- Slow tempo: exceedingly slow, by any standard, and certainly slower than a normal dance tempo. Here, it helps set the mood of the song.
- Understated accompaniment: unlike fast soul songs, where the vocal part fills the register gap between rhythm section and horns, slow songs like "When a Man Loves a Woman" spotlight the voice; everything else is subordinate.
- Sledge's singing: not as gritty as Redding's; the sound is richer, but they are clearly brothers vocally and stylistically.

---

The heyday of southern soul was brief—about four years, from 1965 through 1968. The bullet that killed Dr. King—ironically in Memphis—also seemed to pass through the heart of soul. The major southern soul studios were integrated operations: the Stax rhythm section was half black/half white, and the house musicians at Rick Hall's Fame studio were almost all white. In the wake of the racial tensions triggered by Dr. King's assassination, business ground to a halt at Fame and slowed down at Stax.

Audience attitudes seemed to change as well. Most of the southern soul stars saw their careers nosedive. Only vocalist Al Green had a major career after the glory years, although Isaac Hayes had a brief moment in the sun as a performer. Nevertheless, soul left an indelible imprint on the music of the rock era.

## Aretha Franklin

Sam and Dave, Percy Sledge, Otis Redding, and almost all the other soul acts were southern men. The greatest of the sixties soul singers, however, was Aretha Franklin—neither a man nor a southerner. She was—and is—the queen of soul and one of the great artists in the history of popular music.

If any performer grew up with a destiny to fulfill, it was Aretha (b. 1942). Her father, C. L. Franklin, was one of the most charismatic preachers in the country. Although his home base was in Detroit (interestingly, Berry Gordy recorded his sermons on a Motown subsidiary), he toured the nation, attracting throngs to the black churches where he preached. Reverend Franklin was also a lavish and gracious host. The cream of the black entertainment world, both sacred and secular, passed

Frank Driggs Collection/Getty Images

Aretha Franklin at a recording session in 1961, early in her career. At the time, she was under contract with Columbia. She would move to Atlantic 6 years later.

through his house. Growing up, Aretha heard everyone from gospel star Mahalia Jackson to the virtuosic and elegant jazz pianist Art Tatum.

Although shy as a child (throughout her career, only her singing has been extroverted) and the daughter of a wealthy man, Aretha was anything but sheltered. As a teenager, she went on the road with her father and his entourage; her mother had left when she was 6. She crammed a lifetime of experience into those few years. Before she set off for New York at 18 to begin her secular career, she had repeatedly experienced the discrimination that went with being black in the fifties, endured endless bus rides from town to town, and given birth to two children. So when she sang about love and respect, her feelings came directly from her own experience.

Aretha Franklin's career in secular music began in 1960, when she signed a contract with Columbia Records. Her producer was John Hammond, perhaps the most knowledgeable and sensitive advocate of black music in the music business during the middle of the century. As a pioneering jazz critic, he had signed many top acts for Columbia over several decades. Although he recruited her for the label, the company didn't know how to tap her talent. Some of her recordings show her as a bluesy pop singer, à la Dinah Washington, who was very hot around 1960; others capture her singing pop treacle accompanied by syrupy strings. Jerry Leiber suggested that Aretha was "suffering from upward mobility." Although she produced some good work, her career went nowhere.

In 1966, Atlantic Records' producer Jerry Wexler bought her contract. He took her to Muscle Shoals in January 1967 for what in retrospect proved to be one of the most famous recording sessions of all time. Within seconds after she sat down at the piano to play through "I Never Loved a Man," everyone in the studio knew they were in the presence of someone special. Although put together on the fly—the horns were in the studio's office working out the riffs while Aretha was rehearsing with the rhythm section—the song was recorded in a couple of takes. Its obvious success

CD 2:20

"Respect,"
Aretha Franklin
(1967)

sparked camaraderie among those present at the session, which was fueled by liberal amounts of alcohol. Unfortunately, that proved too rich a mixture: a fight between studio owner Rick Hall and Ted White, Aretha's husband and manager at the time, broke out sometime in the wee hours. With that, the session was called off, Aretha headed back to Detroit, where she all but disappeared for weeks, and Wexler went back to New York with one-and-a-half songs. He finally got Aretha to return to finish the second song, and the rest is history.

Many of Aretha's first hits explored the heartbreak of love, like most soul ballads of the time. However, her first up-tempo hits, most notably her cover of Otis Redding's "Respect" and her own "Think," emotionally redefined fast soul. What had frequently been a forum for men to boast about their sexual prowess became the backdrop to a demand for dignity in "Respect" and a tongue-lashing in "Think." In both songs, the groove is as good as it gets, but it assists a call to arms rather than an invitation to sensual pleasure. "Respect," in fact, took on a meaning beyond the intent of its lyric: it became an anthem for the women's movement, which was just gathering momentum.

The musical formula for "Respect" is much the same as for "I Can't Turn You Loose": interlocked rhythm section, with horns playing riffs or sustained chords. The two major differences are Aretha's singing and the backup vocals, which give the song a churchier sound. The most memorable and individual section of the song is the stop-time passage when Aretha spells out what she wants—"R-E-S-P-E-C-T"—so that there's absolutely no misunderstanding. What had been a straightforward verse/refrain song suddenly shifts up a gear. The remainder of the song features the dense texture previously heard in the refrain: a series of riffs from the backup vocalists—"sock it to me," "just a little bit," and finally the repeated "Re-re-re-re" (not only the first syllable of "respect" but also Aretha's nickname)—piled on top of the beat and horn riffs, with Aretha commenting on it all from above.

---

### ♪ KEY FEATURES

**"Respect," Aretha Franklin (1967)**

- Change gender, change meaning: Aretha's presence brings the woman's point of view to the fore.
- Aretha's singing: unmatched in expressive range, power and sensitivity, and emotional impact.
- Southern soul plus: the song adds a backup vocal group to the typical soul instrumentation of vocalist plus rhythm section and horns. They are integral to the impact of the song.

---

Having quickly established her credentials as the queen of soul, Aretha began to explore other musical territory. She has been one of the very few artists of the rock era who can cover songs convincingly. Her versions of Burt Bacharach's "I Say a Little Prayer," Sam Cooke's "You Send Me," Nina Simone's "Young, Gifted, and Black," and Paul Simon's gospel-influenced "Bridge over Troubled Water" are all standouts. Several of her own songs give further evidence of her expressive range: in "Rock

Steady," she tips her hat to James Brown, while "Daydreaming" is as tender and romantic a song as any released in the early seventies.

Aretha's music is deeply personal and, at the same time, universal. The responsive listener feels her communicate one-on-one, yet her message transcends such a relationship. The best of Aretha's music seems to demand both empathy and ecstasy. We can give ourselves up to the groove even as we listen to her tough-time tales. No one in the rock era has fused both qualities more powerfully and seamlessly than she.

## James Brown

James Brown (1933–2006) was the godfather of soul, the man who had nurtured it longer than anyone else and whose music had more influence than any other soul artist. Brown's career spanned almost the entire history of the rock era. His first hit recording, "Please Please Please," appeared on the R&B charts in 1956. We continue to hear his music today in multiple forms: not only the original recordings but also via samples woven into rap recordings.

CD 2:21

"Papa's Got a Brand New Bag," James Brown (1965)

It took Brown almost a decade to arrive at the original sound heard in "Papa's Got a Brand New Bag," his breakthrough 1965 hit. The majority of his hits in the fifties were typical slow R&B ballads. Other than Brown's singing, there is little in these recordings that anticipates the originality of his work in the sixties.

Brown came to his new sound by subtraction. He gradually eliminated anything not essential to maintaining the rhythmic flow of a song: repeated guitar riffs, repetitive bass lines, keyboard chords, busy drum parts, and the like. With "Papa's Got a Brand New Bag," the process is complete. Underneath Brown's short vocal riffs, the horns play short riffs, the baritone sax a single note, the guitar a chord on the backbeat (except for the double-time repeated chord at the end of each statement of the refrain—a brief moment in the spotlight), the bass short groups of notes separated by silence, while the drummer plays a rock rhythm on the hi-hat and bass drum kicks on the off-beat. The little timekeeping that's audible comes from the drummer.

The drummer's light timekeeping is like aural graph paper, onto which Brown and his band draw their rhythmic design. The open sound that results from this bare minimum texture was not only Brown's new "bag" (in sixties slang, a "bag" is a person's special skill; here, it refers to Brown's new conception of rhythm and texture), but also one of the most original conceptions of the rock era.

"Papa's Got a Brand New Bag" alternates blues-form refrains with sections that don't use blues form. The boundaries between sections are sharply drawn; so are the shifts within sections. Further, each section has its own well-defined character, which usually remains the same throughout. By sharply defining the character of each section and the boundaries between sections, Brown creates forms that seem assembled from blocks. This differentiates them from the Motown songs, which proceed in waves of sound.

In "Papa's Got a Brand New Bag" and "I Got You (I Feel Good)," Brown emphasized rhythm, texture, and the soulfulness of his singing over melody and harmony. In "Cold Sweat" (1967), he goes a step further. The basic approach is the same: riffs layered over light timekeeping. However, there is virtually no harmonic

---

♪ **KEY FEATURES**

**"Papa's Got a Brand New Bag," James Brown (1965)**

- Emphasis on rhythm: like so much of James Brown's music, this song is about rhythm. There is no continuous melody, just fragments tossed back and forth between Brown and the horns. The harmony is a basic blues progression or one chord. The absence of melodic and harmonic interest directs our attention to the groove.

- Percussive sounds: we associate percussive sounds with percussion instruments. However, all of the instruments and Brown's singing are percussive: such as the emphatic consonants (Pa Pa, Bag), the explosive single note on the baritone saxophone, the guitar chord, the fingered electric bass sound, in addition to the drums.

- Teamwork: none of the parts is interesting enough to stand alone. Brown's voice stands out mainly because of the words and the distinctiveness of the sound, but it is not dominant. Collectively, the parts—vocal and instrumental—interlock to create a seamless flow.

- Open sound: because there is just enough activity to maintain the groove, the musical flow is buoyant; there are no thick guitar chords or heavy bass lines to weigh it down. Brown's trademark groove was one of the most distinctive and influential sounds of the sixties.

---

movement: one chord lasts the entire opening section, and the bridge oscillates between two chords. At the same time, the texture is more active. The guitar part adds fast-moving rhythmic counterpoint. Of special interest is the new **choked guitar sound**: the guitarist strums across the strings while holding his hand across the neck, "choking" off the resonance to create a percussive scraping sound. The guitar becomes in effect, a percussion instrument, with more rhythm than pitch. Moreover, its pattern is active and highly syncopated, enriching the rhythmic texture more than any other line. Other strands—drums, bass, baritone sax, other horns—are also more consistently syncopated than in the previous songs. Because the texture is more active, Brown sings less, especially in the contrasting section. Here Brown seems to sing only when he feels like it. He is content to ride the band's rhythmic wave.

The combination of an active, syncopated rhythm texture and harmonic stasis creates a sense of open-ended time: we are immersed in an "eternal present." Because they create and maintain a groove, sections are infinitely extensible: they don't *go* anywhere, they just *are*. This was a huge conceptual breakthrough, anticipated only infrequently by such songs as Bo Diddley's "Bo Diddley." Brown goes well beyond these early efforts.

Brown's music, especially "Cold Sweat" and much of the work that followed it, bring popular music closer to its African roots than it had ever been before. Indeed, John Chernoff reported in his 1971 book, *African Rhythm and African Sensibility*, that

James Brown feeling good, and working harder than the unnamed band member while performing on *The Ed Sullivan Show,* 1966.

African musicians felt more at home with James Brown's music than any other popular musician of the time.

Brown's music has been profoundly influential. With its emphasis on intricate rhythms and de-emphasis of melody and harmony, it would create the blueprint for funk and rap.

With deep roots in gospel, blues, rhythm and blues, and jazz, and its blending and modernizing of these styles, the music of James Brown represents a unique soul synthesis. In its originality and individuality, it stands apart from all the other music of the sixties. It remains one of the most influential styles from that decade.

## The Impact of Black Music of the Sixties

In the film *Good Morning, Vietnam*, Robin Williams portrays Adrian Cronauer, an Air Force disc jockey brought in to improve morale among the troops. Cronauer junks the staff-approved tame white pre-rock pop, replacing it with an integrated playlist that includes James Brown, Motown, and the Beach Boys. While he's on the air, the film cuts away to scenes of the soldiers, on and off duty, listening to the music that he's playing. They are smiling, dancing, moving to the groove. In the film, music is the most powerful symbol of the huge generation gap between the old guard and the young troops.

More than any other aspect of American culture, music—and especially Motown and soul—brought home the arrival of a new generation and the profound changes taking place in American society. The new black music was fresh and it was good. And it was popular, among young people of all races. At least while they listened to it, race no longer mattered, except in a good way. This was no longer "wrong side of the tracks" music. Its broad acceptance was one important sign of the wholesale shift in attitude that would characterize the sixties.

For a brief time in the mid-sixties, it seemed that divisions of race, class, and culture were about to be eliminated. That didn't happen, but the changes that took place during that time were irreversible. The "one-color" world of mid-century film and television was gone forever; the music that was its soundtrack is largely forgotten. The black music of the sixties helped bridge the gap between that world and the multicultural society we now see in both the media and real life. It lives on: the best of it sounds as good today as when it was released.

### Terms to Remember

| | | |
|---|---|---|
| Motown | soul | soul ballads |
| Motown sound | southern soul | electronic keyboards |
| black pop | head arrangement | choked guitar sound |

### Applying Chapter Concepts

In our discussion of Motown's music, we noted that many of the Motown hits from the sixties adhered to a general formula that still allowed for considerable variation in detail. To explore this key point further, consider either or both of the following two projects.

1. Both "My Girl" and "I Heard It Through the Grapevine" use a discreet rock rhythm, and both feature male acts. However, many of the big hits put a new spin on the shuffle rhythm used so widely in fifties R&B, and female acts were, if anything, more popular than the male acts. Listen to one or more of the following songs: The Supremes' "Where Did Our Love Go," "Baby Love," or "I Hear a Symphony," or Mary Wells's "My Guy." Then respond to the following three questions:

    a. How does the shuffle rhythm in the Motown song(s) compare to the shuffle rhythm as used in songs like "Choo-Choo-Ch-Boogie," "Rocket 88," and "Sh-Boom"?
    b. Does the different rhythmic foundation have any effect on the other features of the Motown sound, such as the form, the prominence of melodic material, or the instrumentation?
    c. Do you hear any discernible difference between the Motown approach as applied to female acts versus the approach used for male acts?

2. Gladys Knight's version of "I Heard It Through the Grapevine" was released *before* Marvin Gaye's—it charted over a year earlier. Compare the two versions and account musically for the differences between them. Then discuss the extent to which you feel that the musical differences respond to the different vocal styles of the two artists.

3. Among the many titles that James Brown has accrued are "soul brother no. 1" and the "godfather of soul." However, his music is distinctly different in several respects from southern soul, as represented by the music of Otis Redding, Wilson Pickett, Eddie Floyd, and Sam and Dave. Select one more James Brown song from the sixties and another up-tempo southern soul song, then compare the two James Brown songs to the two southern soul songs to determine similarities and differences between the two approaches to soul music. Focus particularly on rhythm and texture.

# 9

# Rock

In Chapter 1 we described rock's most characteristic features, using a classic song by the Rolling Stones to illustrate these features. Our profile of rock was necessarily static—one-dimensional—because we began without a common frame of reference, and we discussed only one song. In this chapter, we offer a richer and more dynamic view of rock's core style by observing its development through the better part of a decade.

When we think of timeless rock, we expect to hear bands with a core of electric guitar, electric bass, and drums playing songs with heavy riffs over a rock beat at a loud volume. Within these general parameters, there is considerable room for variation: in the music discussed here, we will hear solo- and group-oriented rock, other instruments added to the rhythm section nucleus, and different ways of assimilating the blues—the most profound outside influence on this music.

However, the most exciting aspect of this dynamic view of core-defining rock is hearing the maturation of rock rhythm—from the straightforward rock of the first two examples (released in 1964 and 1965) to the compelling and timeless rhythms of the examples from the early seventies. We will discover that in less than a decade, rock musicians learned to play with rock rhythm: adding other rhythmic layers, most of which conflict with the timekeeping layers; adding faster rhythms; varying the timekeeping, even to the point of completely omitting it for long stretches; and focusing particularly on the rock rhythmic layer. In the process, they transformed rock rhythm from the relatively straightforward rhythms heard in music from the early and mid-sixties into the irresistible groove that is the heart of rock and roll. Most fundamentally, rock is about rhythm; in these examples, we hear rock rhythm assume what has become its most timeless form.

All of this—rhythms, riffs, sounds, virtuosity—was in the service of the defiant, provocative, sexually charged attitude that is conveyed so powerfully in the music. This attitude, present in much of the music heard here but not heard as powerfully in earlier rock, was the result of a second infusion of blues.

## From Blues to Rock

In the early sixties, while the Quarrymen were molting into the Beatles, other young British musicians were hanging out at Alexis Korner's London-based Blues and

Barrelhouse Club. Korner, a **trad** and **skiffle** musician during the fifties, spearheaded the blues revival in Great Britain as the sixties began.

> During the forties and fifties, British popular music consisted mainly of pop stylings and "trad": British-style Dixieland jazz. In the late fifties, "skiffle" was the hot new sound in the United Kingdom. Skiffle mixed American and British folk music, rockabilly (in its use of the drum set), and other sources. It is often viewed as the first British take on U.S. rock and roll.

Korner nurtured a generation of British musicians who had grown up listening to the blues. Their primary contact came from the recordings of Muddy Waters, John Lee Hooker, Howlin' Wolf, and other country and electric bluesmen—highly prized because they were so hard to obtain in Britain. Korner's club, a regular stop for American bluesmen touring England, was a mecca for British blues fans. It was also an outlet for the British blues musicians—a place where they could gain valuable performing experience.

The roster of musicians who played at Korner's club reads like a Who's Who of British rock in the sixties and early seventies. Both the Rolling Stones and Cream were made up of Korner alumni, while key members of Led Zeppelin, the Yardbirds, John Mayall's Bluesbreakers, and other notable bands also paid their dues there.

At first, British musicians were content to play a pale imitation of the real thing. However, when Sonny Boy Williamson visited England, he was accompanied by a very young, very green Eric Clapton. This encounter with a real bluesman transformed Clapton as a musician, as he related some years later to blues scholar Robert Palmer:

> It was a frightening experience, because this man was real and we weren't. We didn't know how to back him up, and he put us through some bloody hard paces. I was very young, and it was a real shock. I realized we weren't being true to the music; I had to almost relearn how to play. But it taught me a lot. It taught me the value of that music, which I still feel.

By the time Clapton and his peers "got real," they had transformed their blues experience into a completely new music: the most essential form of rock. This was music with a hard edge, music that confronted and challenged. Although often popular, it was *not* pop. Nor was it simply heavily amplified blues, although blues attitude and style saturates the music. It was something new.

Another musician who grew up on the American side of the Atlantic had a similar agenda. Jimi Hendrix, following his own path, transformed the blues into the most daring and influential instrumental style of the sixties. Hendrix was born and raised in Seattle, paid his dues touring with blues and rhythm-and-blues artists, got his solo career going in England, made his first big splash in the United States at the 1967 Monterey Pop Festival, and died in London. His powerful and imaginative playing linked like-minded musicians on both sides of the Atlantic.

## Deep Blues and Rock

This rock was the second child of the blues, and it favored a different parent. The music of Blind Lemon Jefferson, Robert Johnson, John Lee Hooker, Muddy Waters, and other blues greats was at most an indirect influence on the rock-era music of the fifties. Electric blues, the most vital and authentic blues style of the postwar era, barely touched rock and roll; its main contribution was instrumentation. Throughout most of the fifties, electric bluesmen lived in their own world, and the old Delta bluesmen who were still alive were all but forgotten.

The blues revival that paralleled the folk revival of the late fifties and early sixties exposed young rock musicians to the power and emotional depth of **deep blues**. The British musicians who immersed themselves in the blues took from it several of its most distinctive features: the attitude and posturing of the bluesmen, often obvious in its sexual challenge; lyrics that told their stories in plain, direct language, often with a nasty edge (Muddy Waters's "I Can't Be Satisfied" and the Rolling Stones' "[I Can't Get No] Satisfaction"); a rough, declamatory vocal style; heavy guitar riffs and string-bending blues-scale guitar solos; a strong beat; and a thick, riff-laden texture. This music is identified variously as **hard rock**, as a hard-rock substyle, such as **heavy metal** or **southern rock**, or simply as "rock." In this small but revealing sampling, we trace the persistence of the defiant and provocative attitude, and the musical features used to convey it, and the dramatic evolution of rock rhythm over an eight-year period.

## Hard Rock in the Mid-Sixties

Among the horde of British bands that invaded the United States in the mid-sixties were blues-influenced groups such as the Animals, the Kinks, and the Rolling Stones. They had a tougher sound than the Beatles: more prominent and more distorted guitar, a stronger beat, rougher vocals, and, behind it all, a more aggressive attitude.

The Animals' interest in the blues resonated with their working-class upbringing in Newcastle. They were the backup band of choice for the American bluesmen who visited there, and they were among the first British bands to score a U.S. hit with "The House of the Rising Sun" (1964). Later that same year, the Kinks also had the first of several U.S. hits: "You Really Got Me."

### The Kinks

Like the Beach Boys, the Kinks were largely a family affair. Two brothers, Ray and Dave Davies, formed the band in 1963—Ray (b. 1944) was the lead vocalist and main songwriter; Dave (b. 1947) was the lead guitarist—by inviting bassist Pete Quaife (b. 1943) and drummer Mick Avory (b. 1944) to join them. The Kinks scored early: "You Really Got Me" and "All Day and All Night," the band's first and most influential hits, charted in late 1964. In them, they laid down a formula borrowed from the blues that would become a hallmark of hard rock styles.

"You Really Got Me," the Kinks (1964)

The idea of building a song over a short, repetitive guitar riff came directly from electric blues: recall the riff that opens Muddy Waters's "Hoochie Coochie Man." In "You Really Got Me," the Kinks transform Waters's approach by harmonizing the riff with a power chord, adding distortion, speeding up the tempo, substituting a rock beat for a slow shuffle, and repeating the riff at successively higher pitches throughout the song. In these changes, we can hear both the connection with electric blues and the differences between blues and blues-drenched rock.

Bettmann/Corbis

The Kinks happily invading America in February, 1965. From left to right: bassist Peter Quaife, guitarist Dave Davies, drummer Mick Avory, and guitarist/lead vocalist Ray Davies.

The guitar/bass riff is the dominant rhythmic feature of the song: it is louder than any other instrumental sound, and it runs continuously through the song. Regular rhythms are either implicit or in the background: The backbeat is a barely audible drum stroke, a tambourine marks the beat, and drums and occasionally piano faintly mark the rock rhythmic layer. In the dominance of the riff rhythm and rhythmic freedom of the bass, the rhythmic texture is clearly rock. But there is not the kind of rhythmic variety or complex interplay that we will encounter in later examples.

The harmony of the song puts a new spin on blues-based harmonies. Recall that a common alternative to the conventional blues progression in Delta blues is a simple one-chord accompaniment: we heard this approach in Robert Johnson's "Come on in My Kitchen." In this song, the Kinks adapt this one-chord approach to a verse/chorus form. They sustain one basic harmony through the first two phrases, then shift up to another chord, and then skip up to still another chord, which underpins the multiple statements of the hook containing the title phrase. This was a novel way to build momentum toward a goal without using standard progressions.

Heavy, distorted riffs set to power chords convey Ray Davies's unbridled lust more powerfully than the lyrics, which in retrospect seem pretty tame. Songs like this formed the bridge between electric blues and heavy metal. Using this sound as a point

♪  KEY FEATURES

**"You Really Got Me," the Kinks (1964)**

- Standard rock-band instrumentation with prominent distorted guitar and occasional piano chords
- Riff is the dominant rhythm; rock rhythm timekeeping mainly in the background
- Terraced harmonies: long sections on a single chord; shifts up between sections; arrival at highpoint coincides with title phrase hook

of departure, heavy metal bands increased the volume and the distortion, as Van Halen's 1978 cover of the song evidences.

However, the song seemed to represent a dead end for the Kinks. Their music went in several different directions (such as the proto-punk of "You Do Something to Me") but seldom returned to the simple but powerful formula of their two early hits. Nevertheless, the Davies brothers have maintained the Kinks in some form since 1963. The only rock band with a lengthier active career is the Rolling Stones.

## The Rolling Stones

That the Rolling Stones' first major hit should be entitled "(I Can't Get No) Satisfaction" is a karmic acknowledgement of the enormous influence of the blues, and Muddy Waters in particular, on the group. Both the band's name and the song title trace back to early Waters's recordings: a 1950 recording entitled "Rolling Stone" and a 1948 recording entitled "I Can't Be Satisfied."

The Rolling Stones grew out of a chance encounter in 1960, when Mick Jagger (b. 1943) saw Keith Richards (b. 1943) standing in a train station with an armful of blues records. It was not their first meeting; both had grown up in Dartford, England, and had attended the same school for one year, when they were 6. Their meeting eleven years later would be the beginning of their band.

Both spent a lot of time at Korner's club, where they met Brian Jones (1942–1969) and Charlie Watts (b. 1941). At the time, Watts was the drummer for Korner's Blues Incorporated, which would also include Jagger after 1961. The band came together in 1962 when they added bassist Bill Wyman (born William Perks, 1936) via an audition. Keyboardist Ian Stewart (1938–1985) was also a member of the band at the time. He stopped performing with the group soon after their career took off but retained a close connection with the Stones and performed on many of their recordings.

Like the other British bands, the Rolling Stones began by covering blues and rock-and-roll songs. Within a year, Jagger and Richards, inspired by the success of Lennon and McCartney, started writing original songs for the band. They had their first U.K. hit in 1963 and reached the top of the American charts for the first time in 1965 with "(I Can't Get No) Satisfaction." By the time they recorded the song, they had pretty well defined their sound, style, and image.

For the Stones, "(I Can't Get No) Satisfaction" was a musical and commercial milestone. No other major band so thoroughly distilled their essence into their first

"(I Can't Get No) Satisfaction," the Rolling Stones (1965)

major hit. Every aspect of the song—the title, its lyric, its melody and form, Jagger's singing and Richards's guitar playing, the sound of the band, and the relentlessness of its beat—embodied the rebellious image the band wanted to project.

"Satisfaction" begins with one of the most memorable guitar riffs of all time. It sounds menacing, because Richards uses **fuzztone** (an effect he seldom used subsequently), situates the riff in the lowest register of the guitar, and places a strong, syncopated accent on the highest and longest note of the riff, which pushes against the beat established in the first two notes. If sound can sneer, then it does so in this riff.

The riff functions not only as an introduction, but also as a refrain. It clarifies both the sequence of events and the underlying meaning of the lyric. Recall that a rock-era song typically begins with a verse, then builds toward the chorus, which includes at least one vocal hook. Here, the sequence is reversed. The title phrase comes where the verse typically appears. The music builds toward a high point, which is sustained for several measures. In a song with a conventional form, this would be the chorus. However, after "I can't get no . . . ," the lyric is verselike: Jagger spews out a litany of complaints. Here, Jagger is dissembling; what is *really* bothering him is that he cannot get sexual satisfaction. Richards's guitar riff mimics the energy and rhythm of intercourse; that it never changes underscores the fact that Jagger never gains sexual release, at least during the song. Here, the music seems to convey directly what the lyrics do not.

> The apparent sexual undercurrent of "Satisfaction" may have emerged originally from the group's subconscious. By Richards's own account, the riff came to him in the middle of a restless night: he woke up from a troubled sleep long enough to play it into a tape recorder, then went back to sleep. The words and the working out of the rest of the song came later.

"Satisfaction" presents a more complex form of rock rhythm than we heard in "You Really Got Me." Watts strongly marks both the beat and the rock beat layer; Jones's rhythm guitar part also reinforces the rock rhythm layer. These steady rhythms serve as a foil for other parts: Richards's guitar riffs, Jagger's vocal line and occasional tambourine rattles, and Wyman's free bass lines. Together they create a dense overlay of conflicting rhythms. The result is a thick, active rhythmic texture that balances heavy timekeeping with strong syncopations.

The songs by the Kings and the Rolling Stones present a rock rhythmic conception that is purged of any transitional elements. In both, the rhythmic texture features a rock beat and strong, persistent syncopations. However, in both cases, the beat is routinely marked, which inhibits the flow of the rhythm somewhat. In the examples that follow, we will hear bands shift the emphasis away from beat keeping to a stronger backbeat and greater emphasis on the rock rhythmic layer.

Neither "You Really Got Me" nor "(I Can't Get No) Satisfaction" is a blues song. Still, this group-oriented music by the Rolling Stones and the Kinks embraced essential aspects of blues style and sensibility. It's evident in the attitude conveyed in both words and music—and in gesture and movement, when seen in live performance. Musically, the strongest connections are found in the rough vocal quality of singers like Jagger, the heavy reliance on repeated riffs, and the dense, dark texture resulting from the interplay of instruments operating in middle and low registers.

# Power Trios: Rock as a Soloist's Music

Among the most compelling new sounds of the late sixties were power trios such as Cream and the Jimi Hendrix Experience. These were bare bones bands—just guitar, bass, and drums—set up to showcase the skills of their exceptionally able guitarists: Eric Clapton and Jimi Hendrix. These and other like-minded guitarists, such as Jeff Beck and Jimmy Page, took one additional element from blues—the guitar as the bluesman's "second voice." They used it as a point of departure as they introduced a new element into rock: virtuosic soloing. We explore the blues connection and the new conception next.

## Blues Guitar and Rock

Throughout the recorded history of deep blues, the guitar had been a melody instrument as well as a harmony and rhythm instrument in support of the voice. From Blind Lemon Jefferson on, bluesmen would answer sung phrases with vocal-like guitar lines, double the vocal line, or showcase the guitar's melodic capabilities in an instrumental solo. This melodic aspect of blues guitar—the guitar as expressive solo voice—resonated deeply with Hendrix, Clapton, and the others, who brought it into rock.

The guitar had been a solo instrument from the earliest days of rock and roll. It was featured in Chuck Berry and Buddy Holly recordings, as well as in instrumentals such as the Ventures' "Walk, Don't Run" and Dick Dale's early surf music. Chuck Berry's solos remain models of their kind, but they are riff-based. Dale's guitar lines contain novel effects, like the low-register scale that slithers and snakes down the fingerboard. However, none are vocally inspired. In retrospect, they seem somewhat limited in their exploration of the expressive potential of the electric guitar.

While Berry and others were creating rock guitar styles, electric bluesmen such as Guitar Slim, Buddy Guy, and Freddie King (one of Clapton's idols) were playing the guitar in a style that paralleled their raw, earthy singing, exploiting such novel effects as severe distortion in the process. Their style served as a direct inspiration for a new generation of rock guitarists, most notably Eric Clapton and Jimi Hendrix.

Because they were the dominant soloists of their time, Clapton and Hendrix are inextricably linked. However, despite their strong connection in time, place, and purpose, they were two quite distinct musical personalities. Some of the differences between Hendrix and Clapton may have grown out of their early exposure to the blues. Hendrix grew up with the blues, hearing it as part of a broad spectrum of black music that also included jazz and rhythm and blues. Clapton approached the blues with the fervor of a convert, especially after his encounters with American bluesmen.

Although they used the blues as a point of departure, Hendrix and Clapton took these new-found capabilities several steps further. In so doing, they helped transform the electric guitar into the transcendental solo instrument of rock.

## Eric Clapton and Cream

During the sixties, Eric Clapton (b. 1945) refined and purified his blues conception, especially during his short stint with John Mayall's Bluesbreakers in 1965 and 1966.

The purity of this conception was important to him: he had left the Yardbirds just prior to joining Mayall when the band moved away from blues toward psychedelic rock.

By the time he formed Cream in 1966, with bassist Jack Bruce (b. 1943) and drummer Ginger Baker (born Peter Baker, 1939), Clapton had developed into rock's premier guitar **virtuoso**. He was the first major rock performer to play extended, improvised solos, especially in live performances. To accommodate his solo excursions, Cream dispensed with the rhythm guitar in live performance, although a second guitar was often added on recordings.

Cream was the first of the **power trios**: lead guitar, bass, and drums but no chord instrument. In live performance, the spotlight was on Clapton, although Bruce and Baker played active roles in support of his solos. They became a different band in the studio. The demands of AM radio airplay, with its 3-minute target, constrained Clapton's solo excursions. Their material gravitated toward the then-fashionable psychedelic rock, although it still retained a strong blues connection. And, through the miracle of overdubbing, the band acquired additional instrumental voices without additional personnel—most notably, Clapton on rhythm guitar.

"Strange Brew," not a singles hit but one of their best-remembered studio recordings, shows the studio side of their musical personality. The lyric has psyche-delic overtones—what *is* the "strange brew"?—but the real story is in the music. Here the blues influence runs deep, yet it's transformed into one of the most influential rock sounds of all time.

Blues influences begin with the form. The underlying harmony is a basic 12-bar blues; the lyric and melodic form use the verse/chorus blues form first heard in "It's Tight Like That." However, the deeper blues influence is in Clapton's guitar playing. Clapton fills three distinct roles in this song. One is the sharp chords that come on alternate backbeats. A second is the rapidly rising riff that runs throughout the song. Third are the solo episodes: during the introduction, answering the vocal, and the brief solo in the middle of the song. The deep blues influence is most evident in the solos, where Clapton adapts many trademark features of electric blues style: the fast vibrato, bent notes, free rhythms, extensive use of the pentatonic scale, and heavy inflection of individual notes. With his impressive command of the instrument, Clapton makes all of this sound easy; his guitar becomes a miraculous prosthetic device that creates vocally inspired musical gestures far surpassing what he could do with his voice.

Clapton's solo playing put him in the vanguard among the rock guitar soloists. Also innovative, however, are Clapton's riff-derived accompaniment, Bruce's synco-pated bass lines, and the loose-jointed rhythm that they create. Clapton's repeated riff is a textural breakthrough for rock. From Chuck Berry on, rhythm guitarists had typically played chords. Usually they surfaced as some kind of boogie-woogie derived pattern (Berry, Holly), strummed (Beatles, Rolling Stones), or arpeggiated (Dylan, Beatles). Clapton's alternative, while certainly based on chords, breaks away from the rhythmic and melodic regularity that are customary in rhythm guitar parts. In this respect, it is more like a repeated riff in an electric blues than anything commonly found in rock and roll.

Similarly, the texture created by the riff, Clapton's lead guitar line, and Bruce's bass line resembles the intertwined melodic strands of the electric blues style heard in

**CD 2:22**

"Strange Brew," Cream (1967)

the Muddy Waters examples. (The connection shouldn't be surprising because Clapton claimed Waters to be his major influence.) At the same time, the concept is considerably updated, not only by the shift to rock rhythm, but also the emancipation of the bass line.

Cream helped loosen up rock rhythm. The basic beat is the eight-beat rhythm of rock, but all three instruments occasionally include patterns that move twice as fast as the basic rock beat. The most persistent and obvious is Clapton's riff, but there are also occasional double-time patterns in the drum part (a variant of the "fatback" beat so popular in soul music) and the double-time break toward the end. The **double-time rhythms** (that is, twice as fast as the rock beat layer) open up new paths toward greater rhythmic complexity.

♪ **KEY FEATURES**

**"Strange Brew," Cream (1967)**
- Power trio instrumentation augmented with a second, active guitar line
- Blues influence in form, texture, and especially in Clapton's adaptation of blues guitar style
- Looser rock rhythm with strong backbeat and active riffs at double-time speed

Clapton's solo work demonstrates how he brought the essence of blues guitar style into rock. Jimi Hendrix would transform it into the most admired and emulated guitar style of the rock era.

## Jimi Hendrix

Jimi Hendrix (1942–1970) grew up in Seattle, Washington, which is about as far away from the Mississippi Delta as one can get and still be inside the continental United States. However, the blues were as close as his father's record collection, which also included a fair amount of jazz. Both would be profound influences on his playing.

After a hitch in the army, cut short by a back injury suffered in a parachute jump, Hendrix began his musical apprenticeship by working in the backup bands of a wide variety of black performers: bluesman B. B. King, Little Richard, saxophone great King Curtis, the Isley Brothers, and Jackie Wilson.

In 1966, Hendrix formed his own band: Jimmy James and the Flames. They were heard in New York by ex-Animals' bassist turned talent scout Chas Chandler, who encouraged Hendrix to come to England. When he arrived, Chandler introduced him to bassist Noel Redding and drummer Mitch Mitchell, who began jamming with Hendrix. Soon, they were performing on the London club scene as the Jimi Hendrix Experience. Their first hit, "Hey Joe," released in the fall of 1966, made Hendrix a star almost overnight. Their first album, *Are You Experienced?*, released early in 1967, secured Hendrix's reputation in England. A spectacular performance at the 1967

Hulton-Deutsch Collection/Corbis

Jimi Hendrix, 1968, captured in live performance.

Monterey Pop Festival spread his reputation in the United States. For the remainder of his too-short career, he cemented his place as rock's most influential and innovative soloist.

Hendrix was one of the most flamboyant performers of sixties rock. Like several of the bluesmen who inspired him, he developed unconventional ways of playing the guitar: between his legs, behind his neck, during a somersault. On stage, his guitar was an erotic instrument as well as a musical one. No rock musician before him had so graphically connected the guitar with male sexual potency.

However, his most memorable visual moment came at the Monterey Pop Festival, when he drenched his guitar in lighter fluid and set it on fire. His red guitar, flickering with flames, remains one of rock's most enduring visual images.

Of course, the most important part of Hendrix's legacy is his music. In his all-too-brief career, Hendrix set the standard for solo improvisation in rock. Hendrix's contribution to rock, and more particularly improvisation in rock, is so substantial because it is multifaceted. He brought to rock guitar playing unprecedented fluency, a new expressive vocabulary, and a dazzling array of new sounds. In all three dimensions, we hear both Hendrix's deep indebtedness to the blues and his thorough transformation of this blues foundation into the most spectacular and influential rock guitar style of the early rock era. These qualities are evident in recordings such as "Voodoo Child," a track from his 1968 recording, *Electric Ladyland*.

"Voodoo Child" is a blues-inspired song, on several levels. The vocal sections of the song inflate and reshape 12-bar blues form. The lyric begins as if it is a conventional rhymed couplet with the first line repeated. But Hendrix adds a

"Voodoo Child," the Jimi Hendrix Experience (1968)

refrainlike fourth line to the lyric, which contains the title phrase of the song. Hendrix also modifies the musical features of blues form by extending the length of the phrases and by using a strikingly different harmonization: static in the first part of the song, then fresh-sounding chords in the latter part. The relationship between voice and guitar recalls the Delta blues of Robert Johnson and Muddy Waters in the hetero-phonic passages (the guitar version of the melody is usually far more elaborate) and the call-and-response between voice and guitar. The vocal sections serve as formal pillars, supporting what is in essence an unbroken 5-minute improvisation. Hendrix ignores the harmony of the vocal section in his solos; they take place over one chord.

Hendrix's brilliant improvisations are the expressive focus of the performance. They are skilled to a degree matched only by jazz in the popular music tradition before rock. Indeed, toward the end of his life, Hendrix immersed himself in the music of John Coltrane, one of jazz's great virtuosos as well as its most progressive voice in the sixties, and collaborated with fusion guitarist John McLaughlin, who also recorded with Miles Davis at this time.

The quality that stands out above all is Hendrix's astounding variety. It is most apparent in his improvisatory strategies and range of sounds. Hendrix does not limit himself to any particular improvisatory style—for instance, a fast-moving single-line melody or variations on a riff. Instead, he roams over the entire range of the instrument, interweaving sustained bent notes, rapid running passages, riffs, and chords in a dizzying sequence.

Just as masterful is the dazzling array of sounds he draws from his guitar—an inventory of the sound possibilities of the instrument. They range from the pitchless strummings of the opening of "Voodoo Child" and the biting sound on the rapid repeated intervals on the bottom strings (at about 2 minutes into the song) to the sustained high-note wails, distorted chords, and hyper-vibrated notes in his solos. And he mixes them together in dazzling sequences that seem completely spontaneous in their unpredictability.

Hendrix plays in Technicolor—there are times when almost every note has a sound that's different from the ones around it. Both the degree and frequency of sound variety far exceed that heard in earlier improvisation-based styles—indeed, such variety was not possible before Hendrix began to exploit the potential of the electric guitar.

Hendrix's solos represent a new kind of genius, one that emerges from the particular demands of rock improvisation. In them, he elevated sound variety to a level of interest comparable to pitch and rhythm, and he enormously expanded the vocabulary of available sounds. In a Hendrix solo, *how* a note sounded became just as important as its pitch and rhythmic placement. In so doing, he built on the expressive sounds of the blues and the artistry and melodic inventiveness of jazz, merging and transforming them into a definitive improvisational style in rock.

Hendrix's legacy is his playing. It not only helped define rock-based improvisation more than the work of any other artist, but it also helped redefine the possibilities of improvisation within popular music. It echoes through much of the music of the seventies and eighties, especially heavy metal and hard rock. Others have built on it, a few have extended it, but none have surpassed it in imagination and originality.

A comparison of Hendrix's solo in "Voodoo Child" with Clapton's solo in "Strange Brew" contrasts two quite different approaches to blues-based improvisation

> ♪ **KEY FEATURES**
>
> **"Voodoo Child," the Jimi Hendrix Experience (1968)**
> - Dazzling new guitar sounds
> - Hendrix's unprecedented virtuosity
> - Strong blues connection/dramatic transformation: in form, hetero-phony, expressive vocabulary
> - Open texture of power trio lineup: strong bass and wide-ranging guitar; no consistent middle-register sound

within rock. Clapton's playing is more focused than flamboyant, whereas Hendrix's solo playing is like a fireworks display, with new sounds firing off in almost random profusion.

The two recordings also highlight the creative tension in rock between individual brilliance and group impact. The instrumental sections in the Cream recording feature three layers of pitched sound: the bass line in the lowest register, the repeated guitar riff in the low middle register, and the solo guitar line in the high middle register. By contrast, there are only two layers of pitched sound in the Hendrix recording: the bass line and Hendrix's guitar, which roams from the lowest notes on the guitar to a high register. For long stretches, there is a void in the low middle register, where one typically hears a guitar playing riffs or chords. Much of rock's impact comes from the dense mass of sound and consistent rhythm produced by bass, rhythm guitar, and drums. It is not present in Hendrix's recording. Indeed, it is hard to imagine adding a rhythm guitar part to the recording that would satisfactorily complement Hendrix's flights of fancy. Nevertheless, there is an emptiness in the texture that is not present in the other three recordings that we have heard in this chapter. How to integrate solo brilliance into a group conception became an issue for rock bands in the wake of Hendrix's expansion of rock guitar resources. We discuss two remarkable solutions later in the chapter.

## The Perfection of Rock Rhythm

What the Rolling Stones began with songs like "Get off My Cloud" and "(I Can't Get No) Satisfaction" was complete less than a decade later in songs like "It's Only Rock 'n Roll (But I Like It)." Although they would explore numerous musical directions in the late sixties (including *Their Satanic Majesties Request*, their "answer" album to the Beatles' *Sgt. Pepper*), their most significant achievement was the perfection of rock rhythm.

The breakthrough came in the late sixties, in songs like "Jumping Jack Flash" and "Honky Tonk Women." It involved two interrelated developments: a change in timekeeping and an enrichment of the rhythmic texture. The new approach to timekeeping involved two major changes: (1) increased emphasis on the rock rhythmic layer and the backbeat and (2) the virtual elimination of steady beat keeping. The enrichment of the rhythmic texture involved adding more layers of rhythm while maintaining an ideal balance between regular timekeeping and rhythms that conflict or play with the regular rhythms.

Consider the very beginning of "Jumping Jack Flash." The song begins with Richards's syncopated guitar riff. Rhythm guitarist Brian Jones enters on the second iteration of the riff, marking the rock rhythm; Wyman also enters playing a bass line that matches up rhythmically with the main guitar riff. On the third iteration of the riff, Watts enters, marking both the rock rhythm and the backbeat, in alternation with a bass drum sound on the first and third beats. At this point, rhythm guitar and drums are marking the regular rock rhythmic layer, while bass and lead guitar play against this regular rhythm. Nowhere in the rhythm do we hear any instrument marking off the beat; our sense of the beat emerges from the interaction of the other rhythms, rather than some kind of steady timekeeping. The absence of beat keeping gives the rhythm a flow that is not present in "Satisfaction" and other songs that evidence a similar approach to rhythm.

"Jumping Jack Flash," the Rolling Stones (1968)

The rhythmic texture is also richer, with several rhythmic layers in the drum part, a steady but occasionally syncopated bass line, plus riffs and insistent rhythms in the guitar parts. The chorus features not only vocal harmony but also a freer bass line and a high obbligato guitar part—all of which produce a rich, vibrant rhythmic texture.

The increased density of the texture and the guitar halo during the chorus are just two of several features that the Stones add to this otherwise straightforward verse/chorus rock song to give it an individual character. Also noteworthy are the addition of piano and maracas, the extended tag, and the alternation between static harmony in the instrumental sections and the verse and active harmony during the chorus. In any noteworthy Rolling Stones song, there are always features—some obvious, some more subtle—that lift the song well above the ordinary.

## ♪ KEY FEATURES

### "Jumping Jack Flash," the Rolling Stones (1968)

- Emphasis on rock rhythm and the backbeat; de-emphasis of the beat
- Rich rhythmic texture, with effective balance between regular rhythms and rhythms that conflict with the beat
- Numerous special features, such as additional instruments and high-register guitar during the chorus

The Rolling Stones' sound was the result of teamwork. What they did best, they did as a group, even though at the time this song was recorded, there was considerable friction between Richards and Brian Jones. Their rock-defining groove grew out of the interaction among all the band members. So did the loose, somewhat unkempt texture. Although Jagger is the visual focus of the band, there is no one musician whose talent dominates the sound. Finally, there are the sounds—most notably Jagger's singing and Richards's guitar playing—that project the Stones' particular kind of insolence. Shortly after this recording was released, the Rolling Stones began billing themselves as "the World's Greatest Rock and Roll Band." It wasn't bragging because they could back it up.

# Heavy Metal in the Seventies

No music of the rock era has been more misunderstood than heavy metal. It has been vilified as cretinous not only by those outside of rock but also by numerous rock critics and musicians. Until the 1990s, surveys of any Top 40/50/100 list of major acts of the rock era generally gave metal groups short shrift. The only names likely to have appeared were Led Zeppelin, a group that quickly transcended the boundaries of the genre, and Van Halen, whose music crossed over to the pop charts fairly early in their career. Seminal metal bands, most notably Black Sabbath, are conspicuous by their absence.

For much of its history, heavy metal has existed with its audience in a largely self-contained world. The music's main outlets have been concert performances and recordings. Metal has received relatively little airplay, especially on mainstream recordings.

For many years, its audience was almost exclusively young males, typically disaffected and from middle- or lower-class environments. (More recently, the audience for heavy metal has broadened to include both older males—those who have grown up with it—and females.) Immersion in heavy metal has been a rite of passage for many teens around the world. Audience members formed powerful bonds with the acts whom they admired, as strong as any in rock.

Critics of metal have targeted what they perceive as its crudeness and cheapness—such as the ponderous riffs of some metal bands or the makeup worn by Kiss and Alice Cooper. Yet metal has been home to many of rock's great geniuses, from Ritchie Blackmore and Jimmy Page to Eddie Van Halen, Randy Rhoads, and Yngwie Malmsteen. Perhaps more than any other rock style, heavy metal values and demands technical excellence.

There is some confusion regarding the source of the term *heavy metal*, as it applies to rock. Everyone agrees that the term appeared in rock as part of the lyric ("heavy metal thunder") in Steppenwolf's 1968 song, "Born to Be Wild." Its history prior to that is less clear. Rock mythology has the term coming most directly from William Burroughs's *Naked Lunch*. That source is myth: Burroughs does not use the phrase anywhere in the book. In any event, it was in common use by the early seventies.

## Sounds and Influences

Metal's sound signature is **distortion**—*extreme* distortion. It has other widely used musical conventions: blues-derived pentatonic and modal scales, often unharmonized; power chords; extended, flamboyant solos; ear-splitting volume; screamed-out, often incomprehensible lyrics; and pounding rhythms, often performed at breakneck speed. Still, the feature that most immediately identifies heavy metal is distortion.

Heavy metal has clear roots in the blues, especially electric blues. Its diabolical overtones, half-sung, half-spoken high-register vocal style, lack of harmonic move-ment, and reliance on riffs easily reach back to Robert Johnson ("Come on in My Kitchen"). Power chords and endlessly repeated riffs trace back to John Lee Hooker ("Boogie Chillen'"), heavy distortion to mid-fifties bluesmen ("Rocket 88"). Blues influence is also indirect. It comes into heavy metal through the early music of the Kinks (for example, "You Really Got Me"), as well as Hendrix, Clapton, and the other blues-based rock guitarists of the late sixties. In transmuting blues rhetoric into heavy metal, bands intensified and stylized these features.

Interestingly, classical music has been another source of inspiration for many metal artists. From it, they have not only borrowed the idea of virtuosity but have expropriated virtuosic patterns from classical works, as we'll hear following. This emphasis on transcendent instrumental skills shows up not only in the guitar solos but also in the tight ensemble (typically, not a feature of blues style) and pedal-to-the-metal tempos.

**Modality** has been another seminal influence. Modes are virtually universal in heavy metal; it is hard to imagine a metal song using conventional harmony. There are several good reasons why metal bands used modes. First, they formed the scales of much English folksong: most of the early metal bands were British, so modality was part of their musical heritage. Second, modes were the basis of a fresh new harmonic language within rock, as we heard in the music of the Rolling Stones, the Beatles, and others. Third, the African American pentatonic scale maps onto most modes. In fact, modes can be understood as an expansion of the melodic resources of the pentatonic scale. Fourth, precisely because it is the basis of so much folksong, as well as medieval and Renaissance classical music, it connotes archaic, even mythical, times. This meshes smoothly with the gothic element in much heavy metal: the beginning to "Stairway to Heaven" seems to turn the clock back about 800 years.

Heavy metal is all of these influences, yet something apart from them and in many cases more than the sum of them. From these influences, metal musicians forged one of the most distinctive styles of the rock era. We will study this style, as realized in the music of the three bands that, more than any others, defined early heavy metal.

Joe Elliot, lead vocalist for Def Leppard, was quoted as saying, "In 1971, there were only three bands that mattered. Led Zeppelin, Black Sabbath, and Deep Purple." His statement summarizes the prevailing consensus. Of the three, Black Sabbath stayed the closest to the musical features that defined early metal. Although they could lay down a riff with anyone ("Smoke on the Water"), Deep Purple strayed far enough from metal basics that some critics considered them an art rock band. From the start, Led Zeppelin was much more than "just" a heavy metal band. Their music covered a broad range of styles, even at times within a single song; indeed, we discuss their music in a different context. The differences among the three bands make clear that heavy metal was anything but a monolithic style.

## Black Sabbath

Take a poll among serious metal fans. Ask them to name the first heavy metal band. Chances are that Black Sabbath will receive the most votes. They were not the first band to play in a heavy metal style. Some writers credit Blue Cheer, a very loud San Francisco band. Others cite Led Zeppelin or Iron Butterfly. But Black Sabbath was the first band whose music consistently laid out the most widely used conventions of the heavy metal world. When you hear Black Sabbath, you're generally hearing heavy metal.

The name Black Sabbath evokes the occult, as it was supposed to. So did almost everything else about them. Black Sabbath's shows would feature crosses burned on stage and other images of devil worship. The lyrics of their songs often sound like they come straight from a gothic horror film. And the music formed the ideal backdrop for the words and images.

Black Sabbath was the third incarnation of a blues band from Birmingham, England. Vocalist Ozzy Osbourne (b. 1948), guitarist Tommy Iommi (b. 1948), bassist Terry "Geezer" Butler (b. 1949), and drummer Bill Ward (b. 1948) first came together as Polka Tuck, then changed their name to Earth. By 1969, they had become Black Sabbath; their first album appeared a year later.

Through relentless touring, they developed an international audience. As a result, their second album, *Paranoid* (1971), sold over 4 million copies. They remained the top metal act for the first half of the decade. With the ascendancy of punk and disco in the late seventies, their popularity waned, and Osbourne left Black Sabbath in 1979 to front his own highly successful and notorious group.

Cultivation of the occult may have been new to popular music but not classical music. The early Romantics (around 1830) also flirted with the diabolical. With his breathtaking talent and cadaverlike appearance, the violinist Niccolo Paganini was thought by many to have made a pact with the devil (long before Robert Johnson). According to his program for the work, Hector Berlioz's *Symphonie Fantastique* depicts a wild opium dream, with goblins, an execution, and a musical citation from the Mass for the Dead.

"Paranoid," the title track of their second album, typifies the sound of Black Sabbath and, by extension, early heavy metal. In its original studio version (there are other recordings of the song), it defines the salient features of early heavy metal. They include:

- Power trio instrumentation: lead vocal, guitar, bass, and drums
- Substantial distortion in both guitar and bass

Black Sabbath early in their career. From left to right: guitarist Tommy Iommi, vocalist Ozzy Osbourne, drummer Bill Ward, and bassist Terry "Geezer" Butler.

- Riffs built from power chords, which are repeated throughout most of the song
- Chord progressions developed from modal scales
- A strong, aggressive, clearly marked rock beat at a fast tempo, with syncopation mainly in the vocal line and the occasional riff
- A dramatic vocal style, in which the boundary between speech and song is often blurred
- A very loud dynamic level

This song offers a reductive approach to rock rhythm. The timekeeping is more prominent—guitar, bass, and drums all mark the eight-beat rock rhythm layer through most of the song. Most of the rhythmic conflict occurs with Osbourne's singing; he is constantly off-beat. There is not the rich interplay that we just heard in "Jumping Jack Flash." Nevertheless, Black Sabbath's approach to rock rhythm in "Paranoid" generates tremendous momentum. It is an approach that grew out of the breakthroughs of the late sixties.

## Sound and Space, Chords and Power in Heavy Metal

The interaction of distortion, power chords, and modal harmony have played a central role in defining the sound of heavy metal. There would seem to be a causal relationship among distortion, the absence of conventional harmony, and the heavy metal esthetic. Consider that rock, like most music, defines a **sound space**. Typically, the main melodic line and the bass line roughly define the upper and lower boundaries of that space; guitar parts (rhythm guitar in the instrumental sections; both guitars during vocals) lie between these boundaries. The extensive use of power chords and distortion fill this space sonically, giving the music enormous impact. We consider how and why this happens.

**Power Chords, Distortion, and Sound Space** **Power chords** are more than melody and less than (conventional) chords. In one respect, they are chords, because they feature several sounds played simultaneously. However, they are not conventional chords because the extra notes do not complete the harmony or even imply a complete harmony. Instead they are essentially **overtones**: other tones that vibrate in simple ratios with the main note. Moreover, the relationship among notes of a power chord never changes. Harmonizing a melody or riff with a series of power chords has the effect of thickening it, as if someone had painted over a line drawn in pencil with a thick-tipped brush. Often, the bass doubles the guitar line, which makes the line sound even thicker.

When enhanced with extreme distortion, power chords—with or without the bass doubled—fill the sound space with overtones and undertones (from the power chords) and **white noise** (randomly vibrating sounds over a wide range of frequency). This creates a mass of sound that stretches from below the lowest notes of the bass to beyond the highest notes of the power chords.

**Power Chords, Power, and the Blues** Power chords imply power on at least two levels. The more obvious is the thickening of a melodic line, which is delivered with extreme distortion at high volume. Its effect is similar to a sumo wrestler invading your space. The more subtle, but just as telling, level has to do with the typical sequences of power chords in heavy metal songs.

In songs like "Paranoid," heavy metal groups like Black Sabbath reject not only conventional chords but also conventional chord progressions. One reason for abandoning conventional chord progressions may have to do with the message of the style. Conventional chord progressions—like the "Heart and Soul" progression heard in pre-rock popular songs and in so much melody-oriented rock-era music—often support songs that talk about romance. Conventional harmony implies movement toward a goal—the return to the **home chord**—via a well-defined path. Because the path is so firmly entrenched, it is possible to create expressive musical moments by deviating from the path and to control patterns of tension (being away from the home chord) and release (arriving at the home chord). This parallels in certain respects the negotiation that is part of a romantic relationship: if arrival at the home chord is marriage, or at least togetherness, then the progression that precedes it is the courtship.

By contrast, harmony in heavy metal is about *power*. Metal songs seldom negotiate harmonically via adherence to conventional progressions; more often they slam from one chord to the next. Particular sequences of chords are more common than others, but they do not create the same kind of musical tension and release as "heart and soul"–type progressions. Indeed, use of conventional chords and chord progressions would undermine the harmonic impact of the style; it would sound like nerd metal.

The roots of this practice seem to grow out of a radical reinterpretation of blues harmony. (Recall that most early heavy metal bands, including Black Sabbath and Led Zeppelin, first incarnated as blues bands.) As practiced by Delta bluesmen, blues harmony was itself a radical reinterpretation of conventional harmony. Bluesmen adapted conventional chords—I, IV, V—to the blues. But instead of arranging them in typical progressions, they simply shifted from one chord to the next, much like heavy metal guitarists shifted from one power chord to the next. In a conventional setting, I, IV, and V are dynamic; they imply a specific kind of movement toward a goal. As used in the blues, however, they become essentially static objects. The sense of directionality all but disappears. As blues entered popular music and jazz, it reacquired more conventional harmonies, which were interpolated between or substituted for the chords that outline the blues progression. This dilutes the elemental power of the blues; one would be hard-pressed to locate a deep blues with conventional harmonies marbled into the progression. By contrast, the harmonic strategies used by heavy metal groups are much truer to the conception of those bluesmen whose music was largely untouched by mainstream popular music. Although the chords and chord progressions are different from the blues progression, they are conceptually more in tune with deep blues, because harmonies simply shift away from the home chord and return.

Black Sabbath songs like "Paranoid" are in essence an introductory course in heavy metal. From them, we can learn the basics of the style. However, when compared to other early heavy metal songs, such as the two discussed following, one element of the style is conspicuous by its absence: virtuosity. Tommy Iommi has neither the technical skill nor the musical imagination to match Ritchie Blackmore, Jimmy Page, and other early guitar geniuses. We explore this and other aspects of heavy metal next, in the music of Deep Purple.

## Deep Purple

Like Black Sabbath and other British groups, Deep Purple went through several incarnations before finding their groove. Theirs involved not only changes in personnel but also radical style changes. Their lineup during their most successful period, from 1970 to 1973, included vocalist Ian Gillan (b. 1945), guitarist Ritchie Blackmore (b. 1945), keyboardist Jon Lord (b. 1941), bassist Roger Glover (b. 1945), and drummer Ian Paice (b. 1948). The inclusion of a keyboard in a metal group was unusual. However, Lord was an important creative voice within the group. Among the first recordings of the newly constituted group was Lord's *Concerto for Group and Orchestra*, which Deep Purple recorded with the Royal Philharmonic. At this point, they were marching in step with classically influenced art rockers like Yes, King Crimson, and Emerson, Lake & Palmer.

However, the band soon shifted direction, focusing more on volume (they were listed in the *Guinness Book of World Records* as the loudest rock band) and heavy guitar riffs. Nevertheless, the classical influence was still apparent in both Lord and Blackmore's playing. Both were expert musicians who borrowed as heavily from the classics as they did from the blues. "Highway Star," a song from the album *Machine Head* (1972), shows how they combined the two influences.

"Highway Star," Deep Purple (1972)

"Highway Star" clearly demonstrates the influence of classical music, and especially the music of the early eighteenth-century composers J. S. Bach and Antonio Vivaldi. Blackmore acknowledged his classical sources: "For example, the chord progression in the 'Highway Star' solo...is a Bach progression." And the solo is "just arpeggios based on Bach." Lord also adapts the melodic patterns and fast even rhythms of Bach and Vivaldi to rock. (Both solos are overdubbed with harmony parts, further evidence of the skill of both players. It's difficult enough to play such fast, intricate passages, but even harder to synchronize a second line perfectly with the first.)

Blackmore's solo shows one way in which classical and blues influences come together in heavy metal: side by side, rather than blended. Blackmore's solo begins with blues-based riffs. After gaining considerable momentum, it reaches a climactic point where more energy is required. It is at this point that Blackmore shifts into classical high gear. The type of figuration that Blackmore uses here, like its Bach and Vivaldi models, is high-energy music. Quite simply, Blackmore wanted speed, and he went to Bach and Vivaldi to get it, because they were excellent models for how to play fast and intelligibly at the same time. After about 30 seconds, the solo returns to less active but more emotionally charged blues-based riffs.

In "Highway Star," blues-based and Baroque-inspired musical ideas coexist happily. That's especially true in Blackmore's solo, because its pacing makes the transition seem perfectly natural. Lord's interpolation of classical figuration has more of a "ready, set, go" quality. In both cases, however, the consistency of sound—both in the guitar and keyboard timbres and in the rhythmic undercurrent—helps link them together smoothly.

Deep Purple's infusion of classical elements into heavy metal brought new dimensions to the music. The most emulated was virtuosity, especially among individual performers. A list of rock's most technically proficient guitarists includes a disproportionately high number of heavy metal players. Indeed, for a handful of top guitarists (and those who wished to play at that level), **Baroque** music became a primary source for musical ideas.

The infusion of Baroque musical elements also led to a more straightforward rhythmic approach: classical music is seldom as syncopated as good rock music. The rhythmic excitement comes primarily from the speed—the fast tempo of the song and the double-time solo lines. As in "Paranoid," the rock rhythm is in the forefront; the primary syncopations occur in the vocal line and the answering riffs. However, there is much more rhythmic variety in this song because of the many contrasts—between vocals and solos and in the periodic breaks between sections.

A final note about virtuosity: in heavy metal it is not just in the solos. As "Highway Star" evidences, heavy metal also places a premium on precise ensemble playing, often at breakneck speeds. This is a different kind of virtuosity, but no less challenging, and it occurs more frequently in heavy metal than in any other important rock substyle.

## Heavy Metal and Early Seventies Rock

Heavy metal took the blues and transmuted them into music of unprecedented power. It was powerful in an absolute sonic sense: no music was louder. But there was also power in the mastery of craft. Like the alchemists of old, heavy metal performers diligently studied ancient formulas: in this case, the musical patterns of Bach and Vivaldi. These they adapted to rock, then juxtaposed them with elemental musical material. Heavy metal evoked supernatural, or at least paranormal, power, especially in the group personas of Black Sabbath and Led Zeppelin. At a time when the women's rights movement was in the ascendancy—bras being burned, NOW being formed—metal bands projected masculine power, to the point where performers could sport skillfully styled long hair, wear makeup, and sing higher than many women without fear of abandoning their sexual identity, à la David Bowie. And heavy metal wielded power over its audience, creating an extremely loyal fan base. Metalheads were not casual listeners or consumers; Black Sabbath's *Paranoid* went platinum on the strength of the group's tours, not airplay.

What heavy metal gained in power, it often sacrificed in subtlety. It was not typically a vehicle for expressing the pain of love lost or the joy of love found. It was not a music of nuance, except perhaps in the blues-inspired inflections in guitar solos. Even songs that talked about man–woman relationships did so in an almost impersonal manner.

Most of the conventions of heavy metal—distortion; massive amplification; use of modes, pentatonic scales, and power chords; basic rhythms; power trio instrumental nucleus—were also part of the vocabulary of all hard rock music in the early seventies. What metal bands did was to take these features and streamline or amplify them to give them more impact. Metal bands used more distortion and played more loudly. They took rock's shift away from traditional harmony several steps further by using conventional chords sparingly or, in some cases, abandoning harmony altogether. Its guitarists played power chords with more "power"—that is, greater resonance—and used them almost exclusively, and they developed more flamboyantly virtuosic styles. Its riffs and rhythms were stronger and more pervasive: at times, vocal lines seemed to ride on the riffs, like a whitewater raft. Indeed, both examples discussed here feature an aggressive form of rock rhythm throughout most of the song, with the rock beat layer hammered out by several instruments.

Above all, the music is *there* more. One quality that distinguishes heavy metal from most other styles is the sheer amount of non-vocal music. Even more important, music is the primary source of heavy metal's overwhelming impact and expressive power. Words serve a largely explanatory role. Most of the audience at a metal concert will know the lyrics to songs, but they *feel* the music. Many writers have observed that rock is ritual. If so, then heavy metal quickly became rock's most ritualistic music.

# The Liberation of Rock and Roll

By the early seventies, the rock revolution was over. It was evident on the charts and in corporate offices. It was evident in the flurry of hastily arranged musical marriages between rock and pre-rock styles: pop rock, rock musicals, jazz fusion. Most fundamentally, however, it was evident in the music itself. It took rock musicians about fifteen years to really get it—that is, to completely assimilate the numerous musical influences and transform them into the now-dominant style and to become comfortable with the conventions of this new style.

In this chapter, we have followed two aspects of this maturation process: the assimilation of deep blues and the evolution of rock rhythm. We have heard how deep blues permeated key aspects of rock, most notably the vocal style, the use of repeated riffs, and the dense, dark texture produced by instruments playing in a low register. And we have heard rock rhythm gain in flow and energy as the musicians purge it of the last remnants of rock and roll. These final two examples, recorded by Led Zeppelin and the Who, illustrate the ways in which musicians could play with rock rhythm when they reached a comfort zone with its essential elements. Unlike the previous heavy metal songs, in which rock rhythm is explicit and in the forefront, these songs feature much more varied textures, including long stretches where rock rhythm is implicit. We begin with the Who's "Won't Get Fooled Again."

## The Who

In 1969, Alan R. Pearlman founded ARP Instruments in order to produce synthesizers capable of creating a variety of electronic sounds. His first synthesizer, released in 1970, was a fairly large machine. His second model, the ARP 2600, which was released in 1971, was portable and flexible enough to be used in live performances, although it was *monophonic*—that is, capable of playing only one sound at a time.

To promote his new instruments, Pearlman gave units to some of the top rock and R&B musicians of the era, in return for permission to use their names in promoting his product. Among his first clients was the Who's Pete Townshend. Judging by the almost immediate results, Townshend was fascinated by the synthesizer and the cutting-edge technology it represented. He featured it on several tracks of their 1971 album *Who's Next*, where it served as the best possible advertising for ARP and its instruments.

The Who had come together as a group in 1964. Vocalist Roger Daltrey (b. 1944), guitarist Pete Townshend (b. 1945), and bassist John Entwhistle (1944–2002) had been part of a group called the High Numbers; they became the Who when drummer

Keith Moon (1947–1978) joined them. A year later, their music began to appear on the British charts. Their early hits, most notably "My Generation" (1965) and "Substitute" (both 1966), speak in an ironic tone: indeed, "My Generation" became the anthem for the "live hard, die young, and don't trust anyone over 30" crowd.

Musically, they were a powerhouse band with a heavy bass sound that betrayed the strong influence of sixties rhythm and blues. Townshend's power chords, Entwhistle's talented bass playing, and Moon's flamboyant drumming gave Daltrey's searing voice a rock-solid foundation. Still, it seemed that they were no more than a singles band, incapable of anything more than a series of good 3-minute songs. That perception began to change with the release of the album *Happy Jack* (1967), which included an extended piece, "A Quick One While He's Away," and it was dramatically altered with the release of the rock opera *Tommy* in 1969.

In 1970, Townshend conceived of a sequel to *Tommy*, which he called *Lifehouse*, that was to be even grander. He eventually put the project aside but incorporated some of the material into an album of singles, entitled *Who's Next*. Unlike *Tommy* and several subsequent efforts (such as *Quadrophenia*), *Who's Next* is not thematic. It is simply a collection of good songs, among them "Won't Get Fooled Again."

In "Won't Get Fooled Again," Townshend spotlights the synthesizer right from the start. A steady stream of kaleidoscopically changing chords marking the eight-beat rhythm emerges from the opening chord. The band returns about 30 seconds later, at first intermittently, then settling into a groove. As the song proper gets underway, it's clear that the synthesizer chords serve a particular purpose: they are, in effect, a futuristic rhythm guitar, pitched in a high register instead of the more characteristic midrange, but providing steady reinforcement of the rock rhythmic layer throughout the song. Musically, there is a direct line between Chuck Berry's transformation of boogie-woogie patterns and the synthesizer chords; both serve the same purpose.

"Won't Get Fooled Again," the Who (1971)

Neal Preston/Corbis

The Who in performance, in 1975, with Townshend in mid-air. From left to right: Roger Daltrey, drummer Keith Moon, and guitarist Pete Townshend. Bassist John Entwhistle is not visible. Note Moon's fully stocked drum kit, with several tom-toms and two bass drums.

> Because the ARP 2600 could only play one note at a time, Townshend must have created the synthesizer chords by overdubbing. In performance, the Who used a tape of the synthesizer part rather than an actual performer.

In this song, the insistent rhythm of the synthesizer chords seems to liberate the rest of the band. Townshend's power chords and riffs, Entwhistle's active and free bass lines, and Moon's explosive drumming all play off of this steady rhythm. It is this interplay between the steady rhythm of the synthesizer and the rest of the group that gives the song its extraordinary rhythmic energy.

Townshend's use of the synthesizer is innovative on two levels. One is simply the use of it—the ARP was a brand-new machine, and the Minimoog with which it competed had only been available for about two years. The more compelling inventiveness is his integration of the synthesizer into the heart of the band—a real novelty at the time.

The synthesizer seems to expand not only the sound world created in "Won't Get Fooled Again" but also the size of the song. It is a sprawling song—over 8½ minutes of music. The long synthesizer introduction and even longer interlude toward the end provide a dramatic contrast to the vocal sections, and its steady rhythm underpins the electrifying group jams in the extended instrumental passages.

---

### ♪ KEY FEATURES

**"Won't Get Fooled Again," the Who (1971)**
- Innovative use of ARP synthesizer as rhythm instrument
- Expansive form with strong contrasts among synthesizer alone, vocal sections, and instrumental sections
- Timekeeping in synthesizer part liberates the band rhythmically

---

Here innovative technology enhances the basic sound and rhythm of a rock band. In both its featured role (where it contrasts with the heart of the song) and in its supporting role, the synthesizer part adds a significant dimension to both sound and rhythm. The groove is so compelling that the lyrics almost seem incidental; we lose ourselves in the sounds and rhythms of the song. It makes clear that the Who never forgot how to rock and roll.

## Led Zeppelin

Most of the most important contributions to the development of rock-era music have come from two kinds of artists: those who help define or affirm its core values by doing one thing supremely well (for example, Chuck Berry, the Rolling Stones, James Brown, the Sex Pistols) and those whose curiosity compels them to explore a wide range of influences and bring them into their music, thereby expanding the boundaries of rock (for example, Buddy Holly, Frank Zappa, Stevie Wonder, the Talking Heads). Few rock-era acts have been capable of contributing in both areas. One that did achieve this was the Who; we will encounter the boundary-stretching side of their musical personality in Chapter 11. Another was Led Zeppelin.

Although often cited as a seminal heavy metal band, Led Zeppelin ultimately defies categorization. From *Led Zeppelin* (1969), their first album, it was clear that heavy metal was just one aspect of their musical personality. Their center is clearly the blues; their version of heavy metal evolved from it. At the same time, there seems to be nothing in their musical world that is not fair game for appropriation. What's particularly interesting in their music, all through their career, is the way in which influences bleed into one another. Their music may cover a lot of stylistic territory, but it is not compartmentalized.

The range of their music came mainly from guitarist Jimmy Page (b. 1944), whose curiosity led him to not only immerse himself in the blues but to seek out exotic musical styles (for example, Flamenco and East Indian music). Led Zeppelin's front man was vocalist Robert Plant (b. 1948), who was Page's second choice as lead singer but who turned out to be an ideal voice for the group. Bassist John Paul Jones (b. 1946) was, with Page, part of the British music scene in the late sixties; drummer John Bonham (1948–1980) was a friend of Plant's from their Birmingham days. Page also produced their albums. His production skills were as important a component of their success as his guitar playing: he brought a wonderful ear for sonority and texture to their music.

Page and Plant shared a deep interest in the mystic, the mythical, and the occult. This interest would increasingly inform their work, from untitled albums to cryptic covers, sparse liner notes, non-referential lyrics, and numerous archaic musical influences.

Another quality that sets their music apart from every other group of the era is their ability to establish, then reconcile, extremes. The extremes are evident in virtually every aspect of their music making. Plant sang higher than most other male vocalists (and many females, too). Their ensemble playing was more daring, their riffs more elaborate and beat-defying, the contrasts within and between songs deeper and more striking. In some of their most memorable music—such as "Dazed and Confused" and "Stairway to Heaven"—they reconcile many of the extremes that characterize their music *within* a single song. These songs cover an enormous emotional and musical range: they can be tender one moment and overpowering the next.

The music of Led Zeppelin evolved considerably from their first album to *Physical Graffiti* (1975). That, coupled with the wide range of their music, makes it difficult to represent their achievement adequately with a discussion of a single album, much less a single song. However, the album that best captures the salient qualities of their music is the untitled fourth album, known variously as *Led Zeppelin IV*, *Zoso*, or the Runes LP. The music on the tracks ranges from the unbridled power of "Rock and Roll" to the delicacy of the acoustic "The Battle of Evermore," which provides clear evidence of the group's mystical/mythical bent. "Stairway to Heaven," perhaps the best-known song on the album, merges both.

"Black Dog," another track from the album, demonstrates Led Zeppelin's connection with heavy metal and their role in the continuing evolution of rock rhythm. From the very beginning of the song, it is clear that they have internalized the feel of rock rhythm. Consider how it begins.

- A noodle on the guitar
- Plant singing without accompaniment
- The band playing an extended, blues-based melodic line, without a vocal

This is a major step forward in rhythmic freedom from typical sixties hard rock songs. Typically, these songs start with a guitar riff that sets the tempo. Other instruments layer in, setting up the groove. That doesn't happen here. Early on, we feel the beat strictly from Plant's vocal line. The silence that follows and the strung-out instrumental line make it difficult to group the beats into measures.

As they demonstrate in "Black Dog," Led Zeppelin became so comfortable with the rock groove that they could play with it—boldly. Even the refrainlike riff under Plant's "Oh, yeah" is completely syncopated. Throughout, the song has a great beat, but the timekeeping that does take place happens very much in the background. Indeed, in much of the song, we do not sense the beat at all, or sense it only from the rhythm of the main melody; what timekeeping there is in this song is purposeful and specific, rather than routine. In terms of freeing rhythm while still retaining the groove, "Black Dog" goes about as far as possible.

The extended instrumental lines in "Black Dog" also point to another feature of Led Zeppelin's approach to rock—one that would profoundly influence heavy metal bands. In effect, they harness solo-like lines within a tight group conception. In rock, guitar solos can be spectacular displays, but they can also undermine the collective conception that is at the heart of a rock groove. Page's solution was to work out these lines and integrate them into a group conception. For future heavy metal bands, this aspect of the recording was key: one of the marvels of good heavy metal performances is the tight ensemble of a band as they negotiate challenging and intricate passages. We can hear its roots in this recording.

"Black Dog" is closer to "pure" heavy metal than any other song on the album. It incorporates many of the features we expect from a metal song: Plant's high vocals, a riff by heavily distorted guitar and bass, loud volume, and a strong beat (some of the time). However, there are several differences from prototypical metal. Plant begins singing without accompaniment. The guitar/bass riff that answers Plant is long, convoluted, and full of rhythmic surprises, instead of short and simple. These and other dramatic contrasts within the song confirm Led Zeppelin's emphasis on extremes.

Despite, or perhaps partly because of, the mystery with which they enveloped themselves, Led Zeppelin gained a large, loyal audience. Their tours sold out and broke attendance records, and all of their recordings went platinum. They are still popular, almost three decades after they disbanded. There is no ambiguity as to why: their music is a rare combination of almost unrestrained power and subtle artistry, of raw emotion and superbly calculated craft. For some, the mix was too heady: the band never attracted the broad-based audience of the Beatles or Elton John. But for a large core, it was just the right strength. Millions of loyal fans remain unsatiated.

"Won't Get Fooled Again" and "Black Dog" show in quite different ways the rhythmic independence achieved by elite rock musicians when they felt comfortable with the rhythmic foundation of rock. The Who use a novel instrument as a substitute for a rhythm guitar, while Led Zeppelin dispense with persistent time-keeping altogether. That they can use this minimal timekeeping as a springboard for great rock is not only a testament to the excellence of both groups but also to the rapid and dramatic evolution of rock rhythm from the mid-sixties through the early seventies.

# The Essence of Rock

At this point, we are back where we began. If we were to include one more song in this chapter, to affirm rock's core values, the Rolling Stones' "It's Only Rock 'n Roll (But I Like It)" would be an ideal choice. As presented in the first chapter, these values were simply an assertion. The examples in this chapter have provided us with a dynamic view of rock style; we can now hear the classic sound of the Rolling Stones' rock and roll as a product of an evolutionary process that began well before *rock and roll* was a musical term. Our discussion has focused on two central aspects of this evolution: the maturation of rock rhythm (the most essential feature of the style) and the assimilation of deep blues (the dominant influence on hard rock).

## Assimilating Deep Blues

Led Zeppelin's "Black Dog" simultaneously demonstrates rock's deep debt to deep blues and its distance from blues style. The blues connection is clear in the rough vocal sound, the dark texture in those passages where the band plays continuously, and the use of riffs—and the nasty attitude that these features help project. The distance is evident in the differences between this song and a conventional blues. Unlike blues singers, who sing in their natural range, Plant sings very high—like doo-wop lead vocalists but with a far more aggressive sound. The extended riff at the beginning, while based on the African American pentatonic scale, is far more elaborate than a typical blues riff. The dark texture is mainly a result of register: low and low middle. However, instead of the riff free-for-all commonly heard in a blues song, the lines are carefully worked out, with guitar and bass moving in tandem.

With regard to rhythm, not only is the basic beat different—a rock beat versus a shuffle beat—but there are long stretches where there is no timekeeping. These are much longer than the stop-time sections one might hear in a blues song. It is as if Led Zeppelin has taken characteristic elements of blues style and pushed them to an extreme: really high vocal, extended riffs, expanded stop-time breaks. In the process, they thoroughly transform the blues elements into something quite new. In this song, and in the other three examples from the early seventies, blues elements have been seamlessly integrated into the fabric of each song.

In the first four songs, the influence of deep blues is more distinct. Still, all four songs—even the two power trio songs, which are based on blues form—are far removed stylistically from a conventional electric blues style. In "Jumping Jack Flash," the blues connection is apparent mainly in the lyric, Jagger's singing, the thick texture, and the attitude that these features project. And it is this attitude—realized far more forcefully in this music than in rock and roll and early rock—that gives hard rock and heavy metal such power. In these songs, we hear the deep blues influence and the evolution beyond blues style.

## The Maturation of Rock Rhythm

The maturation of rock rhythm was largely a process of liberation. Rock rhythm eventually arrived at its now-classic realization primarily by eliminating timekeeping at beat speed and increasing the amount of syncopation and other forms of rhythmic play. We hear this as a point of arrival in a journey that began with Chuck Berry's rock and roll–defining songs. Recall the opening of Chuck Berry's "Johnny B. Goode": in it we hear the key elements of rock rhythm: the eight-beat rock rhythmic layer in his rhythm guitar part, the syncopations in the lead guitar line, and the backbeat in the drum part. However, in terms of rhythm, Berry is swimming upstream. The rest of the band, and especially the bass player, are playing in a swing rhythm. "Rock and roll" became "rock" when the rest of the band—the drummer and the bass player—began emphasizing rock rhythm over the beat. (We noted this in the discussion of Roy Orbison, the Kingsmen, and the Beach Boys.)

In this chapter, we pick up the trail in mid-decade. In "You Really Got Me" and "Satisfaction," the most prominent regular rhythm is the beat, and the dominant rhythmic conflict is a syncopated riff that is repeated throughout. The marking of the beat disappears in the next three songs; at the same time, there is a substantial increase in rhythmic play over the regular rhythms, especially in the songs by Cream and the Jimi Hendrix Experience. The final four songs illustrate contrasting extremes of mature rock rhythm. "Paranoid" and "Highway Star" oppose strong rock rhythm timekeeping with equally strong syncopations—like two rams butting heads. "Won't Get Fooled Again" and "Black Dog" represent the opposite extreme, where rock rhythm timekeeping is in the background or missing altogether, and the patterns that conflict with the regular rhythms are in the forefront.

## A Timeless Music

The years around 1970 were defining for the history of rock; it is during this time that rock emerged as a fully developed style. Up to this point, we hear rock musicians restlessly seeking to discover the optimal approach to rock rhythm; they find it around 1970. As we become aware of this process, we can place songs in time by how far they have come from Chuck Berry's initial efforts to define rock rhythm. Similarly, we can hear the increasing influence of blues style, until the point at which it is completely absorbed into rock. This also occurs around 1970.

From this point on, what the Stones call "rock and roll" becomes a timeless music. Its conventions are clear and widely understood, and they remain substantially unchanged. A "rock and roll" song released in 1980, 1990, or 2000 is likely to have much the same basic sound and feel as the Stones' "It's Only Rock 'n Roll (But I Like It)." The rhythms and sounds of rock-era music would continue to develop beyond this point, as we will discover in the chapters that follow. But the music in the latter part of this chapter defines the core values of rock in a way that neither the rock that preceded it nor the rock that evolved beyond it does. This music is classic rock; it epitomizes the style.

## Terms to Remember

| | | |
|---|---|---|
| trad | fuzztone | sound space |
| skiffle | virtuoso | power chord |
| deep blues | power trio | overtones |
| hard rock | double-time rhythm | white noise |
| heavy metal | distortion | home chord |
| southern rock | modality | Baroque |

## Applying Chapter Concepts

1. Explore the connection between blues and rock discussed in this chapter in two ways. First, compare Robert Johnson's ''Cross Road Blues'' with ''Crossroads,'' Eric Clapton's cover of Johnson's blues. Then compare ''Strange Brew'' and ''Voodoo Child'' to recordings of blues that use a rock beat by blues artists.

2. One main theme in the previous discussion is the maturation of rock rhythm. To hear how this stage of the evolution of rock rhythm connects to earlier stages, sample key songs from earlier chapters. Begin with ''Rocket 88'' to hear the transition from shuffle to rock rhythm, and select other songs from Chapters 4 through Chapters 6, plus the Byrds' ''Mr. Tambourine Man'' in Chapter 7.

You can find playlists for both Applying Chapter Concepts suggestions on the book's website: *academic.cengage.com/music/campbell*.

# 10

# San Francisco and the Diversity of Rock

From the start, rock has been not a single style but a heterogeneous mix of styles linked by common musical features and shared attitudes. This became even more apparent during the latter part of the sixties, when rock became the dominant popular music and simultaneously went in several different directions, musically and geographically.

We may perceive the diversity of rock through geography in two ways. One is to note the numerous regional dialects of rock that surfaced in the sixties: in the United States, there was surf music from southern California, soul music from Memphis, Motown from Detroit, and southern rock from the Southeast. More significantly, rock became the first truly international popular music with the rise of the British bands. Their music added several dialects to the musical language that was rock.

The other way is to observe the activity within a geographical region. During the latter part of the sixties, one good place to do this was the San Francisco Bay Area. The region was the home not only to several important acid rock bands, but also to such diverse styles as Santana's Latin rock, Sly and the Family Stone's proto-funk, Creedence Clearwater Revival's all-American rock, and much more. We sample this diversity after a brief discussion of the culture that supported it.

## The Counterculture

Those who came of age during the latter half of the sixties grew up in a world far different from the world of their parents. A decided majority experienced neither the hardships of the Great Depression nor the traumas of the two mid-century wars: World War II and the Korean War. They were in elementary school during the McCarthy witch hunt; in most cases, it had far less impact on them than it did on their parents. A good number came from families that were comfortable financially, so that as teens they had money to spend and time to spend it.

A sizable and vocal segment of these young people rejected the values of the group they pejoratively called the "establishment." They saw the establishment as excessively conservative, bigoted, materialistic, resistant to social change, obsessed with communism and locked into a potentially deadly arms race, and clueless about sexuality. Fueled by new technologies and drugs—both old and new—they incited the most far-reaching social revolution since the twenties.

227

For college-age youth of the mid-sixties, there were four dominant issues: minority rights, sexual freedom, drug use, and war. A generation that had grown up listening to rock and roll, rhythm and blues, and jazz found it difficult to comprehend the widespread discrimination against blacks that they saw as legitimized in too many segments of American society. They joined the drive for civil rights—through demonstrations, sit-ins, marches, and, for some, more direct and potentially violent activities, such as voter registration in the South. The successes of the civil rights movement created momentum for other minority rights movements: women, Chicanos, gays, Native Americans.

Commercial production of an effective oral contraceptive—the Pill—began in the early sixties. For some women, this was the key to sexual freedom; it enabled them to be as sexually active as males with virtually no risk of pregnancy. It precipitated the most far-reaching revolution in sexual practice in the history of western culture. Moreover, it extended the drive for equal rights from the voting booth—in the United States, women were granted the right to vote only in 1920—into the bedroom and sparked a revival of feminism, which sought, among other things, to extend these rights into the workplace.

During this same period, the recreational use of mind-altering drugs spread to large segments of the middle class. Previously, drug use had been confined to small subcultures: for example, many jazz musicians in the post–World War II era were heroin addicts. Marijuana, always a popular drug among musicians and minorities, became the most popular drug of the sixties among young people, and especially the **counterculture**. However, the signature drug of the sixties was D-lysergic acid diethylamide, a semi-synthetic drug more commonly identified as **LSD** or **acid**. The drug was developed in 1938 by Albert Hoffman, a Swiss chemist; Hoffman discovered its psychedelic properties by accident about five years later. Originally, psychiatrists used it therapeutically, and during the Cold War, intelligence agencies in the United States and Great Britain apparently ran tests to determine whether the drug was useful for mind control. The key figures in moving LSD from the lab to the street were two Harvard psychology professors: Timothy Leary and Richard Alpert. They felt that the mind-expanding capabilities of the drug should be open to anyone; in reaction, Sandoz, Dr. Hofmann's chemical firm, stopped freely supplying scientists with the drug, and the U.S. government banned its use in 1967. Underground use of the drug has continued despite this ban.

In the latter part of the sixties, the Vietnam War replaced civil rights as the hot-button issue for young people. In 1954, Vietnam, formerly French Indo-China, was divided—like Korea—into two regions: the north received support from the USSR and communist China, while the southern region received the support of western nations, especially the United States. A succession of presidents saw a military presence in South Vietnam as a necessary buffer against communist aggression.

As a result, U.S. military involvement gradually escalated over the next decade. Finally, in 1965, the government began sending regular troops to Vietnam to augment the special forces already there. This provoked a hostile reaction, especially from those eligible to be drafted. Many recoiled at the prospect of fighting in a war that seemed pointless; a few fled to Canada or elsewhere to avoid the draft. Massive anti-war demonstrations became as much a part of the news during the late sixties as the civil rights demonstrations were in the first part of the decade. The lies and deceptions of the government and military, which among other things reassured the American people that the war was winnable and that the U.S. forces were winning, coupled with news reports of horrific events such as the My Lai massacre, in which U.S. soldiers killed close to 500 unarmed civilians in a small village, further eroded support for the war.

Civil rights, sex, drugs, and war were issues for many young Americans during the latter part of the sixties. On all of these issues, the gulf between the older establishment positions and attitudes of young Americans widened as the decade wore on. Still, there was a major shift in values: civil rights legislation passed, the role of women in society underwent a liberating transformation, recreational drug use became more common and socially acceptable in certain circles (although it was still illegal), and the war eventually ended in failure. As a result of this revolution, ideas and practices that seemed radical at mid-century—such as multiculturalism and equal opportunity in the workplace—are accepted norms in contemporary society.

## Hippies

A small but prominent minority of young people chose to reject mainstream society completely. They abandoned the conventional lifestyles of their parents and peers; some chose to live in communes. They followed Timothy Leary's advice to "turn on, tune in, drop out." They dressed differently, thought differently, and lived differently. They were the ideological heirs of the Bohemians of nineteenth-century Europe and the Beats of the late 1940s and 1950s. Members of the group were known as **hippies**; collectively they formed the heart of the counterculture.

Throughout the sixties, the San Francisco Bay Area was a center for radical thought and action. The free speech movement led by Mario Savio got started at the Berkeley campus of the University of California in 1964; it led to confrontations between student protesters and university administrators over student rights and academic freedom. In 1966, in Oakland—next to Berkeley and across the bay from San Francisco—Huey Newton, Bobby Seale, and Richard Aoki formed the Black Panthers, a radical black organization dedicated to revolutionary social reform by any means necessary, including violence. Hippies generally followed a less confrontational path.

For hippies, mecca was San Francisco; their counterpart to the Sacred Mosque was Haight and Ashbury, an intersection in a heretofore ordinary neighborhood in San Francisco, near Golden Gate Park, the largest public park in the city. The area became a destination for those who wanted to "make love, not war" and travel the fast route to higher consciousness by tripping on psychedelic drugs. Migration to San Francisco peaked during the 1967 "summer of love," when an estimated 75,000 young people flocked to the city.

Rock music was the soundtrack for the counterculture. Music was everywhere—inside and outside—and especially at the Fillmore. Promoter Bill Graham turned the Fillmore Ballroom, a musty building in a rather seedy part of town, into the main venue for rock bands and their fans. Audiences flocked there for endless concerts; "live at the Fillmore" albums appeared regularly in record stores. The venue was so successful that Graham named its New York counterpart "Fillmore East."

Because of Haight-Ashbury, "flower power," LSD, and the other trappings of the hippie scene, the music most associated with the Bay Area during the late sixties was **acid rock** (or **psychedelic rock**)—a rock substyle defined not by a musical feature but simply by the music's ability to evoke or enhance the drug experience. However, a list of

Ted Streshinsky/Corbis

Jerry Garcia poses at the corner of Haight and Ashbury, the heart of San Francisco's hippie neighborhood, in 1966.

bands active in the San Francisco Bay Area during 1969 makes clear that the Bay Area music scene was far more varied. At the center of it was a trio of acid-rock bands: Jefferson Airplane, Quicksilver Messenger Service, and the Grateful Dead. Of course, the Dead soon ranged far beyond acid rock. But there were also such acts as:

- Janis Joplin, who sang the blues with power and passion, fronting her Kosmic Blues Band
- Creedence Clearwater Revival, one of the great singles bands of the era, playing down-to-earth rock and roll
- Santana, Carlos Santana's one-band foray into Latin rock
- Sly and the Family Stone, whose music provided the crucial link between soul and funk

We sample the music from this special time and place next.

## Acid Rock

The British writer Aldous Huxley, whose book *The Doors of Perception* inspired Jim Morrison to name his band the Doors, described his first acid trip, which he took in 1955, in this way:

> What came through the closed door was the realization—not the knowledge, for this wasn't verbal or abstract—but the direct, total awareness, from the inside, so to say, of Love as the primary and fundamental cosmic fact. These words, of course, have a kind of indecency and must necessarily ring false, seem like twaddle. But the fact remains... I was this fact or perhaps it would be more accurate to say that this fact occupied the place where I had been.

In his thoughtful account, Huxley struggles to put into words the nature of the acid experience. It is clear that for him there was an enormous gulf between everyday reality and the enhanced reality of the acid experience. Words seem inadequate to the task; he all but apologizes for their limitations in the middle of his description. But they are all he has as he tries to translate his heightened experience into mundane, if elegant, language.

As tripping on acid became more widespread, words, images, and music were used to capture the psychedelic experience. Psychedelic art—rich in color, dense and distorted, and often suffused with religious and mystical images—became an important new direction in the visual arts. The images were not confined to canvas, or even album covers and posters. Perhaps the most famous and memorable visual image of the psychedelic sixties was a 1939 International Harvester school bus painted in a rainbow of colors; it was the vehicle for the cross-country tours of Ken Kesey, the patron saint of the psychedelic world, and his Merry Pranksters.

Music was even more integral to the psychedelic experience because it was used not only to evoke but also to enhance tripping on acid. Music could contribute to the experience (as we will learn following), depict the experience (as we heard in the Beatles' "A Day in the Life"), and be a product of it (as was the case of much of the music from the mid- and late sixties). Indeed, the common bond that linked the widely varied music identified as acid or psychedelic rock was the connection to LSD. There was no specific musical feature, or set of features, that identified acid rock. (By contrast, consider the role of distortion in defining the sound of heavy metal, or the combination of horns and heavy bass in defining the sound of soul music.) Examples of acid rock ranged from the sprawling, blues-based improvisations of Jerry Garcia and the Grateful Dead to Jefferson Airplane's tight, flamenco-tinged "White Rabbit," discussed following. The musical products were seemingly as varied as the acid trips themselves. The connection could be in the music, in the words, or both.

## Jefferson Airplane

The band that first directed the spotlight to San Francisco and to acid rock was Jefferson Airplane. Other bands had a more authentic provenance—the Grateful Dead were the house band for Ken Kesey's "Acid Tests"—but it was the Jefferson Airplane that brought national attention to psychedelic rock and to San Francisco as its home base.

Vocalist Marty Balin (b. 1942) and guitarist Paul Kantner (b. 1941) formed Jefferson Airplane in 1965; the next year, Grace Slick (born Grace Wing, 1939) replaced Signe Anderson as the female vocalist with the group and soon became the face as well as the dominant voice of the group. Her good looks and extroverted and uninhibited stage personality were key elements in the success of the group. The rest of the group during the late sixties included lead guitarist Jorma Kaukonen (b. 1940), bassist Jack Casady (b. 1944), and drummer Spencer Dryden (1938–2005).

Slick brought two songs with her from the Great Society, the band she had formed with Jerry Slick, her husband at the time. As reworked by Jefferson Airplane, they became the group's two Top 10 singles: "Somebody to Love" and "White Rabbit." Both songs appeared on *Surrealistic Pillow* (1967), the first album the group recorded with Slick.

Of the two, "White Rabbit" connects more directly to the drug experience. The title of the song refers to the white rabbit in Lewis Carroll's *Alice in Wonderland*. In

CD 2:24

"White Rabbit," Jefferson Airplane (1967)

Carroll's tale, the rabbit, dressed in a waistcoat, leads Alice into a hole and into a fantasy world where she has all manner of strange experiences. The lyric comments on a scene in the story where she meets a caterpillar that seems to be smoking opium. Slick would later remark that the song was an indictment of parents who read stories like *Alice in Wonderland* to their children and then wonder why the children do drugs. However, the connection with LSD was oblique enough that the song made it past the censors, although the drug references (such as "feed your head") seem quite clear in retrospect.

In "White Rabbit," the lyrics (and Slick's singing) are primary; the music plays a supporting role. Among the defining features of the song are the flamenco-inspired instrumental accompaniment (adapted for a rock band) and the sustained crescendo to the final "feed your head." Slick remarked that the inspiration for the accompaniment came from her repeated listening to *Sketches of Spain* while tripping on LSD. *Sketches of Spain* was an adventurous album by the jazz trumpeter Miles Davis; the most extended track was a drastic reworking of a guitar concerto by the Spanish composer Joaquin Rodrigo.

Another remarkable feature of the song is its slow, steady **crescendo** (a gradual increase in volume). The song begins quietly with an extended instrumental introduction in which the instruments enter one by one—bass, drums, then lead and rhythm guitars. Both the rhythm and the chord progression evoke Spanish music. Slick also enters quietly. The music gets louder as the song proceeds, reaching a climax on the line "feed your head." As Slick belts out the lyric, the band shifts from the Spanish-flavored rhythm with which the song began to a straightforward rock rhythm; it is as if music, like the mind and Slick's voice, has been set free from the restrictive Spanish rhythm.

"White Rabbit" has retained its strong association with LSD, and by extension, other mind-altering drugs. To cite just one instance: it has been used in several episodes of *The Simpsons*, especially when the characters have taken hallucinogenic drugs, and they are starting to kick in.

♪  KEY FEATURES

**"White Rabbit," Jefferson Airplane (1967)**

- Importance of the words: the message of the song is mainly in the words; the melody is not a standalone melody, like those found in Motown or Beatles songs, nor is the accompaniment interesting enough to stand alone.
- Spanish flavor: like the string sounds in "Eleanor Rigby," the Spanish rhythms and harmonies connect to rock mainly by association; they are certainly not typical in rock music. In this case, it was Slick's obsession with *Sketches of Spain* that provided the connection; in other respects, there seems to be little connection between words and music.
- Big crescendo: the gradual crescendo makes the final line of the song sound like a call to action—an emphatic exhortation to take an acid trip.

Jefferson Airplane remained one of the leading psychedelic rock bands into the early seventies, when the group reconstituted itself with Slick and Kantner as Jefferson Starship. Although their new name implied that they had become even more adventurous—starships fly higher than airplanes—the band actually became more mainstream and enjoyed even more commercial success during the seventies and eighties.

Both the psychedelic scene and psychedelic rock lost their potency around 1970. The 1967 "summer of love" devolved into a bad trip at the end of the decade. Haight-Ashbury went into decline; it would become gentrified a decade later. For many, LSD lost its status as the mind-expanding drug of choice. The absence of a distinct musical identity made it difficult to sustain acid rock as a vital rock substyle; the style neither evolved (like heavy metal or country rock) nor achieved a more-or-less permanent stasis (like hard rock). It was—and remains—very much a period piece, a sound of a particular time and place.

One important reason that acid rock lacked a distinct musical identity was the fact that the drug experience was an overlay; it was not an integral element of the style. Indeed, most of the major acid-rock acts rooted their style in folk and blues: the Grateful Dead began as a **jug band**; the members of Jefferson Airplane had prior experience in folk, blues, and R&B; and both Jimi Hendrix and Eric Clapton, who were also associated with acid rock, had deep blues roots. For many of the top San Francisco–based acts, this connection with American **roots music** was a stronger musical bond than the drugs. Perhaps the clearest example of this came in the music of Janis Joplin.

## Down to Earth: Janis Joplin and the Blues

The only woman performer in the San Francisco rock scene with a more commanding presence than Grace Slick was Janis Joplin. Like Slick, Joplin fronted a band, had a let-it-all-hang-out stage personality, and wrestled with a severe substance abuse problem. Both looked the part of the counterculture diva—both dressed and undressed. But there were differences. Slick was beautiful and had come from a high-class back-ground. Before joining Jefferson Airplane she had modeled for three years at a high-end San Francisco department store and had begun her undergraduate education at Finch College, a finishing school for young ladies. Joplin had grown up a social outcast in a Texas oil town; music was her escape. Joplin sipped while Slick tripped; Janis's taste for Southern Comfort was legendary. (Ironically, it was Slick who later developed an alcohol abuse problem, while Joplin died of a heroin overdose.) And while Slick took her listeners into a fantastic world in songs like "White Rabbit," Joplin got real by drenching herself in blues and soul.

Like many other young musicians of the time, Janis Joplin (1943–1970) migrated to San Francisco during the mid-sixties. Born in Port Arthur, Texas, Joplin began performing in coffeehouses in her native state before traveling to California in 1965. There, she began performing with a local blues band: Big Brother and the Holding Company. A rather motley crew, the group made an enormous impact at the 1967 Monterey Pop Festival, thanks mainly to Joplin's dynamic stage performance. Signed to Columbia Records, they cut one album that was widely praised for the quality of

Henry Diltz/Corbis

Janis Joplin on stage at the famous Woodstock festival, August 16, 1969.

Joplin's vocals, while the band was criticized for its ragged playing. Joplin soon separated from the band and became an important solo act for the rest of her brief life.

Joplin was rock's original blues diva. Before Joplin, few women sang with anything approaching the supercharged passion and freedom that is inherent in her singing; all of them were black—from Bessie Smith to Aretha Franklin. Indeed, Joplin's singing seemingly owes more to Otis Redding and other male southern soul singers than to any woman, because what distinguishes Joplin's singing from other female singers is the rawness of her sound and the sheer exuberance of her performing style. She had a voice that often sounded like it had been raked over broken glass, although she could also sing as tenderly as any crooner. She combined that with a unique kind of vocal virtuosity. With its stutters, reiterations, rapid-fire streams of words, melismas, interpolations, and the like, it is almost operatic in its exhibitionism.

Although Joplin thought of herself as a blues singer, most of the songs that she recorded were not blues, at least in the formal sense. Unlike the classic female blues singers of the twenties, who recorded mainly conventional blues songs, Joplin recorded a wide range of material. However, she brought blues feeling and style into everything she recorded, blues or not.

"Piece of My Heart" (1968), which she recorded while singing with Big Brother and the Holding Company, was the only song of hers to reach the singles charts during her lifetime. It was a track on *Cheap Thrills*, the band's first album for Columbia and by far their biggest success; the album topped the charts for eight weeks in 1968.

CD 2:25

"Piece of My Heart," Janis Joplin (1968)

"Piece of My Heart" remains the song most closely associated with her, two biographies include it in the title.

"Piece of My Heart" had been a modest R&B hit the previous year for Erma Franklin, Aretha Franklin's younger sister. Her original version was a solid and straightforward slow soul song. Characteristically, the lyric tells the story of a troubled relationship, here from a woman's point of view: she is at once vulnerable and—as the lyric says—tough. Given Joplin's history and personality, it is easy to understand why she would be eager to cover it.

The thorough transformation of the song begins with the band: the instrumental accompaniment features the kind of blues-tinged rock that was characteristic of the San Francisco psychedelic scene, rather than a bass-heavy R&B sound. The instrumentation is standard: two guitars, with some distortion in the lead guitar, bass, and drums. The rhythms are more active and freer than in a straightforward rock song.

All of this is a foil for Joplin's soulful singing, which is considerably more passionate and virtuosic than Erma Franklin's. There is enormous contrast, in volume and vocal quality, from the almost screamed opening ("Come on") to the almost whispered verse ("Didn't I make you feel") to the half-spoken/half-sung ("Each time I tell myself") and the wailed refrain. As she delivers the song, she lays herself emotionally bare—as if she had stripped off all of her clothes. Few singers of any era were willing to throw themselves into a performance the way Joplin did, and fewer had the vocal agility and range to carry it off successfully.

Even more than Grace Slick, Janis Joplin redefined the role of women in rock. It was no longer simply being a pretty face in front of the band; Joplin matched men—black and white—in power and presence. In this respect, she paved the way for a larger role for women in rock: Patti Smith, Annie Lennox, Bonnie Raitt, Madonna, and many others benefited from her trailblazing efforts.

She paid a price for her passion. With her premature death, she joined the not-exclusive-enough club of rock icons who lived too hard and died too young. Ironically,

♪ **KEY FEATURES**

**"Piece of My Heart," Janis Joplin (1968)**

- Blues-influenced rock band with psychedelic overtones: standard instrumentation, blues-inspired riffs, and effects—such as the distortion and the spacey sounds and feedback at the end of the song—all connect the song to blues-oriented acid rock.
- Passionate singing: Joplin's singing is unique, not only for its basic quality, which recalls the voices of the great male soul singers, but also for its uninhibited use of an array of vocal devices and the many shifts of mood.
- Rock that is real: there were dozens of bands that dug into the blues in order to invest their music with the kind of emotional honesty heard in the music of the best blues artists. Few white singers, male or female, could match Joplin's intensity.

she did not live long enough to enjoy her biggest hit; "Me and Bobby McGee," written for her by Kris Kristofferson, one of her ex-lovers, appeared on *Pearl*, an album released after her death. She left the album incomplete; she was to have added vocals to a track entitled "Buried Alive in the Blues" on the day she died.

Joplin and her music embody the tensions of the new womanhood that emerged in the sixties. On stage and in the studio, she is the equal of men, yet vulnerable in a specifically feminine way; she is modern in her sensibility, yet deals with timeless issues in her songs. For a new generation of women, she showed both what they might aspire to and the dangers of getting it.

# Toward an American Rock Sound

Rock, like English, was spoken on both sides of the Atlantic during the sixties; the British invasion simply made North American listeners aware of the British rock scene. British and North American musicians drew on many of the same sources; the influence of the blues was pervasive. They listened to and talked with one another, and at times they played together. To cite just two familiar examples, the Jimi Hendrix Experience included two British musicians, bassist Noel Redding and drummer Mitch Mitchell; and keyboardist Billy Preston played on Beatles' recordings.

Despite the obvious common ground, there was an overall difference in attitude and musical result between North American and British rock. The difference grows out of the division between highbrow and lowbrow, a division that in American music extends back to blackface minstrelsy. There is a strong impulse in British rock to aspire to highbrow status by assuming the trappings of high art. By contrast, Dylan demonstrated that it was possible to create art without being "arty." This difference seems to emerge from a fundamental cultural difference between Great Britain and its former colonies: Buckingham Palace versus blue jeans.

Musically, the biggest difference was the far stronger impact of American folk and country music. Again, Dylan led the way on both fronts—first by his excursion in folk music and then by his extended embrace of Nashville. But country music and, in some cases, folk music helped shape music from all over North America, including the San Francisco Bay Area. The country and folk influence gave this music a distinctly American sound, although it took widely different forms. It shows up particularly in the scales on which many of the songs are based, the spun-out melodies, and the guitar riffs. To experience this, we consider songs by two of the most important Bay Area-based bands: Creedence Clearwater Revival and the Grateful Dead.

## Creedence Clearwater Revival

Unlike many other San Francisco bands, Creedence Clearwater Revival (CCR) was a Bay Area band because its members grew up there. The four band members—John Fogerty (b. 1945), lead guitar; Tom Fogerty (1941–1990, John's older brother), rhythm guitar; Stu Cook (b. 1945), bass; and Doug Clifford (b. 1945), drums—grew up in the East Bay, northeast of San Francisco. Beginning in junior high school as the Blue Velvets, they finally incarnated themselves as Creedence Clearwater Revival in

1967 and released their first album a year later. They were immediately successful; for three years they were the hottest singles band in the country.

In his liner notes to *Chronicle*, an anthology of CCR's greatest hits, Greil Marcus wrote about "Proud Mary" and three other songs that they "literally define rock and roll—as a musical form, as a recurring event, as a version of the American spirit." The values that Marcus—and millions of listeners—seemed to find appealing were the basic, down-to-earth quality of the words and music (nothing fancy and no gimmicks); its independent spirit (CCR stayed away from the "flower power" scene); and its lack of pretense. It was music with a good story, a good beat, and unmistakable riffs.

The opening riff of "Proud Mary," among rock's most memorable 10-second sound slices, perfectly illustrates the fusion of blues and country influences. Fogerty harmonizes each note of the African American pentatonic scale with the three-note chords typical of country music. This apparent country retention makes Fogerty's riff stand apart from many other pentatonic riffs of the period, especially those of British bands. These were typically harmonized with power chords or not harmonized at all, as we heard in Chapter 9.

Like the opening riff, the rest of the song is a seamless mix of black and white roots music. Most of the time, Fogerty's melody noodles around the first three notes of the Anglo-American pentatonic scale, much like the minstrel songs of Stephen Foster: "Oh, Susanna" and "Old Folks at Home" ("way down upon the Swanee

"Proud Mary,"
Creedence
Clearwater
Revival (1969)

Creedence Clearwater Revival, in a posed photo taken in 1970, at the height of their fame. From left to right: Doug Clifford, Tom Fogerty, Stu Cook, and John Fogerty.

River") are good examples. This choice of notes helps give the song an "American" sound. So do the country-ish guitar riffs.

At the same time, there are elements that are clearly black. The texture of the song is dense and highly syncopated: the rhythm guitar pattern plays a key role here. There's a nice **bent note** on the word "Proud"; it is most expressive note in the song, in part because it goes outside the Anglo-American scale. And then there's Fogerty's singing, which resonates with Little Richard's influence.

All of this is in the service of two of the enduring themes in American culture: the rambling man and life along the Mississippi. "Proud Mary" is, of course, a steamboat traveling up and down the river. Fogerty's lyric sketches out a vivid picture of the protagonist finding a comfortable niche in a community of outsiders. The race of its protagonist is unclear: Fogerty is, of course, white, but "the man" is black slang for a boss—and in 1971 the song became a huge hit for Tina Turner. The story connects back to Mark Twain; it brings the myth into the sixties.

---

### ♪ KEY FEATURES

**"Proud Mary," Creedence Clearwater Revival (1969)**

- Basic rock and roll: "Proud Mary" contains the features that we expect to find in a basic rock song: a lyric that tells a story; verse/chorus form; memorable vocal and instrumental hooks; basic rock-band instrumentation (two guitars, bass, and drums); strong, syncopated rhythms; and a thick texture set in a low and middle range. There's nothing fancy, just solid American rock and roll.
- Country flavor: the heartland theme of the lyrics, its clear presentation, and the limited harmony made up of full chords impart a country flavor to the song.

---

From the beginning of "Proud Mary" to the end, Fogerty blends the two folk traditions seamlessly. It is their presence, especially the country elements, that helps Creedence Clearwater Revival achieve their distinctive, hard-driving rock-and-roll sound.

CCR was not a typical San Francisco band. They offered tight singles instead of rambling drug-juiced jams. Their Bay Area base was an accident of birth, not a choice, and unlike the Beach Boys, for instance, they didn't regionalize their sound. Their unique style was all-American.

## The Grateful Dead

Keeping CCR company in the Bay Area were the Grateful Dead. For most of their career, the band consisted of guitarists Jerry Garcia (1942–1995) and Bob Weir (b. 1947), harmonica player "Pigpen" McKernan (Ronald McKernan, 1945–1973), bassist Phil Lesh (b. 1940), and drummer Mickey Hart (b. 1943). Lyricist Robert Hunter (b. 1941), who didn't perform with the band, collaborated with Garcia, Lesh, and Weir on most of their memorable songs.

On the surface, it might seem that the Grateful Dead and Creedence Clearwater Revival were as opposite as two American bands could be, despite their conjunction in time and place. Where CCR was best known for its short singles, the Grateful Dead made their reputation through long concerts—up to 5 hours—which featured extended solos, especially by Jerry Garcia. CCR was on the outside of the San Francisco music scene. By contrast, the Dead were the quintessential San Francisco hippie band: they lived communally for years, ingested copious quantities of trendy drugs, and played all the time, often for free, especially in their early years. CCR had a huge, largely anonymous fan base. The Grateful Dead, who didn't chart a single until 1987 (!), slowly built an extremely loyal cult following, the **Deadheads**, who would travel from concert to concert to hear the band, in part because each concert was likely to be different.

Nevertheless, there is also an American-ness about the Grateful Dead and their music. Like CCR, the Grateful Dead explored America's romantic myths and images in their most highly regarded music. Moreover, the Dead followed their own muse, instead of striving for mass popularity, which exemplified the iconoclastic individualism that is also part of the American character. Their route to success was unique in the history of rock.

*Workingman's Dead* (1970), widely regarded as the Grateful Dead's finest album, offers substantial evidence of the American qualities of the Dead's music. The basic approach is similar in both words and music. And like CCR, they also drew on black and white roots music. But within these overall parameters, the Grateful Dead is yin to CCR's yang. Their music is more exploratory and more diverse in influence and blend than CCR. If CCR were the heart of American rock and roll at the end of the sixties, the Grateful Dead represented multiple directions that American rock music could go. One song cannot give an adequate picture of their range. Still, "Uncle John's Band," one of the most memorable songs from the album, can give some sense of the way in which they combined diverse influences.

"Uncle John's Band," the Grateful Dead (1970)

Like "Proud Mary," "Uncle John's Band" taps into an enduring American image: here, it is the country fiddler as pied piper. And like so many rock songs from the sixties, it conflates the timeless with the current, the universal with the particular. The lyrics are rich in allusions to America's past: for example, buck-and-wing dancing (a popular tap dance at the turn of the twentieth century), as well as a fiddle tune called "Buck Dancer's Choice"; "Don't Tread on Me," a popular motto from the American revolution. However, the lyric has autobiographical undertones—Uncle John's band could easily be the Dead.

"Uncle John's Band" tells a long, slowly unfolding story, à la Woody Guthrie—or the New Lost City Ramblers, a trio that included Mike Seeger and that was among the most conscientiously authentic of the major folk revival groups. Several members of the Grateful Dead, including Garcia and lyricist Robert Hunter, were great admirers of the group and jammed with them on at least one occasion. (Subsequently, Hunter alluded to a connection between the group and the lyrics.)

The old-time music influence of the New Lost City Ramblers is even more evident in the music, at least at the beginning. The acoustic guitars heard at the beginning of the song—two strummed and another almost mandolinlike—recall the Grateful Dead's earlier roots in jug band music. Similarly, the vocal harmonies evoke the early folk revival groups, although more direct precedents were the harmonies of Crosby,

Stills, Nash, and Young. Bass and drums enter discreetly to enrich the sound; Lesh's bass line is the most complex strand of the texture. In addition, the song relies almost exclusively on the major scales and chords of country and folk music, rather than the modal sounds of hard rock. Extra percussion sounds join in as the song unfolds: the persistent scrape of a guiro, then low-pitched drums, claves. Suddenly, about 3 minutes into the song, the song changes character. The harmony grows darker, the drums become more prominent, a riff is repeated over and over, and the rhythm shifts to a pattern of four plus three beats. The original melody returns, without instrumental accompaniment, then the band comes back in. The dark interlude returns briefly as a tag.

The gradual evolution of the song—from simple folk beginning, through mantra-like interlude, to the final section, which combines the two—underscores its autobiographical nature. It is as if we hear the history of the band in less than 5 minutes: its folk roots, its gradual incorporation of other elements (for example, the additional percussion instruments), the psychedelic phase (the dark interlude), and the current (circa 1970) state of affairs, where the group is open to all influences and can blend them effortlessly.

Even a cursory comparison of "Proud Mary" and "Uncle John's Band" reveals significant differences in the two bands' approach to an **American sound**, as well as the underlying similarities. CCR is straightforward rock and roll: the song is memorable, predictable in its instrumentation, form, rhythm, and melodic approach, and well done. There are no frills. By contrast, "Uncle John's Band" is full of subtleties and surprises, such as the acoustic guitars, extra percussion instruments, and rhythmic tricks. They may share a similar heritage, but they rework it quite differently.

It should be noted that this recording is not "trademark Dead": the sprawling, largely improvisational performances that kept the Deadheads on the road with them. Among their many virtues, the Dead were a great boogie band, as they revealed on songs like "Turn on Your Love Light," from *Europe '72*. In their collective persona, the management of their career, and, most of all, in their songs, the Grateful Dead followed the less-traveled road. That it included their own blends of folk, country, and blues influences only makes it that much more American.

## Santana and Latin Rock

If CCR and the Dead represent an almost seamless blend of American roots music, then the music of Santana represents a spectacular instance of the merging of rock with a music with deep roots outside of the United States. The **Latin rock** of Santana was not the first mixing of Latin music and rock: Latin influence has been present from the start, as we noted in Chapter 4. Nor is Latin rock the first instance of the integration of non-rock styles from outside the U.S.–U.K. world into rock. During the latter half of the sixties, rock musicians incorporated elements of such styles as East Indian music, classical music, and French cabaret music. However, these outside influences were, in most cases, used evocatively for a particular song; they were not inherent components of a hybrid style.

In Santana's Latin rock, both the rock and the Latin elements are easily heard: Latin percussion versus electric guitar and bass—a rhythmic conception that draws on rock and Afro-Cuban music but is neither one nor the other. Again, there were styles that drew on rock and non-rock in more or less equal measure: jazz/rock fusion is an early and extensive example. However, Latin rock is the first important *style* to mix rock with an exotic style in balanced proportions. The musician most responsible for the style was Carlos Santana.

## Carlos Santana

Carlos Santana (b. 1947) was born and raised in Mexico. He moved to San Francisco in 1962. He made his first impression as a blues-inspired rock guitarist; his first commercial recording came from a live 1969 performance with blues guitarist Mike Bloomfield. That same year, he acknowledged his Hispanic heritage by forming Santana. Latin music has its roots in Cuba, as we have noted. Most Latin musicians at the time came from Spanish-speaking Caribbean countries, or had roots there; New York was the American home of this music. The music of Mexico (and Santana's father, a mariachi musician) is quite different. Nevertheless, Santana connected with Afro-Cuban music and took a lead role in integrating it into rock.

CD 2:26

"Oye Como Va," Santana (1971)

A prime example of his synthesis of the two styles is his 1971 version of Tito Puente's "Oye Como Va." Here, Santana blends the sounds and rhythmic feel of Latin music into a rock song driven by Santana's guitar and Gregg Rolie's organ. The song begins with an irregular rhythmic pattern, played on the organ (and supported in the bass). It is not the clave rhythm of Afro-Cuban music, but it is similar in that it creates an asymmetrical rhythm over eight beats and serves as the main rhythmic reference. The performance consists mainly of several statements of Puente's simple melodic riffs, wrapped around strong organ and guitar solos.

### ♪ KEY FEATURES

**"Oye Como Va," Santana (1971)**

- Multinational instrumentation: Santana's band includes his rock-style electric guitar, electric bass, and electric organ, plus an arsenal of instruments associated with Afro-Cuban music, including congas, timbales, and guiro (which produces the scraping sound).
- Clavelike rhythm: The foreground rhythm of Puente's song is asymmetrical and syncopated, like the clave rhythm, but the pattern contains six notes, not five, and does not line up with the clave rhythm. The result is a Latin feel but not authentic Afro-Cuban rhythm.
- Rock-based guitar and organ solos: The extended guitar and organ solos in "Oye Como Va" betray no Latin influence; they would sound just as effective in a rock song. The stylistic synthesis occurs because the Latin rhythms and percussion sounds continue underneath the solo.

In Chapter 4, we emphasized that Latin music was the silent partner in the rock revolution. Especially for R&B bands, it became an alternative to rock rhythm. As we listen to the guitar and organ solos in this song, we can hear how seamlessly Latin and rock rhythms merge. Both are built on the division of the beat into two equal parts, so the rhythms align when played together. One could easily imagine the solos of Carlos Santana or Gregg Rolie (b. 1947) taking place over a groove laid down by a rock bassist and drummer. They would not have to adjust the rhythmic feel of their playing to play the same music with a rock band.

Despite this comfortable correspondence between Latin and rock rhythms, those who wish to combine them must reconcile the two, because the beat and the clave pattern are mutually exclusive ways of organizing a steady rhythmic stream. Marking the beat grounds the rhythm, because beat marking divides time into regular intervals. By contrast, organizing the rhythm mainly around the asymmetrical clave pattern helps the rhythm float, because it doesn't come to rest on the beat. Santana's effective compromise is to keep Puente's clavelike rhythm in the forefront throughout most of the song.

What distinguishes Latin rock from more conventional rock? In "Oye Como Va," it is, more than anything else, the sheer quantity of percussion instruments and the persistence of Puente's clavelike rhythm that betrays Latin influence. There is no mistaking the emphasis.

Santana was Latin rock's lone star. New York–based Latin musicians also attempted rock/Latin fusions: *bugalú* was a minor sensation in the Latin community during the sixties and early seventies. But none of this music had the crossover appeal of Santana's early music. In the mid-seventies, Santana gravitated toward jazz fusion; Latin rock faded away. However, the influence of Latin music—especially via Cuba and Brazil—would be even more pronounced, and more seamlessly integrated, in the seventies and eighties.

## Funk and Fun: Sly and the Family Stone

Fun has been part of popular music from the beginning. We encountered it in the music for the minstrel show, and if we were to venture back a century earlier, we would encounter it in John Gay's *Beggar's Opera*, a still-popular British stage entertainment that parodied the grand opera of the time. Ragtime brought a different kind of fun; it grew out of the infectious rhythms that so many found invigorating. This in turn gave way to the frenetic excesses of the animal dances, the high spirits of the Charleston, and the bouncy fox-trot songs of the late twenties. Blues opened up new possibilities: we heard the barnyard humor of "It's Tight Like That" and imagined dancers messing around to "Pine Top's Boogie Woogie." With the emergence of ragtime, jazz, and blues, popular music could be fun—both in what it said and how it felt.

In the rock era, musicians discovered many more ways to have fun. In just the music of the Beatles, we can hear the good clean fun of a "Hard Day's Night," Lennon's self-deprecating humor in "Norwegian Wood," and outright silliness in "Yellow Submarine." Much of the black music of the sixties seemed restrained by comparison: for Motown acts, every move was choreographed. James Brown worked, even when he felt good. It remained for Sly and the Family Stone to reintroduce a completely uninhibited sense of play into black music.

Musicians speak admiringly of a "tight" band: when they do, they are referring to a band that plays with great precision. James Brown's band was tight; he would fine

Jack Robinson/Hulton Archive/Getty Images

Sly and the Family Stone, performing at the Fillmore Auditorium, San Francisco, in 1969. Sly is singing and playing the keyboard.

musicians who missed cues or cracked notes. By contrast, Sly and the Family Stone was a loose band. This too can be an admirable quality; it produces a quite different feel.

The band was the brainchild of Sly Stone (born Sylvester Stewart, 1944), a disc jockey turned producer and bandleader. More than any other band of the era, Sly and the Family Stone preached integration. The lineup included two of Stone's siblings (his brother Freddie and sister Rosie), Cynthia Martin on trumpet, and several others, including trend-setting bassist Larry Graham: there were blacks and whites, and women as well as men.

In a series of hits spanning a five-year period (1968–1972), Sly and the Family Stone created an exuberant new sound. We hear it in "Thank You (Falettinme Be Mice Elf Agin)," one of their three number 1 hits. The music of James Brown is the direct antecedent of this song and this style: like Brown's music, there is a groove built up from multiple layers of riffs, played by rhythm and horns; there is no harmonic movement—instead of two chords, there is only one; and the vocal part is intermittent, with long pauses between phrases.

However, Sly and the Family Stone create a sound that is much denser and more active than that heard in "Papa's Got a Brand New Bag." Although the drummer marks off a rock beat along with the backbeat, the basic rhythmic feel of the song is twice as fast—what is now called a **16-beat rhythm** (by analogy with two-beat [fox-trot], four-beat [swing], and eight-beat [rock] rhythms). We sense this faster-moving

"Thank You (Falettinme Be Mice Elf Agin)," Sly and the Family Stone (1969)

layer in virtually all the other parts: the opening bass riff, the guitar and horn riffs, and—most explicitly—in the "chuck-a-puk-a" vocalization. The more active texture opens up many more rhythmic patterns that can conflict with the beat; Sly's band exploits several of them.

And instead of Brown's spare, open texture, there are plenty of riffs: bass, several guitars, voice, horns. Moreover, there is a spontaneous aspect to the sound, as if it grows out of a jam over the basic groove. It is this quality that gives the song (and Stone's music) its distinctive looseness—looseness that implores listeners to "dance to the music."

If we just listen to the music, it can hypnotize us with its contagious rhythm. However, when we consider the words—the opening lines are "Lookin' at the devil, grinnin' at his gun/Fingers start shakin', I begin to run"—we sense that the band is laughing to keep from crying, or burning down the house. As with many other Sly and the Family Stone songs, there is a strong political and social message: we sense that the music is the buffer between the band and society, a restraint against violent activism.

This is our first example of what would become a growing trend in Afro-centric music, from the United States and abroad: powerful lyrics over a powerful beat. There is an apparent contradiction between the sharp social commentary in the lyrics and the seduction of the beat. They seem to be operating at cross purposes: full attention and response versus surrender to the groove. Perhaps that's so. However, it is possible to interpret this apparent conflict in other ways. One is to view the music as a tool to draw in listeners, to expose them to the message of the words. Another is to understand the music as a means of removing the sting of the conditions described in the lyrics: lose yourself in the music, to avoid simply losing it.

♪ **KEY FEATURES**

**"Thank You (Falettinme Be Mice Elf Agin)," Sly and the Family Stone (1969)**

- Complex 16-beat rhythms: The dominant rhythms move four times as fast as the beat. This is a circa 1970 innovation in popular music.
- Percussive playing techniques: Bass, guitar, and voices cultivate percussive performing techniques.
- Stack of riffs: The song creates a dense texture by stacking several riffs: in the bass, guitars, horns, and voices. The vocal line is the most prominent but not sufficiently coherent or developed to stand alone.
- Static harmony: The song has no harmonic change. The emphasis is on rhythm and texture.
- Potent message carried on the groove: Good-time rhythms support sharp-edged social commentary.

Sly and the Family Stone became popular after the assassination of Martin Luther King and after the backlash from the civil rights movement had built up steam. Civil rights legislation removed much of the governmental support for the racial inequities in American life. It did not eliminate prejudice or racial hatred, as many had hoped it would. Nor have they disappeared in the decades that followed, here and elsewhere. The lyrics of this and other songs by Sly and the Family Stone speak to that.

We find this same combination of strong rhythm and sharp words in Jamaican reggae, seventies funk, calypso from Trinidad, and, from the late seventies on, rap. Increasingly, the musical mood has become darker: rap, for example, often strips away the bright sounds from the horns, guitars, and keyboards. In these styles, there is a hardness to the sound; the fun is over.

The music provided one way to escape the pain of prejudice. Drugs were another. Sly Stone used them to excess and torpedoed his career in the process. He became increasingly unreliable, often not showing up for engagements; promoters stopped booking his band. Once again, drugs had silenced a truly innovative voice.

## The Bass as a Percussion Instrument

Afro-centric musicians—in the United States and elsewhere—have had a long-standing love affair with percussive sounds. As they assimilate an instrument into their culture, they explore ways to make it sound more percussively. Nowhere is this more persistently evident than in the bass instruments of popular music. The first bass instrument in the modern era was the tuba, or brass bass. Although tuba players can sustain long notes, just as trumpeters and other brass players can, the standard tuba part in a dance orchestra was a short note on every beat, in alternation with the backbeat from the banjo. The introduction of four-beat rhythms spelled the end of the tuba as a viable bass instrument: they couldn't "walk" because they had to breathe. As a result, the string bass replaced the brass bass—a sacrifice of power for speed.

In symphony orchestras, bassists usually play their instrument with a bow. Plucking the string with a finger (called *pizzicato*) is a special effect. Plucking the string produces a percussive sound: a sharp attack, followed by a quick decay. This contrasts sharply with the most widely used bowed style, in which notes are sustained and connected smoothly. In jazz and dance orchestras, bass players routinely pluck their instruments; bowing is the special effect. In classical music, the bass instrument typically supplies the foundation note for a harmony. So it is in popular music. But the bass instrument also supplied the rhythmic foundation: it was the percussive sound of the plucked bass that typically provided the rhythmic anchor by clearly marking the beat, even as it outlined the harmony.

The first electric bass players developed a way of plucking the strings that was similar to that used by string bass players. Because of powerful amplification, they didn't have to work nearly as hard as their acoustic counterparts to produce a big sound. James Jamerson and other leading rock bass players liberated the bass from its traditional roles—at least to some extent. The next major step forward in playing style came from Larry Graham (b. 1946), the bass player with Sly and the Family Stone and later the leader of Graham Central Station.

**Larry Graham** Graham created new sounds from the bass by slapping the strings with the side of his thumb or popping the string by pulling it away from the fretboard and suddenly releasing it. Popping, slapping, and other similar techniques made the bass sound even more percussive, as we hear in the opening riff of "Thank You

(Falettinme Be Mice Elf Agin)." Others who followed him—most notably Bootsy Collins, a bassist for James Brown, then George Clinton's Parliament and Funkadelic bands—extended this technique, to the point that the percussive dimension of the sound may overshadow the pitch.

This "**percussionization**" of the bass was part of a general trend toward more percussive sounds in the late sixties and early seventies. Another expression of this trend was the **choked guitar sound**—where a guitarist depresses the strings only part of the way—heard early on in Jimi Hendrix's "Voodoo Child" and persistently in the music for *Shaft* and other early seventies blaxploitation films, and later in disco. A third came from new keyboard instruments, like the clavinet heard on so many Stevie Wonder recordings. In turn, this trend toward more percussive sounds is one aspect of the growing emphasis on rhythm over melody as the century progressed. It would reach its logical end in rap.

## Bridging Soul and Funk

The longest-running evolutionary thread of the rock era is black music with a strong beat. It began in the jump bands of the late 1940s, before rhythm and blues had become rock and roll. By the mid-sixties, it had acquired a new name and a new beat. It had become soul music. The complex and compelling rock rhythms heard in the music of up-tempo soul songs from Memphis and, more influentially, in the music of James Brown had replaced the strong shuffle beat of the 1950s. During the seventies, it would continue to evolve, acquiring even more complex rhythm and gaining a new name: **funk**. The most constant elements in this evolution have been the use of a band made up of horns and rhythm, a rough-edged vocal style, and above all an emphasis on rhythm and riffs.

Sly and the Family Stone played the key role in the transition from soul to funk. By incorporating the more active 16-beat rhythms over a rock beat, they supplied the inevitable next step in the rhythmic evolution of rock rhythm. This rhythmic conception was an innovation in the late sixties; Sly and the Family Stone were among the first to make use of it. It would become far more common in the music of the seventies, not only in funk, but also in disco and a wide range of black music. And it has been the most popular rhythmic foundation in rock-era music since the eighties, most notably in rap but also in a wide range of music, black and white. Sly and the Family Stone increased the density of the musical texture, and they emphasized rhythm and texture over melody and harmony. They stressed more percussive sounds, not only in the rhythm instruments but also in the vocal style.

The influence of the band's style was not limited to funk. Its impact is evident in other music of the seventies and beyond—directly in styles like the art/funk jazz fusion of Herbie Hancock and the film music of Curtis Mayfield and indirectly in styles like disco and the post-disco pop of the eighties.

## Diversity, a Rock-Era Innovation

Our sample of six songs—all from the late sixties and early seventies and all from bands active in the San Francisco Bay Area—highlights an important dimension of the rock revolution: its extraordinary musical diversification. The songs include Jefferson

Airplane's heady, flamenco-tinged evocation of the acid experience; Janis Joplin's blues-drenched rock ballad; CCR's mainline rock-and-roll anthem; the Grateful Dead's cautionary tale, with its eclectic mix of diverse influences; Santana's synthesis of Afro-Cuban music and rock; and Sly and the Family Stone's good-time/dark-message proto-funk. This is only a small fraction of the music produced in this time and place; it is representative only of the fact that rock suddenly became much more diverse.

One remarkable aspect of this diversity is that it happened suddenly; the late sixties saw a veritable stylistic explosion. As late as 1964, even an astute observer of rock music would have needed superior foresight to predict the many directions that rock-era music took in the latter part of the decade. The differences among songs and styles touch every aspect of the music—what songs are trying to communicate and how they communicate their message in words and music.

Another remarkable aspect of this stylistic explosion is that it happened during the same time period that rock-era musicians reached a common understanding about the essential features of this new music. Rock reached maturity during the latter part of the sixties, consolidating its core musical values even as it stretched its boundaries and assumed the dominant position in the music industry. It was as if centrifugal and centripetal forces were applied to the music simultaneously. Especially when compared to the music of the late twenties and early thirties—the last period of stylistic consolidation—rock and black music are far more varied, as even our small sample evidences.

That rock music enormously expanded its stylistic boundaries during a period of consolidation clearly signals a fundamental shift in cultural attitudes and values. The openness of rock musicians to music and ideas of all kinds and their eagerness to blend them with impunity flew in the face of old notions of good and bad, and high and low class. Rock challenged the pecking order of the music world and the assumptions behind it. Before 1965, the music industry in the western world had clearly drawn class boundaries. Classical music represented the aristocracy. Musical theater was the highest form of popular music; jazz was moving up in status, although its dominant venue was still a night club rather than a concert hall or festival stage. *Legit*, a term used by popular and jazz musicians to refer to their classical counterparts—such as, he's a legit (short for "legitimate") trumpet player—underscores the assumption of second-class status of popular music within the larger musical world.

With rock, this changed. Rock embraced classical music and the idea of music as art even as it challenged the notion of the inherent superiority of the established classical tradition, as we discover in Chapter 11. By widening the domain of art and redefining it to some extent on its own terms, rock helped set in motion a thorough re-evaluation of culture and class. More specifically, it cast into doubt the privileged status of Euro-centric culture.

It is stretching the point to say that rock was the cause of multiculturalism; there were enormous changes taking place in virtually every domain—from the work of intellectuals like the Algerian-born literary critic Jacques Derrida (a seminal figure in deconstruction and postmodern thought) and Vatican II, which helped modernize the Catholic Church, to the numerous minority rights movements in the United States. However, it can be argued that rock-era music was the most visible and audible sign of this huge cultural shift and that the kind of diversity—in intent, words, and music—apparent even in this small sample is not only a sign of this shift but also an agent of change.

## Terms to Remember

| | | |
|---|---|---|
| counterculture | roots music | 16-beat rhythm |
| LSD, acid | bent note | *pizzicato* |
| hippies | Deadheads | percussionization |
| acid rock, psychedelic rock | American sound | choked guitar sound |
| crescendo | Latin rock | funk |
| jug band | | |

## Applying Chapter Concepts

1. Confirm or challenge our assertion that acid rock represents a shared experience rather than a musical style with identifiable features by comparing five acid or psychedelic rock songs by different acts. Use consistent parameters in your comparison, including instrumentation, vocal style, tempo, rhythmic foundation, melodic approach, form, and overall length.

2. Explore the idea that an American rock sound in the sixties and early seventies is a fusion of rock, blues, and country either by listening to the music of the Band or the Allman Brothers Band.

Playlists for both Applying Chapter Concepts suggestions are available on the text website: *academic.cengage.com/music/campbell*.

# 11

# Rock as Art

In 1962, *art rock* was an oxymoron. A decade later, art rock was an established rock substyle. As late as the early sixties, it was hard for many to imagine rock-era music as anything more than mindless, if occasionally clever, music for teens. That changed almost overnight in the music of Dylan and the Beatles, as we discussed in Chapter 7. By 1970, art rock and numerous other art-oriented styles were part of a new sound world, all of which contributed to a new understanding of art in music, and in culture.

## Rock and Art

In its broadest meaning, *art* is the product of any human activity done skillfully and creatively. One can artfully manufacture an automobile, bake a soufflé, sew a quilt, or dunk a basketball. However, the artistic aspect of all of these activities is secondary to their function. A Ferrari may be beautiful to look at, but if it won't start, it is only an oversized ornament; a between-the-legs 360-degree dunk may garner style points, but in a game it is as unproductive as an air ball if it clanks off the rim.

## Classical Music: Music as Art

We also use *art* more restrictively to refer to a product of a skilled and creative activity whose main purpose is to stimulate the mind, touch the heart, and delight the senses. This more specific connotation of art is most familiar in the visual arts, for example, the paintings of Rembrandt and the sculptures of Rodin. However, this meaning of *art* has also been used to describe music such as the symphonies of Beethoven and Brahms.

The most established **art music** is what we now call **classical music**. The idea of a "classical" music—that is, the re-creation in performance of the best music of earlier generations—took hold in the middle of the nineteenth century, after the death of Beethoven in 1827 and with the revival of the music of Bach around the same time. Prior to that, the musical world was closer to our own: concerts and opera performances typically featured a composer's most recent works, just as tours by rock bands tend to promote their current recordings. However, by the beginning of the rock era, not much more than a century later, classical music seemed timeless, almost as if it been ordained from the beginning of civilization.

Classical music was, and is, an elite music, not only because of its inherent quality and its purpose—simply to be appreciated and enjoyed as an esthetic experience—but also because of its support system. Through the eighteenth century, the musicians who created the music that we now call classical were able to practice their art because of the patronage of church and court: for most of his career, the Austrian composer Joseph Haydn was in the service of the Esterhazy family, perhaps the richest rulers in Europe during the latter part of the eighteenth century. As church patronage declined in the nineteenth century, other sources of patronage emerged. The wealthy joined the aristocracy in support of the arts. To cite just one example, New York's Carnegie Hall, the most famous North American venue for classical music, was built by the industrialist Andrew Carnegie. During the same time, the marketplace became another source of income for classical musicians, mainly through concert performances and music publishing.

Commerce altered the dynamic between musicians and their audience. With patronage, the relationship was specific: please the patron or look for work elsewhere. With a more diffused and impersonal audience, musicians often had to make a choice between following their muse—that is, creating the music that they felt impelled to create—or composing and performing music designed to attract a larger and more lucrative audience. Suffering for one's art—starving to compose for the ages rather than selling out to put food on the table—is a nineteenth-century idea, a product of this new environment. It too reinforced the idea of classical music as an elite music.

The prestige of classical music continued to grow during the first part of the twentieth century. Conservatories were founded to train classical musicians. Universities trained audiences through courses in music appreciation. So did the media: Leonard Bernstein's Young People's Concerts, in which Bernstein alternately talked about music and conducted the New York Philharmonic, ran for fifteen seasons, beginning in 1958. Universities also became patrons of a sort. Many important twentieth-century composers held teaching positions at universities; indeed, all major universities with serious graduate music programs offer advanced degrees in classical composition, although it has been virtually impossible for a classical composer to make a living wage strictly from the performance and sale of his or her music since World War II.

At the dawn of the rock era, classical music—the substantial and well-documented legacy of works created by generations of European composers, and the institutions that supported it—effectively defined what good music was. Classical music was "highbrow"; classical musicians were "legitimate." Those that did not "appreciate" it were regarded as unsophisticated by the self-proclaimed and well-entrenched cultural elite, in this country and even more in the British Commonwealth. Classical music and the world that had grown up around it was the clearest and most widely accepted measure of art in music.

## Rock as an Art Music

For rock musicians and others who sought artistic status for their work, the existence of an established musical elite created several issues, all related to the notion of quality.

The main issue was not whether the music of Bach, Beethoven, and Brahms was "good." It was—and is. This music has become "classic" as well as "classical" because it has qualities that have touched generations of performers and listeners. Rather, the issue was whether music that was not part of this legacy was somehow inferior and—more important—whether the standards by which commentators evaluated classical music were applicable to other kinds of music. For example, if a musical work was too short, did not use certain forms, or did not develop melodies in certain ways, was it somehow inferior? Complicating the issue was the fact that "good music"—that is, the classics—had accumulated the trappings of high culture: concerts took place in magnificent auditoriums and theaters; musicians dressed in formal wear; well-dressed audiences sat politely through a performance, then applauded enthusiastically at the end. The issue here was whether this concert decorum was the only "right" way to respond to music.

Rock both co-opted and challenged the prevailing view of musical art, often simultaneously. The Who's *Tommy* is identified as a rock opera: opera is among the most elaborate and prestigious classical genres. But *Tommy* is unlike any previous opera—in story, music, and staging. On the liner notes to *Freak Out*, his debut album, Frank Zappa offers a long list of influences. The list includes several important classical composers from the early part of the twentieth century as well as a few from the mid-century avant-garde; they comprise a small fraction of the names on the list, which also includes familiar and obscure jazz, pop, blues, and rock musicians, as well as music industry people and others not directly involved in music. By combining his diverse influences non-categorically in a single long list, Zappa effectively blows away boundaries between musical traditions, as well as the class boundaries that accompany them.

## The Classics and Popular Music Before Rock

The practice in popular music of assuming the musical features and trappings of classical music emerged around the turn of the twentieth century, at about the same time that black music began to have a commercial presence. Scott Joplin and his publisher billed his rags as "classic"; in 1910, Joplin completed *Treemonisha*, an opera for which he received the Pulitzer Prize almost sixty years after his death. Irving Berlin's "That Mesmerizing Mendelssohn Tune" (1909) is a famous early example of a popular song based on a classical melody—in this case, Felix Mendelssohn's "Spring Song."

Both Joplin's opera and Berlin's tune evidence early instances of what would become a recurrent trend in popular music: an attempt to legitimize itself through an association with classical music. The two examples also illustrate the two basic strategies: transforming classical works into popular music (as Berlin did) or composing music using classical music as a model (as Joplin did). The most famous instance of this practice from the first part of the twentieth century is George Gershwin's *Rhapsody in Blue*; there are many others, including Gershwin's "folk opera" *Porgy and Bess*.

There are two main reasons that this has occurred—one social and cultural, the other musical. An association with classical music made musical social climbing possible. Its use, or at least its obvious influence, narrows or eliminates numerous gaps—racial (white/black), generational (old/young), cultural (traditional/novel), economic (rich/poor), class (highbrow/lowbrow)—that separate the new style from established ones. The musical reason is more mundane, yet more compelling. Good musicians are creative. They are eager to explore possibilities or to reinterpret the past in terms of a vibrant new present. To cite only the most spectacular example, Gershwin's music represents an unmatched synthesis of classical and contemporary vernacular music.

As popular genres matured, more musically sophisticated styles and trends emerged. Both jazz and the Broadway musical had attained a kind of art music status by the late fifties: the orchestral albums of Miles Davis; third-stream music, which attempted to fuse jazz and classical music; and Leonard Bernstein's musical *West Side Story* are illustrative. This had the effect of blurring the musical and social boundary between classical and popular.

Classical music was also under siege from above: the most innovative practitioners were severely stretching its expressive boundaries during the years after World War II. Such developments as the chance music of John Cage, *musique concrète*, and the minimalist music of La Monte Young challenged the very definition of music. For many in the avant-garde, the function of art was simply to make a significant statement about something. It didn't necessarily require the conventions or materials of high art (such as a symphony orchestra). Instead, artists took a pragmatic approach to the means. In the case of Cage, for example, it could be no more than sitting quietly at a piano for 4 minutes 33 seconds. Several of Zappa's acknowledged influences came from this avant-garde.

Rock came of age in this turbulent artistic environment. As we noted in the discussion of Dylan and the Beatles, rock bought into the idea that art had more to do with *what* you said than with the *means* you used to say it, particularly in the wake of Dylan's electric music. There were no inherently privileged methods. In fact, one of rock's self-imposed challenges was to create new ways to make a statement. We will encounter this in the music of the Doors and the Velvet Underground.

Other artlike trends emerged in the late sixties and early seventies. One was art as spectacle—what was called glam rock. We experience this through the music of David Bowie. Glam rock also had classical precedents—especially the lavish operas of the Baroque era—if not direct classical models or sources.

Classical/rock fusions were another important direction. These were realized in diverse ways by progressive rock groups such as Emerson, Lake & Palmer, Pink Floyd, and Yes, and heavy metal bands such as Deep Purple. We sample all of these trends following.

## Rock's Dark Side

While the Beatles were singing "All You Need Is Love," other rock groups were exploring the dark side of the rock revolution. Two stand out: the Doors and the Velvet Underground. Each sought out different territory. The Doors visited (in their words) "the other side": nightmarish conflations of sex and death. The Velvet Underground's Lou Reed portrayed the underbelly of life in New York in his lyrics. For both groups, the words, and the way they were sung, were of primary importance. However, they were markedly different in the vocal and instrumental setting of the words.

## The Doors: Rock, Sex, and Death

The Doors came together in 1965 through a meeting of two UCLA film students. After Jim Morrison (1943–1971) read one of his poems to keyboardist Ray Manzarek (b. 1939), they decided to form a band. They soon added drummer John Densmore (b. 1944) and guitarist Robby Krieger (b. 1946). Morrison named the group the Doors after Aldous Huxley's book, *The Doors of Perception*, a reference that was probably lost on much of their audience.

The Doors had a meteoric rise and a slow, painful fall. Their first album, *The Doors*, hit the charts in 1967, reaching number 2 and establishing the group's reputation almost overnight. Less than five years later, it was over. Morrison, who had taken a leave of absence from the group and moved to Paris, was found dead in a bathtub in December 1971. Without Morrison, the group floundered, eventually disbanding two years later.

The band created a distinctive sound world, by late-sixties standards. The dominant sound is Manzarek's organ, for two reasons. First, his melodic parts are most often the most prominent instrumental strand of the texture; Krieger's guitar is mainly in the background, except during his solos. Second, Manzarek is also playing the bass line—at least on their first album. Because the organ effectively replaces both the lead guitar and the electric bass, the sound does not have the fullness that one might expect from a more conventional sixties rock band. Manzarek's playing is certainly skillful, but it is no match for the flamboyance of guitarists like Jimi Hendrix or Pete Townshend, even in his extended solos. Similarly, Krieger's playing is relatively restrained by the standards of guitarists of the late sixties.

"Light My Fire," the Doors (1967)

The Doors performing in Frankfurt, Germany, September 13, 1967. From left to right: keyboardist Ray Manzarek, vocalist Jim Morrison, drummer John Densmore, and guitarist Robby Krieger.

This sets up an interesting tension between hot and cool. Morrison's words and singing are hot—that is, sexually charged. By contrast, the backgrounds crafted by Manzarek are cool. This tension is apparent in "Light My Fire," the biggest hit from their first album. The opening of the song, which features Manzarek's busy, classical-sounding organ introduction, creates an emotionally neutral backdrop for Morrison. In both the original studio version and subsequent live recordings, the instruments are subdued when Morrison is singing. Morrison's lyrics, which he sings in a throaty style, starts as a sexual come-on; the sex will be drug-enhanced ("fire"/"higher"). But in the second section of the song, Morrison rhymes "fire," which is patently sexual in this context, to "mire" and "pyre." In short order, then, Morrison manages to lump together four of the most powerful and enduring cultural taboos: illicit sex, drugs, filth, and death. For Morrison, life would too soon imitate art. Morrison's "accidental" falls into the audience, a routine feature of the Doors' stage show, would be revealed as a ploy; he would expose himself onstage, sometimes to urinate, other times simply "to see what it looked like in a spotlight"; and he died too young because of extreme substance abuse.

## ♪ KEY FEATURES

**"Light My Fire," the Doors (1967)**

- Dark side lyrics: the song juxtaposes references to sex and drugs with wallowing in filth and death by immolation. This adds an element of discomfort to what would otherwise have been an evocation of a pleasant experience for adventurous sixties youths.
- Words versus music; vocal versus instrumental: there is a decided contrast between Morrison's provocative lyrics and singing and the pseudo-classical, organ-dominated sound of the band. It is the opposition of gut and head. Another interesting contrast occurs in the album and live versions of the song: the extended and energetic instrumental solos contrast with the more subdued accompaniments.
- Pop song equals pop success: the Doors were, among other things, a successful pop act: "Light My Fire" (without the solos) was one of two number 1 singles for the group, and it was by far the group's most covered song. One reason for its appeal was the song itself: a melody made up of catchy riffs, with distinctive, slightly quirky harmony supporting it. This gave the song a life apart from its association with the Doors.

Morrison seemingly knew no limits. Apparently, there was no topic so taboo that he would avoid it, no act so outrageous that Morrison would refrain from doing it, no behavior so destructive that he would abstain from it. He poured this into the music of the Doors, in the studio and even more in live performance. Many in his audience must have viewed him with a mixture of admiration and horror. They could experience vicariously his flaunting of social norms and his self-destructive behavior, because he went where they wouldn't dare. They also may have viewed his actions as a cautionary tale, especially in light of his decline and premature death.

The recording that best exemplifies Morrison's willingness to explore theatrically the most difficult and personal issues is the psychodrama "The End," an 11-minute excursion into Oedipal conflict and its most violent resolution. With its East Indian overtones, the musical setting is even more low key than that heard on "Light My Fire." The beginning sounds like background music for an acid trip. The opening of Morrison's long, rambling discourse is histrionic—in the words, if not the music. The middle section offers an extended metaphor ("ride the snake"), abstruse images ("the blue bus is calling us"), and clichés ("the west is the best"). The juxtaposition of images and the musical drone underneath have an almost hypnotic effect. Morrison's switch to clear narrative is like waking up from a nightmare, except that the awakened state *is* the nightmare. The musical chaos of the fatal climax (about 2 minutes after Morrison the narrator announces that "I'm going to kill you") gives emotional credibility to the song's moment of truth.

Morrison's shock-provoking lyrics and his intense, often melodramatic vocal style convinced his audience that he spoke knowledgeably about the confluence of death, decadence, and sex. The emotional detachment of the rest of the band, especially Manzarek, only served to bring Morrison's words and singing into sharper relief. For popular music, songs such as "Light My Fire" and "The End" opened the door to life's underbelly.

From their first album, the Doors, and especially Morrison, were on the edge. In fact, Morrison lived out the dramas he wrote about in his songs: extreme alcohol and drug abuse, increasingly flagrant public obscenity, and finally death at 27, allegedly from a heart attack. Morrison's willingness to go to the limit—to immerse himself in a self-destructive lifestyle and publicize it in his music and behavior, to risk—even invite—spectacular failure and public humiliation (rock critic Lester Bangs once described Morrison as a "Bozo Dionysius")—put him in a category by himself. It made almost everyone else seem tepid by comparison. Morrison embodied contradictions: a curiosity about and commitment to big themes and deep thoughts, such as Jungian psychology and Native American shamanism, and a seeming failure to act upon these ideas honorably. He remains one of the most provocative figures of the rock era.

## The Velvet Underground: Rock and Drugs

The Velvet Underground invites comparison with the Doors. Both took a long walk on the wild side. But the Doors were based in southern California, while the Velvet Underground were part of the New York scene. The Doors were popular; the Velvet Underground was known only to a few. The Doors, and especially Morrison, who fancied himself a major literary figure, aspired to high art. The Velvet Underground started with the support of the high priest of pop art, Andy Warhol, who created the famous peel-able banana cover of their first album. Warhol's backing gave them instant "art" status.

Lou Reed (b. 1942) brought his literary sensibility to the group, as well as his low-key vocal delivery and guitar playing. John Cale (b. 1940), a classically trained violist

Jeff Albertson/Corbis

The Velvet Underground in 1969. Left to right: Doug Yule (who replaced John Cale), Sterling Morrison, Maureen Tucker, and Lou Reed.

"I'm Waiting for the Man," the Velvet Underground (1967)

and composer who had worked with experimental minimalist La Monte Young in the early sixties, was the main architect of its original sound. Guitarist Sterling Morrison (1942–1995) and drummer Maureen "Moe" Tucker (b. 1944) rounded out the rhythm section.

Warhol produced their early records. To promote the group, he set up the "Exploding Plastic Inevitable"—a potent mixture of film, dance, and musical performance. Nico, a blond European-born actress who was part of Warhol's circle at the time, sang with the band for their tour and first album, *The Velvet Underground and Nico* (1967). Given her limited vocal ability, her function within the band would seem to have been visual ornament. In fact, the combination of her icy beauty and lispy, labored singing may have been a Warhol-esque artistic statement: a poor man's Marilyn Monroe for the rock era.

The Velvet Underground owed an obvious debt to Dylan. Both the primacy of words and Reed's flat, largely uninflected delivery recall Dylan. So does the mood-setting accompaniment, which harks back to Dylan's early electric days (just two years previously). However, it's clear that Reed and the Velvet Underground have found their own voice. Reed's lyrics are usually incisive where Dylan's are often elliptical. For example, in "I'm Waiting for the Man," a track on their 1967 album *The Velvet Underground and Nico*, Reed needs only a few short phrases to portray a white guy so strung out that he ventures into Harlem to get his next fix. Each phrase comes to life, as if it were a scene from a film. Where Jim Morrison used a club, Reed used a needle to get his point across.

Reed can afford to be low key because the instrumental accompaniment plays such a powerful role in establishing and sustaining the character of the song. The four instrumental parts—the endlessly repeated guitar riff, the repeated bass notes, hammered drums, and the piano chords—are virtually faceless; they have little inherent musical interest. The piano part is the most distinctive, but that is relative; with the other three parts there is almost no change throughout the song. The minimal musical interest—for instance, no signature guitar riff in the forefront, no complex rhythmic interplay between bass and drums—renders the instrumental background faceless; it is a kind of aural scenery.

For Cale and the rest of the band, the use of rock rhythm—here distilled to its essence—is purposeful, not simply the default option for a late sixties song. The propulsive **proto-punk beat**, a jangly conjunction of sound and rhythm driven by Cale's two-fisted piano playing, surrounds Reed's voice with the nervous energy of the dope-deprived addict. Its very simplicity and almost perverse insistence seems to convey in music the obsessive need of the man waiting for the man.

♪ **KEY FEATURES**

**"I'm Waiting for the Man," the Velvet Underground (1967)**

■ Lou Reed's flat delivery: Reed's vocal line straddles the boundary between highly inflected speech and singing. In his vocal line, rhythm is usually distinct, but pitch is not. The absence of a tune helps draw attention to the words.

■ Proto-punk rhythm: the instrumental parts distill rock rhythm to its essence: the eight-beat rhythmic layer. Everyone except the guitarist reinforces this layer with repeated notes, thumps, or chords. There is no syncopation, except in the moving line in the piano part, a relatively subtle touch. The relentless repetition of the rhythm at a loud volume anticipates punk by more than a half decade.

■ Musical minimalism: the relative lack of musical interest and the repetitive nature of rhythm and melody helps direct attention to Reed's lyric, the main focus of the song.

Even more spectacular is "Heroin," where Cale's viola part mutates from a drone into an inspired frenzy to depict the drug coursing through the bloodstream of its user. In its own way, "Heroin" is just as powerful in its evocation of the drug experience as "The End" is in its evocation of the violent resolution of the Oedipal conflict. Both songs use similar techniques—changing tempos, piling on textural layers—to depict a moment of terror, or, in the case of "Heroin," a moment of terrible ecstasy.

The Velvet Underground's tenure was even shorter than that of the Doors. Cale left after the second album, and the group dissolved soon after. Reed has enjoyed intermittent success as a solo artist and has built a cult following. So did the Velvet Underground, although most of the cult joined after the group's demise. Despite their modest commercial success, the group was a major influence on punk.

# Rock as Serious Satire: Frank Zappa and the Mothers of Invention

We tend to think of art as serious. We sit quietly and respectfully during concerts of classical music; we talk in hushed tones as we stroll through a museum. Our demeanor in these environments suggests that we don't expect art to be humorous. The next guffaw you hear during the performance of Beethoven's *Eighth Symphony* will probably be the first, although it is arguably a cosmically humorous composition. The same is almost certainly true of Debussy's piano prelude "The Interrupted Serenade," which depicts in music an ardent lover's comical misfortunes as he tries to serenade a señorita.

*Serious* can mean solemn; it can also mean important. *Serious music*, like *art music*, has been suggested as an alternative label to *classical music*, as the boundaries of traditional classical music stretch past the breaking point. It can also mean committed: when we say someone is "serious" about playing guitar, or bass, we mean that he or she is willing to work hard to develop mastery of the instrument.

During the heady sixties, the group that took humor most seriously was Frank Zappa and the Mothers of Invention. Their music was seldom solemn and then often mockingly so. However, in terms of importance and commitment, they were certainly dead serious. Zappa and his core group were far more serious about their humor than the album covers would suggest. They remain one of the most innovative and skilled bands of the rock era. Indeed, to identify them as a rock band is too limiting: they were an ensemble capable of shifting styles on the fly; rock and rock-related music was just part of their realm of expertise.

We get some insight into the nature of their humor and their sense of identity from their name. It is a double pun: necessity may have been the mother of invention, but "mother" was also street slang for a highly skilled performer—*and* something else.

Frank Zappa (1940–1993) was rock's great iconoclast. He was an equal opportunity satirist, taking potshots at almost everyone in and out of rock, including himself. At the same time, he was one of rock's cleverest and most knowledgeable minds and one of its great innovators. In addition to using rock as a vehicle for satire, he also pioneered multimedia extravaganzas, which he called "**freak outs**," concept-type albums (McCartney claimed that *Freak Out* [1966] influenced the Beatles' *Sgt. Pepper*), and wholesale eclecticism.

Zappa collected musical influences from everywhere. Among the most important was the French/American avant-garde composer Edgard Varèse. In a Zappa record, one might hear Varèse-influenced music juxtaposed with a fifties rock-and-roll parody. Such jarring contrasts were one of his innovations. He was also one of the pioneers of **jazz/rock fusion**, working with violinist Jean-Luc Ponty.

As with the Doors and the Velvet Underground, words are the main focus—when they are present. You have to listen to Zappa's lyrics; often the music seems to be strictly at the service of the words. Nevertheless, his compositions are in many ways the most sophisticated music of the rock era. They demand great technical proficiency and stylistic flexibility from the musicians who play them. Not surprisingly, his bands included some of the most accomplished and versatile musicians of the era.

Although his first album, *Freak Out*, immediately established him as a unique voice, it is his third album, *We're Only in It for the Money* (1967), that best represents his

*We're Only in It for the Money* excerpts, Frank Zappa and the Mothers of Invention (1967)

early work, in the judgment of many commentators. Zappa's tool was a sharp pin, which he used to pop lots of balloons. Deflation begins with the album cover, a send-up of the cover of the Beatles' *Sgt. Pepper*. On it, the group is wearing dresses, and the wax figures have become mannequins: one is "giving birth" to a baby doll. Their gallery includes Jimi Hendrix, Lyndon Johnson, and assorted cultural icons, many of whose eyes are covered with black rectangles, perhaps to suggest a kind of self-imposed censorship.

We are aware from the outset that *We're Only in It for the Money* is not a conventional album: not just a collection of songs. Although of course there are songs, there are also numerous spoken sections, accompanied by electronic noises (track 1), conventional instruments ("Who Needs the Peace Corps"), or no instruments at all ("Telephone Conversation"). In addition, there are extended instrumental sections.

There is a dazzling virtuosity in the variety. To cite just two examples: the instrumental opening of "The Chrome

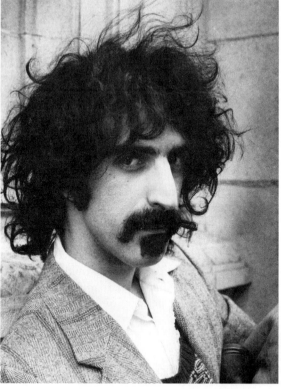

Frank Zappa in 1971, in a candid camera moment.

Plated Megaphone of Destiny" sounds more appropriate for an innovative classical music album than a rock disc, while the opening of "Who Needs the Peace Corps" sounds like a children's song. Zappa's lyrics can be devastating as well as devastatingly funny. The spoken section of "Who Needs the Peace Corps" parodies a definitely uncool guy mapping out his hippie lifestyle in San Francisco.

The biggest zinger, though, is probably "What's the Ugliest Part of Your Body?" The song begins with "Earth Angel"–style background vocals. Their pseudo-innocence only enhances the impact of the punch line. The next few minutes show Zappa's strategy: musical and verbal collage with jarring verbal and musical juxtapositions. He follows the revelation that your mind is the ugliest part of your body with some pompous sermonizing, accompanied by music in an irregular rhythmic pattern (2 + 2 + 3 quick beats, in place of the 2 + 2 + 2 + 2 pattern of rock). A question about "Annie" (who is she and what is she doing in this song, anyway?), accompanied by a slithering melody in waltz rhythm, interrupts the sermon. A piano solo that reaches back to Aaron Copland and ahead to new age music links the sermon with the next song, which begins with a snotty-toned definition of *discorporate*, but not before a woman mutters a snide aside about the limitations of her sexual activity.

It is a dizzying pace, because of the abrupt shifts between segments—the Mothers never miss a beat—and because of the extreme contrast between styles. If it were possible to get whiplash just listening to music, Zappa would be the one to cause it.

Zappa's lyrics were also often intentionally juvenile and scatological, as if to deflate his own high-art intentions. His often silly titles—such as "Peaches en Regalia"—for very sophisticated music was another self-deflating strategy. Many critics missed the seriousness of the music and only focused on the often puerile lyrics—which for Zappa must have been part of the joke. It was if you had to pass through a series of tests to prove yourself a true Zappa fan and listener.

All of this renders Zappa's music, considered as a whole, less accessible than *Sgt. Pepper*. There are certainly straightforward moments: the parody songs and monologues stand out (perhaps this is why Zappa scored his only major hit with the silly parody song "Valley Girl," hardly his most innovative work). But this is not warm and fuzzy music or music that you can groove to. As his album cover makes clear, Zappa demands a commitment from his listeners.

That gives the title of the album a certain irony: it's quite clear that money is not a major motivation for Zappa. He and the Mothers were certainly skilled enough to have created music that would have kept them firmly entrenched in the Top 40 charts. But that would have required some selling out and the sacrifice of his unique vision. Zappa did neither during his lifetime. He took it upon himself to become rock's fiercest social critic as well as one of its most imaginative musicians and its greatest humorist; no one else was even close.

## Rock Opera: The Who

No group of the 1960s merged rock's essence with rock as art more effectively than the Who. Like so many of the important British groups of the sixties, the Who began as a blues-oriented band; their early stage shows mixed original songs with R&B covers, including Motown songs and even an early James Brown hit—Brown was Daltrey's idol. Moon's manic drumming, Entwistle's inventive, soul-inspired bass lines, Townshend's windmilled power chords, and Daltrey's gritty vocals set the group apart from other British bands. So did the absence of a rhythm guitarist; they were among the first power trios, although Townshend was not a virtuosic guitarist. The group quickly gained an enthusiastic following, especially among Mods, a British youth subculture drawn to trendy clothes, motor scooters, and soul—or at least soulful—music.

However, Townshend, the most intellectually adventurous member of the band, had been interested in expanding the Who's musical horizons. The group followed *Happy Jack* (released in the UK in late 1966 as *A Quick One*) with *The Who Sell Out* (1967), a concept album built around the idea of a radio broadcast, interspersed between a diverse group of songs are simulated commercials and public service announcements. The album cover features each band member grotesquely promoting a fake product.

Townshend's next big project would take the group in a dramatically different direction. The genesis of *Tommy* was a casual remark by Kit Lambert, the Who's producer and manager, when he suggested almost off-handedly that Townshend compose a rock opera, he took the idea and ran with it.

Tommy
excerpts, the
Who (1969)

Opera is the most spectacular and prestigious of classical music genres. Labeling *Tommy* a "rock opera" immediately implied its highbrow status, even if the label was misleading. As Richard Barnes points out, "Strictly speaking, [*Tommy*] isn't a rock opera at all. It has no staging, scenery, acting, or recitative." It doesn't have much of a plot, either, and what there is, is difficult to follow. Still, the story—of a deaf, mute, and blind child who becomes a messiah via pinball wizardry—unfolds in the songs, by fits and starts.

The songs don't pull any punches. The list of subjects addressed in *Tommy* includes (again, according to Barnes) "murder, trauma, bullying, child molestation, sex, drugs, illusion, delusion, altered consciousness, spiritual awakening, religion, charlatanism, success, superstardom, death, betrayal, rejection, and pinball." Not typical fare, even for the late sixties, but certainly a logical expansion of the Who's efforts in their previous albums.

Musically, what's remarkable about *Tommy* is not so much the fact that the Who make an artistic statement but *how* they make it. Unlike the Beatles and so many of those who followed in their footsteps, the Who didn't abandon their rock roots, or at least overlay them with classical music trappings. There are no strings, no synthesizers, and no other classical music features associated with so much of the art rock of the period.

Instead, the band remains pretty much self-contained. Rather than adding an orchestra's worth of instruments, they vary the sounds within the group. The most obvious non-rock sounds are Moon's tympani, Entwhistle's French horn, and Townshend's various keyboard sounds. As he shifts from character to character, Daltrey displays extraordinary vocal flexibility, from the soul-drenched grittiness of "Smash the Mirror" to the tenderness of "See Me, Feel Me." Townshend and the rest of the band play classic hard rock in songs like "Sparks," yet the instrumental "Overture" and "Underture" contain steely acoustic guitar playing—alternately gritty and sensitive, and always imaginative.

The other feature that immediately sets *Tommy* apart from standard rock fare is the pacing of the work. The tracks are as long as they need to be—no more, no less. There is no allegiance to the 3-minute song, in either direction. The shortest "song" is "Miracle Cure"; it is 12 seconds long. And it is one of seven tracks well under 2 minutes. The longest track is the magnificent "Underture" (10 minutes 9 seconds), which divides the work in half—like the first and second acts of an opera. The irregular rhythm of the tracks is clear evidence that Townshend is responsive to the dramatic demands of his subject rather than the conventions of popular song.

In *Tommy*, the Who have the best of both worlds—in two ways. They make an artistic statement on a grand scale (75 minutes long) without forsaking, or even downplaying, their rock roots. Moreover, they were able to perform *Tommy* live without hiring a symphony orchestra, because they stayed within the group's basic instrumentation. It was a unique achievement, for the Who, and for rock. Their subsequent operatic efforts, most notably *Quadrophenia*, did not enjoy similar success, and no other band produced anything comparable.

## Glam Rock: Rock as Spectacle

Rock has had a strong visual element since Elvis first combed his hair into a pompadour, curled his lips into a sneer, and twitched his hips. By the late sixties, the visual dimension of rock had become, in its most extreme manifestations, far more flamboyant and outrageous: flaming or smashed guitars, provocative gestures and body movements, even public urination and vomiting. This outrageousness was in part a consequence of larger venues. With arena concerts now increasingly common, performers had to appear larger than life to have visual impact. Bands began touring with elaborate sets, special effects (lighting, smoke bombs, fireworks), and outlandish costuming.

In the first part of the rock era, the most spectacular form of theatrical rock was **glam** (or **glitter**) **rock**. It emerged in the early seventies, mainly in the work of David Bowie and T Rex, a group fronted by Marc Bolan.

## Art as Artifice

As it took shape in the mid-sixties, rock prided itself on being real. It confronted difficult issues, dealt with real feelings, looked life squarely in the eye. The music of the Doors and the Velvet Underground are vivid examples of this dimension of rock. This realism provoked a reaction. The Beatles followed *A Hard Day's Night*, a documentary-style film of their life on the run, with *Sgt. Pepper*, in which they assumed personas, visually and musically. In rock, the mask became the yin to the yang of hyper-real rock.

Steve Wood/Express/Getty Images

David Bowie performing as Ziggy Stardust in 1973.

Rock as artifice—rock behind the mask—found its fullest expression in glam rock, and especially in the music of David Bowie. In Ziggy Stardust, the first of several incarnations, Bowie stripped identity down to the most basic question of all: gender. Was Ziggy male or female, or somewhere in between? With his lithe build, flamboyant costumes, and heavy makeup, Bowie as Ziggy seemed to be a hermaphrodite. Particularly because he was not well known prior to Ziggy—unlike Roger Daltrey before *Tommy*—there was no "real" Bowie to compare with his Ziggy persona. His sexual outrageousness was the mirror image of Morrison's: when Morrison exposed himself, he made explicit his gender. When Bowie pranced around onstage wearing a big feather boa, he put his gender—or at least his sexual preference—seriously in doubt. (With respect to confused sexual identity, Bowie was the rock-era counterpart to *castrati*, singers who were castrated as boys to keep their voices from changing; they sang male roles in a female vocal range in seventeenth- and early eighteenth-century opera.) Add to that a fantastical story, and—when performed live—a spectacular production: glam rock, as exemplified by Bowie, was the opposite of real.

## David Bowie

Bowie (born David Jones, 1947) began his career in the sixties as a British folksinger. Influenced by Iggy Pop, Marc Bolan, and the Velvet Underground, he began to reinvent his public persona. In 1972, he announced that he was gay. (However, he commented in an interview over a decade later that he "was always a closet heterosexual.") Later that year, he put together an album and a stage show, *The Rise and Fall of Ziggy Stardust and the Spiders from Mars.* It featured Bowie, complete with orange hair, makeup, and futuristic costumes, as Ziggy, a rock star trying to save the world but doomed to fail.

Ziggy was Bowie's first and most outrageous persona. For the rest of his career, he has continually reinvented himself in a variety of guises, all markedly different from the others: for example, "plastic soul" man, techno-pop avant-gardist. Bowie has been rock's ultimate poseur. And that has been his art: assuming so many different personas—not only in appearance and manner, but also in music—that he has made a mystery of his real self. Given Bowie's constantly changing roles during the course of his career, it is small wonder that he has been the most successful film actor among post-Elvis rock stars.

Bowie has been intensely involved in all aspects of his roles, including the music. After recording at Philadelphia's Sigma Sound Studios (in the seventies, it was the home of "the Sound of Philadelphia"), he changed his stage show completely—from flair to bare—and incorporated sixties soul classics into his set. Despite his complete immersion in a role—or perhaps because of it—there is also detachment. Listening to his music and to the words of his songs, we hear both first and third person.

***Ziggy Stardust***   The songs from *Ziggy Stardust* provide the musical dimension of Bowie's role playing. Their effect is not as obvious as his appearance, but without them, his persona would be incomplete. The three components of the songs—the words, Bowie's singing, and the musical backdrop—all assume multiple roles, as we hear in "Hang on to Yourself," one of the tracks from the album.

"Hang on to Yourself," David Bowie (1972)

The lyric is laced with vivid images: "funky-thigh collector," "tigers on Vaseline," "bitter comes out better on a stolen guitar." These arrest our ear, without question. But Bowie continually shifts from person to person as he delivers them. He "reports" in the verse—"She's a tongue-twisting storm"—and entreats in the chorus—"Come on, come on, we've really got a good thing going." His voice changes dramatically from section to section. It's relatively impersonal in the verse and warm, almost whispered, in the chorus.

The music is more subtle in its role playing. Bowie embeds vocal and instrumental hooks into all his songs. The instrumental hook is the guitar riff; the vocal hook is the whispered chorus, a shock after the pile-driving verse. Both features make the song immediately accessible and memorable.

But there are also subtle clues woven into the song that seem to tell us that, for Bowie, the hooks are the dumbed-down parts of the music. With such features as the extra beats after the first line of the verse ". . . light machine" and elsewhere, Bowie seems to be hinting that he's capable of a lot more sophistication than he's showing on the surface. Indeed, the spare style of the song was one of the freshest and most influential sounds of the seventies. Like Ziggy, he is descending down to the level of

♪  **KEY FEATURES**

**"Hang on to Yourself," David Bowie (1972)**

- Proto-punk: loud, repeated power chords played on a guitar with some distortion, in a basic rock rhythm and at a fast tempo: these are salient features of punk style. These features inform the basic feel of the song throughout, although Bowie adds a number of sophisticated touches.

- Hooks: the song is loaded with instrumental (such as the whiny guitar riff) and vocal hooks ("come on"), which serve the narrative of the album/stage show (they make the band appealing) and contribute to the appeal of the album/show.

- Sophisticated features: Bowie makes clear musically that this is a song about a rock band rocking out, rather than simply a good rock song, by adding several sophisticated features that were not customarily found in straightforward rock songs of the time. These include the frequent shifts in mood, underlined by the changes in rhythmic texture (such as from verse to chorus), the occasional interruption of the typical four-beat measures through the addition of extra beats, the sporadically active bass lines, and Bowie's ever-shifting vocal sounds.

mass taste (even as he's reshaping it) because he wants the effect it creates, not because that's all he can do.

In *Ziggy Stardust*, Bowie creates a persona that demands attention but is shrouded in mystery. What makes his persona so compelling, both in person and on record, is not only its boldness but its comprehensiveness. Precisely because accessibility and ambiguity are present in every aspect of the production—the subject of the show, Bowie's appearance, the lyrics, his singing, the music—Bowie raises role playing from simple novelty to art. This quality made him one of the unique talents of the rock era.

Bowie was also one of the most influential musicians of the decade. The "lean, clean" sound of "Hang on to Yourself" was a model for punk and new wave musicians; indeed, Glen Matlock of the Sex Pistols remarked that "Hang on to Yourself" influenced "God Save the Queen."

## Rock, Art, and Technology

Rock and music technology are connected symbiotically. Technology is integral to rock in every aspect, from the first steps in the creative process to the final result on recordings or in live performance, as we have noted. More significantly, technology made possible many of the innovations of rock-era music—from a new creative paradigm made possible by multitrack recording and a host of new instrumental sounds to sound systems that filled stadiums.

Because of this dynamic relationship between rock and technology, a revolution in music-related technology occurred in tandem with, and in support of, the rock revolution. And because the new technologies helped make rock sound so different from earlier generations of popular music, it is easy to imagine that these technologies and their uses were exclusively the province of rock-related music, such as the **wah-wah pedal** popularized by Jimi Hendrix.

In addition to such rock-specific devices, rock musicians leveraged rapidly developing technology to explore and expand two sound families: real-world sounds and electronically generated sounds. Both of these sound families were used extensively in art-oriented rock. However, both emerged originally in the most esoteric music of the mid-twentieth-century—avant-garde classical music.

## The Tools of Electronic Music

The practice of incorporating sounds from any source into a musical work took hold only after the tape recorder became commercially available. While it was possible to record sounds not produced by voices or musical instruments prior to the invention of the magnetic tape recorder, everything had to be done in real time. With magnetic tape, however, it was possible to collect sounds on tape, then splice them together. The pioneer in assembling musical works from a wide array of sounds, including those not traditionally associated with music, was the French composer and writer Pierre Schaeffer. Schaeffer called the sound collages that he recorded on tape *musique concrète*, because the composer worked directly (that is, concretely) with the sounds to be heard, rather than relying on notation to convey musical ideas to performers. Schaeffer created his first *musique concrète* work in 1948. Other innovative composers followed suit; by 1967, the year in which *Sgt. Pepper* and *We're Only in It for the Money* were released, it was a well-established if not widely accepted branch of the classical avant-garde.

In rock, it entered almost imperceptibly: crowd noises, alarm clocks, phone conversations, and other "non-musical" sounds were incorporated into songs and compositions to make the atmosphere created in a particular track more vivid. Both avant-garde and rock composers took advantage of multitrack recording to mix real-world sounds with musical elements, rather than simply splice the sounds together in a predetermined sequence.

The first fully electronic instruments, most notably the **theremin** and **Ondes Martenot**, appeared just after World War I. With the theremin, the performer controlled sound by moving his or her hands; the Ondes Martenot used similar technology, but performers could control sound through a keyboard. The most popular and enduring of the pre–World War II electronic instruments was the electronic organ, most notably the Hammond B-3, mentioned in Chapter 3.  This instrument found its way into black churches, cocktail lounges, jazz clubs, basketball arenas, and rock bands, especially after 1945.

The first **synthesizers** appeared in the fifties. The most famous of these early machines was the RCA Electronic Music Synthesizer, introduced in 1955. This synthesizer was a huge machine—and cumbersome and time-consuming to program. The first commercial synthesizers appeared about a decade later; the one released by Robert Moog in 1964 was much smaller and was controlled in part by a keyboard. However, it was not suitable for live performance. The introduction of the **Minimoog**, a portable instrument with preset sounds, appeared in 1970. Rock musicians quickly embraced the Minimoog and other performance-ready synthesizers that also appeared in the early seventies; those willing to master the new instruments gained a much-expanded palette of sounds.

## Pink Floyd

*Dark Side of the Moon* excerpts, Pink Floyd (1973)

Among the most familiar examples to mix real-world and synthesized sounds with more conventional rock was Pink Floyd's 1973 album *Dark Side of the Moon*. At the time of this recording, Pink Floyd consisted of guitarist David Gilmour (b. 1946), percussionist Nick Mason (b. 1944), keyboardist Richard Wright (b. 1943), and bassist Roger Waters (b. 1943); for this album, Waters wrote all of the lyrics and co-wrote most of the songs.

One can argue that the two applications of electrical technology—sounds from the real world and those produced on a synthesizer—used by Pink Floyd in *Dark Side of the Moon* were not only absolutely integral to the intent of the album but also essential to its impact and success. Waters's lyrics paint a bleak portrait of modern life. The tracks describe the stress of living in the modern world—stress that can be so overwhelming that it drives people to insanity. Moreover, he posed for himself the additional challenge of presenting his perceptions in easily understood language. On those tracks where the band plays, the musical setting is comparably direct and anything but cutting edge. Good straight-ahead rock alternates with sensitive rock ballads. There are no histrionics, à la Morrison; no immersion in sound, à la the Velvet Underground; none of the musical complexity heard in the music of Frank Zappa—or Yes (which we encounter later in this chapter). The most obvious deviation from basic rock by the band occurs in "Money": the meter groups beats by seven (4 + 3), rather than by four.

Instead, Pink Floyd relied on the array of "found" sounds—the cash register, the spoken asides (answers given in response to a set of questions prepared by Waters)—and the electronically generated musical ideas and effects—the "running" pattern on the second track, the heartbeat that opens the album—to give weight to the album as a whole. These "concrete" and electronically generated sounds are one dimension of a coordinated plan to support Waters's lyrics with significant-sounding music. Other aspects of this are the strong contrasts from track to track; the variation in pacing, from very slow to very fast; the inventive harmonies—familiar-sounding chords in fresh progressions; the rich reverb, especially in "The Great Gig in the Sky," which features the soaring vocal line of Clare Torry; extended sections featuring instruments without vocals; and the continuous flow of the music from track to track.

Their formula worked: the album remained on the U.S. Top 200 charts for 741 weeks—over fourteen years. No album has ever charted for a longer period of time. Periodic reissues have also sold well. *Dark Side of the Moon* was the first of Pink Floyd's several top-selling albums, almost all of which continued to explore difficult issues. The most acclaimed was the 1979 album *The Wall*. Live performances of the music from the album were spectacular; they ended with the crumbling of a wall constructed at the front of the stage, between the band and the audience.

## Rock as Art and Art Rock

In the late sixties and early seventies, the most self-consciously arty branch of rock was the style known alternatively as **art rock** and **progressive rock**. Progressive rock musicians sought to elevate the status of rock by embracing a classical music esthetic and adapting it to rock. Most often, this meant applying concepts and features associated with classical music, and especially classical instrumental music, into their work: King Crimson's modernist uses of irregular meters and atonality is a notable example. Occasionally, and more specifically, it could involve wholesale borrowing of classical compositions: Procul Harum's "A Whiter Shade of Pale" mixed rock and Bach; Keith Emerson remade the Russian composer Modest Mussorgsky's *Pictures at an Exhibition*. Art rock/progressive rock became the mainly instrumental analogue to concept albums and rock operas, which were typically more vocally oriented.

## From Dance Floor to Concert Hall

In elevating rock from straightforward dance music to sophisticated music for listening, progressive rock musicians accomplished in about a decade what had taken classical music centuries to achieve. The earliest surviving examples of instrumental music are simple dances from the late thirteenth century. Until about 1600, most of the instrumental works published or preserved in manuscript were dances for the court. It wasn't until the early seventeenth century that composers regularly composed idiomatically for instruments—that is, composed in ways that took advantage of the particular capabilities of an instrument. Concertos and sonatas—instrumental compositions not used for dancing—joined dance and dance-inspired compositions as widely used genres.

Nevertheless, despite its growing complexity, instrumental music was considered inferior to vocal music: from the early seventeenth century through the end of the eighteenth century, opera was the most prestigious musical genre. Only in the early nineteenth century, in response to the symphonies and sonatas of Beethoven, did critics begin to regard instrumental music as equal to or even superior to vocal music. These works and others like them had moved far beyond dance music, although they often retained a dance connection: the third movement of a symphony was typically either a minuet or a scherzo—both dance-inspired.

Like classical instrumental music, rock began as music for social dancing. The first requirement of this kind of dance music is a good beat. As rock matured, musicians like Zappa, keyboardists Keith Emerson and Rick Wakeman, and guitarists Ritchie Blackmore (of Deep Purple) and Robert Fripp (of King Crimson) sought to elevate the level of discourse in rock by emulating certain aspects of classical instrumental music: complexity, virtuosity, rhythmic freedom, the grand gesture. This took rock out of the garage and into the concert hall, or at least to the arena. This shift in orientation from dance music to music for listening raised the esthetic bar. Rock had to have more than a good beat. It had to be inherently interesting on several levels, challenging to its audience, and rewarding to those who gave the music the attention that it demands.

Often, this is most evident in the approach to rhythm. A dance-oriented song (such as "The Twist") will typically establish and maintain a consistent, obvious, and danceable beat. By contrast, an art-oriented composition may well feature passages with a great dance beat. But it is also likely to contain rhythmic features that make it virtually unusable as dance music: for instance, tempo extremes and shifts in tempo; suspension of timekeeping; use of irregular meters (like the seven-beat measures in "Money"); active, syncopated rhythms that play off an unheard pulse.

Among the noteworthy progressive rock groups of the early seventies were Emerson, Lake & Palmer; Gentle Giant; Jethro Tull; King Crimson; and Yes. We listen to "Roundabout" by Yes as a commercially and artistically successful example of progressive rock.

Interestingly, almost all of the important progressive rock bands were British. Critic John Rockwell attributes this in part to the relatively greater prestige enjoyed by classical music in British society. In his view, rock musicians who wished to elevate their artistic status could do so by adapting classical values and procedures to rock. He feels that the impetus to do so was far stronger in the United Kingdom.

Another reason might well be the far greater importance of jazz in the United States. Jazz had already attained an artlike status by the late fifties. American musicians interested in following a similar path often turned to jazz/rock fusion. Guitarist John McLaughlin, a Scotsman who recorded with Miles Davis, straddled the two styles.

## Yes

"Roundabout,"
Yes (1972)

Singer Jon Anderson (b. 1944) and bassist Chris Squire (b. 1948) formed Yes in 1968. The band underwent two key personnel changes in 1971: keyboardist Rick Wakeman (b. 1949) replaced Tony Kaye, and guitarist Steve Howe (b. 1947) replaced Tony Banks. Drummer Bill Bruford (b. 1949) was an earlier recruit. *Fragile* and *Closer to the Edge* (both 1972), their first two albums with the new lineup, were their most successful; "Roundabout," from *Fragile*, was their most popular single of the decade.

While not mapped out on the broad scale of their later music, "Roundabout" nevertheless provides a helpful introduction to the qualities that defined progressive rock during this period. First, it's clear that the music is the most important dimension of the piece. There are extended instrumental sections throughout, and the lyric of the vocal sections is so vague and nonreferential as to be virtually meaningless. However, the words do provide milestones for listeners navigating their way through this lengthy song: "Roundabout" is only a third of the length of Yes' longer works (which often covered an entire album side); still, it is over 8 minutes long, about three times the length of the average single.

Its sprawling form, the numerous contrasts, and the flashes of virtuosity also set the song apart from more mainstream rock. "Roundabout" is a big, multisectional piece. An extended slow introduction sets it in motion; its return with an organ obbligato marks the midpoint of the piece. There are several changes of texture and key, and occasionally it shifts away from the regular four-beat measures. The most striking of these shifts occurs in the "choral" section, which has measures with seven beats. Virtuosic ensemble passages, solos, and fills occur throughout: the doubled guitar/bass duet, Wakeman's fast fills, and Squire's well-grooved bass riff under the first vocal section are good examples.

Despite these departures from common practice, "Roundabout" never loses sight of the fact that it is rock. In fact, the gentler sections help the "groove" sections stand

♪  **KEY FEATURES**

**"Roundabout," Yes (1972)**

- Instrumental orientation: vocal episodes make up only a small fraction of the total song, and the lyrics of the song seem almost an afterthought. Most of the interest lies in the musical events.

- Virtuosity: all of the musicians in Yes are fluent on their instruments. The virtuosity of Squire and Wakeman in particular is on display throughout the song. While one can be a virtuoso in almost any kind of music, the kind of virtuosity heard here—the fleet fingers of Squire and Wakeman—is most closely associated with classical music and art-oriented jazz.

- Big conception: the overall length of the song and its sprawling form; the dramatic contrasts, from the pensive opening to the hyperactive interlude; and the rich and varied textures and rhythms—these all give "Roundabout" substance; they suggest that it is a more significant effort than a garden-variety rock song.

out because the contrast is so strong. Indeed, the second melodic idea, which sets "In and around the lake," uncannily anticipates Kool & the Gang's 1981 hit "Celebration"; they even share the same key.

Progressive rock took a good deal of criticism from some quarters as being pretentious, overproduced, and symptomatic of the decline of rock in the seventies. What this song shows, however, is some very capable and inventive musicians at play, stretching rock's boundaries.

# Rock as Art Redux

As this small sample demonstrates, art-oriented rock encompassed an unusually diverse body of music: the dark-side excursions of the Doors and the Velvet Underground; the no-holds-barred/everyone's a target/extremely hip satire of Frank Zappa and the Mothers of Invention; the Who's reconception of opera; art as spectacle—David Bowie masking himself as Ziggy Stardust; Pink Floyd's mix of simplicity and significance, aided by a mix of conventional rock and cutting-edge technology; and Yes' virtuosic progressive rock. Despite their diverse conceptual and musical approaches, these musicians share attitudes and principles that provide a common ground and that distinguish their music from that of most other acts of the era. Most outstanding is a sense of importance: the music is supposed to be significant. This is conveyed in different ways.

- Tackling deep, difficult, or controversial subjects: the Doors, the Velvet Underground, Pink Floyd
- Elaborate artifice: Bowie/Ziggy; the Who/*Tommy*

- Superb musicianship: Zappa and Yes above all, but also the Who, Bowie and Spiders from Mars, and Pink Floyd
- Sophisticated satire: Zappa most obviously; the Who less directly
- Emulating, seeking inspiration from, or co-opting classical concepts, genres, and methods: the Who, Zappa, Yes, Pink Floyd
- Thinking big: concept albums by Zappa, the Who, Pink Floyd; long songs by the Doors, the Velvet Underground, and Yes
- Innovative sounds: Frank Zappa, the Who, Pink Floyd

In virtually all of this music, the divorce from popular song and dance is apparent. Of the examples considered here, only "Light My Fire" (the single version) and "Hang on to Yourself" are similar in length, form, and style to songs of the sixties and early seventies—and Bowie's song is typical because it is dramatically necessary at that point in the narrative to present a more-or-less typical rock song. The departure from late-sixties rock and roll is most apparent in rhythm and sound. Every song or album plays with time: extremes or extreme contrasts in track length (some very long; others very brief); extremes or extreme contrasts in tempo (very fast; very slow); and contrasts in beat keeping and rhythmic play (strong beat marking versus no timekeeping versus highly syncopated rhythmic textures). And while "concrete" and synthesized sounds are not a requirement for art-oriented rock, they occur far more frequently in this music than they do in the music that we will hear in the next chapter.

## The Impact of Rock as Art

The efflorescence of art-oriented rock was brief: its heyday was less than a decade. Among the reasons for its sudden decline were its own excesses, musical and otherwise; the demise of the Beatles; and the rise of a corporate mentality within rock—it seemed that the values of both musicians and audience shifted. Still, this branch of rock demonstrated that it was possible to make significant statements in rock: its impact is evident in such diverse styles as the music of U2, early alternative, new wave, and grunge.

Interestingly, art-oriented rock seems to have had a more far-reaching impact on music from outside rock. We have already noted the emergence of jazz fusion, which combined rock and jazz. The **rock musical** emerged around 1970, most notably in the works of Andrew Lloyd Webber. Both jazz and musical theater had attained a quasi-art status at the beginning of the rock era. Art rock helped them retain their elite status as they merged with rock. And it is possible to view the interaction of classical music and rock as a two-way process: two of the most significant trends in classical music since 1965 have been minimalism and eclecticism. To cite just one noteworthy example, the music of the minimalist composer Philip Glass, the most commercially successful American composer of the latter part of the twentieth century, has more in common with rock than any classical tradition. This is not to claim any direct influence, although there have been instances of that. Rather, it is simply to point out that musical ideas and features expressed in various forms of art-oriented rock were in the air, where they could enter the consciousness of contemporary "classical" composers almost by osmosis.

More generally, art-oriented rock, because it was frequently commercially and artistically important, helped blur the boundaries between high and low culture. It can be seen as an important component of the move toward a more multicultural and democratic view of value in art—and through that, a more open-minded and multicultural society.

Art-oriented rock was about stretching boundaries and saying something significant, in words and music. The music that we hear next takes the opposite approach: it reaffirms the core values of rock.

. . . . . . . . . . . . . . . . . . . . . . . . . . . . . . . . . . . . . . . . . . . . . . . . . . . . . . . . . . . . . . .

## Terms to Remember

| | | |
|---|---|---|
| art music | glam rock (glitter rock) | synthesizers |
| classical music | *castrati* | Minimoog |
| proto-punk beat | wah-wah pedal | art rock |
| freak outs | *musique concrète* | progressive rock |
| jazz/rock fusion | theremin | rock musical |
| rock opera | Ondes Martenot | |

. . . . . . . . . . . . . . . . . . . . . . . . . . . . . . . . . . . . . . . . . . . . . . . . . . . . . . . . . . . . . . .

## Applying Chapter Concepts

1. Explore the similarities and differences between classical music and art-oriented rock by rereading the opening discussion of music as art, becoming familiar with an extended classical composition and all of the music on one of the albums cited previously (*We're in It for the Money, Tommy, Dark Side of the Moon, The Rise and Fall of Ziggy Stardust and the Spiders from Mars*).

After you have become acquainted with both the classical and rock-era works, list three art-related features that you feel the two works share, and three ways in which they are different. Elaborate your observations into paragraphs as appropriate.

Here are some recommended classical compositions. In the case of staged works, try to locate a videotape or DVD of the work.

- Handel: *Julius Caesar* (Baroque opera: the role of Julius Caesar was originally sung by a *castrato*)
- Berlioz: *Symphonie Fantasique* (big romantic symphony in five movements: it depicts an opium-inspired dream)
- Schumann: *Dichterliebe* (a cycle of songs that explore a common theme; the song cycle is an antecedent of the concept album)
- Puccini: *La Bohème* (a Romantic opera about Bohemian life; Bohemians were the counterculturists of the nineteenth century)
- Schoenberg: *Pierrot Lunaire* (a song cycle for voice and several instruments that sets poems about the moon; the vocalist uses a technique between speech and song, called *Sprechstimme* in German)
- Sondheim: *Sweeney Todd* (a musical, but as rich musically and dramatically as most operas; it presents the grisly story of a crazed barber who slays his customers; their flesh becomes the main ingredient in meat pies)

# The Singer-Songwriters
## Rock, Melody, and Meaning

The year 1971 produced some seminal rock works, including *Who's Next* by the Who and *Zoso* by Led Zeppelin. Both are landmark albums, for the bands and for rock. They are two of the six albums released in 1971 that topped *Rolling Stone* magazine's list of the Top 500 albums of all time: *Who's Next* is number 28, *Zoso* is number 66. Just behind *Who's Next* at number 30 is another critically acclaimed album from 1971: Joni Mitchell's *Blue*.

Mitchell recorded *Blue* in the studios of A&M Records, the company founded by Jerry Moss and Herb Alpert (of Tijuana Brass fame), but it could probably have been recorded almost as well in Mitchell's living room. On six of the ten tracks, she accompanies herself on piano or guitar; it is the only instrument we hear. On the remaining four, she is joined by one or two other musicians; only one track, "Carey," features a complete rhythm section.

It is hard to imagine an important rock album from 1971 that is more different from *Who's Next* and *Zoso* than *Blue*. The list of contrasts is extensive. In *Blue*, the dominant voice is a woman's, not a man's—although Mitchell typically sings in a lower range than Robert Plant! The instrumental accompaniment is understated, not dominant. The overall sound level is soft or moderate, not loud. The words and the melodies that support them are primary; Mitchell's delivery makes them easy to understand. The melodies flow out; repetitive riffs are the exception. If we imagine the music performed live, we would probably envision Mitchell busking in a busy park or performing in an intimate club; we would most likely hear the Who and Led Zeppelin in large arenas.

## The Singer-Songwriters

There is no more eclectic subcategory within rock music than **singer-songwriter**. Interpreted literally, *singer-songwriter* identifies those who perform the music they create. That includes almost every rock-era act! However, the term came into use during the early seventies to identify a body of performers who told stories in song, usually by themselves. Their songs were typically supported by a subdued, often acoustic accompaniment that put the vocal line in the forefront.

Within these general parameters, there has been astonishing variety. Some songs are intimate, first-person accounts, confessional in tone. Others are *cinéma vérité*

272

portraits or acerbic social commentary; still others are cryptic accounts that leave the identity of the narrator in question. Most are songs in a restricted sense of the term: they have coherent melodies that help tell the story and make musical sense through an inner logic. They are seldom formulaic; formal and melodic imagination finds its greatest outlet in these songs. The music grouped under the "singer-songwriter" label represented the continued exploration of the path marked off first by Dylan, the Beatles, and the Byrds.

There were old and new faces among the singer-songwriters. Carole King was a Brill Building veteran; she had been a professional songwriter for over a decade before releasing her first album. Neil Young and Paul Simon continued their careers as solo performers. They were joined by a new generation of folk-inspired performers, most notably Joni Mitchell and James Taylor. Randy Newman, by contrast, came from a family heavily involved in traditional pop and film music. A sampling of six songs will give some sense of the extraordinary variety of music grouped under the singer-songwriter umbrella.

## Meaning and Melody

The music of the singer-songwriters of the late sixties and early seventies represents the continuing evolution of the folk/country/pop fusions of the mid-sixties. Bob Dylan was the dominant influence on its development, through inspiration and example. In his acoustic phase, he demonstrated better than any of his contemporaries the power of words set to music. In his electric phase, he showed how the impact of words and music could be amplified with the addition of other instruments. His songs set the tone. In them, he showed a new generation what they could say and how they could say it.

However, there were others within the rock tradition who helped shape its sound and sensibility. Buddy Holly, the Everly Brothers, Roy Orbison, and the Brill Building songwriters were important early sources. The Beatles and the Byrds were the most influential of Dylan's contemporaries. Other influences came from everywhere—folk and country especially, but also jazz, blues, pop, gospel, and Latin music.

## From Ballads to *Blue*: The Deep Roots of the Singer-Songwriters

More fundamentally, the singer-songwriters who began their careers around 1970 can trace their lineage back to the folk music from the British Isles—in principle, if not often in actual practice. ("Scarborough Fair," a British ballad recorded by Simon & Garfunkel, is a familiar, if rare, instance of direct reworking of a folksong.) In their music, as in this timeless folk music, the focus is more on words and melody than on rhythm. The intent is to touch the head and the heart more than the hips.

The impulse to tell a story in song is embedded in the cultures of the British Isles—English, Irish, and Scottish. It remained strong in those who immigrated to the colonies in North America; recall the folk ballad "Barbara Allen" and Henry Russell's "Woodman, Spare That Tree." Storytelling songs remained part of popular music until the turn of the twentieth century. They resurfaced as a commercial music in the 1920s with the emergence of country music and as a modern folk music in the topical songs of Woody Guthrie and his disciples.

For Dylan and the singer-songwriters who followed him, this ancient folk tradition was the point of departure for a new, urban folk-inspired music. They assimilated it and transformed it into a new popular style, much as the rock bands discussed in Chapter 9 assimilated the blues and transformed it into a new, and quite different, popular style. Indeed, they are complementary developments: one of the subtle ironies of the rock era was that North American musicians most fully embraced the musical tradition rooted in the folk music of the British Isles, while it was mainly the British bands that steeped themselves in the blues, the most distinctively American folk music.

## Recapitulating the Sixties

Six examples are discussed in the following: songs by Carole King, Joni Mitchell, a King song performed by James Taylor, Randy Newman, Paul Simon, and finally Neil Young. The songs appear in more or less chronological order; their individual approaches seems to recapitulate the evolution of the singer-songwriter idea. Mitchell and King connect back to the folksingers of the early sixties, and—in King's case—the girl groups for which she wrote numerous hits. Taylor's version of King's song exemplifies the acoustic approach and the collegial environment in which the music developed. Newman and Simon build on the frank, often ironic, attitude of the Beatles; and they expand the sound world to help characterize the lyrics. Young's song, whose message is empowered by the backing of a rock band, grows out of Dylan's electric music. Collectively, they created a new kind of popular song—melodious, like the folk music from which it ultimately derives, yet completely modern in its sound.

# Elevating the Feminine

After a decade of working behind the scenes writing songs for others, Carole King began a solo career after her divorce from Gerry Goffin in 1968. She broke through in 1971 with *Tapestry*, which remained on the charts for almost six years and eventually sold over 22 million units. Similarly, Joni Mitchell's first foray onto the charts came as a songwriter: Judy Collins's version of "Both Sides Now" reached number 8 in 1968; Mitchell's first solo album was released that year.

The rise of King and Mitchell to stardom at the end of the sixties symbolized a new role for women in rock, and in popular music. As we have noted, rock and roll was a male-dominated music: all of its stars, and almost all of its acts, were men. This was due in large part to the sexual undercurrent running through rock and roll and the impact of the double standard in sexually charged behavior. Those who have grown up in the post-Madonna era are used to women performing as provocatively as their male counterparts. However, the movements encountered in music videos and in live performance would have been unthinkable in the early years of rock. Elvis was scandalous enough, by fifties standards; a woman moving like Elvis would have certainly been banned. Women who wanted to front a band like men had to wait for the sexual liberation of the sixties; even then, it required considerable courage.

Further, playing a rock-band instrument was a man's job, or so it seemed. Women rhythm section musicians were almost unheard of during the early rock era. One can count the number of prominent women lead guitarists, bassists, and drummers on the fingers of one hand. The bassist Carol Kaye, who appeared on *Pet Sounds* and several other Beach Boys albums, was in demand throughout the fifties and sixties as a session musician; she had very little female company.

Black music, and particularly black pop, was more open to women, especially in the sixties. There were a few women stars in fifties rhythm and blues; still, most of the acts were male. During the sixties, black women secured a more prominent place, first in the girl groups, then Motown and pop (Dionne Warwick had a string of hits written by Burt Bacharach and Hal David), then soul, most notably with Aretha Franklin. Aretha added to the legacy of strong, soulful yet vulnerable black women, created by singers like Bessie Smith, Billie Holiday, and Dinah Washington.

White female singers fared better in more pop-oriented yet rock-flavored music from the same period: Connie Francis, Brenda Lee, Petula Clark, and Dusty Springfield were among the top solo acts; the Mamas and the Papas were among the most prominent male–female groups.

It was the folk revival that provided women with the most accessible point of entry into rock. With its intimate environment, emphasis on words and melody over rhythm, and understated acoustic accompaniment, the urban folk music of the postwar era was far less macho than rock and roll, jazz, or blues. Indeed, young women folksingers were fixtures in coffeehouses throughout the fifties; Joan Baez was the most notable example of this group. Maybelle Carter, by far the most important member of the Carter Family, was a main inspiration. In the sixties, the repertoire of women performers who came out of the folk tradition, or were inspired by it, mutated from reworked folksongs to contemporary songs in a similar style. Judy Collins's work in the sixties embodies this transition; Janis Ian's "Society's Child" (1965–1967), her first hit, helped mark this new direction, which continued in the music of Carole King and Joni Mitchell.

## Carole King

It took Carole King (b. 1942) the better part of a decade to move from behind the scenes to the front of the stage. Although she had been a successful songwriter throughout the sixties, it wasn't until after her divorce from Gerry Goffin in 1968 that she began a solo career. She broke through in 1971 with *Tapestry*, which remained on the charts for almost six years.

*Tapestry* is, more than anything else, black pop written and sung by a white woman; King sings with real empathy for the sound and style of Motown and soul and speaks candidly about life and love from a woman's point of view. Two of the songs on the album were major hits for black female artists in the sixties. We discussed the seminal role of the Shirelles' "Will You Love Me Tomorrow?" in the creation of a black pop sound in Chapter 6. "(You Make Me Feel Like A) Natural Woman," which came straight out of church, put Aretha Franklin in the Top 10 for the fourth time in 1967.

Most of the new songs on *Tapestry* are cut from similar cloth. "You've Got a Friend" projects the optimistic tone heard in so much black pop. There are also musical parallels: with a form that builds to the title-phrase hook, riff-based melody, and rich but mostly traditional harmony, it echoes hundreds of black pop hits. Not surprisingly, then, the song was almost as big a hit on the R&B charts for Roberta

Evening Standard/Getty Images

Carole King in a moment of inspiration, 1977.

"(You Make
Me Feel Like A)
Natural Wo-
man," Carole
King (1971)

Flack and Donny Hathaway as it was for James Taylor on the pop charts. "I Feel the Earth Move," "It's Too Late," and "Where You Lead"—with their solid grooves, instrumental and vocal hooks, rich harmony, Motown-style backup vocals, and end-weighted forms—could have been hits for the Temptations or the Supremes. Aretha or Percy Sledge could have covered "Way over Yonder," and King's excellent gospel-style piano playing would have provided a first-rate accompaniment.

King's songs have an "everywoman" universality as they describe the ups and downs of love and life. There is ecstasy ("I Feel the Earth Move"), disillusionment ("It's Too Late"), loneliness ("So Far Away"), and the comfort of companionship ("You've Got a Friend"). They are "real," no-frills songs, sending their messages in plain language. There is no sugarcoating—just frank heart-to-heart talk. King's timing was perfect. Her songs found receptive ears, especially among women, just as the women's rights movement was gathering momentum. Aretha Franklin's "Respect" had already been adopted as an anthem; Helen Reddy's "I Am Woman" would top the charts in 1972.

The straightforward lyrics were only part of the appeal. King's songs are skillfully crafted and make use of existing styles and conventions in an imaginative and individual way. "(You Make Me Feel Like A) Natural Woman," a song that King wrote in 1967 with the help of Goffin and Jerry Wexler, reworks two black musical styles: gospel and Motown. The gospel influence is most directly evident in the rhythm. The song features a slow **triple meter** (grouping of beats by three), which is widely used in black gospel (imagine a black congregation singing "Amazing Grace") and also is the underlying meter of "Lift Every Voice and Sing," the black national anthem. King sets the meter with the repeated piano chords; the piano was the most common accompanying instrument in traditional gospel.

The song unfolds like so many Motown songs: it begins simply with a short two-part verse, then slowly builds to the title-phrase refrain through a long transition. The refrain riff is repeated three times; the final statement completes the lyric and the melody. The second verse/transition/refrain section is identical melodically to the first. However, King substitutes a surprising new melody that sustains the intensity of the refrain before returning for the final time to the refrain. This too is a formal strategy in Motown songs: Smokey Robinson's "Tracks of My Tears" is a familiar example.

King's most individual touches come in the curve of the melody and the harmonies that support the melody. The song begins with two melodic drops, which amplify the depressed mood of the lyrics. The melody begins to move back up as the lyric describes the impact of her lover. The close relationship between words and music continues, especially in the new section between the last two refrains. King harmonizes the melody with fresh alternatives to standard chord progressions; they help give the song a distinctive character.

King's spare accompaniment—just two piano parts (both of which she plays via overdubbing), plus a bass for reinforcement in the refrain and overdubbed backup vocals—is much simpler than that used on Aretha Franklin's recording, which features full rhythm section, plus backup singers, strings, and horns. That King can offer a compelling version of the song with minimal instrumental resources points up the primacy of melody in the music of the singer-songwriters. In this song and others like it, the melody carries most of the expressive weight. It is a completely different orientation from the songs we heard in Chapter 9, for instance, that *depend* on the instruments to carry the flow of the song and convey the message.

---

### ♪ KEY FEATURES

**"(You Make Me Feel Like A) Natural Woman," Carole King (1971)**

- Gospel rhythm and accompaniment: triple meter, marked off by piano chords, evoking black gospel
- Motown-style form: verse/transition/refrain form similar to many Motown hits
- Melody is primary: simple setting highlights the focus on melody as the main expressive element
- Woman's point of view: lyric describes the joy of falling in love in language that is mostly simple and direct but with vivid images: "when my soul was in the lost and found/you came along to claim it"
- Easy-to-follow song: no vocal or instrumental pyrotechnics, no unusual effects, just words and melody delivered in a straightforward, expressive way that is easy to understand

---

Dylan has been regarded as the godfather of the singer-songwriter movement, and rightly so. But songs with melody and meaning had been part of rock since Buddy Holly's brief heyday and King's own "Will You Love Me Tomorrow?" in 1961. King's success made clear that the singer-songwriters had roots in pop as well as folk. And it was certainly gratifying to her to step out of the shadows and into the spotlight. She remained there a relatively short time. Her next two albums did well, but neither approached the colossal success of *Tapestry*.

## Joni Mitchell

Although Carole King and Joni Mitchell are linked in time, gender, and style, and share common musical collaborators (not only James Taylor but also several studio musicians), their careers are opposite in several respects. Where Mitchell grew up in the Canadian plains, about as far geographically and culturally as one could be from New York, King was born Carol Klein in Brooklyn. While Mitchell was singing in Canadian coffeehouses, King was at work in the Brill Building, cranking out a string of pop hits with her husband at the time, Gerry Goffin.

Joni Mitchell (b. 1943) was born Roberta Anderson in Fort Macleod, Alberta, Canada, and grew up in Saskatchewan, the neighboring province. As a young girl, she had equally strong interests in art and music. After high school, she enrolled in the Alberta College of Art and Design and played folk music in the local coffeehouse. Like many Canadians in search of a career, she gravitated to Toronto, where she met and married Chuck Mitchell, also a folksinger, in 1966. The couple moved to Detroit. After her divorce a year later, she moved to New York, where she connected into the folk scene, mainly as a songwriter. Tom Rush and Judy Collins recorded two of her early songs: "The Circle Game" and "Both Sides Now," respectively. Within a year, she had moved to southern California.

Mitchell began recording under her own name in 1968. She found her musical voice, and her audience, in a series of albums released between 1969 and 1974. In them, Mitchell uses the folk style of the early sixties as a point of departure, but she transforms every aspect of it—lyrics, melody, and accompaniment—into a highly personal idiom. We hear this in "All I Want," a track from her milestone 1971 album *Blue*.

Like so many of her early songs, "All I Want" has a romantic thread (or at least a relationship thread) woven through it. In this respect, she is right in step with so many other singer-songwriters, and—more generally—popular music, especially black pop. But there the similarity ends. Most love-related songs present their situation in a coherent narrative, through a series of images ("My Girl"), an outpouring of feeling (Buddy Holly's "Not Fade Away"), or a scene that unfolds ("I Heard It Through the Grapevine"), or a combination of these ("Natural Woman"). Typically, both words and music follow a predictable path toward a goal that serves as the expressive high point of the song.

"All I Want,"
Joni Mitchell
(1971)

Joni Mitchell in performance, 1980.

By contrast, Mitchell's lyrics to "All I Want" open the door to her subconscious. There are mercurial shifts in mood: one moment she's high on love ("Alive, alive, I want to get up and jive/I want to wreck my stockings in some juke box dive"), the next, she's licking her emotional wounds ("Do you see—do you see—do you see how you hurt me baby/So I hurt you too/Then we both get so blue"). The only consistent feature of the lyric is the emotional inconsistency of her relationship ("Oh I hate you some, I hate you some/I love you some") It is as if we are inside Mitchell's head, with thoughts and images tumbling over each other in a stream of consciousness. There is no story; indeed, there is no sense even of time passing.

The music amplifies the temporal and emotional ambiguity of the lyric. The accompaniment begins with Mitchell and James Taylor playing guitars—Mitchell playing an erratic series of chords, Taylor a single note. Mitchell deliberately avoids establishing a key or even marking the beat clearly. The song itself is strophic: the same melody serves three stanzas of poetry. It begins tentatively, echoing the indecision of the lyric. The most intense point comes in the middle. Shorter phrases and a more active, wide-ranging melodic contour echo the more active and frequent images in the text. They in turn lead to the heart of the song: "do you want." Like smoke rising from one of Mitchell's ever-present cigarettes, the melody gradually drifts up, reaching its peak on the words "sweet romance": the real issue of the song. It drops down quickly, but not to rest; the final sustained note is not the keynote. The instrumental introduction returns as the outro; it ends limply, as if it is a musical question mark. All of this underscores the message of the lyrics. Mitchell describes a complex, difficult relationship and the emotional rollercoaster that it puts her through; there is no change in it during the course of the song, no resolution at the end.

## ♪ KEY FEATURES

### "All I Want," Joni Mitchell (1971)

- Confessional lyrics: the words reflect the turbulent state of mind of the narrator by jumping from image to image.
- Outpouring of melody: the melody spins out from the opening phrase, finally peaking toward the end.
- Indecisive harmony: the instrumental intro and outro that frame the melody are harmonic question marks; the harmony that supports the melody is also unpredictable and unstable at times.
- Open-ended form: the form of "All I Want" consists of three distinct sections; there is no sense of resolution at the end.

As "All I Want" reveals, Mitchell's songs disdain the conventions of rock and pop. In her songs, ideas shape the forms, not vice versa. Melodies respond to the words, yet follow their own internal logic. Other aspects of the setting—most notably harmony, instrumentation, and rhythm—are individual to a particular song. They remain in a supporting role, the focus is squarely on the words and melody. One measure of

Mitchell's genius is that words and melody are separable yet indivisible. Her lyrics are studied as poetic texts; her songs are performed as instrumentals. Yet the sum is greater than the parts. Those searching for rock's counterpart to the art songs of classical music need look no further than the music of Joni Mitchell.

At the same time, they provide a postmodern perspective on love. In so doing, they bring the love song into the rock era. Scan the playlists of the last several chapters. Note how few of the songs by white artists mention any aspect of a man–woman relationship. And even in those that do, there is no real partner, just Orbison's pretty woman or anonymous females that are not available to satisfy Jagger's lust. There is no emotional interaction. By contrast, Mitchell opens herself up, so that we can experience the turmoil in her troubled relationship with her. It is an emotional breakthrough—for her, for rock, and for popular music.

After 1974, Mitchell turned in other directions. Through the rest of the seventies, she connected with jazz and the avant-garde. This culminated in the collaboration with jazz great Charles Mingus, which was cut short by Mingus's death in 1979. Her seventies experiments anticipated the world music movement of the eighties. In the eighties, she continued to explore what some called "jazz/folk" fusion, as well as to develop her career in the visual arts as a photographer and painter.

# They've Got Friends: The Intimate World of the Singer-Songwriters

The other guitarist on "All I Want" is James Taylor; Taylor also assists Carole King on several tracks on *Tapestry*, including "You've Got a Friend." They return the favor: King by supplying Taylor with one of his biggest hits and Mitchell by singing backup vocals. During the early seventies, the singer-songwriter movement seemed mainly the work of a few good friends: Taylor, King, Mitchell; other singer-songwriters like Jackson Brown and Carly Simon, who Taylor married in 1972 (they divorced in 1983); and the studio musicians who appeared on so many of their recordings, including guitarist Danny Kortchmar (occasionally credited as Danny Kootch).

## James Taylor: A Friend Among Friends

Taylor (b. 1942) seems at the center of these seemingly collegial partnerships, which is in keeping with the persona that he projects through his music. Taylor is rock's first great conversationalist; he sings as if he's talking with you one-on-one. He sings with emotional reserve, not excess, even when he talks about highly personal and obviously painful subjects—as in "Fire and Rain," an account of his reaction to the suicide of a fellow inmate at a mental asylum. In this respect, he is the polar opposite of those rockers who, like Little Richard, were looking for something loud and found it was them.

Taylor was able to project this public persona despite numerous personal problems that nearly cost him his career, and his life. He grew up in Chapel Hill, North Carolina. His childhood was privileged (his father was dean of the University of North Carolina Medical School, and the family was wealthy enough to summer on Martha's Vineyard) and problematic (Taylor committed himself to a psychiatric hospital while in his teens). Through his older brother Alex (all five Taylor siblings—James, Alex, Livingston, Hugh, and Kate—would have professional careers in music), he discovered folk and country music. After working in and around New York in the mid-sixties, he moved to England, where he recorded his self-titled debut album in 1968 for Apple Records. The album didn't do well, so Taylor returned to the United States, while singer-producer Peter Asher, who had produced his Apple recording, negotiated a contract with Warner Bros. Taylor's first two albums for Warner Bros. were enormously successful and established his career.

Taylor's songs are quintessential singer-songwriter material: autobiographical accounts that are nothing less than public confessions of his troubles and desires. These he delivers in a restrained, almost laconic manner—folksy, but also with a grit that comes from the blues (his 1976 hit "Steamroller" is an authentic take on electric blues). He sounds life-size, rather than larger than life: he could be your friend next door who sings and plays the guitar, except that he's really good at it. So it may be surprising to realize that Taylor's biggest hit and most honored recording was his version of Carole King's "You've Got a Friend"; both the song and Taylor's recording won Grammys in 1971.

"You've Got a Friend," James Taylor (1971)

King's song follows much the same general plan that she used in "Natural Woman"—and sends much the same message. The verses, which describe the state of mind of "you," focus around a single note (sung at first to "down and troubled"): like the dark cloud hanging over "you," the melody can't seem to leave the note. Every move up quickly returns to this note; it is like a dead weight that can't be thrown off . . . until the friend enters the picture. In words and music, mood becomes more upbeat; the melody rises, reaching a peak just before the title phrase. And, as in "Natural Woman," a more intense section replaces what would be the third statement of the verse. As with "Natural Woman," King tweaks a well-established form and shapes both melody and harmony so that they respond specifically to the message of the lyric.

The instrumental accompaniment, led by Taylor's imaginative take on Guthrie-style guitar figures, is an acoustic analogue to a rock band: two acoustic guitars, string bass, plus congas and drums. The core instrumentation is intact: guitar, bass, and percussion, but everything is understated. There is a clear rock rhythm, but it is presented gently; the emphasis is on the melody and the chords that support it. Its use here demonstrates two key points about rock-era music. The first is that the song evidences the ever-increasing diversity of rock-era music; this song, as well as the other songs discussed in this chapter, represents a clearly different direction from the

Neal Preston/Corbis

James Taylor on stage, May 1978.

music presented in the previous three chapters. The second and more significant point is the key role of rock rhythm in unifying rock-era music. Taylor's approach to rock rhythm in "You've Got a Friend" is the opposite of much of the music heard in the previous chapters in many respects: it is soft, not loud; the instruments are acoustic, not electric; the melody is more than repeated riffs. The strongest bond is the use of a rock rhythm: Taylor's guitar line and the conga part move at twice beat speed, and the backbeat is subtly present, especially in the chorus. In rock, as in the music of previous and subsequent generations, it is the characteristic rhythm—the style beat—that connects a diverse body of music that differs in so many other ways.

♪ **KEY FEATURES**

**"You've Got a Friend," James Taylor (1971)**

- Melody first: as in the other two songs, melody is in the forefront. Lyrics and melody work together to communicate the message of the song.
- Laconic but gritty style: Taylor's singing is an ideal complement to the melody and message of the song.
- Unplugged instrumentation: acoustic counterparts to standard rock-band instrumentation.
- Rock connection: subtle eight-beat rhythm places the song in the rock era.

Taylor's career peaked in the early seventies, as he scored a series of successes on both album and singles charts. He achieved further celebrity with his marriage to Carly Simon in 1972. He continues to please a sizable audience, and he remains a big attraction, especially on the summer circuit. He seems to have left his personal problems, including heroin addiction, in the past.

Taylor's best songs, and his singing of them, brought to rock an unprecedented intimacy and sense of personal connection with the artist. His music epitomized rock's gentler side. With its acoustic instrumentation, and restrained but expressive vocal sound, it added an important new dimension to the sound of rock.

# Words, Melodies, and Sounds

In 1995, Taylor became divine. Randy Newman cast him in the role of God in his ambitious reworking of Goethe's *Faust*, the classic drama of a man's pact with the devil and its consequences. He recruited other rock stars for important roles: Don Henley, Bonnie Raitt, Elton John, and Linda Ronstadt. Not surprisingly, Newman himself played the devil.

## Pumping Irony: Randy Newman

Randy Newman (b. 1943) has taken an unusual path in his career as a singer-songwriter: he is the genre's true iconoclast. While others were baring their souls,

Newman was inhabiting a string of reprehensible characters: slave traders, rednecks, and assorted other bigots. Unlike almost all the others—Paul Simon is the occasional exception—Newman's songs are usually ironic. They are devastating satires of people he finds deserving of his barbs. What makes them special, and often confusing to simpler minds, is that they are not heavy-handed caricatures but complicated portraits in which Newman assumes the character in the song. Both his satirical humor and his assumption of personas quite different from his own distinguish his music from the other singer-songwriters.

Newman grew up in New Orleans, where he absorbed the sound of Fats Domino and the New Orleans piano professors. He had moved to Los Angeles by the time he was a teenager; he began writing songs for Metric Music while still in high school. He was well-connected: three of his uncles—Alfred, Lionel, and Emil Newman—wrote and conducted film music for Hollywood films, and his long-time friend Larry Waronker, who co-produced his first album, would become president of Warner Bros. Records.

"Sail Away,"
Randy Newman
(1972)

Newman began recording his own music in 1968. New albums appeared intermittently throughout the seventies. Typically they received rave reviews but sold poorly, although *Little Criminals* (1977) went gold, in part because of the controversy surrounding his hit single, "Short People."

"Sail Away," the title track from his 1972 album, offers an even more trenchant instance of Newman's irony. The "voice" in the song is giving a sales pitch about life in America to West Africans during the days of the slave trade. In fact, there are multiple voices. We hear not only the slave trader's perception of the "dark continent" ("lions, tigers, and mama snakes"), but also Newman's own perspective on the various myths and stereotypes regarding life among the slaves ("watermelons and buckwheat cakes").

The instrumental accompaniment is much farther removed from rock than those in any of the previous examples. There are no electric guitars, no bass or drum set. The only rhythm instrument is the piano, which Newman plays. Instead, Newman scores the accompaniment for symphony orchestra. (He performed the song with members of the New York Philharmonic.) The serene winds and sumptuous strings could just as easily be providing background music for a patriotic film. Yet it is precisely this evocative use of style, underscoring the ironic tone of the lyrics, that connects Newman's work to the inspired craft of Zappa and the Beatles. While "Sail Away" may not be a rock song in sound, it certainly is a rock-era song in subject and spirit.

## ♪ KEY FEATURES

### "Sail Away," Randy Newman (1972)

- Ironic lyrics: slave captain's "sales pitch"; a pithy denunciation of slavery
- Documentary-like orchestration: rock instruments missing
- Simple melody, like patriotic song: melody, like lyrics, send an ironic

In "Short People," Newman again assumes multiple personas. To a jaunty accompaniment, the song's protagonist sings "Short people got . . . no reason to . . . short people got . . . no reason to . . ." delaying the tag line "no reason to live." The song is of course a satire of bigotry, but it is also a satire of the mindless, "have-a-nice-day" mentality that infused much commercial music of the seventies. When Newman sings, "Short people are just like you and me," he is satirizing the other side of bigotry: unthinking liberals who offer false sympathy to those who are different. Newman manages to mock bigots and those who profess to oppose bigotry in the same song.

"Short People" was the most notorious example of the confusion his music can cause. Some people took him literally, and the song was banned from a few radio stations. During the controversy, Newman took great pains to explain that the song was not an expression of his personal beliefs but rather his way of putting bigotry in the glare of the spotlight, in the rather forlorn hope that the song might enlighten a few listeners. As he said a few years later, "I don't know why, but bigotry has always bothered me more than war or pollution or anything else."

Newman has been more than just a songwriter: from the beginning of his career, he was also a skilled arranger and orchestrator. In the seventies and eighties, he began to write film scores. Among his credits are the music for *Ragtime*, *The Natural*, and Disney's *Toy Story*. His musical, *Faust*, can be understood as a culmination and synthesis of his work in both areas: as a songwriter and as a film composer.

## Plumbing Psyches: Paul Simon

Paul Simon (b. 1941) had paired musically with Carole King during the late fifties and early sixties, recording several demos, which were picked up by other artists. However, his more significant partner during the first stages of his career was Art Garfunkel (b. 1941), whom he met in sixth grade and with whom he worked while still in high school. The pair billed themselves as Tom and Jerry; they modeled their sound after the Everly Brothers. In 1964, they reformed as Simon & Garfunkel and signed a contract with Columbia Records. They enjoyed remarkable success: providing the soundtrack for the (1967) film *The Graduate* (a rock first), topping the charts with three different albums. Several of Simon's songs from the sixties remain popular, most notably the anthemic "Bridge Over Troubled Water."

When Simon and Garfunkel dissolved their partnership in 1970, Simon immediately embarked on a solo career. The split seemed to liberate Simon musically: it was a case of addition by subtraction. Both Simon and Garfunkel have pleasant voices that do not project a strong and distinctive personality. Yet because there are two voices, usually in harmony, the vocal sound is typically the dominant element, even in a song like "The Boxer," which features a rich instrumental backdrop laced with unusual timbres. Their update of the Everly Brothers' close harmony was one of the most memorable sounds of the sixties.

Simon's voice is true, musically and emotionally, but rather neutral, even when compared to the other singer-songwriters. For example, with Joni Mitchell and Neil Young (heard next), one is almost compelled to react to their voice—to respond to them like one might respond to guitar distortion: with immediate identification or complete turnoff. James Taylor's voice has more grit than Simon's; it would be difficult to imagine Simon singing a blues or a Motown song as convincingly as Taylor does. So Simon communicates his message as much by what he does around his voice as he does in his singing.

Simon usually speaks in the first person in his solo music, and the persona he projects is one of the most distinctive of the time: urban, contemporary, neurotic yet sophisticated and street-wise—a quintessential New Yorker. Right from the start of his solo career, Simon composed songs that were more complex melodically and harmonically than those he wrote during his partnership with Garfunkel. Moreover, all the elements of the accompaniment—the choice of instruments (and, on occasion, voices), the rhythms, the textures—contribute to the meaning of the song. The sound world that envelops the vocal line is a full partner with lyric and melody in conveying the character of a song. As listeners move from song to song, they hear tastes of Latin music, both black and white gospel, and other styles with a strong identity.

A survey of Simon's songs from the early seventies shows the extraordinary range of styles he has at his command and the expressive purposes to which he puts them: "Mother and Child Reunion" is a reggae-influenced song, "Something So Right" is a gorgeous romantic ballad, "Love Me Like a Rock" and "Slip Slidin' Away" have gospel overtones, "Have a Good Time" has a funky chorus, and "Late in the Evening" has a Latin flavor.

Paul Simon, performing in New York's Central Park in 1975, to celebrate the end of the Vietnam War.

Simon's urbane lyrics and subtle evocations of style are two of four key elements in his style. The others are his beautifully crafted melodies and subtle textures, particularly his handling of rhythm. He is expert at controlling the flow of a song by manipulating timekeeping and density: to cite just one example, the light shuffle rhythm, overlaid with sustained keyboard chords and vocal harmonies, helps project the wistful mood of "Slip Slidin' Away." Almost uniquely among the singer-songwriters, Simon's songs derive mainly from the Beatles' revolutionary reconception of song: a sound environment in which the words and melody are central but where the rest of texture also embodies the meaning of the song.

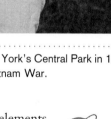

"Still Crazy After All These Years," Paul ?Simon (1976)

Among the most evocative of his songs was the 1976 hit "Still Crazy After All These Years." In it, Simon uses a rich, rapidly shifting instrumental setting to bring the lyric to life. The song begins with spare, gospel-influenced keyboard accompaniment that helps suggest the emptiness of the late-night rendezvous with a former partner. It continues as Simon describes how he generally stays apart from others. It dissolves into a melee of strings and woodwinds after the emotional and musical highpoint of the song—the late-night bout of lunacy, when it all starts to fade. The saxophone solo seems to signify a gradual return to a more normal state of mind; the repetition of the opening phrase of the melody supports the wry comment about his mental state: he may be crazy, but at least he knows it.

**"Still Crazy After All These Years," Paul Simon (1976)**

■ Everyman lyrics: one can imagine sitting next to Simon in a bar, listening to him tell his story.

■ Big, beautiful melody: the melody is expansive, unfolding in long phrases. It is one statement of an AABA form.

■ Setting shifts in response to the lyric: each phrase of the melody has its own setting. The B section (bridge) has the most extensive contrast, including an instrumental interlude.

Perhaps there is some kind of symbolic significance to the dissolution of Simon & Garfunkel in 1970. In musical and cultural importance, it was a distant second to the breakup of the Beatles. However, in his ability to create appealing yet thought-provoking lyrics, engaging melodies, and evocative instrumental settings, Simon builds on the legacy of the Beatles. Indeed, one might argue that his work since 1970 has been close to the spirit of their music. As such, it is some distance, in music and message, from his Everly Brothers–influenced work of the sixties. The spirit of exploration—new ideas, new sounds, new forms—that characterized Simon's music in the early seventies grew bolder in subsequent years.

Both Simon's and Newman's songs are different in kind from the songs by King, Mitchell, and Taylor because the details of the instrumental setting in their songs convey much of the meaning of the song. Unlike a song such as "You've Got a Friend," which retains its meaning in numerous settings (including one by King and a duet version by Roberta Flack and Donny Hathaway), "Sail Away" and "Still Crazy After All These Years" rely on the sound world behind the vocal to communicate their message fully. Words and melody are still the focus, but the setting is as distinctively crafted as words and melody.

## Singer-Songwriters and Rock

The five singer-songwriters discussed to this point established new territory within rock. In many ways, their music is the antithesis of rock, or at least the music that most typifies rock style. But Dylan had made clear that it was possible to write compelling songs and set them to rock accompaniments. The music of Neil Young epitomizes this possibility.

### Neil Young

If a single incident can sum up the restless spirit and unpredictability that has informed Neil Young's music, it's this: in 1983, his then–record label, Geffen Records, sued him for making recordings that didn't sound like Neil Young! Young's songs have overtones of country, rockabilly, rhythm and blues, techno-based pop, not to mention hard rock and punk. He is seemingly open to everything, and because of this, his music defies category—or, better, it is constantly roaming from category to category.

Young (b. 1945) was born in Toronto but grew up in Winnipeg, Manitoba. He made his way to the United States via Toronto, where he met Stephen Stills (b. 1945) and Joni Mitchell, among others. From there, he moved to Los Angeles, where he formed Buffalo Springfield with Stills. After that group broke up, Young embarked on a solo career. Since then, he has occasionally performed with various combinations of David Crosby (b. 1941), Stills, and Graham Nash (b. 1942). However, his most significant work has come as a solo act, usually backed by the rock band Crazy Horse.

Young tells good stories. He paints vivid images in words and music and develops his plots slowly and elliptically. His portraits are typically dark: grays and browns. They are bleak, yet intensely human. They can also be real, in the most specific sense of the term. He wrote "Ohio" (1970) while with Crosby, Stills, and Nash, in response to the shooting of Kent State students. It became an anthem of the anti-war movement.

"Tonight's the Night," Neil Young (1975)

"Tonight's the Night" (1975) is even more personal. The lyric tells the story of Bruce Berry, one of Young's roadies. Like Crazy Horse guitarist Danny Whitten, Berry died of a drug overdose. The song is part eulogy, part cry of despair. Typically, he tells the story in pieces—and allusively, not directly. As we listen to the song, we can visualize with photographic clarity Bruce sitting with Young's guitar, after the gig had finished, doing his best Neil Young imitation. The refrain is even more elusive: does it refer to the night of his death (of course), to getting high (probably), or to something else as well? The contrasts in the musical setting underscore the message of the lyrics. In the refrain, the rhythm floats like Young's voice, perhaps suggesting the suspension of time that is part of the drug experience. By contrast, the verse sections have a nice groove, and Young's singing is much more forthright.

## ♪ KEY FEATURES

### "Tonight's the Night," Neil Young (1975)

- Plainspoken lyric: Young tells the story as if he were talking. It comes out in fragments, as if it were an immediate reaction to Berry's death.
- Melody matches mood of verse: repetition of simple riff in chorus suggests disbelief; more active verse helps characterize flashbacks to happier memories.
- Empty-sounding accompaniment, especially during chorus, reinforces desolate mood of words and melody.

"Tonight's the Night" shows only one side of Young's extraordinarily varied output. Over his long career, he has explored a lot of musical territory. Still, it brings to light essential aspects of his complex, contradictory musical personality. Alone among the major singer-songwriters, Young knew how to rock hard, and did so regularly. Yet, his music may also contain moments of considerable tenderness. Often both dimensions appear within the same song. His quavering voice is not pretty or powerful, yet it is capable of expressing a wide range of emotions. His songs are not obvious, in either words or music, yet their messages have impact and staying power.

# A New Kind of Popular Song

The six singer-songwriters profiled here created a new kind of popular song. Generally, these were songs in the most specific sense: music that set meaningful words to a melody that was the most coherent and prominent element in the texture. In this respect, they were like not only country songs but also pre-rock pop and the art songs of classical music. And the best of them were as beautifully crafted as music from any era. They may have been miles from the power chords of the metal bands or the steam-driven propulsion of CCR. However, in their attitudes and adventurousness, they captured much of the spirit of the rock era.

They were part of a renaissance of melody in the early seventies. It was evident in the music of a new generation of pop rock stars, such as Elton John; in the rise of country rock in the music of the Eagles and others; in the soft rock of the Carpenters, Barbra Streisand, and others; and in new kinds of black pop, some of which we hear in the next chapter. In all of this music, melody comes to the fore: it is the focal element.

An interesting footnote to their earlier music is the varied career directions of several of the singer-songwriters after 1975. Young careened from style to style; Mitchell embraced jazz and non-western music; Simon also explored world music while venturing into film, then onto Broadway. Newman followed in the footsteps of his uncles, scoring (at last count) seventeen films and mounting the production of *Faust*. They were already a heterogeneous group in 1970; they became even more so in subsequent decades.

A final note: if rock needs a beat that moves you, as Lou Reed suggested, then much of the music in this chapter is *not* rock. It fails this most basic test. However, if rock includes music that expresses the feelings and attitudes of its audience in ways that are not dependent on the conventions of earlier eras, then this *is* rock. Granted, Joni Mitchell's "All I Want" is miles away from Led Zeppelin's "Black Dog" in almost every respect. However, rock has always been eclectic; there has always been room for diversity. The message of the music of the singer-songwriters may not be electrically charged, but in its own way, it is powerful. There has always been room in rock for melody and meaningful words.

. . . . . . . . . . . . . . . . . . . . . . . . . . . . . . . . . . . . . . . . . . . . . . . . . . . . . . . . . . . . . . . . . . . . . . . . . . . . . . . . . . .

**Terms to Remember**

singer-songwriter               triple meter

. . . . . . . . . . . . . . . . . . . . . . . . . . . . . . . . . . . . . . . . . . . . . . . . . . . . . . . . . . . . . . . . . . . . . . . . . . . . . . . . . . .

**Applying Chapter Concepts**

1. Revisit the discussion of *singer-songwriter* on page 272. Do you find *singer-songwriter* to be as helpful a style label as *art rock* or *heavy metal*? Can you suggest a more descriptive term? Then consider why the acts considered here are (or, in your opinion, are not) singer-songwriters and why Bruce Springsteen is not usually considered a *singer-songwriter* in this

more restrictive connotation of the term. (Use "Born to Run," discussed in Chapter 14, as a point of reference.)

2. The term *singer-songwriter* came into vogue around 1970. Select one of the artists discussed in this chapter, then listen to a sampling of their post-1980 music. Do you feel that their later music also exemplifies the singer-songwriter approach? Support your answer with at least two reasons.

# 13

# Black Popular Music in the Early Seventies

On May 13, 1971, Stevie Wonder (born Steveland Morris, 1950) turned 21. On that day, his contract with Motown Records expired. The arrangement had been good for both parties: Wonder was a child star, and Motown reaped the rewards. However, Wonder took the $1 million in royalties that Motown had been holding in trust for him, formed his own record and publishing companies (Taurus and Black Bull), and negotiated a new record deal with Motown. For Wonder, the crucial clause in the contract was "complete artistic control." In effect, he made his records and Motown sold them.

Wonder assumed artistic control in an unprecedented way. He immersed himself in electronics, learning how to use synthesizers and electronic keyboards (these were a new, rapidly evolving technology at the time). With these newly developed skills, he played most, sometimes all, of the parts on many of his recordings. On his recordings, a single artist with a lot of equipment replaced the multilevel Motown production pyramid. The string of albums that he produced in the early seventies did well enough that he was able to renegotiate his contract with Motown in 1975. The new deal gave him a $13 million advance and a 20 percent royalty rate.

## Black Music: Change, Context, and Culture

Wonder's emancipation from Motown points up three key features of black music (as well as rock music in general) after 1970. One, this new music had become a big business. Two, important artists were determined to go their own way, no matter which direction it took them. Three, technology would play an increasingly important role. All of these factors reshaped black music during the early seventies. So did musicians' responses to the changing social climate.

## Black Issues, Black Voices

The sixties, which had begun with such promise for blacks, ended dismally. The assassination of Martin Luther King Jr., the riots at the Democratic National Convention in 1968, the legal troubles of the Black Panthers, the election of Richard Nixon and the subsequent shift to more conservative attitudes: all these and more replaced hope with disillusion.

Black music of all kinds, from romantic pop to funk, generally reflected the shifting mood within the black community in response to the retreat from the social advances of the civil rights movement. It also reflected the maturation of its artists and, indirectly, their more secure position in the popular music world. With maturity, they had more to say, and they felt that they could speak more directly without losing their audience: Berry Gordy was extremely reluctant to release Marvin Gaye's landmark album *What's Going On* because of its dark mood and biting social commentary; as things turned out, it was a major success for Gaye, artistically and commercially.

This shift is most clearly evident in song lyrics. Granted that the six tracks discussed in this chapter are only a small sample. Still, only the Jackson 5's "ABC" continues the cheery mood heard in older Motown songs like "My Girl" or Phil Spector's "Da Doo Ron Ron." The other five take a harder look at everyday life: Gaye's "Inner City Blues" is a lament about tough times, misplaced priorities, and social inequities; Stevie Wonder's "Superstition" is a cautionary tale; the O'Jay's "Back Stabbers" rails against infidelity and treachery; Curtis Mayfield's "Superfly" portrays an antihero; Al Green's "Tired of Being Alone" tells the story of a relationship on the rocks.

## Accentuating the Positive: Rhythm, Mood, and Message

In much of the memorable music created by white artists that we have heard (and will hear), there is a clear resonance between words and music: the Beatles' "Eleanor Rigby," Creedence Clearwater Revival's "Proud Mary," the Velvet Underground's "I'm Waiting for the Man," and the Rolling Stones' "Satisfaction" project markedly different moods. In each case, the music and words work together to project the message of the song.

By contrast, such musical responsiveness to a full range of moods in the lyrics seems almost impossible in black music. Upbeat moods come across clearly, but there seems to be a dissonance in meaning between words and music in those songs with more downbeat lyrics. The reason is the rhythm. In all of the songs considered in this chapter, the rhythms are infectious. It is hard to project a dark mood when it is supported by a foot-tapping groove.

However, even though the impulse to create interesting and engaging rhythms seems to work at cross purposes with the specific message of a song, it sends a more fundamental message that is ultimately positive: where there's a groove, there's life and a reason to live. It can take various forms, as we will hear in the examples discussed in this chapter, and it is also present in funk and reggae, as we will discover in Chapter 15. Indeed, it is inherent in the black music of the last hundred-plus years, from ragtime to rap. In all of this music, we hear rhythm not only as an escape from the pain of the present but also as an affirmation of the spirit of a culture.

## Reclaiming a Legacy: The Collective Memory of the African Diaspora

In Chapter 2, we presented a musical example that coupled a field recording of Yoruba tribesmen with a song by Kool & the Gang almost without missing a beat, literally and figuratively. In terms of their fundamental rhythmic approach, there were no significant differences between the two examples. Both marked a rhythmic layer twice as fast as the beat with a repeated sound—strummed note, keyboard chord—then added freely flowing vocal lines and, more significantly, syncopated rifflike figures that map onto a regular rhythm that moves four times as fast as the beat. "Celebration" also has a backbeat, a rhythmic feature virtually unique to music from the African American tradition. (Brazilian samba features a backbeat-like percussive sound, but it is pitched low.)

It is a virtual certainty that Kool & the Gang did not consciously emulate the Yoruba recording. Rather, they shaped their song by drawing on sounds and rhythms that were very much in the air during the seventies, especially in the music of blacks. In the course of our survey, we have heard black music seemingly come out of nowhere: ragtime burst on the popular music scene around the turn of the century, only a few decades after the end of the Civil War. We have heard the rhythms of black (and black-influenced) music become progressively more active and complex: from the two-beat rhythms of the twenties through the swing and shuffle rhythms of the thirties and forties, and finally the rock rhythms of the fifties and sixties. Each stage in the evolutionary process has doubled the level of activity—from two to four to eight "beats": that is, the explicit or implicit marking of a regular rhythm heard twice, then four times, then eight times per measure.

The next stage in this relentless evolutionary progression surfaces in black music, beginning around 1970. Here, the fastest regular rhythm moves four times as fast as the beat, or sixteen "beats" per measure. In most of the examples included here, this new, faster rhythm is heard directly, usually in addition to a rock beat, or implied in the rhythms of the vocal lines and/or the instrumental riffs that support them. This new style beat would enter the mainstream later in the decade, mainly through disco; from there it would become the most widely used style beat in the music of the 1980s and beyond: in dance music, rap, rhythm and blues, and several rock styles.

That this rhythmic evolution has occurred in music from the United States is almost inexplicable. Recall that the emigration of Africans to the United States was different in kind from the emigration of Europeans. The working-class Europeans brought their music with them and re-created it here: singing songs, playing fiddles, fifes, and occasionally other instruments. By contrast, Africans were sold at auction without regard to tribal or family bonds. Too many slaves newly arrived at a plantation would find themselves unable to communicate, because none of the other slaves spoke their dialect; they were deprived of even the most basic human rights, and they had none of the artifacts of the culture that they had left behind. Moreover, attempts to re-create their music were vigorously suppressed by slave masters; drums were not allowed on slave plantations.

In spite of this, blacks have reclaimed their African musical roots, step by step, during the twentieth century. It seems to have happened without any conscious awareness of African heritage: field recordings of African music making were not widely available during the years before 1970, and those that were available were not familiar to most black musicians. Rather, it is as if the music itself has succeeded in peeling off layers of European oppression and in the process activated the collective memory of a culture. It is nothing short of a miracle.

## The Range of Black Music

Driven by the success of Motown and soul, black music gained a firm toehold in the popular music market during the sixties. During the seventies, it expanded its presence. Black pop became more diverse, with Motown artists moving beyond the restrictive vision of Berry Gordy and other writer-producers taking the Motown idea in new directions. Black music found its way into film and television (for instance, Quincy Jones's music for the popular *Sanford and Son*). By contrast, soul, the most powerful expression of a black sensibility during the sixties, continued its late-sixties decline. Al Green was the only major new voice of the seventies; as it turned out, he was the last of the great soul singers. His decision to leave the entertainment world for the ministry effectively closed the book on soul. Funk, the most African black music of the seventies, seldom crossed over to the pop charts. Its impact would occur late in the decade and into the eighties (we discuss it in Chapter 15).

All of this happened even though the largely integrated music scene of the sixties gave way to a more segregated and white-dominated industry. This was true at every level. The audience divided into black and white, to a greater extent than the decade before. The music industry, and especially **AOR (album-oriented rock)** radio, encouraged this. Entire genres—glam rock, art rock, soft rock—lost their connection to rock's roots. Nevertheless, the gains of black music, commercially and artistically, were not curtailed—just as civil rights legislation prevented conservatives from rolling back the progress toward racial equality. The most popular black music of the seventies talked about love, a theme universal enough to blur racial boundaries.

# Motown in the Early Seventies: New Acts, New Attitudes

Perhaps the best way to understand Motown's evolution in the early seventies is generationally. The "Young America" that Gordy had targeted in the early sixties had grown up. At the same time, many of Motown's acts had also matured, and they were anxious to explore new directions. As a result, Motown's freshest sounds came mainly from two sources: new faces (most notably the Jackson 5) and Motown veterans going in new directions (Marvin Gaye, Stevie Wonder, and Diana Ross). The Jackson 5 attracted another generation of young fans, while many of the Motown veterans expanded their audience.

## The Jackson 5

The Jackson 5 was both a Motown product and a product of Motown. Motown's success inspired scores of imitators. Among them was the family of Joseph and Katherine Jackson, living in the industrial city of Gary, Indiana. Joseph Jackson was a crane operator and frustrated musician; Katherine gave birth to nine children, all of whom would eventually have professional musical careers.

Their first successful incarnation was as the Jackson 5. It consisted of the five oldest boys in the Jackson family: Jackie (b. 1951), Tito (b. 1953), Jermaine (b. 1954), Marlon (b. 1957), and Michael (b. 1958). Their father had started them on their career

Bettmann/Corbis

The Jackson 5 performing on their own television special, 1971. From left to right: Tito, Marlon (obscured by the guitar neck), Michael, Jackie, and Jermaine.

as the Jackson 5 around 1964, when Michael was only 6. Within a few years they were opening for major soul acts. In 1969, they came to the attention of Berry Gordy, most likely through Gladys Knight (although Diana Ross was given credit for "discovering" them). He signed them, they released their first single for Motown—the number 1 hit "I Want You Back" (1969)—and they were on their way.

The Jackson 5 were an immediate sensation: they had three more number 1 singles the following year. Among them was "ABC." The themes of the song are as old as rock and roll: school and teen love. However, even more than the teen idols of the late fifties or the Beatles, the Jackson 5, and especially Michael, were speaking *for* their age group rather than *to* it. Michael's pre-puberty sound gave their performance an innocence that it might not have had with a more mature voice. Certainly, when Michael asks the "girl" to "shake it, shake it, baby," there is none of the sexual innuendo heard in, let's say, Ray Charles's line from "What'd I Say," when he remarks that she sure knows how to "shake that thing."

If their lyrics and vocal style projected an air of childlike innocence (they voiced over their own Saturday morning cartoon beginning in 1971 and received a commendation from Congress in 1972 for their "contributions to American youth"), their music was sophisticated and current. Their father had drilled them relentlessly (Katherine's autobiography, released in the late eighties, detailed his abuses), and Motown, since relocated to Los Angeles, supplied topflight instrumental backing and production.

"ABC," the Jackson 5 (1970)

Like sixties Motown hits, "ABC" balanced accessibility and sophistication. The hook, "A, B, C," was simple enough to sink deeply, and the bass line underneath the chorus was a simple scale (the first three notes are A, B, C#!). What made the song current were the rhythm and the texture. An augmented rhythm section—drums, congas, tambourine—laid down an active, highly syncopated 16-beat rhythm that floated effortlessly under Michael during the verse. Partly because of these more active rhythms, the emphasis is more on rhythm than melody. The multiple percussion instruments—spotlighted in the middle of the song—join the Jacksons and electronic keyboards and bass to create a busy and vibrant texture.

---

### ♪ KEY FEATURES

**"ABC," the Jackson 5 (1970)**

- The Jacksons' sound: Michael's teen innocence (his voice hasn't broken)
- Active, syncopated rhythms
- Rich texture, with many rhythmic strands
- Simple and catchy vocal and instrumental hooks
- Throwback to teen-themed rock and roll of fifties and early sixties

---

Songs like "ABC" mark the beginning not only of a new kind of black pop, but also a new kind of pop. In the lyrics and how they are presented, the vocal style(s), and in the active, danceable rhythms, there is a direct link between the music of the Jackson 5 and the pop of Michael Jackson and Madonna in the 1980s and on to Britney Spears, Mariah Carey, and Christina Aguilera around the turn of the century. We trace this connection in subsequent chapters.

The Jackson 5 was Gordy's last big act and Motown's only successful new act in the seventies. By the mid-seventies, Berry Gordy was no longer a major creative force in popular music. His reluctance to cede artistic control led to fractious relationships with many of his acts. From the beginning, he had butted heads with the Jacksons' father. By 1976, they had left Motown and re-formed themselves as the Jacksons, although Jermaine, who had married Gordy's daughter Hazel, remained at Motown. All of the remaining Jackson children had solo careers in addition to their on again/off again collaborations; Michael's and Janet's have been by far the most successful. Their collective and individual success have made the Jackson family pop music's most enduring family dynasty for the better part of three decades.

## Beyond Motown: The Music of Marvin Gaye

From the beginning of their association, Marvin Gaye (1939–1984) had chafed at the tight control Berry Gordy exercised over his career. Gaye, who had a deep interest in jazz, wanted to branch out in that direction. Gordy, who rightfully viewed Gaye as Motown's sexiest male act, wanted him to mine the same vein that had brought him success with songs like "How Sweet It Is (To Be Loved by You)" and "I Heard

Neal Preston/Corbis

Marvin Gaye, 1975. His post-Motown independence included both musical and sartorial freedom.

It Through the Grapevine." After extensive wrangling, Gaye got Gordy's approval to create his own album.

The result was *What's Going On*. Released in 1971, it was a commercial and artistic success. It took a hard look at life in Motown—the city—with songs like "Inner City Blues" and the title track. At the same time, the music behind the words and ideas developed in range and complexity, to support the deepened emotional weight of the songs. Both the album and three singles from it hit the Top 10.

www

"Inner City Blues," Marvin Gaye (1971)

Gaye's lyric in the title track is part lament, part exhortation. It alludes to Vietnam, race relations, and the generation gap—burning issues throughout the country at the time. In the title phrase "What's going on," he simply shakes his head. At the same time, he urges us to find the answer to our problems in love, not hate. The music—with its lush texture, rich, jazz-inspired harmonies, and subtle and active rhythms—sends a similar message.

The darkest song on the album, in words and music, is "Inner City Blues." The song begins with percussion, a soft one-pitch riff on a keyboard, and sustained chords. Other instruments layer in: congas, bass drum, bass, and Gaye's wordless vocal that harks back to the scat singing of Louis Armstrong and Ella Fitzgerald. Despite the multiple instrumental strands and active rhythms, the sound is dark, bleak, and empty. The bass and conga drum are in the forefront; their low pitch helps darken the sound. The piano chords come at widely spaced but regular intervals, like a bell tolling. The static harmony—it shifts once to the IV chord, then returns—is not a blues progression, but it is blueslike in its slow shifts between harmonies. It seems to convey the despair of those trapped in an endless cycle of poverty. The active percussion sounds seem to emulate an urban soundscape: the ambient noises of the ghetto. Even in this context, they are a sign of life.

Gaye's vocal lines—he sings all the vocal parts—start high and finish low, as they typically do in a blues song. Mostly there are snippets of melody: two- or three-note riffs, until the key phrase of the lyric "make you wanna holler." When the strings—the other prominent strand in the texture—enter, they operate in a high register. The open space between violins and bass is filled mainly by Gaye's voices; this spacing reinforces the bleak mood of the song. Just past the middle of the track, Gaye gives up on words and simply scats; this leads to an out-of-tempo reprise of the first part of "What's Going On," which in turn reinforces the underlying unity of Gaye's album.

"Inner City Blues" clearly grows out of the Motown sound. It retains Motown's easy points of entry: straightforward lyrics, melodic hooks, distinctive sounds (the

♪  **KEY FEATURES**

**"Inner City Blues," Marvin Gaye (1971)**

- Bleak texture: well-spaced piano chords, static harmony, active rhythms, and bass, plus Gaye's vocals create a dark sound that matches the lyric.
- Black music as social commentary.
- More active rhythms: clear 16-beat rhythm.
- Jazz influence: most evident in Gaye's scat singing.

piano chords, especially), active rhythms. But it is richer in texture, more purposeful musically, and totally different in mood from most Motown songs—recall that Gordy had grave reservations about the marketability of this album. And it strips away the polish that we associate with Motown acts, just as the cover of the album shows Gaye wearing everyday clothes for a winter day, not the tuxedo that he and other male Motown singers typically wore in performance.

In its depiction of the hard life of inner-city residents in both words and music, "Inner City Blues" is exceptional. There are few examples of black pop that address social issues, and even fewer that succeed in enhancing the message musically as well as Gaye does here. In the previous discussion, we noted the musical influence of the blues on Gaye's song. In an important way, Gaye's song is a bridge between blues and rap, the two black styles that have tackled social issues more frequently than any other. It updates the blues as social commentary and lays the groundwork for rap; Gaye's wordless vocal and the dark, empty texture seem to anticipate early rap tracks, such as the tracks by Grandmaster Flash and Public Enemy, which we hear in Chapter 17.

Gaye's album, and its success, indicated major changes at Motown; so did the music of Stevie Wonder. Wonder, a popular member of the Motown stable since his early teens, assumed artistic control of his music shortly after Gaye did. He would enjoy his greatest success in the seventies.

## Beyond Motown: The Music of Stevie Wonder

There's a certain irony that Motown's most powerful and original talent, and its longest-running success story, is in many ways the antithesis of the Motown image and sound. Stevie Wonder is a solo act; most Motown acts were groups. The visual element was crucial to Motown's success: its groups, dressed in gowns or tuxedos, moved through stylized, carefully choreographed routines as they sang their songs. Our enduring image of Stevie Wonder: a blind man with sunglasses and long braided and beaded hair, dressed in a dashiki, sitting behind a keyboard and rocking from side to side in a random rhythm. Motown recordings were collective enterprises; behind the groups were largely anonymous songwriters and studio musicians. Wonder created his own recordings from soup to nuts: not only singing and playing all the instruments at times, but also performing the technical tasks—recording, mixing, mastering, and so on.

There are also differences in subject and attitude. In the mid-sixties, Motown song lyrics talked mainly about young love, usually in racially neutral, often idealized language. Only reluctantly did they begin to address "real life" in songs like the Supremes' "Love Child." By contrast, Stevie Wonder took on social issues from his self-produced first album; the vignette of an innocent man's arrest in "Living for the City" is chilling. Where Berry Gordy waffled politically and socially, even at the height of the civil rights movement, Stevie Wonder has advocated a long list of causes, from his firm push for a national holiday for Martin Luther King Jr. to rights for the blind and disabled.

Stevie Wonder was born Steveland Morris (some accounts say Steveland Judkins) in 1950. A hospital error at birth left him blind. By 10, he was a professional performer, singing and playing the harmonica (he also played piano and drums). Within two years, he had signed a Motown contract and was being billed as "Little Stevie Wonder, the 12-Year-Old Genius." (The "little" disappeared two years later, but the "Wonder" stuck.) He had a number of hits in the sixties, including "Uptight" (1966) and the beautiful love song, "My Cherie Amour" (1969), but emerged as a major force in popular music only in the early seventies. The reason: when he turned 21 he negotiated a contract with Motown that guaranteed him complete control over his work.

Wonder was the most popular black artist of the seventies. A series of albums, beginning with *Music of My Mind* (1972), established his unique sound and cemented his reputation as a major player in popular music. Each album release was a major event within the black community, and his recordings also enjoyed enormous cross-over success.

"Superstition,"
Stevie Wonder
(1972)

The widespread popularity of Wonder's music grows out of a style that is broad in its range, highly personal in its sound, and universal in its appeal. His music is a compendium of current black musical styles: in his songs are the tuneful melodies and rich harmonies of black romantic music, the dense textures and highly syncopated riffs of funk, the improvisatory flights of jazz, and the subtle rhythms of reggae and Latin music. Yet, even though he absorbs influences from all quarters, his style is unique.

"Superstition," a number 1 single from the 1972 album *Talking Book*, is a funky up-tempo song with a finger-wagging lyric; in it he chastises those who would let their lives be ruled by superstitious beliefs. The melody that carries the lyric grows slowly out of a simple riff. Like so many Motown (and rock-era) songs, it builds inexorably to the title phrase. The harmony shows the two sources of his style: the verse sits on a bed of riffs, all built from the African American pentatonic scale; there is no harmonic change. By contrast, the transition to the hook is supported by rich, jazzlike harmonies.

Graham Wood/Evening Standard/Getty Images

Stevie Wonder performing in London, January 1974. Notice the stacked keyboards.

> ♪ **KEY FEATURES**
>
> **"Superstition," Stevie Wonder (1972)**
> - Lyrics that talk about a real-life issue
> - Multiple catchy riffs
> - Chords appropriated from jazz and popular song via Motown, but applied in a highly imaginative and individual way
> - Dense textures and complex, syncopated rhythms
> - Fresh, new sounds of synthesizers
> - Wonder's resonant, upbeat voice

The most distinctive element of Stevie Wonder's sound, however, is the rich texture that flows underneath the vocal line. The song begins simply enough, with a rhythmically secure drum part. Onto this, Wonder layers multiple lines: the signature riff, a repeated-note bass line, plus several more riffs in the background, all highly syncopated. Stevie played all the lines on synthesizers, overdubbing until he produced the dense, funky texture that became one of his trademarks. (Wonder was one of the first musicians to develop a sound based almost completely on synthesizers.)

**Stevie Wonder and Blacks' Embrace of Technology** Among the people of the African diaspora, the impulse to play with sound seems almost as strong as the impulse to play with rhythm. Two aspects of this impulse that seem especially persistent are the discovery of found sounds and the quest to make multiple sounds at the same time. Found sounds have taken many forms: making instruments out of everyday materials, like the cowbell in Cuban music, the steel drums of Calypsonians, or the turntables of rap DJs; using everyday objects—a toilet plunger, the neck of a beer bottle—to modify the sound of a conventional instrument; or simply inventing new ways of making sound from an instrument, like "patting juba" by tapping out rhythms on various parts of one's body or slapping an electric bass.

The most familiar instance of the tendency to play multiple instruments simulta-neously is the drum kit. More complex expressions of this practice range from jazz multi-instrumentalist Rahsaan Roland Kirk's ability to play the saxophone and two other instruments simultaneously to one-man bands like the obscure Abner Jay, the self-styled "last great southern black minstrel show," who accompanied himself with an electric guitar, bass drum, and hi-hat when he sang or played harmonica.

With his emancipation from Gordy's tight control, Wonder was able to combine both of these practices and take them high-tech. Both the electronic instruments—especially keyboards—that Wonder used on recordings like "Superstition" and the 24-track mixing boards that made the recording possible were new, rapidly developing technologies. Wonder was the first major artist, black or white, to take them to their logical extreme: make a complete recording by not only assembling it track by track but recording each track himself.

Others followed his lead in using high-end technology in the production process, although few filled as many roles as he did—Prince stands out in this regard. But the skillful production of Quincy Jones for Michael Jackson; the house music scene in Chicago and techno in Detroit during the eighties; the sampling of rap producers from the mid-eighties on—all these and more are clear signs of the enthusiasm with which blacks have embraced cutting-edge technology. It is as if they are making up for the generations in which they had little or no access to new technology. From this perspective, we can understand Wonder as a pivotal figure: the person who modernized and combined the practices of playing multiple instruments and finding new sound by using the latest technology.

"Superstition" shows us the rhythmic side of Wonder's musical personality; there is also a romantic side, as evidenced in songs like "You Are the Sunshine of My Life." In either mode, Stevie Wonder is an optimist, a "the glass is half full" person. Even in his darkest songs, hope is implicit, if not in the lyric, then in the bounce of the beat. How can you be down if your hips are shaking and your foot is tapping the beat? Wonder's optimism is remarkable in light of numerous personal problems. Not only has he been blind from birth, but he suffered through a devastating automobile accident in 1973 that left him in a coma for several days. He followed this adversity with some of his best music. He remains one of the icons of rock-era music.

## The Philadelphia Sound—and Beyond

In the early seventies, it seemed as if Motown had opened a branch office in Philadelphia. The most Motown-like records of the period appeared on Gamble and Huff's Philadelphia International label, not Gordy's. The basic formula was the same: lush orchestrations, solid rhythms coming from a rhythm section that had played together for years, jazz-tinged instrumental lines—all supporting vocal groups singing about the ups and downs of love. Only the details were different.

Three men engineered the **Philadelphia sound**: Kenny Gamble (b. 1943), Leon Huff (b. 1942), and Thom Bell (b. 1941). All were veterans of the Philadelphia music scene; they had worked together off and on during the early sixties in a group called Kenny Gamble and the Romeos. By mid-decade, Gamble and Huff had begun producing records together. They enjoyed their first extended success with Jerry Butler, who revived his career under their guidance. Their big break came in 1971, when Clive Davis, the head of Columbia Records, helped them form Philadelphia International Records. The connection with Columbia assured them of widespread distribution, especially in white markets.

"Back Stabbers," the O'Jays (1972)

The artist roster at Philadelphia International included the O'Jays, Harold Melvin and the Blue Notes, Teddy Pendergrass (who left the group to go solo), Billy Paul, and MFSB, which was the house band. Their competition came mainly from Thom Bell, who produced the Stylistics and the Spinners, a Detroit group who went nowhere at Motown but took off when paired with Bell in 1972.

The O'Jays' "Back Stabbers" (1972) shows how Gamble, Huff, and Bell extended and updated the black pop style developed at Motown. The instrumental introduction of "Back Stabbers" runs for 40 seconds—far longer than any of the Motown intros. It begins with a quasi-classical piano tremolo, an ominous rumble that helps establish the dark mood of the song. The unaccompanied piano riff that follows simply hangs in sonic space; there is still no regular beat keeping. Finally, the rest of the rhythm section enters, with the guitarist playing a jazz-style riff.

The rhythm sound is fuller than late sixties Motown records, not just because of the addition of Latin percussion instruments (Motown had been using them for years) but because there are more of them, and the reinforcement of the beat and the eight-beat layer is more prominent. After the conclusion of the opening phrase, the strings and, later, brass enter; all combine to create a lush backdrop for the O'Jays.

The song, co-written by Huff, advises a hypothetical person to guard against "friends" who are out to steal his woman. Like so much black pop, the song is about love, or at least a relationship. What's different about the lyric is that the narrator is an outside observer, rather than the person in the relationship. In effect, it's "I Heard It Through the Grapevine" told from the other side of the grapevine, but up-close and personal. It was the first of a series of such songs by the O'Jays.

♪ **KEY FEATURES**

**"Back Stabbers," the O'Jays (1972)**
- Extensive, multistage instrumental introduction
- Abundance of melodic hooks, in vocal and instrumental parts
- Active, syncopated rhythms played by large rhythm section: piano, guitar, bass, drums, and extra percussion
- Rich orchestration: rhythm, plus strings and horns
- Sprawling form framed by the refrain

As the Key Features list makes clear, the Philadelphia sound, as typified in this song, is the Motown formula—revised, expanded, and modernized. The instrumental introductions are grander; the texture is richer; the songs themselves are more complicated; the spotlighted instruments are more contemporary sounding (in the case of the guitar) or more exotic (in the case of the vibraphone); and there is greater rhythmic freedom, not only in the opening but also in the syncopated riffs that are the instrumental hooks of the songs.

The formula behind the Philadelphia sound worked well for the better part of the decade. By the late seventies, however, it would be largely superseded by a more musically obvious version of itself: disco.

**Barry White** Barry White (1944–2003) outdid both Motown and the Philadelphia producers in the elaborateness of his production and the explicitness of his message, which re-created the sexual experience in music over and over. White might be best described as the "minister of love." Most of his hit songs begin with a spoken erotic fantasy set over a pulsating rhythm track. Like a black preacher whipping his congregation into a frenzy, he lets the music build until he finally breaks into song. The most immediate precedent for his spoken prologues is the music of Isaac Hayes, but the idea of a smooth transition from speech to song goes back to the black church. All this unfolds on an epic scale. The prologue to "I'm Gonna Love You Just a Little More Baby," his first big hit, lasts over a minute and a half, and the song proper doesn't get underway until almost 2 minutes have passed.

The songs themselves are effective, but the prologues are public pillow talk—soft porn in music. As such, they lend themselves to parody. In an early *Saturday Night Live* sketch, Chevy Chase lampooned White: dressed in a white suit, sitting at a white piano, and billing himself as "Very White," he let the spoken prologues build—as if toward climax—but never sang the song: the shtick was all foreplay.

## Black Films, Black Music

Among the most visible consequences of the civil rights movement was the emergence of a film genre created by blacks for a predominantly black audience. Called **blaxploitation** ("black" + "exploitation"), these were a black take on the action films of the sixties. The first two big-budget blaxploitation films were *Shaft* (1971), which is still the signature film of the genre (and which was remade in 2000) and *Superfly*, 1972. In *Shaft* the main character was a hero: Shaft, a private detective, portrayed by Richard Roundtree. By contrast, the main character in *Superfly* was an anti-hero: Ron O'Neal portrayed a drug dealer. Both were set in the ghetto, a gritty backdrop that resonated well with black audiences, rather than a middle-class neighborhood.

To create music in tune with the plot and atmosphere of these films, producers turned to experienced black musicians. For the film score to *Shaft*, producers tapped Isaac Hayes, who helped mastermind the Stax soul sound during the mid-sixties and had just begun a solo career. For *Superfly*, they turned to Curtis Mayfield (1942–1999). In 1958 Mayfield had joined the Impressions, one of the top black vocal groups of the sixties, and he stayed with them throughout the sixties. During this same period, he became increasingly active as a songwriter and producer. He left the Impressions at the end of the decade and released his first solo album in 1970. His score for *Superfly* was his most significant commercial and artistic success. It topped the album charts for a month in 1972. His ability to marry insightful social commentary with compelling grooves would inspire numerous rhythm-and-blues and rap acts: Ice-T, Public Enemy, and Lenny Kravitz cite his music as an important influence.

"Superfly,"
Curtis Mayfield
(1972)

The title track single from *Superfly*, which reached the Top 10, shows how Mayfield told it like it was over music that evoked the setting of the film as it found a funky groove. The lyric is a description of the main character, Youngblood Priest. Singing in his soulful falsetto, Mayfield functions as a one-man chorus in a classical Greek tragedy: a disinterested observer commenting on the drama. He portrays Priest frankly, ticking off his attributes in terse phrases even as he figuratively shakes his head at Priest's errant path.

Musically, "Superfly" finds substantial common ground with Gaye's "Inner City Blues": the prominent role of Latin percussion instruments and the active rhythms they help create; the short vocal phrases; static harmony through long stretches of the song; the bass as the focal rhythm instrument; the open-sounding middle register, occupied primarily by the vocal line. In the early seventies, these seemed to evoke the inner-city landscape. But the tempo is quicker, Mayfield's voice is lighter, the horn riffs are brighter, and Mayfield's wah-wah guitar adds a distinctive color. These and other features help convey a more upbeat mood.

Interestingly, the music for *Superfly* (and *Shaft*) had far more crossover appeal than the films themselves: gross revenue from the soundtrack album exceeded the gross from the film. Indeed, the blaxploitation genre died off in the latter part of the

♪ **KEY FEATURES**

**"Superfly," Curtis Mayfield (1972)**
- Expanded percussion section, with prominent Latin instruments
- Short vocal phrases allow extended instrumental responses
- Open sound, with strong bass, other instruments in higher register
- Active rhythms with lots of syncopation

seventies, due in no small part to the backlash from the black community about the negative role models featured in the films. Mayfield would never match the commercial peak that he achieved with this soundtrack, which remains one of the landmark albums of the seventies.

# Soul in the Seventies

By the early seventies, soul had fallen on hard times. After 1970, the hits stopped coming for most of the southern soul stars. Nevertheless, positive reverberations of the soul style helped diversify the sound of black music in the early seventies. The music of Aretha Franklin and James Brown, soul music's most powerful voices, changed in the seventies. In Franklin's s case it came about through an expansion of her stylistic range; in Brown's case through the continuing rhythmic evolution of his music. Soul music's new voice—and its last great one—was Al Green.

## Al Green

Like virtually all other soul stars, Al Green (b. 1946) grew up singing in church. When he was 9, he and some of his brothers formed a gospel quartet that performed first in and around his Arkansas hometown, about 40 miles west of Memphis, then in Michigan, where his family moved when he was 12. And like many other soul singers, he began his career in his teens. The crucial event early in his professional life was his encounter with Willie Mitchell, who owned Hi Records in Memphis. Mitchell became not only his boss but also his partner: co-producing his records and co-writing many of Green's hits.

"Tired of Being Alone," Al Green (1971)

Although he had an isolated hit in 1967, Green's career effectively began in 1970. Within a year, he had crossed over to the pop charts: "Let's Stay Together," his biggest hit, topped both the R&B and pop charts in late 1971. He remained a presence on the charts for most of the decade.

Green brought subtlety and sophistication to both his songwriting and singing without sacrificing its soulfulness. All qualities are evident in his first big crossover hit, "Tired of Being Alone" (1971). Its basic design is the "refrain-frame" form that dates back to "Maybellene," but the verse is in a different key from the chorus and quite long. In addition, there is an open-ended section where Green simply "goes off." In general design, then, the song is in step with rock-era songwriting, but the details make Green's song distinctive almost to the point of idiosyncrasy.

Frank Driggs Collection/Getty Images

Al Green, performing in 1974; he would retire from pop singing shortly after this appearance.

However, it is his singing—and the man behind the voice—that is the main focus here. Green's voice is a remarkably flexible instrument. He is a tenor: his basic sound is higher-pitched and lighter than most other soul singers. Even more distinctive, however, are the variations in the basic sound. Less than a minute into the recording, we have already heard several different vocal qualities:

- A plaintive sound in the chorus
- A huskier sound for the first phrase of the verse (at about 23 seconds)
- A more matter-of-fact sound on the second phrase (at about 35 seconds)

He even changes sound on a single note: each pulsation on the syllable "me" (at 30 seconds) features a different shade of vocal color.

This variety is evident even before Green goes into high, head-voice singing, or falsetto (his effortless, floating lines anticipate the buoyant sound of the Bee Gees), or begins to use the moans, stutters, melismas, and other devices that are part of his vocal arsenal. All these dimensions make his singing more varied and subtle than the other soul singers, who tended to rely more on brute power. Al Green is Muhammad Ali to the sixties soul singers' Joe Frazier, Sonny Liston, and George Foreman: his voice can float like a butterfly and sting like a bee, as well as punch with authority.

♪ **KEY FEATURES**

**"Tired of Being Alone," Al Green (1971)**
- Richly expressive vocal style
- Enormous range of vocal sounds and effects
- Shifts in mood underscored by changes in singing style and shifts in key and accompaniment
- Great rhythmic freedom over a steady rock beat

As a result, Green's singing was intimate: women took its erotic messages personally. His appearance and stage manner certainly encouraged this perception. During his heyday, he had the svelte physique of a welterweight in fighting trim; photographs show him bare-chested, even in performance. And he teased his audience with his moves as well as his voice. Women, certain that he was singing only to them, showered him with gifts: bras and panties were thrown on stage as a token of his female fans' affection and excitement.

Green's sensuality soon led to tragedy. In 1974, one of his girlfriends poured hot grits on him, burning him over several parts of his body, and then shot herself. Green took it as a sign that he had become too worldly—his father had expelled him from the family gospel group while he was in his early teens for listening to "profane music"— so he turned back to religion. In 1976, he started his own church in Memphis but continued to tour. Another incident in 1979, when he fell off the stage but escaped serious injury, convinced him to retire from secular music, which he has largely done. Since then, Green has devoted himself mainly to gospel music, although he has appeared and recorded occasionally with other rock artists.

Green was the last and one of the greatest of the soul singers. Certain features of his style—especially the stutters, moans, and yelps—recall more directly than any other the singing of Ray Charles, the artist most responsible for the sound of soul. So in effect Green's career completes the circle. And his decision to enter the ministry closes a larger circle. With "I Got a Woman," Ray Charles helped shape soul by expropriating music from the black church; Green helped reinvigorate black gospel music with a large helping of soul.

## Crossroads: The Blues in Black and White

The musicians who began their careers in the seventies represent the first generation of rock-era artists whose music was not shaped directly by the blues. Both fifties rock and roll and rhythm and blues grew out of blues styles, and the core-defining rock of the sixties grew out of a further infusion of blues. By 1970, however, both black and white musicians were far less likely to encounter the blues directly and to bring it into their music.

The diminishing influence of the blues was due principally to two factors: the evolutionary stasis of the blues and the commercial ascendancy of rock and rhythm and blues. During the first half of the twentieth century, blues was not one style but several, as we heard in Chapters 2 and 3. Moreover, blues was the cutting-edge music during this time. From the hot new dance music of the 1910s and 1920s to post–World War II rhythm and blues and rock and roll, blues drove the evolution of popular music; it helped shape the rhythms of the fox-trot, swing, rhythm and blues, and rock.

However, by the early sixties, blues was no longer a current music or an evolving music. For rock-era audiences, blues usually meant either the country bluesmen, living and dead, whose careers were resurrected by the folk revival, or electric bluesmen like Muddy Waters, B. B. King, and Elmore James. And even electric blues had settled into a groove, where it still is. The style is, in essence, frozen in time. As a result, blues would play no direct role in shaping the more active rhythms of the seventies.

By the end of the sixties, rock had become the dominant popular music. The majority of aspiring rock and rhythm-and-blues musicians listened to this current music, rather than more dated roots music, to find inspiration for their music. The next wave of "outsider" styles would find inspiration from outside the United States. Reggae and Latin music would play a more crucial role than the blues in shaping the music of the late seventies and eighties.

Because the direct influence of the blues on rock-era music was essentially complete by 1970, we can assess the extent and nature of its impact. What is most fascinating is that the influence does not divide along racial lines. In previous chapters, we have documented the influence of blues on the rhythms of rock-era music, the extensive use of blues form, the influence of blues style in singing and playing, and the emphasis on being "real" that comes most directly from the blues. The final area of blues influence came from its harmony—not so much in the use of a blues progression, but in the fundamentally different approach to harmony implicit in the most authentic blues styles, such as those of Robert Johnson and Muddy Waters.

There are two features of blues harmony in these styles that found their way into seventies music. One is the slow rate of chord change—indeed, some blues songs have no change of harmony. The other is that chords simply follow one another; they do not leave the home chord, then progress back to it by a conventional path. More specifically, chords that are unstable in a pop song or church hymn because they imply movement to another chord are stable harmonies in the blues. So, although the chords are familiar, they do not operate in the same way that they do in their original context.

The music most influenced by the harmonic aspect of the blues was the rock heard in Chapters 9 and 10; up-tempo soul songs, especially those of James Brown; the music of Sly and the Family Stone; and Marvin Gaye and—to a lesser extent—Stevie Wonder and Curtis Mayfield in this chapter. For rock musicians, blues harmony was a springboard to develop a new harmonic approach, one that abandoned the tension and release present in conventional harmony. For black musicians, it was evident in slowly changing or static harmonies as well as the use of chord sequences that also avoided conventional progressions. In either case, harmony of this kind was capable of projecting a darker mood than conventional harmony, as we heard in songs as diverse as "Paranoid" and "Inner City Blues."

From the mid-sixties on, the influence of blues style on harmony has more to do with the orientation of the music than it does with race. Melodically oriented music—Beatles or Motown, singer-songwriters or Philadelphia—will show relatively little blues influence. By contrast, music more oriented to rhythm and sound tends to make use of blues-influenced harmonies and other features.

## The Continuing Evolution of Black Music

Most of the most popular black music of the seventies built on the innovations of Motown. The music coming from Philadelphia and Motown expanded upon the formula that worked so successfully during the sixties. More innovative music came from the two artists who emancipated themselves from Motown's artistic control: Stevie Wonder's cutting-edge use of technology and musical variety and Marvin Gaye's social commentary. These strands of black pop would continue to evolve. It would help shape disco and eventually lead not only to the black pop of the eighties and beyond but also the dance-oriented pop of Michael Jackson, Madonna, and the wave of rising stars—black, white, and Latin—who followed along this path.

Other contemporary black pop styles also appeared in the early seventies, including the more mature pop styles of Roberta Flack and Bill Withers, both of whom were in their 30s by the time they broke through; and there were the jazz/R&B/pop blends of Grover Washington Jr. and especially George Benson—a first-rate jazz guitarist as well as a fine singer—who became the first artist to have an album top the pop, R&B, and jazz charts simultaneously when *Breezin'* hit number 1 in 1976.

By contrast, soul largely disappeared from the scene with Al Green's decision to give up his career in popular music to return to the church. However, it helped shape several important developments in seventies black music, including the jazz/R&B fusions of groups such as the Crusaders, funk, and a new wave of black gospel music.

The use of black music in a black film genre was a major commercial breakthrough for black music. The success of film scores such as *Shaft* and *Superfly* gave black musicians a toehold in this part of the music industry.

These black music styles were comfortably inside the music industry. Despite the implicit segregation of AOR playlists, black pop artists continued to chart well and tour successfully. Indeed, Stevie Wonder was one of only five acts among the Top 20 recording artists on both the singles and album charts during the seventies. (The others were Elton John, Paul McCartney and Wings, Chicago, and Neil Diamond.)

Two other black musical styles—reggae from Jamaica and funk from the United States—were largely on the outside looking in during the early seventies. Their time would come later in the decade, as we discover in Chapter 15.

- - - - - - - - - - - - - - - - - - - - - - - - - - - - - - - - - - - - - - - - - - - - - - - - - - - - - - - - - - - - - - -

**Terms to Remember**

AOR (album-oriented rock)          Philadelphia sound          blaxploitation

- - - - - - - - - - - - - - - - - - - - - - - - - - - - - - - - - - - - - - - - - - - - - - - - - - - - - - - - - - - - - - -

**Applying Chapter Concepts**

1. In the early years of the rock era, the path from black gospel to secular music had gone in only one direction. However, that changed around 1970, when several contemporary gospel recordings (such as Edwin Hawkins Singers' "Oh, Happy Day" and the Staple Singers' "I'll Take You There") crossed over to the charts. Locate a recording by the Staples Singers and a recording by another contemporary black gospel performer, such as Andrae Crouch. Then consider the extent to which these recordings were influenced by black pop and soul.

2. Locate recordings by Bill Withers and/or Roberta Flack and contrast the lyrics, the vocal style, and the instrumental accompaniment (what instruments are included? how are they used?) with black pop examples. Do you find any correlation between musical setting and musical message?

# 14

# Mainstream Rock in the Seventies

The first gold record was a publicity stunt. In the fall of 1941, Glenn Miller and his Orchestra appeared in the film *Sun Valley Serenade*. One of the featured numbers—a long scene in the film—was "Chattanooga Choo Choo," an especially effective swing tune. Sparked by its exposure in the film, the record sold well over 1 million copies in the first three months after its release. To celebrate Miller's success—and to promote their company—RCA Victor sprayed one of the master discs with gold lacquer and presented the "gold record" to Miller in February 1942, during a radio broadcast. Miller's recording was not the first to sell in the millions, but it was the first to receive a gold record for it.

Sixteen years later, the **Record Industry Association of America (RIAA)**, the trade organization for the recording industry, trademarked "**gold record**" and quantified what it represented: sales of 500,000 singles or albums. In March 1958, the RIAA awarded the first gold record to Perry Como for his recording of "Catch a Falling Star." Four months later, they would award the first gold record to an album: the soundtrack for the film version of Rodgers and Hammerstein's *Oklahoma!*

In 1976, the RIAA added a new category, the **platinum record**, to honor sales of 1 million units of a single or album. The first single to receive a platinum single award was Johnnie Taylor's "Disco Lady"; the first platinum album was the Eagles *Their Greatest Hits, 1971–1975*. The Eagles' album has continued to sell well: it currently holds the record for album sales, at 26 million and counting. The RIAA would subsequently create two more awards: in 1984, the **multiplatinum record**, to recognize sales of 2 million or more units, and in 1999, the **diamond record**, to recognize sales of 10 million or more units.

The Eagles' landmark album epitomizes the transformation of rock and the business that supported it in the space of a decade. The revolutionary music of the sixties had morphed into the establishment music of the seventies. The music that topped the album and singles charts in the mid-seventies was typically pleasant and beautifully crafted. Some of it was quirky or superficially outrageous. However, it was seldom confrontational or innovative, and until disco broke through, it was seldom controversial. The increasing conservatism of rock in the seventies reflected not only musical choices by the most popular acts but also the emergence of a rock-as-product mentality. We survey the transformation of the music business next.

# The Business of Rock

In the seventies, rock traded tie-dyed shirts for three-piece suits. In so doing, it turned its core values upside down. From the beginning, rock had portrayed itself as a music of rebellion; rock took over popular music with a revolution. However, as the market share of rock and R&B grew, so did the financial stakes. It cost more to create and promote a record or to put on a concert or operate a venue. There was more money to be made but also more to be lost.

Not surprisingly, a corporate mentality took over the business side of rock. It was evident to some extent in the music itself, in that there were some artists who seemed to place commercial success as the highest priority and let that shape their music. Elton John, the best-selling rock star of the seventies, was the poster boy for this path.

The impact of profit-oriented thinking was far more telling behind the scenes. It determined to a great extent what music would get promoted and how it would get promoted. Its impact was most evident in the media and in the use of new market strategies designed to maximize sales.

## Media and Money

No medium showed the impact of the big business mindset more than radio. In the early years of rock, radio had been an important part of the music's "outsider" image: Alan Freed and other like-minded disc jockeys in the fifties; "underground" FM stations in the sixties. However, in the seventies, the most significant development was AOR (album-oriented rock). In this format, disc jockeys could no longer choose the songs they played. Instead, program directors selected a limited number of songs designed to attract a broad audience while offending as few as possible. Often, stations bought syndicated packages, further homogenizing radio content. Free-form radio all but disappeared, and so did the adventurous spirit that it symbolized. As a result, distortion was out; tunefulness was in. Acts like Barry Manilow, the Carpenters, Stevie Wonder, Chicago, the Eagles, Fleetwood Mac, Paul McCartney and Wings, and of course Elton John got a lot of airplay and topped the charts.

Another significant trend was the consolidation of the record industry. The scores of independent labels that recorded so many of the early R&B and rock acts were key factors in the story of early rock. During the seventies, many of the independent labels merged or were sucked into a major label. As the eighties began, only six companies produced half of the popular music recordings worldwide.

A major business innovation of the seventies was **cross-marketing**. In pursuit of greater financial rewards, record companies used tours to help promote record sales. With improved amplification, the stadium or large arena concert became common-place. More ritual than musical event, these concerts usually confirmed what the audience already knew about the music of a particular band. As a rule, there was little, if any, spontaneity in performance: typically, bands performed songs—usually from current or recent albums—much as they sounded on the recordings.

Often, the performances were more about show than sound, although there was a lot of both. Flamboyance had been part of rock from the start: Elvis, Little Richard, Jerry Lee Lewis, Chuck Berry. Major acts like Jimi Hendrix and Pete Townshend of the Who raised the stakes: Hendrix by setting his guitar on fire; Townshend by destroying both guitar and amps at the end of a show. However, by the early seventies, spectacle had become part of the business: lights, fog, costumes, makeup, pyrotechnics, and the like. Such productions were almost a necessity, because performers had to seem larger than life in large arenas. Glam, the province of David Bowie and Marc Bolan at the beginning of the seventies, had gone mainstream by mid-decade in the live performances of Elton John and Freddie Mercury with Queen.

Another important reason for increased record sales was the development of new playback devices, which were far more versatile than the phonograph.

## Portable Tapes: Cassettes and Eight-Track Tapes

One of the fruits of the Allied victory in World War II was the acquisition of a magnetic tape recorder that German scientists had developed. When brought to the United States after the war, it served as the prototype for the reel-to-reel tape recorders developed by Ampex and others. These reel-to-reel tape recorders belonged to the production side of the music business. They were expensive, difficult to use, and cumbersome to tote around; these factors outweighed their superior fidelity for all but the most dedicated and well-heeled audiophiles. In an effort to make tape playback devices more accessible to consumers, RCA developed the first tape cartridge in 1958.

In the sixties, two important tape-based consumer formats emerged. One was the **four- or eight-track tape**. These tape players began to appear in cars (and Learjets) in 1965. (Bill Lear had the technology developed for his line of corporate jets.) They remained popular through the seventies. The other, more enduring, playback device was the **audio cassette**. A number of manufacturers, most notably Philips, Sony, and Grundig, worked to develop cassettes and cassette players and to come up with a common standard for them. By the seventies, this new technology had caught on: cassette sales grew much faster than LPs (vinyl); by 1982, they would exceed them.

This new format had many advantages. The units were smaller, and so were the playback devices. Some were portable; others went into car consoles. By the mid-seventies, **boom boxes** had appeared; they offered a low-priced and portable alternative to the home stereo. The first **Walkman** came from the Sony factory in 1979; other companies quickly followed suit. All of these devices made listeners' personal recordings as accessible as the radio.

Cassette players also made it possible for consumers to assemble their own playlists, using blank tapes. With improvements in recording quality, most notably the Dolby noise reduction technology, there was less loss in quality during duplication. People could now take their own music with them wherever they went.

We reap the fruits of these innovations today. It's likely that most of you reading this book can burn your own CDs. Many of you carry around an iPod or other personal playback device, where you store hundreds of songs. This technology is so commonplace that most of us take it for granted. But it wasn't always so, or always so easy. Personal, portable playback became a reality only in the late seventies; it has developed much further since that time.

## Rock: The New Mainstream

In the wake of the turbulent sixties, new music and new technology created a new mainstream. The sounds of the music were different; rock had thoroughly supplanted the pop music of the fifties and early sixties as the dominant music. Modes of dissemination increased: stadium concerts made live performance a grander event; cassettes made the music far more portable and customizable than before. However, the basic premise of the marriage between music and commerce remained: create product for profit by appealing to the largest possible audience. The stakes were higher, because of the expenses of production—studio time was expensive—and promotion. So were the standards. Studio recordings were clearly superior in quality to those of earlier generations: the garage-band mentality that had informed so much music of the fifties and sixties had gone underground, to resurface in punk.

As with the business side during the seventies, the dominant trends in the music were consolidation, expansion, and diversification through recombination. The most popular acts locked in to what worked commercially: the majority of songs had engaging lyrics, tuneful melodies, familiar sounds, good beats, and often a special feature or two that gave them distinctive identities. Songs were often comprehensively bigger: they lasted longer and unfolded more slowly, used more instruments, and featured stronger contrasts. (The quintessential early seventies instance of this trend is Led Zeppelin's "Stairway to Heaven," from their 1971 *Led Zeppelin IV* album [*Zoso*]; the song received extensive airplay on FM radio, although it was never released as a single. We discuss Queen's "Bohemian Rhapsody," a somewhat later example of the same trend.) New sounds continued to emerge mainly through the now time-honored rock practice of bringing together existing styles in new combinations, as we hear following. We begin our survey with two of the most flamboyant rock stars of the decade.

# Mainstream Rock: Inclusiveness, Exuberance, Expansiveness

From its inception, rock has been a diverse music. Over the decades, the openness to diversity has helped drive the expansion of rock from an outsiders' music in the United States during its first years, to an international music in the sixties, to a truly global music by the end of the twentieth century. Its performers have increasingly included musicians of all races, genders, nationalities, and persuasions.

In the seventies, Elton John and Freddie Mercury were two prominent examples of rock's inclusionary nature. Neither looked the part of a rock star, at least out of costume. By their own admission, both were/are gay, although in John's case, he did not acknowledge it until after his marriage failed. John was an Englishman; Mercury was born on the African island of Zanzibar, at the time a British colony. As gay, colorful, piano-playing rock icons, they continued the legacy of Little Richard. Unlike Little Richard, who was a commercial novelty despite his importance, John and Queen, Mercury's band, were definitely in the mainstream: John was the most recording popular artist of the seventies; Queen was a major act from mid-decade on.

Both John and Mercury are of below-average height: John is 5 feet 8 inches; Mercury was 5 feet 9 inches. However, on stage and in costume, they came across as larger than life. They projected bigness in their music as well as their appearance. From the start, John cast his music on a large scale, and Queen's "Bohemian Rhapsody" is an extended and extravagant work.

## Elton John: The Expansion of Mainstream Rock

The career of Elton John (born Reginald Dwight, 1947; his stage name came from the first names of fellow band members in his first band, Bluesology) documents one of the most fascinating professional metamorphoses in rock history. In his first albums, he established himself as a thoughtful singer-songwriter of exceptional talent. However, in the early seventies, John transformed his music into true AOR material by inundating himself in Top 40 songs and adopting an outrageous stage persona. His songs found the middle of the road and he found mega-stardom.

John's career is a testimony to the power of personality. Off stage, he is an unlikely looking rock star: short, chunky, balding, and bespectacled. On stage, his costumes and extroverted style made him larger than life; it rendered his natural appearance irrelevant. He was one of the top live acts of the seventies.

Musically, two of the qualities that enabled him to reign supreme on both the singles and albums charts were his range and his craft. His first hits were melodic, relatively low-key songs like "Your Song," but his albums also contained harder-rocking songs like "Take Me to the Pilot." He retained his ability to tell a story in song while infusing his music with pop elements; they helped expand the range of his music. He followed "Crocodile Rock," a fun take on fifties rock and roll and his first number 1 hit, with "Daniel," a sensitive ballad. For the remainder of the decade, he veered from style to style. At the center of his music was his husky voice, which changed character from the soul-tinged sound in songs like "The Bitch Is Back" to a much more mellow sound in songs like "Little Jeannie." Moreover, because of his considerable skill as a songwriter, he was able to fold external elements into his own conception, rather than simply ape an existing sound.

In "Tiny Dancer," a track from his 1971 album *Madman Across the Water*, demonstrates both the craft and the range of his music at the start of his career. The lyric, written by his longtime collaborator Bernie Taupin, begins as if it is going to tell a story. However, as it develops, it resolves into a collage of vivid images. It is as if we see short video clips, which quickly cut away to another scene. There are oblique first-person references; some of the scenes seem to describe a relationship between John and the tiny dancer ("Piano man, he makes his stand"). But it is not a direct narrative.

"Tiny Dancer,"
Elton John
(1971)

David Ashdown/Keystone/Getty Images

Elton John performing in London, March 1974. The eyeglasses and the dress are conservative by John's standards.

John's setting of the lyric begins simply, with John playing nicely syncopated piano chords, first to get the song underway, then to accompany his singing of the melody. Through most of the opening statement of the verse, it is as if the song will be set simply and intimately, like Joni Mitchell's "All I Want" in Chapter 12. However, other instruments enter in stages: steel guitar at the end of the first large section, other rhythm instruments upon the repetition of the opening section, then a choir at the end of the repeated section. At that point, John shifts gears, using the piano to give a stronger, more marked rhythm and shifting the harmony into uncharted waters. This builds toward the chorus, which adds a string countermelody to the many instruments and voices already sounding. The range of John's music is evident in the gradual shift in mood and style, which are part of an organic whole; the craft is evident in such features as the skillfully paced growth in momentum over the full statement of the song and effective addition of instruments.

"Tiny Dancer" also illustrates the comprehensive expansion of rock style in the seventies. Here, it is most evident in its length, form, and resources. As recorded, it takes over 6 minutes to perform: even at this length, there are less than two complete statements of the song. (In "Tiny Dancer," a complete statement consists of two verselike sections that are melodically identical, a transition and a chorus.) This expands the verse/chorus template used, for example, in so many Motown songs. We can gauge the degree of expansion by noting that one verselike *section* is equivalent to a complete "Heart and Soul"–type *song*.

To realize this larger form, John uses a huge ensemble: his voice and piano, plus bass, drums, guitar, steel guitar, backup vocals, rich strings, and choir. The result is, when desired, a denser and fuller-sounding texture. Moreover, John adds and subtracts instruments to outline the form and accumulate musical momentum through the verse sections to the climax of the song in the chorus. "Tiny Dancer" begins quietly enough, with just voice and piano, but instruments gradually join in: steel guitar at the end of the first verse, drums and bass as the second verse section begins, then choir at the end of the second verse section. The song peaks on the words: "Hold me closer," the melodic high point and hook. The preceding material prepares this climax with a new, more agitated beat pattern, shorter phrases, and more active harmony. Only the interlude set to the text, "softly, slowly," momentarily arrests the momentum.

"Tiny Dancer" sheds light on the fact and nature of rock's continuing expansion in the seventies. The expansion is not one-dimensional: it is not just longer, louder, denser, or whatever. Instead, it is a comprehensive expansion: the supplementary instruments and voices—strings, choir, steel guitar—give shape to the expanded form of the song, articulating sections when they drop out, imparting a sense of movement toward a climax as they enter gradually. Here, the expansion of rock style is artfully managed.

The song illustrates John's musical approach just before his mainstream success. He has always been a gifted melodist, as he showed in this song. In the four albums following *Madman Across the Water*, he often integrated catchier riffs and rhythms into his songs. The result was, among other things, unqualified commercial success: all four were number 1 albums; so was a subsequent "greatest hits" compilation.

John remained active through the eighties and nineties, despite his short and difficult marriage to recording engineer Renate Blauel and his acknowledgement of

♪ **KEY FEATURES**

**"Tiny Dancer," Elton John (1971)**

- Taupin's arty, cinematic lyric shifts from image to image: there is no central narrative holding the lyric together. Even the chorus is deliberately obscure.
- Expansive verse/chorus form: the form of "Tiny Dancer" follows a predictable pattern but unfolds on a much grander scale than a typical sixties rock or Motown song.
- Lavish instrumentation: piano, rhythm-section instruments, steel guitar, strings, and voices added layer by layer for maximum impact.

his sexual preferences—after the divorce, he disclosed that he realized that he was gay before marrying; he also has had numerous substance abuse issues. In the early nineties, he cleaned up his life and directed his energy to film and stage. He won his first Grammy in 1994 for one of the songs from the Disney animated film *The Lion King*, written in collaboration with lyricist Tim Rice. Another of their successful projects was what one reviewer called a "camp" remake of Giuseppe Verdi's famous opera *Aida*.

Two of the most impressive and fascinating aspects of John's career are its longevity—he is still churning out hits—and the range of his collaborations. John Lennon's last public appearance came at an Elton John concert in 1974; about three decades later, John performed with Eminem at the Grammy awards ceremony. The list of those with whom he has performed and befriended reads like a rock-era Who's Who. This speaks to not only his musical flexibility but also his generous nature.

This same bighearted spirit extends beyond his musical career. He has been active in AIDS work since the mid-eighties, and he formed the Elton John AIDS Foundation in 1992 after the death of friend and fellow piano-playing rock star Freddie Mercury. The foundation has raised an enormous amount of money for treatment and research. He remains an active performer and the second highest-selling recording artist of all time, with sales of over 60 million units.

## Queen: The Champions of Camp?

Among the bands keeping John company on the charts was Queen, a band fronted by songwriter-pianist-vocalist Freddie Mercury, born Farrokh Bulsara (1946–1991); the other band members were bassist John Deacon (b. 1951), guitarist Brian May (b. 1947), and drummer Roger Taylor (b. 1949).

Even by rock standards, Mercury was an outsider. His family is Parsi, those based in India who follow the teachings of Zoroaster. Parsis fled to India from Iran centuries ago to avoid persecution by Muslims; they eventually formed a close-knit community around Bombay, where they prospered after the arrival of the British colonists. Mercury's father worked for the British colonial government; Bulsara/Mercury was born in Zanzibar, off the coast of Tanzania. His family returned to India, where he received a proper British education, followed by further training at art college in London.

The band came together in 1971 and released their first album two years later. They waited four years for their first hit, "Killer Queen," and broke through the following year with their fourth album, *A Night at the Opera*, which contained "Bohemian Rhapsody," arguably the band's finest moment and still a top contender for the most outrageous rock track of all time. (There is an "operatic" section in "Bohemian Rhapsody," but the titles of the album and the next one, *A Day at the Races*, were taken from Marx Brothers films.)

Like Elton John, Queen presented dynamic and visually exciting stage shows in large arenas: Freddie Mercury was at least as flamboyant as John. Indeed, a promotional video of "Bohemian Rhapsody" anticipated the music videos of the eighties. And like John, Queen had a chameleon-like musical personality as a songwriter and performer: there are distinct contrasts from hit to hit: "We Are the Champions," "Another One Bites the Dust," "Fat-Bottomed Girls."

In "Bohemian Rhapsody," the hit that catapulted them to stardom and got them out of debt, they packed remarkably varied material into a single track: there are jarring contrasts from section to section within this 6-minute track. It begins with close harmony vocals accompanied only by Mercury's piano playing. A rock-ballad-style section follows; the other instruments join in as Mercury sings alone. Guitarist Brian May takes a brief solo, which is based on the melody of Mercury's vocal. There is an abrupt transition to a spoof of operatic style, followed by a heavy metal-sounding instrumental section, which dissolves into a return to the main vocal material.

Freddie Mercury of Queen, performing in 1977.

"Bohemian Rhapsody," Queen (1975)

The title of the album has a multilevel connection with "Bohemian Rhapsody," the only track on the album that blatantly parodies opera. There is the obvious link: *Opera* in the album title and the operatic interlude. However, this clear connection may mask a more subtle and pervasive connection between the madcap humor of the Marx Brothers and Queen's evocation of it in this song. If the dissonance between words and music is intentional, then "Bohemian Rhapsody" is unashamedly camp. The lush close harmony of the opening recalls the fantasy world of doo-wop love songs: even as the lyrics promise no escape from reality, the music provides it. This sets the stage for the even stronger words–music disconnect of the next section.

Because the words tell the horrific tale so melodramatically and because there is no emotional resonance between words and music (the musical style in this section is associated with love songs, not murder), it would seem that Mercury is crying crocodile tears. Indeed, the entire section would seem to be a send-up. Unlike the previous sections, the operatic section is explicitly silly, and the jarring contrasts between sections simply add to the comedic effect. Like the Marx Brothers' 1935 film *A Night at the Opera*, "Bohemian Rhapsody" is a marvelous parody, created with great skill (and at great cost; it was one of the most expensive albums to record up to that point in time) and combining well-executed slapstick moments (especially the operatic section) with more artfully disguised humor.

Band members refuse to acknowledge whether "Bohemian Rhapsody" was indeed a parody. In a 2005 interview, Brian May said:

> I have a perfectly clear idea of what was in Freddie's mind. But it was unwritten law among us in those days that the real core of a song lyric was a private matter for the composer, whoever that might be. So I still respect that.

His remark is reminiscent of John Lennon's disingenuous denial of any connection between LSD and "Lucy in the Sky with Diamonds"; like "Bohemian Rhapsody," the music of that Beatles' song conveys the mood and message far more clearly than the lyrics. It is difficult to take either statement at face value.

---

### ♪ KEY FEATURES

**"Bohemian Rhapsody," Queen (1975)**

- Wonderful demonstration of rock's openness to music of all kinds: jarring juxtapositions of widely contrasting material, from doo-wop harmony and pseudo-opera to guitar-driven rock ballad.
- Drastic discordance between words and music, plus album title and strong musical contrast, suggest strong humorous undercurrent: song is not to be taken at face value.
- "Bohemian Rhapsody" is cast on a grand scale: it is not so much a long song but a very concentrated large-scale work. The model comes from classical music, not rock.

---

Freddie Mercury described Queen as "the Cecil B. DeMille of rock and roll, always wanting to do things bigger and better." Despite their subsequent success, they never created another track on the scale of "Bohemian Rhapsody." The song returned to the charts in 1992 when music and video were included in the film *Wayne's World*. It is still part of Queen's show; the band now tours with Paul Rodgers taking Freddie Mercury's place.

Elton John and Queen were among the most flamboyant mainstream rock acts of the seventies. Underneath the flash, however, was considerable skill and imagination. Both acts have earned their longevity, even if their music—and their lifestyle—are not to everyone's taste.

Keeping them company on the charts were two less flashy but comparably popular acts: the Eagles and Fleetwood Mac.

# From Country to City

Although initially identified most strongly with surf music, southern California quickly became a desirable destination for rock musicians from all over the United States and—later—Canada and Europe. During the mid-sixties, acts as diverse as the Doors, the Byrds, and the Mothers of Invention used southern California as home base, and by the end of the decade, the area had become the center for a remarkable variety of rock/pop/folk/country fusions.

The first strong evidence of this was the emergence of the Byrds, who pioneered folk rock. In 1967, Arkansas-born singer/guitarist Glen Campbell, who had recorded with such diverse acts as the Beach Boys, Elvis Presley, and the Monkees), graduated from session musician to star with a series of country-ish pop albums. That same year, Joni Mitchell also relocated there, where she played a seminal role in developing the singer-songwriter movement. In 1968, Gram Parsons, a singer and songwriter from the Southeast, moved to southern California, joined the Byrds, and led them into country music. The result was *Sweethearts of the Rodeo.* The music was miles away from "Eight Miles High"; more than anything else, it sounded like conscientious non-southerners playing country. Still, it was significant because it represented a deep immersion in country music by an outsider, much as Eric Clapton and Jimmy Page drank in the blues.

In the early seventies, the fruits of the interchange between rock and its country music roots included not only southern rock, the music of the singer-songwriters, and the "American" rock of bands like Creedence Clearwater Revival and the Grateful Dead, but also a true country/rock synthesis, as in the early music of the Eagles. More generally, there were rock songs in which the lyric told a story in direct language; it was set to a tuneful melody and supported by an understated accompaniment. The surpassingly popular storytelling songs of Fleetwood Mac evidence this more general-ized influence of country music.

## The Eagles and the Rise of Country Rock

Formed in 1971 mainly from Linda Ronstadt's backup band, the Eagles became one of the most successful rock groups of the seventies. The original Eagles were Don Henley (b. 1947), drums; Glenn Frey (b. 1948), guitar; Bernie Leadon (b. 1947), country instruments—banjo, steel guitar, and others; and Randy Meisner (b. 1946), bass. Don Felder (b. 1947), who also played an assortment of country instruments, joined the group in 1974.

The song that helped put both the Eagles and **country rock** on the map was their first single, the 1972 hit, "Take It Easy." It demonstrates their wonderfully effective fusion of rock and country elements. The lyric is all country: women trouble, trucks, small towns (Winslow is east of Flagstaff), but the music smoothly blends rock and country elements. The song begins with a low-wattage power chord, after which it settles into a nice rock groove.

"Take It Easy," the Eagles (1972)

This particular interpretation of a rock beat is a more relaxed version of the honky-tonk/rock beat synthesis noted in Chapter 6 in Roy Orbison's "Oh, Pretty Woman." In both cases, it has two distinct layers. One is a straightforward rock rhythm, played on the drums and acoustic guitar. The other is in essence a modified

Fotos International/Getty Images

The Eagles performing in 1979. From left to right: Don Felder, Don Henley, Joe Walsh, and Glenn Fry.

honky-tonk two-beat rhythm: bass and bass drum mark the first and third beats, in alternation with the backbeat on the second and fourth beats. This would soon become the most common form of rock rhythm in both country rock and rock-influenced country.

Almost everything else also has a country flavor: the guitar licks, the double-time banjo accompaniment, and the singing. The two exceptions are Meisner's occasionally roaming bass lines and the beautiful high-register close harmony, which seems to owe more to the Beach Boys than to the Everly Brothers or any country group.

## ♪ KEY FEATURES

**"Take It Easy," the Eagles (1972)**
- Country-themed lyrics: a contemporary take on the free-lovin' ramblin' man
- Country rock beat: rock rhythmic layer over modified honky-tonk beat
- Banjo figuration and guitar patterns add to country flavor
- Close harmony on the chorus

As their career gained momentum, the Eagles moved toward the mainstream, often shedding country elements along the way. Still, songs such as "Lyin' Eyes"

(1975) retain a strong country flavor. The band shifted direction rather abruptly in 1975, when guitarist Joe Walsh replaced Bernie Leadon. "Hotel California" (1977), their big hit from this later period, borrows from a southern sound of a quite different kind: reggae. It's a skillful adaptation of the reggae feel—as skillful as their earlier assimilation of country—but the Eagles sound like a different band altogether. It was a complete makeover.

## Fleetwood Mac: Old Troubles for New Women

Among the reverberations from the feminist movement was a series of number 1 hits featuring female singers speaking their mind. Helen Reddy's 1972 hit "I Am Woman" became an anthem for women's rights. A year later, "You're So Vain," Carly Simon's diatribe against clueless men, topped the charts; Linda Ronstadt's first big hit, "You're No Good" (1975), mined the same vein with comparable success. In the lyrics, these women vented with a frankness that was virtually absent from pre-rock pop and seldom found in rock. Only in country music had women regularly sung about troublesome issues: songs like Tammy Wynette's 1968 hit "D-I-V-O-R-C-E" were still in the air in the early seventies. Fleetwood Mac's 1977 album *Rumours*, an album that traversed the difficult terrain of fracturing relationships from both female and male vantage points, would enjoy even more success.

Fleetwood Mac was an unusual group for the time, or any time: a rock band with two female lead singers, both of whom had romantic liaisons with other members of the band. This distinctive lineup grew out of a chance encounter, well after the band's career was underway. In 1967, drummer Mick Fleetwood (b. 1942) and bassist John McVie (b. 1945), who had worked together in John Mayall's Bluesbreakers, joined fellow Bluesbreakers alumnus Peter Green (b. 1946) to form Fleetwood Mac. The band went through three incarnations: a blues band in the late sixties, a more progressive group in the early seventies, and a top, thoughtful pop act in the late seventies. Singer-keyboardist Christine Perfect (b. 1943) joined the band after marrying John McVie. After a turbulent period in the early seventies, the band's membership stabilized when Fleetwood was scouting out a recording studio in southern California, heard a demo tape of guitarist Lindsey Buckingham (b. 1949) and vocalist Stevie Nicks (b. 1948), and invited Buckingham to join the band after the departure of guitarist Bob Welch (b. 1946). Buckingham accepted, on the condition that his partner also be part of the group.

This new incarnation of the band, now based in southern California, debuted in 1975 and would—barely—remain intact during the group's most successful period. *Fleetwood Mac*, their first album together would top the charts in 1975. *Rumours*, their next album, released in 1977, would become one of the most successful albums of all time, ultimately selling over 19 million units.

Part of the appeal of *Rumours* was the autobiographical nature of the lyrics, which reflected the turbulent relationships involving all of the band members. The marriage between John and Christine McVie was headed for divorce, Nicks and Buckingham's personal partnership was on the rocks, and Fleetwood was in the process of divorcing his wife. All relationships were strained during the time the group recorded *Rumours*, and the songs on the album speak directly to the problems the couples were having. It was, in effect, the seventies musical counterpart to reality TV.

More than any other major album of the seventies, *Rumours* evidenced the frankness with which rock-era artists could speak about difficult personal issues. In the early years of the rock era, divorce was a dirty word, and problems in relationships were often hidden from public view: one simply didn't discuss such things openly. That would change in the aftermath of the free love of the sixties. What was remarkable about *Rumours* was the willingness of the members of Fleetwood Mac to allude to their troubled relationships in their music.

Their collective experiences, which they explored from both female and male points of view, resonated with the mood of the times. Divorce rates in the United States peaked in the late seventies to 40 per 1,000 married women. The number was almost three times higher than the rate of 15 per 1,000 women during the fifties. Divorce rates have steadily declined since that time.

Another reason for the success of *Rumours* was the way in which the music enhanced the impact of the lyric without overwhelming it. For example, in "Dreams," written by Stevie Nicks and the most successful single from the album, the music creates a dark, unsettled atmosphere underneath Nicks's despairing lyric. In the song, Nicks fatalistically accepts Buckingham's urge to roam but warns him of the likely consequences. She laces her lyric with words like "loneliness" and "lost" and phrases like "drives you mad/In the stillness of remembering what you had/And what you lost." Her vision of his life without her is bleak indeed. The music helps convey this mood. The harmony oscillates between two chords; it is rootless, like a relationship that is going nowhere. In the verse, the background is empty: modest bass and drum parts are the most consistent features. The transition and chorus, where the background vocals and other instruments join in or become more active, do not completely dispel the emptiness of the verse; it is as if there is always something missing—in the music, as well as in Nicks's relationship with Buckingham.

"Dreams,"
Fleetwood Mac
(1977)

---

### ♪ KEY FEATURES

#### "Dreams," Fleetwood Mac (1977)

- Opening her heart: Nicks's highly personal and powerful lyric about a troubled relationship
- Understated background resonates with the mood of the lyric
- Prominent vocal line: words are in the forefront
- Artful touches: oscillating harmonies, spacing of the instruments, widely spaced guitar riffs

---

There is nothing particularly innovative about "Dreams." Both the subject of the song and the musical devices were familiar in 1977. But the song—words, melody, background—was skillfully and imaginatively assembled, in such a way that everything worked synergistically and presented the idea in a fresh way. This was thoughtful pop for adults, many of whom were wrestling with the same problems as the band members or could empathize with them.

*Rumours* was the high point of Fleetwood Mac's career. They have continued to enjoy some success despite the domestic difficulties and substance abuse problems. Still, musically and personally, they remain strongly connected to the seventies.

The Eagles and Fleetwood Mac are linked by their overwhelming success, by the craft and imagination of their music, and by those musical qualities that positioned them for mainstream success: lyrics that engaged their audience, delivered in an easily understood manner; settings that placed the melody and the lead vocalist very much in the spotlight; and imaginative backgrounds that responded to the mood of the lyrics. These shared attributes make the contrast in tone between the two songs even more striking: the irresponsible ramblin' man of "Take It Easy" versus the reflective, despondent woman in "Dreams."

# Jazzing Up the Rock Mainstream

According to chart guru Joel Whitburn, there were five acts active at the beginning of the seventies who were among the Top 20 artists of the decade on both the singles and album charts: Elton John, Paul McCartney and Wings, Stevie Wonder, Chicago, and Neil Diamond. It is a diverse group; at first hearing, there is not a lot of overlap from one to the next—or even in some cases, from one song to the next.

Of these, the most atypical is certainly Chicago. The group, formed as the Big Thing in 1967 and quickly renamed Chicago Transit Authority, then simply Chicago, was not a conventional rock band or pop act. Rather, their most distinctive feature was a tight and agile horn section that typically played complicated lines behind vocals. This was one indication of the substantial jazz influence in their work. Chicago was the most commercially successful of several bands active in the late sixties and seventies that blended rock, jazz, rhythm and blues, pop—and, occasionally quirky lyrics—into a provocative and popular sound. Exploring a parallel path was Steely Dan, a musical entity that existed more as a concept than a working band during the period of their greatest success.

## Chicago: A Rock Band with Horns (and Jazz Chops)

An instrumentation that features a full rhythm section and a horn section containing both brass and saxophones is typical of soul bands: recall James Brown's band or the house band at Stax Records during the sixties. It is also the most common instrumentation in small group jazz. Especially in the two decades after World War II, jazz combos often featured two or three horns (some combination of trumpet, saxophone, and/or trombone) and a rhythm section—most often piano, bass, and drums. The kinship in instrumentation shows their common ancestry in swing-era music: jump bands and jazz combos were two of the important musical currents to develop from swing.

The difference in the roles of horns and rhythm points up their different musical objectives: rhythm-and-blues bands, from the jump bands of the 1940s through the soul bands of the sixties, used horns mainly in a backup role, although most R&B songs featured an almost obligatory honking saxophone solo. By contrast, in jazz, horns were the main melody instruments; rhythm instruments primarily filled a supporting role. In the late sixties, a new generation of musicians with strong interests in both jazz and rock-era music would find a way to fuse the two. In the first part of the seventies, the most commercially successful of these fusions was Chicago, a group that came together in Chicago but made their mark using Los Angeles as home base. Both featured a relationship among horns, vocals, and rhythm that described a middle ground between jazz, R&B, rock, and pop.

Chicago came together in 1967 when saxophonist Walter Parazaider (b. 1945), guitarist Terry Kath (1946–1978), drummer Danny Seraphine (b. 1948), trumpeter Lee Loughnane (b. 1946), trombonist James Pankow (b. 1947), keyboard player Robert Lamm (b. 1944), and bassist Peter Cetera (b. 1944) joined forces to fulfill their ambition of creating a "rock-and-roll band with horns." Parazaider, Kath, and Seraphine had worked together growing up; they connected with Loughnane and Pankow at DePaul University, where Parazaider was enrolled, and they brought in Lamm and Cetera from other contacts. Before forming Chicago, the band members had played in most of the current styles; early on, they covered Beatles' songs and R&B hits as well as presenting their own material. Success came quickly; *Chicago Transit Authority*, their first album, released in 1969, went gold, then platinum (when that measure was introduced in 1976); so did the next twelve albums.

The titles of their first ten albums reveal something of the character of the band: after *CTA*, they were simply numbered: *Chicago II*, *Chicago III*, and so on. Similarly, the band presented themselves as a group: there were no stars, on stage or in the studio. Instead, the focus was mainly on the songs, which charted a virtually unique musical path through the seventies. We sample their approach in "Saturday in the Park." a hit from *Chicago V*, released in 1972.

Walter Parazaider describes the inspiration for the song:

> I was rooming with him [Lamm], and we were in Manhattan on the Fourth of July. Robert came back to the hotel from Central Park very excited after seeing the steel drum players, singers, dancers, and jugglers. I said, "Man, it's time to put music to this!"

Lamm, who filmed his excursions, wrote "Saturday in the Park" as a kind of soundtrack to his edited film, which apparently never went beyond the home-movie stage. (This may provide an extra-musical reason for the shift in tempo and beat in the middle of the song.)

"Saturday in the Park," Chicago (1972)

The song opens with a catchy piano riff: syncopated chords that outline a modified "Heart and Soul" progression. The other rhythm instruments join in; their parts add to the rhythmic play inherent in the piano riff. A nice horn adds another melodic layer, in anticipation of the vocal. The refrain is quite similar to the piano riff and just as catchy. Behind these accessible features are complex features: the extensive rhythmic play, an extended multisection bridge, an instrumental interlude with involved horn lines, a shift to a shuffle rhythm and new melody. This is Chicago's craft coming to the fore.

On the surface, the lyric is simply a depiction of Lamm's visits to Central Park. However, the undercurrent that occasionally surfaces is his joy in experiencing such diversity in happy circumstances and his hope that this is the wave of the future. The upbeat character of the music reinforces that message.

♪ **KEY FEATURES**

**"Saturday in the Park," Chicago (1972)**

- Visual lyric: vivid images help portray an optimistic message
- Unique balance among vocals, active rhythm instruments, and varied horn lines
- Extensive syncopation in all layers, and especially in bass and drums
- Expansive form held together by return of the refrain

*Chicago V* sold very well, topping the charts for nine weeks, the first of five straight Chicago albums to reach number 1. "Saturday in the Park" became the group's first gold single, hitting number 3. Although Chicago's blend of rock, pop, jazz, and soul earned them resounding commercial success during their peak years, it did not gain them critical respect from the rock press. Perhaps because they were unique among white bands in sound and success, the rock press has all but ignored them—as they have most other major seventies musicians who brought together jazz, rock, pop, and rhythm and blues in varying mixes. An almost singular exception was Steely Dan.

## Steely Dan: The Pursuit of Studio Perfection

Although Chicago and Steely Dan shared a common inclination for jazz-flavored horn lines and offbeat lyrics, they presented strongly differing personae to the public. Chicago could be seen and heard. During the early seventies, Chicago toured relentlessly, at one point playing sixteen countries in twenty days. By contrast, Steely Dan was heard but never seen. Although Steely Dan began as a band, it became a popular and critically acclaimed act only after its two creative minds, keyboardist Donald Fagen (b. 1948) and bassist Walter Becker (b. 1950), dissolved the band and made Steely Dan into their studio-driven brainchild.

Becker and Fagen met at Bard College, where they played together regularly in a number of bands, including the Leather Canary. After Fagen graduated, they moved to New York, where they joined the backup band for Jay and the Americans. While in New York, they met producer Gary Katz, who would eventually sign them up with ABC Records—first as songwriters, then as a working band. (The group took their name from a dildo: "Steely Dan" was the name for three dildos used by a character in William Burroughs's *Naked Lunch*.) At ABC, they met recording engineer Roger Nichols; Nichols would record all of their music. For the first three years, Steely Dan was a working band that toured regularly. However, on recordings, Becker and Fagen began using the cream of Los Angeles studio musicians, most of whom had extensive jazz experience. After 1974, Steely Dan became a studio band, in order to better realize Becker and Fagen's distinctive musical vision.

It's difficult to describe their "style" because each of their songs seems so different from the next: among their hits is an electronically enhanced "cover" of Duke Ellington's 1927 recording of "East St. Louis Toodle-oo." The three constants in their music seem to be impeccable production, stream-of-consciousness lyrics that offer

"Peg," Steely
Dan (1977)

slices of life in LA, and sophisticated, distinctive musical settings. There is often a jarring incongruity between the lyrics and the often complex music to which they were set. It is apparent in songs like their 1977 hit "Peg," one of the tracks from *Aja*, their sixth album and one of the first recordings to be certified platinum; *Aja* would win a Grammy for best engineered non-classical recording. The lyric of "Peg" offers a fragmentary account of a film star on the rise, told by someone who knew her when, but who is probably on the outside looking in now. It conveys a bittersweet mood: whatever connection he had with Peg has dissolved now that her career is on the way up.

Although many of their fans have spent long hours trying to decode lyrics to Steely Dan songs, the exercise seems ultimately beside the point, because the songs are mainly about the music. More than anything else, the lyrics seem to serve as window dressing, to entice those listeners who find lyrics important, or at least a necessary point of entry into the song. The lyrics are hip and provocative—Fagen graduated from Bard in 1969 with a degree in English, and Fagen and Becker shared a strong interest in Beat literature. They often offer ironic commentary on life in Los Angeles—"Peg" is typical in that regard. But there is not the sense of connection between words and music that has informed so much of the music that we have heard, from Dylan and the Beatles through Queen and Fleetwood Mac.

The reason may well be Becker and Fagen's abiding interest in jazz. It was strong at the beginning of their career: they met Denny Dias, the original guitarist with Steely Dan, when they responded to an ad he placed in the *Village Voice*: "Looking for keyboardist and bassist. Must have jazz chops!" It remained strong through the seventies.

Jazz is mainly an instrumental music. There have been great jazz singers, but they are a peripheral part of the jazz scene. Given Becker and Fagen's strong affinity for jazz, it is not surprising that the main focus in their songs is on the music—for the guitar solo on "Peg," Becker and Fagen apparently went through four top session guitarists before Jay Graydon recorded the version that they kept. In "Peg," the music is self-contained in a way that makes the content of the lyrics almost incidental, even though vocals are integral to the song.

Steely Dan's songs are not jazz, in the conventional sense: in "Peg," Graydon's one-chorus solo is the only improvised segment. Nor is it much like the jazz/rock fusions of the late sixties and seventies. Rather, Fagen and Becker infused their distinctive music with jazz values: melodic and harmonic complexity, rhythmic play, virtuosity, imagination. For example, the instrumental introduction evokes the angular lines and rich harmonies of bebop, while the harmony under the verse of the song is a clever reworking of a 12-bar blues progression. Throughout the song, there is extensive rhythmic play among the rhythm instruments, especially the bass. At the same time, in its overall design, the song follows the familiar rock-era verse/chorus pattern, and the chorus has a hook carved from a single, richly harmonized melody note: "Peg."

With their particular mix of rocklike accessibility, provocative lyrics, jazz influence, and perfectionist approach to recording, Steely Dan was one of a kind. In their music and their attitude toward music making, they were without any real precedent, and no band has really followed their lead. Becker and Fagen parted ways in 1981. Twelve years later, they came together, resurrected the Steely Dan name, and began recording and touring again. They remain active and productive through the

> ♪ **KEY FEATURES**
>
> **"Peg," Steely Dan (1977)**
> - Words versus music: clever, ironic lyrics with virtually no apparent connection to the music
> - Familiar verse/chorus connects to mainstream rock
> - Infusion of jazz values: rich, varied harmony; rhythmic play; angular instrumental lines; virtuosic playing

early years of the twenty-first century: *Two Against Nature* won four Grammy Awards in 2001, including top album.

Chicago and Steely Dan share common ground in what they are and what they are not. During the seventies, neither was a band of stars; indeed, in the latter part of the seventies, Steely Dan was not a band at all. Their songs, and especially Steely Dan's, favor quirky lyrics. Neither is a conventional rock band in instrumentation or approach. Still, both used rock as a point of departure: with its melodic hooks, underlying rhythms, riff-laden textures, and forms, their music connects directly to rock. Both incorporate a jazz sensibility into their songs, evident in such features as the increased instrumental presence, rhythmic play within the rhythm section, intricate instrumental lines, and complex harmonies. And both found large audiences for their distinctive mixes of rock, pop, rhythm and blues, and jazz.

## The Jazz Renaissance of the Seventies

Although neither Chicago nor Steely Dan qualifies as a jazz band, the strong jazz influence in their music highlights the jazz renaissance that began in the late sixties. Like other established styles, jazz struggled with rock: the first efforts to fuse jazz and rock were awkward and not particularly successful, for the most part. However, jazz musicians—inspired and directed by trumpeter Miles Davis, who abruptly shifted musical directions in order to form "the world's baddest rock band"—soon integrated jazz musicians' instrumental prowess, melodic approach, and improvisational expertise with rock's collective conception, rich texture, and complex rhythmic structure.

The product of this musical marriage, most often called **jazz fusion**, or simply **fusion**, was the most jazzlike branch of jazz-influenced rock-era music. Many of the top fusion artists were alumni of Davis's bands: Joe Zawinul and Wayne Shorter of Weather Report; Chick Corea of Return to Forever; John McLaughlin of the Mahavishnu Orchestra. Other important directions include the Sly Stone–inspired and very popular art funk of Herbie Hancock, the R&B/soul/jazz fusions of groups such as the Crusaders, and the R&B/black pop/jazz fusions of musicians such as guitarist George Benson and saxophonist Grover Washington Jr. In addition, jazz musicians collaborated with rock and R&B artists. For example, Steely Dan used the cream of jazz studio musicians, and Robert Flack and Bill Withers used, and occasionally featured, leading jazz performers, such as Grover Washington Jr. Collectively they made jazz and jazz-influenced pop and rock more popular than it had been since the heyday of the swing era.

# The Future of Rock and Roll

On Thursday, May 9, 1974, Jon Landau went to a concert at the Harvard Square Theater in Cambridge, Massachusetts. The headliner was Bonnie Raitt; opening for her was Bruce Springsteen and the E Street Band. Springsteen had built a small but fervent following among the college crowd throughout the Northeast, but his albums had sold poorly. At the time, Landau was an influential and opinionated critic: he had written record reviews for *Rolling Stone* since their first issue and at the time was also writing for *The Real Paper*, an alternative Boston newsweekly. His review of the concert in the May 22 issue of *The Real Paper*, which begins with a long, rambling account of his relationship with rock music, finally gets to the main point: an ecstatic review of Springsteen's performance. The Springsteen part of the review begins:

> Last Thursday, at the Harvard Square theatre, I saw my rock 'n' roll past flash before my eyes. And I saw something else: I saw rock and roll future and its name is Bruce Springsteen. And on a night when I needed to feel young, he made me feel like I was hearing music for the very first time.

The experience changed Springsteen's and Landau's lives. Landau's oft-quoted review gave Springsteen's career a huge boost. Later that year, Landau developed a friendship with Springsteen that quickly became much more than that. He took over as Springsteen's manager and producer while disentangling him from a messy business relationship with Mike Appel, Springsteen's manager at the time; he still holds that position.

In his review, Landau listed music that he felt passionate about—music that, in his mind, spoke to the head and the gut and that was not pretentious. His personal playlist ranged from James Taylor, Randy Newman, and Stevie Wonder to (good) Rolling Stones and Neil Young. In Springsteen he found music that covered just about that entire range.

The "future" in Landau's review seems to refer to Springsteen's new way of reaffirming what he felt were rock's core values. In this sense, he was prophetic. Springsteen's music has never strayed far from these values, although it has been realized in diverse ways, from all-acoustic music to what Landau called "street trash rockers," and he has been among the most admired rock artists for decades.

Another Northeast-based band would offer another vision of rock-and-roll's future: Aerosmith, formed in 1970, would create music that would connect the good rock of the early seventies with the funk-influenced rock of the eighties and beyond. We consider two memorable songs released in 1975—Springsteen's "Born to Run" and Aerosmith's "Walk This Way"—as part of a discussion of the future of rock and roll.

## Bruce Springsteen and the Rebirth of Important Rock

Asbury Park is a New Jersey beach town about an hour's drive from New York City. Bruce Springsteen (b. 1949) grew up in and around the town. Early on, he forged the musical split personality that has been his trademark: he worked with bar bands close to home and also played solo gigs in Greenwich Village clubs, where he mingled with Patti Smith and other early punk rockers. This helps account for the huge swings in his music, from the all-acoustic *Nebraska* album to the hard-rocking *Born in the U.S.A.*

His enormous success comes in part from his ability to integrate seemingly contradictory aspects of his life and work. He is a superstar and a man of the people, a musician who plays to sold-out arenas and shows up unannounced to sit in with local bands. Throughout his career, he has stayed close to his working-class roots and has written songs that reflect their concerns. At the same time, he is larger than life: he is "the Boss" to his fiercely loyal fans.

This sense of being larger than life emanates directly from his music. In the course of his thirty-plus year recording career, Springsteen has created music that has covered an enormous range of mood, style, and resources: anthems like his "Born" songs and "Counting on a Miracle" from *The Rising*, his response to 9/11; the acoustic *Nebraska*; and more subdued songs like "Streets of Philadelphia," his Grammy-winning song written for the 1993 film *Philadelphia*. If there is a consistent element running through his music, acoustic or electric, early or late, with or without the E Street Band, it is that it sounds big.

Bruce Springsteen performing in 1975, around the time "Born to Run" was released.

Bernard Gotfryd/Getty Images

This sense of bigness is comprehensive and coherent. It touches every important aspect of his music: its message, its sound, its scale. It begins with Springsteen's lyrics, which always have something meaningful to say, whether it's a first-person issue or a social or political statement.

The bigness of the sound begins with his voice. Springsteen's singing—over his band blasting away or in a more intimate setting—is true: in pitch and in the emotions that it conveys. There are no obvious tricks—high falsetto singing, virtuosic melismas, stutters, or other vocal effects—nothing that says "listen to what I can do." Rather, Springsteen sings honestly and expressively, with a rough but resonant voice that delivers words and melody plainly, whether at full volume in front of a band, or more intimately, when he simply accompanies himself on the guitar.

Springsteen often augments this core sound with a large band, strong musical gestures (like the opening guitar riff in "Born to Run"), effective use of registral spacing to give depth and richness to the setting, expansive melodic ideas, and a lot of reverb in the mix. He casts his songs on a large scale: 3 minutes is typically way too short, and in "Born to Run," it takes a full 4 minutes 30 seconds to traverse the form once. This distinctive sense of bigness has been present virtually from the start of his career. We hear how he did it in his first big hit, the 1975 song "Born to Run."

"Born to Run,"
Bruce Spring-
steen and the E
Street Band
(1975)

"Born to Run" is a big song, in every respect. It shows how Springsteen expanded rock style in virtually every important dimension. The song has a strong beat, with the rhythm section hammering out the eight-beat rhythmic layer. There is none of the rhythmic play that we have heard in other rock songs. We might consider this a no-nonsense rock beat: Springsteen seems to use this straightforward version of rock rhythm to convey seriousness of purpose.

On this recording, Springsteen's E Street Band is big: several guitars, saxophone, keyboards, bass, and drums, and so is their range. In this song, moments of great power, such as the reprise of the opening guitar riff right after the instrumental break (and Springsteen's "1-2-3-4") contrast with the more delicate sections in the bridge.

"Born to Run" is cast on a large scale. The opening guitar riff is long; the narrative sections take a while to unfold; the extended interlude before the final statement of the original melody is also more elaborate harmonically, rhythmically, and texturally than good but more conventional rock.

In this song Springsteen connects directly to recent American culture. It builds on Dylan's electric phase: the same concern for the primacy of the words in the midst of a dense, loud accompaniment pervades his music. Springsteen's singing also connects his music with Dylan: his quasi-spoken, rough-edged vocal style borrows directly from Dylan's delivery. The lyric, and the attitude it conveys, goes back another decade, to Hollywood images of rebellion: Marlon Brando astride his motorcycle in *The Wild One* (1954) and James Dean in *Rebel Without a Cause* (1955).

"Born to Run" is at once down home and downtown. It is easy to imagine Springsteen dressed in torn jeans and a T-shirt, wearing his trademark bandanna, seated on a Harley and ready to ride off into the sunset with his girl. Certain aspects of the music—Springsteen's singing, the beat, the big guitar riff—communicate this look in sound. However, such features as the bell-like effects just before the title phrase and the complex harmonies and slithering scale of the instrumental break suggest a level of sophistication far greater than one would expect from the average bar band. Springsteen brings it off: he integrates these contrasting signals into a song with real impact.

♪ **KEY FEATURES**

> **"Born to Run," Bruce Springsteen and the E Street Band (1975)**
> - Rebel with a cause: in the lyric, Springsteen taps into powerful American images.
> - Strong beat, with little syncopation, played by core rock instrumentation, suggests important sound.
> - More background elements, such as synthesizer halo and complex harmony in bridge, balance strength with sophistication.
> - Expansive form matches bold musical gestures, such as the opening riff, heavy rock timekeeping, and reinforced buildup to title phrase.

Springsteen's stature has grown since this early success. He has been one of rock's superstars since the early eighties, and one of the few whose integrity and passion seem unflagging. From *Nebraska* and *Born in the U.S.A.* through the 1995 *Ghost of Tom Joad* (with its allusion to Steinbeck's *Grapes of Wrath* and connection with Dylan's idol Woody Guthrie) and his response to 9/11, *The Rising* (2002), he has continued to express his ideas honestly and powerfully.

## Aerosmith: Bridging Rock's Generation Gap

The video that featured Aerosmith's 1986 collaboration with Run-D.M.C. on the rap group's remake of "Walk This Way" begins with the two parties in adjoining rooms separated by a flimsy and far-from-soundproof wall. As lead guitarist Joe Perry jams away, the rappers yell at the band to turn the volume down, to no avail. So when Aerosmith (bassist Tom Hamilton [b. 1951], drummer Joey Kramer [b. 1950], guitarist Joe Perry [b. 1950], vocalist Steven Tyler [born Steven Tallarico, 1948], and guitarist Brad Whitford [b. 1952]) begins to replay the song, Run-D.M.C. decides to fight fire with fire: we hear the rappers' version of the verse. This in turn sets lead vocalist Steven Tyler off. He begins to throw things at the wall, then hammers away at it with the base of the microphone stand. He breaks through just in time to sing the chorus. The video ends with Run-D.M.C. sandwiching Tyler; the three are moving together to the collective groove of the band and the DJ.

The song and video of "Walk This Way" were a breakthrough for Run-D.M.C. and rap. The collaborative version of the song reached number 4, which was higher than the chart position (number 10) of Aerosmith's 1975 original version. More significantly, it was the first rap video to get extensive airplay on MTV (hard to believe in our time!). It was an important step in bringing rap into the mainstream. The use of a familiar song seemed to give listeners who were new to rap a comfortable point of entry.

The new version of "Walk This Way" also sparked a breakthrough for Aerosmith. The band had seen their career go down the toilet through substance abuse that was excessive even by rock star standards. Perry left the band in 1979, swearing that he would never play with Aerosmith again. Five years later, with all of the band members strung out and broke, the group decided to reunite. Their well-known drug problems made music industry people reluctant to book them, although they toured in 1984 and secured a recording contract from Geffen Records. However, their first reunion record did not sell well. Their collaboration with Run-D.M.C., orchestrated by Def Jam producer Rick Rubin, opened the door to a return to the top. In the wake of the song's success, the band decided to get sober; by early 1987, they were clean.

"Walk This Way" has served as a musical bridge—for Aerosmith, for rock, and for the music industry. For Aerosmith it was the key to their phoenix-like rebirth; they have been even more successful in their second incarnation than they were initially. For rock, Aerosmith's music, most notably in songs like "Walk This Way," was a bridge between the classic hard rock of the late sixties and early seventies and important alternative styles that emerged in the latter part of the eighties. And the cover of "Walk This Way" was a bridge between rock and rap, which inhabited almost completely separate musical worlds at that time. We focus on the bridge between classic and more contemporary rock in the discussion of "Walk This Way" following.

In its first version, "Walk This Way" was a track on the group's third album, *Toys in Our Attic*, which the group recorded in 1975. The album went platinum and helped

"Walk This
Way," Aero-
smith (1975)

establish the band as a top stadium attraction. It was the high point of their career in the seventies.

The original song begins with drummer Joey Kramer laying down a good rock beat with a lot of bass drum and a strong backbeat. Perry enters two measures later with the signature instrumental riff of the song. This leads into Tyler's proto-rap verse—recall that the song dates from 1975. Behind his singing are active guitar parts, Whitford strumming on a chord, and Perry repeating a busy riff. In the first 30 seconds of the song we hear the past, present, and future of hard rock circa 1975. The sound of Aerosmith clearly grew out of the British blues bands that shaped rock and roll and heavy metal. The basic instrumentation of the band, the volume level, the power chords, the complex riffs based on the black pentatonic scale, the heavy distortion—these and other features connect directly to this earlier generation of hard rock. To cite an obvious example: in that both songs begin with a complex line built from a pentatonic scale and are accompanied only by drums, there is an underlying similarity between the guitar/bass riff in Led Zeppelin's "Black Dog" and the opening guitar riff in "Walk This Way." Moreover, the connection was obvious to their audience: early in their career, Aerosmith was derided in the rock press as an American clone of the Rolling Stones.

By contrast, it is the rhythm of the opening riff, the vocals in the verse, and the guitar chords and riffs underneath the vocals that move the sound of hard rock into the seventies and toward the eighties. All three map onto a steady rhythm that moves twice as fast as Kramer's rock beat. As with much of the other music using 16-beat rhythms heard thus far, these faster rhythms make possible a richer, more complex, and more syncopated rhythmic texture. It is this aspect of the music that made it an ideal choice for the rap collaboration and that anticipates the funk-tinged stream of alternative rock that appeared in the latter part of the eighties in the music of groups such as the Red Hot Chili Peppers, Fishbone, and Primus.

All of this supports a lyric that tells the story of a naive young man's introduction to sex via an experienced and promiscuous cheerleader. This reaffirms the erotic element that has underlain good-time rhythm and blues ("Shake, Rattle and Roll" was one of many such songs) and rock from the beginning. And it is in sharp contra-distinction to the other music included in this chapter.

♪ **KEY FEATURES**

**"Walk This Way," Aerosmith (1975)**

- Erotic lyric, sung erotically by Tyler, especially in the chorus
- Core rock sounds: riffs, power chords, distortion, basic instrumentation
- Active 16-beat rhythms that presage an important evolutionary trend in rock

In these recordings by Springsteen and Aerosmith, we hear continuations of two important dimensions of sixties rock: Aerosmith's Rolling Stones–type rock and roll exemplifies what makes rock "rock"; Springsteen's rock exemplifies what makes rock important. Both are exemplars of their particular branch of rock, and each represents an important new synthesis within their particular domain. In their strong connection to the spirit of the sixties, they represent a countercurrent to the other music discussed in this chapter.

At the same time, this pair of examples highlights the seemingly dialectical relationship between rock as a thinking music and rock as an action music—that is, rock that makes a significant statement versus rock as music to rock to—that emerged around the middle of the seventies. For major acts, the challenge was creating music that fed the brain and shook the booty at the same time. This is apparent in the lyrics of the songs. Springsteen's James Dean–like lyrics invite us to engage in their content; the music amplifies their message. In "Walk This Way," only the chorus is easily comprehended on the first listening. The lyrics, learned after the fact, simply explain the erotic thrust of the music.

Musically, perhaps the most significant difference is the ratio of timekeeping to syncopation. In Springsteen's "Born to Run," rhythm guitar, bass, and drums consistently mark the rock-beat layer; what syncopation there is occurs mainly in the lead guitar riff and the vocal line. By contrast, "Walk This Way" is rich in rhythmic play; there is much more rhythmic activity against the beat than there is beat marking. The underlying message seems to be that when the beat is as seductive as it is in Aerosmith's song, it is difficult to detach oneself sufficiently from the groove to think about important things.

In the next several chapters, we will hear this opposition played out in several different styles. Music by white groups such as the Sex Pistols, the Clash, R.E.M., and U2, which has a powerful message in the lyrics, will often have strong beat keeping and little syncopation. By contrast, music that is more syncopated conveys a more good-time message.

## The Diversity of Mainstream Rock

The strongest common denominator among the eight acts discussed in this chapter is their popularity. Elton John and Chicago were popular throughout the decade; the other acts remained surpassingly popular once they broke through, either on record or in live performance. Beyond that, there is little that connects them beyond their age, race, and connection to rock.

On the other hand, the contrasts are striking: Freddie Mercury and Elton John versus Bruce Springsteen and Steven Tyler versus Stevie Nicks and Christine McVie; the reclusiveness of Steely Dan versus the relentless touring of Aerosmith, Chicago, and Springsteen; songs in which the music supported the stories ("Dreams" or "Born to Run") versus songs in which the stories supported the music ("Peg" or "Walk This Way"); third-person songs versus first-person songs; and so on.

That all of these groups were popular is indicative of the steady growth of the audience for rock. Many of those college students who didn't trust anyone over 30 in 1965 were entering, or about to enter, their 30s by 1975. Behind them were those just entering their rock-listening years.

However, despite the homogenizing effects of AOR, the audience for these acts seemed more diverse in its tastes. It is hard to imagine a hypothetical listener feeling equally passionate about Queen and Steely Dan, or Chicago and Bruce Springsteen.

No single artist, white or black, had the almost universal appeal that the Beatles and the top Motown acts enjoyed during the sixties. Moreover, the acts discussed here are represent only one segment of the market for rock-era music during the seventies; black pop, the singer-songwriters, heavy metal, and—later in the decade—punk/new wave, disco, reggae, and funk also claimed a share of the market.

The emergence of a corporate mentality—one far removed from the early years of the rock-era with free-wheeling disc jockeys and independent record companies—inevitably provoked a hostile reaction from those who were marginalized by the pursuit of profit. We discuss some of this music in the next two chapters: reggae, funk, and disco in Chapter 15 and punk and its aftermath in Chapter 16.

## Terms to Remember

| | | |
|---|---|---|
| Record Industry Association of America (RIAA) | diamond record | boom boxes |
| | cross-marketing | Walkman |
| gold record | four-track tape, eight-track tape | country rock |
| platinum record | | jazz fusion, fusion |
| multiplatinum record | audio cassette | |

## Applying Chapter Concepts

1. The country rock of the Eagles was one of several country/rock fusions during the late sixties and early seventies. To develop a broader understanding of country and rock during this time, explore at least one other trend that typically involved country/rock intersections: the country rock of Graham Parsons; the "outlaw" country music of Willie Nelson and Waylon Jennings; southern rock, and especially the music of Lynyrd Skynyrd; contemporary hard country by Merle Haggard and others; country/rock/pop songs by Charlie Rich or Kris Kristofferson.

2. Pick one of the ex-Beatles and compare one of his hit songs to not only the other songs discussed in this chapter but also music from the Beatles' last two years together. In what ways is it similar to and different from the Beatles' music? Which of the acts discussed in this chapter is it closest to in style?

# FIVE

# Beyond Rock:
# The Rock Era, 1977–

■ Christina Aguilera's "What a Girl Wants" was the first new number 1 single of the new millennium on *Billboard's* Hot 100 singles chart. Aguilera might be right behind Aerosmith alphabetically, but her music is so far removed stylistically from Aerosmith's rock-defining music that many of rock's most characteristic features have been turned on end. Among the most prominent differences are these:

• The song was performed by a Latina solo performer who is a multi-talented entertainer, not a white male group of musicians.
• The song was written by someone other than one of the members of the band.
• The backup musicians are virtually anonymous studio musicians, not the band members.

In addition, we find that

• The dominant instrumental sounds are electronically generated, not the standard rock band instruments.
• The "song" exists in components, which have been assembled into several versions: radio version, club version, and Spanish language version.
• The rhythms of the song are based on an electronically enhanced 16-beat rhythm, not a rock beat.

Furthermore, *Billboard's* Hot 100 may represent a plurality in the marketplace, but it is only one moderately sized segment of an increasingly fragmented music industry: the number of *Billboard* charts has more than doubled since 1975. The top-selling recording artist since 1975 is not a rock act but country star Garth Brooks, who has enjoyed sales of more than 116 million units as of this writing. Indeed, with the rise of the Internet, it is no longer possible to use sales as a completely reliable guide to popularity; for a variety of reasons—legal distribution via the Internet, piracy, and peer-to-peer networks—sales can no longer accurately reflect either popularity or chart position.

All of these developments demonstrate not only the continuing evolution of rock-era popular music but significant developments in society, technology, and the music industry. They include the following:

# Globalization and Multiculturalism

The European Community, unimaginable in 1942 but a reality in 1992, is perhaps the most conspicuous symbol of the movement toward a global village. It was made possible politically by the fall of communism, with the attendant dissolution of the Soviet Union and the realignment of eastern Europe, including the unification of Germany. In addition, two media revolutions—cable and satellite television in the late seventies and early eighties, and the Internet in the nineties—have shrunk the planet.

Rock-era music has been both an agent and beneficiary of these changes. Rock has grown from the first truly international popular music style in the sixties into the first truly global expressive language in human history, with rock/regional fusions emanating from almost every corner of the world. The numerous world music genres are the most obvious evidence of this, but the impact is deeper than that. Consider that Christina Aguilera is one of several divas who followed Madonna's lead. What's significant is that race and ethnicity (and gender) are non-issues in their particular domain: Aguilera, Jennifer Lopez, Shakira, Mariah Carey, Céline Dion, Mary J. Blige, Britney Spears, Jessica Simpson, and so on.

Similarly, the basic pop style is a black/white fusion, and it routinely absorbs elements of other styles, for example, a calypso rhythm on top of a disco beat. The ease with which musicians from different cultures dissolve boundaries as they work together has been a model for the world; no other branch of music, and no other art, has been such a force for accommodating diversity within unity.

# Digital Technology

The rapid evolution of digital technology has fundamentally altered every aspect of rock-era music: its sounds, creative process, production, documents, and dissemination. A host of electronically generated sounds and sound effects—some analogues to conventional instruments, others completely new—have enriched rock-era music. Moreover, MIDI technology and instrument controllers have enabled anyone who has mastered one instrument to interface with devices that produce a full range of electronic sounds: a keyboardist can generate the space sonorities of new age music or the distortion of heavy metal guitar with equal ease. With the rapid increase in computing power, and because there is no sound degradation while the music is in digital format, music can be assembled in components: vocal, rhythm track, background harmonies, and so forth. Moreover, it can be delivered in any digital format: CD, online; strictly audio, as part of a video.

# Deconstructing Song

Digital technology has contributed to a major assault on the understanding of "song." In the wake of the Beach Boys' *Pet Sounds* and the Beatles' *Sgt. Pepper*, rock's redefinition of a song was complete: the song was what was on the recording. However, digital technology has helped create a more flexible understanding of song: most pop songs appear in multiple formats, often with different rhythms, different lengths, and different backgrounds. Moreover, songs used in dance mixes have no real beginning or end. And the rise of rap has stretched the boundaries of song: a persistent question during the eighties and early nineties was, "Is rap music?"

## New Media

For pop stars like Aguilera, how one looks and how one moves is as critical to success as how one sings. With the emergence of MTV and other similar television networks, and the phenomenal success of Michael Jackson, popular music acquired an easily accessible visual dimension. This in turn has caused producers to think of music as part of a more comprehensive statement that encompasses several different media forms. Indeed, one can argue that rap videos are a fully integrated, if temporally compact, artistic statement: poetry, music, dance, drama, and visual elements.

## New Rhythms

The new music from the early eighties to the present sounds like it comes from this time, and not from the sixties or seventies, for a number of reasons: the new electronic sounds and effects, new voices, outside influences, and the like. Most fundamentally, however, there is a new approach to rhythm. Rock rhythm got a makeover via punk; 16-beat rhythms became the dominant style beat; and even more active rhythms surfaced in rap, techno, and related styles. These rhythmic innovations help place the music chronologically after 1980.

Because of these significant developments, rock-era music has evolved well beyond what it was in 1975. We chart its evolution as we sample a wide range of music, beginning with three influential outsider styles: reggae, funk, and disco.

### Songs Discussed in Chapters 15–20, Ordered Chronologically

| YEAR | CHAPTER | GROUP | TITLE |
|------|---------|-------|-------|
| 1972 | 15 | Jimmy Cliff | The Harder They Come |
| 1975 | 15 | Earth, Wind & Fire | Shining Star |
|      | 16 | The Ramones | Blitzkrieg Bop |
| 1976 | 15 | Parliament | Tear the Roof Off the Sucker (Give Up the Funk) |
| 1977 | 15 | Donna Summer | I Feel Love |
|      | 16 | The Sex Pistols | God Save the Queen |
|      | 16 | The Talking Heads | Psycho Killer |
|      | 16 | Devo | Jocko Homo |
| 1978 | 15 | Bob Marley | Is This Love |
|      | 15 | Village People | Y.M.C.A. |
|      | 16 | Elvis Costello and the Attractions | Radio, Radio |
| 1979 | 16 | The Clash | Death or Glory |

| | | | |
|---|---|---|---|
| **1980** | 19 | The Police | Don't Stand So Close to Me |
| **1981** | 20 | R.E.M. | Radio Free Europe |
| **1982** | 18 | Michael Jackson | Thriller |
| | 17 | Grandmaster Flash | The Message |
| **1983** | 19 | Van Halen | Jump |
| **1984** | 18 | Tina Turner | What's Love Got to Do with It |
| | 19 | Bruce Springsteen | Born in the U.S.A. |
| **1987** | 18 | Prince | Sign 'O' the Times |
| | 19 | U2 | Where the Streets Have No Name |
| | 17 | Rhythim Is Rhythim | Nude Photo |
| **1988** | 19 | Metallica | One |
| | 20 | Sonic Youth | Hey Joni |
| **1989** | 18 | Madonna | Like a Prayer |
| | 20 | Red Hot Chili Peppers | Good Time Boys |
| **1991** | 18 | Luther Vandross | Don't Want to Be a Fool |
| | 20 | Nirvana | Smells Like Teen Spirit |
| | 17 | Public Enemy | 1 Million Bottlebags |
| **1994** | 19 | Dave Matthews Band | Ants Marching |
| | 20 | Nine Inch Nails | I Do Not Want This |
| **1995** | 20 | Ani DiFranco | 32 Flavors |
| | 17 | Tupac Shakur, featuring Dr. Dre | California Love |
| **1996** | Outro | Afro Celt Sound System | Whirl-Y-Reel 1 |
| **1997** | 20 | Radiohead | Paranoid Android |
| **1999** | 17 | Moby | South Side |
| | 18 | Christina Aguilera | What a Girl Wants |
| **2004** | 20 | Green Day | Wake Me Up When September Ends |

# 15

# Reggae, Funk, and Disco

## Views from the Outside

"Rapper's Delight" was arguably the surprise hit of 1979. Released in the fall of 1979 as a 12-minute single, it reached number 4 on the R&B charts and crossed over to the pop charts early in 1980. It would become the first rap record to go gold. The recording was the brainchild of record executive Sylvia Robinson. She had become aware of block parties in the South Bronx where enterprising blacks hotwired into the streetlamps to get power for their sound systems, then rapped over prerecorded music. So she had her son Joey recruit the three rappers who would become the Sugarhill Gang—Wonder Mike, Big Bank Hank, and Master Gee—then brought them into their studio. Then, while a studio band re-created the instrumental accompaniment to Chic's 1979 hit "Good Times," the trio rapped for almost 14 minutes.

It is worth noting that the first hit song of the most significant new style during the last part of the century is a synthesis of three Afro-centric styles that came to prominence in the seventies. The most easily detected connection in "Rapper's Delight" is with disco. The borrowing from "Good Times" anticipates the sampling that would become common practice by the mid-eighties. Rapping is a black adaptation of "toasting": a Jamaican practice of talking over a recording, often a rhythm track without vocals. And most generally and most directly, rap connects to funk; it is the seemingly inevitable continuation of the increasing emphasis on rhythm and sound over melody that has characterized one stream of black music throughout the twentieth century.

Reggae, funk, and disco share much common ground. All three are musical styles created mainly by members of the African diaspora. All have their beginnings in the sixties and emerged as mature styles in the seventies. All three began very much outside the mainstream: reggae is Jamaican music; funk found most of its audience among blacks; disco was part of the largely underground dance club scene in the United States and Europe before the release of *Saturday Night Fever*. These styles would enjoy varying degrees of crossover success; disco was briefly a mainstream style.

Collectively, the three styles have had enormous influence on rock-era music since 1980. Many of the important innovations of late twentieth-century and early twenty-first-century music—most notably, more active and free rhythms, the extensive use of electronics, the use of musical quotation, the practice of mixing songs into a larger musical entity—have their roots in these styles. In this respect, they played a role comparable to the blues in the early years of rock. Indeed, they replaced the blues as the primary influences on a new musical generation; the music of the last quarter century was the first generation of twentieth-century popular music *not* to be shaped by an infusion of the blues.

Despite their obvious affinities and mutual influence, they were distinct musical styles, with different audiences, different esthetics, and different expressive objectives. We consider each in turn, then discuss their impact on the music of the eighties and beyond.

## Reggae

Most Jamaicans are of African descent—about 90 percent at the turn of the twenty-first century. Most trace their roots back to slavery: like the United States, Cuba, and Brazil, Jamaica was a destination for the slave traders. More than 600,000 slaves arrived in Jamaica between 1665 and 1838, the year in which the slave trade ended. British colonial rule continued for more than a century. Great Britain gradually transferred authority to Jamaicans, with the final step—independence—taken in 1962. However, the economic and social inequities of colonialism did not keep pace with the political changes. One result was a great deal of social unrest in the sixties. Two mid-century movements that emerged in response to Jamaican social conditions stand out: Rastafarianism and "rude boys."

**Rastafarianism**  An important consequence of Marcus Garvey's crusade to elevate the status of people of African descent is **Rastafarianism**. Garvey, born in Jamaica, agitated for black power in the United States during the twenties, in response to the dire poverty and discrimination that the vast majority of blacks living in the New World faced. His efforts blended church and state: even as he pressed for an African homeland to which former slaves could return (it never materialized), he prophesied that Christ would come again as a black man. After serving half of a five-year sentence for mail fraud in an Atlanta prison (the charge was almost certainly politically motivated), he was exiled from the United States and returned to Jamaica.

For centuries, African slaves and their descendants had been confronting the historically inaccurate image of Jesus as a pale-skinned Caucasian. Moreover, it was inevitable that they would connect this image with the colonial empires that brought it to them. At the same time, those slaves who had become Christians saw parallels between the Jews' enslavement by the Egyptians and the slavery of Africans in the New World. Black spirituals are rich with such connections. In this context, Garvey's prophecy about Christ's second coming and his emphasis on the Jewish/African slavery connection was a logical, if controversial, extension of these circumstances. In effect, they were the religious analogue to his black nationalism.

Rastafarians took Garvey's ideas several steps further. They claimed that Jesus had indeed come again, in the person of Haile Selassie (Prince Ras Tafari), the former emperor of Ethiopia. Selassie claimed lineage back to King Solomon, which Rasta-farians have taken as further proof of Selassie's divine status. In line with Selassie's personal genealogy, Rastafarians also claim to be descendants of the twelve tribes of Israel.

These beliefs, which have never come together as "official" doctrine—as has happened in organized religions—are the religious dimension of Rastafarians' efforts to promote a more positive image of Africa and Africans. This has largely come from within the movement. For those on the outside, the most vivid impressions of Rastafarianism are images and sounds: dreadlocks, ganja (marijuana that they ingest as part of their religious practice), and the music. To Jamaican music, they gave a sound, Rastafarian drums, and reggae's one superstar: Bob Marley.

**Rude Boys** The other response to the social unrest during the transition to independence was more violent: it came in the form of **rude boys**, young black Jamaicans who grew up in the most disadvantaged sections of Kingston. They were stylish dressers and often carried sharp knives. For many Jamaicans, including the police, they were outlaws. However, others saw them as heroes, much as the James Brothers and Billy the Kid were heroes to earlier generations of Americans, or as today's gangsta rappers are heroes to some of today's youth.

## From Ska to Reggae: The Evolution of Rock-Era Jamaican Music

It is no coincidence that a distinctive Jamaican popular music during the drive for independence often had a political orientation. Nor is it a coincidence that this music drew heavily on the American rhythm and blues popular in the years around 1960: the proximity of the two countries made it available in multiple ways.

**American Radio in Jamaica** Rhythm and blues reached Jamaica in two ways: through radio broadcasts and via sound systems used to create impromptu block parties. Since the development of networks in the twenties and clear-channel stations in the thirties, radio has been able to ignore borders; it is limited only by distance and wattage. So it should not surprise us that Jamaicans tuned in their radios to American stations in the years after World War II. Kingston, the capital city, is just over 500 miles from Miami as the crow flies, and about 1,000 miles from New Orleans. Stations from all over the southern United States were within reach, at least after dark. Like Buddy Holly, many young Jamaicans listened to rhythm and blues; for them, it replaced **mento**, the Jamaican popular music of the early fifties; some would transform it into ska.

**Sound Systems and Street Parties** Sound systems, the mobile discos so much a part of daily life in Jamaica, offered another way to hear new music from America. **Sound systems** were trucks outfitted with the musical necessities for a street party: records, turntables, speakers, and a microphone for the DJ. Operators would drive around, pick a place to set up, and begin to play the R&B hits that enterprising operators had gone to the United States to fetch. Between songs, DJs delivered a steady stream of patter. Much of it was topical, even personal: they would pick out, and sometimes pick on, people in the crowd that had gathered around.

This practice was called **toasting**. It became so popular, and so much a feature of the sound system party, that Jamaican record producers like Lee "Scratch" Perry began releasing discs in which the "B" side was the "A" side without the vocal track. The instrumental track would then serve as the musical backdrop for the DJ's toasting.

As we noted earlier, toasting is a direct forerunner of rap: both initially featured topical, humorous commentary over pre-existing music.

**From Ska to Reggae**  By the end of the fifties, Jamaican music had begun to absorb, then transform, the R&B brought to the country. The first wave of new Jamaican music was **ska**. Ska emerged around 1960 and was the dominant Jamaican sound through the first part of the sixties. The most distinctive rhythmic feature of ska is a strong afterbeat: a strong, crisp "chunk" on the latter part of each beat. This was a Jamaican take on the shuffle rhythm heard in so much fifties R&B. It kept the basic rhythm but reversed the pattern of emphasis within each beat. In the standard shuffle rhythm, the note that falls *on* the beat gets the weight; the afterbeat is lighter. In ska, it is just the opposite, at times to the extent that the note on the beat is absent—there is just the afterbeat. Whether this was an intentional decision by ska musicians such as Derrick Morgan and Prince Buster, a product of the relatively primitive recording studios in Jamaica during this time (recall that early electrical recording did not pick up bass sounds very well), or the lack of bass instruments and people to play them, we don't know; perhaps it was a combination of all of these factors. Whatever the reason, the strong afterbeat remains the aural trademark of ska and part of the rhythmic foundation of reggae.

**Rock steady,** a new Jamaican style that emerged in the latter part of the sixties, combined the persistent afterbeat of ska with a backbeat. The backbeat is typically played on a different instrument, so that the two layers—the afterbeat and the backbeat—are distinguished by timbre.

Both off-beat layers stand out because the beat is either marked lightly or not at all. In particular, the bass, which was the main beat-keeping instrument in rhythm and blues, now roams freely, typically playing a line not tied to a timekeeping role.

With the creation of the composite afterbeat rhythm and the addition of the bass, the rhythmic foundation of **reggae** was in place. In reggae, the basic rhythmic texture of rock steady is treated more flexibly, and with greater complexity, much as late-sixties rock treated rock rhythm more flexibly than early-sixties rock. In the music of its biggest stars, reggae's rhythmic texture is typically denser and more subtle, often with several additional rhythmic layers. In addition, the backbeat is generally stronger, which then establishes the trademark "ka-CHUN-ka" pattern.

The distinctive rhythm of reggae is typically a pattern of emphasis: light or no sound on the beat, strong afterbeats, even stronger backbeats. It works equally well with any rhythm that divides the beat into two parts: we will hear it superimposed on rock rhythm–like even division of the beat in Jimmy Cliff's "The Harder They Come" and on a shuffle rhythm–like uneven division of the beat in Bob Marley's "Is This Love." In this respect, reggae rhythm is different in kind from a style beat like rock rhythm, which describes a more fundamental relationship.

In about a decade, the rhythms of Jamaican music had mutated from an adaptation of the shuffle rhythm of post–World War II rhythm and blues into a rhythm that was unique in the early seventies. Early on, its development went largely unnoticed outside of Jamaica. Jimmy Cliff's film *The Harder They Come*, released in 1972, attracted attention in England, then in the United States when it was released there the following year. But it wasn't until Eric Clapton scored a number 1 in 1974 with a cover of Bob Marley's "I Shot the Sheriff" that reggae got real mainstream exposure.

## Jimmy Cliff and Reggae as Protest Music

Jimmy Cliff (born James Chambers, 1948) was one of reggae's first stars. Born in Jamaica, he emigrated to England in 1964. By the time he landed the lead role in the film *The Harder They Come*, he had gained a modest international reputation as a singer and songwriter. His appearance in the film, and the songs that he recorded for the sound, cemented his place in popular music history.

In *The Harder They Come*, Cliff played Ivanhoe Martin, a naive musician who becomes a dope dealer after being ripped off by his record producer and hassled by a corrupt police force. Cliff wrote several songs for the film, including the title track. Although his character is loosely based on a real-life person from the forties, the film is set in the present: Martin is a reggae singer. The film, widely acclaimed at home and abroad, helped introduce reggae, still a new sound at that time, to an international audience. It also exposed the difficult conditions under which so many Jamaicans lived.

The lyric of the title song sets the tone of the film. It resonates with overtones of social injustice and police oppression and brutality, even as it outlines how the character will respond: "I'm gonna get my share now of what's mine." Cliff does not sugarcoat his message at all. Lines like "But I'd rather be a free man in my grave/ Than living as a puppet or a slave" brutally clarify the options he saw.

In "The Harder They Come," the characteristic reggae rhythm is embedded in a dense rhythmic texture. Two keyboards outline the rhythm: an abrasive-sounding organ chord occurs on the backbeat, while another keyboard plays the afterbeats more faintly. All of this happens over a muted rock rhythm in the drums; an active bass line and other percussion sounds enrich the rhythmic texture. The rhythm serves as a cushion for Cliff's lyric, set to a gently flowing melody that is harmonized with basic chords and that follows the familiar verse/bridge/refrain form heard in many Motown songs and much other rock-era music.

"The Harder They Come," Jimmy Cliff (1972)

---

♪ **KEY FEATURES**

**"The Harder They Come," Jimmy Cliff (1972)**

- Scathing lyrics give voice to the "outlaw" point of view
- Cliff's buoyant voice, riding on a smooth and simple melody, presents words clearly: performing style at odds with the message of the lyrics
- Infectious reggae rhythm, with active rhythms around the characteristic "ka-CHUN-ka" pattern

---

## Topical Tropical Music: Reggae and Music with a Message

In "The Harder They Come," we are faced with the seeming contradiction between words and music. The lyrics are dark, even menacing. But the music can't help bringing a smile to one's face and a body movement somewhere. This is happy music: in its rhythm, in the lilt in Cliff's voice, in the Motown-inspired form, and in the gently undulating melody. Is the music the candy that entices us to listen to the message of the lyrics, or is it a way to forget for the moment the situation that the lyrics depict, or something else altogether? What we do know is that many of the songs that put reggae on the international musical map—like this one and Bob Marley's "I Shot the Sheriff" and "Get Up, Stand Up"—embedded hard messages within reggae's infectious rhythms and sounds.

The use of popular song as a vehicle for social commentary was largely a rock-era phenomenon. There were isolated examples in modern-era popular songs—Andy Razaf and Fats Waller's 1929 song "Black and Blue," a lament on the disadvantages of dark skin color, is a memorable example; so was Billie Holiday's 1939 recording of "Strange Fruit," a powerful song about lynching. But songs like these were the exceptions. What topical music there was in the thirties and forties came mostly from singer-commentators like Woody Guthrie and, to a lesser extent, the blues (for example, some maintain that Nat Cole's "Straighten Up and Fly Right" is an allegory on race relations).

The music of Dylan and the other folksingers of the early sixties brought topical song into popular music, and reshaped it in the process, as we have seen. During the sixties and early seventies, a few black performers—most notably James Brown and Sly Stone among popular musicians and jazz saxophonists John Coltrane and Archie Shepp—dealt powerfully with racial issues and their emotional consequences in their music. But the efforts of all these musicians represented only a fraction of their total output, and an even smaller fraction of the musical activity in rock and soul.

Reggae was different, in that it first became known outside of Jamaica as a music with a message. The music of Marley, Cliff, and other early reggae stars called attention to the social inequities in Jamaica. Moreover, it came at a time when rock had largely forsaken its role as a vehicle for social commentary. Marley would help fill that void, becoming a powerful voice on social issues. In this respect, reggae anticipated both punk and rap. And like these later styles, its musical features soon found their way into songs that had no literal or emotional connection to the social issues that the first hits introduced. Marley would lead the way in this respect as well.

## Bob Marley

Bob Marley (1945–1981) was born in Nine Miles, a small Jamaican village. His recording career began in the early sixties and took off in 1964, after he formed the first edition of his backup group, the Wailers, which included longtime associates Bunny Livingston (b. 1947) and Peter Tosh (1944–1987). By the early seventies, he was extremely popular in Jamaica. However, it wasn't until he signed with Island Records that his reputation spread throughout the world.

His success on record and in concert gave him and his country's music unprecedented exposure. For many people, Bob Marley *was* reggae. Worldwide, he was its most popular artist. He was also the decade's most visible spokesperson for peace and brotherhood, carrying the torch of sixties social activism and idealism into the seventies. He also made clear his affiliation with Rastafarian practice, which he had begun in the mid-sixties. While Marley's stance didn't completely legitimize Rastafarianism, it certainly raised its status in Jamaica and elsewhere.

Bob Marley performing in 1980, shortly before he passed away.

However, Marley's music left the deepest impression. It made possible his popularity, which in turn gave him the leverage to work for meaningful change in Jamaican society. His first hits, most notably "I Shot the Sheriff" and "Get Up, Stand Up," both recorded in 1973, show his political side. Both were recorded with the original version of the Wailers, which dissolved in 1974. Marley re-formed the Wailers with the Barrett brothers (Aston "Family Man" Barrett [b. 1946] on bass and Carlton Barrett [1950–1987] on drums), plus several other musicians and the I Threes, a backup vocal group that included Marley's wife Rita (b. 1946). In addition to politically charged songs, Marley also scored with gently themed songs, including the lilting 1978 hit, "Is This Love." In keeping with the content and tone of the lyric, the form of this song sprawls lazily through time, moving at a relaxed tempo.

A comparison of the rhythm in the two songs suggests the flexibility of reggae rhythm: in "Is This Love," Marley adapts the characteristic reggae afterbeat/backbeat pattern to a shuffle rhythm, rather than a rock rhythm. Combined with a slower tempo, it projects a quite different rhythmic feel from Cliff's "The Harder They Come." Note that in both songs the slower offbeat rhythm is the same: a backbeat. It is only the faster-moving layer that is different.

The gentle pulsations of the drum and tambourine, prompted by the fast shuffle-based reggae rhythm in the keyboards, keep the rhythm afloat, while the vocal parts—Marley's slow-moving melody and the sustained harmonies of the I Threes—and in-and-out bass slow the beat down to a speed below typical body rhythms, even the heartbeat at rest or the pace of a relaxed stroll. As a result, the rhythm of the song is buoyant and lazy at the same time. All of this evokes a feeling of languid lovemaking in the tropics, a perfect musical counterpoint to the lyric of the song.

"Is This Love,"
Bob Marley
(1978)

> ♪ **KEY FEATURES**
>
> **"Is This Love," Bob Marley (1978)**
> - Shuffle-based reggae rhythm, with "ka-CHUN-ka" created by two keyboards
> - Large band: Marley, backup vocals, several percussion instruments, including Rastafarian drums, bass, guitars, and keyboards, saxophone
> - Free bass line, light beat keeping
> - Song about love, not politics, set to a flowing melody at a leisurely tempo

Bob Marley was reggae's greatest ambassador. With his death in 1981, reggae lost an important world presence. Reggae is still a dominant music in Jamaica, and its sounds and rhythms have shaped diverse styles in the last quarter century—and so has its look: Rastafarian dreadlocks are still fashionable. However, it is ska, its antecedent, that has enjoyed a resurgence in popularity in both the United Kingdom and the United States.

## Reggae as an International Music

Within popular music, and particularly within rock-era music, patterns of influence have often had a geographic component: the long journey of deep blues from the Delta to England via Chicago and Memphis, then back to the United States, is the most spectacular of numerous examples. In the process, the music undergoes a thorough transformation, coming back to its original home significantly changed and profoundly influential. In the seventies, the most dramatic instance of a long and winding pattern of influence was reggae. Like the blues-based rock of the late sixties, reggae also drew heavily on the music of black Americans, flourished in Great Britain, then returned to the United States via England.

Reggae's popularity outside of Jamaica owed much to the heavy concentrations of Jamaicans in England. As part of the transition from colonialism, Great Britain opened its doors—or at least its ports—to people from its colonies. During the fifties and early sixties, around 250,000 people arrived from the Caribbean, more than from any other former colonial region. By the end of the sixties, the British government had enacted legislation that severely restricted immigration. By that time, however, several generations of Jamaicans were already in England, where they re-created much of their culture. All the types of Jamaican music of the sixties and seventies found a supportive audience in England, among Jamaicans eager for this link to their homeland and among British whites intrigued by this quite different music.

For a new generation of British musicians in search of "real" music, reggae (and ska) provided an at-home alternative to the blues. Eric Clapton, who had immersed himself so deeply in the blues during the sixties, led the way with his cover of Marley's "I Shot the Sheriff"; the recording topped the charts in 1974. A wave of new British acts—among them the Clash, Elvis Costello, and the Police—wove the fresh sounds of reggae into their music.

Reggae's path to America seems unnecessarily roundabout: the music didn't find a substantial audience in the United States until after it had become popular in England. Once known, however, its influence was in some respects even more widespread and more divorced from the social context of the music. For example, we hear echoes of the distinctive rhythm of reggae in the Eagles' huge 1977 hit "Hotel California." It had a deeper and more sustained impact on black popular music in two quite different ways. One was its influence on rap: the toasting of Jamaican DJs soon evolved into rapping, as we have noted. The other was the continuing liberation of the rhythm section in black pop. Because reggae embedded the pulse of a song in the distinctive rhythms played by mid-range instruments, bass players were free to roam at will, largely independent of a specific rhythmic or harmonic role. Because of this, reggae offered eighties black romantic music the next step beyond the advances of Motown and the Philadelphia sound. We hear its influence in such diverse hits as "Sexual Healing," Marvin Gaye's 1982 ode to carnal love, and "What's Love Got to Do with It," Tina Turner's 1984 cynical rejection of it.

# Funk

Like *blues*, *jazz*, *rock*, *soul*, and *rap*, *funk* is a one-syllable word from African American culture that began as non-musical slang, then found its way into music, and eventually became a style label.

"Funk" originally targeted not the ears but the nose. As far back as the early years of the twentieth century, "funky" meant foul or unpleasant: a person who neglected to bathe for several days usually gave off a funky odor. Over time, it acquired another meaning: hip. Stylish clothes were funky threads. When James Brown sings "Ain't It Funky Now," he is referring to the ambience, not the smell.

Funk and funky came into popular music through jazz. Beginning in the mid-fifties, **funk** referred to a simpler, more blues-oriented style—a return to roots and away from the complexities of hard bop. By the sixties, it had also come to mean soulful. (It also retained the other meanings; context and delivery determined which meaning was appropriate.) By the early seventies, it had come to identify a particularly rhythmic strain of black music.

James Brown was the father of funk as well as the godfather of soul—and the grandfather of rap. Funk musicians built their music on both the basic concept of Brown's music and many of its key musical features. Whether he was talking about feeling good or exhorting his listeners to get up and get involved, Brown embedded his message in a powerful groove. Those who followed his path—first Sly and the Family Stone, then the funk bands of the seventies—expanded both the range of messages and the musical resources. Brown's music was relentlessly upbeat; Sly and the Family Stone and funk bands occasionally expressed the gloomier side of the black experience. Funk bands used the same basic lineup—vocal, horns, rhythm instruments—but they were bigger. Not surprisingly, textures thickened and rhythms became even denser and more complex.

## George Clinton and Funk

Nowhere are these developments more evident than in the music of George Clinton (b. 1940). Clinton was the mastermind behind two important funk bands: Parliament and Funkadelic. While still a teen, he formed Parliament, but as a doo-wop group. They signed on with Motown in 1964 but did not break through. When Clinton left Motown, he had to relinquish the Parliament name to them. So he formed Funkadelic while battling to regain ownership of his group's name. Funkadelic represented a major change of direction. As the group's name implies, it brought together funk and psychedelic rock: James Brown and Sly Stone meeting Jimi Hendrix. When Clinton regained control of the Parliament name in 1974, he used two names for the same band. He recorded the more outrageous material under the Funkadelic name and the tighter, more polished material as Parliament.

The formation of Funkadelic signaled Clinton's transformation into Dr. Funkenstein (he also referred to himself as Maggot Overlord); the title of his 1970 album *Free Your Ass and Your Mind Will Follow* shows another side of his funky sense of humor. While Clinton certainly enjoyed being provocative and playing with words, there is in many of his songs a sense that he is laughing to keep from crying. He tucks his darker messages inside humorous packages, set to a good-time groove. When he asks people to "Tear the Roof Off the Sucker," he could be urging them to party hard—or riot.

Without question, there is an escapist aspect to his work: his many aliases, the flamboyant costumes he and his bands wore in performance, the sci-fi world he created (the Mothership Connection), the spectacular stage shows that were a major attraction during the seventies.

In a very real way, this is the opposite of punk, in attitude and music; there is no doubt about the message of a punk song like "God Save the Queen," either in words or music, which hammers the listener. By contrast, Clinton seems to invite listeners to become "one nation under a groove"; surrendering to the rhythm offers momentary relief from the pain of daily life as a black person in the United States. Whatever the motivation, there is no question that Clinton's groups could create a groove. We experience this in his 1976 hit "Tear the Roof Off the Sucker (Give Up the Funk)," which his band recorded as Parliament.

"Tear the Roof Off the Sucker (Give Up the Funk)," Parliament (1976)

**"Tear the Roof Off the Sucker (Give Up the Funk)"** The song shows both Clinton's debt to James Brown and Sly and the Family Stone and the ways in which his music went beyond theirs. The instrumentation is similar: vocal, horns, and rhythm, but the sound is fuller than either James Brown's or Sly Stone's because there are more instruments and all of them are busy. Clinton's debt to Brown goes beyond these general features; after 1975, his roster included two important James Brown alumni: bassist Bootsy Collins (b. 1951) and saxophonist Maceo Parker (b. 1943). They were key members of his large band, which included as many as twelve musicians.

Like Brown and Stone, Clinton creates the groove over static harmony: this is a one-chord song. The texture is dense. There are riffs and sustained chords from both horns and keyboards, high obbligato lines from a synthesizer, an active but open bass line, lots of percussion, and voices—both the choral effect of the backup singers and Clinton's proto-rap. Clinton gives Collins a chance to stretch out. Collins's lines are active, syncopated, and melodic; they call attention to the increasingly prominent role of the bass in this branch of black music. (Within another generation, hip-hop artists would take this direction to its logical end, by creating backgrounds that emphasized bass and percussion sounds to the exclusion of almost everything else.)

The rhythm has a 16-beat feel over the eight-beat rhythm laid down in the drum part. Clinton's raplike introduction moves at this faster rhythm; so do the horn riffs, the bass line, and guitar parts. This is the same approach heard in the music of Brown and Stone; it is a thicker sound because there is more going on. It is a darker sound, mainly because of Clinton's voice and the prominence of the bass.

Clinton's various bands—Parliament and Funkadelic were recording for two different labels, and there were other offshoots in addition to these two—ran into trouble in the late seventies, mainly because of bad money management, sloppy business practices, and drug abuse. By 1981, Clinton consolidated the two versions of the band under one name: the P-Funk All Stars. Around the same time, Clinton began to concentrate on producing, not only his own music but also groups like the Red Hot Chili Peppers.

Henry Diltz/Corbis

George Clinton performing in 1979 at the "World's Greatest Funk Festival." He is characteristically outrageous: his "outfit" features a blond wig.

♪  **KEY FEATURES**

**"Tear the Roof Off the Sucker (Give Up the Funk)," Parliament (1976)**

- 16-beat activity in vocal line, horn riffs, and bass line over eight-beat drum part
- Large band: with extra percussion, more chord instruments, synthesizers added to soul band
- Dense, syncopated texture, with activity in low, middle, and high registers
- Static harmony supporting a series of repetitive melodies

Funk, by Clinton's band and other groups, never crossed over to the pop mainstream in its pure form. "Tear the Roof Off the Sucker" was Parliament's highest-charting song; it made it only to number 15. However, the music would prove to be enormously influential; most immediately, it helped shape disco and other black styles. And with the advent of digital technology, rappers sampled Clinton's music mercilessly. Among the bands that borrowed heavily from funk was the leading black act of the late seventies: Earth, Wind & Fire.

## Earth, Wind & Fire: A Black Music Synthesis

Like *rock*, *rhythm and blues* has been an inclusive term. Precisely because it has identified such a wide range of music, it has not been—indeed, cannot be—completely precise. From the time Jerry Wexler coined the term, *rhythm and blues* has also embraced not only rhythmic and bluesy music, but also black pop, which emphasizes melody and harmony over strong rhythm and deep blues feeling.

**Two Streams in Rock-Era Black Music**   From doo-wop through Motown to the several streams of black romantic music in the early seventies, black pop had grown dramatically—in presence, in variety, and in market share. During the same time-frame, more rhythm-and-blues-oriented black music had also grown, musically and commercially: from the big-beat music of the fifties through soul in the sixties and funk in the seventies.

These two paths were the most significant trends in black music during the third quarter of the twentieth century. And throughout these twenty-five years, there has been a clear distinction between the two—at least in retrospect. James Brown didn't sing black pop; Diana Ross didn't sing soul. Similarly, Roberta Flack and George Clinton inhabit different musical worlds.

Few artists have successfully fused these two streams. Among the few are two truly great performers: Ray Charles and Aretha Franklin. Both brought soul into pop, and vice versa. In the early seventies, Marvin Gaye and Stevie Wonder, the two newly independent Motown artists, found a fruitful middle ground between funk and romantic pop. Gaye's music in the seventies ranged from the bleakness of "Inner City Blues" and "Trouble Man" to the rapture of "Let's Get It On" and "Got to Give It Up." Wonder's music ranged from funky songs like "Superstition" to romantic ballads like "Send One Your Love." In the latter part of the decade, Earth, Wind & Fire joined them: all three acts moved easily between the two styles and at times blended them within a single song.

**Earth, Wind & Fire**   Maurice White (b. 1941), the founder and leader of Earth, Wind & Fire, named the group after his astrological sign. He is a Sagittarian: the sign contains three of the four elements—earth, wind, and fire—but not water.

After a successful career as a session drummer at Chess Records and with jazz pianist Ramsey Lewis, White set out in 1969 to create a new kind of group. By 1971, they were Earth, Wind & Fire. The next year, they moved to Columbia (now Sony) Records and continued to climb up the charts. By 1975, they had become one of the elite groups of the decade, both on record and in live performance, and remained a top act through the end of the decade.

Earth, Wind & Fire was a big group. In this respect, they were in step not only with black acts like George Clinton's funk bands, Barry White's Love Unlimited Orchestra, and the various Philadelphia groups, but also some of the rock groups encountered in Chapter 14. As many as fourteen musicians could be on stage; the nucleus of the band was White, who sang and played a kalimba, an African thumb piano: his brothers Verdine (b. 1951) on bass and Freddie (b. 1955) on drums, plus singer Philip Bailey (b. 1951).

The group was comparable in many respects to George Clinton's groups: Both were big bands; they created great grooves by layering piles of riffs on top of 16-beat rhythms. But there was a marked difference in attitude, as we hear in their first number 1 single, the 1975 hit "Shining Star."

The title and refrain line of this song projects the optimistic, hopeful mood that runs through so many of the group's songs: "Shining star for you to see, what your life can truly be." The song itself has a clear division between verse and refrain. The verse sets up a complex funk-style groove over a single chord, much like that heard in "Tear the Roof Off the Sucker (Give Up the Funk)." However, the refrain underpins a more coherent, riff-based melodic line with rapidly changing harmonies. As in gospel and love songs, rich harmony is used to send a message of hope; that also seems to be the case here.

---

### ♪ KEY FEATURES

**"Shining Star," Earth, Wind & Fire (1975)**

- Inspirational message: both words and music emphasize the power of positive thinking.
- Funk/pop mix: the verse of this song is Earth, Wind & Fire's take on funk. By contrast, the chorus is more melodic and has active harmony, although it retains the groove.
- 16-beat rhythm: it is marked in the guitar and conga drum. Other rhythms map onto this faster rhythm; most are syncopated.
- Stacks of riffs: a dense texture is comprised of riffs in the horns and rhythm instruments.

"Shining Star," Earth, Wind & Fire (1975)

---

Earth, Wind & Fire's ability to meld funklike grooves with more melodious material is one key to their crossover success. This versatility is evident in the range of their hit songs, from soulful ballads like "That's the Way of the World" to uptempo songs like "Serpentine Fire." Few seventies acts were at home in both funk and black pop styles; fewer still succeeded in blending the two. Earth, Wind & Fire was one of them.

## Disco

*Disco* is short for *discothèque*. *Discothèque* is a French word meaning record library (by analogy with *bibliothèque*, meaning book library). It came into use during World War II, first as the name of a nightclub—Le Discothèque—then as a code word for underground nightclubs where jazz records were played. Because of the German occupation, these clubs were run like American speakeasies during the Prohibition era.

**The Roots of the Club Scene** Discothèques survived the war, becoming increasingly popular in France. The first of the famous discos was the Whiskey-a-Go-Go, which featured American liquors and American dance music, both live and on record. Others sprang up in the postwar years, eventually becoming a favored destination of jet setters. By 1960, the idea of a discothèque had moved to New York. The Peppermint Lounge, where Chubby Checker and the rich and famous did the twist, opened in 1961.

This rags-to-riches-and-back-to-new-rags story would become the recurrent theme of dance music in the latter part of the century. As dance fads like the twist moved out of the clubs into mainstream society, the original audience sought out new music in different, less exclusive, and less pricey venues.

By the end of the sixties, a new club culture was thriving. It was an egalitarian, non-restrictive environment. The new, danceable black music of the late sixties and early seventies provided the soundtrack: Sly and the Family Stone, Funkadelic, Stevie Wonder, Marvin Gaye, Curtis Mayfield, Barry White, and above all the Philadelphia acts. Clubbers included not only blacks but also Latinos, working-class women, and gays, for whom clubbing had become a welcome chance to come out of the closet and express themselves. Despite the gains of the various "rights" movements in the sixties and seventies, these were still marginalized constituencies.

**The Mainstreaming of Disco** By mid-decade, however, **disco** had become not only a venue but also a music for the venue. Integrated bands like KC and the Sunshine Band, which exploded onto the singles charts in 1975, began making music expressly for discos. *Saturday Night Fever* was the commercial breakthrough for the music. Almost overnight, what had been a largely underground scene briefly became the thing to do.

In New York, the favored venue was Studio 54, a converted theater on 54th Street in Manhattan. It became so popular that crowds clamoring to get in stretched around the corner. It was the place to see and be seen. Writing about Studio 54 at the end of the seventies, Truman Capote noted, "Disco is the best floor show in town. It's very democratic, boys with boys, girls with girls, girls with boys, blacks and whites, capitalists and Marxists, Chinese and everything else, all in one big mix."

**Disco and Electronics** Meanwhile, the discothèque scene continued to flourish in Europe. The new element in the music there was the innovative use of synthesizers to create dance tracks. Among the most important figures in this new music were Kraftwerk, a two-person German group, and Giorgio Moroder, an Italian-born, Germany-based producer and electronics wizard who provided the musical setting for many of Donna Summer's disco-era hits.

Kraftwerk and Moroder exemplified the increasingly central role of the producer and the technology. Disco became a producer's music, even more than the music of the sixties girl groups. Just as Phil Spector's "wall of sound" was more famous than the singers in front of it, so did the sound of disco belong more to the men in the studio than the vocalists. Here, the wall of sound was laced with electronic as well as acoustic instruments. Singers were relatively unimportant and interchangeable; there were numerous one-hit wonders. We hear a seminal example of electronically driven disco in Donna Summer's "I Feel Love."

## Donna Summer: The Queen of Disco

If there is one performer whose career embodies disco—its brief history, its geography, and its message—it is Donna Summer (b. Donna Adrian Gaines, 1948). Summer grew up in the Boston area and moved to Europe while in her teens to pursue a career in musical theater and light opera. While working as a backup vocalist, she met Giorgio Moroder (b. 1940), who would collaborate with her on her major seventies hits. Her first international hit, "Love to Love You Baby," was released in 1975; it was a hit in both the United States and Europe. The most striking feature of the song was Summer's erotic moans. In its graphic evocation of the bedroom experience, it is in spirit an answer song to Barry White's orgasmic episodes.

As the song title suggests, "I Feel Love" (1977), her next big American hit, explores the erotic dimension of love, although not as blatantly as in the earlier song. Here Summer's deliberately wispy voice floats above Moroder's sea of synthesized sound. Summer's vocal may be the most prominent element of the music, but the background is certainly the more innovative. The innovation begins with Moroder's

"I Feel Love,"
Donna Summer
(1977)

use of electronic counterparts to a traditional drum set; there is not one conventional instrument on the track. Even more noteworthy is the idiomatic writing for synthesizers. Moroder creates a rich tapestry of sound by layering in a large quantity of repetitive patterns, some constantly in the foreground, others in the background and often intermittent. None of them really corresponds to traditional rock guitar or bass lines: it is not only the sounds that are novel, but also the lines that create the dense texture behind Summer's vocal.

Rhythmically, the song converts the 16-beat rhythms of funk and black pop into an accessible dance music by making the beat and the 16-beat layer more explicit. From the start we hear the steady thud of a bass drum–like sound on every beat and an equally steady synthesized percussion sound moving four times the speed of the beat in a mid-range register. Other parts, most obviously the synthesized ascending pattern that runs through the song, also confirm regular rhythms. Compared to previous examples that used this more active rhythm, "I Feel Love" is far less syncopated and much more obvious in its timekeeping. This is certainly due in large part to its use as dance music.

The busy rhythms of the accompaniment contrast sharply with Summer's leisurely unfolding vocal line and the slow rate of

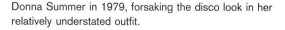

Donna Summer in 1979, forsaking the disco look in her relatively understated outfit.

Bettmann/Corbis

harmonic change. These two seemingly conflicting messages about time in fact invoke two aspects of the disco scene: the activity of the dancers to the throbbing beat and the endlessness of the experience, as one song mixes into the next. (The abrupt ending of the song suggests its use in a disco: the DJ would fade it away before the end as he brought up the next song.)

---

### ♪ KEY FEATURES

**"I Feel Love," Donna Summer (1977)**

- Accompaniment created exclusively from synthesized sounds
- Obvious 16-beat rhythm: bass drum on the beat; other regular rhythms moving four times as fast
- Contrast between Summer's gradually unfolding vocal line and slow harmonic change and active rhythms in many parts

---

Summer's career started before disco went mainstream, then crested during the late seventies. Perhaps anticipating the imminent commercial decline of disco, she took her music in new directions in songs like "Bad Girls." This helped sustain her popularity through the end of the seventies; her last three albums of the decade went number 1.

Among the most loyal members of Summer's fan base were gays. Their connection to disco took on a public face in the music of the Village People.

## The Village People: Disco out of the Closet

The Village People was the brainchild of Jacques Morali (1946–1991), a French producer living in New York. Morali's various accounts of the formation of the Village People are conflicting, but what is certain is that he recruited men to front his act literally from off the street and from gay clubs.

The public image of the Village People is six guys dressed up as macho stereotypes: the Native American (in full costume, including headdress), the leather man (missing only the Harley), the construction worker, the policeman, the cowboy, and the soldier. These expressions of hyper-maleness were, in effect, gay pinups. Their look was more important than their sound, although after a disastrous appearance on *Soul Train*, Morali fired five of the six men and replaced them with new recruits.

The whole act was an inside joke. Morali and gay audiences laughed while straight America bought their records by the millions and copied the look—mustaches, lumber jackets, and the like. Many listeners were not aware of the gay undertone to the lyrics—or if they were, they didn't care.

The group's song "Y.M.C.A.," their biggest hit on the singles charts (number 2 in 1978), shows the macho men at work. In most cities and towns around the United States, a Y.M.C.A. is a place for families to participate in an array of activities. Some are athletic: basketball, swimming, gymnastics. Others are social and humanitarian, such as meals for senior citizens. In larger cities, a Y.M.C.A. can also accommodate residents. In cities like New York, these became meeting places for gays.

"Y.M.C.A.,"
the Village
People (1978)

The Village People, dressed in their macho-stereotype outfits: cowboy, construction worker, Native American, policeman, biker, and soldier.

The lyrics of the song have fun with this situation. Seemingly innocuous lines like "They have everything for men to enjoy/You can hang out with all the boys" take on a quite different meaning when understood in the context of the Y as a gay gathering spot.

The music is quintessential disco. Here are some of its characteristic features:

- The tempo: most disco songs had a tempo right around 120 beats a minute—the same speed as a Sousa march—so that the DJ could seamlessly mix one song into the next.

- The four-on-the-floor bass drum: many disco songs featured a rock-solid beat, marked on the bass drum (or its drum-machine counterpart). This song is no exception.

- Active, 16-beat-based rhythms: the conga drum most clearly marks the 16-beat rhythmic layer. Often the bass line and drums add a "dum-diddy" rhythm. And the drummer plays on the off-beat of every beat. The rhythm in disco songs like "Y.M.C.A." derives its density and activity from both funk and dance-oriented black pop. The biggest difference is that the beat is much more obvious, not only from the beat-keeping bass drum, but also the bass line and other rhythm parts. Compared to funk, there is not much syncopation.

- A rich, almost orchestral, accompaniment, featuring an augmented rhythm section, electronic instruments, and strings: here, there is all of that, with brilliant string lines, horn parts, plus "solos" for the synthesizer in the disco mix version.

- A catchy tune, delivered in chunks and sung without much finesse: this is a simple verse/refrain song, put together in short phrases. The vocalists are enthusiastic but not terribly skilled.
- Repetitive harmony: disco songs often cycle familiar progressions endlessly, the better to suggest the endless disco experience—with continuous music, no clocks on the wall, or any other method of marking time. Here, the harmony is a stretched-out version of that perennial favorite, the "Heart and Soul" progression, in both verse and chorus. When simply recycled, as it is here, it loses its sense of direction to a home chord; it recontextualizes the progression into something quite different in meaning: from clear boundaries to no boundaries.

## Dance Fads and the Influence of Disco

Disco was widely popular during the last part of the seventies. During that three-year window, it spread from urban dance clubs to the suburbs, and its audience grew considerably. While it had clear and strong gay associations, as "Y.M.C.A." makes clear, it was more than music for gays and blacks. In this respect, *Saturday Night Fever* was a slice of life: there were many working-class urban youth who used disco dancing as an outlet.

Disco was more than the music, or even the culture that had produced it. For many, it became a lifestyle. It was hedonistic: dancing was simply a prelude to more intimate forms of contact. It was exhibitionistic: fake Afro wigs; skin-tight, revealing clothes; flamboyant accessories; platform shoes; everything glittering. It was drug-ridden: with disco, cocaine became a mainstream drug; the logo for Studio 54 showed the man on the moon seemingly ingesting cocaine from a silver spoon.

**Reactions Against Disco**  All this, plus the inevitable stream of mindless disco songs (the ratio of wheat to chaff in any genre is low; disco was no exception) gave disco's detractors plenty of ammunition. They trashed the music and the culture. Ostensibly, it was simply a reaction against disco's many excesses, but there was also a strong homophonic undercurrent. Perhaps the most notorious disco-bashing incident occurred in Chicago during the summer of 1979. Steve Dahl, a disc jockey at a local rock station, organized Disco Demolition Night. Fans who brought a disco record to a Chicago White Sox doubleheader got into the park for 98 cents. They spent the first game chanting "Disco Sucks"; after the first game, they made a pile of records in center field. An attempted explosion turned into chaos.

Dahl's attack came around the time the disco fad was losing momentum. His voice joined the chorus of critics who decried the disco lifestyle and the seeming superficiality of the music. Homophobia was the unspoken undercurrent. When disco disappeared from the charts and the radio, there was an "I told you so" response from those who hated it. But in retrospect, it would have been surprising if it had lasted much longer, given the history of earlier dance fads.

## Disco and Twentieth-Century Dance Fads

The major dance fads in the twentieth century have had short lifespans: the Charleston and black bottom in the early twenties; jitterbugging and lindy hopping around 1940;

the twist and other rock-and-roll dances around 1960. The Charleston and the twist were dance fads that caught on somewhat after the introduction of new rhythms: the two-beat fox-trot in the 1910s and early 1920s, and the eight-beat rhythm of rock and roll in the 1950s. Disco, like the jitterbug, was a dance fad that came with the division of popular music into two related rhythmic streams. In the thirties, it was sweet (two-beat) and swing (four-beat). In the seventies, it was rock (eight-beat) and disco (16-beat).

Both swing and disco were brief windows when the more active rhythms of black and black-inspired music became a truly popular music. In both cases, much of the music was rhythmically more obvious than the music that had spawned it. Many of the hits of the swing era, especially by the white bands, laid down the beat but lacked the rhythmic play of music by Basie, Ellington, or Goodman. Similarly, disco was more straightforward rhythmically than funk or black pop, as we have discussed. This made it accessible to a greater number of dancers, but sacrificed musical interest in the process.

So it shouldn't be surprising that disco faded away so quickly. It was following much the same path as the other dance fads that signaled the arrival of a new beat. And it should not be surprising that the new beat took root following disco's demise. In this way, disco was an influential music, far more so than its brief lifespan would suggest.

## Moving Beyond Rock

It's a long way geographically and culturally from the ghettos of Kingston, Jamaica, to the glitz of Studio 54 in New York. Jimmy Cliff's pointed commentary in "The Harder They Come" sends a strikingly different message from the Village People's puckish humor in "Y.M.C.A." Reggae, funk, and disco inhabited largely independent worlds during the seventies, although some funk bands tried to hop on the disco bandwagon in an attempt to cross over to the pop charts. And only disco had a significant commercial presence, however brief.

Nevertheless, they are linked not only temporally, but also musically and socially, despite their differences in message, milieu, and musical substance. Each was a minority music: reggae took shape outside the U.S.–U.K. axis; funk was less popular than other forms of black music, even within the black community; disco's original fan base included multiple minorities: race, ethnicity, and sexual preference. And each represented a significant departure from mainstream rock—in subject, style, and sound.

Their musical common ground is extensive. Most fundamentally, it includes an emphasis on large bands (or their electronic counterparts); more active and often more syncopated rhythms, typically based on a 16-beat rhythmic foundation; dense, multi-layered textures; and a predilection for electronic sounds. Collectively, these style features laid the foundation for the most far-reaching developments in post-1980 rock-era music. We have already noted rap's debt to these styles. However, other distinctive trends—including the new pop of the eighties and beyond, the numerous forms of dance music, and world music fusions—also connect directly to this music. In particular, disco was the gateway for the wholesale infusion of electronica. And it created a new kind of underground dance club culture, which would continue through the eighties and flower in the nineties. Funk, especially that of George Clinton, became a sampling ground for rap and a primary source for an important direction in alternative rock. Reggae was arguably the first world music with a significant commercial presence: similar rock/R&B/regional fusions emerged elsewhere in the Caribbean (for example, soca, zouk) and in Africa (such as new forms of juju, Afro-pop, mbalax).

In the remaining chapters, we will hear rock-era music evolve far away from the core rock discussed in earlier chapters. These three styles—reggae, funk, and disco—and the cultures that they represented contributed more to this evolutionary momentum than any other music of the seventies.

. . . . . . . . . . . . . . . . . . . . . . . . . . . . . . . . . . . . . . . . . . . . . . . . . . . . . . . . . . . . . . . . . . . . . . . . . . . . . . . . . . . . . .

**Terms to Remember**

| | | |
|---|---|---|
| Rastafarianism | toasting | funk |
| rude boy | ska | disco |
| mento | rock steady | |
| sound system | reggae | |

. . . . . . . . . . . . . . . . . . . . . . . . . . . . . . . . . . . . . . . . . . . . . . . . . . . . . . . . . . . . . . . . . . . . . . . . . . . . . . . . . . . . . .

**Applying Chapter Concepts**

1. Using the six songs discussed here as your primary resources, compare the rhythmic approaches used in reggae, funk, and disco. In particular, describe the following:

   a. What instrument(s), if any, are marking the beat? How prominent is the beat marking?

   b. What instrument(s) are marking eight-beat and/or 16-beat rhythms? How prominent are they?

   c. What rhythms conflict with the beat and other regular rhythms? How prominent are they? What is the balance between timekeeping and rhythmic conflict?

   d. In what registers does the rhythmic activity take place? How dense is the rhythmic texture?

   Present your information in table form.

2. In this chapter, we noted that disco was, from one perspective, a more rhythmically obvious line form of funk. Confirm or challenge this point by exploring the music of late seventies/early eighties acts such as Chic, the Brothers Johnson, Rick James, and Kool & the Gang. In particular, comment on the role of the bass, the rate of harmonic change (fast/slow/not at all), and the prominence of timekeeping.

# 16

# Punk and Its Aftermath

CBGB is a small club located in the Bowery section of New York City. Originally, it was the bar in the Palace Hotel. By 1973, the year that CBGB opened, the hotel had gone from palatial to poverty-stricken: it was a cheap rooming house for the alcoholics and druggies that inhabited the neighborhood.

The full name of the club is CBGB & OMFUG: Country, Blue Grass, and Blues, and Other Music for Uplifting Gormandizers. Owner Hilly Kristal's original plan was to book these kinds of acts into his new club. However, an encounter with Richard Hell, Richard Lloyd, and Tom Verlaine of Television—Kristal was repairing the awning over the club entrance when the three band members walked by and struck up a conversation with him—led Kristal to hire the band for a gig at Kristal's club, followed by another with another newly formed band: the Ramones. Neither date attracted much of a crowd.

Nevertheless, Kristal persevered and promoted. After some success with Patti Smith early in 1975, he decided to present "A Festival of the Top 40 New York Rock Bands." He scheduled it in the summer to coincide with the Newport Jazz Festival, a big-time event. It was a gamble—he spent a lot of money on advertising—that paid off. Critics came to hear the bands, and the audience for punk exploded almost overnight.

Among Kristal's customers was Malcolm McLaren, who came to New York in 1974 to attend a boutique fair. Three years earlier, McLaren had opened a clothing boutique in London with Vivienne Westwood called Let It Rock, which featured vintage and retro styles; he and Westwood also created theater costumes. However, McLaren saw himself as a political provocateur. He wanted to be able to thumb his nose at the establishment and make money on it at the same time. McLaren viewed rock music as a vehicle for his politics; bands would make a statement with images as well as sound.

While in New York, McLaren persuaded the New York Dolls, who had just been dropped by Mercury Records, to let him manage them and design their outfits. He costumed them in red leather and had them perform in front of a hammer and sickle. For the Dolls, the shock strategy backfired: the blatant nod to the Soviet Union apparently turned off other labels, and the band broke up the following year. For McLaren, it was simply the prelude to an even bolder statement. After hearing early punk bands like the Ramones and Neon Boys (who would become Television) and seeing Richard Hell's torn clothing and studded collars, McLaren returned to England, changed the name of his boutique to SEX, and started carrying fetish clothing and original punk-inspired items. This in turn attracted a clientele from which McLaren would eventually assemble the Sex Pistols.

That a boutique storeowner and fashion designer would form and manage the U.K.'s seminal punk band says a lot about the movement. At least in McLaren's realization of it with the Sex Pistols, punk was part of a larger package. It was only one component of a presence designed to stand out, outrage, and affront those on the outside. Hand in hand with the noise of punk went the hostile attitude and—even more obvious from a distance—the look: spiked hair in a rainbow of colors, tattoos and body piercings, torn clothes ornamented or even held together with safety pins.

**Punk** was an extreme form of a wave of new music that emerged in the mid-seventies, first in New York, then in other parts of the United States and in England. Rather than stadiums with thousands listening and watching, it flourished in small clubs like CBGB, with audiences in the hundreds. In the sense that it sought to recapture the revolutionary fervor and the relative simplicity of early rock, it was a reactionary movement—a counterrevolution against what its adherents saw as the growing commercialism of mainstream rock. However, in its reconception of these values, it established an important and influential new direction in rock, which continues to the present.

# The Punk Movement

The most powerful and enduring image in rock has been the rebellious outsider as hero. From Elvis, Little Richard, and Jerry Lee Lewis to the latest flavor of indie band, rock has glorified those who outraged a complacent, corporate-minded establishment while delivering their message loudly, if not always clearly. In rock's early years, it was rock on the outside versus the pop establishment. However, when rock became the dominant commercial music, the rebellion happened on the inside. As before, it was David and Goliath; with punk, however, Goliath was the rock establishment. The power of this image can be gauged by the ratio of commercial success to critical attention. Few punk or new wave bands enjoyed much commercial success; nevertheless, far more has been written about the early years of punk than about more mainstream rock in the seventies.

## The Roots of Punk

Punk took shape in New York. Much like the folksingers of the sixties, bands performed in small clubs located in Greenwich Village and Soho. CBGB, the most famous of these clubs, launched the careers of a host of punk and new wave bands. Among the CBGB graduates were Patti Smith, Richard Hell (in the Neon Boys, then Television, and finally as Richard Hell and the Voldoids), the Ramones, and the Talking Heads. Ohio was another spawning ground: Pere Ubu, from Cleveland, and Devo, from Dayton, both had careers underway by 1975.

Among the major influences on punk in New York were the Velvet Underground and the New York Dolls. The Velvet Underground embraced the New York City subculture sensibility and nurtured it in their music. Their songs (for example,

"Heroin") were dark, which foreshadowed punk's "no future" mentality, and the sound of their music was often abrasive and minimalist. They presented an anti-artistic approach to art, which was a rejection of the artistic aspirations of the Beatles and other like-minded bands. In addition, their impresario was an artist, Andy Warhol, who packaged them as part of a multimedia experience (the famous Exploding Plastic Inevitable); this presaged McLaren's vision of punk as a fusion of image and sound in the service of outrage.

The New York Dolls, led by David Johansen, were America's answer to David Bowie, Marc Bolan, and the rest of the British glam bands. They lacked Bowie's musical craft and vision; their musical heroes were not only the Velvet Underground but also the MC5 and Iggy Pop and the Stooges. In effect, they dressed up the latter groups' proto-punk and made it even more outrageous, wearing makeup and cross-dressing outlandishly—they out-Bowied Bowie in this respect—and taking bold risks in performance. Brinksmanship came easily to them, as they were, in the words of one critic, "semi-professional" at best.

Patti Smith, a rock critic turned poet-performer, was the first major figure in the punk movement to emerge from the New York club subculture. Smith was its poet laureate, a performer for whom words were primary. There is nothing groundbreaking in the sound of her music. Indeed, she wanted to recapture rock's brief glory period in the mid-sixties, to have her music make a statement, not a spectacle. Her work had much of the purity and power of punk: purity in the sense that it returned rock to its garage-band spirit, and power in the outrage. But it was not outrageous, at least not by the Sex Pistols' standards. Smith was also important because she was a woman in charge: she played a seminal role in the creation of this new/old style. Partly because of her presence, punk and new wave music were much more receptive to strong women than conventional rock.

In the United Kingdom, punk was a music waiting to happen. All the components were in place, except the sound. Disaffected working-class youth wanted an outlet for their frustration: pierced body parts, Technicolor hair, and torn clothes made a statement, but they weren't loud enough, and they didn't articulate the message. Following McLaren's return to London and the Ramones' 1976 tour, punk took off in England as well as in the United States, most notably in the music of the Sex Pistols. Elvis Costello quickly became the bard of the new wave. The Clash, the Pretenders (fronted by Akron, Ohio, native Chrissie Hynde), and the Buzzcocks were among other leading U.K. bands in the late seventies.

The attitudes expressed in the punk movement reflected deeply rooted contradictions in everyday life during the seventies. The "we" mindset of the sixties—the sense of collective energy directed toward a common goal—gave way to a "me" mindset, where everyone looked out for themselves. The various rights movements and the move toward a more democratic society eroded class distinctions at a rapid rate. Still, there was a strong conservative backlash in both Britain and the United States. At the same time, a prolonged recession, fueled in part by the absence of fuel due to the Arab oil embargo, gave working- and middle-class people little opportunity to take advantage of their new social mobility. And sky-high interest rates and inflation created the fear that today's savings would be worth far less in the future. "No Future," the nihilistic battle cry of the Sex Pistols, was in part a product of this bleak economic outlook.

# The Power of Punk

Although the look screams outrage and the words scream rebellion, the power of punk is in the music; it is the sounds and rhythms of punk that most strongly convey its energy and attitude. Especially when experienced in its native environment, a small club overflowing with people, the music overwhelms, injecting the crowd with massive shots of energy.

Punk is to rock and roll what heroin is to opium: it gains its potency by distilling its most potent elements and presenting them in concentrated form. "Pure" punk songs are short: they say what they have to say quickly and move on. In their mid-seventies heyday, the Ramones would play 30-minute sets, in which all of the songs lasted about 2 minutes. Within such brief timespans, punk offers songs that intensify the dangerous aspects of rock and roll: the loudness, the sounds, the rhythms.

Punk is loud. Typically, subtlety is not part of the equation; neither is contrast in volume. It's full-bore volume from beginning to end. Punk is noise: guitarists and bassists routinely use heavy distortion. Punk singing is the triumph of chutzpah over expertise. Indeed, the lack of vocal skill or sophistication was a virtual requirement; one couldn't credibly croon a punk song. Part of the message was that anyone could sing a punk song, if they had the nerve. Punk is fast: tempos typically exceed the pace of normally energetic movement—walking, marching, disco dancing. However, the most compelling feature of punk is its approach to rock rhythm.

## Saturated Rock Rhythm

A brief recap of twenty years of rock rhythm: Recall that what distinguished rock and roll from rhythm and blues was the eight-beat rhythm. We heard it in the guitar lines of Chuck Berry and the piano playing of Little Richard and gradually in other rhythm instruments, as musicians caught on to this new rhythmic conception. Move ahead to the late sixties and early seventies: as rock musicians became comfortable with rock rhythm, the basic rock beat became a springboard for rhythmic play, as we heard in the music of the Who, Led Zeppelin, and others.

Punk restored the essence of rock rhythm. Punk bands extracted the eight-beat rock rhythmic layer, sped it up, then intensified it by isolating its defining feature, making it the most prominent feature of the rhythm and saturating the rhythmic texture with it. In punk, the "default" way of playing the rock rhythmic layer was simply to repeat a note, a chord, or a drum stroke over and over at rock-beat speed. Musicians could graft riffs onto this rhythm to create variety and interest, but this was an overlay; typically, the eight-beat rhythm continues through the notes of the riffs. By contrast, Chuck Berry's rhythm guitar patterns typically oscillate every beat between two chords. This oscillation creates slower rhythms that attenuate the impact of the faster rhythm. Punk strips away these slower rhythms, presenting rock rhythm in a purer form.

Punk made this "purer" form of rock rhythm stand out through a two-part strategy. First, the entire rhythm section typically reinforced it: guitar(s), bass, and drums all hammer it out. Indeed, depending on the speed of the song and the skill of the drummer, the reinforcement could be heard on the bass drum as well as the drums or cymbals. Second, it favored explicit timekeeping over syncopation and other forms of rhythmic play. This reverses the prevailing direction of the evolution of rock rhythm, which was toward greater rhythmic complexity—more syncopation, more activity, more implicit timekeeping—as we heard in Chapter 9. We sample the power of punk in songs by the Ramones and the Sex Pistols.

## The Ramones

The Ramones—vocalist Joey Ramone (Jeffrey Hyman, 1952–2001); guitarist Johnny Ramone (John Cummings, 1951–2004); bassist Dee Dee Ramone (Doug Colvin, 1952–2002); and original drummer Tommy Ramone (Tommy Erdelyi, b. 1952)—were the poster boys of punk. With their trademark look— torn jeans, T-shirts, leather jackets, and long dark hair—and electrifying half-hour sets that consisted of a nonstop string of high-voltage songs, they put punk on the map, first in New York, then in the rest of the United States and in England, where they inspired groups such as the Sex Pistols and the Clash.

The Ramones were brothers only on the bandstand. All had been students at Forest Hills High School in Queens, New York, but were not related. They formed the Ramones in 1974 and quickly reclaimed the spirit of early rock and reworked it into punk. They

The Ramones performing in 1977. We see guitarist Johnny Ramone and vocalist Joey Ramone.

began with the essence of the garage band: a singer backed by guitar, bass, and drums playing three-chord songs built from simple riffs. However, they jacked up the tempo to breakneck speed: a typical Ramones song has a tempo of over 170 beats per minute, well above the 120 to 126 beats per minute of a disco song. Such fast tempos tax any drummer's physical ability, and certainly approached the limit of Tommy Ramone's skill and endurance. A set of ten or twelve songs at maximum tempo and volume was exhilarating for band and audience.

Partly because of the extremely fast tempo, Ramones' songs are not rhythmically subtle. The three essential layers of rock rhythm—the beat, the backbeat, and the rock-rhythm layer—are in the forefront during the instrumental sections and clearly audible underneath the vocals. There is little syncopation, and they are basic. Compared to pre-punk rock, a set of Ramones' music amounts to mainlining rock rhythm.

"Blitzkrieg Bop" was the Ramones' first single: it was released in November 1975 in the United States and in July 1976 in England. The song, which also appeared on the band's first album, introduced the sound for which the Ramones would become famous and which would outline the key elements of pure punk.

"Blitzkrieg Bop," the Ramones (1975)

The title of the song is worth a comment: "Blitzkrieg" ("lightning war") was a term that the German military used during World War II to identify a quick strike; it has a clear association with Nazis. Although there are no obvious neo-Nazi overtones in "Blitzkrieg Bop," Nazi images were a big part of the punk scene in the United Kingdom. Among the provocative fashions sold at McLaren's shop was a short leather skirt with a swastika in studs on the back panel, and Siouxie (of the Banshees) regularly sported an armband with a swastika.

The song begins by repeating a three-chord pattern: I, IV, and V, with a syncopation on the V chord. We hear distorted guitar, bass, and drums, all at full volume, and all hammering out the rock beat. The first vocal chorus is a primer on the punk take on rock rhythm. Underneath the famous "Hey ho/let's go" we hear Tommy Ramone beating out a straight rock rhythm and the backbeat. Soon, Dee Dee joins in, playing the same note over and over at rock-beat speed. Johnny joins in next, playing a repeated chord, also at rock-beat speed. In these 10 seconds, we can hear the role of each rhythm-section instrument in creating the distilled essence of rock rhythm: everyone pumps out the rock rhythmic layer—on a drum, on a single note, on a single chord. The only other rhythmic feature is the backbeat, the other main component of rock rhythm. No other rhythms are implied. This is as pure, and as energetic, as rock rhythm gets.

In several other respects, the song recalls early rock. The melody consists of simple riffs that lead to the short hook that is the title riff. It uses the AABA form typical not only of pre-rock pop but also those many rock-and-roll songs that emulated the older style. The lyric seems teen-themed ("climbing in the back seat/ ...steam heat"), but with an edge ("shoot 'em in the back now"); but the overall effect is disconnection—between the title phrase, the events described in the lyric, and the exhortation ("Hey ho/let's go"). This has the effect of focusing attention on the music: the real message of the song is its unbridled energy.

## ♪ KEY FEATURES

**"Blitzkrieg Bop," the Ramones (1975)**
- Garage-band instrumentation: guitar, bass, drums, vocals
- Saturated rock rhythm: everyone hammering out the rock rhythmic layer
- Pop song form and riff-based melody
- Catchy lyrics ("Hey ho/let's go"; "Blitzkrieg bop") with no real narrative

The Ramones were one of the most prolific punk bands, playing over 2,000 performances during their twenty-plus years and recording fourteen studio albums. They were also punk's premier ambassadors, fueling the punk revolution in Britain with their appearance there in 1976. Among the bands that heard them perform were the Sex Pistols.

## The Sex Pistols

We think of rebels as independent figures standing apart from the crowd. So there is an uncomfortable irony to the fact that the most rebellious act in the history of rock music was part of perhaps the most complex and manipulative relationship between a major rock act and its management. Malcolm McLaren, a radical and an entrepreneur, made the Sex Pistols: vocalist Johnny Rotten (John Lydon, b. 1956), guitarist Steve Jones (b. 1955), bassists Glen Matlock (b. 1956) and Sid Vicious (John Ritchie, 1957–1979), and drummer Paul Cook (b. 1956); he also made them an instrument that enabled him to realize his own provocative ends.

McLaren found the Sex Pistols in his shop. Glen Matlock, the original bassist with the group, worked for McLaren. When he let McLaren know that he and two of his friends, guitarist Steve Jones and drummer Paul Cook, were putting together a band, McLaren found them rehearsal space, took over their management, and recruited a lead singer for them. John Lydon, who became Johnny Rotten (allegedly because of his less-than-meticulous personal hygiene), had been hanging around SEX for a while. McLaren had gotten to know him and felt that he had the capacity for outrage that he'd been looking for. (Another SEX shop hanger-on, Sid Vicious [John Ritchie], would eventually replace Matlock.)

In fact, none of the four had much musical skill at the time they formed the band. Jones was more adept at thievery than guitar playing: he stole the group's first sound system. McLaren booked the group into small clubs, where they acquired more of a reputation for outrageous conduct than for musicianship. Word spread about the group through word of mouth, newspaper reviews, and subculture fanzines. (*Punk*, a fanzine started by two high school friends from suburban Connecticut, gave the new movement its name.)

The Sex Pistols found their musical direction after hearing the Ramones and learning the basics of their instruments. What they had from the beginning, however,

The Sex Pistols performing in Atlanta in 1979. The photograph shows bassist Sid Vicious and Johnny Rotten in characteristic poses.

was the ability to shock, provoke, confront, and incite to riot. When they added the musical energy of the Ramones to this stew, they were ready to overthrow the ruling class, a stance that is evident in two of their best-known songs, "Anarchy in the UK" and "God Save the Queen." Johnny Rotten opens "Anarchy in the UK" with "I am an Anti-Christ; I am an anarchist" and ends with a drawn out "Destroy." The opening line lances both church and state; the final word makes clear their agenda. Rotten, a skinny kid who knew no bounds, sings/screams/snarls the lyrics. In "God Save the Queen," we can imagine the sneer on Rotten's face as he delivers the opening line, "God Save the Queen, the fascist regime."

All of this was music to McLaren's ears. He hated the liberal attitudes of the sixties and was canny enough to exploit their openness, so that he could take aim at both the ruling class and the "peace and love" generation. In his mind, punk was nihilistic: "no future" was the motto. For McLaren, the Sex Pistols were another expression of his business philosophy. The bondage gear sold in McLaren's boutique promoted sex as pain, not pleasure. Although Rotten railed against the "fascist regime," punk's use of the swastika image evoked the ultimate fascist regime. And the Sex Pistols' sets often ended in some kind of fracas: their attitude was more than words and symbols.

The music behind the words was, if anything, even more provocative. It was not just that it was loud—particularly when heard in the small venues where the punk bands played. Or simple—power chords up and down the fretboard. It was the beat. Punk fulfilled the confrontational promise of the very first rock-and-roll records. Rock-and-roll's signature was a repetitive eight-beat rhythm, whether pumped out by Chuck Berry or hammered out by Little Richard and Jerry Lee Lewis. It was the subversive element that got the revolutionary message across loud and clear, even when the lyrics didn't (after all, what is "Tutti Frutti" about?).

In "God Save the Queen," guitar and bass move in tandem to hammer out a relentless rock rhythm almost all the way through; only the periodic guitar riffs that answer Rotten's vocals give it a distinctive shape. The drummer reinforces this rock rhythm by pounding it out on the bass drum and either a tom-tom or hi-hat. Like the Ramones, the band distilled and intensified rock and roll's revolutionary rhythmic essence. There is no way that a rock beat could be more pervasive or powerful.

As expressed in the Sex Pistols' music, the beat is the primary source of punk's power, but its impact ultimately grows out of its remarkable stylistic coherence. Every aspect of the song—the lyrics, Rotten's vocal style, the absence of melody, simple power chords, the heavily distorted sounds, and the relentless, fast-paced beat—conveys the same basic message: they are mutually reinforcing.

www

"God Save the Queen," the Sex Pistols (1977)

---

### ♪ KEY FEATURES

**"God Save the Queen," the Sex Pistols (1977)**
- Incendiary lyrics
- Abrasive vocal style: more than loud speech; less than singing
- Distilled, intensified rock rhythm
- Nuclear rock band: vocals, guitar, bass, drums
- Distorted power chords outline simple riff, played by guitar and bass

The message of the Sex Pistols resonated throughout the United Kingdom. Many working- and middle-class youths were tired of the rigid class system that they inherited and foresaw a bleak future. The Sex Pistols' songs encapsulated the frustration and rage they felt.

The group achieved their main ambition—to be rock-and-roll stars. So did McLaren: through the band, he made a statement, although the fact that he made a statement seemed to be far more important than its message. McLaren had his cake and ate it, too: he made a lot of money off the Sex Pistols, some of which he had to turn over to the band after they sued him. His dishonest management certainly suggests that punk, for him, was more a business proposition than a matter of political principle.

Despite their meteoric rise and fall (Lydon announced the breakup of the group in January 1978), the Sex Pistols were enormously influential: no group in the history of rock had more impact with such a brief career. They embodied the essence of punk in every respect. No one projected its sense of outrage and its outrageousness more baldly. The Ramones were comparably influential, not only because their fast and loud sound inspired the Sex Pistols and countless other groups, but also because their facelessness—assumed names and punk "uniform" (torn jeans, T-shirts)—and cryptic lyrics projected a different form of nihilism: loss of identity and meaning.

# New Wave

The punk of the Ramones and the Sex Pistols was an extreme form of a new wave of music that began to emerge around the middle of the seventies, mainly in New York and London. Other bands, most notably, the Talking Heads and Devo in the United States and Elvis Costello and the Attractions and the Clash in England found a similar audience.

These diverse acts shared considerable common ground. Most obvious, perhaps, were the venues and the audiences who filled them. Both bands and audience assumed an anti-mainstream position: with few exceptions, their music, whatever form it took, was a reaction against prevailing tastes. The reaction could be rage, weirdness, cleverness, humor, and more; but it was typically a reaction. Musically, their shared values included such features as the directness of the rhythm and instrumentation that was typically limited to the nuclear rock band: vocalist, guitar, bass, and drums. The varied musical products reflected their equally varied responses to mainstream rock. Most of it was called either punk or **new wave**, often interchangeably.

In retrospect, one of the significant distinctions between punk, or at least the "pure" punk of the Ramones and Sex Pistols, and the new wave styles that emerged at the same time is the aim of the music: punk aims for the gut; new wave aims for the brain or perhaps the funny bone. The Sex Pistols' biggest songs express rage. The lyrics of Ramones' songs seem calculated to deflect attention away from the words to the high-energy sounds; we hear them, but we don't always process them as a coherent statement. By contrast, the songs of new wave acts such as the Talking Heads and Elvis Costello demand attention to the words, and the musical setting puts the lyrics in the forefront.

To support clear delivery of the lyrics, bands favored a stripped-down, stream-lined sound. Many groups were garage-band graduates. They kept their basic three- or four-piece instrumentation: guitar(s), bass, and drums, with the occasional keyboard.

(Elvis Costello seemed fond of cheesy-sounding synthesizers.) The rhythmic texture was relatively clean, with little syncopation or rhythmic interplay. This energized the songs without overpowering or deflecting attention from the vocals. Instrumental solos were at a minimum; the primary role of the music was to enhance the words.

Within these relatively general boundaries, there was considerable variation in content and result, which we sample following in the music of the Talking Heads and Elvis Costello and the Attractions.

## The Talking Heads

Like so many British rock musicians, the Talking Heads started out in art school: lead singer David Byrne (b. 1952) and drummer Chris Frantz (b. 1951) attended the Rhode Island School of Design together before moving to New York. They formed the group in 1975, with Tina Weymouth (b. 1950), Frantz's then-girlfriend (and later wife), playing bass, and added guitarist/keyboardist Jerry Harrison (b. 1949) two years later.

Although they operated in the same CBGB milieu as the Ramones and other similar punk bands, the Talking Heads came from an opposite place conceptually. Where the Ramones' sound remained remarkably consistent from song to song, the Talking Heads' music, beginning with their debut album *Talking Heads '77* and continuing throughout their sixteen-year career together, offers considerable variety. In their earlier albums, this is especially remarkable, given their limited instrumental resources and Byrne's vocal limitations.

Lynn Goldsmith/Corbis

The Talking Heads "on the road." From left to right: Chris Franz, Tina Weymouth, Jerry Harrison, and David Byrne.

Their music reflects both their seemingly insatiable curiosity regarding the world of music and their art-school training. Byrne would become one of the leaders of the world music movement in the eighties; *Naked*, their last studio album, released in 1988, featured African musicians. Many of their early songs draw on the rock and rhythm and blues with which they were surrounded in their formative years. However, they process it in their songs much as cubist painters like Picasso and Braque processed the scenes and objects that they portrayed in their paintings. These once-familiar sounds often occur as distorted or fragmented in the Talking Heads' music, to the extent that the connection with an earlier style is all but broken. This manipulation of familiar sounds provided an instrumental setting that enhanced the impact of Byrne's quirky lyrics and quavery voice, which was ideally suited to convey a person who has drunk way too much coffee or is simply over the edge.

"Psycho Killer," the Talking Heads (1977)

"Psycho Killer" (1977), a surprise hit from their first album, evidences salient features of their sound: lyrics and Byrne's singing in the forefront, varied accompaniment, with several subtle features in support. Rhythm and texture are simple and clean: the bass line marks the beat with a repeated note, while guitar and keyboard move at rock-beat speed. The jangly guitar—first in the arpeggiated accompaniment of the verse, then in the chords under the chorus—echoes Byrne's words and sound. This spare backdrop—perhaps a musical counterpart to the white cell of the psycho ward—is an ideal foil for Byrne's vocal. The lyric is inflammatory. Byrne announces quite clearly that he's crazy ("a real live wire"), and his neutral delivery makes his portrayal especially effective: as if he's a time bomb waiting to explode. In contrast to the punk songs heard previously, which go full bore from beginning to end, there are numerous changes in accompaniment, from the edgy beginning to the brutal beat-by-beat chords in the interlude where Byrne shifts to French.

---

## ♪ KEY FEATURES

**"Psycho Killer," the Talking Heads (1977)**
- Prominent lyrics describe a person about to lose it
- Byrne's quavery voice: untutored and uninhibited, and an ideal voice for the lyric
- Modest instrumentation: guitars, bass, and drums, but with evocative special effects, such as guitar harmonics
- Spare texture, with considerable variety: does not overpower the vocal line

---

As "Psycho Killer" demonstrates, the sound of the Talking Heads was fueled more by imagination than craft. There is nothing particularly challenging in any of the instrumental parts, nor is Byrne a vocalist with a wide expressive range. There is none of the virtuosity heard in such diverse acts as Steely Dan, Yes, or Led Zeppelin, nor is there the rhythmic complexity heard in hard rock or funk, or the lavish instrumentation of much black pop or disco. Yet, the Talking Heads created one of the most innovative sound worlds of the seventies.

## Elvis Costello

In the United Kingdom, the most distinctive new voice of the new wave belonged to Elvis Costello (born Declan McManus, 1954). Costello began with the great singer-songwriter's storytelling gift and a fertile musical imagination. He nurtured it in an early-seventies apprenticeship with pub rock bands, which fueled his ambition to obtain a recording contract. Punk and reggae gave his music an edge, evident in some of the tracks from his first album, *My Aim Is True*. Flush from the success of this album, he recruited the Attractions, who would be his collaborators for the better part of a decade. The group included keyboardist Steve Nieve (born Steve Nason, 1960), bassist Bruce Thomas (b. 1948), and drummer Pete Thomas (b. 1954) (the two are not related). The group helped him realize songs that grew out of what Costello acknowledged in an interview as his main motivations: revenge and guilt.

The anger in his music was more complex than that of the Sex Pistols, whose music inspired him. Instead of a frontal assault, Costello would often seduce his listeners, in words and music, then gradually reveal the underlying message of the song. We hear this in one of his first hits.

"Radio, Radio," Elvis Costello and the Attractions (1977)

"Radio, Radio" was originally released as a single in 1977 and later included on Costello's second album, *This Year's Model*, which was released in 1979. The storyline is easy to follow, and the music, from the opening organ hook on, is as accessible as a mainstream rock song. Costello's genius becomes apparent as the song unfolds. What seems like a simple paean to radio in the verse develops Orwellian overtones (1984 was less than a decade away!) by the chorus. And the complexity of his ideas is matched by the complexity of the form of the song. Although it is a verse/chorus song, with sections clearly marked off by restatements of the opening organ hook, the chorus goes through a tunnel full of twists and turns before returning to the verse.

The setting is likewise a complex realization of the basic punk/pop sound. Costello's texture is almost orchestral. The opening organ hook is thickly textured, the punk band equivalent of a full orchestra. As Costello enters with the verse, the texture thins drastically with only the three rhythm instruments playing a bottom-heavy version of rock rhythm. The organ returns in the chorus, along with some special effects, and there is a nice stop-time section at the end. The basic texture has a clear affinity with punk, but the orchestral-like variation in rhythm and texture has much more in common with the Talking Heads than it does with the Ramones or the Sex Pistols.

---

♪ **KEY FEATURES**

**"Radio, Radio," Elvis Costello and the Attractions (1977)**
- Frightening lyrics that describe mind control through the media
- Punk-inspired rhythms and textures, with considerable variation from section to section
- Complex form, especially in the middle of the song
- Catchy organ sounds, especially the hook of the song

Both Costello and the Attractions and the Talking Heads explored dark and difficult themes (a demented killer; oppressive control through the media). They did so through songs that put the words in the forefront and that backed them up with musical settings that helped evoke the ominous lyrics, despite relatively modest instrumental resources. Like punk, new wave often projected rage or frustration, but it did so with more finesse: a sharp stick instead of a bludgeon.

# Punk: Devolution and Evolution

The next two examples offer additional perspectives on the punk/new wave movement of the late seventies. In the music of Devo, we hear the humorous side of the new wave movement; in the music of the Clash, we hear the rapid evolution of punk beyond the raw, manic energy of the Ramones and the Sex Pistols.

## New Wave Humor

If there are emotions that seem to dominate punk and new wave music, they are rage and frustration. They spill out from the words and even more from the music. It is explicit in the music of the Sex Pistols and present, albeit more obliquely, in the music of the Ramones, the Talking Heads, and Elvis Costello and the Attractions. However, a small minority of new wave bands, some emerging from such unlikely locales as Athens, Georgia, and Akron, Ohio, rechanneled the energy and streamlined simplicity of punk and new wave into music that revisited humor in rock. The B-52s, the first of several noteworthy bands to get started in Athens, brought kitsch into rock—in image (their name came from the beehive hairdos popular in the years around 1960), words, and sound. Devo, like Pere Ubu, was formed in Ohio; the three founding band members were students at Kent State University.

**Devo** The founding members of Devo were bassist Gerald Casale (b. 1948), lead singer and keyboardist Mark Mothersbaugh (b. 1950), and guitarist Bob Lewis (b. 1947). The band quickly evolved into a two-family affair: Casale's brother Bob joined the band shortly after its formation as a rhythm guitarist, as did Mothersbaugh's brothers Bob and Jim: Bob (Bob II) replaced Lewis on lead guitar, while Jim replaced original drummer Rod Reisman. Alan Myers would soon replace Jim Mothersbaugh.

Devo the band was the vehicle created mainly by Mark Mothersbaugh and Jerry Casale to convey their response to the senseless shootings at Kent State in 1970. After the incident, the two friends began formulating a Dada-esque theory of devolution, which they promulgated in an obscure journal. They maintained that at the end of the twentieth century, man was devolving, not evolving. They expressed this viewpoint not only in their music but also in a short film entitled *The Truth About De-Evolution*, which caught the attention of David Bowie and Iggy Pop when presented at the 1976 Ann Arbor Film Festival. This led to a recording contract with Warner Bros. and an association with Brian Eno, who produced their debut album: *Q: Are We Not Men? A: We Are Devo!* (1977). By this time, their anger at the absurdity of modern life had devolved into weirdness, as is evident in their first hit, "Jocko Homo," a single taken from the album.

"Jocko Homo,"
Devo (1977)

The weirdness is apparent from the start: The sound of the opening instrumental riff is a blend of distorted guitar and other rock band instruments and synthesizer. The mix gives the distortion an eerie quality that evokes the soundtracks to underfunded science fiction films. (**Synthesizers**, or **synths**, always a key element in Devo's sound, would become the dominant instrumental resource in the eighties.) The rhythm is even more unusual than the sound: the riff lasts seven equally spaced notes per measure, rather than the eight used in conventional rock rhythm. This necessarily creates an asymmetrical pattern (4 + 3 notes), which puts the song off-balance from the start. The asymmetry is maintained through much of the song; a familiar rock rhythm occurs only in the interlude. This almost minimalist setting supports the almost mechanical delivery of the lyric, which the vocal distortion simply underscores in the answering phrase of the refrain: ("Are we not men?) We are DEVO." The absurdist element continues in the interlude, which interrupts their succinct account of human evolution and social commentary with the riddle "What's round at the ends and high in the middle? (O-hi-o)."

---

### ♪ KEY FEATURES

**"Jocko Homo," Devo (1977)**

- Instrumental and vocal effects: distorted voices, synthesizer/guitar mix
- Basic setting, with recurring instrumental riff; only the interlude breaks away from the repetitious riff
- Asymmetrical rhythm: seven quick beats per measure, not eight, as in a conventional rock song
- Absurdist lyrics

---

Devo would carve out a niche for themselves, both on disc and on video, that sustained their career into the eighties. Their videos, which typically featured them in "uniforms" of various kinds (the geek analogues to the Ramones' look) and wearing unusual headgear, like flowerpots, enjoyed a brief vogue in the early years of MTV. Their commitment to weirdness may have cost them popular success but preserved their special place in the history of punk.

## The Clash

Like the Rolling Stones, the Clash grew out of a chance encounter. However, the meeting between guitarists Mick Jones and Joe Strummer took place not in a train station over an armful of blues records, but while waiting in line for an unemployment check. As in the United States, rampant inflation in the United Kingdom had had a devastating effect on the economy. An influx of people from the former British colonies (Jamaicans, East Indians, Nigerians, and others) strained social services and heightened racial tension. At the same time, the class distinctions that had been part of British life for centuries were under assault—as was made manifest in "God Save the Queen." All of this fueled the punk movement in the United Kingdom.

The Clash came together in 1976, when Strummer (1952–2002) and Jones (b. 1955) teamed up with bassist Paul Simonon (b. 1955) and drummer Terry Chimes

(b. 1955). Topper Headon (b. 1955) soon replaced Chimes. Simonon gave the group its name, which suited the confrontational personality of the group and their on-stage persona. In the summer of 1976, Strummer and Simonon found themselves in the middle of a riot between Jamaican immigrants and police. "White Riot," the song that they wrote in response to the incident, was the group's first major hit. It not only got the group noticed but also set the tone for their career: many of their songs railed against political and social injustices.

"White Riot" and many other early songs follow the lead of the Ramones: they are fast, loud, and crude. However, the group quickly evolved into a much more skilled and versatile band. By 1979, the year in which they released *London Calling*, the highpoint of their recording career, the Clash were at home in a variety of styles. However, they never lost the passion that informed their first work. It is evident in virtually all of their music, regardless of subject.

"Death or Glory," the Clash (1979)

"Death or Glory," a track from the album, comments on a central issue for the group: whether money will motivate a group to sell out. The lyric reeks attitude: The cast of characters includes a "cheap hood" and a "gimmick hungry yob" ("yob" is British slang for a young working-class male). The images are brutal: the hood beats his kids; bands who haven't got it should give it up. The refrain sums up the disillusionment that pervades the song.

The music that supports it is simply good rock, rather than high-energy pure punk. The song uses the conventional verse/chorus form; the refrain features catchy melodic hooks that embed themselves in listeners' ears. Once underway, the song

Roger Ressmeyer/Corbis

The Clash, newly arrived in the United States for their first American tour, 1979. From left to right: Joe Strummer, Topper Headon, Paul Simonon, and Mick Jones.

maintains a driving beat enriched with rhythmic interplay among the rhythm section players, except for an adventurous interlude that spotlights Headon. The texture is dense in a way that is typical of rock, with melodic lines in both guitars and bass, and there is an array of timbres, from the distorted chords that announce the refrain to the more mellow bass and guitar sounds in the introduction.

---

### ♪ KEY FEATURES

**"Death or Glory," the Clash (1979)**

- Lyric with brutal images
- Rock song conventions and features: verse/chorus form and melodic hooks make the song easy to follow and appealing
- Strong contrasts from section to section: musing introduction, straight-ahead verse, active interlude

---

"Death or Glory" is not representative of *London Calling*, a double album with nineteen tracks. Neither is any other track on the album; each song has a distinct character and musical setting; they range from swing-evoking "Jimmy Jazz" and reggae-inspired "Revolution Rock" to the clever punk-style "Koka Kola" and the more conventional rock of "Death or Glory." However, throughout the album, the Clash infuse their music with the power and passion of punk. Regardless of the style or influences of the music, the songs matter—because of the lyrics and because the music backs up the lyrics.

More than any other group of the late seventies, the Clash demonstrated by example how to revitalize rock with words and music that mattered, because, unlike the "gimmick hungry yob," they refused to compromise. (Interestingly, their record company undermined their integrity by marketing them as the "The Only Band That Matters," a phrase created by their fans.)

## The Reverberations of Punk

Many commentators regard *London Calling* as the most significant album of the decade: for example, it is the only album by a band formed after 1970 to make the Top 10 of *Rolling Stone*'s list of the 500 greatest albums of all time. That the most significant music would be released in the United Kingdom in December 1979, the last month of the last year, is the ultimate comment on rock in the seventies. It was as if rock in the seventies had to wait until the last possible moment to be reminded of its ability to send a strong message.

Punk and new wave restored the soul of rock and roll. The important bands resurrected rock's sense of daring and amped it up well beyond what had gone before. As with Dylan's pre-electric and early electric work, the anthemic sixties songs of the Who and the Rolling Stones, and reggae, there is a powerful message: political, social, personal. However, in punk it is embedded not in a simple acoustic setting, the coming-together rock of the mid-sixties, or the transparent rhythms of reggae; in punk, the rock can be as brutally blunt in its musical message as in the lyrics. There is a synergy among attitude, words, and music that gives both punk and new wave unprecedented impact. Once again, this is rock music that sought to change the world.

In its intent, punk stands apart from almost all other music of the seventies that we have heard, in that the music is not an end in itself but a means to convey a meaningful message. It is not music for dancing, like disco; for entertainment, like mainstream rock; for expressing personal feelings and experiences in an almost private way, like the singer-songwriters' melodies; or for appreciation as an art artifact, like the music of Yes. Instead, the message is primary, whether it is expressed directly, as in "God Save the Queen" or "Death or Glory," or more obliquely, as in "Blitzkrieg Bop" or "Radio, Radio." This helps account for the relative simplicity of the musical materials—whether presented as a soundblitz (as in the Ramones' music) or with imagination (as in the music of the Clash and the Talking Heads): if the musical setting were too elaborate, it would deflect attention away from the underlying intent of the song.

As with any significant new music, punk and new wave would reverberate through the music of the next generation. Punk, and especially the music of the Clash, served as a bridge between the significant rock of the sixties and the significant rock of the eighties, most notably the work of U2. It introduced a new conception of rock rhythm that would filter into numerous mainstream and alternative styles: this was one reason that much of the rock from the eighties sounds as though it is from that decade and not from an earlier time. It sharpened the edge of much rock-era music, even the pop of Michael Jackson and Madonna. It opened the door for those outside corporate rock: the alternative movement that began in the early eighties continues the independent spirit that typified the punk and new wave music of the late seventies. That spirit lives on most fully in the post-punk bands that have emerged since 1980.

. . . . . . . . . . . . . . . . . . . . . . . . . . . . . . . . . . . . . . . . . . . . . . . . . . . . . . . . . . . . . . . . . . . . . . . . .

**Terms to Remember**

punk                           new wave                        synthesizer (synth)

. . . . . . . . . . . . . . . . . . . . . . . . . . . . . . . . . . . . . . . . . . . . . . . . . . . . . . . . . . . . . . . . . . . . . . . . .

**Applying Chapter Concepts**

1. In the discussion of punk, we noted that the punk movement was a revival of the garage-band spirit of the late fifties and early sixties. We also noted that punk's approach to rock rhythm, as evidenced in the songs of the Sex Pistols and the Ramones, was a particularly intense form of rock rhythm. Using examples presented in earlier chapters, trace the development of rock rhythm from Chuck Berry through the Beach Boys and the Kingsmen to the first part of the seventies, with particular attention to the difference between the approach used by the Rolling Stones (and others) and the approach used by the Velvet Underground and David Bowie. Then contrast the approach to rock rhythm used by Aerosmith and that used by the Ramones.

2. Rock critics have noted that the Talking Heads' influences go beyond rock to minimalist classical music (for example, Philip Glass), funk, and African music; Greil Marcus suggests that Costello's music has elements of Randy Newman, Bob Dylan, Buddy Holly, and John Lennon. Explore the *new* in *new wave* by documenting the connections between either of these acts and their influences. How evident is the influence of these sources? How novel is their use by the act?

# Electronica and Rap

The welcome page of Joseph Saddler's website (*www.grandmasterflash.com*) features a video in which Saddler, better known as Grandmaster Flash, explains how DJs from the seventies never put their hands on the grooves of the vinyl discs they played. He goes on to say that he was the first to put his hands on the grooves, which enabled him to develop an array of innovative techniques, including cutting, scratching, backspinning, and flaring. Soon, he would mark particular spots on a disc with tape or crayon so that he could access a particular spot on the fly. Armed with two turntables, a mixer, and a stack of discs, including doubles of the tracks he planned to use, Flash could transform the playback of a song—to this point as predictable an event as the sun rising in the east—into a unique, spontaneously crafted experience.

In the sense that it became a device in which one could shape musical sound in the moment, Flash turned the turntable into a musical instrument. But because the musical sounds involved an extra layer of creativity—the sounds had already been recorded—the turntable was different in kind from more conventional instruments, such as those used in a rock band. Although the use of pre-recorded sounds in live performance was not new, Flash's techniques brought a new, richer, and more improvisatory dimension to the experience. They were one sign of a movement that would radically transform cutting-edge rock-era music in the eighties and beyond.

It should be noted that there was a good reason that other DJs handled recordings by the edge: bringing the grooves into contact with anything—fingers, crayons, errant tonearm needles—would damage the disc and eventually render it unplayable. While Grandmaster Flash was perfecting his novel techniques, another revolution was underway that would render them all but obsolete. In this chapter, we discuss the digital revolution and consider its impact on electronica and rap, the two styles that would benefit most directly from it.

## The Digital Revolution

What made electronic technology—the microphone, the radio, and improved recording quality—possible was the ability to convert sound waves into electrical signals and electrical signals back into sound. What made digital audio possible was the ability to encode the waveform generated by the electrical signal into a binary format. This was

374

accomplished by **sampling** the wave at regular intervals, with several possible gradations. On a standard CD, the wave is sampled 44,100 times a second; there are 65,536 (16 x 16 x 16 x 16) possible gradations of the wave. What happens is that this high sampling rate, coupled with the thousands of gradations, makes it possible to simulate the shape of the wave so closely that the original waveform and the digital sampling of it are virtually identical.

Digital audio fools our ears in much the same way that digital images fool our eyes. Open a visual image on your computer and magnify it. You'll notice that it is a grid of squares, each a single color or shade of gray. However, the size of each square is so small that our eyes are fooled into seeing color blends, curves, and other continuous images. (By contrast, dot-matrix printers typically have a resolution of only 200 dots per inch, so curves seem more jagged, especially in larger font sizes.)

This ability to encode waveform data digitally has had several benefits. First, it eliminates signal degradation. In analog tape recording, there were inevitably some unwelcome sounds: one can hear tape hiss on pre-digital recordings that have not been remastered or on cassette copies of recordings. The more a tape is copied, the more pronounced the extraneous sounds become. By contrast, digital information can be copied an infinite number of times with no loss of audio quality, as anyone who has burned a CD or used a file-sharing service knows.

Second, it became possible to maintain quality despite unlimited use. Because of the physical contact of a stylus with a record groove, or tape with the tape head, the quality of sound degraded over time. A recording played for the one-hundredth time on a turntable or cassette player will sound worse than the first time, no matter how much care is taken. This problem disappeared with digital audio.

Third, the high sampling rate has enabled those working with computer audio to isolate musical events with a precision that earlier generations could only dream about. Instead of shuttling a tape head back and forth to find the right starting point, those working in the digital domain can quickly identify and mark the beginning and end of a musical event. Once isolated, they can manipulate it at will—compressing or expanding it, changing its pitch higher or lower, changing its timbre, enhancing it with special effects.

## The New Digital Technologies

It was one thing to have the capability of using digital technology; it was quite another to actually have the hardware that made it possible. After years of research and development, two crucial technologies emerged in the early eighties: audio CD and MIDI.

**Audio CD**  The **audio CD** required more than the ability to convert sound into digital data; it was also necessary to apply laser technology to encode and decode the data from the storage medium (hence "burn" a CD). Research on the laser dates back to a 1958 paper by a physicist at Bell Labs. By the early seventies, lasers were being used to read digital data stored on discs. By 1980, Philips and Sony, two of the leaders in audio research, had agreed on a standard for CD audio. They agreed that a CD should use 16-bit sampling and a 44.1K sampling rate. Other sampling precisions and sampling rates have also come into use; streaming audio generally uses less precise sampling (8-bit sampling produces 1/16 the data of 16-bit sampling) and slower sampling rates.

In 1984, the first CD pressing plant in the United States—in Terre Haute, Indiana—started producing CDs. The first CDs were expensive because the production process was seriously flawed; only a relatively small percentage of the CDs produced were good enough for release. As a result, the cost of a CD was high— higher than cassette or vinyl. (Not surprisingly, given the nature of the music business, the cost of a CD has remained higher than that of a cassette, even though production costs are now much lower.)

This initial audio CD format remains the most widely used method for delivering sound digitally, although that may change soon, with the emergence of portable MP3 players, DVD audio, online music services, and other formats.

**MIDI** Musical instrument digital interface or **MIDI** is an industry standard that allows electronic instruments to communicate with one another and with a computer. In theory, this seems like a natural and modest step. In practice, it was a tremendous breakthrough, for two main reasons. First, it enabled a single person to simulate an orchestra, a rock band, or a swing band, using just one instrument. Using a MIDI-enabled electronic keyboard or other similarly configured device, musicians could choose from an array of MIDI-out sounds—usually no less than 128. They could play the passage, as if playing a piano or organ, but the sound coming out would be like a trumpet, or bells, or violins, or a host of others.

Second, MIDI devices could interact with sequencers. A **sequencer** is a device that enables a person to assemble a sound file, track by track. Using a sequencer that can store eight tracks, a person can re-create the sound of a band: one track for the bass, another for the rhythm guitar, and so on.

Sequencers can also be used to create loops. A **loop** is a short sound file—such as a drum pattern or a bass line—that can be repeated and combined with other loops or freely created material to create a background for a song, whether it's rap, pop, techno, house, or something else. To make this process easier, loops are usually a standard length: eight beats (two measures), sixteen beats (four measures), and so on. With these kinds of resources, assembling the rhythm track to a song can be like building with Legos: users simply snap them into a track in their digital audio software.

**Sampling** A **sample** is a small sound file. (Please note that this meaning of *sample* is different from the sample of a waveform; the two meanings are related but different, much like the multiple meanings of *beat*.) There are two basic kinds of samples in common use. One is the recorded sound of a voice or group of voices, an instrument (for example, a grand piano) or group of instruments (such as a violin section), or some other sound. This sound can then be activated through some other device. For instance, one can buy a disc with the sampled sound of several cellos playing every note on the usable range of the instrument, recorded in many different ways. Then the buyer can install it on a computer, activate it inside the appropriate software, and produce a passage that sounds like a recording of the cello section of a first-rate symphony orchestra.

This kind of sampling has been available since the sixties. The first commercial "sampler" to achieve any kind of currency was the Mellotron. It was a keyboard instrument in which depressing a key would activate a looped tape of a string sound.

It was not very flexible, but it was a cost-efficient alternative to hiring violinists. However, sampling didn't really become practical until digital technology.

Now, sampling has reached such a level of sophistication that it is often impossible to determine whether a passage was recorded live or created using samples. In effect, this kind of sampling is a more advanced version of MIDI playback, because the sounds are rendered more accurately.

The other primary kind of sampling involves lifting short excerpts from existing recordings to use in a new recording, much like a visual artist will use found objects to create a collage or assemblage. It has been a staple of rap background tracks since the technology became available in the mid-eighties.

**Computer Audio**  In 1965, Gordon Moore, one of the founders of Intel, predicted that the number of transistors on a computer chip would double every couple of years. Moore's law, as it has been called, has largely held true. What this has meant is that the amount of computing power one can buy for $1,000 has doubled every eighteen months or so.

Because CD-quality digital audio requires over 1 million samples per second, the first personal computers could not handle audio processing in real time. Fast-forward to the turn of the century, though, and it's a different story. One can burn CDs at . . . I hesitate to write a number here, because by the time this book gets into print it will be out of date. Digital audio workstations, sequencers, special effects plug-ins, notation software: there is nothing in the process of creating and producing a recording that cannot be done on a computer, supported with the right software and peripherals, except the invention of original material.

Those who have come of age with this technology in place may not find it to be unusual. However, for those of us who have seen it emerge, it is awe-inspiring. For just a few thousand dollars, anyone can create a home studio that can do just about anything that could only have been done in a million-dollar studio less than a generation ago. One of the images of this time that is sure to endure is the creative person sitting not at an instrument or a desk, but at a workstation, surrounded by displays, keyboards, CPUs, and other computer audio equipment.

The advances in computer-based digital audio have put high-end music production within almost everyone's budget. For the aspiring creative artist, the financial investment is a fraction of what it once was. The larger investment is time: not only to develop the necessary musical skills but also to master the applications necessary to create the desired result. And there are plenty of role models, from Stevie Wonder, Brian Eno, and Grandmaster Flash to Trent Reznor, Moby, Juan Atkins, Richard James, and hundreds more. And it will only get better.

Digital technology has made it easier to make well-crafted music, both for those with well-developed musical skills and those with little or no skill. But it has also allowed for a less-immediate kind of music making. In performance or recording, there can be a world of difference between having a drummer playing and having a drum loop playing, simply because the drummer can respond in the moment. For those who want to keep their music real, the challenge is to use the technology in ways that enhance the personal dimension of their music, rather than undermine it. Another option is to create a radically new esthetic, one that builds naturally on the innovations of digital technology. We explore this new esthetic in a discussion of electronica.

# Electronica

Among the most enduring images in twentieth-century music is the singer with guitar. The image transcends style, race, gender, locale, theme: Blind Lemon Jefferson, Jimmie Rodgers, Gene Autry, Maybelle Carter, Robert Johnson, Woody Guthrie, Bob Dylan, Joan Baez, Joni Mitchell, and countless others—country and city, traditional and topical.

Now imagine a sound that is its complete opposite. There is little or no singing—and what vocals there are have been filtered through an electronic device. There is no melody with accompanying chords; instead there might be wisps of riffs or some sustained notes. Instead of the simple rhythm of the accompaniment, there is the thump of a low percussion sound marking the beat, several fast-moving patterns, plus other electronically generated loops. Instead of the strumming of an acoustic guitar, there is an array of electronic sounds, complete with special effects (fx). Instead of a story with a beginning and end, there is total immersion in a sound world with no apparent time boundaries. Instead of a single performer singing and playing while a few others listen, there is a DJ in a booth, surveying a dance floor filled with bobbing and weaving bodies as the DJ mixes the music.

You will find examples of this totally opposite sound in the dance/electronica section of your favorite record store—on the street, in the mall, or online. **Electronica** has become the umbrella term for a large and varied family of styles: house, techno, trance, ambient, jungle, drum 'n' bass, industrial dance, and many more.

The almost total contrast between electronica and the folk/blues/country singer underscores how radically different the electronic-based music of the eighties, nineties, and the twenty-first century is from so much earlier music, including much of the music of the early rock era. The differences begin with its origins, continue with its venues, its performance, and ultimately its intent.

## The Antecedents of Electronica

Most popular music genres have evolved through the influence of music from "below": that is, music from "plain folk" who live outside and beneath the realm of high culture. We use the word *roots* to convey this. Electronica is different. Its origins are in the most cerebral and esoteric music of the mid-twentieth century, the classical music avant-garde.

During the middle of the twentieth century, composers in Europe and the United States, using equipment as sophisticated as the first tape recorders and synthesizers and as everyday as nuts and bolts, explored virgin musical territory. Shortly after World War II, the French composer Pierre Schaeffer began creating music using recorded sounds, rather than musical ideas inside his head, as raw material. The recordings could be of any sounds at all, and they could be modified or transformed before being assembled into a music event. Schaeffer called this process *musique concrète* (concrete music).

Others—among them the German composer Karlheinz Stockhausen, the French American composer Edgard Varèse, and the American John Cage—assembled compositions completely from synthesized sounds, recorded, then spliced together to form a complete composition. In 1958, Lejaren Hiller set up the first computer-music studio, at the University of Illinois. Among these new electronic works were the first examples of the recording as the creative document—with no performer involved in the creative process.

Much of this music was conceptual: it grew out of a particular idea that the composer wanted to explore. The results explored every possible extreme. American composer Milton Babbitt created works in which every musical parameter was regulated by a predetermined series: total serialism. In effect, his compositions using this procedure were pre-composed. At the other end of the spectrum were works by John Cage. One famous work required the performer to sit perfectly still for 4 minutes 33 seconds; the composition was the ambient sounds in the performing space. Stockhausen composed a work for piano in which fragments of music were printed on an oversized score; the performer determined the sequence of the fragments during the performance. Cage created works in which events were determined by chance. Varèse created *Poème électronique*, an electronic piece that mixes synthesized and *concrète* sounds, for the 1958 World's Fair in Brussels. It was played over 425 loudspeakers.

All of these concepts have found their way into the various electronica styles. For example, the loudspeaker setup for *Poème électronique* anticipates the "total immersion" sound systems of dance clubs. Stockhausen's piano piece, where the performer switches arbitrarily from fragment to fragment, anticipates the DJ mixing on the fly. *Musique concrète* anticipates the found sounds that appear in so much electronica and related styles, like rap. And totally electronic pieces anticipate the millions of synthesizer-generated dance tracks.

This is not to say that there is a straightforward causal connection between mid-century avant-garde music and the electronica of the last twenty-five years. Rather, it is to suggest three things. First, even the most esoteric ideas and concepts have a way of filtering down; in this case, they made it all the way to the underground—the club scene that has nurtured this music. Second, electronica could blossom only when the necessary equipment became accessible and affordable. Third, electronica involves more than simply making dance music on computers. Its most imaginative creators have radically altered or overturned conventional assumptions about music making.

## Music for Dancing, Places to Dance

The dance club is the home of electronica. The dance scene that has nurtured the music since the early eighties has been an underground continuation of disco: the music of Donna Summer and Giorgio Moroder were among the best and most successful examples of early electronica. In essence, there were people who still wanted to dance after disco declined in popularity; the club scene, and the music created for it, gave them the outlet.

During the eighties, two major club scenes emerged in the Midwest: **house** music in Chicago and **techno** in Detroit. Both would have a profound influence on dance music throughout the world. House music was a low-budget continuation of disco; DJs like Frankie Knuckles would use bare-bones rhythm tracks as part of mixes that included disco hits and current disco-inspired songs. The Detroit scene was almost exclusively the work of three friends and colleagues—Juan Atkins, Derrick May, and Kevin Saunderson—who had known one another since junior high. Despite their

Detroit base, they were more interested in techno pioneers like Kraftwerk than Motown. Atkins said in an interview that "I'm probably more interested in Ford's robots than in Berry Gordy's music." As DJs and producers, they delivered a stark, dark kind of dance music under numerous guises, including Atkins's Model 500 and May's Rhythim Is Rhythim.

By the mid-eighties, the music had migrated to Great Britain. The event that brought the music, the culture, and the drugs up from the underground and into the public eye was the 1988 "Summer of Love," a rave that went on for weeks. A **rave** is a huge dance party conducted in a large space: outdoors, an abandoned warehouse, or even a large club. Ecstasy and other designer drugs were very much part of the scene; they suppressed the need to eat or sleep. (Never mind that the drugs are dangerous— even deadly—especially when consumed with alcohol.)

**Ambient music**, a quite different branch of electronica, dates back to the seventies. Its early history includes Pink Floyd, Kraftwerk, and Tangerine Dream. The father of ambient music, though, is Brian Eno; his recording *Ambient I: Music for Airports* (1979) is seminal.

As its name suggests, ambient music is more atmospheric and less dance driven, with more attention to texture and less emphasis on rhythm. As a genre within electronica, it hasn't had a home, but it has merged with both house and techno, introducing a more varied sound world into both. In these hybrid genres, it began to catch on in the late eighties and early nineties.

Fueled in part by the growth of the club scene, a host of other styles have emerged in the nineties and the first years of the twenty-first century. The proliferation of styles came about not only through the combination and recombination of existing styles (such as ambient house) but also through the absorption of outside influences, which led to an array of hardcore techno substyles. Electronica has begun to appear on the pop charts, in the music of acts such as Bjork, Chemical Brothers, and Moby.

## Hearing Electronica

Dance music has defined a new performance paradigm for popular music. The nature of the venue—the dance club, rather than the arena, auditorium, night club, or coffeehouse—has fundamentally altered what is performed, how it's performed, how it's created, and how it's experienced.

The obvious difference, of course, is the use of recordings, rather than live musicians, to create the music being heard. That doesn't mean that there isn't the spontaneity and performer–crowd interaction that can be part of a live performance; it's just that it comes from a different source: the DJ.

The idea of stringing together a series of songs has a long history in popular music. From the thirties on, dance orchestras and small dance combos would occasionally play a **medley**, a group of songs connected by musical interludes. Often medleys were slow dance numbers; bands would play one chorus of each song, rather than several choruses of one song. But they could be any tempo.

Medleys were harder to create in the moment during the early years of the rock era, because the identity of a song was more comprehensive. It was more than just the melody and harmony; it included every aspect of the song, as preserved on the recording. It was more difficult to alter songs so that one would flow easily into the next. Still, the idea of connecting songs did not disappear, as landmark albums such as *Sgt. Pepper* and *The Dark Side of the Moon* evidence.

Still, it wasn't until disco that the idea of creating medleys resurfaced, in a much updated form. It was the DJ who transformed the practice of connecting songs into an art. A DJ with a two-turntable setup was able to **mix** a series of songs into a **set,** an unbroken string of songs that could last longer than even the most extended Grateful Dead jam.

The art of the DJ begins with music that he or she selects. For this reason, many DJs create their own music: it helps them develop a signature style. In performance—in the dance club—skilled DJs string together a series of dance tracks with seamless transitions. It is not just that they blend one record into the next without dropping a beat—unless they plan to. They orchestrate the sequence of songs, how much they'll use of each song, and the kind of transition they'll use to give a sense of architecture to the set. It is in this context that they can respond to the dancers' energy, building to a climactic moment or moments as the set unfolds.

In the discussion of rock and rhythm and blues in the sixties, we noted that the record had become the document, the fullest and most direct expression of the musicians' creative intent. This changes in dance music. The musical unit is no longer the *recording*—which is seldom if ever played in its entirety—but the *set*. The recording is the raw material for the set; recordings are the building blocks—much as riffs are the building blocks of so many songs.

This in turn changes the nature of a dance track. It is not just that it is music for dancing. It is that the dance track is often created with the idea that it is a component of a larger structure—the set—rather than an entity complete unto itself—the song. This is a radical departure from mainstream rock; rock gave the song an integrity that it could not have had in earlier generations.

Moreover, music for club use employs a different sonic spectrum. Since the early sixties, popular music designed for airplay concentrates on mid-range frequencies, because these come across better on radio than high or low frequencies do. By contrast, dance clubs typically have good sound systems, so producers can take advantage of the range of audible frequencies. Electronica styles typically make full use of this, especially low-end frequencies.

This combination of a full sonic spectrum and relentless dance beat, all in an enclosed space, produces a kind of sensory inundation. It is virtually the opposite extreme of sensory deprivation, and it seems to have many of the same mind-altering consequences.

## Electronica and Dance Music

We hear an influential example of electronica: "Nude Photo" by Rhythim Is Rhythim (Derrick May, b. 1963), is a good early sample of Detroit techno. "Nude Photo" establishes a characteristic techno groove almost immediately. The heart of it is the beat: a bass drum–like sound on every beat, a strong backbeat, and a fast-moving percussion part. Layered over that is some more melodic material: complicated, syncopated synthesizer figures, one in mid-range and two in a lower register. After the track gets underway, a slow-moving melodic fragment comes in and out. There is some variety: a short raplike vocal, some other vocal sounds, addition and subtraction of the various layers, some new versions of the melodic figures toward the end. These are the musical counterparts to the disco ball: rotating, and slightly different because of that, but essentially the same throughout. The track begins and ends abruptly; one can imagine it as part of a mix where we would never hear beginning or end.

This example can only hint at the range of sounds, rhythms, and textures possible within the world of electronica. Still, it highlights key features of the genre: a steadily marked beat at about 120 beats per minute; rich, complex textures featuring electronically generated percussive and pitched sounds; very little singing; subtle changes within a generally repetitive, modularly constructed form; and little sense of beginning or end. These tracks are not telling a story; rather, they're sustaining a mood.

♪  **KEY FEATURES**

**"Nude Photo," Rhythim Is Rhythim (1987)**

- Electronic sound generation: where's the band? Instrumental sounds are completely electronic. Some replicate conventional instruments; others present new sounds.
- Mixing: tracks like "Nude Photo" effectively have no beginning or end, because the very beginning and very end are mixed with the surrounding tracks.
- A new way of making music: creating dance tracks electronically eliminates the need for performers and the need to record in real time.
- Rhythim's rhythm: "Nude Photo" mixes obvious beat- and backbeat-keeping with several layers of active rhythms, often in complex patterns, all at 16-beat speed.

"Nude Photo," Rhythim Is Rhythim (1987)

Electronica has been the most faceless music of the last twenty-five years. Its creators work anonymously in studios—often alone. They assume aliases: Aphex Twin is Richard James; Rhythim Is Rhythim is Derrick May. The music they produce—largely instrumental and without the melodic points of entry common to other kinds of popular music—does little to encourage the listener to identify with them in the same way that they would identify with the lead singer or lead guitarist of a rock band. In many ways, this recalls the structure of the music business at the turn of the previous century, when largely anonymous songwriters turned out reams of songs for Tin Pan Alley publishers. For the most part, DJs are the stars of electronica, but it is a very localized form of stardom. However, there are signs that the music, as a genre, is beginning to develop a larger audience and a more mainstream presence.

## Electronica as Popular Music: Moby

In a 1993 review, Jon Pareles, the contemporary popular music critic of the *New York Times*, wrote:

If techno music is going to make the leap from dance clubs to the pop charts, its starkly propulsive dance rhythms are going to need melodies, identifiable stars or both. Moby, a one-man band from New York City, could be the techno performer whose showmanship carries him to a wider audience without turning techno tracks into pop songs.

Nine years later, Moby made the front covers of *Spin*, *Wired*, and the *New York Times Magazine*. In the United States, Moby (born Richard Melville Hall, 1965—he took his professional name from the famous novel *Moby Dick*, by Herman Melville, a distant relation) has put a face on electronica, in part by bringing his music closer to a mainstream pop style. This of course has provoked cries of outrage from hardcore clubbers who feel that he's selling out. Nevertheless, the genre has significantly broadened its audience base.

Moby began his professional career in 1982, playing guitar in a punk band called the Vatican Commandos; he left a year later. By 1989, he had redirected his energies to electronic music. Over the next decade, he attracted a loyal following, first in Great Britain, then in the United States, among dance club audiences as a recording artist and DJ. His first hit was "Go," a single from his 1993 album *The Story So Far*. His breakthrough came in 1999, with the release of the album *Play*. Although sales started slowly, by 2002 the album had sold over 10 million units, earning it diamond album certification. Several singles, including "South Side," also charted. More tellingly, every one of the eighteen tracks on the album has been licensed for commercials, films, and soundtracks. With this album, electronica, as represented by Moby's music, found mainstream success.

Moby originally recorded "South Side" with Gwen Stefani (b. 1969), the vocalist with No Doubt, a Jamaican-influenced alternative band. The version that featured her did not appear on the first release of the album. However, the single version and the reissue of the album did include her. That she was present, and a key component of the song, indicates a significant difference between "South Side" and "Nude Photo." "South Side" assimilates the electronic elements into a traditional rock song format:

"South Side," Moby (1999)

the song has a beginning and an end; an instrumental introduction; a (rap-inspired spoken) verse; a sung chorus with a can't-miss hook; and a vintage-style guitar solo. In this format, the song is clearly directed toward radio airplay, instead of being confined to use within a club. Indeed, the song reached number 3 on *Billboard's* Modern Rock Tracks and number 14 on their Hot 100 chart.

The electronic elements—including the rhythm track, the orchestral strings-inspired sound cushion under the chorus, and numerous other subtle effects—are merged with rock and rap elements to create a new fusion for the turn of the millennium. However, the song follows a time-honored pattern in popular music that we first observed in the music for the minstrel show: create a new sound by assimilating outsider styles (fiddle music/techno) into the prevailing style.

Moby performing on his Area: One tour, 2001.

> ♪ **KEY FEATURES**
>
> **"South Side," Moby (1999)**
> - Active, funky rhythms, with the 16-beat layer clearly marked by percussion sounds
> - Rock/rap elements: verse/chorus form, with rap-influenced spoken verse, sung chorus; guitar solo
> - Electronic elements not only in rhythm parts but also sustained sounds behind vocals in chorus

It is clear that "South Side" owes much of its success to the incorporation of rock and rap elements. Historically, when a new sound emerges, audiences have first embraced versions of it that contain familiar elements: the cover versions of R&B songs in the fifties are a noteworthy example. However, it is also clear that by incorporating these familiar elements into "South Side," Moby has abandoned the esthetic of techno, as exemplified in tracks such as "Nude Photo." It is a song, not a dance track. Whether this is good or bad—or neither—depends on your point of view: those who preferred their techno "pure" would be turned off by the song (and many of Moby's longtime fans felt betrayed by his move to the mainstream); those who were not ready to take their electronica straight welcomed the more familiar features.

Moby's *Play* has been a rare exception; the large family of electronica styles commands a relatively small market share. Nevertheless, its influence on popular music has been profound. Rap, pop, rock, world music—there is hardly a contemporary sound that does not show at least some influence of the technology and tools of dance music.

# Rap

Several years ago, students at the university where I was teaching asked me to participate in a discussion titled "Is rap music?" To get the discussion started, one of the students read a definition of *music*. As it turned out, rap would not have been music according to the dictionary definition. However, at no time in the discussion did anyone challenge the question itself. For me, the correct answer to the question "Is rap music?" is simply "It doesn't matter." Rap is rap. **Rap** is a form of creative expression that uses musical sounds to get its message across. (Indeed, one could argue convincingly that the rap video is the first total-arts genre, since it combines poetry, drama, visual arts, dancing, and music!) Whether it's music should be a non-issue, and it is a non-issue to the millions who enjoy it.

## Forerunners of Rap

The practice of talking over a musical accompaniment has a long history in popular music. Al Jolson used to talk over instrumental statements of the melody in the twenties; bluesmen and contemporary folk artists like Woody Guthrie would routinely strum and talk. Within the popular tradition, the practice of reciting poetry over a musical accompaniment goes back to the fifties, when Beat poets such as Kenneth Rexroth presented their work backed by a jazz combo. Somewhat later, black poets such as Amiri Bakara (LeRoi Jones) often delivered their work with jazz in the background. In the sixties, acts as different as Bob Dylan and James Brown delivered words that were both rhymed and rhythmic, using a vocal style that fell somewhere between everyday speech and singing.

However, the most direct antecedent of rap was the toasting of the Jamaican DJs who ran the mobile sound systems and who kept up a steady stream of patter as they changed discs. Recall that some Jamaican record companies began issuing the instrumental background of a recording as the "B" side of a song, so that the DJs could prolong their toasts. The Sugarhill Gang's "Rapper's Delight," the single widely acknowledged as the first commercial rap, uses a similar approach: much of the rap takes place over a sample of Chic's "Good Times." Another source of rap, this one closer to home, was George Clinton's funk; we heard a proto-rap at the beginning of "Tear the Roof Off the Sucker (Give Up the Funk)."

## Rap and African American Culture

There are numerous parallels between the Mississippi Delta in the first half of the twentieth century and the South Bronx in the latter half. Both regions are heavily black. Both are heartbreakingly poor: there is either no work or work at such low pay that one cannot make ends meet. They are violent, even lawless places. Health and living conditions are closer to life in a Third World country than the suburbs of New York or Memphis: out-of-wedlock children born to young teens; rats and roaches everywhere; segregated, underfunded schools, where the playground may become a battleground.

There are differences, of course. The Delta was—and is—rural. Geography, prejudice, and poverty kept the people who lived there thoroughly isolated from mainstream culture. The South Bronx is urban. Fifth Avenue in Manhattan is a short subway ride away. But it might as well have been another world for those who lived in the ghetto. In effect, there has been, in both cases, an invisible barrier that has prohibited meaningful contact between blacks and whites. However, television brought the rich and famous into the living rooms of South Bronx residents; they had a much sharper sense of what they didn't have than their Delta counterparts.

Both are depressing, demoralizing environments, environments that can suck hope out of one's mind, body, and spirit. So it is a testament to the resiliency of African Americans and the vitality of their culture that the Delta and the South Bronx have been home to two of the most vital, important, and influential forms of artistic expression to emerge in the twentieth century. Just as the Delta is the spiritual home of the blues, so is the South Bronx the home of rap.

Ask those who listen to rap what draws them to it. Chances are they'll say, "It's real." Like the blues, the realness of rap is not just in what it says, but how it says it. Rap gives us a window into life in the ghetto: the good, the bad, the ugly . . . and the beautiful. There is humor; bleak visions of the past, present, and future; posturing; misogyny, and responses to it; slices of gang life and pleas to bring an end to it; brutal depictions of current conditions and forceful demands for action. Like other roots music—blues, folk, country—this is music by and for its constituency. That rap has found a much wider audience is great but incidental to its original mission. The power comes from its emotional urgency: as with the blues, we can feel it's real. It has much more of an edge, in words and sound. It's as if blacks are saying, "We're tired of this s@#t."

Rap is a contemporary instance of a popular style speaking to and for its audience. In a 1992 *Newsweek* article, Public Enemy's Chuck D called rap "Black America's CNN." In his view, it provides information and opinions for the inner city, viewpoints not available through conventional media. Chuck D feels that rap and rap videos give whites exposure to a side of black life that they could not get short of living in a ghetto.

**Rap and Hip Hop**  Rap emerged as one artistic dimension of **hip hop** culture, along with break dancing and graffiti. All three were unconventional forms of expression that required considerable skill and preparation. **Break dancing** is extremely athletic; its vigorous moves parallel the energy of the music to which it's performed. Graffiti artists prepared their work much like a military campaign. They would plan the graffito through a series of sketches, scout out the train yards, sneak in and paint the cars, then sneak out. Their use of trains and buses as "canvases" suggests that graffiti was another way to get their message out of the ghetto.

There is a kind of defiance built into all three: rap, graffiti art, and break dancing. The implicit message is "You can put us down, but you can't keep us down." You— the man, the establishment—can subject us to subhuman living conditions. You can ignore us. But you can't break our spirit. We can create something that comes from us, not you, and you can't do what we do, even though you want to. (Keep in mind that before Eminem there was Vanilla Ice.)

**Rap and Technology**  Rap is a fascinating blend of low- and high-tech; and of the creative use and reuse of whatever is at hand. One can rap without any accompaniment at all. In this sense, it is about as low-tech as one can get. The first raps happened over existing music, but it wasn't long before DJs such as Grandmaster Flash found ways to put a new (back)spin on playing discs. With Grandmaster Flash, the turntable went from simple playback device to musical instrument. Equipped with two turntables, each with a copy of the record being played, DJs would **scratch** (move the turntable in a steady rhythm while the needle was still in the record groove to produce a percussive sound) and create breaks by repeating a segment of a song over and over on alternate turntables. In order to do this, DJs had to know exactly how far back to spin the turntable. Affordable samplers have rendered this technique obsolete.

These techniques were two more in a long string of found sounds within black music: the bottleneck for the guitar, the toilet plunger for the trumpet and trombone, the diddley bow and washtub bass. The resources may have been more sophisticated, but the principle remains the same: an imaginative search for new sound resources.

## Grandmaster Flash: Messages and Techniques

Rap evolved quickly from this point—in content, style, and appeal. Among the pioneers was Grandmaster Flash. Flash (born Joseph Saddler, 1958) was born in Barbados but moved with his family to the Bronx at a young age. He grew up with passionate interests in his father's jazz records and electronics, which he merged as a budding DJ at block parties and in public parks.

### Performing Aliases

In the twentieth century, there have three groups of musicians who have routinely assumed performing aliases: rappers, rural bluesmen, and calypsonians. For every Grandmaster Flash, Ice-T, or Notorious B.I.G., there were bluesmen like Leadbelly, Lightnin' Hopkins, and Howlin' Wolf, and calypsonians from Attila the Hun and Lord Kitchener to Mighty Sparrow and Lord Stalin. Calypso is an Afro-centric genre associated with the Carnaval celebration in Trinidad. Soca is a more modern offshoot.

Inspired by Kool Herc, the first great hip hop DJ, Flash developed the array of turntable techniques that would revolutionize rap. Even more significantly, he translated these techniques into a radically new musical conception: the **sound collage**. In the visual arts, an artist creating a collage assembles found materials (artifacts such as print materials, photographs, or machine parts) or natural objects (such as seashells, flowers, or leaves) into a work of art. The collage can consist exclusively of the pre-existing materials, or it can be integrated into the work of the artist. What the visual artist does with found materials, Flash did with sound. In effect, he cut and pasted sound clips from recordings into his music. The clips could range in length from a fraction of a second to several seconds; in either case, Flash completely recontextualized them.

The first song in which he showcased these skills was "The Adventures of Grandmaster Flash and the Wheels of Steel," which he recorded with the Furious Five, featuring Melle Mel (Melvin Glover) and ex–Sugarhill Gang percussionist Duke Bootee (Ed Fletcher). The song, a minor R&B hit in 1981, included excerpts from

Grandmaster Flash (Joseph Saddler), performing in 1981, shortly before he released "The Message."

Chic's "Good Times," Blondie's "Rapture," and Queen's "Another One Bites the Dust," as well as samples from other songs and sources; it would become a textbook for the creative possibilities of sampling.

This was a radical transformation of the age-old practice of musical quotation. Instead of inserting snippets of melody, Flash mixed in the entire musical event, as preserved on record. The result was a redefinition of "song."

"The Message,"
Grandmaster
Flash (1982)

Flash's other major contributions came with "The Message," which reached number 4 on the R&B charts in 1982 and also crossed over to the pop charts. It was innovative in both subject and setting. "The Message" presents a brutal picture of life in the ghetto. Its impact begins with the rap itself, which describes the oppressive and parlous circumstances of everyday life for those who live there. Another noteworthy feature was "arrest" at the end of the track, a "slice of life" interpolation that interrupts the musical accompaniment for several seconds. When the accompaniment resumes, it is as if the arrest was barely a blip on the radar screen—a virtual non-event in the ongoing misery of life in the ghetto. Such real-life non-musical sounds were not an innovation with rap; in rock-era music they date back to the Beatles. However, rap captured more powerful clips and used them more extensively. Both the rap and the arrest scene convey a much more serious message. With "The Message," rap graduated from party music to serious social commentary.

The other major innovation in "The Message" is the coordination of the musical setting with the message of the rap. There are many layers of activity, most of it generated on synthesizers and drum machines. The most prominent are the strong backbeat and the high synthesizer riff, the closest thing to melodic material on the entire track. However, none of the many layers establishes a consistent, active rhythm: the bass part, percussive guitarlike mid-range part, and the multiple percussion parts dart in and out of the texture; the overall effect evokes James Brown's music, but it is much emptier-sounding than the textures typically heard in his music. The 16-beat rhythm that is implicit in the instrumental sections becomes explicit only when the rap begins. An abrupt change in the rhythm of the rap, from the 16-beat stream to a variant of the clave pattern, signals the arrival at the "chorus": "Don't push me cuz I'm close to the edge."

## ♪ KEY FEATURES

**"The Message," Grandmaster Flash (1982)**

- Lyrics paint a dismal portrait of ghetto life
- Rapping (no singing) plus electronically generated pitched and percussive sounds
- Open texture with wide registral gaps between bass and high synthesizer riff
- 16-beat rhythms kept mainly in the rap; no consistent timekeeping in the instrumental setting

The spare, widely spaced sounds, and the way in which the synthesizer riff trails off seem to communicate the desolation of the ghetto environment; the lack of change in the setting seems to imply the difficulties faced in ameliorating this depressing environment.

Rap crossed over to the mainstream with Run-D.M.C.'s version of "Walk This Way." As with earlier rap songs, "Walk This Way" built the rap on a pre-existing musical foundation, in this case, Aerosmith's 1976 hit, "Walk This Way." The new twist was that Aerosmith members Steven Tyler and Joe Perry participated in the recording session. This new version made the charts exactly a decade after the original, in 1986. A year later, LL Cool J and the Beastie Boys (who were signed to Def Jam Records, the most prominent rap label) found the charts; with their emergence, rap burst out of the ghetto and into the 'burbs.

## Public Enemy: Rap as a Political Music

Among the major rap acts of the late eighties and nineties was Public Enemy. The group's key figures were Chuck D (born Carlton Ridenhour, 1960), Flavor Flav (born William Drayton, 1959), and DJ Terminator X (born Norman Rogers, 1966). They surrounded themselves with a substantial posse, some of whom contributed to their work.

Public Enemy was the most political of the rap acts to emerge during the late eighties. Their look kindled memories of the black radicals from the sixties: paramilitary uniforms, Black Panther evocations, fake Uzis carried by their entourage as they appeared on stage. The look was the smaller part of the equation. Far more telling were the raps themselves.

In "1 Million Bottlebags," a track from their 1991 album *Apocalypse 91...The Enemy Strikes Black*, Public Enemy takes on everyone. The rap is an indictment of

Public Enemy in 1995, in their paramilitary uniforms.

S.I.N./Corbis

alcohol abuse. It takes on all of those responsible for the problem: not only those who consume it and can't stop, but also the companies that prey on blacks by advertising their liquor products heavily in the ghetto. The language is powerful and direct; it is from the street. The frustration and anger behind it are palpable.

The rap begins with a collage of sounds: a bottle breaking, a "news bulletin" about target advertising by liquor companies in the black communities, the rhythm track, the sound of beer (or malt liquor) being poured, a beer belch, then hornlike synthesizer chords. The rap begins. Sirens and more prominent rhythm sounds signal the arrival of a refrainlike section. The end of the track simulates changing stations on a radio. Juxtaposed are a long statement about the immorality of making money off the impoverished and a scathing critique of the way in which racist corporate types dismiss the problem.

There are five kinds of sounds here: the rap, the spoken elements, the real-world sounds (for example, the bottle breaking), the rhythm tracks, and the pitched sounds, such as the siren screeches that mark the refrain. Collectively, they amplify the message of the rap through the sharp juxtaposition of sounds and images. The siren screeches are at once a musical sound—a two-note riff—and an evocation of a too-familiar real-life sound. There is complexity in the density of information, which matches the multiple levels of commentary.

The rhythm track, which combines a strong backbeat with interlocked patterns that collectively mark the 16-beat rhythm, serves several purposes. It is the glue that holds the track together, through the changes of voice, the spoken clips, and other sounds. It reinforces the delivery of the rap. Because both move at 16-beat speed, the percussion sounds give the rap support and strength. And it creates a groove: even more than in funk, you can move to the groove even as you take in the message.

"1 Million Bottlebags" is even less melodic than "The Message": the only easily identifiable melodic elements are the siren-like sound and the repeated chord: in both cases, the same pitch is repeated again and again. The absence of melody is a strength, not a shortcoming. Its presence would dilute the impact of the rap. It would soften the edge that is present everywhere else: in the delivery of the rap, in the rhythm track and other musical sounds, in the sound clips.

"1 Million Bottlebags," Public Enemy (1991)

---

## ♪ KEY FEATURES

### "1 Million Bottlebags," Public Enemy (1991)

- Rap indicts both the abusers and the producers of alcohol: the former for their unwillingness to clean up, the latter for targeting the black community in their advertising.
- Rich sound world formed from five different sound sources: rap, spoken elements, real-world sounds, percussion sounds, and pitched sounds—the sirenlike sounds and the synthesizer chords.
- Rap delivery and rhythm create a 16-beat rhythm at a fast tempo, which conveys the anger and frustration of the rap.
- Aggressive sounds (percussion sounds, siren) and use of non-musical sounds amplify the message of the text.

The moral high ground staked out by Public Enemy in tracks like "1 Million Bottlebags" was undermined by incidents such as the 1989 *Washington Post* interview with Professor Griff (born Richard Griffin, 1960), Public Enemy's "minister of information," in which he made numerous provocatively anti-Semitic remarks, including claiming that Jews were responsible for the majority of wickedness that goes on throughout the world. It was the most flagrant of several anti-Semitic public incidents in Public Enemy's career; others included an endorsement of Nation of Islam leader Louis Farrakhan. The controversy surrounding such incidents created dissension within the group and a sudden decline in their fortunes. By 1993, Chuck D put the group's career on hold; he would revive Public Enemy later in the decade, where they recaptured some of the success that they had previously enjoyed. Still, their most substantial contribution came in the late eighties and early nineties; more than any other group of the era, they made rap relevant—the black CNN—to both blacks and non-blacks and created sound worlds that amplified the impact of the lyrics.

## Mainstreaming Rap: The Case of Gangsta Rap

In rap, the boundary between life and art is all but invisible. The work of rappers often comes directly from their life experiences; the raps may simply document them. Nowhere has this been more evident than in gangsta rap. **Gangsta rap**, which emerged in the latter part of the eighties, brought the violence of inner-city life into the music and out into the world.

Gangsta rap might well be written gang-sta rap, because its strongest under-current was the association with gang life. A visual image of this life was the 1988 film *Colors*, starring Robert Duvall and Sean Penn as police officers trying to control violence between the Bloods and the Crips, two rival Los Angeles gangs. Ice-T, among the first of the gangsta rappers, recorded the title track of the film.

Although Schoolly D, a Philadelphia-based rapper, is credited with the rap that sparked the genre (the 1986 single "P.S.K."), gangsta rap has been perceived as a west coast phenomenon because of the success of rap artists and groups such as N.W.A. and Ice-T, then Dr. Dre (a former N.W.A. member), Snoop Doggy Dogg, and 2Pac (Tupac Shakur). The success of these groups escalated the territorial animosity from rival gangs within a community to the communities themselves. Bad blood developed between west coast gangsta rappers and New York hip hop artists; both groups used lyrics to dis the opposing camp. The violence portrayed in the lyrics often spilled over into real life: Snoop Doggy Dog and Tupac Shakur were among the notable gangsta rap artists who served jail time ("California Love" was Shakur's first recording after his release from jail); the shooting deaths of Shakur and Notorious B.I.G. are commonly regarded as gang retribution for earlier offenses.

The violence was not the only controversial aspect of the music. Raps were often pornographic and misogynistic, and richly scatological. Most recordings routinely earned the "parental advisory" label from the RIAA (Recording Industry Association of America). For suburban whites, gangsta rap must have seemed like forbidden fruit; the genre would enjoy a large following among whites, most of whom experienced the rappers' world only vicariously.

Although its audience had grown steadily throughout the late eighties and early nineties, gangsta rap crossed over to the mainstream in large part because of a musical decision: to work pop elements into hardcore rap in an effort to give the music more widespread appeal. It first appeared in the music of New York hip hop artists such as Notorious B.I.G. and Nas and quickly spread to the west coast: Tupac Shakur's "California Love," which topped the pop, R&B, and rap charts in 1996, epitomizes this new approach.

**Tupac Shakur**   If ever an artist seemed destined to live and die by the sword, it would be Tupac Shakur (1971–1996). His parents were active in the Black Panthers; his mother was acquitted on a conspiracy charge only a month before Shakur's birth; his father is currently incarcerated in Florida; and others close to his mother during his childhood were either in and out of prison or fugitives.

What made his too-short life doubly tragic was the terrible conflict between the sensitive and violent sides of his personality. He was intelligent and curious—reading Machiavelli during his prison term—and creative and multitalented, with obvious gifts as an actor, poet, dancer, and musician. Yet in his personal and professional lives, he gave vent to the violent side: run-ins with the law; a sexual abuse lawsuit and scandal; the track "Hit 'Em Up," a personal attack on Notorious B.I.G., in which he claimed to have slept with B.I.G.'s wife. That his life would end prematurely as a result of the ultimate violent act seems in retrospect almost a foregone conclusion.

Shortly before his death, Shakur recorded "California Love" with Dr. Dre for Death Row Records, the label headed by Suge Knight, who was also repeatedly in trouble with the law. Both the video and the song evidence the mutation of rap from an outsiders' music flourishing in inner-city parks to a big business. Both the opening scene and the action during the song itself seem inspired by the Mad Max films: it purports to present a desolate, lawless world a hundred years in the future. Although it is skillfully produced, the video has no obvious thematic connection with the song, which is very much in the present—the "'95" that Dr. Dre mentions is clearly 1995, and Tupac's first words are "out on bail fresh outta jail." What is obvious is that the video took a lot of money to produce; it is a clear sign that rap has become big business.

The song shows how rap found a mainstream audience by bringing in non-rap elements. It begins with a striking processed vocal riff; the instrumental introduction that follows spotlights the bass. The next section features a tuneful melody with a rich accompaniment; this becomes the main refrain of the song. The refrain returns after Dr. Dre's rap. It is followed by another sung section "Shake it," which gives way to Tupac's rap.

"California Love," Tupac Shakur, featuring Dr. Dre (1995) (music and video)

Getty Images/Getty Images

Tupac Shakur in a pensive moment, in 1991.

The rap lyrics offer a sizeable dose of gangsta rap posturing: there are references to violence, gangs, prostitution, money, clothes, and jewelry. But the prevailing mood, in both words and music, is party hard, because "we keep it rockin'!" Especially in the refrain, it sounds more like a promo for the chamber of commerce than an incitement to riot.

Its most surprising feature, and undoubtedly one of its most appealing features, is its melodic and textural richness. The vocal melodies are the most apparent evidence of this, but woven into the texture behind both the sung sections and the raps are lush synthesizer harmonies and multiple fragments of melody. The return of the refrain features even more supplementary melodic activity, both vocal and instrumental. Almost all of this activity, and especially the synthesizer chords and lines, occurs in middle and high register, above the vocal range of the rap. This counterbalances the characteristic dark bass sound that runs throughout the song.

Additionally, several layers of percussion sounds mark the backbeat and 16-beat rhythms or play against these regular rhythms: the whistle stands out as a source of rhythmic play. The rhythmic texture of the song is even denser than that heard on "1 Million Bottlebags," although the tempo is considerably slower.

The sound world of the song, and the genre, is defined most fundamentally in the brief instrumental interlude just after the title-phrase riff. For a brief moment, there is only the active bass line and several percussion sounds, most prominently the high-pitched percussion sound marking the 16-beat rhythm. It is a sound that we associate with rap: we hear it above everything else emanating from car stereos. In Motown, soul, seventies black pop, and funk, the bass is the dominant rhythm instrument. In rap, it has become the dominant instrument, period. This sound—strong, freely moving bass and active percussion—distills the most characteristic elements of black music to their essence and pushes them into the forefront, much as the saturated rock rhythm played by a punk rock band reduces, intensifies, and projects the most basic elements of rock rhythm and sound.

In particular, the bass sound, made dark and fat by stripping away the overtones so that only low-frequency sounds remain, is a logical extension of the dark sound of electric blues. Electric blues made rural blues darker by adding a bass instrument and guitar riffs in a low register; the characteristic bass-driven sound of rap simply continues this progression.

In "California Love" we hear this essential sound by itself for about 7 seconds. During the course of the song, the other elements of the song—vocal refrains, raps, other instrumental sound—covers over this foundation, which continues through the song. Especially in light of the fact that the more tuneful elements were added as a conscious effort to enhance the appeal of the style, the effect is striking; it is as if we get a glimpse of a public figure in an unguarded moment and see him as he really is, not as he portrays himself.

The rich texture created by the numerous melodic fragments and sustained chords are an important source of the enormous crossover appeal of the song. It makes the song more accessible and more familiar, and there is more to connect to—not only the two raps and the beat, but the melodies and the sound variety. The strategy to mainstream rap through melody succeeded on both coasts, and it has remained a common practice up until the present.

> ♪ **KEY FEATURES**
>
> **"California Love," Tupac Shakur, featuring Dr. Dre (1995)**
> - Raps mix a salute to California with personal remarks: jail, jewelry, clothes, and the obligatory commentary on street life
> - Strong 16-beat rhythm runs through the song; raps line up with this rhythm
> - Variety of sounds, including dark bass sound and high-register percussion and synthesizer sounds
> - Sung refrain frames the two rap sections
> - Melody in sung sections, plus instrumental melodic fragments underneath sung vocals and raps

Fortunately for Death Row Records, Shakur had recorded a substantial amount of unreleased material. Six albums were released posthumously, the last in 2004. All went platinum. His legacy extends beyond his recordings. Following his death, his mother Afeni Shakur established the Tupac Amaru Shakur Foundation to "provide training and support for students who aspire to enhance their creative talents."

**The Future of Rap**   Gangsta rap has been the most visible rap style since the late eighties, because of its appeal and because of its notoriety, but it is one of many rap styles to emerge during this period. Because it is so integral to hip hop culture, it may be hard to divorce rap from its trappings and particularly the baggage that it carries: the controversial pronouncements, the violent world it portrays and realizes, the hedonistic lifestyle it projects. So it is not surprising that rap, like so many other genres with aggressive postures and outsider status (heavy metal, punk, techno), has gotten its share of bad press. Its critics focus on the language, the lifestyle, the lyrics, and the emergence of substyles like gangsta rap to condemn the entire genre. There is no denying rap's edge; the speed and tone of the rap and the busy rhythms underneath virtually guarantee it.

However, the act of rapping is inherently value neutral. It can be, and has been, used to deliver a variety of messages—not only dark gray portraits of life in the hood and expletive-filled rants but also humor and hope. Whether the message is negative or positive depends on the content, not the genre. A case in point: Christian rap (or, more alliteratively, holy hip hop) also emerged in the nineties. The music of groups such as the Gospel Gangstaz sends a message far different from that heard in "California Love," "Hit 'Em Up," and other gangsta rap tracks.

At the beginning of the twenty-first century, rap—in all of its manifestations—is an enduring and significant part of the rock-era musical world. The numerous rap/ rock syntheses—such as rapcore, rap-rock, and rap-metal—offer one more indication of its strong presence in popular music. At the same time, some have looked back almost nostalgically to "old school," the rap from the late seventies and eighties, when the message, whether it talked about good times or bad, seemed purer.

# Beyond Rock

In the summary of rock's core values that appeared at the end of the first chapter, we listed features that one expects to hear in a classic rock song. A comparison of that style profile with the features found in the examples of "pure" techno and rap—"Nude Photo," "The Message," and even "1 Million Bottlebags"—offers compelling evidence of the way in which electronica and rap, arguably the two most progressive musical styles since 1980, have moved beyond rock. Here are key differences:

- 16-beat rhythms, instead of a rock beat
- A good beat of far greater complexity, because of the more active rhythms and a richer texture
- Electronic instruments and samples, instead of a core rhythm section of guitar, bass, and drums
- Few if any sung riffs, and no melody to speak of; no hooks in a sung refrain or in a lead guitar part

And while there is a sense of verse/chorus form in the two rap songs and recurring musical ideas in the techno track, there is little sense of arriving at the chorus and highlighting it with a memorable melodic hook.

Moreover, the very *idea* of a song as a fixed, discrete document contained on a recording comes under attack in both styles. Tracks like "Nude Photo" are pieces in a larger puzzle, a single element in a DJ's mix. And in both techno and rap, remixing songs into new versions is standard practice. We consider the historical context of these changes next.

## The New Rhythmic Foundation of Popular Music

In our discussion of rock and roll, we noted that the feature that most distinguished rock and roll from rhythm and blues was the rock rhythmic layer. In our discussion of the maturation of rock rhythm, we outlined the purging of transitional features, such as insistent marking of the beat. And in our discussion of punk, we highlighted the saturation and distillation of rock rhythm.

Even as rock rhythm assumed its classic realizations, more active 16-beat rhythms began to emerge, beginning with the black music of the late sixties and early seventies. Disco brought them to the fore in the late seventies. By the early eighties, 16-beat rhythms were the rhythmic foundation of electronica and rap, as we discovered in this chapter; in part because of the influence of electronica and rap on other styles, 16-beat rhythms became the dominant rhythmic foundation of post-eighties rock-era music, just as rock rhythm pervaded the music of the sixties and early seventies.

Rhythmically, this is a paradigm shift. It is not as dramatic as the shift from swing rhythm to rock rhythm, because rock rhythm can be mapped onto 16-beat rhythms, while swing and shuffle rhythms are incompatible with rock rhythm. Nevertheless, the rhythmic textures that are based on these more active rhythms—whether heard in rap, techno, pop, or even the music of U2 and Nirvana—place this music in the more recent past.

## Rap and the "Percussionization" of Popular Music

In the larger view of things, we can understand rap as the logical end result of a process that had been going on for most of the twentieth century: the "percussionization" of popular music. It began shortly after the turn of the century, with the formation of the syncopated dance orchestra, which included a drummer. It continued with the development of the drum set and the more percussive approach to banjo playing—the crisp backbeat of the fox-trot. Next was the plucking of the string bass, instead of bowing it, as was customary in orchestral playing. (Plucking—*pizzicato*—is exceptional.) R&B and rock musicians soon found ways to extract percussive sounds from new instruments of the rock era: slapping techniques on the electric bass and choked guitar. Rhythm-and-blues recordings often featured extra percussion instruments, especially conga drums. New keyboard instruments, such as the clavinet (heard on Stevie Wonder's "Superstition") produced a percussive sonority. Synthesizers and drum machines expanded the range of percussive sonorities.

With rap, the voice becomes a percussion instrument. Like many other percussion instruments, a rapper's voice has resonance (more so than normal speech) and a general sense of high or low. But the rapper does not sing definite pitches, as a singer does. James Brown was a primary source for this because even his singing is percussive—listen to how syllables explode, then die away quickly, when he sings a phrase like "I Feel Good." As an all-percussive genre, rap has taken this trend about as far as it can go. In this respect, it is the sound parallel to the increased activity in the style beats of popular music.

## Deconstructing Popular Song

When the album version of "South Side" was released as part of a "single" in England on Mute Records, it was one of seven versions of the song on the CD. The others were:

- The single version
- The "Hybrid Dishing Pump Remix" version
- The "Peter Heller Park Lane Vocal" version
- The "Ain't Never Learned" version
- The "Hybrid Dishing Pump Instrumental" version
- "The Sun Never Stops Setting" version

The many versions of the song highlight one of the most fascinating postdigital developments in popular music: the **deconstruction** of a song. Recall that one of the significant developments of the early rock era was the emergence of the "record as document." That is, the song was what was recorded on the album or single. Still, even then, multiple versions of songs occasionally appeared: the single version of the Doors' "Light My Fire" is much shorter than the album version, which features long instrumental solos by Ray Manzarek and Robby Krieger. As mentioned earlier, Jamaican record companies took this a step further when they would issue the instrumental backing of a song as the "B" side of the record, so that DJs could toast over it. Still, musicians and producers were limited, because of the relative difficulty in isolating and recombining tracks and song components and segments in analog mixing.

Digital technology liberated music creators from both the signal degradation and ease-of-use issues in analog recording. As computers gained speed and audio workstation software developed, it became possible to construct a song out of several components, which could be modified, added to, and otherwise manipulated to create other versions of the song, some of which can be quite different. For example, the "Peter Heller Park Lane Vocal" version of "South Side" is 5 minutes longer than the album track, and one track is an instrumental.

Because the track or song's components for "South Side" were in digital format, it was possible to, in effect, deconstruct them and reassemble them into different forms. Increasingly, releasing multiple versions of a song or track, either simultaneously or in subsequent remixes, is now common practice in techno, rap, and pop. As a result, what a song is has become far more fluid than it was in the sixties and seventies.

One significant consequence of all of these changes—the more active rhythms, the increase in percussive sonorities, and the assembling and reassembling of songs—was a relative neglect of melody. That melody remains important to mainstream audiences is evident not only in the crossover success of Moby and Tupac Shakur, whose music is far richer melodically than the other three examples, but also in the relative popularity of techno, rap, and other styles influenced by this music—most notably the new pop styles that emerged in the early eighties. We consider these next.

## Terms to Remember

| | | |
|---|---|---|
| sampling | house | rap |
| audio CD | techno | hip hop |
| MIDI | rave | break dancing |
| sequencer | ambient music | scratch |
| loop | medley | sound collage |
| sample | mix | gangsta rap |
| electronica | set | deconstruction |

## Applying Chapter Concepts

1. Explore the idea of deconstructing a song by comparing multiple (at least three) remixes of a techno song. Create timed guides similar to the ones prepared for the musical examples and describe the activity within each section of each track. Summarize the differences in length, form, and instrumental resources.

2. Run-D.M.C.'s cover of "Walk This Way" not only sparked rap's move to the mainstream but also established a precedent for merging rap with other musical styles. Today there are numerous rap/rock, rap/R&B, rap/whatever fusions. Create a profile of a rap fusion through the following process:

a.  Select a rap hybrid style that you like.

b.  Choose at least three tracks by different acts that you feel represent the hybrid style.

c.  Identify five common features among the three tracks: one can be lyric content, but the other four should be some feature of the music.

# 18

# The New Sound of Pop in the Eighties

Perhaps it's karma. Coincidence or not, it is certainly intriguing that the three biggest pop acts of Ronald Reagan's presidency were Michael Jackson, Prince, and Madonna. In an era of political and social conservatism, all three have presented complex, provocative, and at times confusing images of race and gender. Michael Jackson's gradual metamorphosis to paleness, questions about his sexual and generational preferences, and his erratic behavior have been tabloid fodder for over two decades. Prince alternated between blatant eroticism in performance and total withdrawal from the public eye—to the extent that he even retracted his name. Madonna broke down barriers on stage, in the media, and behind the scenes. People noticed what she did and what she thought; both were often controversial. More tellingly, she was the first female pop star to chart her own career path. Two of them have ascended to one-name celebrity status. Michael Jackson might well have if it weren't for another prominent celebrity named Michael J.

All three have been extraordinarily visible; what people can see has been very much part of their success. Michael Jackson broke through first. He appeared as the scarecrow in the 1978 film *The Wiz*, a black take on *The Wizard of Oz*. There he met Quincy Jones, who was instrumental in shaping his career. He made his mark in a series of landmark music videos, which displayed the full range of his talents. In 1984, Prince had a surprise hit with the semi-autobiographical film *Purple Rain*. By that time, Madonna's career was well underway; she would star in music videos, films (such as the 1985 *Desperately Seeking Susan*), and stage musicals. All three, and especially Michael Jackson and Madonna, capitalized on a newly emerging genre (the music video) that became a staple on a new network (MTV) in a new medium (cable television).

## MTV and Music Videos

Those who have grown up with hundreds of networks may find it difficult to imagine a time when television viewing options consisted almost exclusively of three networks: NBC, CBS, and ABC. Larger metropolitan areas had public television and perhaps a few independent stations. But until the early seventies, most viewers had only NBC, CBS, and ABC to choose from. That would change with the emergence of cable television.

Cable TV is almost as old as commercial broadcasting. The first cable TV services were launched in 1948; a well-situated antenna brought television signals to homes in remote rural regions. There was some growth during the fifties and sixties; however, cable TV as we currently know it didn't get off the ground until the seventies. Two key developments—the launching of communications satellites and significant deregulation of the broadcast industry—made cable television economically viable.

Cable changed the economics of the television industry and transformed it in the process. Prior to its emergence, networks relied exclusively on advertising for their revenue. The signal was free. Cable TV services charged subscribers a fee. In turn, they passed on a percentage of the fee to the channels that they offered their subscribers. This new source of revenue made possible the fragmentation of the television market. A network that could command only 1 or 2 percent of the market would have no chance for success against the major networks. But that same 1 or 2 percent of the cable market could provide enough income to keep the network on the air and make money for its owners.

## MTV

Among the first of these new cable networks was **MTV**. The network began broadcasting on August 1, 1981. Symbolically, the first music video that MTV broadcast was "Video Killed the Radio Star." The original format of the network was analogous to Top 40–style radio stations: videos replaced songs, and VJs (video jockeys) assumed a role similar to radio disc jockeys.

Perhaps because cable originally serviced mainly rural parts of the country, MTV took an AOR-type approach to programming. For the first couple of years, programming targeted a young, white audience: bands were almost exclusively white—Duran Duran, a British pop group with a keen visual sense, was one of the early MTV bands. Black acts cried "racism," with some justification. The most notorious incident involved jazz keyboardist Herbie Hancock, whose song "Rockit" was a hit in 1983. The video for the song received airplay on MTV. It features a Dali-esque collage of white mannequins—some whole, some only partly present—moving to the music. Hancock appears fleetingly, as if he were on a television show. Later, it was revealed that MTV insisted on his limited visibility, because of their white orientation. However, change was in the air: that video would win awards in five categories at the first MTV Video Music Awards ceremony the following year.

It was Michael Jackson who obliterated MTV's color barrier. The demand for his spectacular music videos—made in conjunction with his 1982 album *Thriller*—was so overwhelming that the network changed their policy. Race was suddenly a non-issue.

The Cable Act of 1984 effectively deregulated the television industry. In its wake, the cable industry wired the nation. With new revenues came new and improved programming. MTV started VH1 in 1985 and diversified their programming in several ways, adding documentaries, cartoons, and talk shows and continuing to broaden their programming. In particular, their segments on rap helped bring it out of the inner city.

MTV has affected both consumers and creators. The network has become a key tastemaker for young people around the world. It has influenced not only whom they listen to but also many other aspects of youth culture: dress, looks, body language, vocabulary, attitudes. The emergence of MTV has also reshaped the sound of pop, as we consider shortly.

## Music Videos

From the start, rock had been a look as well as a sound. Elvis was a sensation on television, then in films. Other rock-and-roll stars made their way into films as well, although not as stars; the 1956 film *The Girl Can't Help It*, which starred Jayne Mansfield, featured Little Richard, Gene Vincent, and Fats Domino. The Beatles' breakthrough film feature, *A Hard Day's Night* (1964), showed the power of film to enhance music, especially when the visual element was so well in tune with the music and the spirit of the band.

During the late sixties—the twilight of the Beatles' career—the idea of using videos as promotional tools began to emerge. At the same time, live performances were captured on video, or on film: documentaries of the Monterey Pop Festival in 1967 and Woodstock in 1969 remain treasures. With its opening scene clearly differentiated from live performance, Queen's video of their 1976 hit "Bohemian Rhapsody" was an important step in moving music video beyond capturing a live performance. Further experiments, especially by new wave acts like Devo, moved closer to the integration of sound and image that characterizes contemporary music video. In their hilarious video of "Jocko Homo," they make no pretense of performing the song.

## The Impact of Music Videos

Sparked by the emergence of MTV, the music video producers of the early eighties inverted the conventional relationship among sound, story, and image. In music theater and film musicals, songs were written for the story. Ideally, songs enhanced those moments when what the character felt was too much for mere words. In early music videos, the relationship was the opposite: the visual element was designed to enhance the song. However, because MTV provided an important and attractive new outlet for videos, the music video became more than a promotional tool. Songs could be conceived with their potential as videos in mind. Acts could create song and video as an integrated and balanced whole, where the song is more than a soundtrack, and the visual elements are more than enhancements of the song. Music videos were a new genre.

## The Transformation of Pop

The most obvious, and most widely discussed, consequence of MTV's new-found importance as an outlet for music videos was the suddenly increased emphasis on the look of an act, and the look of the video, as a determinant of success. However, its impact went beyond that, especially in the work of Michael Jackson and Madonna, the two stars who defined music video in the eighties. Jackson is a sensational, innovative dancer, and Madonna began her career as a dancer. Both were in touch with the new dance music; Madonna started her career in the New York club scene. *Off the Wall* (1979), Michael Jackson's first big post-*Wiz* success, drew on disco, and much of his eighties music had a punk/funk/disco-derived edge. With both of them, movement became an expressive third element in the music video, joining words and music.

The new sound of pop that emerged in the eighties was the confluence of three developments: the emergence of MTV and music videos; the more active rhythms and richer textures of dance music; and the return of the all-around performer, whose skill as a dancer more than matched his or her vocal ability. (Michael Jackson's most direct predecessor would be Fred Astaire.) The result was a new kind of pop, where much of the momentum in the song shifted from the melody to the dance-track rhythms. At the same time, dancer–singers like Michael Jackson and Madonna put on exhilarating displays. The songs were still tuneful, but they left room for plenty of movement.

Today, the pop singer who simply stands in front of a microphone and sings a tuneful melody is the exception, not the rule, especially at the top of the pop charts. Vigorous movement is in, whether it's groups like the Backstreet Boys and 'N Sync or solo acts like Mariah Carey, Britney Spears, Christine Aguilera, and Mary J. Blige. The music matches the movement. Much of it draws on the 16-beat rhythms heard in dance music and rap. An overlay of tuneful melody and pleasant voices cannot obscure the fact that the major new pop acts of the eighties took rock-era music in a new, visually exciting direction.

# Michael Jackson and Madonna: Redefining Pop in the Eighties

Both Michael Jackson and Madonna integrated image and movement into their performing persona to an unprecedented degree. For Jackson, song and dance were complementary components of the same conception. In his videos, we experience them as a unified expressive gesture, even though we are well aware that he lip-syncs the vocal. For Madonna, song and dance were components of the mini-dramas that she compressed onto video and disc.

## Michael Jackson

Although only 24 when *Thriller* (1982) was released, Michael Jackson had been a professional entertainer for three-fourths of his life and a star for half of it. He had released solo singles in the early seventies, but Jackson's solo career didn't take off until 1978, when he starred in the film *The Wiz*. During the filming, he met composer/arranger/producer Quincy Jones, who collaborated with him on *Off the Wall* (1979), his first major album, and *Thriller*. Jones's skill and creativity proved to be the ideal complement to Jackson's abilities.

There are precedents for Michael Jackson's exuberant dancing in rock-era music: for example, Elvis's stage and film performances; the stylized choreography of the Motown groups, including the Jackson 5; James Brown's stage shows, which featured "the hardest working man in show business" moving and grooving all over the stage; and the dance scenes in such films as *Saturday Night Fever*. However, it was the musical that offered a more direct precedent for the integration of song, dance, and story. This connection is evident in the video of "Thriller": the group dance scene recalls the marvelous dance scene to the song "Cool" in the film version of Leonard Bernstein's landmark musical *West Side Story*.

As with so many other rock artists, Michael Jackson was fortunate to be in the right place at the right time. MTV had gone on the air in 1981; *Thriller* was released a year later. Jackson helped transform the music video from a song-with-video into a mini-film that used a song as the focal point: for example, the video of "Thriller" is over twice the length of the track on the album. Jackson made it work through his dancing: no earlier rock-era performer had danced with his virtuosity and expressiveness.

The title track to *Thriller* shows the musical side of these changes. It is a long song by pop standards, in part because of the long buildup at the beginning and the voice-over at the end by Vincent Price, one of Hollywood's masters of the macabre. But the heart of the song is a Disney-esque version of scary: Michael's voice, the skillful orchestration, the security of the four-on-the-floor bass drum and heavy backbeat, and the busy rhythms all ensure a cartoonish kind of spooky music more reminiscent of *Scooby Doo* than *Friday the 13th*. The video reinforces this as each of the nightmarish scenes dissolves into fiction. This is not to say that it wasn't well done, or deserving of its enormous popularity. But compared to the Black

Michael Jackson showing off his glove, 1984.

Bettmann/Corbis

Sabbath version of a scary night, this one is safe—at least until the music drops out and Price has his last laugh—or Jackson's cat eyes return.

"Thriller" also reveals several distinctive characteristics of post-1980 pop. One is the extensive use of electronic instruments in combination with conventional instruments. Among the most prominent electronic sounds are the repeated bass riff, the sustained harmonies behind Michael's vocals, and the brash chords of the opening: all are played on synthesizers. The basic rhythm grows out of disco: we hear a strong backbeat, a relentless bass-drum thump on each beat, and several layers of percussion marking off a 16-beat rhythm. However, the other instrumental parts, especially those played on rhythm section instruments or their electronic counterparts, create a texture that is denser and more complex than that heard in a conventional disco song. (This is certainly appropriate, since the dancing of Jackson and his cohorts is more expressive and complex than social dancing to disco.) Jackson's vocal line is simply one strand in the texture: in the verse, it is in the forefront, but in the chorus sections the backup vocals and instruments playing the title-phrase riff all but drown him out. It floats on the busy rhythms and riffs that provide much of the song's momentum—indeed, in the video, the basic rhythm track sustains the flow through the graveyard scene, and, after a short break, through the first part of the extended dance number that is the heart of the video.

"Thriller," Michael Jackson (1982) (music and video)

---

♪ **KEY FEATURES**

**"Thriller," Michael Jackson (1982)**

- Extensive use of electronic sounds: sustained chords, hornlike sounds, bass riff
- Dense texture, with several instruments playing riffs and multiple percussion instruments
- Expansive form: allows the action in the video to unfold
- Active rhythms, with 16-beat rhythms over a strong beat and backbeat

---

Although only three of the tracks were shot as music videos, all of the songs on *Thriller* have a distinct identity. There is considerable contrast from song to song, as the musical settings capture the tone and content of the lyric. For example, the hard-edged riffs that open "Wanna Be Startin' Somethin'" anticipate the lyric's school-yard-style provocation. The punk-inspired beat and Eddie Van Halen's guitar underscore the message of "Beat It." The loping rhythm (a shuffle beat on top of a rock beat), the use of pre-rock pop harmony, and the soft synth sounds reinforce the friendly rivalry between Michael and Paul McCartney in "The Girl Is Mine." And a setting that mixes an open middle range—just a simple synthesizer riff—with the irritation of a persistent bass riff and percussion sound characterizes the emptiness of the groupie-style relationships in "Billie Jean." Both the songs and Quincy Jones's masterful settings give the album an expressive range that compensates for the one-dimensional quality of Jackson's singing.

There is no doubt that *Thriller* would have been a successful album without the videos. But it also seems certain that the videos, and the fact that the songs were so "video-ready," played a crucial role in its overwhelming success. *Thriller* has been the crowning achievement of Jackson's career; nothing before or since matched its success.

## Madonna

In Renaissance-era Italian, *madonna* was originally a variant of *mia donna*, or "my lady." The term eventually came to refer more specifically to Mary, the mother of Jesus: for example, the phrase "madonna and child" identifies those works of art that depict Mary with the infant Jesus. In the eighties, "Madonna" acquired an even more concrete image: the pop star whose given name soon was enough to identify her to the world at large.

Madonna (born Madonna Ciccone, 1958) was born the same year as Michael Jackson. In 1978, while Jackson was starring in *The Wiz*, Madonna moved to New York to further her career as a dancer. She soon became active in the club scene, while she struggled to pay the rent. Her star rose quickly. Her first records, released in the early eighties, gained her a following mainly among clubbers. Although these songs didn't cross over, they created enough of a buzz that she received a contract to record her first album, *Madonna*, which was released in 1983.

In 1984, she took one of the many bold steps that have characterized her career, releasing the video of "Like a Virgin." Shot in Venice, Italy, the video rapidly juxtaposes images of Madonna in a white wedding dress with her in street clothes and a provocative evening dress—attire that suggests she is anything but a virgin. The video established a formula that would set the tone for her subsequent work: combine provocative, shocking, and controversial themes and images with bright, accessible music.

Among her most controversial projects of the eighties was the video "Like a Prayer"; the song was the title track from her 1989 album of the same name. The video conflates religious images (for example, a scene in which she grasps a knife, and it cuts her in a way that evokes the stigmata of the crucified Christ); symbols of racism (burning crosses); numerous incongruities and impossibilities (a black gospel choir in a Catholic chapel; the statue of a black saint who comes to life, then doubles as the black man wrongly accused of murdering a woman); and the one constant: Madonna in a revealing dress. All of this outraged numerous religious groups, who threatened to boycott Pepsi, which had recruited Madonna as a spokesperson. The controversy served as free publicity: the album topped the charts.

Madonna performing in 1987 dressed in a relatively modest outfit, by her subsequent standards.

The video of "Like a Prayer" dramatically evidences the emergence of the music video as an entity distinct from the song that spawned it, and from other expressive forms that merge song, image, and movement. The messages of the song—among them, racism is wrong, we are all brothers and sisters in Christ, and Madonna is sexy—come through mainly in the rapid-fire series of images/scenes/song fragments. There is little sense of continuity in the narrative, visually or in the lyric, and there are long stretches where Madonna makes no attempt to sing in the video, even as we hear her voice in the song. This shows the rapid evolution of the music video, not only in Madonna's own work but also in the medium overall. It has moved well beyond simply capturing a live performance, as was the case in "Everybody," her first video; at this point in her career and in the brief history of the medium, such videos seem a distant memory.

"Like a Prayer," Madonna (1989) (music and video)

Musically, Madonna's winning formula has been to combine a simple, catchy melody with trendy sounds and rhythms and skillful production. The melody of "Like a Prayer" flows in gently undulating phrases, with little or no syncopation. When isolated from its setting, the melody bears a closer resemblance to a children's song or a folk melody than to a dance-inspired song from the eighties. And like a folk melody, it is easily absorbed and remembered. The support for this melody oscillates between sustained chords sung by a choir and played on an organ and a Caribbean-flavored background that bears a striking resemblance to Steve Winwood's 1986 number 1 hit "Higher Love." As with much post-1980 pop, the active accompaniment is dense, rhythmically active, and rich in both electronic and conventional instrumental sounds. The steady flow of Madonna's melody allows her to alternate between the dancelike sections and those sections with only sustained harmonies and extremely light percussion sounds.

---

### ♪ KEY FEATURES

**"Like a Prayer," Madonna (1989)**

- Striking contrasts in sound and texture: melody plus sustained chords from dense texture with Madonna, choir, and lots of rhythm, including distorted guitar
- Basic rhythm: a complex 16-beat rhythm with a strong backbeat, active bass line, and layers of riffs and percussion
- Straightforward, simple melody runs through most of the song

---

"Like A Prayer" breaks no new ground musically, but it does merge disparate and seemingly contradictory musical features into an effective song, just as the video does.

Artistically, Madonna has not been an innovator. The most ground-breaking aspect of Madonna's career has been her ascension to a position of complete control of her career: writing her songs, producing her recordings, choreographing her performances, and making the key decisions about every aspect of its production and promotion. This owes more to her ambition, business acumen, and chutzpah than it does to her talent. In achieving elite celebrity status (single-name recognition, constant tabloid fodder) as she directed her career, she has become a role model for a new generation of women performers.

Many have found her public persona liberating. Without question, her success added a new dimension to sexual equality within the pop music business: women, or at least women like her, no longer had to be front persons for men. Cynical observers have dismissed the provocative images that she presents, such as those encountered in the "Like a Prayer" video, as attention-getting stunts whose shock value obscures a lack of talent and imagination. It is true that Madonna is not spectacularly creative in any artistic dimension of the music business: she is not Michael Jackson's equal as a dancer, Prince's equal as a songwriter or an instrumentalist, or Tina Turner, Luther Vandross, or Christina Aguilera's equal as a vocalist. However, to dismiss her talents out of hand would be to ignore the sense of conviction with which Madonna presents these controversial juxtapositions, and to dismiss their role in challenging value systems that have grown rigid over time.

# Post-Punk/Post-Disco Fusions: The Music of Prince

Punk and disco seem as easy to blend as oil and water. As they emerged in the late seventies, they seemed to demarcate contrasting ideologies and musical approaches. Punk was real while disco, as experienced in a club, was an escape into a timeless world. Punk was about grit; disco was about glitter. Punk was performed by live bands on conventional rock instruments, hammering out a concentrated rock rhythm; disco was performed by DJs mixing a string of recordings, most of which combined a strong beat with active 16-beat rhythms. The lyrics of punk songs usually said something; disco lyrics often descended into banality.

However, in *Christgau's Record Guide*, his 1990 survey of 3,000 recordings from the eighties, Robert Christgau, the dean of American rock critics, described "post-punk/post-disco fusion" as a key development of the decade. He described a synthesis of the two in what he called **DOR**, or **dance-oriented rock**, an umbrella term he coined to identify an array of eighties styles. What Christgau called DOR was just one of several new sounds that emerged in the eighties that showed the joint influence of punk and disco. The most significant pop musician to draw on both styles in his music was Prince, a multifaceted musician who, more than any other figure of the decade, forged a new middle-ground consensus from a broad spectrum of sixties and seventies musical styles.

## Prince

It would be difficult to find any rock artist who embodies more confluences and contradictions than Prince (born Prince Rogers Nelson, 1958). His music is a rock and rhythm-and-blues melting pot: one hears elements of funk, punk, hard rock, disco, black and white pop, and more, in varying proportions. His touring bands, like Sly and the Family Stone, have included blacks and whites, women and men. His particular syntheses came to be known as "the Minneapolis sound," after the city where he was born and where he continued to make his home base (he opened Paisley Park Studios there in 1987). The confluences extend to his personal life: the unpronounceable symbol that he used in lieu of his name from 1993 to 2000 (when he became "the artist formerly known as Prince") reputedly represents a merging of the symbols for male and female.

The contradictions are present in his life and his music. He created a public persona so blatantly erotic at times that his music sparked the campaign to put parental advisory labels on recordings, but he has led an extremely reclusive private life, which has a strong spiritual dimension. (He claimed that God directed him to change his name to a symbol.) He has been an artist sufficiently drawn to the spotlight that he co-authored and starred in a quasi-autobiographical film (*Purple Rain*) and a musician who willingly and anonymously writes for, produces, and accompanies other artists. (Prince often uses aliases when he appears on others' recordings.) His music has been deeply rooted in the valued music of earlier generations: in a 1985 *Rolling Stone* interview he acknowledged artists as diverse as Stevie Wonder, Joni Mitchell, Miles Davis, Santana, and George Clinton. Yet his music has grown by absorbing

Frank Micelotta/Getty Images

Prince in an inspired moment during a 1985 performance.

numerous contemporary influences some distance from his musical roots—such as new wave—and by blending sounds produced by cutting-edge technology—for example, drum machines in the early eighties—with more conventional instruments, all of which he plays masterfully.

One measure of Prince's greatness as an artist has been his ability to reconcile the contrasting, even contradictory, elements of his musical life into a personal style that retains its identity despite its great stylistic and emotional range. Most songs exhibit qualities, particularly in the approach to texture and rhythm, that give evidence of a consistent musical conception, despite considerable differences from song to song. Listening to a Prince album can be like taking a course in rock history. Prince has mastered virtually all rock-era styles. For Prince, style mastery is not simply the ability to cover a style; he seldom does just that. Instead, he draws on disparate style elements and mixes them together to evoke a particular mood. For him, beat patterns, sounds, and rhythmic textures are like ingredients in a gourmet dish; they are used to flavor the song. More importantly, he also adds original ideas to create the nouvelle cuisine of eighties pop.

Prince is the son of musicians: jazz pianist John Nelson and singer Mattie Shaw. To escape his parents' troubled relationship (they divorced when Prince was 10), Prince sought refuge in music. By his teens, he had mastered not only the full array of rhythm instruments, but he had begun writing his own material and had learned production skills. Although not a child star, he was more precocious in some respects than Michael Jackson as both musician and producer. He played all the instruments on his first five albums and produced them as well. Stevie Wonder had pioneered this electronic version of the one-man band in the early seventies; Prince grew up with it.

He secured his first recording contract, which gave him total freedom in the studio, in 1977. The hits began coming two years later, beginning with "I Wanna Be Your Lover." The success of *Purple Rain* (1984) brought him commercial success (sales of 13 million units; three hit singles) and critical recognition (the soundtrack won three Grammy awards); in its wake, he became one of the few superstars of the eighties. His subsequent work continued to explore new territory. As he remarked in the *Rolling Stone* interview, "I always try to do something different and conquer new ground." He reached what many commentators feel was an artistic high point in 1987 with the release of the double album *Sign 'O' the Times*. We consider the title track following.

"Sign 'O' the Times," one of three singles from the album to chart, presents a bleak vision of contemporary life: gangs, AIDS, drugs, natural disasters, interlaced with anecdotal accounts of the fallout from drug use. The music is correspondingly bleak. The track begins with an intricate rhythm formed from a syncopated synthesizer riff and two electronically generated percussion sounds. This texture continues throughout the song. In the larger context of Prince's music, the repetition seems purposeful: it seems to suggest a despair that knows no end. In effect, it serves as a substitute for a standard rhythm section, and it is the accompaniment for Prince's vocal in the verse section. Other consistent elements include a strong backbeat and a synthesized bass riff, which often provides a response to the vocal line. Funky, jazz-influenced guitar figures, then sustained synthesizer chords, which provide the first harmonic change, highlight the buildup to the crux of the song: one finds happiness only in death. To underscore this difficult idea, the music returns to the empty sound of the opening—an abrupt and disconcerting return to reality. Only a blues-tinged guitar solo, again over the relentless synthesizer riffs and intricate percussion rhythms, provide relief from the misery portrayed in the lyric; this is interrupted by percussion sounds that evoke the fire of a machine gun. (Shades of U2?)

"Sign 'O' the Times," Prince (1987)

"Sign 'O' the Times" gains its impact as much from what's missing as from what's present. There is no rhythm guitar, no bass line, and no routine timekeeping on a drum set. There is no hook at the highpoint of the chorus to latch onto. There are no familiar chord progressions and few other clues that help us navigate through the song. The rhythms are complex, as in funk, but disciplined; the texture is spare, not dense. These features help create a sound world that is as vivid and powerful as a black and white photograph of a gray day in the ghetto.

## ♪ KEY FEATURES

### "Sign 'O' the Times," Prince (1987)

- Depressing lyric that describes ills of contemporary society
- Heavy reliance on synthesized sounds, in combination with voice and more conventional electric guitar style
- Spare texture, with only intermittent harmony and no routine timekeeping
- Absence of conventional rock band sounds: no rhythm guitar, electric bass, drum set
- Verse/chorus form that subverts the arrival at the chorus by subtracting instruments and returning to bleak opening texture

"Sign 'O' the Times" shows how Prince mixes disparate elements into a coherent and effective whole. From punk, via rap, he took realness: there is no fantasy, or escape, in this song. From funk, he took complex layered rhythms, which he pared down to convey the mood of the song. He adapts blues-influenced rock guitar to the context, supporting it unconventionally with the minimalist synthesizer riffs and rhythms.

Almost any other Prince song will sound quite different in many respects; that is one reason for his commercial and critical success. The most consistent elements are likely to be the mix of synthesized and conventional instruments; an open-sounding, intricately worked-out texture that puts a different spin on the conventional interplay between regular timekeeping and syncopated patterns; and a few distinctive features that help set the song apart from the sources that inspired it. In this song, it is the absence of bass and drum set and the rich sustained harmonies in the first part of the chorus. But the distinctive element can be anything: "U Got the Look," another top hit from *Sign 'O' the Times*, offers a radically transformed version of the 12-bar blues progression.

Even by rock standards, Prince is an eccentric. Still, the odd, often contradictory aspects of his personal life cannot obscure or diminish Prince's remarkable musical achievement: there has been no more multitalented, multidimensional musician in the history of rock.

## The Maturation of Black Pop

The more traditional black pop, the one that charted the ups and downs of romantic love, got a makeover in the eighties. A new generation of singers—among them Lionel Richie, Natalie Cole (daughter of the great Nat Cole), Whitney Houston, and Luther Vandross—were among the brightest stars of the eighties and nineties. Top acts from the past continued to make great music: Tina Turner, Marvin Gaye (until his untimely death in 1984), Aretha Franklin, Stevie Wonder, and Diana Ross stand out.

Tina Turner was 44 in 1984, when she scored her first number 1 hit as a solo act with "What's Love Got to Do with It." At 44, she was the most senior of the prominent black pop singers, but most of the others were not far behind. Of the singers just mentioned, only Whitney Houston was not yet 30 in 1984. By contrast, the Shirelles were still in their teens when they first hit the charts, and Diana Ross had just turned 20 when the Supremes' "Where Did Our Love Go" reached number 1 on the pop charts.

Not surprisingly, these artists sang about love in a more mature and real way than the black pop artists from the sixties usually did. They and their audience had grown up in the intervening years; in most cases, the tone of the lyrics connected more directly to the mature black romantic music of the early seventies, most notably the music of Roberta Flack and Bill Withers, than it did to the bright-eyed, more innocent lyrics of sixties black pop.

The music is comparably more mature. In the songs of the early sixties girl groups and early Motown recordings, there is a sense of discovery; the occasional rough edges in conception and production evidence that it is hard to get everything right when you're inventing a dramatically new style and sound. By contrast, the black pop of the eighties is exquisitely produced, not only because of the improved technology but also because of the improved skill of the recording engineers and producers. And like the pop of Michael Jackson and others, the songs make use of the new rhythms and synthesized sounds of the late seventies and eighties.

However, these are songs about love—or more accurately, about the problems of relationships— and the singers deliver them in a manner that makes the lyrics credible.

For example, in the video of "What's Love Got to Do with It," Tina Turner alternates between simply standing and singing and walking. Her walk is stylish and in the rhythm of the song, but it is light years away from the elaborate dance numbers seen in "Thriller." And the song is not in the service of a larger message that is evident only when the video is viewed. Here, the video simply presents an enhanced version of the song; the song is the defining element.

## Musical Features of the New Black Pop

The sound of the eighties black pop resulted mainly from two significant changes: the use of synthesized sounds to replace most, if not all, of the traditional instruments, and more adventurous rhythms. The sumptuous backgrounds that were so much a part of the sound of later doo-wop, Motown, Philadelphia, and Barry White are part of this updated black pop sound. The difference is that producers use electronic analogues to the strings, horns, and even rhythm instruments. Their function is much the same, but the sounds are new. This fresh sound palette gives the music a more contemporary flavor.

The other major change had to do with rhythm. By the beginning of the eighties, 16-beat rhythms were the norm throughout much rock-era music, and especially black music: we hear these more active rhythms in all of the songs discussed in this and the previous chapters and in much of the music in the subsequent chapters. At comparable tempos, 16-beat rhythms offer many more opportunities for rhythmic play than rock rhythm, simply because there are so many more combinations of sound and silence. When applied to a Motown-style conception of rhythmic texture, the results are liberating.

Recall that one of the distinctive features of Motown songs was subtle timekeeping, except for a strong backbeat. Generally, only the drummer (and conga player, if present) kept the rock rhythm; no instrument marked the beat. In the black pop of the eighties, timekeeping became not only more active, but also often more implicit. Any regular timekeeping was generally in the background, and at times it was dispensed with altogether. The dominant rhythms moved either much slower (for instance, sustained chords) or faster than the beat; the faster rhythms typically played against the beat, with irregular patterns or syncopations.

In this connection, it is worth noting the impact of reggae on this new kind of rhythmic freedom. Recall that the black pop and R&B of the late fifties and early sixties was a major influence on Jamaican music in the sixties, which developed into reggae by the end of the decade. The characteristic sound of reggae comes largely from the off-beat rhythms in the middle of the texture and the free bass line underneath. In the late seventies and eighties, both black and white acts wove reggae rhythms into other styles. Its impact on black music can be heard in such songs as Marvin Gaye's "Sexual Healing" (1982) and Tina Turner's "What's Love Got to Do with It" (1984). With this development, the exchange between black pop and Jamaican music has come full circle, much as Ray Charles's fusion of gospel and blues closed the connection begun by Thomas A. Dorsey/Georgia Tom. We hear the influence of reggae in "What's Love Got to Do with It."

## Tina Turner

If anyone was entitled to be cynical about love, it would be Tina Turner (born Annie Mae Bullock, 1939?). In 1956, as a young woman still in her teens, she connected with Ike Turner, eight years her senior and already a music business veteran. (Recall that he was the musician behind the seminal "Rocket 88," which came out under Jackie Brenston's name in 1951.) The connection soon became personal as well as professional: they married in 1962, and for more than a decade, they prospered professionally as the Ike and Tina Turner Revue; they had a huge hit in 1971 with a cover of CCR's "Proud Mary."

However, for much of their relationship, Ike abused Tina emotionally and physically. The abuse grew worse as their career declined; Ike's alleged drug use and almost paranoid distrust of outside management was a main factor in their career decline. Their professional relationship complicated any personal breakup. When she finally broke free of Turner—in the middle of a tour—she also broke contractual obligations. Because of this, the divorce settlement devastated her financially; she retained only her name.

It took Tina the better part of a decade to get her solo career on track. Her break came in 1983, when she covered Al Green's "Let's Stay Together" for B.E.F. (British Electric Foundation), the production side of a synth-pop group doing some serious soul searching. (B.E.F. would eventually record with not only Turner but also Chaka Khan, Mavis Staples, and other major black artists.) The next year saw the release of *Private Dancer*, an album that included "What's Love Got to Do with It" among its three charting singles. The song would win three Grammys the following year.

Turner's song and her singing are in tune with each other. Both project an embittered view of love: any excitement found in the physical aspects of a relationship is tempered by the foreknowledge that the relationship will never mature into love. She sings from the heart: close to two decades of pain spill out in her soulful singing.

"What's Love Got to Do with It," Tina Turner (1984)

The song uses the verse/chorus template as a point of departure: the verse builds inexorably to a magnetic hook, which Turner's gritty voice invests with deep feeling. By contrast, the musical setting is muted—almost arid. Synthesizer sounds are prominent: sustained synthesizer chords and obbligatos. The rhythm shows the influence of reggae in the persistent rebound pattern on the off-beat, the open texture, and a free-roaming bass in the chorus. The accompaniment never matches the intensity of Turner's singing; it is almost as if the accompaniment is indifferent to her pain. This has the effect of casting Turner's pain into relief: in the song, she grieves alone.

Turner's song blends the urgency of soul singing with an accompaniment that connects directly back to Motown. The next example surrounds one of the great black pop voices of the late twentieth century in a rich, and synth-rich, setting.

## Luther Vandross

Like so many black pop singers, Luther Vandross (1951–2005) grew up singing gospel. He began his career largely out of the limelight, composing jingles and doing session work as a backup singer for numerous top acts. A guest appearance on an album by Change, *The Glow of Love* (1980), led to a recording contract and a jumpstart

---

### ♪ KEY FEATURES

**"What's Love Got to Do with It," Tina Turner (1984)**

- Lyric speaks directly and honestly about the hurt of a broken heart
- Turner's singing is comparably direct; it makes the lyric emotionally credible
- Instrumental accompaniment dominated by synthesized sounds
- Rhythm features open texture with light rock-rhythm timekeeping, more active rhythms darting in and out, and reggae-influenced rebound off-beat

---

to a solo career. By the middle of the decade, he had become one of the most prominent of the new generation of black pop singers.

"Don't Want to Be a Fool," a track from his successful 1991 album, *Power of Love*, continues the evolution of the black pop style that began with Motown and continued through the seventies. The song updates form, rhythm, and sound, while retaining its most timeless elements: lyrics about love, set to an appealing melody and sung by a singer with a rich, pleasing voice.

"Don't Want to Be a Fool" is a more expansive version of a classic Motown song form: a verse/chorus format where the first part of the chorus builds to the hook, plus an intense bridge that replaces the final verse. There are no real surprises in the form, except perhaps that the form itself continues to be viable after over twenty-five years. However, it unfolds more slowly than typical Motown songs: once through the form takes over 4 minutes.

The rhythmic texture of "Don't Want to Be a Fool" has its roots in the black pop of the sixties but also evidences the greater rhythmic complexity of post-1980 music. There is a strong backbeat and a discreet rock beat most of the time. Other rhythms, mostly at 16-beat speed, dance over this basic backdrop; in particular, the bass line is free and very syncopated.

The introduction and the first phrase of the verse have almost no timekeeping from percussion instruments; we hear mainly electronic keyboards and Luther's voice. Things get busier as the song builds to the refrain. By the refrain, the fast rhythm is present but spread out among several different percussion sounds. The bass line moves occasionally in these quicker rhythms, but there is never a time when the 16-beat rhythm is hammered out, as it so often is in rap and dance music. Indeed, the heart of the song—Luther's vocal, the background vocals, the background instrumental harmony and melodic riffs—are in the eight-beat rhythm of a rock song for most of the song.

"Don't Want to Be a Fool," Luther Vandross (1991)

This combination of the two rhythmic levels—eight- and 16-beat rhythms—plus the more implicit approach to timekeeping seem to match the mood of the song better than the more explicit, active rhythms of dance music. It would be harder to focus on the words and the story they're telling if they had to compete with insistent dance rhythms.

We can hear this rhythmic texture as a more sophisticated continuation of the rhythms heard in the black pop of the sixties and seventies. Recall that one of

Motown's innovations was a more implicit approach to rock and shuffle rhythms: the bass was strong, but free, while the mid-range timekeeping was very much in the background: the song still had a great beat, but rhythm did not overpower the melody and rich accompaniment. The rhythms heard in "Don't Want to Be a Fool" take this innovation several steps beyond. Such a sound was possible only in the eighties, after the textural possibilities of the new 16-beat rhythms had been thoroughly assimilated.

"Don't Want to Be a Fool" also updates the sound world of rock-era black pop. A classic Motown song had a full orchestra behind the singer(s): rhythm section, horns, and strings. Vandross and bassist Marcus Miller (b. 1959), who collaborated with Vandross on this song, not only create electronic counterparts to most of the conventional instrumental sounds (such as the sustained chords that sound like strings, the shaker-like percussion sounds in the background), but also add an array of new timbres (for example, bell-like timbres). They provide evidence of the way in which electronic sound generation and sampling have enriched the sound world of contemporary popular music.

---

♪ **KEY FEATURES**

**"Don't Want to Be a Fool," Luther Vandross (1991)**
- A song about love, in words, melody, and vocal style
- Active, often implicit rhythms update the open rhythmic texture of Motown
- Rich accompaniment: strong, active bass line; discreet percussion sounds; backup vocals; and synthesized counterparts to the strings and horns of pre-digital black pop
- Form follows well-established black-pop model as it expands it

---

## The Persistence of Love

Songs such as "What's Love Got to Do with It" and "Don't Want to Be a Fool" continue black pop's romance with romance. It dates back to the very beginnings of the rock era, with the first doo-wop songs from the late forties. The constants that have informed this music throughout its history have been not only the focus on love, but gospel-tinged vocalists singing tuneful melodies with rich accompaniments that featured harmonies typically found in pre-rock pop.

Among the reasons for this continuity is the strong connection with gospel music: so many of the black pop stars came out of the gospel tradition. The correspondences in the message of the words and the musical means to support it continued through the seventies. In fact, gospel acts occasionally crossed over to the pop charts in the years around 1970: "Oh Happy Day" was a surprise number 4 hit for the Edwin Hawkins Singers in 1969, and the Staples Singers' "I'll Take You There" topped the charts in 1972.

Another reason might have been the relative novelty in black music of connecting not only the song but also the singer to romance. Ever since Bing Crosby began to croon into a microphone, audiences, or at least those of the opposite sex, personified their relationship with the singer: they could imagine Crosby and other crooners singing to them alone, and meaning it. Frank Sinatra would soon become the first pop-singing heartthrob; thousands of adoring fans swooned during his performances, much as they would for Elvis fifteen years later. Sinatra, Crosby, and several other singers parlayed their pop success into film careers; even Fred Astaire, in appearance an extremely unlikely leading man, succeeded in winning the affection of Ginger Rogers, at least on the screen.

By contrast, Ethel Waters, the top black pop singer, could sing "my man and I ain't together" (from Harold Arlen's bluesy standard "Stormy Weather") to Cotton Club audiences and on disc, but her most significant film role before 1950 came as Petunia (!) in the 1943 all-black film *Cabin in the Sky*. In it, she sings another great pop standard, "Taking a Chance on Love," to Eddie Anderson, who would later become famous as Jack Benny's servant Rochester. She is dressed dowdily, and simply rolls her eyes back and forth as she sings. The song and the singing are great, the message is romantic, but their interaction is anything but romantic. Indeed, the scene reminds contemporary viewers that minstrelsy was not ancient history in 1943; Hollywood would not portray blacks romantically. In the late forties and fifties, Nat Cole thrilled black and white audiences with beautiful love songs like "Unforgettable." but his appeal was limited to his voice, at least among white audiences.

The personification of romantic song in popular music began to transcend race in the sixties, as we noted in Chapter 6. This wholesale shift in attitude was evident by the time Tina Turner recorded "What's Love Got to Do with It." Turner's sex appeal was certainly not delimited by her ethnicity in North America, and even more in Europe, where she has had an ardent fan base (and where she currently resides): her video won MTV's Best Female Video Award in 1985.

By the end of the century, race and ethnic heritage were a complete non-issue in romantic music, as we note in a discussion of the pop divas of the 1990s and 2000s.

# The Divas

*Diva* is the feminine form of the Latin word for God or God-like; it shares a common etymology with *divine*. *Diva* came into English through Italian, where it identifies a female opera singer performing a leading role. More recently, it has come to refer to female pop singing stars, and even more generally, to any woman with star quality (and too often the attitude seems to be part of the baggage).

## The Emergence of the Divas

In 1998 VH1 sponsored its inaugural Divas concert, an all-star event presented to raise funds for the station's "Save the Music" foundation. The concert brought together two rock-era queens—Aretha Franklin (the queen of soul) and Gloria Estefan (the queen of Latin pop)—and three rising stars: Mariah Carey, Céline Dion, and Shania Twain. The Divas concert series ran for six more years; the last concert took place in 2004. The format remained much the same: bring together established stars and new talent; younger invitees included Christina Aguilera, Mary J. Blige, Faith Hill, Jewel, Beyoncé, Brandy, Shakira, and Jessica Simpson.

These and other young female performers, such as Alicia Keys, Jennifer Lopez, and Britney Spears, formed a new generation of pop singers. Their numbers show Madonna's enormous impact; it is clear that her unprecedented commercial success paved the way for their entry into the music business. Not surprisingly, in light of this connection, image has been as important as sound. Most look as good as they sing, and all are portrayed as glamorous on album covers and in the media. A few—for example, Britney Spears, Jennifer Lopez—enjoy a tabloid-driven celebrity apart from their music.

The diva label was not simply show-business hype: for the most part, they are skilled singers with pleasant, accessible voices and, in some cases, distinctive, even unique, vocal abilities. For example, Mariah Carey's vocal range is more than twice that of a typical pop singer (her songs have often included extensive reminders of this fact), and the fluency of Christina Aguilera's melismatic singing deserves comparison with not only great black singers like Aretha but also opera singers.

They are a diverse group: Shania Twain and Céline Dion are Canadian. Twain took the name Shania, an Ojibwa word, to affirm her connection with Native Americans: her stepfather is a full-blooded member of the nation. Dion is from French-speaking Canada. Shakira is Colombian. Jennifer Lopez is a child of Puerto Rican parents. Christina Aguilera's father is from Ecuador. Beyoncé, Mary J. Blige, and Brandy are black; Mariah Carey has white, black, and Latino blood. Several gravitated toward pop from their "home" styles: Twain and Hill began as country singers; Dion's first songs were in French; Alicia Keys, Beyoncé, and Mary J. Blige have strong R&B roots.

Their common ground extends beyond gender, appearance, success, and on-stage compatibility. They and their producers have incorporated the defining elements of eighties/nineties pop into their music. Their music may retain features of their home style—Jennifer Lopez singing in Spanish, rapper Jay-Z on a Beyoncé track, steel guitar in a Faith Hill song. Still, the use of rich textures with synthesized instruments and active rhythms in support of a tuneful melody that sets a lyric about love brings much of their music into the pop middle ground. Their chart success evidences that.

It is fitting that Aretha was one of the five artists invited to perform at the first Divas concert. Clearly, she was the dominant musical personality, although she only sang with others, and she has been the dominant influence on the vocal style of many of the younger divas—black, white, or Latina. Indeed, the prevailing vocal style of these performers might be described as Aretha-lite.

Geiger Kraig/Corbis Sygma

Christina Aguilera performing in Florida, September 2000.

Her influence is evident in the singers' diction, which has something of the intonation and cadence of black speech; in the vocal quality, typically a more restrained echo of her soulful sound; and in the forms of expressive nuance, especially the use of melisma. Each has personalized her style to some degree, but most share a connection to the more soulful black vocal style of the sixties and beyond, which Aretha's singing epitomizes. The young divas may have modeled their image and performance style after Madonna, but their musical and vocal conception derives most directly from Aretha and her peers. We hear evidence of both influence and individuality in Christina Aguilera's hit, "What a Girl Wants."

## Christina Aguilera: "What a Girl Wants"

If *American Bandstand* was required after-school viewing for teens in the late fifties, then the *Mickey Mouse Club* was the must-watch show for their younger siblings. Both shows aired on ABC every afternoon. The *Mickey Mouse Club* was one of Walt Disney Productions' first excursions into television programming. The show featured two older men guiding a group of perky kids through an hour of kids' news, singing, dancing, cartoons, and stories. All sported the mouse-eared beanies that were as required an accessory for pre-teens as coonskin caps had been a few years previously (the Davy Crockett fad) and that a single white sequined glove would be for Michael Jackson fans in the early eighties. The show ran from 1955 to 1959, when Disney elected to cancel it.

In 1989, thirty years after its initial cancellation, the Disney Corporation revived the show for a second time. (The first attempt, which went on the air in 1977, was a failure.) This time the show aired on the Disney Channel, a premium cable channel that commenced in 1983. This would prove to be the longest-running version of the show; *MMC*, as it was called, would air for seven seasons. It would also help launch the careers of three top pop acts: the male vocal group 'N Sync and two pop divas, Britney Spears and Christina Aguilera.

By the time Christina Aguilera (b. 1980) joined the *Mickey Mouse Club* in 1992, she had been an active performer for half of her life. By 6, she was performing in talent shows around Pittsburgh, where she grew up; she competed on *Star Search* at 9. Aguilera's star rose quickly. In 1998, she was chosen to sing "Reflection" for the animated Disney feature *Mulan*; this led to the release of her self-titled first album, which quickly went to the top of the album charts in 1999; so did "Genie in a Bottle" and "What a Girl Wants"—the top two singles from the album.

"What a Girl Wants" puts a contemporary sheen on the well-established rock-era black pop style even as it showcases Aguilera's considerable vocal ability. The lyrics impart a postfeminist flavor to a discussion of love: Aguilera asks her significant other to give her some space as she looks around (but never touches). That she asks for it and that he assents to her request show that, in song at least, relationships should offer equal opportunity to both parties.

"What a Girl Wants," Christina Aguilera (1999)

The story unfolds in typical fashion: a series of verses build smoothly to a catchy chorus with a can't-miss hook. The melody unfolds in smooth undulations, and at a pace that allows the words to be easily understood; Aguilera saves most of her vocal acrobatics for interludes and obbligato flights during the chorus.

Although the song is based on the familiar verse/chorus model, "What a Girl Wants" is anything but formulaic. From the introduction that features just Aguilera and percussion sounds through the pseudo-classical synthesizer interlude through the chorus that never really ends (to suggest that Aguilera's looking-but-not-touching will not stop anytime soon?), the song evidences the considerable skills of songwriter-producer Guy Roche, who co-wrote the song with Shelley Peiken. Both have supplied numerous hits for Aguilera and other leading pop acts.

Roche created a rich setting for Aguilera's singing: it combines backup vocals plus synthesized percussive and pitched sounds, with subtle colors added via conventional instruments: the strummed acoustic guitar gives warmth to the largely synthesized accompaniment.

The rhythms of "What a Girl Wants" belong to the new century; they show the influence of post-Motown black pop and dance music. From the pop of the eighties, it takes the largely implicit beat keeping and highly syncopated patterns; its especially active rhythms show the influence of dance music. The basic tempo of the song, which we sense from the alternation of bass note and backbeat, is quite slow: about 75 beats per minute, or just over half the speed of a disco track or rock song. In the verse, both Aguilera's vocal and the strummed guitar move at 16-beat speed. The dance music influence becomes most evident in the rhythms that move twice this fast: that is, eight times as fast as the beat. These especially animated rhythms include synthesizer noodles, percussion bursts, and most spectacularly, Aguilera's flawless melismas, which are the contemporary pop counterpart to not only the melismatic flourishes of Aretha Franklin, Patti LaBelle, and other top black singers but also the florid embellishments heard in operatic arias for sopranos. (Especially in these moments, Aguilera earns her diva status.)

The stylized melismas are one dimension of Aguilera's black-influenced vocal style. Her delivery of the verse sounds black, or at least beige; it is quite different in inflection and intonation from her everyday speech, as heard in television interviews, for example. The basic quality is rich and resonant, although not as gritty as Aretha or Tina Turner. The inflection of the vocal line—for instance, the occasional bluesy bent note—also betrays black influence.

Especially when considered in the context of the pop music landscape at the turn of the century, Aguilera's vocal sound and style seem not so much a case of Aguilera deliberately trying to sound black as singing in the prevailing popular style. Pop singing, like so many other aspects of the style, evidences the profound influence and the continuing evolution of the black pop tradition that took shape in the early sixties. By the end of the century, it was so thoroughly assimilated that the music of black, Latino, and white pop performers represented a smooth stylistic continuum, rather than several distinct styles.

The infusion of dance rhythms into pop virtually demands movement on video and in live performance. With Michael Jackson as the quintessential role model, elaborate choreography became the norm in music videos; the video of "What a Girl Wants" is typical in this respect. This sets up a curious dissonance between the song's subject and its presentation. The lyrics read like an intimate conversation. If they had been set to music in the sixties or seventies, the song would probably have been a slow rock ballad. And although there are brief scenes where Aguilera lies in the lap of her video heartthrob, the bulk of the video features her dancing with her crew.

> ♪ **KEY FEATURES**
>
> **"What a Girl Wants," Christina Aguilera (1999)**
> - Lyric: freedom and understanding in a relationship from a feminine perspective
> - Expanded but familiar verse/chorus form with appealing title-phrase hook
> - Rich setting with multiple percussion part, synthesized riffs and sustained chords, and strummed guitar, all behind lead and backup vocals
> - Complex, syncopated rhythmic texture, with a slow-moving beat overlaid with extremely active (8 times beat speed) rhythms
> - Aguilera's black-influenced vocal includes fluent, flawless melismas: virtuoso pop singing

The dissonance becomes clear if we think of singing in popular music as a more urgent and compelling form of speech. The great women singers, from Bessie Smith and Billie Holiday through Aretha Franklin and Tina Turner, conveyed their feelings mainly through their voices. They stood and sang their songs; vigorous movement wasn't necessary to get the message across. However, the conventions of pop and music videos virtually preclude such a presentation; there has to be activity, especially when the rhythms of the song all but require it. The song is effective in spite of the conflict between the message of the lyrics and the musical setting, rather than because of it.

Aguilera and the numerous other young divas were a commanding presence in pop music at the end of the twentieth century and the beginning of the twenty-first. They joined an earlier generation of stars that included Whitney Houston and Janet and La Toya Jackson. No group of pop performers was more frequently heard or was more in the public eye. They reaped the fruit of the efforts of Madonna and the many other women who worked to break down the gender barrier in popular music. Their success evidenced the fact that the pop music world was a level playing field with respect to race and gender.

# Beyond Rock: The Legacy of Motown

The early eighties ushered in a new generation of pop stars. In many respects, their music was dramatically different from the music of the previous decade. Six qualities distinguish it:

- *It made gender, race, and sexual preference a non-issue.* During the eighties, its leading acts were Michael Jackson, Prince, and Madonna. None of them are heterosexual, white males. Other successful performers during that decade included Boy George, Cyndi Lauper, and Tina Turner.

- *It exploited new media resources.* Michael Jackson was not the first to make music videos, but he raised the music video to an art form. Video and film were essential in boosting both Prince and Madonna to superstardom; the three set the tone for the pop music videos of the next decades.

- *It brought back the multifaceted entertainer.* It was no longer enough to be just a good singer or musician; one had to be able to move well, although no one topped Michael Jackson in skill or imagination. Conversely, those who could present themselves well, dance expressively, and use the music video as a new meaningful medium (think Madonna) could achieve stardom with more limited vocal ability.

- *It was a musical melting pot.* Although the new pop of the eighties and beyond connects most directly to the black pop tradition of the sixties and seventies, the music was certainly open to other influences: disco, punk, reggae, funk, Latin music, and, more recently, dance music and rap.

- *Synthesizers played an increasingly important role in the sound of the music.* Some replaced guitars, basses, and conventional keyboards as the main sources of harmony; synthesized percussion sounds enriched, or even replaced, drum kits and other acoustic instruments; and sustained synth sounds put a lot of string players out of work.

- *It has been extraordinarily popular.* Michael Jackson's *Thriller* album easily surpassed the sales of the previous best-selling album. Prince and Madonna also had impressive sales figures. As rock critic Robert Christgau pointed out, the sheer volume of sales was part of its significance.

Precisely because its artists drew from so many sources, there has been no single "middle-ground" style. It has not been defined by a distinctive kind of beat keeping, like punk; or a rhythmic feel, like funk; or a special sound quality, like the distortion of heavy metal. Indeed, all three are used in middle-ground music: the opening of Prince's "When Doves Cry" or Eddie Van Halen's solo in Michael Jackson's "Beat It" are familiar examples of metal-style guitar playing.

Instead, it was a set of principles that defined the music that topped the charts during the eighties. The songs typically have intelligible lyrics that tell a story— usually about love or its absence or about a slice of life. They are set to a singable melody. The melody in turn is imbedded in a rich, riff-laden texture; most layers—if not all—are played on synthesizers. The songs typically have a good beat—easy to find and danceable, neither too monotonous nor too ambiguous.

This set of principles is, more than anything else, an updated version of the Motown sound. The lyrics are more worldly, the rhythms are more complex and usually based on the more active 16-beat rhythms, and synthesizers replace many of the conventional instruments. Novel elements, most notably rap, give this more recent music a different sound. Still, the basic approach is clearly the same.

The Motown middle ground connection extends beyond the music. The elaborate movement and dance made possible by the music video production process upgrade the choreography of the Motown acts, and Motown's pyramid-like creative structure evolved into the elaborate production of post-eighties pop.

Michael Jackson is the direct link between the two traditions: as a member of the Jackson 5, he was part of the last great act in Motown's heyday. As a solo performer in the late seventies and early eighties, he helped define the new pop middle ground musically, revive the all-around performer, and establish the music video as a new, integrated mode of expression. Moreover, his dancing raised the bar to a virtually unattainable height. His growth as an artist parallels the evolution and transformation of the Motown paradigm into the new pop of the eighties.

Berry Gordy's vision was a black pop style whose appeal transcended the black community. One branch of its legacy was the post-eighties pop middle ground marked out by Michael Jackson, which continues to flourish in the music of women and men of many races and ethnic heritages. Motown was not a force for social change during the sixties drive for civil rights; however, the fact of Motown—the enduring appeal and popularity of the music—has helped bring us to a musical world where the boundaries between black and white—and Hispanic—are all but invisible, and inaudible. This is in turn both cause and consequence of more open attitudes with regard to race and gender, not only in music but in society.

This openness, which we take for granted at the beginning of the twenty-first century, was unthinkable half a century earlier. Nat Cole was the first black performer to host a network television show. It would air for only thirteen months, from November 1956 to December 1957, because NBC could not convince potential sponsors to advertise their products on a show headlined by a black man. Today, blacks and Hispanics not only attract sponsors but also help sell their products. This stream of rock-era music, from Motown to the divas, has helped bring us to this far more open society.

### Terms to Remember

| | |
|---|---|
| MTV | DOR (dance-oriented rock) |

### Applying Chapter Concepts

1. Our discussion of Prince necessarily provided only a hint of the range of Prince's music. Explore the range of styles and sounds present in his music by comparing four or five contrasting songs released between 1984 and 1990. Your comparison should include, but not be limited to, the following categories:

   a. Style beat used, and the way in which it is presented
   b. Instruments used
   c. Basic form
   d. Connection that you hear between the lyric and the overall mood of the song

2. Explore contemporary pop in more depth by surveying the music of one or more male pop acts, such as 'N Sync, the Backstreet Boys, or Ricky Martin. Seek out similarities and differences between the musical approach of these acts vis-à-vis the divas. Do any seem to be gender related?

19

# Renewing Rock
## Rock Since 1980

Ethiopia is a country in northeast Africa. The vast majority of its citizens depend on farming for their livelihood. In the seventies, the Soviet-backed government instituted a land-reform program that limited the acreage that individuals could farm. In 1984, drought, overcultivation, and the government's poorly conceived and ineptly executed marketing program created a famine that devastated the country.

British journalist Michael Buerk, aided by Kenyan cameraman and journalist Mohammed Amin, traveled to Ethiopia in the fall of 1984. On October 24, the BBC broadcast a 7-minute film that showed thousands of people dying from starvation. The other major news agencies quickly picked up the film. Over a billion people around the world soon saw Buerk and Amin's account of the Ethiopian famine.

## The Relevance of Rock

Among those who saw Buerk's broadcast was Bob Geldof (b. 1954), the lead singer with the Irish new wave band the Boomtown Rats. Geldof was so moved that he resolved to organize a musical event to raise money for famine relief and to raise people's awareness of the crisis; he would call his project Band Aid. He enlisted the help of Midge Ure (born James Ure, 1953), a member of Ultravox, another U.K. new wave band. Together they wrote the song "Do They Know It's Christmas?"; then they recruited an all-star cast to perform it and obtained 24 hours of free studio time to record it. Among the guest performers on the recording were Paul McCartney, Bono, Sting, Boy George, and Phil Collins. The recording was released on December 15, less than two months after Geldof viewed Buerk's broadcast. It would become the best-selling single in the United Kingdom. Geldof donated all the revenues from its sale to assist the Ethiopian people through the Band Aid Trust, which he formed for that purpose.

Around the time "Do They Know It's Christmas?" was released in Great Britain another equally bleak news report of the famine aired in the United States. After viewing the news report, Harry Belafonte (b. 1927)—a singer and actor who had parlayed his spectacular success as a calypso singer in the fifties into a long and distinguished career in entertainment—called his manager Ken Kragen, who also managed several other top entertainment stars, about organizing a project for famine relief. Within short order,

Lionel Richie, Stevie Wonder, and Michael Jackson were on board; Jackson and Richie wrote the song "We Are the World." The principals scheduled a recording session right after the American Music Awards ceremony. An all-star cast—including Paul Simon, Tina Turner, Diana Ross, Willie Nelson, Bruce Springsteen, Bob Dylan, and Ray Charles—recorded the song on January 28, 1985; Quincy Jones, who included Jackson's *Thriller* album among his numerous significant credits, produced the session. The single came out in March. On Good Friday (April 5 that year), 5,000 radio stations played the song simultaneously. The single and an album spun off from the single both went multiplatinum. The project, called USA (United Support of Artists) for Africa, raised over $50 million for famine relief.

Capitalizing on the goodwill generated by the Band Aid project, Geldof organized Live Aid, the most massive fund-raising event in the history of the music business. His idea was to create a "global jukebox" with broadcasts of concerts from stadiums in London and Philadelphia. The concerts—over 22 hours between the two venues—and live performances from other venues throughout the world—for example, Moscow, Sydney, the Hague—would be broadcast throughout the world via satellite. The roster of acts performing at the multiple venues reads like a Who's Who of rock. Live Aid, performed July 13, 1985, drew a worldwide audience estimated at over 1 billion viewers; at one point during the broadcast, Billy Connolly, a Scottish comedian and actor who was opening for Elton John, announced that he had been informed that 95 percent of the world's television sets were watching the event. Live Aid eventually raised over $260 million for famine relief in Africa. Even more important, the events and the recordings called attention to the plight in Africa; shipments of grain surpluses from the United States and elsewhere soon alleviated the suffering in Ethiopia.

These events and others like them (such as Farm Aid) put the "we" back in rock. In the sixties, rock had defined itself as a "we" music: first in the bands themselves (names like the Beatles, the Beach Boys, the Who, the Rolling Stones gave bands a collective identity), then in the bond between music and audience. The "we" in rock was a generation that didn't trust anyone over 30. The seventies, by contrast, have been dubbed as the "me" decade: in music, self-involvement (what about me?) and the pursuit of success seemed to negate the sense of community created in the sixties. There was no Woodstock in the seventies.

The massive fund-raising events of the eighties signaled the return of rock's conscience, but with a huge difference. In the sixties, rock gave voice to a generational revolution. It provided the soundtrack for an assault on the establishment, and by overthrowing the pop music establishment, it led by example. In the eighties, rock *was* the establishment, the dominant segment of the music industry. As a result, it could leverage the celebrity of its artists in projects that served a greater good. In the eighties, "we" in rock not only included the musicians, the music industry, and the audience, but also those whom they sought to help. The success of their efforts was a strong signal of the enormous cultural presence of rock-era music in the latter part of the twentieth century.

The sense of purpose that these events symbolized was one sign of a renewal in rock. Some of the most memorable music of the decade shone a light on contemporary problems; we will hear songs about the problems of Vietnam War veterans and the devastation in Africa. Other signals were more strictly musical. The energy and attitude of punk gradually filtered into other rock styles. Synthesizers became more integral to the sound world of rock. A new generation of virtuoso guitarists sparked a heavy metal renaissance; the style would grow in range, significance, and popularity. Old and new stars would revive the heart of rock and roll, often by infusing new elements into it. We consider all of these developments in our survey of music by the Police, Van Halen, Bruce Springsteen, U2, Metallica, and the Dave Matthews Band.

# A New Pop Rock: Mainstreaming Reggae and Punk

From the start, rock has been a musical melting pot. It has seamlessly absorbed markedly different musical styles and produced vital new music; during the sixties alone rock absorbed folk, pop, classical music, jazz, Latin music, musical theater, and traditional country. It made no difference whether a style began on the opposite side of the cultural fence: rock assimilated it. Rock's openness to outside influences and sources, regardless of provenance, has been one of its hallmarks.

As rock became the dominant popular music, the dynamic between inside and outside changed. It was no longer rock and non-rock styles coming together, but mainstream and non-mainstream styles. In the seventies, both punk and reggae began outside the mainstream—reggae mainly because of geography and culture, punk by choice. That rock would eventually assimilate and transform both styles was all but inevitable; it occurred in the years around 1980. In both cases, a new generation of rock musicians borrowed musical features from punk and reggae. As they recontextualized them, they often divorced the music from its original message. Particularly in the case of punk, there are songs that clearly betray the influence of punk but whose message perverts the original intent of the music. We explore the impact of reggae and punk on mainstream rock in songs by the Police and Van Halen.

## Reggatta de Blanc: The Police

"Reggatta de blanc" translates as "white reggae." *Reggatta de Blanc* (1979) was the title of the second album by the Police. With this title, the group positioned themselves in the musical world of the late seventies.

For almost all of their decade-long career together, the Police was a trio: drummer Stewart Copeland (b. 1952), bassist and lead singer Sting (born Gordon Sumner, 1951), and guitarist Andy Summers (b. 1942). Although linked with the new wave movement in Great Britain, the group traced a different trajectory from the start. At the time the group formed in early 1977, its members were 24, 25, and 34—long in the tooth by punk standards. In particular, Andy Summers was an experienced musician whose credits included a stint with Eric Burdon and the New Animals as well as extensive session work in the early seventies. In part because of their wide-ranging backgrounds, their career as the Police lasted well into the eighties, peaking during the early eighties, well after the first wave of punk and new wave bands gained notoriety and commercial success. Each member has enjoyed success since they dissolved the band in 1986: Sting as a solo artist, and Copeland and Summers mainly in film scoring.

Lynn Goldsmith/Corbis

The Police, in 1982. From left to right: Stewart Copeland, Sting, and Andy Summers. Their blond hair came from a bottle; early in their career, they were asked to dye their hair for a TV commercial.

The pared-down, reggae-influenced style that served them so well throughout their time together was a choice, one that enabled them to project the words effortlessly and explore subtle nuances in rhythm and sound. Although linked to the punk and new wave movement, their music is different temperamentally from both. For them, reggae was not a way to project a political message, as it was with the Clash, but a point of departure for a new pop style.

In their first recordings, the reggae elements are distinct: in "Roxanne," a hit single from their first album, the off-beat bass and repeated guitar chords connect directly to the Jamaican music. However, they quickly transformed the reggae elements into a new approach—one that captured the airy texture and floating rhythms of reggae without precisely replicating its rhythmic features. We hear this sound in a 1980 recording, "Don't Stand So Close to Me."

Before forming the Police, Sting was the British equivalent of a high school English teacher. His background in literature helps explain the prominence of the lyrics in the songs of the Police; his prior teaching experience certainly sheds some light on the subject of the song. Much later, Sting claimed the experience described in the lyric was not autobiographical, although he was a young man when he taught secondary school. If in fact he were not dissembling, he almost certainly would have

"Don't Stand So Close to Me," the Police (1980)

witnessed it happen to a colleague. Certainly, he found it all too easy to imagine the tensions felt by the teacher who is the protagonist in the lyric.

Rather than relating a story, Sting's lyric simply describes a dilemma. It is deliberately inconclusive; he leaves it to our imagination to determine whether lust or honor wins out. The musical setting connects to this tension in numerous ways— some obvious and some more subtle. The obvious ones include the suspenseful opening and the voiceless final statement of the verse: instead of another installment of the lyric, where we would certainly learn which path the teacher and student took, we hear synthesized washes of sound.

The more subtle touches include the harmony and the rhythm. The harmony oscillates between two keys: one in the verse and the other in the chorus. Neither resolves conclusively; the end of the song leaves listeners hanging—in this respect, it's a musical analogue to the teacher's emotions. The rhythmic texture uses reggae-inspired rhythms to convey a sense of uncertainty. It begins with the sustained synthesized bass sound and the guitar noodle, continues with the off-beat guitar chords, then settles in to a pattern that features little or no sound on the first beat of every measure, in both verse and chorus. The timekeeping is subtle; the most prominent rhythm is the guitar riff, which always starts on the second beat. This is an adaptation of the reggae off-beat rhythm; it has the similar effect of making the rhythmic texture buoyant. Here, it underscores the unsettled state of mind of the young teacher who may ask the student to keep her distance but wish her next to him as he says it.

♪ **KEY FEATURES**

**"Don't Stand So Close to Me," the Police (1980)**

- Unresolved lyrics about an unresolved situation
- Words and melody in the forefront
- Oscillating harmony: indicating oscillating emotions?
- Reggae-inspired rhythms avoid the first beat

The combination of buoyant rhythms, prominent words and melody, and an open texture dominated by single-line parts rather than chords exemplifies one of the freshest rock sounds of the eighties. It was a sound that listeners found especially appealing; a 1983 *Rolling Stone* feature article declared them "today's best-loved band."

The Police offered a distinctive realization of the new pop-oriented, punk- and reggae-influenced rock of the eighties. More common was the post-punk pop rock sound heard in the next example and in much other music from the first half of the decade.

## Punk-Inspired Pop

Rock got a "beatlift" around 1980. The new sound was lean, clean, vibrant, and colored with an array of synthesizer timbres and effects. It harnessed the energy of punk, but its most direct antecedent was the music of David Bowie, himself one of punk's seminal influences. From these sources, it distilled a purer form of rock rhythm, typically spread throughout the texture, from bass and kick drum to high-pitched percussion and synth parts. Its leanness and cleanness came in large part from an open-sounding mid-range: crisp single-note lines and sustained chords replaced thick guitar chords and riffs.

Bowie himself was a major contributor to this new sound. So were new wave artists such as Elvis Costello, Blondie, the Pretenders, the Talking Heads, Devo, and the B-52s. However, there were also groups that had neither punk's rage nor new wave's weirdness.

The Go-Go's' "We Got the Beat" (1981) could easily be the signature song of this new rock sound. Like a typical Ramones' song, it has a simple lyric, mostly the repeated title phrase. And it has punk's saturated rock rhythm—not only in the drum part but also in repeated notes and chords from top (high piano chords) to bottom (bass and low guitar). But the spirit of the song is completely different: it is almost mindlessly happy—much closer to fifties rock and roll than it is to punk or new wave. However, the rhythmic approach clearly places it in the eighties.

So does the makeup of the band. The Go-Go's were among the first of the all-girl rock groups. "We Got the Beat" also shows how the point of punk's rhythmic innovation had been turned completely on its head within five years. In the Sex Pistols' music, the rhythm was aggressive and confrontational. Here it's simply bouncy: lead singer Belinda Carlisle (b. 1958) had been a cheerleader in high school. It's as if someone put one of those yellow smiley faces on Johnny Rotten.

Among the bands to utilize this new approach was Van Halen, an excellent second-generation heavy metal band. Two brothers, drummer Alex (b. 1953) and guitarist Eddie (b. 1955) formed the band with bassist Michael Anthony (b. 1954) and lead vocalist David Lee Roth (b. 1954). Their 1978 debut album, simply titled *Van Halen*, showcased Eddie Van Halen's breathtaking virtuosity. The appropriately titled "Eruption," a free-form solo by Van Halen, immediately raised the bar for guitarists. The album was an immediate success and one of the most spectacular debut albums in rock history. It would be the first of an almost unbroken string of platinum albums by the band.

Although associated with heavy metal because of the guitar-centric songs and Eddie Van Halen's playing, Van Halen was, from the start, more than a heavy metal band. During the early eighties, in the latter part of Roth's tenure with the band, Eddie Van Halen sought to move more toward the mainstream, in part by incorporating synthesizers into their sound—he is also a skilled pianist. Among the fruits of this particular direction was "Jump," from their sixth album, *1984*; it was the band's first number 1 single.

"Jump," Van Halen (1983)

"Jump" (1983) exemplifies the new sound of punk-inspired and pop-oriented rock that emerged in the early eighties. The features that most clearly identify this sound are the prominent place of synthesizers, the open texture, and the rhythmic conception. For most of the song, including the opening signature riff, synths rule: in addition to replacing the lead guitar as the source of the opening instrumental hook, they provide most of the accompaniment for Roth's vocal. Van Halen plays guitar only in the contrasting section and in a brief tantalizing solo, which only hints at his technical mastery and sonic imagination. This soon gives way to a synthesizer solo that is more extended but less virtuosic. The synth riff lies mainly in a medium-high register; it is in a higher range than Roth's vocal line much of the time. By contrast, the bass line, played by Anthony (on bass) and Van Halen (on a synthesizer—synthesizers are now polyphonic and can play several parts simultaneously), is in a low register. What's missing—or very much in the background—most of the time are chords played by a rhythm guitarist. By omitting this typically prominent part of the texture, Van Halen gives the song a more spacious sound. This sound is a defining characteristic of the new rock sound of the eighties.

Underpinning Roth's vocal and the synthesizer and guitar parts is a bass line that is mostly a single note repeated at rock-beat speed. It changes infrequently in the heart of the song: mainly at the end of phrases, in the contrasting section, and during Van Halen's guitar solo. By presenting the rock-rhythm layer most prominently in a repeated-note bass line, Van Halen (and the other eighties bands that also used this strategy) further concentrates this already distilled form of rock rhythm. Here, the bass part turns rock rhythm into a musical trampoline, on which the rest of the texture bounces. In this form, the rhythm is vibrant, not aggressive and confrontational. Indeed, "Jump" is a good-humored song; we can almost see Roth smirking as he sings the song.

---

### ♪ KEY FEATURES

**"Jump," Van Halen (1983)**

- Prominent synths: main solo voice, as well as bass line support, dominant riff, and background color
- Open-sounding texture, because of the large gap between bass line and synth and vocal ranges
- Bouncy rock rhythm focused mainly in the repeated-note bass line
- Good mood in lyrics echoed by syncopated riff, guitar and synth solos, and clearly outlined rhythm at a moderate tempo

---

Shortly after recording *1984*, Roth left the band. Sammy Hagar (b. 1947) replaced him for the better part of a decade. He too left, in 1996. Gary Cherone (b. 1961) then began his brief tenure as lead vocalist. The band has been inactive since 2004. Although Roth claims that a reunion is "inevitable," it remains (as of this writing) a dream for Van Halen fans pining for a return to the glory days of the early eighties.

The sounds and rhythms popularized in songs like "Jump" were one of the freshest trends in rock during the eighties. Other acts—including the Eurythmics, Cyndi Lauper, and the Smiths—also featured it in their music. It is these qualities—the livelier, cleaner rhythmic textures and the expanded sound palette created by the new synth timbres—that make the music sound distinctly different from almost all of the music of the seventies and before.

Elements of this approach also contributed to **significant rock**, as evidenced in music by such acts as Bruce Springsteen and U2. We consider their music next.

## Significant Rock

Music, like the musicians who produce it, can mature; and maturation, in music as in life, is ideally a never-ending process. The discussion of the maturation of rock rhythm in Chapter 9 described an early stage in the musical development of rock, comparable to changes from adolescence to young adulthood. The music that we explore next is a markedly later stage in this process. We might think of it as a successful response to a mid-life crisis: as if a man asked himself where the idealism of his youth had gone and resolved not only to recapture it but also to convert those ideals into positive actions.

Idealism and altruism came into rock via the folk tradition, most notably in the early music of Bob Dylan. In this music, the words delivered the message—whether it was a trenchant critique of contemporary life or a call to action. The music amplified its impact because the words were sung, not spoken, but melody and accompaniment were, for the most part, expressively neutral. As in the songs of Woody Guthrie, there was little or nothing in a guitar accompaniment that resonated directly with the message of the lyrics. By contrast, electric Dylan and those he influenced moved away from the idealistic, socially involved themes of early sixties folk. It often took an extraordinary event to prompt a musical response: "Ohio," which Neil Young wrote for his supergroup Crosby, Stills, Nash, and Young in response to the shootings at Kent State, is a well-known example.

Significance returned to rock at a time when rock had matured to the point that it could convey importance in music as well as words. This is the musical corollary to the fund-raising events created to help those in need. Celebrity was a resource for these artists that they could leverage to gain support for a good cause. The folkies of the early sixties could have only dreamed about the huge amounts of money that Geldof and others raised. And for a few eighties acts, a generation of musical development provided resources to create a music that sounded significant before the first phrase of the lyric. The opening seconds of a song by Bruce Springsteen or U2 send a message far more powerful than even the most artfully constructed acoustic accompaniment, a point that we explore in the following discussion.

## Springsteen in the Eighties

After "Born to Run," Springsteen's career was primed for takeoff. However, a drawn-out legal battle involving Jon Landau, his new manager, and Springsteen's first producer, Mike Appel, kept Springsteen out of the studios for about three years. He returned with a string of critically acclaimed and mildly (for 1980) popular albums: *Darkness on the Edge of Town* (1978), *The River* (1980), and the acoustic *Nebraska* (1982). He finally broke through to a mass audience in 1984 with *Born in the U.S.A.* It was in this album that Springsteen fully realized the big conception first expressed in songs like "Born to Run."

"Born in the U.S.A.," Bruce Springsteen (1984)

In the title track, as in "Born to Run," Springsteen mixes a strong story line, simple riffs and rhythms, and subtle details. However, in this song, Springsteen adopts a less-is-more approach, with telling effect. The lyric paints a brutal portrait of a Vietnam War veteran through powerful, almost posterized images: "sent me off to a foreign land/to go and kill the yellow man." The verses telegraph defining moments in the protagonist's life, from early childhood to his inability to get a job and the insensitivity of the government in supporting veterans. Springsteen's words put an ironic spin on the title phrase. In this context, what could be a prideful affirmation of patriotism becomes a jingoistic mantra—a badge of shame for a country that sends its less fortunate off to fight in a senseless war, then does little to help those who return.

Springsteen sets his trenchant lyric in an almost minimalist musical environment. The song begins with only a single octave on the piano, a heavy backbeat, and a synthesizer riff. The spacing of these three elements—low, middle, high—and a judicious amount of reverb (which makes the backbeat sound uncomfortably close to a rifle shot) give the introduction a big sound by defining a wide open space waiting to be filled in. As the song unfolds, Springsteen fills in the middle; the most prominent of the additional parts either strengthen the bass or fill in the upper range—most notably, the piano part presents a more active version of the synthesizer riff. These and other instruments weave in and out of the texture, but the riff and backbeat are constants—even through Max Weinberg's "war zone" drum solo.

♪ **KEY FEATURES**

**"Born in the U.S.A.," Bruce Springsteen (1984)**

- Lyric a scathing indictment of war and its costs
- Heavy backbeat, signature riff dominate through the entire song
- Open texture with Springsteen's raspy voice in the middle conveys a sense of importance
- Springsteen strategy: combine easily grasped features (riff, backbeat) with subtle touches (piano doubling synth riff)

In "Born in the U.S.A.," Springsteen is at once simpler and subtler than he was in "Born to Run." The prominent elements in "Born in the U.S.A." are even simpler than the driving rhythm and opening guitar riff of the earlier song, whereas the spacing of the texture and the balance between the prominent features and background support is more sophisticated, because it is less obvious. Springsteen has maintained this strategy in his subsequent music, most notably in *The Rising*, his response to 9/11. He remains one of the few artists in rock music with a truly powerful presence.

Springsteen's "significant" sound, as evidenced in "Born in the U.S.A.," was one of several musical options that he would employ in his music from the early eighties on. Other tracks on the album range from the punk-drenched "No Surrender" and the country-flavored "Darlington County" to the synth rock of "Dancing in the Dark" and the moody ballad "My Hometown." Another significant band of the eighties would define themselves musically with one of the distinctive styles of the decade.

## U2

From the start, U2—lead vocalist Bono (born Paul Hewson, 1960), guitarist-keyboardist The Edge (born David Evans, 1961), bassist Adam Clayton (b. 1960), and drummer Larry Mullen (b. 1961)—have had a sense of their destiny. In 1981, three years after the group came together, Bono told *Rolling Stone*, "Even at this stage, I do feel we are meant to be one of the great bands. There's a certain spark, a certain chemistry, that was special about the Stones, the Who, and the Beatles, and I think it's also special about U2." They have fulfilled their destiny because they have stayed together and because they have never lost their passion for rock and what it can be. As recently as 2000, after more than two decades of touring, recording, and sending their message out into the world, Bono told *USA Today* that "There is a transcendence that I want from rock. . . . I'm still drunk on the idea that rock and roll can be a force for change. We haven't lost that idea."

U2 soon made Bono a prophet. In their first two albums, *Boy* (1980) and *October* (1981), the group addressed personal issues, among them relationships and their faith. By 1983, the year that they released *War*, their third album, the band had defined its purpose, found its audience, and had begun to define its sound. With this album, their music took on the politically and socially aware edge that would characterize it through the rest of the eighties. "Sunday Bloody Sunday," a track from the album and their first number 1 hit in the United Kingdom, for example, recounts an especially bloody incident in the ongoing strife between Catholics and Protestants in Northern Ireland, and the musical setting reinforces the message of the lyrics: the five-note bursts played by the entire band underneath Bono's vocal line evokes the sound of gunfire.

The following year, they began their long and fruitful collaboration with Brian Eno (b. 1948)—a founding member of Roxy Music, an electronica pioneer, the father of ambient music, and by 1984, a much-in-demand producer. (More recently, Eno has identified himself as a "sonic landscaper," a label that also applies readily to his work with U2.) Eno brought a polish to U2's music, while preserving the distinctive sound world that they had begun to create. Their first album together was the 1984 release *The Unforgettable Fire*; he would collaborate on four of their albums. By 1985, *Rolling Stone* had dubbed them the band of the eighties, but it wasn't until *Joshua Tree* (1987) that they achieved the overwhelming commercial success to match their critical acclaim.

Virtually from the start of their career, U2 cultivated a sound world that made their music sound significant. They put the essential components in place in their first albums, enhanced them with the help of Brian Eno, and maintained them through the eighties. The sound grows out of punk but already has a distinct identity in songs like "Gloria" (1981) from their second album. Surrounding Bono's vocals is a four-strand texture, separated into low, middle, and high:

- Two low-range sounds: repeated notes at rock-beat speed in the bass and beat-keeping on the bass drum
- A mid-range percussion sound: a rock-rhythm layer on the sock cymbal
- A medium-high-range sound: the angular guitar line, also moving at rock-beat speed

The insistent rock rhythmic layer, played by the entire band, derives from punk, but U2 has already put their personal stamp on it, in the spacing of the instruments and in The Edge's asymmetrically patterned single-line guitar figures. Because of the registral openness and the angular guitar lines, the effect is quite different from punk: whereas the sound of Ramones'-style punk rams the listener head-on, the sound of U2, even at this early stage, envelops the listener.

This distinctive sound world is built on contrast: between high and low and between slow and fast. As the band's music evolved during the eighties, the contrast

"Where the
Streets Have
No Name,"
U2 (1987)

deepened. One significant change came from within the band: the active rhythms doubled in speed, from rock rhythm to the 16-beat rhythms of disco, while such features as chord rhythm often moved at even slower speeds. In his work with U2, Eno enriched the "sonic landscape" by deepening the contrast between slow and fast with sustained synthesizer sounds and introducing stronger textural contrasts. These changes gave U2's music an even more sharply defined profile, as we hear in "Where the Streets Have No Name," a hit track from their 1987 album *Joshua Tree*.

"Where the Streets Have No Name" continues U2's predilection for meaningful words encased in meaningful-sounding music. The lyrics describe a universal longing for the harmony that can be created when divisions by class, race, and wealth disappear. They are general enough to have spawned multiple interpretations. Some connect the song's message to Ethiopia, where Bono and his wife had done relief work. Others link it to Los Angeles, where the video of the song was filmed. Still others associate it with Dublin, where the street one lives on could identify one's social and economic status. And most connect it to the world beyond.

Bono presents the lyric through a melody whose simplicity is obscured by the rich instrumental backdrop. If we tune out the instruments and simply listen to Bono's voice, we hear a folksong-like melody: short phrases that gently rise and fall within a narrow range. Like "Barbara Allen," the Scottish folksong heard in Chapter 2, this melody is coherent even without accompaniment, and it would work with a simple folk guitar accompaniment.

It is U2 and Eno's grand setting that relocates this simple melody from the front porch to the stage. The extended instrumental introduction—almost 2 minutes in

U2 performing at Live Aid in 1985. From left to right: The Edge, Bono, Adam Clayton.

length—begins with sustained organ and synthesizer sounds. The Edge's busy guitar pattern slowly emerges out of this sound cushion. At first it is in a rhythm that oscillates once for every six notes, like a jig in slow motion. Imperceptibly, he converts the pattern to the 16-beat rhythm that is sustained through the rest of the song. The rhythmic patterns range from the sustained synthesizer chords, which may last four measures before changing, through the beat-speed thump of Mullen's bass drum, Clayton's rock-beat-speed repeated note, and the 16-beat rhythms of the guitar(s)—there are two guitar sounds much of the time—and drums. All of this encases Bono's singing in a musical halo.

♪ **KEY FEATURES**

**"Where the Streets Have No Name," U2 (1987)**

- Lyrics that send a message of hope: for a world that is not divided by class, wealth, race, or any other arbitrary criterion
- A simple folklike melody
- Bono's singing: an Irish tenor with the grittiness of the blues
- Persistent rhythms at several speeds, with very little syncopation
- Rich, synthesizer-enriched texture, with parts widely spaced

The sound world that U2 created in "Where the Streets Have No Name" was the band's musical signature during the eighties. It is heard in many of their hits during that decade, and it becomes progressively more sophisticated from album to album. It has the effect of elevating the simple melody that lies at its center, investing it with a power and impact that it could not have had in a simpler setting. In this sense, the music of U2 is the ultimate folk rock: one in which the power of the words is matched by the power of the music.

## Significant-Sounding Rock

For many, Bruce Springsteen and U2 were the only two truly important acts of the eighties. Above all, their music signaled a return to the spirit of the sixties, when rock meant something. Both confronted difficult problems in which they had a deep personal involvement: the Vietnam War; the conflict in Northern Ireland; and the suffering in Africa. And both wore their hearts on their sleeves: they would rather be too passionate than too reserved.

The power of their music comes from applying two principles: simplifying and highlighting basic rhythms and creating a full, yet open sound. By emphasizing regular timekeeping over syncopation, and maintaining the same basic texture with only subtle variation through long stretches of time, the instrumental settings convey both simplicity and seriousness. Their function is to enhance the power and presence of the lyric.

The rhythmic approach used by both Springsteen and U2, while realized in strikingly different ways, has the same effect: it cuts the cord with good-time rock. As we have noted in earlier chapters, the rock groove that makes people want to get up and dance grows out of the interplay between regular rhythms and rhythms that conflict with it or transcend it. Both of the songs discussed in this section minimize or all but eliminate this interplay: in "Born in the U.S.A." it is confined almost exclusively to the dominant riff and the backbeat; in "Where the Streets Have No Name" it occurs only in the irregular *patterns* of The Edge's active accompaniment, not in the rhythm itself, which is regular. It is as if both Springsteen and U2 are saying that they want listeners to hear the message in the lyrics. Listeners can draw power from the music, but they should not be distracted by rhythms that are too playful for the lyric. In post-punk rock, a serious message virtually demands music with minimal syncopation.

# Extreme Virtuosity: Heavy Metal After 1980

Heavy metal, such a powerful force in rock during the early seventies, seemed to be merely a cartoon parody of itself by mid-decade. The most visible metal band was Kiss, who made their reputation on their clownish makeup and over-the-top stage show. However, metal didn't go away; it simply went on the road.

Although dismissed or ignored by rock critics—Lester Bangs pronounced it all but dead in the late seventies—heavy metal developed a loyal and steadily increasing fan base through the late seventies and eighties through frequent touring. Fans packed arenas to hear their favorite bands, bought their recordings, and kept up to date through fanzines. Exposure on radio and MTV was minimal, especially early in the decade.

## The Revival of Heavy Metal

By the end of the decade, it was clear that heavy metal was the most popular genre in a heavily segmented rock marketplace. To cite just one piece of evidence, Guns N' Roses' debut album, *Appetite for Destruction* (1987), has sold over 20 million units. Numerous other metal bands, among them Van Halen, Def Leppard, Metallica, and Living Color, also racked up platinum/multiplatinum record sales.

Male teens and males slightly older made up most of the heavy metal fan base in the eighties. In the wake of the economic hard times in both Great Britain and the United States, many faced a bleak future. They felt out of the loop, especially during the eighties, when the gap between rich and poor widened so dramatically. They responded to the recurrent themes in heavy metal: the occult, sexual dominance (often to the point of misogyny), rage, frustration, protest, and—above all—power. Band names tell the story—Megadeath, AC/DC, Motörhead, Judas Priest, Iron Maiden, Twisted Sister, Scorpions—all were worthy sequels to the original: Black Sabbath.

And it was the music above all that conveyed the power. Most characteristically, it was loud to the point where a listener *felt* it as much as heard it. And the sound was heavily distorted, a sign both of power (distortion originally came from overdriving amplifiers) and defiance (distortion was originally an undesirable byproduct of amplification, to be avoided if possible).

Performances were a communion between musicians and their audience. Bands preached to the converted. Fans knew the words to songs, even though they were often unintelligible (fans learned the lyrics from record jackets). Stage shows were typically spectacles on a grand scale, comparable to an elaborate pagan ritual. In response, metalheads engaged in **headbanging**, heavy metal's version of dancing. In the familiarity of the audience/congregation with the songs, in their involvement in the performance, and in the sense of power that they experienced during the event, a heavy metal concert was more like a religious rite than anything else.

All of this occurred outside the purview of the mainstream media. Few "unconverted" listeners were willing to go past the distortion, the lyrics, and the visual images. The music, and what it stood for, was almost universally misunderstood and underappreciated. Those who attended the symphony would probably have been horrified to learn of the wholescale expropriation of classical music by metal guitarists such as Eddie Van Halen, Randy Rhoads, Yngwie Malmsteen, James Hetfield, and Dave Mustaine. They might well be scandalized at the suggestion that Eddie Van Halen expanded the sound possibilities and raised the level of virtuosity on his instrument more than any performer in any genre—classical, jazz, rock, or country—since the diabolical nineteenth-century violinist Niccolo Paganini and his pianist counterpart, Franz Liszt. For the most part, heavy metal remained insulated in its own world: the bands and their fans. Indeed, Van Halen's 1978 self-titled debut album helped bridge the gap between the early seventies and the metal renaissance of the eighties.

Heavy metal was never a monolithic style, as we have seen, but in the eighties it became even more diverse. Substyles, often based on a single feature, proliferated. By the end of the decade there was speed metal, thrash metal, death metal, industrial metal, and more. Its diversity was also due to its blending with other styles; during the eighties, heavy metal came in several grades of purity. Distortion remained metal's sound signature, but "pure" heavy metal was far more than a rock song played with distortion.

As evidenced in the music of top eighties bands such as Metallica and Megadeath, a heavy metal song is a far cry from standard rock, rhythm and blues, or pop fare. Here are some of the most striking differences:

- *Distortion is typically more extreme.* Because it is the most easily borrowed feature of heavy metal style, serious metal bands compensated by increasing the distortion to the point that the notes being played may be almost impossible to discern because of the halo of white noise around them.

- *Instrumentation is basic.* It consists of one or two guitars, bass, and drums. Use of additional instruments—synths, saxes, extra percussion—is a stylistic impurity, as we noted in the earlier discussion of Van Halen's "Jump."

- *It is not tuneful music.* This is especially evident in the vocal line, which is typically more incantation than melody. The vocalists chant, wail, even spit out the words. They seldom sing a catchy melodic phrase.

- *The ratio of instrumental sections to vocal sections is much higher than in most other rock-based styles.* In addition to extended solos, where lead guitarists show off their prowess, there are also long passages with no vocal lines. These typically consist of a series of intricate riffs.

- *It typically avoids conventional harmony.* Bands may play power chords, but complete harmonies and chord progressions are the exception rather than the rule. Instead, the music tends to be linear, with both solos and group riffs built on modes. Variety in pitch choice comes about through shifts from one mode to another, or shifting the central tone of a mode. (It should be noted that the avoidance of conventional harmony in heavy metal is a choice, not a limitation. Numerous metal songs begin with delicate slow introductions; these often contain sophisticated harmony. Apparently, eighties metal bands, like their predecessors from the early seventies, felt that the use of standard or even alternative chord progressions would undermine the power of their music.)

- *The best metal bands are virtuosic.* This applies not only to the guitarist(s) who solo, but to the entire band, who create and perform intricate riffs, often at breathtakingly fast tempos, with a level of precision comparable to a fine string quartet or jazz combo.
- *Metal "songs" tend to be long, sprawling, multisectional works.* They avoid the standard verse/bridge/chorus formula of rock-era music. Instead, the work typically consists of blocks of sound, often in different tempos and with different key centers, all arranged in complex, unpredictable sequences.

These features occur in heavy metal tracks undiluted with other stylistic elements. What passed for heavy metal in the eighties ranged from mainstream rock covered with a metal sheen (for example, Def Leppard's "Photograph") to the music of high-minded bands such as Metallica. We consider "One," a track from their 1988 album *And Justice for All*. The song was released as a single during the following year; it was also the song used for the band's first music video.

## Metallica

Metallica began the eighties toiling in relative obscurity. The group, formed in 1981 by guitarist-vocalist James Hetfield (b. 1963) and drummer Lars Ulrich (b. 1963), built an ardent cult following during the first part of eighties even as they went through a string of guitarists, including Dave Mustaine (b. 1961), who would later form Megadeath. In 1983, Hetfield and Ulrich recruited Kirk Hammett (b. 1962); Hammett remains the lead guitarist with the group. Cliff Burton (1962–1986), the bassist for Metallica's first three albums, died in a freak accident during a 1986 Swedish tour. Jason Newsted (b. 1963) replaced him; he would remain with the group through 2001.

Like those of other top metal bands, Metallica's record sales were brisk, although the band got almost no exposure on radio or television. The group eventually broke through on radio in 1988 with "One," a single from their fourth album (and first with Newsted), *And Justice for All*, which peaked at number 6 on the charts.

Even a cursory listening to "One" makes clear that the market came to Metallica, not the other way around. "One" is a grim anti-war statement that unfolds on a large scale: the work is well over 7 minutes long. It makes few concessions to mainstream rock—in lyrics, music, or length. The form of the song takes its shape from the images in the lyrics; it is an especially graphic depiction of the horrors of war, as experienced by one of its many casualties.

"One," Metal-lica (1988)

The song unfolds slowly, and gently at first, after the faint chatter of machine guns and other war noises: the extended instrumental introduction features a guitar duet. The first flash of typical metal comes about 2 minutes later, in the chorus; the burst of

Metallica performing in 1994 at Woodstock. From left to right: Jason Newsted, Kirk Hammett, James Hetfield, and Lars Ulrich.

distortion seems to depict a flashback by the protagonist. For the next 2 minutes, the track alternates between the gentler Flamenco-tinged music and the more aggressive and distorted music of the chorus, as the protagonist moves back and forth from faint memories to the painful present. About halfway through, the music abandons the gentler music of the opening section. With the entry of the "machine gun" rhythm—first on drums, then with the entire band—it is as if the scene shifts from the hospital ward to the battlefield. The action escalates, first in an ensemble section dominated by the "machine gun" rhythm, then in a guitar solo. The song ends abruptly.

## ♪ KEY FEATURES

### "One," Metallica (1988)
- Grim anti-war message in the lyrics
- Sprawling form highlights elements in the narrative: images and emotions
- Strong contrast between gentle guitar duets and powerful war scenes
- Frequent shifts in rhythmic organization between three- and four-beat measures
- Updated metal sounds: intense distortion, tight ensemble (especially in the latter half of the song), fluent guitar solo

In its sprawling form, relatively little emphasis on vocal lines, musical sophistication (for instance, there are several shifts from four-beat to three-beat measures), deep contrast from dark, and moody beginning to powerful conclusion, "One" demands a lot from its listeners. The music is as uncompromising and grim as its message.

"One" has more in common with a film soundtrack than a conventional rock song. Indeed, after recording the song, Metallica discovered the similarities between their song and *Johnny Get Your Gun*, a 1939 anti-war novel that author Dalton Trumbo later turned into a film. The music video of "One" juxtaposes scenes from Trumbo's film with footage of the band and adds dialogue from the film to the music. Curiously, many of Metallica's fans objected to the video, the band's first. Perhaps it was the fact of the video that troubled them, because the video, with its skillful mixing of band scenes with film footage, makes the anti-war message of the track even more compelling.

Like the two previous songs, Metallica's "One" is significant rock. With its long narrative-based form, dramatic shifts in mood, masterful playing, and vivid sound images, "One" makes its statement through a style that is in many ways more complex than that heard in the songs of Springsteen or U2. It exemplifies Metallica's uncompromising approach to music making; there is nothing in "One" that suggests any effort to accommodate more mainstream tastes. Despite this, the band has enjoyed commercial success as well as critical acclaim.

### Heavy Metal and Bebop

There are intriguing parallels between heavy metal in the eighties and another counterculture music: bebop. Bebop was the avant-garde jazz of the forties. Although developed mainly by black musicians, bebop and "pure" metal have several noteworthy correspondences, musical and otherwise.

Both were true outsiders' music, supported initially by a relatively small but loyal fan base. Both challenged prevailing standards of appearance: metal stars' ratted hair, makeup, bare chests, tattoos, and the like were anticipated by the zoot suits of the bop hipsters. Both cultivated aggressive, confrontational sounds: the heavy distortion of metal bands has its parallel in the hard, penetrating sound of Charlie Parker's saxophone playing. Both required considerable technical skill to negotiate intricate solo and ensemble passages. Both borrowed heavily from classical music: the "sampling" of Baroque figuration by metal guitarists was preceded by the harmonic sophistication of bebop, which had its most direct precedents in the music of the French composers Debussy and Ravel. And both were largely misunderstood during their emergence.

Despite its growing popularity, no rock music of the eighties was less understood or less appreciated than heavy metal. However, even though critics and audiences may have scorned it early on, musicians didn't. Not only did it develop into one of the important directions of the late eighties and nineties, but it bled into the exciting new fusions of the alternative bands that began to surface at the end of the decade. It remains a significant part of the rock music scene.

# Renewing Rock and Roll

Among the most important debuts of 1988 was a group known as the Traveling Wilburys. They presented themselves as half-brothers of the late Charles T. Wilbury Sr.: Lucky, Otis, Charles T. Jr., Nelson, and Lefty. In fact, the Traveling Wilburys were one of the great supergroups of any era: on their first album, released in the fall of that year, the Wilburys included Bob Dylan, Jeff Lynne, Tom Petty, George Harrison, and Roy Orbison. This recording was the only one to include all of the original members; Orbison passed away later that year.

Lynne (b. 1947) was the catalyst for the formation of the group. After leading the Electric Light Orchestra throughout the seventies and into the eighties, Lynne dissolved the band in 1986 to move into solo work and production. While at lunch, Harrison and Lynne called Bob Dylan to ask if they could use his home studio to record a song. Orbison was in town and agreed to sing on the track. Petty (b. 1950) and Dylan joined in. The good times led to an album assembled over a ten-day period.

There is symbolic significance to the coming together of Dylan, Orbison, and Harrison just before Orbison's death. The road from Anglo-American folk music to rock divided with the birth of country music in the twenties and the reclamation of the folk heritage in the thirties. Until the sixties, they evolved along largely separate paths. Rock-and-roll acts found little common ground with folk counterparts other than their shared heritage and a mostly young audience: Buddy Holly and the Kingston Trio were in different worlds musically. Their intersection with—and through—rock began in the early sixties, in large part because of the work of Orbison and Dylan. By the late eighties, the schism was ancient history; the formation of the Wilburys celebrated that fact.

## Neo-Traditional Trends of the Eighties

The Wilburys' collaboration was one branch of a **neo-traditional** movement within rock during the eighties and nineties. The Rolling Stones breathed life into their career in the early eighties, while boogie bands such as ZZ Top kept trucking along. Also, many newer rock acts—such as John Mellencamp, Tom Petty and the Heart-breakers, and Dire Straits—carved out a niche in the rock marketplace.

Flashing back to an even more distant past was a rockabilly revival led by the Stray Cats; it would gain momentum in the nineties in the music of groups such as the Brian Setzer Orchestra. Fresh voices breathed new life into two of rock's most influential antecedents: the blues and the socially conscious song. The blues revival that began in the mid-eighties gave a boost to the careers of established bluesmen and introduced new stars, such as Stevie Ray Vaughan and Robert Cray. Later in the decade, a new generation of socially aware female singer-songwriters, among them Tracy Chapman and Suzanne Vega, would evoke the spirit of early Bob Dylan.

## The Dave Matthews Band

One of the freshest takes on rock and roll at the end of the century came from the plainly named Dave Matthews Band. The Dave Matthews Band is a "what you see is what you get"–type name: Dave Matthews and four others. Its simplicity harks back to the fifties when rock-and-roll acts were identified by their names: Elvis, Jerry Lee Lewis, Little Richard, Chuck Berry.

Dave Matthews (b. 1967) was born in South Africa, but his parents moved to New York in 1969. In 1986 he moved to Charlottesville, Virginia; by the end of the eighties, he was tending bar in a jazz club, admiring musicians like saxophonist LeRoi Moore, and keeping his music to himself. After a trip home to South Africa, he returned to Charlottesville and decided to record some songs that he'd written. To help make a demo, he recruited jazz musicians, among them several he'd heard in the club where he tended bar. Four of the musicians on his demo—violinist Boyd Tinsley (b. 1964), saxophonist LeRoi Moore (b. 1961), drummer Carter Beauford (b. 1957), and bassist Stefan Lessard (b. 1974)—remain the nucleus of his band. Guitarist Tim Reynolds (b. 1956?), while not an official member of the band, has remained a long-time collaborator.

The Dave Matthews Band played their first gig in 1991 and quickly built a large and enthusiastic fan base. Their first album, drawn from a live performance and issued on the group's own label, Bama Rags, was released in 1993. From start to finish, it showed the kind of energy and enterprise for which the band is famous. It sold well enough that the band could choose which of the majors they would sign with: they opted for RCA—now BMG as of this writing (there are rumors of yet another big merger). By the end of the decade, their albums started at the top of the charts. In the fall of 2003, they played to over 85,000 people in New York's Central Park to raise money for the New York City school system.

Mitchell Gerber/Corbis

The Dave Matthews Band with their Grammy awards, 1997. From left to right: Dave Matthews, Carter Beauford, Boyd Tinsley, Stefan Lessard, LeRoi Moore.

The musicians that Matthews chose for his band set it apart from so many other bands on the outside looking in. It has the guitar/bass/drums nucleus. But both Beauford and Lessard are skilled jazz musicians, who brought a jazzlike freedom to their playing. The two lead instruments, saxophone and violin, are the trademark solo instruments of rhythm and blues and country music, respectively. Both get plenty of space to solo. The influence of jazz, not only in the instrumental interludes but also in the interplay of the rhythm section, plus the R&B and country connections give the Dave Matthews Band an all-American sound, as we hear in one of the fan favorites from their early years: "Ants Marching."

"Ants March-ing," the Dave Matthews Band (1994)

The song begins with three sharp raps by the drummer. Only when violin and saxophone enter with the song's signature riff do we discover that Beauford has been playing the backbeat, not the beat. Bass and guitar join in with a complementary riff; the four oscillate between two chords for the verse of the song.

"Ants Marching" follows a familiar rock path: alternating verse and chorus, with a climactic section toward the end where the marching ants make their debut. The solos and the wonderfully expansive final section help separate the song from the run of the mill; so does the great groove. It doesn't seem to matter that the lyric is a somber commentary on those who go through life without reflection or growth—the kind that words-first singer-songwriters seem to write. It's a safe bet that many more left Matthews's concerts humming the signature riff than pondering the connection between ants marching and inflexible personalities. One can understand why it has been a favorite on tour.

♪ **KEY FEATURES**

**"Ants Marching," the Dave Matthews Band (1994)**
- Instrumentation features nuclear rock band plus instruments that suggest country (violin) and R&B (saxophone) connections
- Rhythmic play within band revives groove of classic rock
- Interesting contrast between serious tone of lyrics and the exhilaration of the music
- Violin and saxophone (but not guitar) are the dominant solo voices

The music of the Dave Matthews Band offers compelling evidence of the continued vitality of rock and roll. It demonstrates not only that rock and roll is still full of life, but also that it is possible to bring new sounds and ideas into the basic conception without losing its essence.

## Reinvigorating Rock

The six acts whose music has been discussed in this chapter are an infinitesimal fraction of the rock bands active after 1980 and a small fraction of those that achieved commercial success. Moreover, they inhabit musical worlds that are, for the most part, mutually exclusive: no one would confuse a song by the Police with a Dave Matthews song, or even Van Halen's pop-oriented metal with the music of Metallica.

Still, there are connections beyond their shared rock heritage that link them together. One is their undiminished stature: each enjoys as much esteem in the early twenty-first century as they did during their first career highpoint. At this writing, only Van Halen is inactive. Another is that each has contributed to the renewal of rock during the eighties and nineties. Unlike the mainstream rock of the seventies, which seemed to evolve continuously from the music of the sixties, the more mainstream rock of the eighties and nineties discussed previously involved a reorientation, in purpose and in music. This could mean reviving old ideas that seemed to be forgotten: here it was the sixties idea that rock mattered, that it could sharpen the awareness of those who take it seriously, and that it could be a force for positive change. It could also mean the infusion of non-mainstream elements: punk and reggae elements in the music of the Police, Van Halen, and U2 stand out early on; the Dave Matthews Band's violin and saxophone front line is more recent. It often leveraged new technology: not only the expanded sound palette that synthesizers provided, but also the greater control in production made possible by digital technology. All of this produced a body of music that remains as vital today as it was when it was released.

## Terms to Remember

| significant rock | headbanging | neo-traditional |
|---|---|---|

## Applying Chapter Concepts

1. To bring into focus the range of heavy metal music, contrast a song by Pantera, Slayer, or other similar band with a song by Bon Jovi, Def Leppard, or another like-minded band. Your comparison should touch on the following subjects:

   a. Tempo
   b. Degree of distortion used by guitarist(s) and bassist
   c. Vocal style (including intelligibility of the lyric)
   d. Ratio of instrumental to vocal sections
   e. Accessibility of the form
   f. Rhythmic texture

2. Explore the neo-traditional dimension of eighties rock by sampling the music of Bonnie Raitt, John Mellencamp, or the Traveling Wilburys. In particular, focus on connections to country and/ or blues in the music of the act that you choose.

# 20

# Alternatives

Aberdeen, Washington, is a town of about 16,000 people. It is situated at the eastern end of Grays Harbor, an inlet along the Pacific Coast in the west-central part of the state. The town bills itself as the gateway to the Olympic Peninsula, a beautiful temperate rainforest. However, timber, not tourism, is the main industry. It is not a wealthy town. Unemployment runs high, especially among younger residents.

The dominant colors in Aberdeen are green and gray. As in other towns along the coast in northern California and the Pacific Northwest, the climate is relatively mild: not too cold in the winter and not too warm in the summer. Trees and other plants thrive there. However, it rains frequently—about 85 inches a year—and fog and overcast skies are far more common than sunshine, especially in winter.

While it is difficult to establish a causal connection between artists and the environment in which they were raised, one cannot help but wonder whether Kurt Cobain's music would have taken a radically different form had he been born in Miami, Florida, which is about as far southeast as Aberdeen is northwest. As it happened, grunge, the alternative music that Cobain and Nirvana helped bring to a mass audience, seems to reflect the depressed circumstances and depressing weather one encounters in Aberdeen.

Grunge brought alternative music into the mainstream and made Seattle a rock hotspot during the nineties. However, by the time Nirvana crossed over in 1992, the alternative movement was a decade old and rapidly diversifying from its punk base.

## The Alternative Movement

**Alternative** is an umbrella term for a large family of rock-related, punk-inspired styles that began to develop in the early eighties and continues to flourish in the early twenty-first century. Like "rock" (rocking and rolling = having intercourse; rock and roll = code for R&B; rock = the continuing evolution of rock and roll) and punk (a worthless person or criminal; punk rock = an aggressive seventies rock style), "alternative" has lost its original connotation as it has become more familiar as a musical term. However, the alternative movement began as a musical alternative to not only the pop of Michael Jackson and others but to the more commercial MTV-oriented rock of the eighties.

## The Alternative Ecosystem

The elevator-trip version of alternative rock: in the sixties, rock mattered; in the seventies, it sold out—except for punk; in the eighties, alternative bands mattered; in the nineties, they sold out.

Such a simple paradigm cannot but distort the reality of the situation. Integrity is not incompatible with popular success, as the Beatles and many other acts have demonstrated. Nor is all pop necessarily bad. But there is no question that the bottom-line mentality of the major players in the music business has made mainstream pop more calculating and less daring. In this respect, the paradigm rings true.

What the paradigm does describe, with greater accuracy, is the us-versus-them attitude of those who inhabited the world of alternative rock. As the movement took shape, musicians and audiences believed passionately that their music mattered. For them, rock was a way of life, as it had been in the sixties. Like the punk and new wave music from which it developed, early alternative flourished in a largely closed ecosystem. Control was the key. Bands sought the artistic freedom to make the music they wanted to make, uncorrupted by a corporate mindset.

Alternative was a grassroots movement to restore integrity and importance to rock. Bands toured relentlessly, going from one small club to the next. (The Bird, Seattle's first punk rock club, had an official capacity of ninety-nine people, although twice that many routinely crowded in the club.) They recorded low-budget albums on independent labels and sold many of them at performances. Some got airplay on college radio stations; during the eighties, commercial stations seldom programmed songs by alternative bands. Many developed loyal, even fanatic, followings; some fans published or wrote for fanzines. Occasionally, bands attracted attention from outside critics and fans: *Rolling Stone* selected *Murmur*, R.E.M.'s first album, as the best album of 1983.

Because it started out on such a small scale, the world of alternative music was far more personal. Fans, writers, and others who supported the music felt a sense of ownership. Usually, they had gone the extra mile or two to seek out bands to follow. They bought their recordings. Perhaps they had gotten to know members of the band, done some of the grunt work, or written for a fanzine. The sense of connection went beyond the music: as the Minutemen, one of the pioneer alternative bands, sang, "Our band could be your life." So when a band caught on—signed with a major label; played on big, well-organized tours; made videos; appeared on MTV—fans felt betrayed, or at least marginalized.

Success was also a concern for the musicians: the experience of becoming a rock star helped drive Kurt Cobain to suicide. His suicide note alludes to this:

> I feel guilty beyond words about these things, for example when we're backstage and the lights go out and the manic roar of the crowd begins. It doesn't affect me in the way which it did for Freddie Mercury, who seemed to love and relish the love and admiration from the crowd, which is something I totally admire and envy. The fact is, I can't fool you, any of you. It simply isn't fair to you, or to me. The worst crime I can think of would be to pull people off by faking it, pretending as if I'm having one hundred percent fun. Sometimes I feel as though I should have a punch-in time clock before I walk out on-stage. I've tried everything within my power to appreciate it, and I do, God believe me, I do, but it's not enough.

It is painful to read how fame caused Cobain to lose the thing that he valued the most. In 1994, he cancelled Nirvana's appearance at Lollapalooza, the Woodstock-like touring festival that helped catapult alternative into the mainstream, then took his life.

It is ironic that "rock that mattered" became an alternative to mainstream music, rather than the heart of it, in less than two decades. Even though many of the sixties artists whose music mattered the most—such as Bob Dylan, Frank Zappa, and the Velvet Underground—were never mainstays on the singles charts, there was a sense of common purpose between them and acts, such as the Beatles and the Rolling Stones, who did have a real pop presence. Moreover, they had the support of those behind the scenes, from major labels eager to book the next important act to free-form radio and festivals like Woodstock.

That was not the case in the eighties. For the most part, the mainstream had evolved away from this change-the-world attitude. Acts like Springsteen and U2—acts that said something important to a lot of people—were the exception, not the rule. Most of the other integrity-first bands were simply an alternative to the mainstream.

## Alternative, a Neo-Traditional Trend

Alternative began as a neo-traditional movement: recapturing the sense of importance that characterized rock in the sixties and punk and new wave music in the seventies was its primary goal. However, the message was different. Alienation replaced the heady optimism of the sixties as the dominant theme. Musically, alternative derived most directly from punk and new wave music: tempos were fast, rhythms busy, sound levels were generally loud—and sounded louder because of the small spaces in which they played. The point of departure was the garage band. The core instrumentation was typically vocals, a guitar or two, bass, drums, although bands often went beyond this basic lineup.

As the movement gained momentum in the latter part of the eighties, it diversified by infusing elements of other rock-era substyles—such as funk, metal, or electronica—into its punk core or by imparting a more modern sensibility to genres that had come and gone, such as ska and the music of the early seventies singer-songwriters. Common ground became more a matter of attitude and commercial presence (or lack of it—bands flew under the radar of big music) than musical similarity. The first Lollapalooza tour—**Lollapalooza** was an important outlet for alternative music in the nineties—featured such diverse acts as Jane's Addiction (the festival was band member Perry Ferrell's idea), Nine Inch Nails, and Ice-T and Body Count. None is a "pure" post-punk band.

With the sudden and surprising success of grunge in the early nineties, alternative music wrestled with the tension between high-mindedness and commercial success. A few bands, such as Radiohead, have charted their own course and still enjoy commercial success and critical acclaim. Others, such as Green Day, have introduced mainstream elements into their music; it has been one component of their long-term success. As the music of these two bands demonstrates, alternative, like the sixties rock that ultimately inspired it, has continued to diversify, while holding on, at least to some degree, to the values that brought it into being and gave it importance. Still, in the early twenty-first century, alternative is as much a music industry label as it is a statement of purpose.

# The Transformation of the Recording Industry

If Keith Richards and Mick Jagger had been born forty years later, chances are the Rolling Stones would never have come together. It's not just the musical changes, but also the circumstances of their chance encounter. Most likely, Jagger would be wearing earphones, and he would not have been clutching his treasured, hard-to-find blues LPs. He might still have treasured them, but they wouldn't have been hard to find; he could go online and find Robert Johnson, Muddy Waters, Elmore James, and most of the other great bluesmen. He could hear excerpts from their recordings, buy their albums online, or access them through file sharing, both legal and illegal. And they would be stored on his iPod; there would be no album covers in sight.

The growth of alternative music is due in part to the increased ease with which musicians can create and distribute their music. This in turn is the product of such post-1980 developments as the emergence of the personal computer and the Internet.

## Music and the Personal Computer

In 1985, music making on a computer was a cumbersome task. Apple had just sold its first Macintosh computers the year before. Windows and Sound Tools, the first iteration of Digidesign's Pro Tools digital audio workstation, would not appear until 1987. By 1995, both Windows and Mac had several software companies offering digital audio workstations and other computer audio software. However, users often took coffee breaks during processor-intensive tasks. CD drives that enabled users to play, then burn, audio CDs were moving from high-end accessory to standard equipment. By 2005, computers could serve not only as the heart of inexpensive but high-end recording studios but also as performance instruments. At contemporary concerts, laptops are almost as common on stage as electric guitars.

The rapid increase in computing power predicted by Moore's law (that the complexity of integrated circuits, with respect to minimum component cost, doubles every 24 months) has made high-quality recording affordable for almost everyone. For a penny of the seventies recording dollar, enterprising independent bands can now record, mix, burn, and package their music, using a PC, software, and a few peripherals. They no longer need to go to expensive studios to record; even Garage Band, Apple's entry-level digital audio workstation, can accommodate dozens of tracks and make available a wide range of special effects. Computers have also created new modes for distributing music, both legal and illegal, because of the rise of a corollary phenomenon: the Internet.

## The Internet

The first attempts to create an Internet, or network of networks, dates back to the seventies. By 1980, a protocol that enabled different networks to communicate with one another was in place. During its early years, the Internet was mainly under government supervision and control; the National Science Foundation managed it in the United States. However, in 1993, the Internet backbone was opened to the private sector in the United States, and Mosaic, the first browser, became available. (Mosaic became Netscape the following year.) Browsers simplified access to the Internet by providing a graphical user interface, similar to those found on Windows and Mac operating systems. Rapid development in every aspect of the Internet experience, from increased bandwidth to faster computers and more capable browsers, has made downloading and—more recently—uploading audio and video routine.

For listeners, the Internet has collapsed time and space. Users can listen to music from around the world, and from most of the century. By way of example, before writing this paragraph, I listened to two complete songs online. The first was "Vahsi" (pronounced "wah-shee"), a song recorded by Kesmeseker, a Turkish alternative band. It's very much in the international rock style; only the language of the vocals gives its country of origin away. The second song I heard was Cole Porter's 1928 hit "Let's Misbehave," recorded by Irving Aaronson and his Commanders. Aaronson led one of the top dance orchestras of the late twenties and early thirties. That I could do this would only have been imagined as recently as the early nineties.

The Internet is in the process of turning back the clock to the first half of the century. Before 1965, the single was the unit of currency in pop and rock. Before the long-playing record became standard, an album was literally that: several 78 rpm discs collected in a folder. Most pre-LP albums contained classical music. It wasn't until the fifties that the long-playing "album"—which put the equivalent of an album's worth of 78 rpm recordings on a single disc—came into widespread use, and it wasn't until the mid-sixties that the album became the preferred format for rock music, as we noted earlier. For decades, listeners had to buy an entire album, even if they were interested in only one or two tracks. Now, with the emergence of iTunes and other Internet-enabled delivery services, buyers can choose between buying an album or buying an individual track. In this way, it has ushered in a return of the single, while preserving the album as an option. Similarly, subscription services such as Rhapsody are in effect an online jukebox—with millions of choices and a monthly fee instead of three plays for a quarter.

## Consolidation of the Majors and the Rise of Indies

These developments have provided a paradigm-shifting counterpoint to the continuing consolidation of the record industry. In 1980, there were six major record labels: Columbia, RCA, EMI, Polygram, MCA, and WCI. Collectively, they sold about four-fifths of the recordings released that year. By 2005, there were four majors, with the possibility of only three on the horizon. Seagram acquired MCA in 1995 and Polygram in 1998; they became the Universal Music Group. Columbia (bought by Sony) and RCA (bought by BMG) merged in 2003. An attempted merger between EMI and Warner in 2000 was called off; it may still happen. The four companies continue to control a decided majority of recorded music, although they market it under numerous labels: in 2005, about 82 percent of the recordings sold in the United States came from one of these majors.

The **majors** are as international as the music they sell. By 2006, three of the four companies had headquarters outside of the United States. Their operations have been similarly diverse. They have served, in effect, as large holding companies, providing administrative structure for numerous smaller labels targeted to specific markets. As a result, the recording industry has continued to diversify.

What the majors lack is the flexibility to respond to variation and change. This has opened the door for independent labels, and even independent artists, to market quickly and specifically, using all available resources. Computers and the Internet enable them to do so at a fraction of the conventional marketing costs. The use of a website for promotion, distribution, and online delivery eliminates upfront production expenses, such as pressing a large quantity of CDs and the need for middlemen and conventional channels of distribution. At the same time, it makes music immediately available to a global audience. Because of these technological advances, artists and entrepreneurs have been able to create their own independent labels—including **netlabels** that only deliver music online, launch personal websites, start online artist cooperatives, and establish interest groups. All of this has enabled artists and labels to extend the sense of personal connection to a potentially much wider audience and return more revenue to the artists themselves. Ani DiFranco, whose music is heard following, is the "poster girl with a poster" for this kind of entrepreneurship: she formed her own label, Righteous Babe, rather than wait for a major label to offer her a contract, and she created a flashy website to promote it.

Computers and the Internet have served as an underground stream that has continued to nourish the alternative movement even as major labels co-opt promising alternative acts. In effect, it has extended the garage-band ethos through the entire creator-consumer cycle: with a broadband connection and a reasonably current computer, bands can distribute from the den as easily as they can rehearse and record in the basement.

# From Punk to Alternative

The boundary between punk and new wave on the one hand and alternative on the other seems more geographic than temporal or musical. The formation of the first alternative bands occurred around 1980, when the careers of bands like the Clash, Elvis Costello and the Attractions, and the Talking Heads were at a high point. Their music represents a stylistic continuation of punk and new wave; there is no radical difference between the two at the beginning, although alternative would soon diversify into a much more varied music.

However, alternative took root in college towns throughout the United States, rather than in major metropolitan areas. Small clubs were its first venues, and college radio stations were among the first to broadcast the music of alternative bands. The size of the town was not as important as the size of the university: it was the student body that provided the most enthusiastic support for these bands. Active regional scenes, in the United States and ultimately throughout the world, would become a hallmark of alternative music.

## Early Alternative

The two bands most responsible for starting the alternative music movement were Hüsker Dü, based in Minneapolis (the home of the University of Minnesota), and R.E.M., formed in Athens, Georgia (the home of the University of Georgia). Both locales were well outside the New York–London axis where punk and new wave flourished. Hüsker Dü (the group took their name from a Danish board game) began as a hardcore punk band trying to out-Ramone the Ramones. Their music occasionally ventured beyond this frenetic-paced music toward a more moderate and melodic style. Although admired as an important influence on the new alternative movement, Hüsker Dü never crossed over to a more mainstream audience. That was not the case with R.E.M.

**R.E.M.**  R.E.M. formed in 1980 by guitarist Peter Buck (b. 1956) and vocalist Michael Stipe (b. 1960); they began as one of the numerous do-it-yourself groups that sprang up in punk's wake. Buck and Stipe recruited bassist Mike Mills (b. 1958) and drummer Bill Berry (b. 1958), agreed on a name (R.E.M. is the acronym for rapid eye movement, a defining characteristic of the lightest stage of sleep), then performed relentlessly. They quickly became favorites of the local underground rock scene, playing college bars and parties while waiting for their break, which came quickly.

"Radio Free Europe," R.E.M. (1981)

"Radio Free Europe" (1981), their first hit, helped put the band on the rock music map and establish the essentially retrospective orientation of alternative music. It has the bright tempo, clean rhythm, and lean sound associated with David Bowie and new wave bands. The texture is spare in the verse; by contrast, the chorus features a much richer texture because of the jangly, reverberant guitar figuration and the active bass line underneath Stipe's vocals.

Characteristically for R.E.M., the lyric is as elliptical as the music is clear. The words are intelligible but what do they mean? By their own admission, the band has deliberately written nonspecific lyrics. As Michael Stipe said in a late-eighties interview, "I've always left myself pretty open to interpretation."

---

♪ **KEY FEATURES**

**"Radio Free Europe," R.E.M. (1981)**
- Non-narrative lyrics whose meaning is abstruse at best
- Clean, prominent rock rhythm in drums at a fast tempo
- Sharp contrast between open sound of the verse and warmer, guitar-enriched texture of the chorus
- Active bass line and harmonies in the chorus go beyond punk basics

---

The sharp and sudden contrasts between verse and chorus provide a foretaste of what would become a defining feature of alternative music: dramatic, often jarring contrasts within songs. And Buck's flashback to a guitar sound directly descended from the Byrds' Roger McGuinn provides an early instance of the infusion of alternative's punk base with elements from other retro styles.

By the late eighties, R.E.M. had begun to bring alternative into the mainstream: "The One I Love" (1987) was their first Top 10 single. They would remain a popular band through the nineties, although Berry retired from performing in 1997.

In their determination to follow their own creative path, even if it circled back to the past instead of toward the future, the group set the tone for the alternative movement. And the simplicity of their sound—basic instrumentation, clear textures, little if any electronic wizardry—was a model for the alternative bands that followed.

## Beyond Punk: Infusions of Funk and Metal

Among the most eclectic and electric new sounds of the late eighties and early nineties alternative scene was the music created by bands such as the Red Hot Chili Peppers, Primus, Jane's Addiction, Living Colour, and the Spin Doctors. Like the pop middle ground surveyed in Chapter 18, this alternative music thoroughly integrated black and white music. But all of it was almost militantly anti-pop.

The songs expressed wildly different attitudes, from rage to razor-sharp humor. However, they shared stylistic common ground, which comes mainly from two features. One was deep roots in soul and sixties hard rock. This connection is evident in the complex, active, syncopated rhythms and the reaffirmation of the basic rock-band instrumentation. The other was the infusion of elements from important non-pop styles of the late seventies and eighties, most commonly funk, heavy metal, and rap. From funk, they took complex, active 16-beat rhythms. From heavy metal, they took bold guitar playing, extreme distortion, and virtuosity: Les Claypool of Primus is a strong candidate for the Van Halen of the electric bass. They occasionally overlaid these mixes with rap-inspired voice parts, more spoken than sung.

In 1985, none of these sources was new. Neither was the idea of forging new styles by mixing black and white sources: that is rock's most time-honored tradition. What gave the music a late eighties sound was its thorough integration of rock and soul, and punk and funk, and the currency of its sources. We hear this interplay in "Good Time Boys," a track from the Red Hot Chili Peppers' 1989 album *Mother's Milk*.

**The Red Hot Chili Peppers**  The Red Hot Chili Peppers was formed in 1983 by four alumni of Fairfax High School of West Hollywood, California. Two of the original four, bassist Michael "Flea" Balzary (b. 1962) and vocalist Anthony Kiedis (b. 1962), are still band members. Hillel Slovak (1962–1988), the original guitarist, died of a heroin overdose in 1988; his death prompted drummer Jack Irons (b. 1962) to leave the band. Drummer Chad Smith (b. 1961) and guitarist John Frusciante (b. 1970) replaced Irons and Slovak.

"Good Time Boys," the Red Hot Chili Peppers (1989)

The Red Hot Chili Peppers received their training in funk from the highest authority. George Clinton produced their 1985 album *Freaky Styley*, which also featured Maceo Parker and Fred Wesley, both veterans of James Brown's band. Neither their self-titled debut album nor *Freaky Styley*, their second album, went anywhere commercially, but their next album, *The Uplift Mofo Party Plan* (1987), did. *Mother's Milk* (1989), with new band members Smith and Frusciante, did even better: it would become the group's first platinum album, eventually selling over 2 million units.

In "Good Time Boys," the Red Hot Chili Peppers merge the edge of punk with the strong bass lines of funk, the distorted guitar sounds and prominent and complex riffs of hard rock and heavy metal, and raplike vocals. Among the most innovative features of the song is the presence of both a strong bass line and a prominent guitar part. In the music that we have heard, typically either guitar or bass is dominant—guitar in rock, bass in R&B. Here they are virtually equal partners. Flea's bass lines stand out beneath the rap-style verse; Frusciante's complex guitar riffs take over in the instrumental interludes. And with its chanted, pentatonic vocal line, sung in unison by the band and doubled on the bass, the chorus recalls Parliament-style funk. All this supports an upbeat, self-promoting lyric, much closer to rock and roll and early rap in style and spirit than it is to the anger of punk or the weirdness of new wave. A simulated spinning of the radio dial interrupts the song just after the midway point. The final radio clip ends with the phrase "She's a white girl . . ." sung to a vanilla accompaniment; the abrupt return to the funky groove underscores the strong black influence in this song.

The influence is especially evident in the rhythm. From the very opening riff to the end of the song, the rhythms are complex, active, and highly syncopated. Smith lays down a rock beat, but Frusciante's riffs, Flea's bass lines, and Kiedis's rap-style vocals in the verse all move at 16-beat speed.

♪ **KEY FEATURES**

**"Good Time Boys," the Red Hot Chili Peppers (1989)**

- "Good Time Boys" has a good-time lyric, rapped in the verse, sung in the chorus
- Both bass and guitar have prominent roles: fusion of R&B and rock instrumental roles
- Thick texture because of active guitar and bass lines and low- or mid-register placement
- Complex 16-beat rhythms over a rock beat in both vocal and instrumental lines

"Good Time Boys" illustrates the punk/funk fusion of the latter part of the eighties and early nineties. The infusion of funk and rap elements helped introduce a different tone in alternative music and broaden its horizons. The success of the Red Hot Chili Peppers helped put alternative on the music industry's radar and blur the musical, commercial, ecological, and ideological boundaries that distinguished alternative from other genres.

The band's well-documented problems with drugs—Kiedis, Frusciante, and Flea were addicts—crippled the band during the nineties; Frusciante left the band in 1992 and was invited to return in 1998 after quitting drugs. They are now the leading "modern rock" act in the music industry. Like other acts that have moved from the fringes of the industry to stardom, they have left the alternative world behind. And they were never at the center of it, as were R.E.M. and Nirvana during their early years. For the Red Hot Chili Peppers, "alternative" is increasingly just a label.

## Women's Voices

Women quickly found a home in the alternative movement. Their growing presence can be understood as still another dimension of the more prominent place of women in popular music: the eighties were the decade not only of Madonna but also Joan Jett, the Go-Go's, and the Bangles. What made the work of women in alternative music distinctive was that their voices were not constrained in any way by the expectations of more mainstream music. Alternative gave feminists a forum and enabled women of every persuasion to speak their mind.

The women's movement within alternative music took root in the latter part of the eighties and flourished in the nineties. Among the important trends was the **riot grrrl** movement, which supported a militant feminist agenda with post-punk music that favored confrontation over chops (that is, musical skill). The music was part of a self-contained subculture: Bands such as Bratmobile and Bikini Kill played in clubs and at music festivals that promoted feminist solidarity. Feminist fanzines nurtured and promoted them and other acts, and independent labels released their recordings The **queercore** movement, which reacted against the more mainstream gay and lesbian views, found a musical voice in the work of bands such as Sister George, Tribe 8, and Team Dresch, whose founder Donna Dresch also created the fanzine *Chainsaw*, which she spun off into a still-active record label.

Alternative music also supported a revival of singer-songwriters, many of them women. Even as artists such as Tracy Chapman, Suzanne Vega, k.d. lang, and Alanis Morrissette garnered major label contracts and the occasional Grammy award (Tracy Chapman's "Give Me One Reason" won a Grammy in 1996 for Best Rock Song), other singer-songwriters such as Patty Larkin, Dar Williams, and Ani DiFranco also toured and recorded extensively.

That the music of women within the alternative movement would take these two directions should not be surprising, because they have their roots in the two seventies styles most open to women. Patti Smith was a punk pioneer, and musicians like Talking Heads bassist Tina Weymouth made women instrumentalists less exceptional—Kim Gordon, the bassist with Sonic Youth, followed in her footsteps. Similarly, singer-songwriters like Joni Mitchell and Carly Simon brought a feminine perspective to the forefront of popular music; the music of contemporary artists such as Ani DiFranco continues that tradition.

**Ani DiFranco**  Although her music has evolved away from what she calls the "folk punk" of her early recordings, Ani Di Franco (b. 1970) embodies the entrepreneurial spirit of alternative music as fully as any artist. She started her own record company, Righteous Babe Records, in 1989 and put out her first album the following year. While in college at New York City's New School, she began touring actively, performing in small clubs and other venues where she built up a loyal following. As she and her label grew more successful (it now offers all of her recordings, plus recordings by twelve other acts), she established the Righteous Babe Foundation, to give support to causes in which she believes, including queer visibility, opposition to the death penalty, and historic preservation. (The new headquarters of Righteous Babe is a formerly abandoned church in Buffalo.)

Like Joni Mitchell, whose music has reflected a similarly wide-ranging curiosity and a from-the-heart perspective, DiFranco's music has ranged from contemporary takes on the urban folk style to collaborations with major artists such as Prince, Janis Ian, Maceo Parker, and the Buffalo Philharmonic Orchestra. The three constants have been incisive lyrics, which usually speak either to social and political issues dear to her heart or the current take on her personal life; her affecting voice; and her fluent and imaginative acoustic guitar playing. We hear her mordant view on a failed relationship in "32 Flavors," a track from her 1995 album *Not a Pretty Girl*.

"32 Flavors" is the product of just two musicians: DiFranco and percussionist Andy Stochansky, a longtime collaborator. Together, they update the work of the great singer-songwriters of the early seventies. DiFranco's guitar accompaniment, which remains consistent throughout the song, is more elaborate and melodic than the accompaniments typically heard in the folk and folk-inspired music of the sixties and seventies. Guitar(s)—DiFranco added a discreet bass guitar part—and percussion provide a buoyant cushion for DiFranco's scathing indictment of a former partner. Lines like "cuz some day you are going to get hungry/and eat most of the words you just said" cut like a scalpel because they are funny and true. DiFranco's warm, low-key vocal style in this song resonates with the gentle accompaniment; its understated quality gives the lyrics even more bite, because of the contrast between the message and its delivery. The extended percussion outro is a nice bonus, although not connected thematically to the lyric.

The gently flowing music of Ani Di-Franco heard here is some distance stylistically from the punk-inspired sounds that typify alternative music. However, her do-it-yourself approach to all aspects of her career—performing, recording, managing, promoting, and support for other grassroots efforts in causes that are important to her—embodies the spirit of alternative music; so does her high-mindedness. Her enterprise and determination in charting her own career path, unbeholden to authority figures in any branch of the music industry, has been an inspiration to numerous young musicians.

Ani DiFranco performing at a rally for Green Party presidential candidate Ralph Nader.

♪ **KEY FEATURES**

**"32 Flavors," Ani DiFranco (1995)**

- Sharp-edged lyric that describes a relationship gone bad with vivid images and imaginative, occasionally humorous wordplay
- Compelling low-key vocal style an ideal foil for lyrics
- Rhythmically active and melodically imaginative guitar/percussion accompaniment create a buoyant cushion for words and melody

"32 Flavors,"
Ani DiFranco
(1995)

Interestingly, just as DiFranco's career began, alternative began its move into the mainstream, in the music of groups such as Nirvana. We consider their music, and the generation to whom they addressed it.

# Alienation

The next three tracks discussed in this chapter are Nirvana's "Smells Like Teen Spirit," Nine Inch Nails' "I Do Not Want This," and Radiohead's "Paranoid Android." One typically finds them identified as representative examples of grunge, industrial, and **art rock** or **prog rock**, respectively. The musical resources used on each of these recordings differs markedly. Still, there is an undercurrent that connects them despite their obvious musical differences.

All project a sense of alienation. It pours out of the lyrics and the music. And it comes from and speaks to a group dubbed Generation X.

## Generation X

*Generation X* is a term popularized by the Canadian novelist Douglas Coupland: it identifies the children of the baby boomers—those born mainly in the latter part of the sixties and the seventies. Most were born during the hangover from the sixties, with race riots, the squalid end to the Vietnam War, the rise of the "silent majority," the impeachment of Nixon, and rampant inflation all but obliterating the optimism with which the decade began. The members of Generation X, some of whom came from counterculture families, came of age during the "greed is good" eighties. Many, and especially those stuck in service-industry "McJobs" (another term coined by Coupland), felt completely estranged from their baby-boomer parents and the world portrayed in the media. They saw little hope for advancement in their work; many felt that their odds of enjoying the lifestyle of the rich, if not the famous, were about as good as winning the lottery. They were more in tune with the "no future" mindset broadcast by the disaffected youth in Great Britain and North America and the punk bands that set it to music. The "X" used to identify them underscored their lack of identity and power. As a result, they turned away from mainstream society and turned toward the music that expressed their anger, frustration, and alienation. Their anthem was Nirvana's 1991 hit "Smells Like Teen Spirit."

## Grunge

The pivotal song in the history of alternative rock as a commercial music was Nirvana's "Smells Like Teen Spirit," from their 1991 album, *Nevermind*. For this recording, Nirvana consisted of singer-guitarist Kurt Cobain (1967–1994), bassist Chris Novoselic (b. 1965), and drummer Dave Grohl (b. 1969). Grohl replaced the drummers on Nirvana's first album, *Bleach* (1989), which the group made for just over $600. In the wake of its surprising success, Nirvana signed with Geffen Records. As a result, *Nevermind* was a far more elaborately produced album.

The album soared to number 1, dethroning Michael Jackson's *Dangerous* album, which had been on top of the charts. "Smells Like Teen Spirit" got incessant airplay from MTV. All of a sudden the nineties had an anthem: it is still among the best-known songs of the decade. Alternative had crossed over.

Nirvana's particular brand of alternative was called **grunge**. Grunge fused punk disaffection with the power and distortion of heavy metal. Like so many other alternative styles, it started on the fringes—literally: Cobain and Novoselic formed Nirvana in Aberdeen, Washington, which is on the fringe of North America. The group's first single appeared on one of the many indie labels: the appropriately named Sub-Pop, which was based in Seattle. Nirvana's sudden success made Seattle the mecca for grunge, but the sound had already surfaced in several locations around the United States.

In retrospect, it is easy to understand the enormous appeal of "Smells Like Teen Spirit," especially to its target audience: angry young people who were not ready to buy into the system. The lyrics jerk from image to idea, like a trigger-happy video editor. Their power comes not from their coherence but from the jarring juxtapositions—mulatto, albino, mosquito, libido; hello, how low.

The music amplifies this sense of dislocation. The song begins with a distinctive four-

Nirvana in 1991, while performing at the Warfield Theater in San Francisco. From left to right: Chris Novoselic (in back), Dave Grohl, Kurt Cobain.

chord pattern. It is barely amplified; it sounds almost as if Cobain is trying it out for a song he's writing. Suddenly, we hear the same riff, this time with the whole band in heavy metal mode. Just as suddenly, the middle falls out—we are left with just bass, simple drum timekeeping, and a haunting two-note riff, which serves as an introduction to the verse; it continues underneath Cobain's singing. The two-note riff speeds up under the "hello/how low." The two-note vocal riff that sets "hello" then becomes the raw melodic material for the climactic section of the refrain. Here Cobain sings as if his throat is being ripped out. A short instrumental interlude, which interrupts the four-chord progression, bridges the refrain and the verse that follows.

We hear this same sequence of events, then a loud instrumental version of the verse and "hello" section. Instead of the refrain, however, the song shifts to a third verse; we hear the entire verse/bridge/refrain sequence again, followed by primal screams on the word "denial."

"Smells Like Teen Spirit" is a dark song. Everything about it conveys that message; its enormous impact comes in part from the reinforcement of this mood on so many levels. The chord progression does not follow a well-established path; because of this we respond more to its rise and fall. It is like a hole that one cannot climb out of: every time the band arrives at the fourth and highest chord, they drop

"Smells Like Teen Spirit," Nirvana (1991)

back down. Because the bass line/outline runs through almost all of the song, despite all of the contrasts, it seems to suggest a depressed state of mind that's impossible to shake. In this context, the instrumental break following the refrain sounds absolutely demonic; it is purposefully ugly, even mocking.

The big innovation—and perhaps the biggest stroke of genius—is the schizo-phrenic shift from section to section. Nirvana creates sharply defined sound worlds within each section of the song. They are haunting, mocking, and angry in turn. They create sharp contrasts from section to section: the kind one would more likely encounter between one song and the next, rather than within a song. When combined with the relentless chord progression and the repetition of the two two-note melodic fragments, they project a mood of utter despair: one can rage against the wind—or the machine—or fall into an almost apathetic state, but it is impossible to shake off the dark mood.

"Smells Like Teen Spirit" is a remarkable synthesis of several different, almost contradictory, elements. The melodic material—especially the several instrumental hooks, the "hello" section, and the vocal refrain—embed themselves in the listener's ear; they offer immediate points of entry. At the same time, they don't sound like music calculated to be appealing. Rather, they seem to be a direct expression of the mood of the song; that they are catchy at the same time is a bonus.

The sharp contrasts and abrupt shifts from section to section help "Smells Like Teen Spirit" portray the darkest depression: an oppressive weight that cannot be thrown off. It is easy to understand why "Smells Like Teen Spirit" was the song of the nineties. And it makes Cobain's subsequent suicide even harder to take; it is as if he let us into his mind so that we can feel his despair.

"Smells Like Teen Spirit" is a punk song in spirit: it expresses rage, alienation, and frustration in both words and music. But the eclectic mix of styles—power trio intro, understated verse, metal breaks—serves an expressive purpose here. It extends the emotional range of punk, if only because the quiet of the verse makes the louder sections, especially the chorus with its short vocal riffs, more powerful by contrast. Classic punk drove in only one gear; here, Nirvana shifts back and forth between several.

## Industrial Rock

The **industrial rock** movement in rock has its roots in two avant-garde trends in classical music: *musique concrète* (the assembling of musical compositions from pre-recorded sounds) and electronic music. In the seventies, industrial pioneers such as Throbbing Gristle melded electronic and concrete sounds and noises with percussion sounds and used it as a backdrop for provocative lyrics that explored subjects, such as deviant sexual practices, widely regarded as taboo. Within a decade, adventurous bands had begun to incorporate industrial sounds into other genres, most notably heavy metal and rock.

Among the most creative minds fusing industrial music with rock has been Trent Reznor (b. 1965). Reznor, who studied computer engineering at Allegheny College before dropping out and moving to Cleveland, found work as a handyman at Right Track Studio and received permission to record his own music when the studio was not in use. This solitary work was a prelude to the rest of his career: several demos from his time at Right Track appeared on *Pretty Hate Machine*, his first Nine Inch Nails album.

Nine Inch Nails came into being in 1988, if only in Reznor's head. The name of the group was a seemingly whimsical choice. As Reznor acknowledged in a 1994 interview, Nine Inch Nails was chosen for its appearance—it was easily abbreviated and the reverse *N* made a striking visual image; Reznor claimed it had no literal meaning. Nine Inch Nails has had a schizophrenic existence: in the studio, the "band" is Reznor and his equipment; on tour, it is a working band that Reznor assembles for that purpose. In a 2002 interview with rock journalist Anthony de Curtis, Reznor contrasted his meticulous production in the studio with what he called the "chaotic" experience of performing his music live. It is in the studio that Reznor crafted his distinctive fusion of industrial, punk, and heavy metal. We sample it through "I Do Not Want This," a track from *The Downward Spiral* (1994), his third complete album as Nine Inch Nails.

"I Do Not Want This," Nine Inch Nails (1994)

A common complaint about the music of Nine Inch Nails by "pure" industrial acts and their fans was that Reznor had diluted the impact of industrial rock by shoehorning it into conventional pop songs. If we listen to "I Do Not Want This" reductively, we can hear how the various sections coalesce into the familiar verse/chorus form: there is an instrumental introduction, two verselike sections, and a two-part chorus, which is repeated. What seems like an instrumental outro transforms into an extended interlude that leads to the shattering climax.

However, if we look at this familiar form not as a mold but as a point of departure, we can hear how Reznor has crafted the form to portray a person perpetually on the edge, and one who occasionally loses it. From the start, Reznor blends industrial and conventional sounds: initially, the mix pairs an electronically generated percussion sound in a distinctive rhythm with a lonely, discordant piano riff that would have sounded completely at home in the atonal music of the early twentieth century. The vocal part—more than spoken, less than sung—enters over this bleak backdrop. The second segment of the verse abruptly shifts to a new, more complex texture, with wordless singing, whispered text, and several layers of electronic percussion sounds. The piano riff returns at the beginning of the chorus, as Reznor sings "I Do Not Want This" in a quavery voice that sounds on the verge of hysteria, as well as preserving the wordless vocal of the previous section. More electronic sounds, including an insistent repeated note in a low register, produced on a synthesizer, ramp up the tension.

It all boils over in the second part of the chorus, where Reznoz screams "Don't you tell me how I feel" over heavily distorted power chords played in an irregularly accented 16-beat rhythm. The second pass through the form features consistently more activity, as if the protagonist of the lyric is inside a pressure cooker and someone has turned up the heat.

By using industrial sounds and the heavy distortion of heavy metal, and contrasting it with the fragile piano figure, Reznor seems to convey in music as well as words and voice the alienation of the individual in contemporary culture. The juxtaposition of the relentless and impersonal industrial sounds with the vocal parts and piano riff suggest that the distress conveyed in the lyric derives at least in part from the essential impersonality of technology.

The sense of alienation created by technology has been a familiar theme throughout the twentieth century. Its repeated refrains include not only its impersonality, but also its potential for evil—even though the Big Brother world depicted in George Orwell's *1984* never materialized—and the increasingly rapid pace of its evolution. Precisely because the industrial elements are so prominent and persistent in "I Do Not Want This," and because the contrast between those sounds (and the distorted power chords) and the piano figure and vocal sounds is so jarring, it is hard *not* to create a causal relationship between those sounds and the distress projected in the lyric and its spoken/sung/chanted/shouted delivery.

This connection between technology and alienation is reinforced by the contrast in sound world between "I Do Not Want This" and the other tracks on *The Downward Spiral*. By incorporating industrial elements into his music and mixing them with more conventional instruments, Reznor has expanded his sound palette enormously. Not surprisingly, he creates a sound world that is as distinctive as the lyric for each track on his albums. This is one of the most striking and appealing features of his music, especially his later releases.

*The Downward Spiral* did for Reznor and industrial alternative what *Nevermind* did for Nirvana and grunge. The album peaked at number 2 on the *Billboard* Top 200 chart and eventually went multiplatinum. Critics continued to laud it: it eventually made top-album lists by *Rolling Stone* and *Q*.

Reznor has continued to develop his technological skills in step with the rapid developments in music-related computer technology, and to share them with those who enjoy his music, sometimes in unusual ways. He has begun sharing multitrack sessions via his website; these have been available in various file formats. Fans can download the file, open it in the application of their choice, and remix it as they choose. In this endeavor, he joins other music/technology pioneers such as Todd Rundgren, whose 1995 album *The Individualist* was among the first to be released via the Internet and an early enhanced CD.

## The New Art Rock of the Nineties

Like the original members of the Red Hot Chili Peppers, the members of Radiohead all went to the same high school: Abingdon School, a private school outside of Oxford. Drummer Phil Selway (b. 1967), guitarist Ed O'Brien (b. 1968), guitarist-vocalist Thom Yorke (b. 1968), bassist Colin Greenwood (b. 1969), and multi-instrumentalist Jonny Greenwood (b. 1971)—Colin's younger brother—formed the band On A Friday in 1986. They went to different universities but continued to practice together over vacations during their college years and came together again as Radiohead in 1992.

Their first album made it quite clear that the group would find their own direction. The album name *Pablo Honey* came from a bit by the Jerky Boys, a comedy group whose CDs consist of irritatingly funny phone calls. "Creep," the single that got them noticed, is very much in the spirit of the times: it is Buddy Holly, deeply depressed. Musically, however, it does little to predict the group's future.

The alienation that marked Radiohead's early work becomes even more apparent in subsequent albums. This may be evident before the first sound: The booklet that comes with *OK Computer* (1997) contains the lyrics displayed almost randomly amid collage-like images. Both words and images are hard to decode. *Kid A* (2000) is even more frugal with content: there are simply fragments of images and no lyrics. It is as if the group is challenging its audience: we have something of value to say to you, but

Radiohead in Oxford, 1999. From left to right: Ed O'Brien, Thom Yorke, Jonny Greenwood, Phil Selway, Colin Greenwood.

you have to work hard to discover what it is. This attitude extends to their songs, as we hear in "Paranoid Android," from *OK Computer*.

> Among the most formidable challenges facing newly-formed bands is coming up with a name. This challenge first surfaced in the early sixties when bands began using group names like the Beach Boys instead of individual or "star + sidemen" names. Radiohead, like the Beatles, began with a false start: they originally called themselves On A Friday, because it was the only day that they could rehearse. However, after a critic found their name too mundane, they changed it to Radiohead after the 1986 Talking Heads' song "Radio Head."

**"Paranoid Android"**  "Paranoid Android" was a boundary-stretching single: this is apparent on even the first hearing, because the song is almost $6^{1}/_{2}$ minutes long, more than double the length of a typical single. The lyrics are at once unremittingly depressing and incoherent. We have the impression of someone (human or android) holding his head and screaming "I can't stand this any more" as he goes mad.

The song is profoundly disturbing, not because the music is as dark as the lyrics, but because it so often so beautiful. It begins with a pan-Latin sound: intricate guitar figuration outlining exotic harmony, plus the shaker associated with Brazilian music and the claves of Cuban music, then a higher-pitched classical guitarlike line. There is no bass yet; the music floats. Yorke delivers the lyric slowly and in measured fashion, which directs our attention more to the haunting, plaintive quality of his voice. The refrain of this part has only two syllables: "what's then"; because there are only two words, our attention goes even more to the sound of his voice. A beautiful halo of sound surrounds it, as bass and a high synthesizer part enrich the texture. All this seems to resonate with the melancholy that is so much a part of Latin culture. Radiohead seems to have captured its essence in this part of the song, although they apply it to a quite different end.

A long transition to a new section begins with a guitar riff set against the Latin percussion. The riff appears on two levels and in two forms. The first statement lines up with four-beat measures. The higher-pitched restatement has a beat removed (4 beats + 3). The sense of imbalance that the foreshortened riff creates helps set up the next vocal section, which has no apparent connection to the previous section. We get a spark of distortion, then another statement of the riff with full-bore distortion. It gains in power because of the contrast with the two previous sections. After a brief guitar solo, we get a sustained chord, then a slower section with wordless vocal harmonies. Yorke sings over these simple but beautiful harmonies. Little by little, other layers are added; by the time the guitar riff interrupts again, the sonority is rich with vocal parts and sustained stringlike synthesizer sounds. The reprise of the guitar riff is strictly instrumental; with its abrupt ending, it seems to signal a descent into madness.

## ♪ KEY FEATURES

### "Paranoid Android," Radiohead (1997)

- Dark lyric, rich in obscure allusions, and as violently contrasting as the music
- Expansive, multisectional form that does not follow a familiar outline
- Strong contrasts in character between sections: haunting opening and third sections, bridged by unsettling instrumental interlude
- Remarkable variety in instrumentation, texture, and rhythm: Latin percussion, synthesizer sounds, plus rock band instruments: all supporting Yorke's quavery voice

The facts of the song—its sprawling length; the three distinct sections, plus the reprise of the second section; the strong contrast in character within and between sections; the deliberate delivery of the lyrics—are there. The reading of it is necessarily subjective. I have offered one response to "Paranoid Android"; your response might be quite different.

The more significant point is that the conflicts and discontinuities within the words, within the music, and between the words and music demand that listeners engage with the song in more than a casual way. In particular, the music is complex and rich enough—even though it is also quite accessible—to admit multiple levels of meaning. Not since the Beatles' demise has a group blended accessibility, challenge, sound imagination, and sound variety so artfully. This is rock aspiring to significance.

## Alienation and Fragmentation

The three songs discussed in this section create different sound worlds with different resources. "Smells Like Teen Spirit" is built around the sound of a basic rock band, although Cobain's two-note supporting riff introduces a fresh timbre. "I Do Not Want This" mixes conventional piano and distorted guitar with industrial sounds. "Paranoid Android" adds beautiful synthesized sounds and Latin percussion to the core rock band. These varied sound worlds in turn reflect the different tone and content of the lyrics.

Despite these differences, the songs have two common elements that place them in the nineties. One is the sense of alienation that the lyrics project. In all three there is palpable tension between the outside world and the world inside the protagonist's head. The other is sudden and jarring contrasts. In each song, the abrupt shifts from soft to loud seem to suggest a sudden loss of control: flying into a violent rage because the person can't stand it anymore. These shifts magnify the message of the words; as used here, they provide the most consistent and powerful expression of the alienation depicted in the lyrics.

The strong sectional contrasts—sometimes to the point of discontinuity—describe a formal approach that is precisely the opposite of that used in more conventional rock songs. There, the refrain establishes the mood of the songs; the function of the verses is to amplify and explain that overall mood. Here, the various sections create their own moods; we are violently whipped from one to the next. This kind of sonic fragmentation within a song is common in recent alternative music, in part because of the critical and commercial success of Nirvana, Nine Inch Nails, and Radiohead.

# The Persistence of Punk

Even as reverberations from the punk movement touched much of the new music of the eighties, "pure" punk—that is, the music that was most in tune with the attitude and sound of late seventies punk—went underground. With its breakneck tempos, screamed-out vocals, loud and crude riffs, and confrontational, politically charged lyrics, **hardcore punk** (or simply **hardcore**) was the most direct continuation of the punk esthetic established by the Sex Pistols. Bands such as Hüsker Dü, the Dead Kennedys, and Bad Religion were among the leading hardcore bands of the eighties.

The movement known as **post-punk** identifies a family of styles that merged the aggressive elements of punk with more experimental elements and outside influences, such as synthesizers. Joy Division, which dissolved in 1980 after the suicide of lead singer Ian Curtis, is generally regarded as a seminal post-punk band. The early industrial group Throbbing Gristle is often associated with post-punk. Other noteworthy bands include Public Image, Ltd. (fronted by John Lydon), Sisters of Mercy, and Sonic Youth.

The proliferation of punk-related sub- and sub-substyles in the eighties and nineties—for example, hardcore (leading to thrashcore, emo, and skate punk); post-punk (leading to gothic rock); and no wave—highlights the seemingly causal relationship between the number of styles and the enthusiasm and isolation of the fan base. Since 1980, the three most subdivided genres have been the second waves of punk, heavy metal, and dance music. Each has relatively small but extremely supportive followings, and each exists in a cocoonlike world well outside the mainstream. The profusion of labels is certainly due in part to the desire of fans and commentators (who are often one and the same) to provide the bands that they support with something that quickly and easily distinguishes them from other similar bands. In practice, the labels often overlap, and bands often find the distinguishing feature of a substyle (for example, breakneck tempos or extremely loud power chords) too confining.

## Enhancing Punk

From the start, the fundamental creative tension in punk has been between power and expressive range. The challenge for bands was to broaden the range without dampening the impact. In the seventies, this tension was manifested in the different paths of punk and new wave music. In the eighties, it was evident in the numerous punk offshoots, most notably in the numerous post-punk substyles, such as **no wave**. The most successful no wave band, critically and commercially, is Sonic Youth.

**Sonic Youth**   Sonic Youth is a four-person band formed in 1981. During the peak of its career in the latter part of the eighties and early nineties, the band members were guitarists Thurston Moore (b. 1958) and Lee Ranaldo (b. 1956), bassist-guitarist Kim Gordon (b. 1953), and drummer Steve Shelley (b. 1963).

Like other no wave bands, Sonic Youth brought a rock-as-art sensibility to their work. Using the basic instrumentation, fast tempos, and clear timekeeping as a point of departure for their style, they overlaid it with unusual guitar sounds, noise, exotic harmonies, and sharp contrasts in texture. This sound world supported lyrics that put a fresh spin on familiar themes, sung/shouted accessibly to a simple melody. We hear these qualities in "Hey Joni," a track from their critically acclaimed double album *Daydream Nation* (1988).

"Hey Joni,"
Sonic Youth
(1988)

"Hey Joni" begins with a low synthesizer drone that is gradually surrounded by extraneous noises. This abruptly gives way to the refrain of the song, in which both the connection and the distance from punk are evident. Drummer Shelley raps out a fast, straightforward rock rhythm—the kind that one expects to hear in a typical punk song. However, both guitarists alternate between conventional power chords and more dissonant and intricate figuration. An alternative effect comes to the forefront during the interlude between refrain and verse: syncopated riffs in one guitar part compete with high-register figuration that uses the more delicate sound of **harmonics** (musicians create the sound of harmonics on a stringed instrument by depressing the string only partway at certain points; this creates higher-pitched sounds with a distinctive ring). Other similar effects, such as the "Wipeout"-inspired glissando,

Steve Jennings/Corbis

Sonic Youth in 1990. From left to right: Lee Ranaldo, Thurston Moore, Kim Gordon, and Steve Shelley.

follow in the verse and subsequent instrumental interludes. The changes in texture, which are concentrated in the middle registers, create a kaleidoscopic effect.

For Sonic Youth, sonic variety is key. Although they start from a basic rock-band instrumentation, they create magical sounds with the interplay of often discordant riffs and figuration and by employing special effects, such as the harmonics used here. The song melds the energy of punk with the glorious guitar sounds and noises for which the group is known.

♪ **KEY FEATURES**

**"Hey Joni," Sonic Youth (1988)**
- Punk tempo and rhythm, marked clearly by the drummer
- Unusual texture: dense in the middle range because of multiple riffs and figuration, often with little or no bass
- An array of guitar effects, from conventional distortion to harmonics and the "noise-halos" that surround guitar pitches
- Jarring, often discordant harmonies, often layered on top of each other

Although *Daydream Nation* remains their most respected and best-known album, Sonic Youth has continued to evolve and explore new directions. Their tour with then barely known Nirvana was captured on the DVD *1991: The Year Punk Broke*. Their work, and especially the innovative guitar sounds and noises, have influenced more recent alternative bands.

## Pop Punk

Of all the challenges facing punk bands, perhaps the most complex was creating a viable fusion of punk and pop. As we have noted in previous chapters, punk reshaped rock and pop during the eighties and nineties. However, punk was a reaction against rock and pop; in attitude and musical substance, it was in direct opposition to mainstream music. As a result, the difficulty for punk was reconciling punk values with a pop sensibility. The danger was that the David and Goliath opposition of pop and the rock music establishment would morph into Jonah and the whale—punk being swallowed by pop.

Pop punk caught on in the mid-nineties, principally on the strength of albums and tours by bands such as Green Day, the Offspring, and Rancid. Other bands, such as Weezer and blink-182, followed in their wake. Its rise can be understood as both a product of and a reaction to grunge. Grunge brought the hard edge of alternative music into the mainstream, thus laying the foundation for a more aggressive tone in mainstream music. At the same time, those who were not ready for a steady diet of Nirvana-style doom and gloom welcomed music that blended punk's edge with a more upbeat tone.

**Green Day**  No band has done this more successfully than Green Day: guitarist-vocalist Billie Joe Armstrong (b. 1972), bassist Mike Dirnt (born Michael Pritchard, 1972), and drummer Tré Cool (born Frank Wright, 1972). The group, which has its roots in the East Bay region of northern California, was precocious: Armstrong and Dirnt played their first gig in 1988 as Sweet Children; Green Day, with drummer John Kiffmeyer, released their first record and completed their first nationwide tour in 1990. In 1991, Tré Cool replaced Kiffmeyer. Three years later, the group signed a contract with Reprise Records and released *Dookie*, which put them and pop punk in the mainstream consciousness.

Their career since that time has been a steady ascent. Their 2004 album *American Idiot*, which won a Grammy as Best Rock Album in 2005, reached the top of the charts in both the United States and abroad and received favorable reviews from the mainstream press. We sample their fusion of punk and pop in "Wake Me Up When September Ends," one of the tracks from the album. (The album and the video of the song include the unofficial fourth member of the band, guitarist Jason White [b. 1973], who has toured with the band since 1999.)

Since they signed a contract with a major label, Green Day has been castigated by the alternative and punk diehards for selling out. The discontent surfaced with *Dookie* and resurfaced strongly with *American Idiot*. One component of their discontent is the extraordinary success of the album, which has already sold well over 10 million units worldwide, including 1 million digital downloads. Those who feel that the band has put aside the attitude and atmosphere of punk in order to embrace pop will find plenty of ammunition in "Wake Me Up When September Ends."

"Wake Me Up When September Ends," Green Day (2004)

The lyric of the song is personal, not political. It alludes to Armstrong's pain as he recalls the death of his father, who died in September when Armstrong was 10. More generally, it is a bittersweet lament over the loss of innocence. (Interestingly, the video for the song completely recontextualizes the lyric: it depicts the relationship of a young couple that is torn apart when the man enlists in the military and is sent to Iraq.)

Musically, the song has more in common with the Everly Brothers' "All I Have to Do Is Dream" than any punk or alternative song on the playlist. The tempo is slow, and the tone is nostalgic, although the objects of nostalgia are distinctly different. In both, a tuneful melody is the dominant element. This holds true in "Wake Me Up When Spetember Ends" even in its restatement, where pounding punk power chords and drumbeats replace the gentle guitar accompaniment of the opening. Further, both the development of the opening phrase of the melody from a simple riff and the use of AABA form turn back the clock even more; this is the most characteristic melodic style and form in the Tin Pan Alley songs of the twenties and thirties. Finally, the delicate bell-like sounds that complement Armstrong's acoustic guitar during the opening are far removed from punk's characteristic sound world. By contrast, the punk elements seem to be an overlay: they are certainly not essential to the message of the song or its identity, which is all but complete after a full statement of the melody.

## ♪ KEY FEATURES

**"Wake Me Up When September Ends," Green Day (2004)**
- Tin Pan Alley–style pop song form: multiple statements of an AABA form
- Simple, memorable melody in the forefront
- Sharp contrast between voice and guitar setting in first statement of the

Those who value the song and the album—and there are many—can point out that accusing Green Day of selling out because they incorporated pop elements is simply a matter of putting theory before practice. The more appropriate issue is whether lyric and music work together to convey a consistent musical message. From this perspective, the pop elements are more relevant to the lyric than punk.

## Alternatives

Green Day's "Wake Me Up When September Ends" makes clear how nebulous "alternative" has become—in attitude, audience, and music. In its history of over twenty years, alternative music has evolved from the alternative to mainstream music into—at least in the case of Green Day and other popular "alternative" bands—one of many mainstream alternatives.

The blurring of the boundaries is an almost inevitable result of the nature of the alternative movement. As it took shape, alternative involved the intersection of three independent but interrelated domains: the us-versus-the-world attitude of punk; the alterative ecosystem of bands, indie labels, club owners, and the fans who followed the bands and wrote about them; and the punk-derived music that was the focus of the bands and their fans. Music is most clearly "alternative" when attitude, environment, and music overlap, as they did in R.E.M.'s "Radio Free Europe" and the songs on Nirvana's first album. However, each of these domains is inherently confining. Lyrics may keep their confrontational tone, but they shift the focus from the political and polemical to the personal: that was the case in Ani DiFranco's "32 Flavors."

The alternative world explodes when bands cross over—obtain a major label contract, perform for tens of thousands rather than a few hundred, make videos for MTV. It can become a source of distress not only for the fans but for the musicians, as Cobain's suicide evidences. From the start, bands strayed from the most basic musical features of punk: its volume level, simplistic but supercharged rhythmic approach, core rock instrumentation, and so on. Their challenge was to retain punk's spirit as they enriched or modified the punk essence. In this respect, there is a difference in kind, for example, between Van Halen's "Jump" and Sonic Youth's "Hey Joni." Both are clearly influenced by punk, but only "Hey Joni" sustains the punk spirit.

As even our miniscule sampling evidences, alternative music mushroomed from an underground movement into a major force in the music industry. Through these changes it retained a strong link to the past: no contemporary music has provided such a fresh take on the spirit and substance of rock.

. . . . . . . . . . . . . . . . . . . . . . . . . . . . . . . . . . . . . . . . . . . . . . . . . . . . . . . . . . . . . . . . . . . . . . . . . . . . . . .

## Terms to Remember

| | | |
|---|---|---|
| alternative | queercore | hardcore punk |
| Lollapalooza | art rock | post-punk |
| majors | prog rock | no wave |
| netlabels | grunge | harmonics |
| riot grrrl | industrial rock | |

. . . . . . . . . . . . . . . . . . . . . . . . . . . . . . . . . . . . . . . . . . . . . . . . . . . . . . . . . . . . . . . . . . . . . . . . . . . . . . .

## Applying Chapter Concepts

1. Alternative music includes a profusion of substyles. To explore the meaningfulness of these style labels, try the following activity. Select two substyles, using the Internet for substyles and bands whose music exemplifies them. Then choose at least two songs that are representative of the substyle and identify five features that, taken together, distinguish the substyle. Summarize your findings in a profile of the substyle. Then compare your profiles, noting the common ground and distinguishing features of the substyles.

2. Identify an act that was formed after 2000 that you think charts an important future trend in rock music. Select a song or two by the act and, using the song(s) as a reference, explain why you think the act is charting an innovative path.

# Rock in the Twenty-First Century:
## Issues and Opportunities

■ As we write this, rock is over fifty years old, and there is substantial evidence that it is here to stay. From the overwhelming success of the Rolling Stones' A Bigger Bang tour to the slew of new acts aspiring to rock-and-roll stardom via the Internet, rock and roll is in the air and up-to-date.

## The Future of Rock

The unavoidable question at this point is the future of rock: where does the music go from here? In the spirit of exploration that informs this text, we address this question by identifying three aspects of the contemporary rock scene that present both issues and opportunities, and we provide a historical perspective on the current state of rock-era music.

### Technology

I "prepared" for the writing of this paragraph by listening to Bob Dylan's "Someday Baby," a track from his new (2006) album *Modern Times*. My first two reactions were that Dylan still has something to say after over forty years in the business and that the band behind him sounds so much better than the bands he used in the sixties. The kinds of sloppy mistakes that one finds on the earlier albums—such as the bass player playing the wrong chord—are absolutely unthinkable here. The musicians provide flawless support for Dylan's gritty voice, and contemporary recording technology makes the removal of even the slightest flaw a relatively easy process.

Digital technology and the Internet have made affordable perfection a reality for musician and audience. Musicians in almost any economic bracket can edit their recordings and videos in the most detailed way without leaving any trace of their editorial work. Any imperfections—a slightly out-of-tune note, a vocal crack, an accent that is too loud or too soft—can be smoothed over by someone thoroughly familiar with a digital audio workstation application. Moreover, musicians can access

467

an ever-expanding library of pre-recorded sounds and loops, perfectly realized. Those who use these resources never have to worry about the drummer speeding up or the guitar player playing the wrong chord.

Song delivery and use is comparably perfect. Audiences can acquire a song for 99 cents or less and be assured that it will never degrade over time: it will always sound just as the artist intended.

The issues:

• "Perfection" in the studio is difficult, if not impossible, to replicate in live performance.

• In the use of pre-recorded materials and multistage recording, calculation replaces the spontaneous combustion that can result from the creative interaction of musicians performing together.

The opportunities:

• Sound synthesis, special effects, and sampling have enormously expanded the range of sounds that artists can incorporate into their music.

• Technology makes including them more efficient and more affordable: one can imagine string parts, then record them onto a track via a sampler and a keyboard, instead of writing out the parts and hiring musicians to perform them.

## Globalization and Regionalization

Rock is the first living expressive language that reaches to every corner of the world. It is not just that the international style that emerged in the sixties is all but universal. Other musical traditions, most notably classical music, have also found audiences on every continent. It is because local musicians have mixed the music of their culture with these international styles to create regional fusions: Pakistani techno, J-pop from Japan, zouk from the French Caribbean—the list is endless. It is not just a matter of importing a musical genre from another culture, but also reshaping it when it arrives. This is without precedent in human history. Never before has an expressive language of any kind been so close to universal. We are lucky to be alive at this moment in time and in a position to experience it!

The issue:

• Contact with the musical world outside the culture can marginalize or eliminate the authentic elements of the regional style.

The opportunity:

• Both the regional style and the prevailing international style can be enriched by contact with each other.

## Fragmentation and Fusion

In 2003, *Billboard* began producing a "comprehensive" album chart. This year-end chart ranks albums according to the number of units sold; genre is a non-issue. In 2005, the Top 10 artists on the chart were 50 Cent, Eminem, Green Day (with *American Idiot*), Mariah Carey, Kelly Clarkson, Gwen Stefani, Destiny's Child, U2, Shania Twain, and Rascal Flatts. These acts represent widely varying genres: rap, pop, R&B, modern rock/alternative, and country.

*Billboard*'s decision to create a comprehensive album chart was a tacit, if belated, acknowledgement of the extraordinarily fragmented musical landscape that we enjoy at the beginning of the twenty-first century; no one genre is dominant, as it was at the beginning of the rock era. The more than thirty charts through which *Billboard* monitors the sales of genres as diverse as dance, rap, bluegrass, Latin, and new age offer further evidence of the stylistic variety of contemporary music.

Cable television, satellite radio, and the Internet have made catering to niche markets economically viable: indeed, one can reach a global audience for the price of a server and domain name registration.

The issue:

• There is an absence of a body of music that a large segment of the population knows. Today, there is no music even remotely comparable in widespread popularity to the Beatles or Motown songs of the sixties.

The opportunity:

• Those working in different genres can become more aware of one another's music and can come together in new and intriguing ways. Ray Charles's *Genius Loves Company*, a duet album with artists ranging from fifties pop crooner Johnny Mathis to Willie Nelson and Norah Jones, was number 21 on the 2005 comprehensive album charts; a collaboration between Jay-Z and Linkin Park was number 25.

"Whirl-Y-Reel 1," Afro Celt Sound System (1996)

> To illustrate these aspects of the contemporary music scene, we offer "Whirl-Y-Reel 1," by the Afro Celt Sound System (or simply the Afro Celts). The Afro Celts include Celtic musicians playing such instruments as an Irish harp and a tin whistle; African musicians playing a battery of percussion instruments, including talking drums; and tech-savvy musicians who mixed modern dance rhythms with these timeless sounds. It is global—bringing together old and new and African and European. It leverages the new technology in both sound generation and production. And it is, without question, a successful fusion of strikingly dissimilar musical traditions.

# Rock at the Crossroads: Rhythm, Melody, and Innovation

The most surprising development at the turn of the twenty-first century was what didn't happen: there was no revolution. Recall that there were two revolutions in twentieth-century popular music. The first occurred in the teens and twenties, when a wholesale infusion of black music—ragtime, hot dance music, blues, and jazz—and new technology transformed the sound of popular music and changed American culture. The second was the by-now-familiar rock revolution of the fifties and sixties, in which a further infusion of black music and new technology transformed popular music and changed the world.

A third revolution was "due" around the turn of the century, but it hasn't happened—although new technologies that impacted both the creative process and music delivery were in place, another important new black music emerged, and lively underground scenes eventually crossed over to more mainstream audiences. One reason for the non-revolution is rock's inherent openness to new styles; another is the diversity of contemporary music. In the two previous revolutions, there was a dominant popular music establishment supported by a mainstream culture that viewed minorities, and especially blacks, as inferior and as a source of moral degradation. Rock changed the attitude toward minorities—of all kinds—and their culture: multi-culturalism is a rock-influenced and rock-era phenomenon. Moreover, the diversity of the music and the numerous outlets for it have made it impossible for the dominant players in the industry to concentrate their efforts in support of one particular style. Still another reason was that, unlike the previous two revolutions, the future direction of the music was not at all clear.

Minstrelsy opened the door for blacks to enter mainstream culture. They walked through it—first as minstrels, then as ragtime pianists, dance musicians, jazzmen, blues and pop singers, then as major players in rock-era music. Their music set in motion two evolutionary trends that have now run their course. One was a shift in musical emphasis from melody to rhythm; the other was a regular—even predictable—progression of style beats.

At the turn of the twentieth century, the most popular songs were flowing melodies set to a piano accompaniment in a bright waltz rhythm: the evergreen "Take Me Out to the Ball Game" remains the most familiar example. The musical interest in these songs resided almost exclusively in the melody; accompaniments were typically generic. There was none of the rhythmic interest that we associate with popular music, certainly since the twenties. Ragtime, a rhythmically interesting music, was on the fringes of the music business: its notoriety far exceeded its popularity. By the turn of the twenty-first century, the pendulum had swung to the other extreme: rhythm is the dominant element in contemporary music, often to the exclusion of melody. Rap and dance music are familiar styles, and active rhythms are a prominent feature in pop, rock, and R&B, as we have noted.

More specifically, ever since a black-based rhythmic conception became the rhythmic foundation for popular music, the speed of the defining rhythmic layer has doubled every twenty years or so: from the two-beat rhythms of the fox-trot in the twenties and thirties to the four-beat rhythms of swing in the thirties, forties, and early fifties; the eight-beat rhythms of rock in the latter part of the fifties, sixties, and seventies; and the 16-beat rhythms in a variety of styles, mostly since the mid-seventies.

The logical next step in this progression, 32-beat rhythms, occurred right on schedule, in the dance music of the nineties; however, drum machines were required to produce them at all but the slowest tempos. (There were occasional bursts of them in "What a Girl Wants.") They have not caught on in other kinds of music, nor are they likely to, because of their speed. In the earlier style beats, melodies and other supporting parts moved at the same speed as, or faster than, the style-beat-defining layer: in rock-era music, Chuck Berry's vocal line moves in step with his rhythm guitar part; the cadence of a rapper lines up with the 16-beat rhythms supporting the rapper. By contrast, 32-beat rhythms are simply too fast to be usable at a dance tempo. A melody with lyrics that moved at 32-beat speed would be all but impossible to deliver, and even harder to understand. For this reason, 16-beat rhythms represent the last stage in this rhythmic progression.

Where do rock and popular music go from here? It's clear that innovation *within* the music of a generation is still possible: Radiohead's "Paranoid Android" is hauntingly beautiful and without significant precedent. However, innovation on a larger scale—creating a new musical vocabulary for a new generation—may prove to be more problematic. The current imbalance between rhythm and melody and the exhaustion of usable new style beats suggests that further innovation in popular music may well require a completely new paradigm, created from a source other than black music. It would seem that the forces that impelled the evolution of popular music during the twentieth century have reached the evolutionary end of the line: they can no longer generate a revolutionary new music.

Rock will always be here, just as the best music of the past in other genres—for example, classical music, jazz, musical theater—remains very much a part of our cultural life. It will continue to come alive not only through the rich recorded legacy of its greatest artists but also through fresh interpretations of this legacy by subsequent generations. We await with considerable interest the new directions in music over the next several years and will report back then.